The Genesis of Kant's <u>Critique of Judgment</u>

The Genesis of KANT'S Critique of Judgment

JOHN H. ZAMMITO

THE UNIVERSITY OF CHICAGO PRESS   *Chicago & London*

J O H N H. Z A M M I T O is lecturer in the Department of History at
Rice University and chairman of the Department of History at St. John's
School, Houston.

The University of Chicago Press gratefully acknowledges a grant from
Rice University in partial support of the costs of publication of this
volume.

The University of Chicago Press, Chicago 60637
The University of Chicago Press, Ltd., London
© 1992 by The University of Chicago
All rights reserved. Published 1992
Printed in the United States of America
01 00 99 98 97 96 95 94 93 92   5 4 3 2 1

ISBN (cloth): 0-226-97854-0
ISBN (paper): 0-226-97855-9

Library of Congress Cataloging-in-Publication Data

Zammito, John H., 1948–
    The genesis of Kant's critique of judgment / John H. Zammito.
        p.   cm.
    Includes bibliographical references and index.
    ISBN 0-226-97854-0. — ISBN 0-226-97855-9 (pbk.)
    1. Kant, Immanuel, 1724–1804. Kritik der Urteilskraft. 2. Kant,
Immanuel, 1724–1804—Aesthetics. 3. Aesthetics. 4. Judgment
(Aesthetics) I. Title
B2784.Z36   1992
121—dc20   91-32390
                                                                    CIP

⊗The paper used in this publication meets the minimum requirements
of the American National Standard for Information Sciences—Perma-
nence of Paper for Printed Library Materials, ANSI Z39.48-1984.

To Martin Malia, mentor and friend

 *Contents*

✒ *Acknowledgments*

There are several individuals whose assistance I would like to acknowledge as this work comes to press. As the dedication suggests, I owe a great debt of gratitude to Martin Malia for his confidence and solicitude. His careful reading of various versions of this study and his conviction of its significance helped keep the project alive. Laurence Dickey and Dallas Clouatre read earlier versions of my work and I benefitted from their insights. Steven Crowell read the ultimate draft, argued out some of the more technical philosophical issues with me, and provided generous and timely counsel. Gershon Shafir helped me cope with the academic publishing system.

I wish to thank T. David Brent and the readers and editors associated with the University of Chicago Press for their consideration and professional execution, and Dean Allen Matusow and Rice University for a subvention to support the publication of the book.

Finally, I want to thank my wife, Katie, for abiding—in all its senses.

🐾 *Introduction*

I mmanuel Kant's *Critique of Judgment* of 1790 marked a water-shed in German intellectual life, proving a conduit through which the most important ideas and ideals of the German eighteenth century passed to the generation of Idealism and Romanticism. So rich is the *Third Critique,* however, that it can threaten to overwhelm the reader with the heterogeneity of its philosophical and cultural burden. One way to grasp this complexity is through a reconstruction of the text's composition which contextualizes Kant's philosophizing amid the manifold impulses animating Germany at the time. In particular, Kant's allegiance to the Aufklärung in its struggle against the *Sturm und Drang* for dominance in German culture proves crucial to the evolution of his intentions.

Kant revised the work substantially from his embarkation upon a "Critique of Taste" in late summer 1787 to the publication of the finished *Critique of Judgment* at Easter 1790. The major thrust of this study is to establish the shifts in conceptualization and argument that shaped the *Third Critique,* and to relate these to Kant's earlier works of philosophy of the 1780s. There have been many efforts to approach Kant's works in terms of the archaeology of their arguments. The so-called "patchwork" theory of the *First Critique* is the most famous.[1] A similar effort has been undertaken with reference to the *Third Critique* by such scholars as Michel Souriau, Gerhard Lehmann, James Meredith, and Giorgio Tonelli, and my analysis will set out from theirs. Weaving together the genetic development of Kant's versions of the *Third Critique* with considerations of the context to which they represented Kant's response sheds light on the meaning of textual passages at their more problematic junctures. Hence it proves worthwhile on immanent grounds. But since

1

readers judged Kant's *Third Critique* against the backdrop of that wider context, this approach also illuminates the major impact of the work on its epoch. In reconstructing this process of growth and change certain possibilities come to light which Kant at one point took seriously, though after reflection or change of orientation eventually abandoned. These left vestigial traces in the final product which aroused the speculative interest of his Idealist successors, who would follow out the trail of these neglected possibilities. To retrieve this historical sense of the openness of Kantian philosophy and of vast metaphysical possibilities which seemed latent within it is one of the most important tasks this study sets for itself.

The hermeneutic problem posed by the *Third Critique* is why Kant should have brought his treatments of aesthetics and teleology together with systematic intent. Since he had a longstanding interest in aesthetics and it was on this project, his "Critique of Taste," that he embarked once he completed his *Second Critique* in September 1787, the issue is: Why did teleology intrude? Kant had to think this connection in a creative manner, and therefore could not simply have put these two topics together casually. That Kant might act in a manner undeliberate in anything should strike those familiar with him as man or thinker as suspect from the outset. All the more so in one of his major enterprises. Some effort to grasp the work as a whole is therefore essential.

While the *Third Critique* has become the object of intense study in recent years, the concerns of much of this literature lie elsewhere. Disdaining teleology and even Kant's concern with the sublime, a good deal of contemporary Anglo-American interpretation chooses to neglect the unity of the work for the sake of a few currently interesting arguments about beauty.[2] Clearly, one can read the "Critique of Aesthetic Judgment" as an argument largely conducted in the "Analytic of the Beautiful" and in the "Deduction of Aesthetic Judgments." It then takes on a delimited and coherent character, pointing to the issue of "intersubjective validity" and culminating in the deduction of a *sensus communis* as the ground for the validity of the judgment of taste. That was the original ambition which led Kant to undertake a "Critique of Taste" along transcendental lines. It is also what Anglo-American philosophy almost without exception tries to salvage from Kant.[3] Undoubtedly the transcendental deduction of the judgment of taste is a landmark in the history of aesthetics, and one which has ever since served as the starting point for new efforts. However, this study is devoted to proving that only when we pass beyond the transcendental deduction of the judgment of taste do we enter the true heart of the *Third Critique.*

The thrust of a good deal of recent German interpretation has been to retrieve the work as a whole, recognizing the rigorous propensity to closure with which Kant developed his philosophy.[4] These insights point to a major systematic importance for the *Third Critique.*[5] I have drawn heavily on this approach, and also on German studies of earlier vintage, stressing the coherence and architectonic relevance of the *Third Critique* in Kant's system, in seeking to establish the unity of the work.[6]

I wish to pursue Kant's effort to extend his theory of aesthetics into the "metaphysical" domains of the sublime and the symbolic, culminating in the bold claim that "beauty is the symbol of morality." By drawing the aesthetic and the ethical into this analogical relation, Kant essentially established that aesthetics was only a propaedeutic concern leading to anthropology, and set the stage for a transition to reflections on man's ethical destiny in the natural world, which would form the most important part of the "Critique of Teleological Judgment."[7] A considerable interest in this idea of teleology has developed among scholars of Kant's ethical, historical, religious, and political philosophy.[8] On the other hand, analytic philosophers have considered the issue of teleology only as part of Kant's methodological writings on natural science.[9] As against this, George Schrader has offered a view of the place of teleology and unity in Kant's thought which is more in keeping with that presented in this study, and which has been a very important source for it.[10] For a good sense of the different potentials of these two approaches one might compare the work of John McFarland with that of Klaus Düsing. Of course, this teleological interpretation has met with predictable resistance.[11] Nevertheless, Kant's teleology did offer potent insights into issues of complex human experience.[12] This has been emphasized especially by those who see Kant as concerned with "philosophical anthropology."[13] This study will uphold the validity of that interpretation.

Archaeology of the Text

The "Critique of Taste" was begun in late 1787 on the basis of massive previous writing on the empirical problem of aesthetics, but with a new and crucial idea for a transcendental grounding. With that new idea, Kant could readily marshal a considerable body of material in rather short order (or thought he could) into a new *Cri-*

tique. Kant claimed in December 1787 that much of his envisioned "Critique of Taste" was "already in writing, but not quite prepared for the press."[14] He promised it for Easter 1788. But for a decade Kant had assured his correspondents that the *First Critique* was already in writing, but not quite prepared for the press. Indeed it was, but in numerous drafts and folios of widely varying orientation, which Kant was only able to pull together with the most grueling difficulty at the end of a decade's gestation. The *Third Critique* was not so labored a birth, but it, too, went to full term. Yet in the autumn of 1787 Kant did have a burst of writing, based on a burst of insight, whereby the very idea of the possibility of a "Critique of Taste" first arose in his mind. Into that project Kant threw himself the moment he completed the *Second Critique*, around September 1787, and he was in the high tide of this "aesthetic" phase when he wrote his memorable letter of December 1787 describing his new work and its motivating insight.

In order to organize our archaeological investigation into the genesis of the *Third Critique,* let us consult previous efforts to develop a chronology of its composition and revision. The scholar who inaugurated the investigation—and had the richest sense for its implications—was Michel Souriau. It was he who first recognized the revolutionary implications of Kant's theory of the faculty of judgment for the entire transcendental philosophy. The editors of the Prussian Academy edition of the *Third Critique* and its *First Introduction,* Wilhelm Windelband and Gerhard Lehmann respectively, made some very useful contributions as well.[15] James Meredith, in his work—far more than a mere translation—on the *Critique of Aesthetic Judgement,* offered a remarkable proposal for the archaeology of the original "Critique of Taste."[16] But the most compelling analysis of the chronology of the composition of the text is that of Giorgio Tonelli.[17] While I will draw on the others to supplement Tonelli's interpretation, it is from his results that any further interpretations of the genesis of the *Third Critique* must take their point of departure.

Like Souriau, Tonelli finds the key to the evolution of the *Third Critique* in the notion of reflective judgment. Tonelli shows that the distinction of determinant from reflective judgment—and therewith a clear sense of the faculty of judgment as such—only arose midway through the composition of the text. It did not inform the original treatment of the aesthetic—what has come down as the "Analytic of the Beautiful" (§§1–22 of the *Third Critique*) and the early and properly termed part (§§31–40) of the very hodgepodge "Deduction of Aesthetic Judgments." These are the most likely components of the "Critique of Taste" in its original form. Indeed, Tonelli connects the discovery of reflective judgment with the *First Introduction to the Critique of Judgment,* which he dates to sometime prior to May of 1789. Only after working out the implications of the new idea of a faculty of judgment could Kant have undertaken the "Critique of Teleological Judgment," which Tonelli therefore dates after May 1789.

That leaves substantial sections of the "Critique of Aesthetic Judgment" still to be accounted for. As to the body of material on art (§§41–54) and the extremely important "Dialectic of Aesthetic Judgment" (§§55–60), Tonelli dates them before the *First Introduction*—that is, before the clear conception of the faculty of judgment. Hence he assigns these sections of the work roughly to the year 1788. I will suggest some modifications of this interpretation, especially concerning the "Dialectic." Finally, Tonelli contends that the "Analytic of the Sublime" (§§23–30) was only composed after and in the light of the *First Introduction* and then inserted, with the necessary transitional sections, into the already composed "Critique of Taste."

Kant's "aesthetic" phase of composition, which began as the "Critique of Taste," carried into the new year of 1788, as he drew upon a massive body of material he had accumulated on aesthetic questions over the years and arrayed these ideas in terms of his new transcendental approach. Kant proceeded, in 1788, to bring his manifold reflections on art and his specific grievances against *Sturm und Drang* notions of artistic genius into formulation in terms of his newly established transcendental philosophy of taste. As he did so, he surveyed and revised the prevailing critical theory of the late eighteenth century, and his work can only be grasped against the context of that "conventional wisdom" he was correcting. Hence in order to make his work clear, it will be necessary to discuss key issues in eighteenth-century aesthetics, both in their English origins and in their German adaptations. Yet this material was, for Kant, very much "old business." What quickened his attention was rather a latent implication in his aesthetics (which he called an "intellectual interest in the beauty of nature"), namely, that nature itself seemed to show artistic design. That led him to the consideration of teleology as a cognitive judgment, and to the composition of the *First Introduction to the Critique of Judgment* by May 1789.

With the idea of "reflective judgment," Kant's work took a decidedly *cognitive* turn. The time of the writing of the *First Introduction* was the high point of Kant's confidence in the systematicity of his whole philosophy, and of his notion that the *Third Critique* should articulate this systematicity. In this context the work changed names, becoming the *Critique of Judgment*.[18] This turn has been the object of the greatest scholarly attention, not just among those interested in a genetic reconstruction of the whole text, or in the specific content and significance of the *First Introduction*, which is a most remarkable fragment in Kant's opus, but above all among those interested in the very notion of a "unity of reason" or systematic totality in Kant's entire philosophy.

But something led him to retreat from his synthetic enthusiasm. Something led him to suspect an excess of reason, and therefore to perceive the need for a "Critique of Teleological Judgment." That danger was the idea of immanent purpose in nature: "hylozoism" or pantheism, especially as it was being propagated by Johann Herder in the late 1780s—which brings us to the decisive matter of the Pantheism Controversy and its impact on Immanuel Kant. Teleology could be linked to his two most crucial metaphysical commitments: to moral freedom and to theism. The renaissance of Benedict Spinoza and outburst of pantheist ontology in the late 1780s seemed to challenge these very convictions fundamentally. The ultimate fabric of the *Third Critique* was profoundly shaped by Kant's reaction to the threat of this new "dogmatic metaphysics" in the very midst of the assimilation of his antidogmatic "critical philosophy." Therefore, the "Dialectic of Teleological Judgment" and especially Kant's confrontation with Spinozism and pantheism in §§72 and 73 expresses the ultimate concerns of the *Third Critique*.

Kant's struggle with pantheism brought on what I should like to call an *ethical* turn. He undertook to formulate his theory of the "supersensible" as a rebuttal to pantheism. This new and decisive turn in the composition of the *Third Critique* occurred in late summer 1789. In working out the full implications of this new, ethical turn, Kant undertook the substantial revisions of the text which intervened between his announcement to his publisher François de la Garde in October 1789 that the work was finished, and his delivery of the first installment of the manuscript, running roughly through §50, in January 1790.[19] In early 1790, as part of this same turn, he revamped the concluding segment of the "Critique of Teleological Judgment." Tonelli notes that Kant "tripled the volume" of this final segment between February 9 and March 8, 1790.[20] Finally, in March 1790, Kant revised the Introduction in crucial ways along similar lines.

The key to this ethical turn was the articulation of the idea of the "supersensible," a concept one can use in a textual analysis analogous to Tonelli's with "reflective judgment" to distinguish the revisions throughout the entire text which attended the ethical turn. This suggests that the final form of the "Dialectic of Aesthetic Judgment" must be dated to this final phase. With this ethical turn, Kant recognized further possibilities latent all along in his idea of beauty and of reflective judgment more generally. The result was an intense revision of the entire work, now toward the elaboration of the notion of the supersensible and the effort to make over the *Third Critique* into a vindication of Kant's notions of theism, moral freedom, and the "highest good." This was a very metaphysical turn in Kant, and one with momentous implications for the genesis of Idealism.

The segment on the ethical turn will demonstrate how the analogy of the deductions of the judgment of beauty and of the pure moral choice became a more intimate and important association, how beauty now became conceived as a "symbol of morality," and how this made relevant the consideration of the sublime, completely transformed the "Dialectic of Aesthetic Judgment," and, of course, found consummate expression in the "Methodology of Teleological Judgment" in considerations of the historical culture and religious destiny of mankind.

In sum, we must demarcate three phases in the composition of the *Third Critique.* The first, which launched the venture, was the breakthrough to a transcendental grounding of aesthetics, which occurred in the summer of 1787, during, and on the basis of, Kant's work on the *Second Critique*. That breakthrough made possible a "Critique of Taste," an idea which Kant had long considered beyond the reach of transcendental philosophy. The second phase, the most famous, came with Kant's formulation of the idea of reflective judgment, and it is most aptly considered a cognitive turn. He embarked upon it in early 1789, and it occasioned the transformation of the "Critique of Taste" into a full-fledged *Critique of Judgment*, i.e., a work which considered both aesthetics and teleology. But my most important claim is that there was yet a third turn, occurring in late summer or early fall 1789, which I designate the *ethical* turn. That ethical turn resulted directly from Kant's struggle with pantheism, and introduced a much more metaphysical tone into the whole work, emphasizing the idea of the supersensible as the ground of both subjective freedom and natural order. It resulted in the inclusion of a discussion of the sublime, a complete reformulation of the "Dialectic of Aesthetic Judgment," and, in 1790, an elaboration of the "Methodology of Teleological Judgment" and a revision of the Introduction to the whole book.

The Context of the Third Critique: Kant and Aufklärung

The contextual origins of the *Critique of Judgment* lie in the polemical concern of Immanuel Kant to drive the forces of the *Sturm und Drang* from their prominence in German intellectual life in the 1780s and to establish the complete hegemony of the Aufklärung, the mantle of whose leadership had fallen to him with the deaths of Gotthold Lessing (1780) and then Moses Mendelssohn (1786).[21] The Aufklärung must be understood not simply as a period but as a movement, and one struggling on several fronts for intellectual eminence in Germany. As its leader, Kant felt compelled to rebuff the "excesses" of the rival *Sturm und Drang* movement.[22] Earlier in his career Kant had ventured a more literary thrust at the rival movement in *Träume eines Geistersehers*. But the current had not abated. Indeed, in the 1770s it seemed to have swollen to flood tide, and, in the great stature accorded Herder in German literary and aesthetic circles during the 1780s, it still seemed to be the prevailing point of view. Under Herder's leadership the *Sturm und Drang* paraded its claims to privileged insight as the inspiration of "genius." This Kant could abide neither personally nor philosophically. The project of enlightenment itself appeared to be at stake.

Kant's life has seemed so little enmeshed in the matter of his thought that many of the biographies which have become standard, rather than seeking to explore the motivating interests of the person, read more like summaries, in chronological sequence, of his works.[23] Yet Kant's concerns and values, indeed even his weaknesses, played a significant role in his writing, especially in the 1780s.[24] The years 1781–90 constitute the decade of Kant's struggle for recognition and the beginning not only of his renown but also of his conflicts with religious, philosophical, and even political authorities. In 1781 Kant published what he knew to be one of the world-historical monuments in philosophy. Yet the *Critique of Pure Reason* largely fell on deaf ears.[25] The only review of substance, the so-called Garve-Feder review of January 1782, thoroughly garbled his meaning. So anxious was Kant for some wider response that he published a more "popular" version, the *Prolegomena to Any Future Metaphysics* in the spring of 1783. Not only did it fail to achieve its goal, but Kant now faced criticism for ostensible inconsistencies between the *First Critique* and the new *Prolegomena*.[26] In the 1780s, Kant's letters reveal his sense of time's foreclosure. Acutely aware of his advanced years, he felt pressed to complete his monumental labor and begrudged distraction, yet he also had an urgent and certainly unexceptionable need to be understood. In a letter to Mendelssohn dated August 16, 1783, Kant expressed regret that his colleague could not grasp his arguments, and ascribed the difficulty to his own lack of stylistic elegance. It troubled him, however, that he could find none among the first rank of Germany's philosophers—neither Mendelssohn nor Johann Tetens nor Christian Garve—who evinced any sympathetic understanding of his new work and might aid the general public in recognizing its importance. It mattered so much to him that he considered writing a popular course book on the *First Critique*. First, however, he planned to work up his moral philosophy, which he hoped would be "more popular" *(mehrer Popularität fähig)*.[27]

Other letters from the same period echoed this concern with the reception of his works and, behind it, a growing frustration.[28] That frustration had its element of human weakness. His publisher Johann Hartknoch, who had the good fortune also to publish Johann Herder's *Ideen zur Philosophie der Geschichte der Menschheit*, paid a visit to Herder in Weimar late in 1783. At that time he informed Herder that Kant believed he could trace the "neglect" *(Nichtbeachtung)* of his *Critique* to Herder's influence.[29] Kant's longstanding hostility to the whole of the *Sturm und Drang*, of which Herder was by the mid-1780s the dominant intellectual product, made their situation one of rivalry, however little either of them wished self-consciously to recognize it. That Kant was concerned with "rivals" is clear from his sensitivity to reviewers in the 1780s.[30]

The origins of the *Third Critique* lie in Kant's bitter rivalry with Herder. In his published works, with the obvious exception of the direct reviews of Herder's book, Kant scrupulously refrained from mentioning Herder by name, but he referred to him, as I will demonstrate, regularly and disparagingly. It is particularly important to attend the language of Kant's comments on Herder, for there turns out to be a remarkable consistency in the very words Kant used when he thought of Herder. That *Sturm und Drang,* and specifically Herder, irked Kant is evidenced through some withering *Reflections* from the 1770s, the decade of his laborious silence and the height of the *Stürmer*'s volubility. This hostility can be traced through the original edition of the *First Critique* with its veiled references in the preface to "indifferentists."[31] Throughout the early 1780s critics harped on Kant's lack of literary grace in the *First Critique* and the obstacles to popular understanding it presented. With exasperation Kant protested in his preface to the *Prolegomena to Any Future Metaphysics* that philosophy must sacrifice such glib accessibility for the sake of clarity and penetration. It is not too farfetched to suspect an implied contrast with Herder and even a little Kantian jealousy.[32]

The *Third Critique* was almost a continuous attack on Herder. At each stage in the genealogy of the *Third Critique* we can discern a clear and self-conscious aggression on the part of Kant against the positions adopted by Herder. Herder and the *Sturm und Drang* were the main targets of Kant's theory of art and genius. Indeed, Kant's hostility to the *Sturm und Drang* was one of the most important motives behind his entire enterprise of a treatise on aesthetics. Similarly, Kant's differences with Herder on history were substantial and crucial. Not only did Kant develop his ideas on history and culture in the "popular essays" of the mid-1780s in explicit rivalry with Herder, but he took them up again in 1789–90 in the context of the "Critique of Teleological Judgment." One can find fewer more intimate connections than that between "Idea for a Universal History" and §83 of the *Critique of Judgment.*[33] At both moments Kant self-consciously challenged Herder's primacy in this field. The battle between Kant and Herder over the meaning of history, or more precisely over human destiny and the tension between nature and culture, was one of the most important literary events of the late 1780s in Germany. The controversy had enormous impact upon subsequent German thought, especially Friedrich Schiller.

The decisive continuity, however, is that of Herder's thoughts on *Naturphilosophie* from Volume 1 of his *Ideen* to his *Gott: einige Gespräche* of 1787, on the one hand, and of the observations in Kant's reviews of Herder from the mid-1780s to his remarks in the "Critique of Teleological Judgment" of the *Third Critique* of 1790, on the other. Indeed, the key provocation for the final turn in Kant's composition of the *Third Critique* was Herder's *Gott: einige Gespräche*. Herder proves to be the unnamed antagonist of most of the "Critique of Teleological Judgment."[34]

At each step of our analysis, then, this relationship with Herder will play a crucial role. While it will appear useful in treating Kant's aesthetics, and familiar in treating Kant's philosophy of history, the real power of this connection lies in its illumination of the contextual sources of Kant's "Critique of Teleological Judgment" in the Pantheism Controversy.

For some time, aggressive, secularizing rationalists, centered in Berlin, had enjoyed the protection of that erstwhile skeptic in matters religious, King Frederick II. But theological innovation was still politically dangerous. Not only the established churches, but even the Pietist movement, which had once been a major reform movement within orthodox Christianity, had by the late eighteenth century become alarmed at the trend of theological rationalism in German high culture. Earlier in the century, this had led to the notorious persecution of Christian Wolff at the University of Halle, which was only reversed by the succession of Frederick II in 1740. More recently, in the 1770s, the controversy generated by Lessing's publication of the *Wolffenbüttel Fragments* of Hermann Reimarus showed the seriousness of the situation. Lessing had taken, by the end of his life, a very bold and provocative stance on the issue of the rationalization of religion which troubled and even offended the orthodox adherents of Protestant Christianity.[35] When orthodoxy assailed Lessing, the spokesman of theological rationalism, the entire Aufklärung saw its political and intellectual liberty jeopardized. The mobilization of the forces of repressive orthodoxy proves the indispensable backdrop for Kant's concern with Aufklärung.

Kant's intervention in the Pantheism Controversy (1785–89) must be linked to these considerations. The Pantheism Controversy brought about a revival and vindication of the philosophy of Spinoza in Germany in the later 1780s, but its ideological furor revolved around Lessing and his stature as the leader of the German Aufklärung.[36] Kant became deeply embroiled in the controversy because he saw Spinoza and pantheism as a great threat to the security and stability of the cultural milieu in Germany. Kant could sense the shift in the political-religious atmosphere, and he worried for the kind of "enlightened" attitude toward religion which he advocated. King Frederick II was approaching his death as the Pantheism Controversy broke out. He was succeeded by the more orthodox, indeed reactionary, Frederick William II in the midst of the affair.[37] Since the coronation ceremony traditionally took place in Königsberg, and since Kant happened to be serving as rector of the University of Königsberg at the time, he came into personal contact with the new king, but the latter's attentiveness to him was not an unmixed blessing. Frederick William II's Minister of Justice,

Johann von Wöllner, would confirm by his Edict of 1788 the appropriateness of the Aufklärung's anxiety over religious backlash. Indeed, Kant himself would feel the lash, and Fichte would be driven out under it.[38]

Kant's immediate comment on the pantheism affair, ["Was heißt: sich im Denken orientieren?"] of 1786, maintained an almost Olympian indifference to the respective substantive concerns of the disputants, and confined itself for the most part to calling both sides to order from the vantage of the critical philosophy. Why did he intervene at all? A footnote late in the essay provides the answer. It sets out with a protest from Kant: ["It is hard to conceive how thoughtful scholars could find support for Spinozism in the *Critique of Pure Reason*."[39] Only because such a link had been intimated did Kant feel compelled to enter the bitter controversy. His primary objective was to distance himself from such dangerous divagations, to defend reason against *Schwärmerei*, and, if possible, to shift attention to his soon to be reissued *First Critique*. This was, after all, the very time when Kant's "critical philosophy" was struggling painfully for recognition.[40]

However, Kant soon discovered that the pantheist stream was too strong to be so quickly diverted. With the appearance of Herder's *Gott: einige Gespräche* in 1787 the whole issue reopened in a new and, for Kant, still more provocative light. His bête noire, the *Sturm und Drang*, seemed once again to be stealing center stage just at the time that he was sensing a ground swell of interest in his own critical philosophy. It was at this point that the Pantheism Controversy exerted its most important influence on Kant—affecting his major critical works, especially the *Third Critique*.

Because his own disciples seemed enamored of these notions, Kant could only find the continued indulgence in pantheism profoundly dangerous, and hence he determined to take a personal hand in debunking Spinozism and pantheism. He began that campaign in the *Second Critique*, but it was primarily into the *Third Critique* that he channeled these concerns, decisively shifting its orientation in its final stages of composition. Placing Kant's intervention in the Pantheism Controversy in the context of the latest trends in eighteenth-century science as well as in the context of German theology, however, it becomes apparent that Kant's *Third Critique* only succeeded in provoking his own most adept disciples to take up Spinoza and "hylozoism" against him and thus led directly to the new metaphysics of nature which is one of the cornerstones of German Idealism.

While this work focuses on the *Third Critique* itself, it is worthwhile briefly to consider its key audience, the generation of Idealism, and what shaped their reading. Young German intellectuals of the 1790s, in order to ratify their emergent cultural identity, wished to see theirs as preeminently "Das Land der Dichter und Denker."[41] German Idealism appears, in this light, as the expression of a powerful intellectual movement of cultural nationalism in late eighteenth-century Germany, which German historiography has termed the "deutsche Bewegung."[42] A ripening pride in language and in poetic gift, and a cultivated attentiveness to the unique and outstanding aspects of the central European setting combined with the aspirations for social and political prominence in a particular group of educated commoners to create a very potent nationalism.[43] German intellectuals found cultural identity in resisting the dominance of French language and style in German courts, especially Potsdam. The struggle to get free from Latin dominion led them to a new theory of ethnic uniqueness and creativity as well as of the Greek, as opposed to the Roman, origins of ancient grandeur.[44] Both the ethnic and the Greek orientation promoted the idea of "culture" in the anthropological sense, linking language with ecology, religion, and politics.[45] This vastly deepened the German sense of history and its process, and gave Germany a distinctive model for its own self-invention as a nation.[46]

This emergent German culture had a serious problem, however. It seemed to be divided at the very core. On the one side, stressing the project of assimilating the new rationalism of the West in questions of religion, politics, and history, stood the German Aufklärung, led first by Lessing and later by Kant. Kant's "Idea for a Universal History with Cosmopolitan Intent" and "What Is Enlightenment?" (both 1784) formulated the typical Aufklärung stance on many of the key issues of the epoch. On the other side stood the *Sturm und Drang*, stressing linguistic uniqueness, literary genius, ethnic and religious tradition, and a staunch aversion to Western rationalism and its Latin classicist aesthetic. Its key figures were Herder and Goethe. If Herder offered a theory, Goethe personified the spirit of a German national literary culture.

Thus for Friedrich Schiller, who sought to place his own and his nation's identity in the frame of a grand and unified culture, the project seemed to reconcile the two traditions, and join Germany's foremost *Dichter*, Goethe, with its foremost *Denker*, Kant. Schiller himself was, in the 1790s, a student of the Kantian philosophy as well as the closest to a poetic peer and ally Goethe had. In his effort to define German greatness in terms of a synthesis of these two figures, Schiller drew heavily on Kant's *Third Critique.*[47] It was the one work by Kant which Goethe recognized and accepted with enthusiasm.[48] Schiller's effort to reconcile the two currents culminated in *On the Aesthetic Education of Mankind* (1795), a decisive anticipation of and inspiration for the young Idealists who emanated out of the Tübingen seminary: Hölderlin, Schelling, and Hegel. They expressed their initial vision in the crucial document "Earliest System-Program of German Idealism."[49]

If they declared themselves Kantians, it did not mean they took Kant as their only lodestar. Many of the disciples Kant recruited in Germany simultaneously reverenced Lessing and Goethe, read Herder with attentiveness and appreciation, and found Spinoza and pantheism fascinating. Indeed, one of the crucial facts that must be retrieved from the context is the widespread conviction of the incompleteness of the Kantian system and of the agenda for philosophy which that created.[50] Kant contributed substantially to this sense of the openness of his system and to the idea of its possible completion, and only very late, when it became apparent that what his disciples had made did not suit him, would he give public notice that his own works constituted an altogether complete system, and that his heirs had utterly misunderstood him.[51]

What fascinated this new generation in the *Third Critique* was the metaphysical potential it seemed to suggest. In Kant's association of beauty with morality, nature with art, history with the achievement of a just society, they saw the prospect for a consummate vision of the order of the world as well as a cultural mission for their generation. Some possibility which glimmered in the *Third Critique* seemed to them to cry out for retrieval. Nature, art, and history needed to be welded into a grander synthesis than Kant himself had dared. This quest for an "aesthetic solution," in the phrase of Schiller and Hölderlin, preoccupied the brightest minds of Germany in the 1790s and resulted in the genesis of German Idealism.[52] This "aesthetic idealism" found systematic articulation in Schelling's writings of the late 1790s, and contributed greatly to the rise of Romanticism.[53] Yet for all that, this project, undertaken by Schiller, Wilhelm von Humboldt, Hölderlin, Schelling, and Hegel (as well as others like Fichte and Novalis) took form under the aegis of the Kantianism of the *Third Critique.*

Part One

THE GENESIS OF THE "CRITIQUE OF AESTHETIC JUDGMENT"

One

KANT AND THE PURSUIT
OF AUFKLÄRUNG

As an *Aufklärer*, Kant saw himself part of a movement not only in his nation but in Europe as a whole. Yet the German Aufklärung should not simply be assimilated into the Western Enlightenment along cosmopolitan-secularist lines.[1] Germany had a very distinctive tradition.[2] German culture in the eighteenth century was still very Christian: Christian piety persisted vigorously in the urban laity, and university culture remained distinctly Christian in outlook.[3] The German Aufklärung was inextricably involved in the theological controversies of the Protestant faith in Germany. Kant was not alone in being "roused from his dogmatic slumbers," yet if he and other Germans surrendered some of their dogma*tism* in the face of criticism from beyond the Rhine (and the channel), they struggled to preserve as much of the *dogma* as they could. While this meant a strained relation with orthodoxy, it never approached the radical hostility to religion of a Voltaire or a Hume in the West.[4] If we are to ascertain how Kant came to identify himself with Aufklärung in its distinctive German sense, we have to look to Frederick II and his effort to inaugurate a new cultural epoch for Prussia upon his accession to the throne in 1740. His two key innovations were the reinstatement of Wolff to his chair at the University of Halle and the creation of the Berlin Academy.[5]

The conflict between the rationalists around Wolff and the Pietist successors of Christian Thomasius within the German university system had driven Wolff from his chair in 1723.[6] With the restoration of Wolff's chair, the old struggle between rationalism and Pietism resumed. Against the resurgent Wolff, the Pietists brought forth a new champion: Christian August Crusius. Crusius raised the level of philosophical sophistication in the Pietist campaign.

Professor of philosophy and later of theology at Leipzig starting in 1744, Crusius published his most influential work, *Weg zur Gewißheit und Zuverläßigkeit der menschlichen Erkenntnis*, in 1747.[7] In the 1750s, his disciples were active in the circles of the Berlin Academy, where they joined forces with the French anti-Wolffians in the Newtonian-positivist tradition.[8]

Wolff maintained that all knowledge was grounded in the principle of identity, even Leibniz's famous principle of sufficient reason, and since it was possible to deduce the law of sufficient reason from the principle of identity, formal logic served as an adequate ontology. Actuality, in his view, was not nearly so important as the two forms of possibility, necessary and contingent. Rational argument established necessity and this warranted reality. Hence Wolff subscribed to the ontological argument for the existence of God. A corollary of this faith in the analyticity of all knowledge was Wolff's conviction that all forms of human activity could be grounded in a single faculty, which was cognitive. Ethical and sensual discriminations could be derived from this single cognitive faculty, even as specific cognitions could ultimately be grounded in the principle of identity. The result was a methodical but indiscriminate rationalism.

While Wolff acknowledged allegiance to Leibniz, he was by no means fully in sympathy with the latter's philosophy. He adopted, for example, a firm dualism in his theory of substance, as between mind and matter. He rejected Leibniz's monads and the idea of pre-established harmony, and conceived of the material universe in strictly mechanistic terms far closer to Descartes than to Leibniz. He accepted the Cartesian geometric method as appropriate for physical science, and found it completely consistent with the method used in philosophy and metaphysics. This Cartesian element in his thought provoked the revisionism stirring against Wolff in eighteenth-century German philosophy.

Crusius attacked Wolff on all these fronts. He denied that the principle of sufficient reason could be derived from the principle of identity. Thus formal logic and ontology remained distinct. Indeed, Crusius argued that formal logic was not particularly useful in the latter, since it dealt merely with the possible, while philosophy's real problems were with the actual, with the blunt and intractable existence of things. Consequently, mathematics and metaphysics did not operate with identical methods. By emphasizing the disjunction between formal logic and the problems of existence, Crusius maintained that metaphysical issues were not soluble through analytic logic.[9] The ontological argument could not be upheld in this light, and that restored the importance of Scripture and revelation, an explosive proposition in eighteenth-century German theology. Crusius furthermore stressed the limitations of human knowledge, using arguments from skepticism to uphold fideist commitments in Pietism.[10] He directed attention to the concrete human project of making sense of experience, outward and inward. In this light Tonelli observed that Crusius's Pietism "allowed his successors to be much more receptive to English and French empiricism, sensationalism, and common-sense philosophy than were orthodox Wolffian rationalists."[11]

As Lewis Beck has argued, Kant was never an orthodox Wolffian.[12] Tonelli has elaborated on this heterodoxy by linking it to the influence of Crusius.[13] The issues that Crusius introduced into German philosophy—the distinction of logic from actuality, the limitations of human understanding, and the distinction of the metaphysical from the mathematical method—proved decisive for Kant. He began as a philosopher of natural science, concerned above all with the conflict between Newton and Leibniz over the structure and metaphysical implications of the natural universe. In 1755, when he began his lectureship at the University of Königsberg, Kant's main interest remained the relation between philosophy and natural science, and especially the issues which had been inaugural for eighteenth-century German metaphysics—those of the Leibniz-Clarke debate and the meaning of Newtonianism.[14] Kant published *Allgemeine Naturgeschichte und Theorie des Himmels*, his most significant scientific contribution on this theme, in the same year that he began his university teaching.

That space, existence, and the distinction of natural science and mathematics from philosophy were crucial questions for Kant in the late 1750s and early 1760s is clear.[15] What they led him to investigate was the relation of actuality to sensibility, and thus the role of sensibility in valid knowledge. And it is in this context that we must place his reception of the very different philosophical project of Alexander Baumgarten and Georg Friedrich Meier. Alfred Bäumler set the study of the *Third Critique* on a new path by connecting the issue of aesthetics to the epistemological concerns of German "school philosophy" in the eighteenth century.[16] German school philosophy, inspired by Leibniz, sought a logic adequate to induction, by focusing on the nature of concept formation at the level of individual empirical entities and the role of sense in knowledge.[17] Baumgarten revised Wolffian philosophy with a new theory of human knowledge through sensibility, which he called the "science of aesthetics."[18] He and his disciple, Meier, investigated beauty and the fine arts for their cognitive potential.

Baumgarten made the claim that beauty or sensuous perfection *(perfectio phaenomenon)* consisted in a perfect clarity even in the absence of distinctness. Clarity and distinctness had become prominent in the lexicon of modern philosophy from the time of Descartes and played an important role in Wolff's system. For Wolff, clarity involved the ability to discriminate an object of attention from its background. It was a recognition of specificity. Distinctness involved the precise analysis of the marks which characterized that object. In traditional language, clarity discerned entities, distinctness analyzed their properties. The process of distinguishing involved the comparison of properties at a more abstract and universal level. That entailed reason or logic. What Baumgarten, among others, noted was that this abstracting process lost purchase on the unity and concreteness of the entity as a whole. Baumgarten proposed to revise Wolffianism on this important question, and he introduced some distinctions which were to prove stimulating to German philosophers of the second half of the eighteenth century, and to Kant in particular.

Baumgarten distinguished "extensive" versus "intensive" clarity in conceiving of an individual entity, i.e., the unity of a manifold in its actuality. No logical analysis of the particular properties could account adequately for their combination in a whole. This unity or "perfection" seemed to require a different approach. Baumgarten linked "extensive" coordination or "perfection" in the sensuous realm of actuality with beauty. Beauty therefore took on a cognitive function. Aesthetic perfection was an inferior kind of objective knowledge, rather than an entirely distinct and self-sufficient mode of experience.

"Extensive" clarity was to be achieved by finding the most complete articulation of the properties which joined together to form the individuality of any entity. Beauty represented the quantitative maximum of this extensiveness—"richness." For Baumgarten the essential quality of extensive clarity was its "vivacity."[19] By contrast, Baumgarten associated "intensive clarity" with "purity."[20] But Baumgarten did not get very far with the idea of "intensive clarity" because he meant by it that logical unity which Leibniz had articulated but could not specify, and which Kant was to find one of the most intractable problems of his own epistemology, the idea of a singular "intuition." While vivacity or richness might express the quantitative completeness of properties in any individual entity, this "perfection" gave no real purchase on the logical, or better ontological, problem of its integral or systematic unity. Hence the admission that it was "confused." "Confused" meant lacking distinctness, i.e., the logical-analytic discrimination of properties through which understanding might make precise what distinguished that particular entity from both similar and different objects of possible experience. While Baumgarten recognized the inadequacy of Wolffian analytic rationalism, he could not resolve the issue of the relation of rational determination to sensible actuality. Kant was to take issue with the Baumgarten-Meier position precisely there.

Kant considered Baumgarten the foremost Wolffian and took him as a foil in developing his own approach to the problem of sensibility and understanding. That meant Kant had to follow him into the question of beauty and its place in philosophy. Kant's concern with aesthetics, then, must be grounded in this epistemological interest. What first interested Kant in the Baumgarten-Meier project was strictly this epistemological issue regarding the laws of sensible knowledge, this problem of "confusion" and the relation of the aesthetic and the logical in the cognition of an actual individual entity. Kant was primarily and professionally enmeshed in the Aufklärung's epistemological project. He was not interested in fine art, in its system, in creativity or artistic taste. In a *Reflection* from the mid 1750s, Kant put this quite clearly: "The beautiful sciences are those which make ready to hand the rules for the inferior capacities of knowledge, that is, confused knowledge [*die unteren Erkenntniskräfte, d.i. die verworrene Erkenntnis*]."[21] But the German Aufklärung must be seen as much in an *ideological* as in an epistemological light.

Frederick II, the Berlin Aufklärung, and Cosmopolitan Taste

Frederick II's effort to bring Prussia into the cultural mainstream of the European—which for him meant the French—Enlightenment stimulated cosmopolitanism in central Europe. The official language of the Potsdam court was French; the King of Prussia declared German inept for literary or cultural expression; and French language and Frenchmen dominated his new academy in Berlin. He even selected Pierre Maupertuis as president (1746–59) of this academy.

Maupertuis's allegiance was to a positivist program of natural science along the lines of Jean d'Alembert's *Preliminary Discourse to the Encyclopedia*. At the instigation of the king, Maupertuis employed a series of prize competitions in the Berlin Academy in the mid-1750s to debunk German "school philosophy" (Leibniz and Wolff) as well as German religion (Pietism). The academy's program was quite simply Newton's physics without Newton's God. Ironically, such "French" thought had its origins in Britain. Indeed, Voltaire himself acknowledged a "new trinity" for the continent: Bacon, Newton, and Locke.[22] The British impulse towards sensationalism, set off by Hobbes and Locke, had progressed by midcentury into the writings of Hartley and Hume. The latter's works became available in Germany in the 1750s through a four-volume translation of his essays, and they were widely read.[23]

While a cultural-nationalist reaction eventually threw off this tutelage to foreign thought, a number of Germans sought urgently to bring themselves abreast of the more sophisticated culture from abroad, though in their own language and in terms of their indigenous philosophical, religious, and literary concerns.[24] The leaders of this discriminating assimilation of foreign elements into a German Aufklärung were the so-called "popular philosophers" of Berlin: Friedrich Nicolai, Lessing, and Mendelssohn.[25] In the 1750s, without and perhaps even against Frederick II's programmatic guidance, the indigenous Aufklärung found its first articulation in the journals this trio founded for German literary life. They distilled and broadcast the European Enlightenment to the rest of central Europe, including Kant's Königsberg.

The Berlin Aufklärung brought to Kant a whole new set of interests. Kant took very seriously his status as a Prussian official obliged to implement Frederick's program, but it was also a matter of personal cultivation. In a German of that epoch, the mark of "taste" was Aufklärung, a cosmopolitan acquaintance with the best of foreign thought and discrimination. Not only was Kant in contact with the Berlin Academy and the upper echelons of the cultural bureaucracy in the capital, but he was also voracious in his reading of the learned and critical journals that emanated from there.[26] The publicity of the Berlin Aufklärung, both through the academy and through the "popular philosophy," conveyed to Kant the vivacity of intellectual discourse in the wider world.

Kant was an utterly untraveled man, living in a remote East Prussian city. Yet from the very first he strove to achieve cosmopolitanism, to widen his intellectual horizons if he could not widen his physical ones. Kant wished to bring himself abreast of distant environments, to feel at home in a wider world than his provincial city. We find evidence of this cosmopolitanism in Kant's announcement that he would give lectures in physical geography, starting in 1757.[27] He announced that such a course would be appropriate "for the rational taste of our enlightened times."[28] The wording is very important. Kant had a very strong desire, in those early years, to be a fashionable man, to show his "taste." Beck notes that "during the years that he was *Dozent* he was often called 'the galant master'—a spruce dresser, a popular teacher, and a welcome guest in the best society of his city."[29] Herder, who was Kant's student from 1762 to 1764, has given us a magnificent portrait of this Kant:

> Playfulness, wit, and humor were at his command. His lectures were the most entertaining talks. His mind, which examined Leibniz, Wolff, Baumgarten, Crusius and Hume, and investigated the laws of nature of Newton, Kepler, and the physicists, comprehended equally the newest works of Rousseau . . . and the latest discoveries in science. He weighed them all, and always came back to the unbiased knowledge of nature and to the moral worth of man. The history of men and peoples, natural history and science, mathematics and observation, were the sources from which he enlivened his lectures and conversations. He was indifferent to nothing worth knowing. No cabal, no sect, no prejudice, no desire for fame, could ever tempt him in the slightest from broadening and illuminating the truth. He incited and gently forced others to think for themselves; despotism was foreign to his nature.[30]

He made a very strong effort in the case of students like Herder, and also Jakob Lenz, and even with his recalcitrant contemporary and friend Johann Hamann, to make them as acquainted with the wider intellectual world as he could, and to take up from them whatever they might bring to his attention of this wider world as well.[31]

Kant compensated for his Königsberg provincialism not only with a good dash of Prussian francophilia, but also with a taste for things English. The crucial medium for this fascination in Kant was the Berlin Aufklärung. A fascination for things English was all the rage among the "popular philosophers" of Berlin with whom Kant entered into very lively exchange.[32] Moses Mendelssohn looms as especially influential in mediating the foreign Enlightenment, and especially the British, for German philosophy, fusing the new English and French aesthetics with the work of Baumgarten and Meier.[33] Mendelssohn helped naturalize into German discourse three crucial notions from abroad: feeling, genius, and the sublime.

Mendelssohn enjoyed one signal advantage over Kant: he could read English. As Frederic Will has noted, he devoted an entire year to the study of Edmund Burke's *Enquiry Into the Original of Our Ideas of the Sublime and the Beautiful*.[34] He was also conversant with the French literature, particularly Jean Dubos and Charles Batteux. His greatest utility, from Kant's vantage, was that he put all their insights directly into the context of German school philosophy and particularly related them to the issues raised by Baumgarten and Meier with which Kant was already wrestling. Kant came into intellectual contact with Mendelssohn in the Berlin Academy Prize Competition of 1761–63, which Mendelssohn won and in which Kant's submission was accepted for publication by the academy. Shortly thereafter they entered into a correspondence which lasted until the death of Mendelssohn in 1786. Their relationship was from the first warm and sympathetic, despite wide differences in their philosophical orientation. They were allies on a more general level: the program of indigenous Aufklärung in Germany.

Mendelssohn's effort to integrate foreign aesthetic theory into the German approach led him, perhaps somewhat unintentionally, to shift the discourse in a psychological and empirical direction away from Baumgarten, or at least the prevailing view of Baumgarten's project as a cognitive approach to beauty. By incorporating a more psychological approach into his essays, especially the later ones, Mendelssohn helped bring the sensationalist and naturalistic viewpoint of Dubos, Batteux, and the French Enlightenment, and the related British school of Hume and eventually Burke, into fashion in Germany.

One of Mendelssohn's goals was to establish a hierarchy of gratifications. Foremost he placed intellectual satisfaction in pure ideas. Such a delight had no sensual content whatever and belonged to the tradition of "intelligible beauty."[35] In addition, Mendelssohn discerned a separate gratification in the cognitive perfection of an empirical object. The pleasure in beauty Mendelssohn raised from mere sensuality by claiming it aroused no desire. This notion of "disinterestedness" would have a great impact on Kant.[36] In the essays of the 1750s, Mendelssohn did not succeed, however, in distinguishing clearly between the good, the beautiful, and the pleasant.

Having already written on the problem of the sublime, Mendelssohn felt obliged to come to terms with Burke's major work in the field. The result, the essay "Über die Mischung der Schönheiten" (1758), summarized the arguments of Burke quite effectively, making them accessible to a German reading audience long before Lessing's translation of the work in 1773. But Mendelssohn was not content merely to summarize; he went on to make a telling criticism: "He piles observation upon observation, all of them fundamental and insightful; only every time it comes down to explaining these observations in terms of the nature of our souls, his weakness becomes obvious. One realizes that he is unaware of the theory of the soul of German philosophy."[37] In arguing thus for a more spiritual interpretation of the sublime, Mendelssohn made the same argument which informed his response to the foreign theory of genius.

The principle of the innate activism of the subject is perhaps the most distinctive feature of German as opposed to British philosophy in the eighteenth century. Its source was Leibniz.[38] But Leibniz had not published some of his most important work, and so Germany's school philosophy carried forward only a partial formulation of Leibnizian metaphysics, and Wolff's Cartesian and Newtonian modifications with respect to the material world had served further to weaken or render perplexed these potentialities from Leibniz. Mendelssohn and all the other, lesser figures of German school-philosophy sought reinforcement from abroad for their fundamentally Leibnizian intuition that the active powers of the subject lay at the core of human experience, and therewith transfigured the world from mere mechanism. It was in that context, i.e., before the "great light" which the publication of Leibniz's *Nouveaux essais* brought to them, that the German philosophers stood open to the ideas of activism in the subject originating in Britain and France associated with "genius."

In his essay on the sources and linkages of the fine arts and sciences, Mendelssohn had adhered firmly to Baumgarten's theory of *ingenium* as formulated in §648 of the *Metaphysica*, i.e., that genius was the perfect harmony of the human faculties, but no separate faculty of its own. But in his reviews for Nicolai's journal, the *Briefe, die neueste Literatur betreffend,* starting in 1759, Mendelssohn began to move away from the strictly Baumgartian theory. The first sign of this is Mendelssohn's defense, in the sixtieth letter, of the "unschooled" genius against those who insisted that genius must always be tutored by taste and regimen, as Johann Gottsched and Christian Gellert had made the premise of German criticism.[39]

Mendelssohn's revision of his theory of genius was part of a whole series of reconsiderations taking place within the Berlin Aufklärung. His colleague in Berlin, Friedrich Resewitz, had delivered a lecture on the subject of genius in 1755.[40] And in 1757, Johann Sulzer had addressed the Berlin Academy with a very important "Analyse du genie," which had then been published in the academy yearbook.[41] Sulzer was active in the Berlin Academy starting from the 1750s, and his academy lecture on genius made a very important contribution to the new trends, as did the topics he proposed, as leader of the section for philosophy, for the prize essays sponsored by the academy. It was Sulzer who raised the issue for the famous prize competition of 1761–63 on the relation of metaphysics and morals for which Mendelssohn and Kant submitted important contributions.[42] Sulzer wished to naturalize the German ideas and bring them into coordination with the Encyclopedist tradition.[43] Mendelssohn recognized that Sulzer was trying to achieve the same integration his own essays had sought, between the foreign, naturalistic interpretation of genius and the indigenous tradition of Leibniz. Indeed, that was the most important element in Sulzer's essay.[44]

The idea of the "unschooled" as opposed to the "learned genius" came from Joseph Addison's celebrated essay on genius in the *Spectator* in 1711, which had been translated into German in 1745. The issue had come to a head in Britain in the revolt of the new emotional school against Augustan taste. In 1756, Joseph Warton had published his manifesto against Alexander Pope, and in 1758 Edward Young's famous essay on "original composition" came out.[45] Mendelssohn and his colleagues were already quite familiar with Young's view, and had published an earlier essay by the poet in the second volume of their *Sammlung vermischter Schriften zur Beförderung der schönen Wissenschaften und der freyen Künste* (Berlin, 1759).[46] It is important to retrieve the entire controversy in British aesthetics at that pivotal moment, for it profoundly stamped the last and most decisive sense of Aufklärung for Immanuel Kant, the struggle of reason against the impulse toward irrationalism he detected in the emerging *Sturm und Drang* movement.

Starting roughly around the midcentury in Britain, a new school identified with "sensibility" challenged neoclassicism, offering a new approach to taste: the assertion of the "sublime" against the beautiful and of "genius" against rule.[47] Sensibility was shifting all across Europe in the course of the eighteenth century, at different but related moments in Britain, France, and Germany. This manifested itself in changes in attitudes towards gardening, travel, and painting ("picturesque" landscapes), as well as in preferences in architecture (the revival of appreciation for Gothic) and literature (the enthusiasm for Shakespeare and "Ossian").[48]

The fascination with the sublime was perhaps *the* symptom of this new sensibility. As David Morris argues, the impulses behind the revival of interest in the sublime were "scientific, physicotheological, epistemological, and literary."[49] The subjective experience of the grandeur of the universe—indeed the grandeur of the very earth, in all its variety and potency—had about it a religious reverence and awe, which came, via literary criticism, to be identified with what Longinus called the sublime. The heart of this notion was the aesthetic confrontation with infinity, or with the vastness and potency of the universe.[50] No longer did the world appear bounded, mathematical, simple, and static. It now appeared boundless, dynamic, complex, changing. That is the crucial notion behind the "natural sublime."[51] The mediation between natural grandeur and the literary trope was the similar subjective emotion which they aroused, which was, for that epoch, religious in its fundamental texture.[52] While that religious texture may have abated in the course of the eighteenth century, with the rise of Enlightenment and Deism, the emotional linkage remained firmly established.

The mid-eighteenth-century appreciation of nature had changed; men saw nature differently, and thought of themselves differently for having done so. The sublime was the decisive term through which to articulate the new appreciation of the world of nature as an aspect of human consciousness. Scientists were enthusiastic about the complexity of nature, her variety and dynamism.[53] No longer would the mechanical vision of Descartes suffice. Newton's own *Opticks* had created far vaster and more intricate possibilities. An energized nature seemed too lively for reductively mechanistic thinking on the lines of seventeenth-century thought. Indeed, scientists expressed enthusiasm concerning possibilities of an expanded physics which was not so mechanistically determined, but which took up the mysterious question of "force." Not only scientists but also poets were swept up in this new physics of "force" and its attendant metaphysics.[54] Consequently, after 1740, and in terms of this new sense for the complexity and dynamism of nature, the "sublime" came to be applied directly to natural phenomena.[55]

X   The linkage of the strong feeling within the subject with imaginative responsiveness to grandeurs in the outer world of nature provided all the elements of a theory of human creativity. The fate of the sublime and its elevated emotions came to be linked, as a consequence, with the issues of spirituality, freedom, and creativity in the crucial notion of "genius."[56] The Earl of Shaftesbury (A. Cooper) set this relation in motion by linking genius with the "principle of pure aesthetic intuition," or "the process of pure creation."[57] He shifted the inquiry into beauty "from the world of created things to the world of creative process."[58] Shaftesbury sought to articulate a notion of human creativity and spontaneity of a sort which, while immanent, was not material or mechanical.[59] That notion, which had strong parallels with Leibnizian metaphysics, seemed all too metaphysical to the British of the eighteenth century.[60] Instead they fought it out in terms of the conflict of genius with rule, that is, in terms of the relation of creative freedom to conventional neoclassical standards.

Addison's famous essay on genius in the *Spectator* strove, with an eye to Shakespeare, to use the contrast between Homer and Virgil to make a distinction between the natural or "unschooled" genius and the "learned genius."[61] While Addison celebrated the natural genius for the originality and power of his work, he also warned that this was exceedingly rare, and that it was highly dangerous to emulate such figures. Addison implied that genius could quite comfortably be schooled in taste, learn rule and reason, and emerge the better for it. Virgil epitomized such genius among the ancients, the Augustans believed, but they also ascribed it to Pope among the moderns.

→   It was against this that Warton rebelled in *Essay on the Genius and Writings of Pope* (1756). He denied that Pope was a genius at all. Genius meant for him precisely the mysterious and unschooled "originality" of a Shakespeare. And he insisted not only that Shakespeare's originality was unschooled, but also that schooling destroyed originality. The irrational note had clearly sounded. Spontaneity here took on another tone.[62] The stress on the emotional involved a total rejection of rules, a Promethean rebellion.[63] The very notions of craft, technique, and taste went by the boards. Genius was like nature. In what was the most famous manifesto in this vein, *Conjectures on Original Composition* (1758), Edward Young put this quite bluntly: "An Original may be said to be of a vegetable nature, it rises spontaneously, from the vital root of Genius; it grows, it is not made."[64] Works of art developed as an organic consequence of the genius's soul.[65] Indeed, the artist exerted no conscious control at all, it seemed.[66]

Finding a response to this "enthusiastic" theory of original genius preoccupied the most serious philosophical minds in Britain in the late 1750s. In Edinburgh, the prize-winning aesthetic philosopher Alexander Gerard delivered a new and very important series of lectures on genius.[67] Hume's essays on taste and tragedy from the late 1750s touch on this topic. Henry Home, Lord Kames, addressed the question as well in what many take to be the culminating work of this whole period, *Elements of Criticism* (1762). They worked to develop a carefully naturalistic theory of genius based upon the premise that the imagination was limited to what the senses had provided. There could be no creation *ex nihilo*, no divine analogy in mortal genius.[68] The conflict which raged between these two schools in Britain would be taken up with equal or greater ferocity in Germany, with the *Stürmer* on the side of the irrationalists and the Aufklärung on the side of reason.

In light of all this, while Alfred Bäumler's argument is crucial to the proper contextualization of the *Third Critique*, it is also incomplete. As Ernst Cassirer pointed out in a long and incisive note to his *Philosophy of the Enlightenment*, Bäumler, perhaps out of a misguided national pride, rejected altogether the influence of British thought on Kant.[69] That is as unlikely as the opposite view, professed by Edgar Carritt, that "Kant's philosophy of beauty owes nearly everything but its systematic form to English writers."[70] The issue is not even, as a more recent commentator has put it, to find the balance of "Kant's shifting debt to British aesthetics."[71] The question is rather what Kant took to be the contribution the British made to Baumgarten's question of the role of sensibility in valid knowledge. As we will see, for a long time Kant believed that the British had the final—negative—word on that score.

Kant could not read English. That makes the question of Kant's assimilation of the British Enlightenment problematic on the most basic level. Accordingly, it is important to establish when, what, and how British material reached him. Few modern interpreters would dispute the importance of British thinkers for the Kant of the 1760s. Beck goes so far as to write that "in 1763 Kant was as much a disciple of Shaftesbury and Hutcheson as Mendelssohn was— perhaps more so."[72] Both Mendelssohn's and Kant's submissions for the Berlin Academy prize show this strong British influence, though Mendelssohn remained more conventionally German and hence won the prize.[73] Kant articulated the key influence of British thought in the second part of his essay: "In these times we have first begun to realize that the faculty of conceiving truth is intellection, while that of sensing the good is feeling, and that they must not be interchanged."[74]

The major theory of moral feeling, articulated by Hutcheson in 1725, became available in a German translation in 1762. Other works by Hutcheson had appeared in translation even earlier.[75] Kant acknowledged Hutcheson in the published version of his *Prize Essay* as the founder of the school of moral feeling.[76] Not only Hutcheson but especially Hume proved influential in this period.[77] Hume's major essays had been translated into German in a four volume collection in the late 1750s, and his subsequent essays came swiftly into German.[78] The consistency and brilliance of Hume's skeptical distinction of matters of fact from relations of ideas, of empirical from necessary connections, made an impression on all serious philosophers in Europe in the 1750s and 1760s.[79] To be sure, the full scope of Hume's radicalism was not apparent to many, and Kant would only realize it after 1772, when he read in the translation of James Beattie's work a sustained attack on Hume which had the misfortune of presenting the superior arguments of its opponent in sufficient detail to refute itself.[80]

But perhaps equally important for Kant in the early 1760s was the *Elements of Criticism* by Henry Home, Lord Kames. It appeared in English in 1762, and a year later became available in German. The reviewers praised it, and it proved influential in German aesthetic thought from that point forward. The early essays of Herder, which date from the mid 1760s, consider Kames equal in stature to Baumgarten in the question of aesthetics.[81] That parallel, there is reason to suppose, he learned from his teacher, Immanuel Kant. Kames served as the crucial expositor of the principle of the British method in aesthetics: criticism.

For the Kant of the 1760s, "science" and "criticism" stood juxtaposed as alternative methods for aesthetics. Kant used the two names, Baumgarten and Home (Kames), as personifications of the two methods. In his lectures in *Logic,* for example, he observed: "The philosopher Baumgarten in Frankfurt had the plan to make an aesthetic as science. More correctly, Home has named aesthetics criticism, since it gives no rules a priori that sufficiently determine the judgment, as does logic, but takes its rules a posteriori and only makes the empirical laws general through comparisons, by which we know the imperfect and the perfect (beautiful)."[82] The distinction of science and criticism is linked, here, with the distinction of a priori and a posteriori (Hume) and applied to the concept of "perfection," which Baumgarten associated with the idea of beauty.

The lectures which serve as the basis for the published *Logic* stem from the 1770s, though Kant had been giving the course since the late 1750s. The juxtaposition of Kames with Baumgarten dates, as attested by *Reflection* 1588, from the mid-1760s: "Fine art allows only critique. Home. Therefore no science of the beautiful."[83] Without Kames's name, but with just the same content, are several other crucial *Reflections* of the 1760s.[84] In *Reflection* 626, Kant distinguished knowledge according to three methods: science, discipline (instruction in doctrine), and critique. The first operated on a rational, a priori basis. The second worked historically, a posteriori, toward principles which could be converted ultimately into science.[85] The third worked only with *Beurteilung*, or judgment, and it was inevitably and incurably subjective. Aesthetics fell under this last category, and, Kant wrote, "for this reason the school term 'aesthetic' should be avoided, since it permits no instruction in schools."[86] Kant had abandoned the rational approach to beauty altogether. He wrote tellingly: "We do an injustice to another who does not perceive the worth or the beauty of what moves or delights us, if we rejoin that *he does not understand* it. Here it does not matter so much what the *understanding* comprehends, but what the feeling senses."[87]

Kant adopted the British argument that "knowledge of beauty is only criticism . . . [I]ts proof is a posteriori."[88] The British had come to the conclusion that the only plausible standard would be an empirical consensus among gentlemen of breeding and cultivation. If there could be no a priori proof, no science, Kant realized, then the standard of taste could be no more than "general agreement in an epoch of rational judgment [*Beurteilung*]."[89] Taste, as distinct from appetite, mattered only in society, and therefore, while aesthetic pleasure might be felt in all contexts, it would only call for the reflection and judgment involved in taste in the context of a community which valued such discrimination. This notion of a *sensus communis* remained one of Kant's most important borrowings from the British discussion of taste even in the *Third Critique*.[90]

After his *Prize Essay*, Kant began changing rapidly from the "moral sense" approach of Hutcheson towards his own ultimately rationalist ethics. It would not be too farfetched to see his *Observations on the Feelings of the Beautiful and the Sublime* (1764) as a kind of data-gathering in connection with the new approach to ethical phi-losophy which, in his *Nachricht von der Einrichtung seiner Vorlesungen in dem Winterhalbjahre 1765–1766*, Kant proposed to teach: "eval-uating historically and philosophically what *happens* [with men] before demonstrating what *ought* to happen."[91] There is, in short, an anthropological and moral purpose behind the little essay, far more than an aesthetic one. Kant realized that feelings involved in aesthetic appreciation had significance for his philosophy of morals.

The question remains: What led Kant to concern himself pre-cisely with the two kinds of feeling called "sublime" and "beautiful"? The juxtaposition evokes, of course, not just the general discussion which had been transpiring in Britain since the turn of the century, but the specific title of Edmund Burke's key work, *Enquiry into the Original of our Feelings of the Sublime and the Beautiful,* which ap-peared in English in 1757. The work was only translated in 1773 (by Lessing). Kant did eventually read it, to be sure, because he referred to Burke's work in the *Third Critique,* but there is a good deal of con-troversy over whether the work had any influence on his *Observa-tions.* Theodore Gracyk has most recently argued that if there was any influence, it passed via the mediation of Mendelssohn's writings on Burke.[92] That is, I think, almost certain. Kant knew of Burke's work, and probably found the idea of echoing its title very appealing in terms of the popularity of his own work. But he did not by any means intend to give any serious analysis of Burke's arguments.

Significantly, the sublime receives clear pride of place in the es-say. Kant identifies it with *Rührung,* emotion, and especially move-ment of the mental faculties. More importantly, Kant associates the sublime with "true virtue." He argues that only "that which rests on principles" deserves both the appellations of genuine virtue and sublimity. "As soon as this feeling has arisen to its proper univer-sality, it has become sublime" because "now, from a higher stand-point, it has been placed in its true relation to your total duty."[93] Hence the sublime for Kant was clearly a feeling with moral and spiritual elements.

If Kant was fascinated with the "sublime" in the 1760s, he did not show the same interest in "genius." In the 1760s, Kant found genius neither provocative nor problematic.[94] He accepted it as a term appropriate for the conception of the distinctive practice in the fine arts which corresponded to the term "judgment" *(beur-teilen)* in the appreciation or "criticism" of aesthetic experience.

The key link between them, for Kant, was that they could not be taught.[95] They required a natural talent.[96] Beyond that, Kant merely assimilated the foreign theories of genius, along the lines of Mendelssohn's commentaries, to the *Psychologia empirica* of Baumgarten's *Metaphysica*, which he began to use as his text for courses in the mid 1760s. Baumgarten, in §648 of that work, had already defined *ingenium* as that harmony of all the cognitive faculties which results in a heightening and enlivening of their function.[97] This was the idea from which Kant would always start out in his approach to "genius." Indeed, it would become the key to his whole theory of aesthetic experience.

If the issue of "genius" did not become philosophically significant for Kant until the 1770s, the related issue of "imagination" did, a good deal earlier.[98] From the outset, Kant conceived of aesthetic imagination as a dangerous capacity to project the unreal upon the actual.[99] In *Reflection* 313, from the mid-1760s, Kant wrote: "Imagination [*Einbildung*] is actually the illusion [*Täuschung*] in which one believes he sees something in the object which is actually the creation of our own brains. That is how an enthusiast [*Schwärmer*] comes to believe he can find all his phantoms [*Hirngespinsten*], and every particular sect its dogmas, in the Bible. It is not that they learn these things in the Bible so much as that they read them into it."[100] These associations of imagination with "enthusiasts" (*Schwärmer*) and "phantoms" (*Hirngespinste*) and with religious sectarians reappear across Kant's work for the next several decades, and they form a decisive contextual backdrop for the *Third Critique*.[101] Shaftesbury had formulated the issue for Europe as a whole when he set forth the case for England in his celebrated and widely read *Letter on Enthusiasm* (1708).[102] He recognized in "enthusiasm" not only the creative mystery of genius, but also the dangers of frenzy and madness in religious fanaticism. That set of connections overshadowed many eighteenth-century estimations of genius, and later still the connection of genius with madness became the favorite vein of nineteenth-century thinkers.[103]

The dangers of "enthusiasm" (*Schwärmerei*) were not merely abstract and conjectural for Kant. They were concrete and tangible, personified in one of the most remarkable and disturbing of his personal acquaintances: Hamann. Hamann was an unmitigated "enthusiast," whose powerful religious sensibility merged with a poetic sensitivity and a personal hypochondria to create a charismatic but difficult personality whose influence upon the age was not small.[104] Hamann was able to draw out of Kant's powerful orbit one of his best students, Johann Herder, in the course of the early 1760s, and he communicated many impulses to Herder which Kant found extremely dangerous. That the subversion of Herder from Aufklärung to *Schwärmerei* by Hamann in the early 1760s may have been a contributing factor in Kant's ironic essay, *Träume eines Geistersehers* (1766), is something that has not been sufficiently considered.[105] To be sure, the essay focuses primarily on the fascination for the occultism of Swedenborg, but that was the very stuff Hamann found worthwhile. To be sure, the broader target was metaphysicians without method or self-restraint, who projected images of the natural order into the transcendent. Yet once again, Hamann most emphatically believed in the continuity of realms, and the validity of the most sensual, even sexual experiences as testaments of divinity. If Kant universalized the argument, as he always sought to do, that does not mean that there might not have been a very particular goad to make it. The irritation Hamann and Herder caused in Kant's life and thought proves to be crucial.

Kant warned Herder, in a letter of 1768, against the excesses of "genius."[106] That Kant sensed an excess of "genius" already in the late 1760s is significant. For Kant it was clear enough already in the writings of Edward Young, in Hamann's personality and writings of the 1760s, and in the "enthusiastic" poetry of Friedrich Klopstock.[107] For Kant, the "cult of genius" was already an issue by the late 1760s, before the *Sturm und Drang* had in fact emerged. He was already predisposed to reject it, before it had even begun to intrude on his cultural world, as it would in time.

Kant's empirical skepticism reached its high point with the writing of *Träume eines Geistersehers*. He turned to extreme skepticism not only because of the offensiveness of *Schwärmerei* but also because of the powerful arguments from Hume which Kant received via the new work of Johann Basedow.[108] In the new work, his tone as much as his argument alarmed his friends in the Berlin Aufklärung. Mendelssohn began his correspondence with Kant by expressing concern over this precise issue. Mendelssohn already began to fear that Kant was embarking on a kind of Pyrrhonism which would undermine all rational metaphysics. Kant sought to reassure him that this was not the case. While he believed that all earlier metaphysics, and especially the self-indulgent metaphysics so common in their day, was misguided, he claimed to be committed to metaphysics and proposed to find the correct way to ground it.[109]

Aufklärung vs. Sturm und Drang

The ultimate sense of Aufklärung for Immanuel Kant would be the defense of reason against what he took to be the dangerous impulses of *Sturm und Drang* irrationalism, especially as carried forward by Johann Herder. Herder first entered Kant's life in 1762 as a poor student at the University of Königsberg, disenchanted with medicine and interested in a clerical career. Kant allowed him to attend his lecture courses for free, and he took a particular interest in Herder, allowing him to read several unpublished manuscripts of his own and opening up his library to the young man. Through Kant, Herder came to learn for the first time of such European eminences as Hume, Montesquieu, and Rousseau. Of all this, Herder's description of Kant has given us evidence. But the young Herder was drawn to another mentor at Königsberg, the "Magus of the North," Hamann, both by the charisma of his personality, with its strange blend of mysticism and poetry, and by the skill he had to offer: knowledge of the English language. Studying with Hamann, Herder fell under his spell. Hamann himself responded by putting on paper many of his ideas on themes of mutual interest, in particular poetry, language, genius, and their relations to the mystical-metaphysical ground of being. The work *Aesthetica in nuce*, Hamann's most sustained aesthetic philosophy, was composed while Herder was his student, and presumably with the young man as ideal reader.[110] For Kant, this influence upon the young and talented Herder could only be baleful.

In 1764 Herder left the university; the next year he was ordained and took up the ministry in Riga. But his intellectual interests remained primarily literary, not theological, and he worked up a first critical effort, *Über die neuere deutsche Literatur: Fragmente*, which he published in 1767. This work, which dealt with problems of language and stylistic development in literature, showed clearly the predominance of Hamann over Kant as inspiration: the theme, the texts, and the methods all suggested Hamann's approach and interests. Kant, while he congratulated his former student for his first publication and praised his style by comparing it to Pope, his own favorite poet (but hardly Herder's!), nevertheless warned against some tendencies he saw in the work towards an excessive indulgence of "genius"—i.e., *Schwärmerei*.[111]

But Herder went his own way. In 1769 he left Riga, sailing to France to come to closer grips with the philosophy of the Enlightenment. He swiftly withdrew to Strassburg, where he met a young

→ law student from Frankfurt, Johann Wolfgang von Goethe, in 1770. Together they launched a literary revolution in Germany, the *Sturm und Drang*.[112] Herder composed three crucial essays in literary criticism and aesthetics in the immediate aftermath of the Strassburg friendship. The first dealt with "Ossian" and the question of folk poetry. The second dealt with Shakespeare and his significance for modern literature. These two, together with an essay by Goethe on the Strassburg cathedral and Gothic architecture, were eventually published, in 1773, in a volume entitled *Von deutscher Art und Kunst*, the great manifesto of the *Sturm und Drang*.[113] The third essay was submitted to the Berlin Academy in competition for the prize for the best essay on the origins of language. Herder won the prize. The result of all this was that by the mid 1770s Herder and Goethe, who meanwhile published *Götz von Berlichingen* and the enormously successful *Leiden des jungen Werther*, had become the new lions of German letters.

The incongruity between Herder's career and his publications continued, however. In 1771 he was appointed court preacher in Bückeburg. He held this position until 1776, when Goethe secured him the office of *Generalsuperintendent* of Lutheran clergy in Weimar. This "Bückeburg period" was Herder's most intensely religious, a time when he came closest to the mystical, fundamentalist "enthusiasm" of Hamann, and of a new and notorious friend, Johann Caspar Lavater, a Swiss mystic and student of physiognomy.[114] Lavater had occasioned an enormous scandal in 1769 by challenging Mendelssohn either to refute the arguments of Charles Bonnet for Christianity or to convert.[115] Hamann and Herder defended Lavater in this controversy.[116] Kant, as might be expected, sided with Mendelssohn and Lessing.[117]

X Religion was, from the first, part of the constellation of dangers involved in *Schwärmerei* for Kant. All expressed themselves clearly in the Lavater-Mendelssohn affair. Herder, for Kant, took on all the blemishes of his friends Lavater and Hamann. Indeed Kant found these blemishes in Herder's own works, above all in *Älteste Urkunde des Menschengeschlechts* and, perhaps less immediately, in *Auch eine Philosophie der Geschichte*, both published in 1774. Kant read what Herder wrote. Of that we can be quite confident. We know that he read Herder's first publication, because he wrote to Herder about it. We know for certain that he read *Älteste Urkunde*. We know that he read *Ideen zur Philosophie der Geschichte der Menschheit*. We must assume Kant read almost everything

Herder wrote, and we may therefore connect specific *Reflections* from Kant's "silent decade" with his reading of particular essays by Herder. If we do so, we can weave a story out of Kant's *Reflections* of the 1770s with decisive importance for the contextualization of his *Third Critique*.

The earliest *Reflection* in which we can trace Kant's uneasiness over the new tendencies in German culture which were associated with the *Sturm und Drang*, and hence with Herder, is 767, which dates from 1772–73. It is important for its disparagement of *Rührung* (emotional agitation) and *Reiz* (charm):[118] "Charms and emotions move one against one's will; they are always impudent because they rob others of their peace. (To storm [*stürmen*] against my sensibilities is rude [*unartig*]. I may want to have my emotions stirred, but only in a way in which I keep these under my own control. When that line is crossed over, then others are playing with me rather than letting me into their game . . .)."[119] That this refers to the style of the *Sturm und Drang* is unquestionable. It suggests that Kant knew about the new trends in German literature, but that, as we would expect, he did not like them.[120] Kant claimed that "this sort of disturbance puts many off and is therefore not likely to be popular."[121] He was wrong.

Sturm und Drang surged into high gear in the years 1773–74. Herder published two works of extreme self-indulgence and impudence in which he trod on the toes of eminences and authorities in many fields.[122] Kant, observing this from afar, and himself deeply enmeshed in the most demanding and rigorous philosophical investigations, found the new trend in his former student utterly offensive. The result was great irritation. It expressed itself in a series of *Reflections* and in some heavily ironic correspondence with Hamann. The center of it all was Herder's work *Älteste Urkunde des Menschengeschlechts*, the study of Genesis as a historical source for the origins of the human race. In the work, Herder sought to apply the new historical methodology which he had developed in his essays of the early 1770s, and to follow in the footsteps of the powerful work by Bishop Robert Lowth of England on the poetry of the Hebrews.[123] But he also plunged into some highly self-indulgent tirades against others and glorifications of himself and the mystical insight of which he as a self-proclaimed genius was capable.[124] This grated on the ears not only of those he attacked, but even of those who were his friends.[125]

It was all too much for Kant. In *Reflection* 771 he exploded:

[Whoever sets any sort of intuitions in the place of ordinary reflection by understanding and reason (puts that sort of thing which is a matter strictly of concepts and of which we have absolutely no intuition . . . [lined out]), *raves* [*schwärmt*].] He has to set his feelings, his mental agitations, images, the half-dreamed, half-thought notions which play about in his swirling mind, before the matter at hand [*die Sache selbst*], for these appear to him a unique [*besonderen*] power in himself. The less he can make himself understood, the more he criticizes the limitations of language and of reason and is an enemy of all distinctness because he is entertained not by concepts, not even by images, but by mental agitation. Even writers of feeling actualize their caprices. They may one and all have genius, be full of sensibility and spirit, even some taste, but they are without the dryness and laboriousness and cold-bloodedness of judgment. Everything that is distinct presents itself one aspect after another and then in a concept of the understanding; they want to be able to intuit all aspects at once. Everything mystical is welcome to them; they see unheard-of things in enthusiastic writings or best of all in ancient texts; the newer writing, just because it is precise and sets bonds upon their shrieking spirits, seems to them short-sighted and shallow.[126]

In this *Reflection,* Kant clearly associates genius with *Schwärmerei* and contrasts it with "cold-bloodedness of judgment." The former is self-indulgent and trusts in a mystical-mysterious subjective power rather than in the orderly discrimination of understanding. The former denies the power of language and reason to give clear expressions of truth. It disparages the rationality of the Aufklärung, and opts instead for the esoteric wisdom of occult writing, modern (e.g. Swedenborg) or especially ancient.

Kant identifies himself, in this as in other *Reflections,* with "dryness and laboriousness and cold-bloodedness of judgment" and with the logical approach of the Aufklärung. In *Reflection* 775, for example, Kant despairs of making any of the *Schwärmer* ever attend to a rational argument. "They have to delude themselves and others in order to appear to be fully endowed with insight which only shallow pates may disentangle. They cannot let their genius stiffen and grow cold by tarrying. Flashes of wit are the gift of genius . . . If they were to condescend to join the ranks of cold scholars, they would play a very menial role. But now they can flash like meteors."[127] The edge of resentment on Kant's part is even clearer here than in the *Reflection* we cited in full. The question is: can we specify exactly whom Kant is describing? We can, and it is Herder.

Herder's *Älteste Urkunde* emphasized the vividness and immediacy of the poetic imagery of the Hebrews in the Old Testament as a ground for their greater validity than rational arguments could provide.[128] We can find several revealing *Reflections* from the early 1770s in which Kant shows his extreme displeasure with this idea. In *Reflection* 765, Kant argued that there was a difference between those who preferred the particular and unique and those who preferred the principle of harmony and order. He left no question as to his own allegiance in that question, and then went on to make the contrast in ethnic terms. Northern Europeans, he argued, preferred a more rational approach, while "Oriental peoples" tended to be more sensual.[129] It is clear who these "Oriental people" are from *Reflection* 789:

> Would to God that we could be spared this Oriental wisdom; nothing can be learned from it; the world has received no instruction from them but a kind of mechanical artifice, astronomy and numbers. Once we had Occidental education from the Greeks then we were able to lend some rationality to the Oriental scriptures, but they would never have made themselves understood on their own. To be sure there was once a wise man, who was entirely different from his nation and taught a healthy, practical religion, which, for the sake of the times he had to dress up in images and old parables; but his teachings fell swiftly into hands which spread the whole Oriental nonsense [*den ganzen orientalischen Kram*] over them and once again set a stumbling block for reason.[130]

The editor of Kant's *Reflections on Anthropology*, Erich Adickes, cites two passages from Kant's lectures on anthropology from the early 1770s which supplement this discussion. In one, Kant argued that Oriental people were totally unfit for rational thought, and thus incapable of clarifying morals or law. He therefore warned against the effort of "some, who wish to improve European style by a richness of imagery." They threatened the conceptual rationalism of Europe, and meant to think in images rather than ideas. In the other passage, Kant noted that in Germany there were those who wished to introduce Oriental rhetoric, but he rejected this, because Oriental peoples indulged in "bombastic ideas which went beyond the bounds of reason." Europe was too used to "purity" of thought, too "enlightened." Kant insisted that the whole manner of the west-ern peoples was such that they were more interested in understanding than sensibility. Adickes adds: "There is no doubt [that as the German advocates of this 'Oriental style' Kant] meant Hamann and Herder."[131]

The confirmation of this connection is to be found, finally, in the letters exchanged between Kant and Hamann over Herder's *Älteste Urkunde* in April 1774. Kant's first letter ended with a very ironic appeal:

> If you, dear friend, can find a way to improve my grasp of the main intention of the author I ask that you give me your opinion in a few lines, but if possible in the language of men. For I, poor son of the earth that I am, find myself utterly unconstituted for the godly language of intuitive reason. On the other hand, what one spells out for me with common concepts according to logical rules I can handle perfectly well. Also, I want merely to ascertain the theme of the author, for to comprehend it in its entire worth according to the evidence is not a matter I would dare to undertake.[132]

Hamann answered with equal irony, mocking some of Kant's phrasing in a way which made Herder sound more provocative. Hamann mystified, rather than clarified Herder, and glorified him just for this element of mystification.[133] The result was to estrange Kant still further. In his rejoinder, Kant made a shrewd and telling criticism of the approach to the Old Testament that Herder was advocating:

> If once a religion is placed in the position that critical competence in ancient languages, philology, and antiquarian scholarship are necessary to set the foundations upon which it must build for all times and all peoples, then the person who has familiarized himself best with Greek, Hebrew, Syrian, Arabic, etc., and with the archives of antiquity, will be able to manipulate all orthodox believers about like children, no matter how sourly they react.[134]

This point of view evokes resonances with Lessing's challenge to orthodoxy over the Reimarus fragments, which would rip Germany apart over the issue of theology in the later 1770s. That issue will concern us in detail at a later juncture, but it is crucial to note here that for Kant, the religion controversy, especially as conducted by these strange mystagogue-fundamentalists, Hamann and Lavater and—in his view—Herder, was part and parcel of the *Sturm und Drang*. That connection was reinforced in Kant's mind at just this moment, for he received a typically "enthusiastic" letter from the notorious Lavater, dated that very same day, identifying himself as a good friend of Herder.[135]

Kant's irritation with *Schwärmerei* was shared by others of the Aufklärung. Lessing, for example, was deeply offended by Lavater's treatment of Mendelssohn and devoted the last ten years of his life to a sly campaign to debunk the pretensions of fundamentalists and mystagogues and salvage some rational meaning from the thousand years of Christian civilization in the West.[136] Mendelssohn, obviously, had to deal with the issue, and he did in *Jerusalem*, his great defense of Judaism and Enlightenment and plea for civil rights for Jews.[137] The issue of *Schwärmerei* and its association with genius found massive exposition in the work of a Zürich professor, Leonhard Meister, *Über die Schwärmerei* (2 vols.; 1775–77). Meister connected passion with imagination as the source of the frenzy of visionaries and poets.[138] Back in England, where the concern about "enthusiasm" dated all the way back to the mid-seventeenth century, the "cult of genius" had drawn similar criticism, and a more rational approach to genius developed. Perhaps the most important figure in this effort was Alexander Gerard. He sought to avoid the "enthusiastic" theory of genius by offering a more mundane version. In his prize-winning *Essay on Taste* he had already addressed the question of genius. But in a series of supplementary lectures in 1758–59 he elaborated on his interpretation. Both works made their way into German translation, and it is highly probable that Kant read them in the same years that we are examining. The *Essay on Taste* was translated in 1766; the *Essay on Genius* appeared in German translation in 1776 and we know with certainty that Kant read it just about as soon as it arrived. He was also reading the new translation of Burke's *Enquiry*, with its no-nonsense sensationalist approach to human emotions, for Lessing's translation appeared in 1773. Armed with this level-headed interpretation, Kant set about devising a theory which could explain the excesses of the *Stürmer*, on the one hand, and give adequate recognition to true genius, on the other. The result was a theory of genius which asserted the firm conviction that genius had no place in science.[139] We will take up that theory in its final form, as articulated in the *Third Critique*, later in this work. What is important to grasp is that the exclusion of science from genius was not a disparagement of science but rather of genius, and was grounded in Kant's disdain for the *Sturm und Drang*. That became absolute in his mind after a second, even more extreme bout of anger at Herder, this time from the very late 1770s.

We must recall how strenuously Kant was working across this "silent decade," how long it was taking for him to come up with his new "critique" of metaphysics and morals, which he kept promising his correspondents would soon be at hand. We must recall the epochal nature of the work Kant was accomplishing, then with a Kantian eye survey the literary scene of the late 1770s and see what Germany found exciting. Take, for example, Lavater's *Physiologische Fragmente* (1775–78), with contributions from Goethe and Herder. Wieland's new journal, *Teutsche Merkur,* established in 1773, actually credited such authors as Goethe and Lenz with the renovation of tragedy and comedy in the German language. Justus Möser had the temerity to defend such literature against the criticism of the king of Prussia. People flocked to Frankfurt to meet the "universal genius" Goethe as though he were Mohammed in Mecca. Closer to home, take the questions posed by the Berlin Academy. The topic for the prize essay in 1775 was: "What is Genius, of what elements is it composed, and do these permit themselves to be distinguished within it?"[140] Sulzer posed it, after having given his own *schwärmerisch* answer in his *Allgemeine Theorie der schönen Künste* (2 vols., 1771–74), and it was an obvious opportunity for the *Stürmer* to advertise themselves. For this prize Herder composed his essay, *Von Erkennen und Empfinden,* published in Riga in 1778. The winner, however, was Johann Eberhard, an orthodox Wolffian.[141] Still, the year before Herder had won his second prize from the academy in the decade; the theme had been on the decadence of taste in peoples.[142] The *Sturm und Drang* was, as far as Kant could tell, continuing along its mad course.[143]

Herder's prize essay submission, *Von Erkennen und Empfinden,* and a subsequent essay, "Über den Einfluß der schönen in die höheren Wissenschaften," which appeared in 1779, had to do with philosophy. They argued against dividing human experience into abstract faculties and insisted upon the wholeness which art and poetry above all evoked.[144] In these essays Kant could not help but read an attack on his concept of philosophy and hence on himself. In his *Reflections,* Kant defended himself:

> Herder is very much against the misuse of reason through an utterly abstract kind of thinking, in that one thereby neglects

the *concrete*. That was the habit of the ancients in their natural philosophy. But the general is not always merely abstract; rather, there are many things which are independent universals. That is the nature of all judgments which even *in concreto* are not dependent on experience, but where such judgments of experience themselves require *principles* a priori. Here there is no place for the *concrete*.[145]

In yet another *Reflection*, Kant continued his attack: "Herder corrupts minds because he gives them encouragement to make universal judgments using merely empirical reason without any thorough consideration of principles."[146] This was the Kant of the *Critique of Pure Reason* writing, and his disdain was grounded in a philosophical sophistication Herder could never approach.

Having rebutted the criticism of his own position, Kant undertook a sustained debunking of the weakness of the approach fostered by Herder. "The adepts of genius, who must lay claim to genius and can only count on the approval of people of genius, are those who cannot communicate but must count for comprehension only upon a communal, sympathetic inspiration . . . The artifice consists of scraps [*Brocken*] of science and learning sewn together with the prestige of an original spirit, criticism of others, and a deeply hidden religious sense, to give the laundry [*Gewäsche*] dignity."[147] Kant denied that one could have intellectual intuitions, and he denied that images served better than universal concepts. "There are only two sources of valid insights: rational science or critical clarity. And then someone comes along with a thrown-together bag of scraps from both, without method and science, but animated [*beseelt*] with a spirit of inspiration. All such enthusiasts talk religion."[148] Reason was the only vehicle for true communication, for general validity. It was human nature to grasp the particular only through the universals of reason. For Kant, the pride of Aufklärung was its advancement of reason, not its indulgence in occult symbolism.[149] Authentic genius sought universality of access and meaning. Those who insisted upon mystification, who refused to be examined in the clear light of reason, were not practicing genius but illusion.[150]

Kant carried this criticism forward into a series of *Reflections* on the new literary style. He argued that Klopstock, for him the first of these *schwärmerisch* authors in Germany, had not nearly the authentic genius of a Milton, and could easily be imitated.[151] On the other hand, he conceded that *schwärmerisch* authors could be of value—

such authors as Rousseau and Plato, for example. Even Lavater could be used by a critical mind to indicate the excesses which more discreet believers might conceal from scrutiny in their orthodoxy. But to be useful, they had at least to be wrestling with an important matter.[152] On the other hand, what did not contribute to entertainment (fine art), invention (technology), or understanding (scholarship) should not be considered a matter of genius, but rather of the "fantastical" [*Phantasterei*]. That style Kant equated with the alchemical and mystical writings of Jacob Böhme.[153]

Kant linked this criticism with his longer-standing suspicion of imaginative excess—fantasy—as the phrase *Phantasterei* suggests. In several *Reflections* from the late 1770s, he returned to the question of imagination and fantasy, stressing this connection with *Schwärmerei*. Above all, he cautioned against the loss of self-control which indulgence in fantasy ("ecstasy") could entail. "One should never be beside oneself, but rather in *possession* of oneself [*Man muß niemals außer sich, sondern bei sich selbst sein.*]"[154] He made a set of associations with this excessive fantasy: with hypochondriacs, with the superstitious, with Oriental peoples. Hamann had to figure in that set of associations.[155] For Kant, imagination had to be disciplined if it were to be productive. Otherwise one risked losing track of the actual by crediting the unreal.[156]

The volume of observations on these matters, the consistency of the language which he used, and the vehemence of Kant's commentary suggest the seriousness with which Kant responded to Herder and the *Sturm und Drang*. And yet all this was in private. Publicly he said nothing across the entire decade of the 1770s. He patiently went on building his world-historical monument of reason. But when he published it, no one cared. Herder remained the darling child of the age. And that was the last straw. Kant was ready for a public showdown.

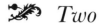

Two

KANT'S RETURN TO AESTHETICS: TRANSCENDENTAL ARGUMENTS AND THE "CRITIQUE OF TASTE"

To situate the *Third Critique* within the "critical philosophy," it is necessary to establish how it relates to the *First Critique*'s articulation of the limits of philosophical reasoning and its criteria for valid knowledge. There are those who, as Mary Gregor has put it, suspect that "Kant sometimes writes, in the third *Critique*, as if he had not read the *Critique of Pure Reason*."[1] In the light of such observations, it is important to consider whether the *Third Critique* does flagrantly violate the constraints of the *First Critique;* i.e., are its innovations contradictory or developmental? To be specific, was Kant justified in conceiving of a transcendental principle a priori for *noncognitive* human experience? That was the whole idea behind the attempt at a "Critique of Taste." And, with his strong emphasis on a subjective judgment apart from the categories, was Kant's very conception of a "judgment of taste" in utter violation of his rules for the possibility of experience? These two questions pose the immanent philosophical problem of Kant's decision to compose the *Third Critique*.

Moreover, as he wrote on it, he came to conceive a philosophical viewpoint for the *Third Critique* which extended—and therefore modified—the cognitive theory of the *First Critique:* the theory of reflective judgment.[2] This was the essence of the "cognitive turn" that reshaped the "Critique of Taste" into the full-fledged *Critique of Judgment*. To grasp the evolution of the *Third Critique*, accordingly, it is inevitable that we must consider it in relation to its predecessors. This chapter will consider the problem of transcendental argumentation. The next will explore the problem of the phenomenology of subjective consciousness. Later, in part 2, we will take up the "cognitive turn" and the theory of reflective judgment.

X   [Kant's return to aesthetics in 1787 had both a contextual and an immanent origin.] The contextual origin lay in Kant's hostility to Herder and the *Sturm und Drang*. Kant had a score to settle with them on the question of art and genius, as we have seen. The immanent origin lay in a crucial innovation in Kant's theory of transcendental argumentation. When he took up the "Critique of Taste" in September 1787, Kant returned to a question he had judged fruit-
→ less in the *Critique of Pure Reason* of 1781: [could taste be grounded transcendentally?] For some time Kant had not believed taste eligible for inclusion within the conspectus of critical philosophy because it seemed inevitably empirical. He stated this clearly in a footnote to the "Transcendental Aesthetic":

> The Germans are the only people who currently make use of the word 'aesthetic' in order to signify what others call the critique of taste. This usage originated in the abortive attempt made by Baumgarten, that admirable analytical thinker, to bring the critical treatment of the beautiful under rational principles, and so to raise its rules to the rank of a science. But such endeavors are fruitless. The said rules or criteria are, as regards their sources, merely empirical, and consequently can never serve as *a priori* laws by which our judgment of taste must be directed.[3]

X   But by 1787 Kant had changed his mind. The discovery of a transcendental grounding for aesthetics finally set Kant free from Kames and British empiricism and allowed him to incorporate taste into his critical philosophy. That is reflected in the changes he introduced into this footnote in his revision of the *First Critique*. It is reflected even more clearly in a very famous letter.

In December of 1787, Immanuel Kant wrote to the man who had successfully popularized his philosophy in Germany, Karl Leonhard Reinhold, announcing himself at work on a new study, a "Critique of Taste." That letter is a crucial document in the history of the genesis of the *Third Critique*, and it can be used to establish not only the nature of the original impulse of that work, but also the novelty of its argument. Even the context of the letter is of interest, but first let us focus upon its text.

> My inner conviction grows, as I discover in working on different topics that not only does my system remain self-consistent but also, when sometimes I cannot see the right way to investigate a certain subject, I find that I need only look back at the

general picture of the elements of knowledge, and of the mental powers pertaining to them, in order to discover elucidations I had not expected. I am now at work on the critique of taste, and I have discovered a kind of a priori principle different from those heretofore observed. For there are three faculties of the mind: the faculty of cognition, the faculty of feeling pleasure and displeasure, and the faculty of desire. In the *Critique of Pure* (theoretical) *Reason,* I found a priori principles for the first of these, and in the *Critique of Practical Reason,* a priori principles for the third. I tried to find them for the second as well, and though I thought it impossible to find such principles, the systematic nature of the analysis of the previously mentioned faculties of the human mind allowed me to discover them . . . so that now I recognize three parts of philosophy, each of which has its own a priori principles. We can now, therefore, securely determine the compass of knowledge, which is possible in this way, as including the three departments of theoretical philosophy, teleology, and practical philosophy, of which, it is true, the second will be found the poorest in a priori grounds of determination. I hope by Easter to be ready with this part of philosophy, under the name of the *Critique of Taste,* which is already in writing, but not quite prepared for the press.[4]

At the outset of the *Third Critique,* then, Kant was seeking a priori principles for the "faculty of feeling pleasure and displeasure" even though for some time he had "thought it impossible to find such principles." Kant claimed to have now found "a kind of a priori principle different from those heretofore observed." And he came to it, significantly, via "the systematic nature of the analysis of the . . . faculties of the human mind." Since his system was "self-consistent," he could trust it to aid him "when sometimes I cannot see the right way to investigate a certain subject." It would present him with "elucidations I had not expected." What aided him, specifically, was "the general picture of the elements of knowledge, and of the mental powers pertaining to them." The idea of faculties of mind and the idea that there are different kinds of a priori principles, of which the sort he had now before him was unique, prove crucial to Kant's procedure in late 1787, at the genesis of the "Critique of Taste."

To grasp how he had come to this new turn in his thinking, we must consider what Kant meant in the *First Critique* by "transcendental philosophy." ["Transcendental argument"] has been the storm center of controversy in Kant scholarship for the past thirty years.[5] There has never been anything approaching consensus on these issues. Dieter Henrich pointed this out eloquently in one of the most widely acclaimed efforts to achieve coherence.[6] Many years later, Karl Ameriks richly documented the variety of views that still remained.[7] We are no closer to closure today. A part of this problem is, no doubt, obscurity in Kant's text. Another part is the inherent difficulty of the task he set himself. But there is a third difficulty, which is the disposition to treat Kant in terms of contemporary philosophical concerns and standards, and thus to lose any hermeneutical sense of what Kant himself sought to achieve. In this study the philological-historical question takes precedence over the epistemological one. Methodologically, we must try to establish what sense *Kant* had of his terms, his project, and his result before we begin to assess their "correctness" by contemporary standards.[8]

Kant's Pre-Critical Notion of "Discursiveness"

Kant broke with Baumgarten by insisting upon a dichotomy between the logical and the aesthetical, between understanding and sense, between concept and intuition. As sensibility and understanding were his terms for the "faculties" constituted in this duality, intuition and concept were his terms for the specific content which pertained to each, and aesthetics and logic were the modes or processes which obtained in these faculties in relation to their specific contents. For Kant, the distinction of sensibility from understanding was not one of degree, as in school philosophy, but one of kind. Sensibility was particular, while understanding was universal. Sensibility was subjective or private, while understanding was objective and generally valid. Finally and crucially, sensibility was passive in contrast to the activity of the understanding. This discrimination was to be the foundation of the entire critical philosophy, Kant's principle of "discursiveness."

Baumgarten had contended that a different criterion of objective validity could be applied to sensibility: individual wholeness (coordination, "extensive clarity") rather than logical articulation (subordination, "intensive clarity"). What Baumgarten sought to interpret as an objective, if inferior manifestation, Kant insisted upon reading merely subjectively. Aesthetics had to do with intuitions as presence in sense. Objectivity (universal validity) belonged exclusively to the other side of the duality, the side of understanding, concept, and logic, and so aesthetics by definition was a subjective mode.[9] At first, Kant had tried to operate with the language of Baumgarten, using "extensive" versus "intensive" clarity.[10] Yet clarity and distinctness did not express the aesthetic versus logical distinction sharply enough.[11] Both understanding and sensibility could be confused. Both understanding and sensibility could be distinct. "As to distinctness, it is perfectly compatible with intuition. For distinctness has to do with the differentiation of the manifold in a whole representation. In so far as these pieces for cognition can be thought through universal concepts, distinctness is a consequence of reason; if it occurs through particular [concepts], then it is a form of sensibility. The first occurs through *subordination*, the second through *coordination*."[12] Baumgarten's distinction between "extensive" and "intensive" clarity did not help much. Kant quickly threw off the whole language of clarity and distinctness as distracting, though he retained the contrast between coordination and subordination.[13]

Leibniz's *Nouveaux essais*, which finally appeared in print in 1765, helped Kant sort out from Baumgarten's approach the sound elements in a cognitive approach to sensibility by stimulating Kant's thought toward two new distinctions. Logically and ontologically, what mattered far more than clarity and distinctness was the distinction of matter from form. Epistemologically, what mattered most was the distinction between active understanding and passive sensibility. Kant took the act of form-giving as the essence of understanding or reason. This was the great legacy of Leibniz to German school philosophy. Once Kant had adopted the two discriminations of passivity/activity and matter/form, he was in a position to make a much more complete and powerful account of the process of representation.

Kant argued that all form resulted from spontaneity, from "the soul's own activity."[14] He distinguished sharply between the mere givenness of material in sensation and the active representation of an appearance as a figure [*Gestalt*] in space and time by developing the two technical terms *Empfindung* (sensation) and *Erscheinung* (appearance).[15] His first impulse was to discriminate the subjectivity of *Empfindung* from the objectivity of *Erscheinung*.[16] "Sensation" referred strictly to a subjective state, while "appearance" involved the reference to an object as the putative source of the passive impressions.[17] But this original distinction, which came later and more effectively to be formulated as that between *Gefühl* and *Sinn*, quickly developed into one between matter and form.

Not only were sensations subjective, in that they entailed passive responses of the subject, but they provided merely the "matter" for, and were not themselves representations of, objects.[18] Before they could be thought about, they had to be formed, shaped.[19] Only that process of forming them into representations-of-objects resulted in *Erscheinungen*. An *Erscheinung* differed from an *Empfindung* not only in that it referred to an object, but in that it was formed into a determinate figure [*Gestalt*]. Kant equated that formal dimension of sensibility with *Anschauung*, or intuition. He wrote: "Sensibility can be considered in terms of its matter or its form. The matter in sensibility is sensation, and its faculty is sense; the form of sensibility is appearance, and its faculty is intuition."[20]

But of even greater significance to him was the distinction of activity from passivity in mental process. Within sensibility itself he tried to discriminate, along with form and matter, passivity and activity. This he did in the contrast between *Sinn* and *Einbildung*: "Our sensible faculties are either senses or formative powers [*Sinne oder bildende Kräfte*]."[21] What Kant was groping toward was a sense of form-giving in which beauty was a "subjective principle" which conformed to the "laws of intuitive knowledge." He argued that the form provided by intuition could not be reduced to or derived from the form provided by reason. Two equally formal approaches could be taken to the "matter" provided in a whole representation of an object, i.e., an *Erscheinung*. One could analyze it in terms of its elements in so far as they were universal, i.e., common to other objects, or in terms of the specific bond among them in a particular entity. The first operation would be a logical one, involving subordination, the second an aesthetic one, involving coordination.[22] Both, however, would be impositions of "form."

The so-called "subjective deduction" in the *First Critique* was the result of a prolonged effort to discriminate the preconceptual synthesis associated with imagination. Kant was already trying to differentiate the subjective process of individual concept formation in *Reflections* dated around 1769, hence prior to any influence by the psychology of the "three-fold synthesis" of Tetens.[23] Kant identified a representation eligible for judgment with several features. First, it had to be synthetic, though not through reason, hence it had to unify a manifold of sense.[24] It created a shape or figure [*Gestalt*] which involved "not only the form of the object according to the relations of space in the appearance, but also the matter, i.e. sensation (color)."[25] Second, it had to be "intuitive." Kant did not define this term. Third, it had to be immediate in terms of the proportionality of the sensations. Kant's phenomenology of subjective consciousness clearly recognized the presence to consciousness of representations [*Vorstellungen*] which could not yet be considered cognitions [*Erkenntnisse*].[26]

Kant broke down the process of representation into a series of operations: differentiation [*Abstechung*] of the manifold; comprehension [*Begreiflichkeit*]; synthesis [*Zusammennehmung*]; and discrimination from other possibilities [*praecisio*].[27] He argued that the synthesis he described as *Zusammennehmung* was not yet sufficient to provide "determinate form" [*bestimmte Form*].[28] Rather, this required what he called *Zusammenordnung*, that is, a "connection by coordination, and not of subordination [via reason]." This connection by coordination had to take place in terms of the form of space in intuition. "All objects can be known sensibly or via intuition only in a given figure [*Gestalt*]. Other appearances cannot form an object, but are merely [subjective] changes [involving succession in time]."[29] But Kant had yet a further level of synthesis: *Zusammenstimmung*. It had two forms: parts to a whole, or ground to consequence. The second, he argued, was a matter of subordination. The former, while clearly a matter of coordination, could very well fall under the logical rubric of disjunctive judgments as well. Already in the late 1760s, then, Kant conceived of the building of a particular representation-of-the-object in terms of three stages: a material one, *Zusammennehmung* or the apprehension of a manifold of sensation; a formal one, *Zusammenordnung* or the representation of this manifold as a *Gestalt* or figure in space (and time); and a rational one, *Zusammenstimmung*, which involved conceptions of a cognitive-evaluative nature.[30]

Kant wished to associate this form-giving in intuition with the objectivity of the representation, i.e., its reference to the object and hence its validity. He was moving toward the notion that objective validity was grounded in the form which the mind, either in sensibility through intuition or in understanding through concepts, applied to the merely given in sensation. In conceiving of intuition strictly as the form of sensibility, Kant was in fact detaching it from its function as the source of objective actuality, or reality. That remained inertly given in sensation. We have come upon one of the fundamental problems of Kant's commitment to "discursiveness."

"Discursiveness" entailed three difficulties from the outset which would beset Kant throughout the so-called "critical" period of his philosophy. First, Kant had committed himself to the idea that form-giving was an active process, associated with the spontaneity of the subject, hence associated with the understanding. Yet he had developed a theory of intuition as similarly form-giving and spontaneous, but within sensibility. As formal and active, intuition did not fit comfortably into the passive concept of sensibility. Was it part of the passivity of sensibility or part of the activism of understanding? Let us call this the problem of imagination.

The second difficulty presented by discursiveness is, if sensibility and understanding are different in kind, how can understanding determine the particulars given in sensation with logical and especially with ontological necessity? How are objective actuality, that mere, "material" givenness in sensation, and objective validity, that formal construction under rule by the understanding, to be unified? *Could* reason have a "real use"? This is the problem of transcendental deduction. In the year 1772, under the impact of the full radicalism of Hume's skepticism, Kant recognized the enormity of this problem. It would take him a decade to formulate a position on it in the *Critique of Pure Reason*.[31]

But there is a third problem which has to do with a certain duplicity in Kant's notion of subjectivity: passive/active; private/general; singular/universal. Kant had a very strong penchant to think of these three discriminations as interchangeable. But they are not. Once again, his notion of intuition evidences this. There is only one space, for everyone, and necessarily. It is singular, not a composite, but it is an all-encompassing totality.[32] It resides in sensibility, the ostensibly subjective and private aspect of human experience, but it is not subjective or private. That raises the question: How is it that everything subjective is not necessarily private? Conversely, what sort of general concept can one develop to discuss what is utterly particular and private? Is there even a subjective access to such matters, i.e., can they be thought? Let us call this the problem of subjectivity.

These three epistemological problems drove Kant to a continual reworking of his phenomenology of consciousness not only up to the *First Critique* but onward through the *Third*. It would be an utter misapprehension to believe that Kant considered all the epistemological—or, more broadly, cognitive—issues in his philosophy to have been resolved in the first edition of the *Critique of Pure Reason* in 1781. Rather, he continued to reflect and to revise over the entire balance of his philosophical career, and some of the revisions proved major. The *Third Critique* represented a major effort to resolve these epistemological difficulties. Kant concentrated, in his "critical" breakthrough, on resolving the problem of the transcendental deduction. As a consequence, his solution left unresolved several subtle difficulties in his notions of imagination and intuition and others, more blatant, in his notion of subjectivity.

The "Critical" Breakthrough: Transcendental Philosophy

Kant explained what he meant by "transcendental philosophy" in the Introduction to the *First Critique*: "I entitle *transcendental* all knowledge which is occupied not so much with objects as with the mode of our knowledge of objects insofar as this mode of knowledge is to be possible *a priori*."[33] And in the *Prolegomena* he elaborated: "the word *transcendental* . . . for me never means a reference of our cognition to things, but only to our faculty of cognition."[34] In both contexts Kant stresses the *procedural,* not merely the objective character of knowledge: *how,* not just *what* we (can) know.[35] The question is not simply: "What is an object?" but "How can our experience of the object be valid?" That, Kant insists, can only be answered by considering the mind's active participation in knowledge, the noetic, not simply the noematic dimension: "the *mode* of our knowledge . . . insofar as [it] is to be possible *a priori*." It is this active, procedural dimension that is the domain of "transcendental philosophy."[36]

The mind takes an active role in cognition, but it does not always do so through a self-conscious choice. This necessity which is prior to volition and yet inherent in subjectivity is Kant's most distinctive philosophical discovery, which might be called the "involuntary spontaneity" of the subject in experience.[37] According to Kant, the subject is active in cognition, as against the viewpoint of empiricism (but not arbitrary, as against the view of skepticism.) To the extent that a subject necessarily structures perception in a manner beyond conscious control and hence antecedent volition, there is more to subjectivity than one is immediately aware of.[38] Philosophically it is possible to account for that involuntary spontaneity and to show its necessary rationality. That is precisely what transcendental arguments seek to do.

The subject may perform this reconstruction from the vantage of a higher level of self-consciousness. However, one will never be in a position voluntarily to execute those involuntary acts of spontaneity at the ground of his consciousness, and thus that aspect of his own subjectivity will always remain objective to him, though still spontaneous vis-à-vis the object of consciousness. This is what Kant meant by "transcendental idealism."[39] In the B-version of the

"Transcendental Deduction" he put it in perhaps the most straight-forward manner: "This peculiarity of our understanding, that it can produce *a priori* unity of apperception solely by means of the categories, and only by such and so many, is as little capable of further explanation as why we have just these and no other functions of judgment, or why space and time are the only forms of our possible intuition."[40] While the subject may comprehend the transcendental structures of his own subjectivity, he is not in a position to change them or to produce them by an act of will. This primordial givenness is a dimension of reality which man can only recognize, not command. It is for the philosopher to speculate and if possible to explain persuasively the foundations of such activity.

Transcendental philosophy starts from the fact of experience, the act of empirical judgment. Given that there is experience, i.e., that a judgment gets made claiming objective reference, what can be done to establish its objective validity in terms of the noetic procedure that it logically must presuppose in light of the discursiveness of human nature? Kant wanted to secure the coherence of empirical experience through the idea of conceptual determination: the understanding imposed categorial "form" through judgment upon sensory "matter" and constituted experience as objectively valid. The alternative to be eliminated was some "stream of consciousness" which really offered no security against disintegration into "blooming, buzzing confusion" and dissolution of any cognitive identity, i.e., coherent experience.

Kant hardly meant that every empirical judgment had to be true. He merely wished to establish that a judgment could make a claim to truth based upon criteria that were validating. These criteria, the categories, determined with necessity and universality the form of all possible judgments about an object-in-general (*Objekt*).[41] This warrant had to be shown to apply to the only actual content humans experienced—sensory intuition in space and time—and hence to actual objects (*Gegenstände*). How categories of pure understanding could apply with validity to sensory intuition was *the* question of transcendental philosophy.[42] The problem lay precisely in the separation of these two elements (concepts and intuitions) in two distinct faculties. That made "transcendental reflection" indispensable.

Kant claimed in his "Transcendental Deduction" that the constitution of the object-in-general in a "transcendental synthesis," whose spontaneity was distinctly *involuntary*, provided the necessary foundation for all voluntary acts of synthesis: empirical judgments with claims to validity.[43] A "pure" transcendental synthesis must be presupposed as the foundation for any and every act of empirical judgment.[44] This "original synthesis" is not the act or invention of the empirical subject. It is part of subjectivity, to be sure, but it is *involuntary subjectivity*. But Kant is interested, beyond the establishment of this *originary* synthesis, in the conscious act of (empirical) judgment. That "applies" the categories, in the sense of finding instantiations in a "syllogistic" rather than "judgmental" sense of subsumption under rule.[45]

How can we establish that the pure concepts of the understanding, as categories, have objective validity with reference to sensibility? While this was the particular focus of the chapter entitled "Transcendental Deduction," the whole *First Critique* is Kant's answer, and only the whole *Critique* could be an answer, because it alone offered scope to establish the "transcendental" or "critical" consequences of discursiveness for knowledge. Nonetheless, the kernel of the "critical" philosophy has always been found in the "deduction." No piece of modern philosophical writing has provoked so much study and controversy. Many contemporary interpreters claim it impossible to *find* a deduction there.[46] Part of the difficulty, as Henrich and others have noted, is that Kant's concept of deduction is not ours; it had a definite historical source that colored its usage.[47]

Contextual reference also clarifies the question of "empirical psychology" and its relation to transcendental philosophy. There were, for Kant, two ways of going at mental activity and the concepts which were its elements. One, which he designated "psychological," traced the historical evolution of empirical concepts in consciousness.[48] For Kant, Locke was the primary model of this. One could easily add Hume (and Tetens in Germany).[49] The other way sought not the origins or development of a concept but the warrant or right to it—its validity. That was the properly "transcendental" project.[50]

We thus need to be clear about the meaning of "a priori" and the purpose of transcendental philosophy. A priori means not derivative from experience. It does not mean completely apart from it. Consequently, a transcendental argument is, as Ameriks argues, necessarily a *regressive* argument, not a "presuppositionless deduction."[51] It cannot be, nor did Kant ever intend to make such a claim, however much some interpreters ascribe this intention to "transcendental arguments" and Kant's in particular.[52] A transcendental argument sets out *from* experience, but that does not—

for Kant—in any way reduce its a priori validity to something "empirical" or a posteriori. To be sure, if the philosophical inquiry is to establish anything with necessity and universality—which is what Kant meant by the term "a priori"—then it will have to achieve a purity of articulation which will not depend for its cogency upon anything empirical. Everything hinges on exactly what is meant by "purity" and the "empirical," however. We cannot even begin to discuss the validity of knowledge without acknowledging that empirical experience occurs. Philosophy cannot sensibly question the occurrence of experience, but only whether it can be reckoned valid knowledge.[53] Kant proposed to avoid taking what any specific empirical experience concretely entailed—its "matter"—into account in explaining how it was possible in general for experience to occur. To explain why, or how it is possible that, empirical experience can occur, we must look to the "form" of that experience, to its structure.[54] A "pure" analysis is not one which has no connection whatever with empirical experience. How can it be, when it is supposed to ground the validity of that experience? Rather, it is one which is not dependent on the content of any particular experience for its argument.

That this was exactly what he meant by the crucial term "pure," Kant explained in an essay, composed in 1787, which he sent under the cover of the very letter to Reinhold we began by analyzing. He offered his explanation of the term as a supplement to Reinhold's widely recognized exposition of his philosophy, the *Briefe über die Kantischen Philosophie*. Indeed, Kant's letter and the essay enclosed with it were his public acknowledgment of Reinhold's contribution in popularizing Kant's complicated system. Hence the observation on "purity" in the essay should be taken as canonical. Kant wrote:

> I would like to take this opportunity to devote just a little attention to the charge that ostensible contradictions have been discovered in a work of considerable length [the second edition of the *First Critique*], before [the discoverer] had a real grasp of the whole . . . [This critic charged that] in the first place I said those cognitions a priori are *pure,* with which absolutely nothing empirical is *mixed* [*denen gar nichts Empirisches beigemischt ist*], and as an example of the opposite presented the proposition: all that changes has a cause. By contrast . . . [a few pages later] I present this same proposition as an example of a pure a priori cognition, that is, one which is not dependent on anything empirical [*die von nichts Empirisches* abhängig

ist]—two distinct meanings of the term *pure*, of which, however, in the whole work I dealt exclusively with the latter.[55]

"Pure" transcendental philosophy was not dependent on the empirical, but it was not utterly unrelated to it. Kant claimed that the method he pursued in the *Second Critique* was in fact identical to that of the *First:* "We come to know pure practical laws in the same way we know pure theoretical principles, by attending to the necessity with which reason prescribes them to us and to the elimination from them of all empirical conditions, which reason directs. The concept of a pure will arises from the former, as the consciousness of a pure understanding from the latter."[56] The mark of rational determination as such is the modality of necessity. In all mental acts, the presence of this modality is the crucial indicator of an a priori transcendental principle.[57] Kant believed that without this primordial and determining modality of necessity, even what we assessed cognitively could never advance beyond Hume's conception of contingent-customary association, i.e., it would remain merely assertoric, never apodictic. In the case of cognitive experience, Kant argued in the *First Critique,* without this modality in fact any possibility of experience—even Hume's—became incoherent. That was the only sense in which Kant could and did "answer" Hume.[58]

Hence transcendental philosophy had to grasp the capacities of "pure reason." Kant wished to introduce as the decisive distinction between his philosophy and all other philosophy the claim that his was not grounded on mere general logic but rather on what he called "transcendental logic." General logic, Kant insisted, amplifying a point first made by Crusius against the rationalist-essentialist tradition in Germany, could never proceed from the mere form of the judgments to any assertion about the actuality *(Wirklichkeit)* of the terms in those judgments, for general logic was only a set of rules about the forms of judgments, not a vehicle for the establishment of actuality.[59] Transcendental logic, he asserted, dealt with the problem of synthetic judgments a priori, and synthetic judgments a priori had as their specific difference from judgments in general logic precisely their entailment of existence.[60] General logic could not in any way yield ontology.[61]

Existence is extra-logical: *onto*logical. To enter that domain, philosophy had not only to reckon with the *forms* of judgments (the *logical* use of reason) but to discriminate the two kinds of *matter* (concepts and intuitions) in judgments by tracing them to their disparate *sources*—i.e., the cognitive faculties—in order to establish the possibility of their synthesis in valid knowledge (the *real* use of reason). Kant conceived transcendental reflection to entail not simply the comparison of concepts with other concepts—not merely the logic of judgments—but comparison with the faculties which constituted their possibility.

well...

> Reflection *(reflexio)* does not concern itself with objects themselves with a view to deriving concepts from them directly, but is that state of mind in which we first set ourselves to discover the subjective conditions under which [alone] we are able to arrive at concepts. It is the consciousness of the relation of given representations to our different sources of knowledge; and only by way of such consciousness can the relation of the sources of knowledge to one another be rightly determined. Prior to all further treatment of our representations, this question must first be asked: In which of our cognitive faculties are our representations connected together?[62]

The passage deserves the most careful exegesis. "Reflection" is termed a "state of mind" [*Zustand des Gemütes*]. In that state, Kant continues, "we set ourselves to discover"—hence he is describing an intentional act, or, in his own language, a *Handlung*, which implies conscious (and presumably rational) choice—"the subjective conditions [*subjectiven Bedingungen*] under which [alone] we are able to arrive at concepts."[63] Kant explains that reflection provides the "consciousness of the relation of given representations to our different [faculties] of knowledge [*Erkenntnisvermögen*]." That is, reflection seeks to know whence a given representation arises, by reference to the faculty which is its "source." That process is essential, Kant continues, because it is "only by way of such consciousness" that philosophy can then correctly establish the essential transcendental issue of "the relation of the [faculties] of knowledge to one another."

Kant referred to this process of reflection in his letter to Reinhold when he wrote of "the general picture of the elements of knowledge, and of the mental powers pertaining to them."[64] For Kant these were not elements of a "merely empirical" psychology. They were fundamental structures of mental activity apart from which it was impossible even to begin to philosophize. That subjective conditions are the only basis upon which we can arrive at philosophical knowledge is one of the most important principles of transcendental philosophy. Only on this basis is it possible to appraise the validity of knowledge, or secure a *real* use of reason. I take this discussion to be among the most straightforward and decisive Kant ever made regarding the procedure of transcendental philosophy, and therefore as decisive for the interpretation not only of the *First Critique* but also of the later ones. Ours is a *determinate* noetic structure, discursiveness; and that determinacy must figure as the foundation of the epistemological enterprise. It is discursiveness that makes human knowledge problematic. It is discursiveness, then, that a transcendental argument must reckon with if "objective validity" is to be secured.

This project could not dispense with reference to faculties of cognition. Discursiveness cannot be articulated except in terms of faculties of mind and without discursiveness there can be neither a "transcendental" problem nor a transcendental solution. If *pure* concepts sufficed, the "Metaphysical Deduction" would have been complete—and, moreover, the whole Kantian project would have been irrelevant: Leibniz, Wolff, or Baumgarten could just as well serve. Nor could strict empirical psychology suffice, or Hume would have been the finish of philosophy. The best expositions of Kant's "transcendental deduction," therefore, recognize that there are two problems superimposed upon one another: first, how the objective validity of the categories in cognitive judgments is to be established; but second, how synthesis between the faculty of understanding and the faculty of sensibility is to be possible.[65]

The interpretation of transcendental procedure that makes sense in the light of all three *Critiques* is one which sees Kant regressing from the complexity of empirical experience (cognitive, moral, or aesthetic) to a pure, rational principle a priori. This establishes transcendental validity. But he must then return to the complex case by offering a constitutive account of the operation of the pure principle with reference to empirical experience (application/subsumption). In the case of the *First Critique*, the analysis set out from complex (logical and actual) empirical judgments, seeking the warrant for their claims to validity. Such a claim, Kant argued, could only be warranted by a priori categories of the understanding. He demonstrated that these pure categories "applied" to "pure" intuition— *that* they did, preeminently in §26 of the B-version of the "Transcendental Deduction"; and *how* they did in the "Transcendental Schematism" chapter. The "Analysis of Principles" then proceeded to explain how the "original synthesis" could warrant applications to an empirical object *in general* in an objective cognitive judgment.

The *First Critique* did not end with the "Transcendental Analytic." Kant's point was not simply to defend the coherence of judgment and the possibility of objectivity from a skeptical-solipsist dissolution into streams of impressions. He also wished to limit reason's pursuits to the sphere of actuality, i.e., to defend against "speculative metaphysics." This was the project of the "Transcendental Dialectic." There Kant discussed, among other things, (1) the question of "rational psychology," or the substantive interpretation of the self; (2) the question of "practical reason," or ethics; and (3) the question of religion, since the *Critique*'s purpose was to "make room for faith." It was not that Kant disputed the importance of such concerns to reason. These were perennial interests of reason because they were concerns humans could not avoid.[66] Nevertheless, he disputed reason's competence cognitively to resolve these concerns.

The point to consider is that transcendental principles for noncognitive dimensions of human experience found little scope—indeed, on some readings, were denied any *valid* scope—in terms of the *First Critique*. But that did not remain the case in the later *Critiques*. Therefore, Kant changed his conception of transcendental philosophy between 1781 and 1789. However, we must reckon with the prospect that not all the changes in his thought over the decade worked in the same direction. There were at least two crucial motives at work: first, a desire to extend the transcendental philosophy into the moral sphere; and second, a need to avoid the charge of idealism. The first concern led Kant to seek transcendental principles for the wider human faculties. The second led him to an even more acute suspicion of "psychologism" and subjective as opposed to objective reference. These two concerns were not entirely harmonious. While scholars interested above all in the "Transcendental Deduction" of the B-version of the *First Critique* (1786) have fastened upon Kant's concern with the charges of idealism and psychologism and accordingly stressed the "progress" from 1781 to 1786 in terms of his "Refutation of Idealism" and his "suppression" of the "Subjective Deduction" and with it much "faculty-talk," it is by no means clear that this was the preponderant shift of the decade, or even that it was such a pronounced shift as these interpreters wish to believe.[67] Kant felt a concern that even within his strictly cognitive philosophy there remained a certain indeterminacy, a "gap" in the system, which I will term later the problem of empirical entailment.[68] Even with reference to cognition, depending on one's reading of the task (to say nothing of the success) of the "Transcendental Analytic," a great deal might well remain to be done in the matter of constituting a valid empirical concept. Kant himself promised to demonstrate the "metaphysical" application of his transcendental principles in terms of a philosophical foundation of natural science.

From these considerations it is possible to formulate at least four projects that would animate the later critical period:

1. ethics (practical reason)
2. aesthetics (subjective consciousness)
3. metaphysics (God, the soul, and immortality)
4. natural science (methodology).

Most fundamentally, to keep coherence at the core of his transcendental philosophy, Kant had to pursue all these concerns under the principle of the *unity* or *sytematicity* of reason. The desire to find a legitimate extension of his "transcendental philosophy" into noncognitive areas of human experience led him to considerations which complicated or indeed revised his earlier positions in a more metaphysical—"transcendental psychological"—direction.

The *First Critique* simply set aside vast reaches of philosophical concern (because it set aside essential dimensions of human experience) in its relentless pursuit of a warrant for the objectivity of empirical cognition. Kant did not give a full phenomenology of subjective consciousness in the *First Critique* because he systematically abstracted from all nontheoretical elements in that experience in order to establish what would make objective knowledge possible. Moreover, in 1781 Kant had no plans for either of the later *Critiques*, because their matter did not appear to him amenable to transcendental argument.[69] He only turned to this phenomenology in the later *Critiques*.[70] To put it in terms of the problems of discursiveness, Kant may have addressed the narrow issue of the "transcendental deduction," but only to some degree at the expense of his resolution of the problem of imagination and the problem of subjectivity. That did not escape his own self-criticism.

Above all, Kant came, over the 1780s, to see transcendental philosophy not simply as a question of epistemology but rather as the system of philosophical understanding of man.[71] Hence the impulse of his work in the later *Critiques* was to carry forward the same transcendental quest for a priori principles which grounded or warranted complex (rational and actual) human experience not only narrowly in the question of the cognitive faculty *(Erkenntnisvermögen)* but more widely in all the distinctively—i.e., essentially—human faculties *(Gemütsvermögen)*. He took such a project to be quite distinct from "empirical psychology" or "heteronomous (empirical) ethics." He stressed, in what may be for us uncomfortably antiquarian terms, the primacy of reason in human nature.

The important result to retrieve from this complex set of considerations is that transcendental philosophy necessarily entails reference to the faculties of human experience. Consequently, in the later *Critiques* Kant would expand his "transcendental philosophy" in terms of reference to the faculties of human nature. In his letter to Reinhold, Kant very emphatically stated "there are three faculties of the mind: the faculty of cognition, the faculty of feeling pleasure and displeasure, and the faculty of desire."[72] In the later *Critiques* Kant clarified how transcendental philosophy approached the problem of the "psychologism" of faculties of the mind.

By 1787 Kant believed one could promote certain concepts from empirical status through explanations "according to transcendental determinations," reformulating them in a way which did not presuppose anything empirical, but referred only to the elements of the transcendentally grounded cognitive situation: the subjective faculties and their representations taken in general, not concretely.[73] In an important footnote to the preface of the *Second Critique* Kant clarified the nature of "transcendental explanations."[74] A transcendental explanation, he wrote, "consists only of terms belonging to the pure understanding, i.e., categories, which contain nothing empirical." That is, the terms in his definitions were perfectly general and logical, having no specific material content. And he insisted: "I need no more than this for the purposes of a critique of concepts borrowed from psychology; the rest is supplied by the *Critique* itself."[75] Kant believed these transcendental explanations were entirely legitimate elements in transcendental philosophy, that they did not violate its "purity," and, therefore, did not undermine its a priori claim. Moreover, if we take seriously the argument in "Amphiboly of Concepts of Reflection" in the *First Critique,* it is precisely these which enable transcendental philosophy to take place at all.[76] A historically grounded characterization of Kant's procedure must take seriously his faculty framework—not as a mere empirical psychology but, especially through the device of transcendental explanation, as transcendental psychology or, better, phenomenology. Such a methodological premise underlies the interpretation which follows.[77]

Transcendental explanations made possible the extension of the critical enterprise beyond the strictly theoretical, permitting the transcendental grounding in reflective reason of those key aspects of human consciousness which Kant identified with choice and with feeling.[78] That, in turn, considerably widened the scope of possible propositions of "transcendental logic" over against what was permitted under the far stricter terms of the first edition of the *First Critique.*

Kant's concern to demonstrate that reason constitutes and regulates the wider human faculties *(Gemütsvermögen)* most immediately determined his approach to the *Third Critique,* and most tellingly revealed his ultimately *rationalist* commitments in metaphysics. For Kant, only in the measure that reason governed, even in the sphere of feeling, was there any validity or truth in human comprehension, or, more broadly, any vestige of dignity and value in human experience. The *First Critique* had demonstrated reason's self-legislation in the sphere of cognition. The *Second Critique* demonstrated reason's legislation of the faculty of desire. The Introduction to the *Third Critique* announced that reason, through the faculty of judgment, would now be shown to provide an analogous legislation for the faculty of feeling. Of course, as Kant indicated in his letter to Reinhold, the scope of that transcendental legislation was narrowest in the sphere of feeling, where mankind was at its most "natural," but it was for Kant a triumph nonetheless that even there reason demonstrated its sovereignty.[79] If, as I infer, the object of transcendental explanation is to transpose into a cognitive key all (or as much as possible) of human experience, then to find any rendering of pleasure—for Kant the most recalcitrantly irrational component of that experience—in a transcendental form must have been an extremely heady accomplishment, and one that would indeed confirm Kant in his view of the aptness of his system. To be in a position to understand it, however, we must develop a more rigorous conception of Kant's phenomenology of subjective consciousness. That will require us to plunge very deeply into Kant's theory of mental activity and into a serious problem with his notion of "objectivity."

Three

VALIDITY AND ACTUALITY: TOWARD KANT'S PHENOMENOLOGY OF SUBJECTIVE CONSCIOUSNESS

K ant associates objectivity with actuality marked by "mate-rial" sensation given involuntarily to subjective con-sciousness. But at the same time Kant claims that objec-tivity is a question of validity, which can only be secured by understanding in its constitutive determinacy. The result is a perplexing ambiguity about the concept "objectivity" in Kant's epistemology. How does he relate objective validity to objective re-ality (actuality)?[1] In the paradigmatic instance of an empirical judg-ment, the two conceptions coincide: objective validity simply *is* objective reality (actuality), i.e., the judgment is *about* the object. There are, however, important instances in which validity and actu-ality do not coincide. Thus validity without actuality would have to be ascribed to general logic, to be sure, but in a radically different sense also to some propositions of transcendental logic.[2] Con-versely, and of more immediate concern, actuality without validity would have to be ascribed to subjective states that are not fully con-ceptual (e.g. animal or infant consciousness). The question of sub-jective states prior to cognition is crucial to the problem of aesthe-tics for Kant.

Kant moved from his relatively unproblematic notion of objec-tive judgment in the *First Critique* through the distinction of "judg-ments of experience" from "judgments of perception" in the *Prolegomena* (1783) to his ultimate discrimination in the *Third Cri-tique* (around 1789) between "determinant" and "reflective" judg-ment.[3] The point of this evolution was to distinguish a form of *subjective* judgment, with its own references, rules, and validity. If, as some specialists in *First Critique* issues have persuaded them-selves, Kant reverted to the original notion of judgment in his revi-sions of the *First Critique* (1786), then these efforts could only have been senseless. Given the historical fact that these efforts did not seem senseless to Kant, the only option is to interpret the B-version of the *First Critique* as consistent with these impulses. This means that a consistent construal of what Kant meant in §26 of the B-version of the "Transcendental Deduction," when he claimed that all sensory experience is subject to the categories, even if *not yet* in a judgment, is that some contents of consciousness are preconceptual.[4]

Objective Judgment: Toward a Phenomenology of Empirical Concept Formation

In his *Logic*, Kant argues that making a concept distinct and making a distinct concept are by no means the same. While making a concept distinct belongs in the sphere of analytic logic, making a distinct concept is a synthetic project, and one which requires that givenness of matter in intuition which is the focus of our concern.[5] He then explains the process of constituting an object. This constitution in Kantian epistemology is an extremely complicated project to decipher. For one thing, Kant is far more concerned with establishing *that* objective judgment is possible in general and valid in principle than he is with explicating *how* it is accomplished concretely. Empirical judgments apply (schematized) categories to actual sensible intuition to generate judgments with claims to "objective validity." This second or empirical synthesis needs to be transcendentally analyzed no less than the originary, "transcendental" or pure synthesis. All sensible intuition is in space and time, and space and time as pure intuition are subordinated to the (schematized) categories, but that does not yet establish that particular regions of space and time should be vested with particular material predicates, designated accordingly as an instance of some general rule, and given a name (empirical concept).

Empirical concepts are results, not foundations. The unity in a concept that results from an empirical judgment is *made*, not found. But that procedure of constituting an empirical concept does draw on the primordial, structuring categories and hence upon (schematized) concepts. There is, accordingly, a crucial ambiguity that must always be borne in mind in considering Kant's discussion of concepts. When Kant speaks of concepts being always indispensable for judgment, he must be taken to mean the categories and only the categories. Empirical concepts, the products of judgments, are objects constituted, not presupposed, in these judgments.[6]

They are fashioned in a complex phenomenological process Kant calls generally "synthesis."[7]

In the *Prolegomena* and in the "Transcendental Analytic" of the *First Critique* Kant gives a more detailed account of it. He writes of appearances *(Erscheinungen)* involving sensation which "*does not itself occupy any part of space or of time.*"[8] In §vii of the *Third Critique*, Kant describes "space" as a form of intuition internal to consciousness; consequently, "objects" as we represent them by deployment in that space are merely phenomenal. Yet he insists these spatial representations nevertheless refer to empirically real (external) objects. Kant terms sensation a similarly subjective element, but one which provides the "matter" for objective reference. Actuality as givenness-in-intuition requires not merely the "form" of space but existence, or "matter" provided in "sensation." The Introduction to the *Critique of Judgment* defines sensation in §vii as the "subjective side of our representations of external things, but one which is properly their matter (through which we must be given something with real existence)."[9]

"Appearance" we might call "figure" *(Gestalt)*, and the mental activity which necessarily responds to sense data by projecting such figures in space and time, "configuration" *(Gestaltung)* or "delineation" *(Zeichnung)*.[10] To configure in space and in duration is the first mental activity associated with the givenness of experience in sensibility. It constitutes "extensive magnitude" and is precisely what we mean by the word "outer" in its most simple sense, which Descartes would have called "extension." But perception also contains ("besides intuition") what is "real" in appearances: sensation.[11] Sensation, however, occupies no part of space and time.[12] It is entirely a modification of the subject. Kant thus terms sensation an "intensive magnitude" and denies it as an objective representation. Nevertheless it "refers" to the reality in appearances; consciousness ascribes this content or "matter" to these figures based entirely upon internal response. Assigning color, flavor, texture, or warmth to these figures (which we necessarily associate with given volumes for given durations in a unitary field of space and time based on sense data) "fills" the appearances configured in space.

What Kant is offering is a new twist on the contrast of primary and secondary qualities.[13] In Kant's version, the element of "appearance," the disposition of intuitions in space and time, is as subjective as the qualities of taste, color, and so on, and even these latter, though merely modifications of the subject, nevertheless offer data concerning, and hence "refer" to, objects external to the subject. But space and time are "ideal," whereas sensation is merely "private." Contrast the necessary singularity and identity of space and time, not only for one subject but for all, with the utter plurality of sensation, for example, the shade of blue or the taste of honey. There is no guarantee that all such sensations are identical intersubjectively. Indeed, there is even evidence on the other side.[14]

Internality to consciousness, therefore, must not be identified with "mere"—i.e., idiosyncratic or private—subjectivity. The distinction of the ideal from the private is what makes space and time empirically real in a way that is more primordial (they are, in that sense, "primary qualities") than the simple givenness of a certain, individually modulated degree of sensation—color, warmth, flavor, and so on (which are, hence, secondary qualities). It is just by virtue of this distinction of the necessary universality, i.e., intersubjectivity, of the ideal structure of space and time, that Kant claims he is a transcendental, not a solipsistic idealist.[15]

Kant seems to contend that neither appearance nor sensation suffices for the experience of the existence or "externality" of an object. It seems to lie in its independence of subjectivity, its public character, or universality, but that is not sufficiently clarified yet. The decisive element for true reference to the object is still missing. Kant writes:

> Everything, every representation even, in so far as we are conscious of it, may be entitled object. But it is a question for deeper enquiry what the word "object" ought to signify in respect of appearances when these are viewed not in so far as they are (as representations) objects, but only in so far as they stand for an object. The appearances, in so far as they are objects of consciousness simply in virtue of being representations, are not in any way distinct from their apprehension, that is, from their reception in the synthesis of imagination.[16]

What is attended does not change; everything hinges on a change in how we attend it. "Object," in its rigorous Kantian sense, must, then, be constituted out of—and promoted from—this mere subjectivity of the representations. We must construe as object what is "nothing but the sum of these representations."[17] That is what it means to recognize existence, Kant claims. Objective reference requires postulation of the existence of such "appearances and their *relation* to one another in respect of their existence."[18] Accordingly, he reformulates his notion of the synthesis in a cognitive judgment in three levels: "of mere intuition (that is, of the form of appearance), of perception (that is, of the matter of perception), and of experience (that is, of the relation of these perceptions)."[19] Note the sequence *form-matter-relation.* Experience is a higher order integration than appearance or sensation, and only at that level is the object truly constituted as external existence.

This promotion can only result from "regarding the formal conditions of empirical truth."[20] That is: "appearance, in contradistinction to the representations of apprehension, can be represented as an object distinct from them only if it stands under a rule which distinguishes it . . . and necessitates some one particular mode of connection of the manifold."[21] This formulation is exactly that of a determinant judgment, which entails subsuming the manifold under a definite concept or rule.[22] A "judgment of experience," in the language of the *Prolegomena,* posits what Kant asserted in the "Analogies of Experience" of the *First Critique:* "I render my subjective synthesis of apprehension objective only by reference to a rule."[23] Again, Kant privileges the sense of objectivity as validity (subsumption under a universal rule) as against the sense of objectivity as givenness. What is given is still *in* the subject, and only conceptualization lifts it to objectivity.

Consequently it is in our appraisal of the relation of the representation to the universal rules of the understanding that the decisive question of objectivity is addressed. Note that nothing is added to the content of the concept; only the validity is reappraised. That, precisely, is the domain of the modality of judgment. It is via the modality of judgment that the distinction is first made between merely possible objects and objects to which we ascribe actuality.[24] Indeed, it is only because within this modality we have access to an even higher criterion, necessity, that the operation has any prospect of viability. Because the modality of necessity is efficacious in the schematization of an object-in-general, the modality of actuality is efficacious in empirical judgments, and we have the right to posit existence in a judgment of experience.[25]

All objective judgments employ empirical concepts and ground their claim in the transcendental warrant of the categories, but they also need that *through which* the judgment can relate immediately to its object: intuition. Intuition provides the requisite features of singularity ("this one specific") and immediacy ("actual" or given). But what exactly is an intuition?[26] Kant equivocates severely between a receptive and a spontaneous—i.e., passive versus active—interpretation of intuition. As sensibility, intuition is associated with receptivity and passivity. As imagination, however—and there is a very important connection between imagination and intuition—it is spontaneous and active. There is a very significant degree of overlap between the strictly "receptive" conception of intuition (the discussion in the "Transcendental Aesthetic") and the "synthetic" sense of it in the "Transcendental Analytic," not only in the so-called "Subjective Deduction," but in the "Schematism" chapter and in the "Analytic of Principles."

Formal and *formative* are words which Kant invariably assigns to the spontaneous side of his discursive dichotomy, to the mind or the understanding broadly conceived. One can simply hold Kant guilty of an "error" for thinking of intuition or imagination in this way.[27] The role of imagination in knowledge has been controversial especially in the light of the analytic effort to "update" Kant. Perhaps one of the most powerful initiatives in that direction came from Peter Strawson.[28] Moreover, there is a serious difference between the two versions of the *First Critique* on the question of imagination. While the original edition of the *First Critique* assigns to imagination not only the capacity for a synthesis of intuition but almost the whole responsibility for synthesis as such, the B-version seems to withdraw most such credit from imagination and assigns synthesis exclusively to the understanding.[29] The project to liquidate imagination altogether from "acceptable" Kant materials was carried forward by Jonathan Bennett, and especially by Eva Schaper.[30] Their resistance to any "transcendental psychology" or "metaphysics" in Kant's notion of imagination is perhaps the counterpart of an excess of enthusiasm precisely for those aspects by the Heideggerian camp.[31]

Far more interesting is the effort to see in imagination/intuition, in this formative sense, a phenomenological moment in the synthesis of an empirical judgment, and to break this moment out for closer examination. Instead of seeing the claims of synthesis as a matter either of narrowly conceived understanding (judgment involving objective concepts) or of narrowly conceived imagination (without any connection with concepts), it might be wise to see each as elements in Kant's general approach to the synthetic-spontaneous participation of mind in knowledge. Indeed, there may well be grounds for argument that the first schematizations of the categories, those of quantity and quality, tend in a very substantial measure to merge rather than to differentiate the properly intuitive and the properly conceptual projects. Might it not be more fruitful to recognize in these initial moments of the construction of empirical concepts a far more complex symbiosis of imagination and conceptualization than recent analytic philosophers find comfortable?

Kant tends to think that ordinary consciousness simply *is* judgments, i.e., voluntary synthesis-acts of the understanding. Accordingly, the "Transcendental Deduction" is frequently taken to hold that nothing can be in consciousness that is not the product of a conceptual synthesis.[32] All representations—even those not already in a unified intuition—*must* be determined by the categories in order to be a matter of judgment, i.e., to be available for consciousness at all.[33] This interpretation is not only *prima facie* implausible, it runs afoul of very important textual evidence.[34] The scholarship on Kant has moved very firmly toward an alternative interpretation. Perhaps the most powerful influence has been Gerold Prauss, with his work, *Erscheinung bei Kant*.[35] Another important influence was Beck's essay, "Did the Sage of Königsberg Have No Dreams?"[36] A wide range of scholars have, in a typically disparate manner, acknowledged this issue of subjective immediacy.[37]

Moltke Gram and Graham Bird both distinguish a "strong" from a "weak" sense of experience or objectivity for consciousness. Gram notes: "if objects can appear to us without standing under the categories, then we can have experience of objects without synthesizing intuition according to the categories."[38] This problematic result made sense given two distinct notions of "experience," only the stronger of which would merit "objective validity." As Bird sees it, we can have more experience than we can recognize. He makes much of Kant's line that "appearances can certainly be given in intuition independently of the functions of the understanding."[39] This weak sense of object, however, still allows the subject to recognize the object as being of a determinate sort, and thus achieve the "strong" sense.[40]

Henrich and Paul Guyer pursue this problem in terms of two senses of the term "mine," drawing on the obvious importance for Kant of the "unity of apperception." As Henrich puts it: "Sensibility is distinct from self-consciousness . . . [A]s long as it is only *available* to be taken up into consciousness, it is not at all 'mine'; but only 'in relation to me.'"[41] Guyer finds Henrich's formulation unclear, but not the point he is trying to articulate, and offers a variant which he thinks puts it better: "There might be cases in which one is conscious without recognizing it . . . [O]thers may recognize me to be in a state which I do not or cannot recognize as mine."[42] Even Daniel Kolb, who is much closer to the old interpretation, acknowledges that "it is always possible to distinguish between the way in which a thing seems in perception and the way the thing actually is."[43] Guyer, evaluating Henrich's most extended effort to make sense of the "Transcendental Deduction," made what many take to be the most promising move: "Every transition in consciousness [is] explicable by judgments employing the categories but not expressible solely in such judgments."[44]

Ameriks, indeed, contends that "Kant was quite aware of and quite concerned with accounting for items that initially are not taken explicitly as fully unified and determined by the categories."[45] He goes on to claim that "Kant was phenomenological enough to believe in a difference between an appearance in the general sense of any kind of idea before the mind, and an appearance in the specific sense of a self-manifesting given . . . [I]t is the latter kind of appearance that is Kant's main concern in §26 . . . [with] its demonstration that the categories apply 'even' for 'perception' (B161)."[46] Ameriks acknowledged "the importance of Prauss' general idea for developing a sophisticated Kantian account of the subjective side of our perceptual life . . . [A] Kantian theory cannot ignore this issue . . . [but] it . . . must construe the realm as also subject, in some kind of derivative way, to judgment and the categories."[47]

For Prauss, the essential nature of Kant's objective judgment is a *Deutung*—a process of "metamorphosis" of subjective data of consciousness into *objects*.[48] There is in that process no pause to consider the subjective data in themselves. He notes that such givens are not, as *such*, matters of cognitive attention for ordinary consciousness. They are worked through—*verwandelt* (Kant) or *gedeutet* (Prauss)—as the letters and indeed words of a text are worked through and abandoned for the meaning they betoken. Consciousness finds itself always already in the language of the judgment of experience.[49] It can perform a transcendental analysis upon that language, however, and that will lead it retrospectively to realize the necessary existence in consciousness of appearances as such. But the problem that faces such a transcendental analysis is how ever to talk about appearances in their own right, *prior* to the object into which they have been constituted.[50] To focus on them is a consequence either of some problem of reading (e.g. "deciphering" a corrupt text, to stay with the metaphor), or of an interest in the *process of reading* (i.e., how is it actually that letters and words *make* a text which can be read?).[51]

This last question is phenomenological. It, too, can be broken out into two aspects. First, it can be seen as a regression from fully objective judgments into their constitutive moments for the sake of reconstructing or validating that objective procedure. Second, it can be conceived as an inventory of subjective *states*: an effort to catalog all the possible contents available to consciousness, whether or not they become elements in a cognitive judgment. In the first of these inquiries, the judgments that are generated are properly *transcendental*, not subjective. In the second, the judgments seem to be merely psychological. While they are about the subject, however, it does not follow that all such judgments are themselves subjective (as concerns validity). Thus, to claim that colors are subjective qualities—that, e.g., "green" is a sensuous content of my perception—says nothing about the objective validity of the judgment. Green is a property, however subjectively registered, that features into objective judgments.[52] What is it, then, that constitutes the *subjectivity* of judgments, and how can they still be *judgments* in the Kantian sense of the term?

Prauss identifies three decisive features such an analysis must explicate. First, there must be a *judgment*, and judgments require the categories. Yet it cannot refer to the object since that already bypasses the appearances in their own right. To qualify as a judgment, some categories must obtain, yet others, equally essentially, must not, for the *full* application of the categories necessarily constitutes an object, and the subjective appearance as such gets annulled. Second, this judgment must be of a particular form: it must be a first person judgment in the sense not only that it is by but also that it is about the subject, and as such it must make a claim to validity (*Gültigkeit*), which while subjective in scope is nevertheless compellingly actual.[53] Finally, and logically in light of the genesis of the problem, a judgment of perception must correspond to each and every judgment of experience, since its "object" (*Objekt*) is precisely the "appearance" (*Erscheinung*) out of which the "object" (*Gegenstand*) was constituted by the judgment of experience.[54]

Prauss takes subjective judgments to signify *acts* of judgment about—hence *conscious attention* to—*pre-objective* data of consciousness (*Erscheinungen* as representations eligible for constitution into objects). Prauss correctly claims that, as such, a *judgment* of perception can be possible only in light of, indeed parasitically compounded from a prior judgment of experience in a kind of reversal or suspension of part of its process. Thereby it borrows the (conceptual) language of the judgment of experience, i.e., it applies the conceptual "names" of objects to what are only their subjective concomitants. More importantly, it borrows the *form* of the judgment itself, rendering it "problematic" and subjective by reversing the objective reference through the suspension of the categories of relation which alone constituted an objective order external to the subject.[55]

It follows that judgments of perception cannot literally be taken as constitutive in the genesis of judgments of experience.[56] It is rather that the elements *appraised* in a judgment of perception are the elements metamorphosed *(gedeutet)* into an object by the judgment of experience.[57] Nevertheless, Kant did use language in the *Prolegomena* that suggested a sequential structuring of the two judgments. That usage fits into a reconstruction of Kant's theory of empirical concept formation which takes an empirical judgment as a "synthetic act" in the unconventional sense that it is not simply a compound of active understanding and passive sensibility, but rather the outcome of an initial *intuitive formation* (by imagination) "taken up" into a cognitive judgment: i.e., a subjective synthesis compounded, or more precisely validated, by conceptual generalization.

Richard Aquila has argued for such an interpretation vigorously in a series of works. Setting out from the serious ambiguity in Kant's notion of synthesis, he recognizes the impulse in the scholarship to seek to resolve the conflict by a reduction of synthesis either to understanding or to imagination. Neither resolution is plausible, however. Therefore, Aquila opts for a constructive or sequential approach to empirical concept formation. Citing the "Vienna Logic," Aquila suggests that the issue is, in Kant's own words, "how it comes about that *repraesentatio singularis* becomes *communis*."[58] In his own terms, "in some sense or other, empirical conceptualization is an operation by which empirical *intuitions* are themselves converted, if not literally into concepts, then into determinate empirical conceptions."[59] This sense of "promotion" is the key to his reconstruction of Kant. He writes of "intuition's elevation, through the elevation of some material in it, to a specifically conceptualized status." The crucial point, however, is that some of the synthesis must already have transpired at the level of intuition/imagination: "at least part of the job of imagination is to 'synthesize' the material . . . an intuition must *contain*, quite in itself, the manifold of all the material that is merely 'associated' with it."[60] Hence Aquila argues that we must recognize "the need that Kant might have felt for a genuinely preconceptual and precategorical form of imaginative representation, appropriately 'associated' with any intuition to which concepts are supposed applicable."[61] Hence "we must think of the conceptualization of an intuition in terms of some sort of internal *alteration* of that very intuition . . . something that happens to it *together with* whatever intuitional expectations it already contains."[62] He concludes: "at least part of what conceptualization adds to the work of mere imagination involves elevating the *level of consciousness* involved in the imaginative expectations in question,"[63] hence "an objective judgment involves an objective relationship *among the very same representations* that a purely associative 'judgment' connects in a merely subjective manner."[64] It is precisely the presentation of an intuitively integrated 'object' to the faculty of understanding as a whole, the transcendental structures of consciousness, that promotes mere subjective experience to objectivity.[65]

Henry Allison has made an argument along a similar line. He starts from the proposition that "an intuition is itself a representation of an individual object, quite apart from any conceptual determination," drawing support from the note Kant made upon receipt of a letter from Jacob Sigismund Beck in 1791: "To make a concept, by means of intuition, into a cognition of an object, is indeed the work of judgment; but the reference of intuition to an object in general is not."[66] Allison continues: "having a set of sensible impressions that are associated with one another is not the same as having a concept . . . [That] is produced by a series of 'logical acts' of the understanding that Kant terms 'comparison,' 'reflection,' and 'abstraction.'"[67]

This approach, which will be closely paralleled in my own account, can be linked to Kant's strategy in the *Prolegomena*. While Prauss would not find this line of interpretation acceptable, he did offer some important leads that can be taken up into it. First, he noted that the so-called mathematical categories in fact appeared indifferent as to the question of the external reference or objectivity of their "objects."[68] He noted, further, the very close connection between these categories of the understanding and the pure forms of intuition.[69] He then concluded that the categories of quantity and quality very likely had to be involved in what Kant called a "judgment of perception," but that the "dynamic" categories did not.[70] With the suspension of the categories of relation, however, all claims to objective validity are suspended and the judgment is rendered problematically subjective. That is to say, such judgments can "only be made by myself about my own—by any subject only about his own—sensible appearance [*Erscheinun-gen*]."[71] A similar recognition that judgments involving only the (schematized) categories of quantity and quality but not carried through to the categories of relation or modality might be at the heart of Kant's notion of subjective judgment is to be found in the crucial essays of Lewis Beck, Mary Gregor, and J. Michael Young.

Beck starts from a clear stance on the problem of subjective immediacy: "Kant does not anywhere say that the 'I think' must accompany all of my representations; he says merely that it must be able to accompany them . . . A perception that *could not* be accompanied by 'I think' 'would not belong to any experience, consequently would be without an object, merely a blind play of representations, less even than a dream.' (A112)"[72] Beck argues that what cannot serve in a objective judgment might nevertheless be relevant for subjective reckoning, and he asserts that this is the precise sphere of "empirical psychology." In such reckonings, data could be "*categorized* without being *objectified*."[73] Nevertheless, for such reckonings to be "judgments" in the Kantian sense, certain rules must apply. Some categories prove indispensable. But "if all even tacit reference to objects were excluded from the judgment of perception the mathematical categories would still apply to the intensive magnitude . . . The Anticipation of Perception applies."[74] Therefore, Beck concludes, "aesthetic judgments do not employ the dynamical categories and principles of substance, causality, and existence . . . But the mathematical categories and principles certainly do apply . . . The concepts which Kant holds do *not* play a role in the construction of (pure) aesthetic experience are not categorical concepts but empirical."[75] Beck then suggests that "the *Critique of Aesthetic Judgment* seems to have grown out of the doctrines of the *Prolegomena* which were rejected in the second edition of the *Critique of Pure Reason*."[76] I agree with the first point, but not the second: indeed, because of the connection between the *Critique of Judgment* and the *Prolegomena* on this issue, we may not take the second edition of the *First Critique* as a rejection of these ideas.[77]

Gregor, too, begins with the apparent conflict between the *Prolegomena* and the *Third Critique*, on the one hand, and the ultimate form of the *First Critique* on the other: "The *Prolegomena*'s theory about judgments of perception which do not subsume sense data under the categories, together with Kant's insistence that the pure judgment of taste does not subsume under a concept, might suggest that the representation 'this,' in 'this is beautiful,' escapes the categories."[78] Gregor argues that any judgment, even the judgment of taste, must, on the most indisputable reading of the *First Critique,* involve a relation to the unity of apperception possible only via the categories. What she then does is develop the argument that the "mathematical categories" feature centrally in Kant's notion of form in aesthetic judgments.

Young notes that "concepts of a highly empirical sort . . . to a large extent simply mirror the functions of the imagination."[79] And later in his essay, in considering the crucial problem of schematism, he develops the point even more strikingly: "I take Kant to hold that the concept of quantity—whether of quantity in general, or of a specific, determinate quantity—is the concept of a feature that can be adequately represented only by means of intuition."[80] What I, in turn, take Young to mean is that in the initial schematization of the categories of quantity and quality it is not at all clear that it is understanding and not imagination (as intuition) which is the primary formative or "synthetic" agent.

The initiation of the empirical judgment is conducted in intuition—by *imagination.* The *coordination* of sensation into a singular intuition cannot be the function of concepts. That work must be done—to be sure in accordance with the requirements of the understanding—by imagination.[81] Concepts are rules which apply to several possible instantiations. All concepts, therefore, whether pure or empirical, are general. If all judgments involve concepts and all concepts are general rules, then the singular individual, in its unique determinacy and coordination, becomes problematic. The reference of any concept to a particular ("numerically singular") instance is simply indeterminate at the level of the concept itself. Accordingly, Kant calls concepts without intuitions *empty.*[82] Empty does not mean false or contradictory. In formal terms, judgments using such concepts are perfectly lucid. It is when we move from formal to real use of judgment that this problem arises.

At the level of concepts, "*this* tennis ball" never makes any advance over "tennis ball." The modifier is pointless unless it can point beyond language—beyond concepts to existence. To be sure, the language can try to offer predicates that differentiate this *kind* of ball from other balls (e.g., hollow, elastic) or from other *tennis* balls (e.g., white). But there are a lot of tennis balls that fit the most exhaustive description (there can be no lowest level of specification of concepts).[83] One can only specify ultimately in intuition. Moreover, nothing in the concept can fully specify the similarly particular version of each of its predicated properties (e.g, which white? how elastic?) or, more crucially, the *coordination* of these properties into an integral whole. An empirical concept *names* something that concepts cannot fully constitute. And, of course, the *concept* of a tennis ball, however determinately specified, can never be played on a tennis court. One needs the *actual* ball. This problem can be resolved only by the extension of concepts through schemata into the field of spatio-temporal intuition, where numerical singularity can be constituted as a region of extension and duration.

Subjective Judgment: States and Appraisals,
Another "Kind of Judging"

If we take it that for Kant judgment is simply the form of all conscious attention, such that there can literally be no conscious attention without an explicit judgment, that does not mean that there cannot be a great deal available for conscious attention that does not get attended, that does not enter into judgments. One would, accordingly, need to distinguish between an *awareness* which encompassed all presence-to-consciousness, and a *conscious attention* proper, which involved what achieved recognition in judgment. To be even available to consciousness is to be "mine," but mine in a far weaker sense than it is when it is appropriated into consciousness by an act of judgment. One can still acknowledge that conscious attention requires an act of empirical judgment.

The point is, however, that there can be more than one kind of empirical judgment: not simply the objective reference of cognition, but the subjective reference of aesthetics and reflection. Kant clearly recognized three forms of "subjective judgment" over the course of the 1780s:

1. "judgments of perception"
2. "judgments of taste"
3. "(logical) reflective judgments."

How it is possible for Kant to use the word "judgment" in this context—and what the implications may be—proves essential to the understanding of the *Third Critique.* Indeed, as a *Critique of Judgment,* it is dedicated to the examination of this problem.

We need to distinguish "subjective objects" *(subjektive Gegenstände),* to use Prauss's phrase, from subjective *judgments.* One might ask whether there are representations which can never become elements in an objective cognition. The question needs to be rephrased: what *about* a representation can never become an element in an objective cognition? Not the *matter* in it, but the specific *reference* of it: not the *Sinn* but the *Gefühl*—how it was *for* me, i.e., about me, not just in me. What would examples of such a judgment be? The essential point about such judgments is that they are explicitly restrictive: they assert a private situation, *for me alone*. Thus, Prauss's prefatory-transformational phrase "It seems (to me)" works to privatize the *scope* of the claim of the judgment. Subjective judgments about objects are judgments about the subjective response to objects: valuations. Such valuations can be of quantity, not just quality: e.g., "that ski run looks steep to me."

About contents of my consciousness I am more than cognitively aware. I am also affectively and pragmatically embroiled in them. "Subjective objects" are simply contents of consciousness *(Vorstellungen)* taken as *for* me, *when* they are taken that way, i.e., in judgments of *that* sort. These same subjective objects remain simply elements of objects—including myself as one—in judgments of *that* sort. The content does not change; all that changes is the reference of the judgment. The issue that remains, of course, is the validity claim of judgments that are self-referential in this sense. What then does subjective validity mean? Late in the *First Critique* Kant used "subjective validity" to signify a *belief* which was not yet confirmed as objective knowledge.[84] That use of "subjective validity" does not quite get at the interesting sense of the conception, however. It makes absolutely no sense to think of a "subjective principle a priori" in that light.[85] Nor does it really illuminate the three essential forms of subjective judgment that Kant developed over the course of his critical philosophy.

Accordingly, it will be necessary to examine in some detail Kant's phenomenology of subjective consciousness. Kant took up this problem in at least three salient discussions: the discussion of imagination in the *First Critique,* the distinction of "judgments of perception" from "judgments of experience" in the *Prolegomena to Any Future Metaphysics,* and the section on aesthetic judgments in the *Critique of Judgment.*

The key to Kant's phenomenology lies in the notion of "reference" *(beziehen).* In §vii of the Introduction to the *Critique of Judgment* Kant sets out by discriminating the "logical validity" of representations from their "aesthetical character" by associating the former with "reference to the object" and the latter with "reference to the subject." Immediately thereafter, he notes: "In the cognition of an object of sense both [references] are presented conjointly [*kommen beide Beziehungen zusammen vor*]."[86] What does it mean that both references occur together? The representation-of-an-object is itself at one and the same time aesthetical and logical, i.e., available for reference either to the subject or to the object. What is referred is always just the representation. And as representation—as presence-to-consciousness—it is always for the subject. This is Kant's point in the "Transcendental Aesthetic" of the *First Critique:* representations "contain nothing that can belong to an object in itself, but merely the appearance of something, and the mode in which we are affected by that something."[87]

Kant writes in §vii of a representation-of-an-object *(Vorstellung eines Objekts).* That is a particular kind of representation, namely, one which requires givenness-of-matter in sensation. Representations are possible without such sensuous intuition, without materiality, and hence without objective reference. Examples of such representations are ideas of reason (God, the soul, the world-whole), or abstract universals like the idea of virtue, or transcendental faculties. Insofar as we can think of "pure" intuition as a representation in itself, and not simply as the form of sense-derived representations, there, too, we have representations without objective ("material") reference. The same would be true of mathematical constructions in "pure intuition."[88] But the case that concerns us is precisely representation-of-an-object, both as a matter for conscious consideration and as this consideration itself—both as a what and as a how.

In a famous passage in the *First Critique,* Kant presents a hierarchy *(Stufenleiter)* of terms relating to *Vorstellung:*

> The genus is *representation* in general *(repraesentatio).* Subordinate to it stands representation with consciousness *(perceptio).* A *perception* which relates solely to the subject as a modification of its state is *sensation (sensatio),* an objective perception is knowledge *(cognitio).* This is either *intuition* or *concept (intuitus vel conceptus).* The former relates immediately to the object and is single, the latter refers to it mediately by means of a feature which several things may have in common.[89]

It would appear the genus representation is wider than representation-with-consciousness. In his *Logic,* Kant writes of "presenting something to oneself [*sich etwas vorstellen*]" in a way that leads his translators to note that "any implication of a *conscious* act is to be excluded."[90]

That seems absurd, for how can there be presence-to-consciousness without consciousness? Yet here is precisely where we must distinguish between that which is present and that which consciousness discriminates or attends.[91] In a letter to Marcus Herz, dated May 26, 1789, the very time Kant was completing the *First Introduction to the Critique of Judgment* and developing his most complex conception of the faculty of judgment, he wrote:

> For if we can demonstrate that *our knowledge* [*Erkenntnis*] of things, even experience [*Erfahrung*] itself, is only possible under those conditions [i.e., the categories and space-time as the form of intuition], it follows that all other concepts of things (which are not thus conditioned) are for us empty and utterly useless for knowledge [*Erkenntnisse*]. But not only that; all sense data for a possible cognition [*Erkenntnis*] would never, without those conditions, represent objects. They would not even reach that unity of consciousness that is necessary for knowledge [*Erkenntnis*] of myself (as object of inner sense). I would not even be able to know that I have sense data; consequently for me, as a knowing being [*als erkennendes Wesen*], they would be absolutely nothing. They could still (I imagine myself to be an animal) carry on their play in an orderly fashion, as representations connected according to empirical laws of association, and thus even have an influence on my feeling and desire [*auf Gefühl und Begehrungsvermögen*], without my being aware of them (assuming that I am even conscious of each individual representation, but not of their relation to the unity of representations of their object, by means of the synthetic unity of their apperception). This might be so without my knowing the slightest thing thereby, not even what my own condition [*Zustand*] is.[92]

It is critical to discern the strategy of this frequently cited passage. It clearly takes up the issues adumbrated in §26 of the B-version of the *First Critique*. It reasserts firmly that *in a cognitive light* (hence the frequent use of the word *Erkenntnis*), the presence to consciousness of *data* (Kant used the Latin word to signal strict givenness) would be utterly meaningless apart from the transcendental structures. But it also asserts with equal clarity that such data would still be ordered ("according to the empirical laws of association") and even more importantly that such data could "have an influence on my feeling and desire [*auf Gefühl und Begehrungsvermögen*], without my being aware of them," i.e., that we *respond* to stimuli in more than cognitive ways and that these noncognitive responses would be operative even in the absence of the transcendental structures. The issue that the passage poses, and which is at the heart of any sophisticated discussion of subjective immediacy, is not whether such data can have significance for *cognition* apart from the transcendental structures, but whether they can even have significance for subjective awareness in these other dimensions. Kant concludes his passage with the statement "without my knowing the slightest thing thereby, not even what my own condition [*Zustand*] is," yet it is typical of him in the *Critique of Judgment,* as also in the *Prolegomena,* to assign precisely to an awareness of subjective condition [*Zustand des Gemüts*] the *judgmental* features associated with presence to consciousness of such data. Kant is using "knowing" in this last phrase in a sense more rigorous than he would in much of his consideration of subjective judgment. But the reason may well be that he wishes to stress that level of consciousness which is entirely animal, without any possibility of harmony with rational-transcendental structures.

In the *Stufenleiter* passage we come to representation-with-consciousness with "perception" *(Wahrnehmung)*. But what exactly does that betoken? Kant places at the level of perception both what "relates solely to the subject as the modification of its state"—which he calls sensation *(Empfindung)*—and "objective perception"—which he calls cognition *(Erkenntnis)*. How is the attention involved with sensation distinguished from cognition? Does what is attended change, or only how we attend it? Kant does not here provide an account of how one moves from *Empfindung* to *Erkenntnis*.[93] The issue is precisely to articulate the difference between what is given to consciousness in representation and how we come to note it, i.e., develop a phenomenology of the different moments in conscious attention.

In his *Logic,* Kant suggests that *Wahrnehmen,* perception as the mere consciousness of the representation, is separated by at least several mediations from the kind of consciousness we normally understand him to mean by "objective knowledge." The *Stufenleiter* does not break the matter out in enough detail. The *Logic* offers more discriminations.[94] A new step, *kennen,* is introduced, which entails a capacity of comparison, discernment of identity and difference, yet clearly without recourse to concepts. Indeed, Kant holds animals to be cognizant in this sense.[95] He juxtaposes to this the idea *erkennen*—"to be cognizant with consciousness"— as distinctly human and rational, and yet he reserves to a higher level still, *verstehen,* conception through concepts.[96] What are *kennen* and *erkennen* in this account, as distinct from *wahrnehmen* on the one

hand, and *verstehen* on the other? Is Kant indulging in idle discriminations? Or is it not, rather, that both in what we share with animals
(kennen) and in what we exceed them by *(erkennen)*, Kant seems to
endow human consciousness with the capacity for a *judgment of perception?*

In the *Prolegomena* Kant writes: "All our judgments are at first
merely judgments of perception; they hold only for us (i.e. for our
subject), and we do not till afterwards give them a new reference (to
an object)."[97] This subsequent judgment—of "experience"—has
claim to objectivity. In one sense, this is because it "expresses not
merely a reference of the perception to a subject, but a quality of
the object." One might take this "quality" to be existence or givenness. But Kant privileges a second sense of objectivity: validity
grounded in the logical universality of the concepts of understanding. Kant means to secure "objective reference" through "logical
validity." Only this promotes judgments of experience to objectivity.

Nevertheless he conceives of *two* judgments in a sequence (note
the "at first" and the "afterwards" in the passage). Indeed, he
speaks of two different "kinds of judging": "first, I may merely compare perceptions and connect them in a consciousness of my state;
or secondly, I may connect them in consciousness in general. The
former judgment is merely a judgment of perception and is of subjective validity only; it is merely a connection of perceptions in my
mental state, without reference to the object."[98] Kant seems to link
the more primitive kind of judging with the sorts of processes he
termed *kennen* and *erkennen* in the *Logic*. That kind of judging has
the power to unify representations through reference to "a consciousness in one subject only."[99] This unification is by means of
comparison, discerning likeness and difference.

This "kind of judging" is undertaken by the understanding,
but it is hardly Kant's standard idea of the understanding (e.g., his
"determinant judgment" in the *Third Critique*).[100] It is rather a
mode of judging which, like the notion "judgment of perception"
itself, would not seem to have been developed yet in Kant's *First
Critique*—except, perhaps, in Kant's notion of "imagination." In
the *Stufenleiter* passage of the *First Critique*, Kant characterizes "intuition" as an objective perception, a cognition, though it "refers
immediately to the object and is single." That is extremely problematic, not only vis-à-vis Baumgarten but vis-à-vis modern skeptics of
his notion of intuition. Intuition of singular objects, not according
to universal rules, as an immediate and unique reference to the ob-

ject, fails to satisfy the decisive criterion of a judgment of experience. How is intuition [*Anschauung*] as "objective" perception to be distinguished from sensation [*Empfindung*] as merely "subjective"? It is not subsumed under any universal concept. The relation between sensation and intuition as "objects" of attention raises all the issues entailed in the incongruity of validity and actuality in Kant's notion of objectivity. We could, as many recent interpreters have contended, simply hold Kant to have erred in claiming objective status for this sense of intuition.[101] Yet there is a crucial sense of external reference involved with intuition.[102] We need a clearer phenomenology of this perception. Imagination is the decisive link in this whole inquiry.

Kant's characterization of imagination in empirical cognition in the *First Critique* proves very important in reconstructing his phenomenology. Different perceptions "occur in the mind separately and singly" and they cannot be combined by sense. Kant characterizes sense as "the power of intuiting when the object *is* present," whereas imagination is not so restricted. Sense is momentary or immediate; the presence has no duration. Only imagination has the power to hold past and present perceptions together and by that synthesis "produce an *intuition.*" That is the sense of reproduction or "presentation" *(Darstellung; exhibitio).* That is what imagination must do: "bring the manifold of intuition into the form of an image."[103] While imagination is an act of consciousness, and clearly part of its spontaneity, it acts by rules and proceedings "of which we are scarcely ever conscious."[104] Imagination is generally taken by Kant to be part of the spontaneity of consciousness, and hence, of "understanding" as conscious activity on a much wider range than his *First Critique* usage.[105]

In his *Anthropology,* Kant distinguishes between "attending" and "abstracting" as powers of "understanding (in the most general sense of the term)." He identifies with *attentio* "the power of apprehending given representations to produce an *intuition,*" and with *abstractio* "the power of abstracting what is common to several of these to produce a *concept.*"[106] Note that both are productive activities. Kant elaborates on the power of imagination in §31 of the *Anthropology.* He discriminates three powers: "*forming* intuitions in space *(imaginatio plastica),* associating intuitions in time *(imaginatio associans),* and connecting our representations because of their affinity for one another, in so far as they have a common ground *(affinitas).*"[107]

The last of these powers holds our attention. Kant elaborates his meaning: "By affinity I mean the connection of the manifold by virtue of its origin from one ground." What does that signify? He attempts to elucidate by contrast with "a succession of representations having no objective connection" so bemusing that we "wonder whether we have been dreaming."[108] That *cannot be,* though we can only clarify why that cannot be, only find the necessary transcendental law for it, when we leave this stage of consciousness and rise to the higher power of the understanding. Yet what is crucial to note is that "the play of imagination still follows the laws of sensibility, which provides the material, and this is associated without consciousness of the rule but still in keeping with it. So the association is carried out *in conformity with* understanding, though it is not derived *from* understanding."[109]

Imagination "produces" such an intuition independent of conceptual universals, Kant suggests in the *Anthropology.* He characterizes the kind of unification of which imagination is capable as constituting a discernible individual by coordinating the heterogeneous properties that belong in it. One must discriminate from mere particulars of sense perception, which are the truly simple things for Kant, the object in its singularity, which is a composite, i.e., contains a manifold, but is nonetheless individual, i.e., determinate enough to be distinguished. That determinacy is constituted not by the application of universals in a conceptual construction, but rather by contrast *(oppositio)* which "arouses our attention by juxtaposing contrary sense representations under one and the same concept."[110]

Obviously, more than mere contrast is discriminable. The imagination must also be able to find similarity. Kant characterizes these two capacities as "judgment" *(iudicium)* and "wit" *(ingenium).* "Judgment's task is to note the differences in a manifold that is identical in part; that of wit is to note the identity of a manifold that is different in part."[111] Judgment and wit are talents—natural gifts. They belong to understanding in the broad sense, to be sure, but they "depend on the subject's natural predisposition" and in that measure cannot be taught or learned.[112] Kant adds a very important characterization of wit: "When wit draws comparisons, its behavior is like play."[113] Imagination, with its percipience of affinities, seems very close to the *kennen* and *erkennen* of the judgment of perception.

Young argues that imagination must be rescued from a simple association with imaging and seen rather as involving reconfiguration *(umbilden, umgestalten),* a taking as other or as more than is given.[114] In this sense, imagination is inherently *interpretative*, not receptive.[115] Indeed, Young goes very far toward identifying imagination with functions that Kant is conventionally held to assign to the understanding via concepts. There is no question, for Young, that imagination belongs to the spontaneous functions of the mind in Kant.[116] He sees it functioning in terms of discerning in the sensibly given configurations which "might also appear in other ways and on other occasions," which seems to come close to the conceptual sense of "falling under a rule." Young pushes so hard in this direction that he seems close to Schaper's project of dissolving imagination entirely into understanding and reducing Kant's epistemology to two faculties, with no mediating third.[117] But Young is not ultimately disposed to follow Schaper that far.

He makes a crucial distinction: "to construe or interpret something sensibly present as an F and to discriminate it from things of other types . . . is a function of imagination," but "to have the discursive representation of a thing of kind F, the *concept* of such a thing, and to be able to *judge* that what is sensibly present is an F . . . are functions of the understanding."[118] The first function has to do with that recognition or naming associated with *kennen* and *erkennen* as in acquaintance, not knowledge [*wissen*], while the second is involved with what Kant called *verstehen* (understanding), or more generally objective judgment. Young points out that some of the things imagination discerns as F's find no conceptual correlate, while some of the things understanding conceives as F's find no sensible correlate.[119]

Young means to draw imagination very close to the *faculty* of judgment *(Urteilskraft)*.[120] Both entail "subsuming particulars under rules." However, judgment is concerned with validity in a crucial way that imagination is not. While imagination functions as subsumption in accordance with a rule, judgment functions as subsumption in accordance with the *conception* of a rule, i.e., with explicit reference to the validity of the claimed subsumption. This distinction is decisive. Kant writes of imagination acting in accordance with the rules of understanding but not for the sake of these rules in a crucial passage of the *Anthropology* which will prove essential to the whole idea of aesthetic judgments. That it is possible for imagination to act in accordance with the rules of the understanding but without explicit acknowledgement of them makes the freedom of the imagination conceivable and permits of Kant's crucial concept of "harmony" in the *Third Critique*, whereas in *constitutive judgment*, imagination is not free, but is precisely *determined*.[121]

Young concludes that the key is to "distinguish between a merely subjective linking of appearances and a linking of the appearances in truth . . . between a merely subjective unity and an objective unity."[122] With this language he comes amazingly close to the distinction between the judgment of experience and the judgment of perception, but he mentions neither the *Prolegomena* itself nor Prauss's famous exegesis of it. Nevertheless, his analysis of imagination shows how profoundly close imagination and the judgment of perception are, and how close both are to the faculty of judgment. It is that coherence that I wish to push to its ultimate conclusion.

Kant recognizes that existence is a matter about which nothing can be "anticipated" a priori. If there are rules for promoting actuality via concepts to validity, they must start from and reinterpret what must already be given. That raises once again the question of the reference involved in intuitive synthesis. Is the "common ground" or "origin" produced by imagination—Kant at one point calls it "intuition" and at another "image"—not approaching the sense of an object? Kant seems driven to concede at least a restrictive sense of this: "the power of intuition (pure or empirical) is limited to objects in their singularity, whereas the power of concepts contains the universal element of [representations]."[123]

If we exploit fully the sense we have been garnering both of the core ambiguity in Kant's notion of objectivity and of the peculiar "kind of judging" we have discriminated, we can suggest that Kant could mean that objective reference only has a claim to validity when conceptually constituted, but that some prospect of plausible, merely subjectively valid, reference to the object might be associated with the judgment of perception: perhaps a descriptive rather than a scientific reference. In the imaginative synthesis, then, we could discern *(kennen)* a unity of the manifold (image) as referring to something existing external to the subject in the most primordial sense of givenness: an involuntary modification of the subjective state, to be sure found in the subject, but not made by it.

Let us sum up the capacities we ascribe to this other "kind of judging." Insofar as it has all those powers of attending involved in imagination, it can form intuitions in space, and associate them in time. It can compare and contrast, and thereby discern identity and difference, agreement and opposition. That is to say, it can find whether and which sensations are given as connected with, or are about, distinct forms as their proper matter. And it can find the affinities of mere representations and ascribe them to a unified ground. It can constitute an image of an object.[124] But what imagination cannot do, nor this form of judging either, insofar as they are identical, is "bring forth a sense representation that was never given to the power of sense."[125] Insofar as the subject can recognize this involuntary givenness of sensation and ascribe it to an intuition as external to itself, this kind of judging can discriminate "inner" and "outer"—even if all that it contemplates is present as inner sense. It does this, it must be stressed, ultimately in accordance with, but without explicit recourse to, the rules of the understanding.

It is just here that the *Third Critique* takes up and decisively advances the argument. In what is very likely the oldest section of the work, §10, Kant makes the following crucial observation: "Again, we are not always forced to regard what we observe (in respect of its possibility) from the point of view of reason. Thus we can at least observe a purposiveness according to form, without basing it on a purpose (as the material of the *nexus finalis*), and remark it in objects, although only by reflection."[126] "The point of view of reason" in the text should be taken to refer to theoretical or cognitive operation in the technical sense of subsuming representations under universal concepts: "judgments of experience" or "determinant judgments," in other words. Thus we are concerned in this passage with that "other kind of judging." Twice in the passage Kant calls that activity "observation" *(beobachten)*. In addition, he uses "remark" or "recognize" *(bemerken)*. Both are words that appear in some sense cognitive. To observe *(beobachten)* and to recognize *(bemerken)* are very likely the senses of *kennen* and *erkennen* in the *Logic* passage. Kant claims now that they are possible only "by reflection." What, then, is reflection?

In the "Amphiboly of Concepts of Reflection" of the *First Critique,* Kant defines reflection as "that state of mind [*Zustand des Gemütes*] in which we first set ourselves to discover the subjective conditions under which (alone) we are able to arrive at concepts." Hence it "does not concern itself with objects themselves with a view of deriving concepts from them directly," but rather considers "the relation of given representations to our different sources of knowledge."[127] Kant goes on to argue that all judgments require this reflection. He intimates that it is a commonplace in all acts of consciousness, not merely judgments but "all comparisons" *(alle Vergleichungen).*[128] Every interpretative encounter with experience involves reflection, and he characterizes its operations in just the terms which we have connected with that other kind of judging: "Now the relations in which concepts in a state of mind can stand to one another are those of *identity* and *difference,* of *agreement* and *opposition,* of the *inner* and the *outer,* and finally of the *determinable* and the *determination* (matter and form)."[129]

In discussing reflection under these "four headings of all comparision and distinction," Kant provides the seal to the argument I have been trying to elaborate: "They are distinguished from categories by the fact that they do not represent the object according to what constitutes its concept (quantity, reality), but only serve to describe in all its manifoldness the comparison of the representations which is prior to the concept of things."[130] Reference to the object in this "other kind of judging," I maintain, is the essential structure of the "reflective judgment" upon which the entire *Third Critique* is grounded.

Kant's association of "purposiveness" with this emergent notion of reflective judgment is the consequence of his attunement to the cognitive potential in this other kind of judging, and it is in pursuing this cognitive extension of his language of purposiveness that Kant would come to make his breakthrough to the theory of reflective judgment as such, with its attendant discrimination from determinant judgment and modification of the faculty scheme of rationality. But before he could follow out that potential, Kant had still to use what he already grasped about purposiveness to solve his problem in aesthetics.

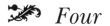 *Four*

THE TRANSCENDENTAL
GROUNDING OF TASTE:
PURPOSE AND PLEASURE

As he turned to the composition of his "Critique of Taste" in late 1787, Kant believed that some form of transcendental grounding was possible. He believed he had found that elusive and unique a priori principle in which he could ground the faculty of feeling transcendentally in a critique of taste. But how did he come to that principle? How was it distinctive? And why, above all, did he term that department of philosophy which would explicate it "teleology?" With those questions we get to the heart of the specific genesis of the "Critique of Taste." Kant found his key just as he intimated in the letter to Reinhold, namely, by reflecting on his previous success along the line of a systemic extension of the critical philosophy in terms of the faculties of mind, i.e., the *Second Critique*. The genesis of the "Critique of Taste" lies in the adoption of the model of the *Second Critique* for the resolution of the transcendental problem of the *Third*. Kant began the "Critique of Taste" on the premise that the structure of the judgment of taste was analogous to that of the pure moral choice. Both had sensuous outcomes, but both were determined entirely by form, and thus by a universal rational principle, and they could both therefore be taken to be autonomous and a priori. To work out the analogy it is necessary to understand what form meant in the context of the judgment of taste, hence what the structure of the judgment of taste had to be, and what purity of such a judgment would entail. Kant needed to follow the procedure he outlined for the transcendental deduction of pure principles: first, to attend to the modality of necessity that reason itself introduced into these propositions, and second to eliminate all the particular, empirical content and isolate the pure form of the propositions.[1]

Kant was interested exclusively in the idea of finding "a kind of a priori principle different from those heretofore observed" which would ground feeling in reason, and this guided the whole flow of his argumentation. His procedure proved very intricate, and I propose to reconstruct it exegetically through the sections which, on the basis of Tonelli and the other scholars, we can date earliest, and hence as the original "Critique of Taste" of fall 1787: §§1–22, 31–40. We must not assume, however, that they were composed—much less conceived—as they now stand. Here Meredith steps forth as an extremely ingenious guide.[2] He suggests that the marvelous piece of architectonic, whereby the "Analytic of the Beautiful" was ultimately structured in terms of the general characteristics of all logical judgments, came somewhat late and was imposed on a text that had developed in an altogether different manner. He further suggests that the earliest segments of the work were, accordingly, §§10ff. and §§31ff. He includes §1 as introductory and §9 as, in Kant's own words, "the key to the Critique of Taste."[3] It is in these sections that we must locate that breakthrough which made possible the transcendental grounding of the "Critique of Taste."

Kant began §10 of the *Critique of Judgment,* "Of Purposiveness in General," with no less than five transcendental explanations. Purpose, purposiveness, pleasure, pain, and will all received transcendental explanations. That these explanations are in large measure assumed in the argumentation of the rest of the analytic, including sections which precede it, supports Meredith's conjecture that this may have been the starting point of the original "Critique of Taste." Connecting the transcendental achievement represented by §10 with the account Kant gave in his letter to Reinhold in December 1787 enhances the plausibility of Meredith's suggestion.

Purposiveness—"teleology"—served as the vehicle for the development of a "Critique of Taste." Kant acknowledged in his letter to Reinhold that teleology had little to offer, that it was the "poorest in a priori grounds of determination."[4] But that there could be any a priori principles grounding feeling was already a revolutionary insight. The link between pleasure and purposiveness is the grounding insight of the "Critique of Taste." In §10 Kant takes pleasure, transcendentally described, to be the causality of a representation in "*maintaining* the subject in the same state."[5] Kant characterizes purpose and purposiveness with crisp economy: "Purpose is the object of a concept in so far as the concept is regarded as the cause of the object (the real ground of its possibility); and the causality of a *concept* in respect of its *object* is its purposiveness *(forma finalis)*."[6] Purpose is the *relation* between a concept and an object whereby the concept acts as cause of the actuality (existence) of the object.

What is caused is "not merely the cognition of an object but the object itself (its form and existence)."[7] But even more important is the fundamentally distinctive kind of cause: causality through a concept. In the Kantian framework, the relation of purpose involves intelligent agency, or "will." That is why Kant presents a transcendental explanation of will in §10. He describes it as "the faculty of desire, so far as it is determinable to act only through concepts, i.e. in conformity with the representation of a purpose."[8] Causality through intelligent will is "noumenal causality"; it constitutes an event which cannot be accounted for within the strict categorical system of the world of phenomena.[9] The essential idea of this mode of causality arises in the human consciousness of moral freedom and responsibility. In reflecting on the idea of will in the context of the *Second Critique* Kant found the clue to a transcendental deduction of the *Third.*[10]

It remains to see exactly how Kant thought he had achieved his transcendental deduction of taste. Kant first analyzed (to "analyze" or "expound" is the first step in "Critique") the essential elements in the judgment of taste as a type of proposition.[11] He discerned that it was a singular, not a universal logical judgment, i.e., it referred to a single instance.[12] The judgment "This tulip is beautiful" was a judgment of taste, while the judgment "Tulips are beautiful" was a cognitive judgment.[13] A judgment of taste had always to be an immediate, first-hand response to an unanticipatably unique stimulus.

Second, the judgment of taste was grounded not in any conceptualization but rather in the mere feeling elicited by the presence of the representation-of-an-object. Here Kant found it necessary to discriminate repeatedly between "sensation" *(Sinn)* and "feeling" *(Gefühl)*, that is, objective and subjective reference.[14] More specifically, he discriminated between cognitive use involving conceptualization, and mere aesthetic contemplation.[15] He associated the former with objectivity and the latter with subjectivity. Thus the judgment of taste was subjective, had to do with feeling, and ostensibly had no cognitive use whatsoever.[16]

But despite these two features, the judgment of taste claimed on the one hand universal consent and on the other, necessity. It claimed, in short, features which Kant associated with a priori judgments. Kant was careful to discriminate the sort of universality and the sort of necessity claimed in the judgment of taste from those claimed in cognitive judgments. The universality of consent claimed in a judgment of taste, Kant observed, had to do not with the true universality which could reside only in logical validity, but rather with the intersubjective validity of the judgment, namely, its claim on all observers.[17] Similarly, the kind of necessity claimed in the judgment of taste was not the necessity of a universal logical category but rather the "exemplary" necessity of a singular instance.[18] Yet, for all that, in the measure that the judgment of taste made these claims, it seemed to suggest a rational a priori principle at its foundation.

The key point is that in the sorts of propositions involved in aesthetic judgments some modality of necessity seemed involved. Thus, Kant wrote: "In this modality of aesthetic judgments, namely their assumed necessity, lies what is for the *Critique of Judgment* a moment of capital importance. For this is what makes an a priori principle apparent in their case, and lifts them out of the sphere of empirical psychology."[19] These lines come from one of the transitional sections added to the "Analytic of the Sublime" to accommodate it into the "Critique of Aesthetic Judgment," and the use of the phrase "Critique of Judgment" confirms that it cannot have been written before the spring of 1789. But the idea had to be present to Kant's mind before he could embark at all on any transcendental grounding of a "Critique of Taste."

Thus Kant felt that establishing the ground whereby the singular judgment could be recognized as universal and necessary, a priori, in this sense constituted the philosophical challenge and the reward of a consideration of taste as a transcendental issue. In §8, he noted that while the formal category was not particularly problematic for general logic, it was quite another matter for the transcendental philosopher: "It brings to light a property of our cognitive faculty which, without this analysis, would have remained unknown."[20] It was this discovery which enabled Kant to write his "Critique of Taste," and this which he identified as the a priori principle of a kind unlike any other discovered.

In the case of the pure moral choice, the purpose of the action could not be its material outcome, but only the internal dynamic of rationality in the subject. Similarly, the judgment of taste had to be pure of such connection. Purity in the case of the judgment of taste meant that pleasure could not be connected with the materiality of the object represented to consciousness. Hence Kant argued that "every interest vitiates the judgment of taste and robs it of its impartiality . . . where instead of, like the interest of reason, making purposiveness take the lead in the feeling of pleasure, it grounds it upon this feeling. . ."[21] To be sure, in both moral choice and the judgment of taste, a material pleasure might accompany the mental process. "Happiness" in the case of a pure moral choice was not excluded as a result, only as a cause. Similarly "charm" in the case of a judgment of taste was not excluded as attending the experience, but only as the determining basis.

Kant distinguished, in strict analogy to the moral problem, between empirical (heteronomous) and pure (autonomous) judgments: "A judgment of taste . . . is only pure so far as its determining ground is tainted with no merely empirical delight. But such a taint is always present where charm [Reiz] or emotion [Rührung] have a share in the judgment by which something is to be described as beautiful."[22] Rather, a "pure" form of delight was associated with the immanent determination of the mental process expressed in the propositions: in the case of the pure moral choice, "respect," and in the case of the judgment of taste, beauty. These two feelings, in their purity, i.e., their abstraction from any determining interest in the material gratification that might empirically be bound up with them, betokened or "marked" the intrinsic and rational determination of the mental activity which occasioned them.

Thus, as from the feeling of respect we can necessarily infer the pure moral choice as its only possible cause, so from the feeling of beauty we should be able necessarily to infer a pure rational process as its only possible cause: "an autonomy of the subject passing judgment on the feeling of pleasure (in the given representation)."[23] Autonomy is the decisive idea. Again, in striking analogy to the argument of the *Second Critique,* Kant insists that "taste lays claim simply to autonomy."[24] It is a free choice. Indeed, Kant argues, it is the freest choice possible for man, and a kind of freedom which man alone enjoys, just by virtue of his complex nature.[25]

In analyzing the judgment of taste, just as in analyzing the pure moral choice, transcendental philosophy is "concerned with the a priori principles of pure judgment . . . those in which it is itself, subjectively, object as well as law."[26] The way in which we ascertain whether such purity or autonomy is attained in the judgment of taste is strikingly parallel to the manner in which any given maxim of choice is appraised for its conformity to the categorical imperative:

weighing the judgment, not so much with actual, as rather with the merely possible, judgments of others . . . by putting ourselves in the position of every one else, . . . letting go the element of matter, i.e. sensation, in our general state of representative activity, and confining attention to the formal peculiarities of our representation or general state of representative activity.[27]

It is only insofar as the subject has no reason to suspect that his judgment can be merely private that he is emboldened to speak with a "universal voice" and express what he takes to be a "common sense" (sensus communis).[28] This is the basis for his claim to universality and necessity.

Previous philosophers of aesthetics had sought the basis for the judgment of taste in a property of the object, but their search had been vain.[29] Instead, Kant proposed that it be sought in the conformity of the representation of the object to our judgment, i.e., we must find in the rules given by the judgment the ground of the beauty ascribed to the object. This was, as it were, Kant's "Copernican revolution" in aesthetics, which made possible a transcendental philosophy of taste. Kant argued, in view of all the essential features of the judgment of taste, that the rational a priori principle which grounded it could only lie in a relation of the faculties themselves. In §9, which he called the "key to the Critique of Taste," he articulated this as the idea of "harmony of the faculties."

A "Critique of Taste," undertaken transcendentally, had to be "an investigation of the faculties of cognition and their function in these judgments, and the illustration, by the analysis of examples, of their mutual subjective purposiveness, the form of which in a given representation . . . constitute[s] the beauty of their object."[30] Here, finally, "purposiveness" [Zweckmäßigkeit] or "teleology" enters into Kant's account, and justifies his contention about the grounding transcendental principle of this faculty of mind.

The strategy of the "Critique of Taste" appears to have been to superimpose the language of reflection, as a kind of judging indispensable for cognition in general, upon human capacity for feeling, as a "real" aspect of finite-rational subjectivity in general. The "Critique of Taste" can be construed as a project of grounding at least some feeling in a rational principle a priori. The core argument, working from pleasure and purposiveness to the intersubjective validity of the judgment of taste, found articulation ultimately in the "Critique of Aesthetic Judgment" in the Third Critique, especially in the "Analytic of the Beautiful" and in the "Deduction of Aesthetic Judgment." Kant formulated the view that there was an intrinsic aptitude peculiar to human beings for grounding feeling in reason through beauty.[31] He called this a "common sense" *(sensus communis)*. With that he tried to incorporate not only the German rationalist tradition, but also the British "critical" approach to aesthetics.

Not objectivity but subjective response—specifically "mutual subjective purposiveness"—is the key to the nature of beauty and of the judgment of taste, "a thing being called beautiful solely in respect of that quality in which it adapts itself to our mode of taking it in."[32] The crucial locus of Kant's analysis of aesthetic experience is within consciousness, in its own operations, and for him the crucial condition is that "the mental state in this representation must be one of a feeling of the free play of the powers of representation in a given representation for a cognition in general."[33] Kant goes on to elaborate the meaning of this "free play." He writes: "The quickening of both faculties (imagination and understanding) to an indefinite, but yet, thanks to the given representation, harmonious activity, such as belongs to cognition generally, is the sensation whose universal communicability is postulated by the judgment of taste."[34] Why did Kant call this "mutual subjective purposiveness?" In §12, Kant wrote that "this pleasure is in no way practical." Yet he claimed that it "still involves an inherent causality." This he characterized as "*preserving the continuance* of the state of the representation itself and the active engagement of the cognitive powers without ulterior aim."[35] Thus Kant conjoined his transcendental explanations of pleasure and purpose to generate this notion.[36]

The Language of Purposiveness

Purpose has its coherent and literal sense in the willed act. Kant immediately asserts, however, that we may discriminate the form of purpose from its reality. The form of purpose is design, i.e., the relation of an idea as cause of the actuality of an object. That is the explanation of "purposiveness" offered in §10.[37] But if we abstract from this relation and think only of the form, then we attend to the *appearance* of design, which does not necessarily entail its actuality. And thus we derive the explanation of purposiveness given in §iv and anticipate the phrase Kant introduces in so many words in §10: "purposiveness without purpose."[38] The notion of "formal" purposiveness invokes similarity or analogy to purpose. It is a figurative use of the language.

Why does Kant transpose the language of purposiveness from literal to figurative use? The answer lies in the peculiar opportunity it provides for accounting for events. The form of purpose is a possible cognitive order. This emerges clearly in §10: "But an object, or a state of mind, or even an action is called purposive, although its possibility does not necessarily presuppose the representation of a purpose, merely because its possibility can be explained and conceived by us only in so far as we assume for its ground a causality according to purposes."[39] Such a representation is patently figurative, a subjective recourse to make the matter "intelligible to ourselves." But the occasion for this account is nonetheless the perplexity of empirical cognition. We are struggling to "explain" and to "conceive." Purposiveness is a cognitive language to which we resort in the extremity of empirical anomaly.

If we have cognitive recourse to this language, what validity can it claim? Purpose, Kant emphatically assures us, is not a category. It is not part of the constitutive framework whereby the understanding determines objective knowledge.[40] Heuristic "maxims" in general are certainly "useful" (*zweckmäßig* has that sense in German) in investigations, but they are, according to Kant, strictly subjective. This subjective usefulness, though cognitive, might be construed in terms of human practical purposiveness—in its "technical" rather than its "moral" sense—reading cognition as a mode of human technical practical purposiveness. This idea comes to articulation in Kant's *First Introduction to the Critique of Judgment,* especially in §i. All of this notwithstanding, nothing about this sort of usefulness renders its cognitive results "objective." The Introduction discriminates logical from aesthetic reflective judgments, yet Kant never ascribes objectivity to logical reflective judgment. He restricts his entire discussion to subjective purposiveness.

Kant wished to equate subjective with formal, and objective with material purposiveness, but the exigencies of his exposition did not permit this.[41] Had he held to a tighter line, Kant could not have conceived of a purposiveness which was at once objective and formal or of one which was at once subjective and material. But in fact he did. In §62 Kant gave an account of the purposiveness of geometrical constructions as objective and formal. And Kant accounted for the agreeable or pleasant *(das Angenehme)* in his *First Introduction* as subjective but material purposiveness. Only by virtue of our account of the disjuncture of Kant's notions of validity and actuality can we make any sense of this. Objective formal purposiveness proves to be a form of validity without actuality, while subjective material purposiveness involves actuality without validity, especially in Kant's conception of the "animality" of man. It remains that the other two types of purposivess prove far more significant for Kant: objective material purposiveness and, above all, subjective formal purposiveness.

In contrasting the formal "purposiveness in general" of geometrical figures with "real" or "material" purposiveness in §62 of the *Third Critique,* Kant stressed that the latter was to be found in "*things,* external to myself," whose "order and regularity [as] existing things must be given empirically in order to be known."[42] He used as his example a garden laid out in geometric regularity. Encountering this empirical garden, one discovered purposiveness. It was given, the result of an empirical cognition, as something about the object. Yet purposiveness could only be given problematically, for it was an interpretative inference from, not a property immediately in, the given. Thus Kant wrote: "The purposiveness of a thing, so far as it is represented in perception, is no characteristic of the object itself (for such cannot be perceived) although it may be inferred from a cognition of things."[43] First the thing had to be recognized. That seemed to require an empirical cognitive judgment.[44] That judgment, moreover, led to the conjecture that the thing as recognized could not plausibly be taken as a mere natural happenstance; it stood out as anomalous in nature. It appeared as an *artifact,* as the consequence of some design.[45]

Recognizing the purposiveness of things does not appear problematic if they result from our own particular practical activity.[46] It is alien purpose that poses interpretative difficulty. Encountering such a thing, we have to make an inference about its genesis, having recourse to our own practical purposiveness as a model. We are in the realm of empirical judgments. To take the example Kant suggests in §62, we might find ourselves in yet another kind of garden, not one on the model of Versailles and geometry, but one modeled in the Oriental fashion to imitate the spontaneity of nature, and fail to recognize the artifact for one.[47] Or we might recognize it as purposive and yet still take it to seem natural, and enjoy it as a work of art: a "dependent" beauty, because we shall have had to recognize, hence conceptualize, it as a garden before we can judge it as art.[48] But the converse is also possible: we may take a natural occurrence as an artifact because it *seems* so designed.[49] The point is, discern-ment, discrimination—in a word, judgment—is requisite here. It is a cognitive situation in which one may easily err.

And *more* than cognition is involved. There is also usefulness, and the connection of usefulness with existence. "Material pur-posiveness" has a strong sense of an object available for use. In §10, in defining purpose Kant made a great deal of distinguishing the object itself from its mere cognition. He characterized the object it-self as "form and existence."[50] The existence of the object in this sense seems to go beyond the cognition of it. Its form and existence must have some additional meaning. The meaning of the actual ex-istence of an object in terms of its availability for use is encompassed in Kant's term "[material] interest."[51] It extends the relation of the subject to the object from a cognitive to a practical one, and entails not only the material existence of the object, but also the material existence of the subject (as *Willkür*). A purpose always entails inter-est, a concern for the existence or actualization of the object. That is exactly what "material purposiveness" signifies.

In §15 Kant introduces the notion of "objective purposive-ness."[52] The connection of "objective" with "material purposive-ness" is twofold. It involves, in the first regard, a determinate object of cognition to be appreciated by the subject as an occasion for mere gratification. "Material purposiveness" is promoted to "objec-tive purposiveness" in reference to an object constituted by con-cepts and elected by a rational process of will (not moral, in this case, but simply prudential, i.e., pleasure-seeking). As such it would be useful or, in Kant's words, a "relative" purpose (or relative good). Objects become "relative" purposes only via their utility for an in-trinsic purpose, an agent or "end." They are, precisely, "means." Consequently, purposiveness remains merely "external," not in the object itself but in its utility to a separate "end" or *intrinsic* purpose.

Hence the essential contrast between "material" and "objec-tive" purposiveness only comes to full articulation in terms of this notion of *intrinsic* (self-determining) purpose. An intrinsic *purpose* is an agent capable of means-ends choice, or at least an actual entity whose empirically observed behavior cannot be accounted for by human understanding otherwise than by analogy with such an agent. Thus "natural purposes" have imputed to them a form of action analogous to that of a true agent. Yet Kant is unequivocal that the effective mechanism in the case of natural purposes is not means-ends choice, not rational will, but merely instinct. Hence "natural purposes," or organic forms, have only an imputed "intrinsic *purposiveness.*" As a consequence they do not merit the full status of an "end-in-itself."[53]

Kant identified the notion of "intrinsic purposiveness" with the concept of "perfection." Baumgarten had used the notion to refer to the completeness of a thing in terms of its distinguishing marks. To be perfect in that sense was to demonstrate all the requisite marks of a particular kind of thing. This sense of completeness after its kind Kant termed "quantitative perfection." He argued against Baumgarten that it was only possible to use perfection in its "quantitative" sense if one already could posit what "kind" a thing was supposed to be. But the idea that an entity *ought* to be any kind was not a simple judgment of experience, not a cognitive judgment presided over by the understanding, but a judgment of (practical) reason. It presumed a concept of the thing, and more specifically, an idea of what the purpose of the thing should be. This was the explanation of his own notion of "qualitative perfection" which Kant offered in §15 of the *Third Critique*. Where moral judgments are concerned, the faculty at work is reason, and reason functions not in the realm of the actual, but in the realm of "intelligible form." The judgment of "qualitative perfection," insofar as it is a moral appraisal, that is, insofar as the terms "good" and "perfect" correspond, translates the object of such a judgment from the world of the senses into the noumenal order. Perfection as he uses it, *qualitative* perfection, entails immanent purposiveness or entelechy.[54]

The most essential link between Kant's philosophy and that of Baumgarten is the problematic consideration of this idea of *Vollkommenheit,* or perfection. Perfection, in this context, refers to the objective quality of a thing. The notion of intrinsic perfection has, for Kant, not merely a cognitive but an evaluative aspect. Kant developed this notion in the 1750s and 1760s. "All perfection appears to consist in the accordance [*Zusammenstimmung*] of a thing with freedom, hence in its purposiveness, general utility, etc."[55] For Kant the objective perfection of a thing had to do with its purpose.

Kant initially, under the influence of Baumgarten, sought to use beauty as an access to this objective perfection. In a *Reflection* from the 1750s, Kant made this clear in explaining the meaning of *judicium.* "If one notes not only the similarities and differences of things, but also how a manifold merges into a unity and forms its ground, then one recognizes perfection. This is called judging [*beurteilen*] . . . Such judgment is quite certainly possible through the lower faculties of knowledge."[56] What Kant wished to resolve, vis-à-vis Baumgarten, is "whether beauty and perfection, including their causes as well as the rules for judging them, stand in secret connection."[57] Kant wished to believe that the recognition of the objective quality of a thing—a cognitive-evaluative judgment—had an aesthetic concomitant. "The inner perfection of a thing has a natural relation to beauty. For the subordination of a manifold to a purpose requires its coordination according to common laws. Therefore the same property through which a building is beautiful contributes as well to its perfection [*bonität*]."[58] But sometimes, with certain sorts of phenomena, Kant believed it possible that this aesthetic aspect could arise even when there were difficulties with the cognitive-evaluative judgment. "In all products of nature and of art there is something which relates exclusively to the purpose, and something that merely has to do with the agreement of the appearance with the state of mind, i.e. the manner [*Manier*], the wrapping. The latter, even when one cannot grasp the purpose, is often quite sufficient [for beauty], e.g. the shape and color of flowers."[59] The mere manner in which such things affect our sensibility suffices for the experience of aesthetic pleasure.[60] "We recognize of many things in nature that they are beautiful, but we do not know their purpose; one should believe not that it was nature's intention to please us, but that we are pleased nature seems to have intention."[61]

Yet, while the feeling of beauty might be aroused merely by the *Manier,* Kant believed it was tied to the objective purpose. Kant went quite far along this line:

> One notes that almost everything in nature which has the property of shaping itself distinctly from the general clump of matter is beautiful in the eyes of man. From this one can see that beauty must involve a consequence [*Folge*] of perfection, while perfection itself must be a matter of concepts. Perhaps the recognition of perfection comes first in man; recognized sensibly, it is beauty; as a mere matter of sensation, the pleasant.[62]

In some obscure remarks that follow, Kant insisted that something must be given in sensation which pertained to the "absolute and real" in the object, even if understanding could not grasp this absolute quality perfectly [*in der Vollkommenheit*]. Kant thus introduced a distinction between a perfection in the thing itself, which was intimated only obscurely in sensation, and a perfection in comprehending the thing, which was a matter of cognitive process in which the obscurity of sensation intervened.

In all sensibility there is a perfection which human under-standing does not possess, namely, intuition, and an imper-fection: sensation and the form of appearance. Reason represents only relational concepts [*verhältnis Begriffe*]; in in-tuition, however, what is absolute and internal in an object is thought. Except the imperfection is that our intuitions con-cern only the relation of things to our senses.[63]

In the *Reflection* Kant argued that it was in intuition that the "abso-lute and internal"—the reality—of an object was thought. That clearly suggested a cognitive-evaluative level of discourse.[64] Over against that, Kant claimed that "the synthesis of a manifold for a determinate purpose is relative perfection."

In Kant's thinking of the 1760s, "perfection" pointed in too many directions. He tried to integrate under it cognitive, ethical, and aesthetic components of judgment. The load was simply too heavy, and the enterprise collapsed under the impact of British em-piricism. Kant gave up his notion of beauty connected to objective perfection in *Reflection* 676, in which he recognized two distinct sorts of perfection. One involved the nature of the object, and was cognitive and evaluative.[65] The other involved the nature of the subject, and perfection in this sense was what the aesthetic, what beauty, was all about. It involved "liveliness," i.e., expanding the consciousness of life.[66] "That the form of an object facilitates the activity of the understanding is what makes something beautiful pleasurable and this is subjective; what is objective, however, is that this form is universally valid."[67] Kant described aesthetic experi-ence as a sort of play, a use of the mind without specific purpose merely for the sake of entertainment, in which "all the powers of the mind are set into harmonious play."[68] This notion of harmony of the faculties was directly drawn from the school-philosophy tra-dition.

While Kant believed that beauty was a matter of subjective per-fection and involved the heightening of the mind, he had to deter-mine whether he could explain beauty entirely by this enhancing function or whether it required a supplementary account in terms of merely sensuous pleasure. In *Reflection* 638, Kant formulated the issue in the following way: "The question is whether the play of sensations or the form and shape of intuition is immediately plea-surable or only pleases because it provides understanding with comprehensibility and facility in gathering into a whole the manifold and giving distinctness to the whole representation."[69] In the first case, Kant believed, beauty would be indistinguishable from sensual "charm" [Reiz]. Since Kant came to reject this identification, his theory of beauty as subjective perfection had to be oriented toward a harmony of the faculties, and beauty grounded in this utility for understanding. That was the meaning of his most fruitful notion of purposiveness: "subjective formal"—i.e., *aesthetic*—purposiveness.

"Aesthetic" Purposiveness

In §vii of the Introduction Kant wrote: "If pleasure is bound up with the mere apprehension *(apprehensio)* of the form of an object of intuition, without reference to a concept for a definite cognition, then the representation is thereby not referred to the object, but simply to the subject . . . and hence can only express a subjective formal purposiveness of the object."[70] We have, then, to construe "subjective formal purposiveness."

> The subjective (element) in a representation, *which cannot be an ingredient in cognition,* is the *pleasure* or *pain* bound up with it . . . The purposiveness, therefore, which precedes the cognition of an object and which, even without our wishing to use the representation of it for cognition, is at the same time immediately bound up with it, is that subjective (element) which cannot be an ingredient in cognition. Hence the object is only called purposive when its representation is an aesthetical representation of purposiveness.[71]

There are few more essential or more difficult passages than this one in the *Third Critique.* Consider the peculiarities of the exposition. It is the *object* which is "called" purposive. That suggests a judgment very akin to the one involved in the figurative extension of the term in empirical interpretation.[72] But in this new context this signifies only that the representation of the object is "immediately combined" with a feeling of pleasure. Does this mean they are the same or different? Is the "reference" *in* (i.e., an aspect of) or *about* (i.e., an assessment of) the representation-of-the-object? The issue only gets muddier when Kant redefines this representation, which as such had to have available in it matter for reference to the object, into an "aesthetic representation of purposiveness." Is the materiality and distinctiveness of the object utterly annulled? In addition, is an aesthetic representation of purposiveness the same as or different from purposiveness itself?

Kant does well to ask, at this juncture, "whether there is, in general, such a representation of purposiveness."[73] At the outset of §vii, in dealing with logical validity as reference to the object, Kant discriminated between the "form" of the representation and its "matter": space and sensation respectively. Now it would appear that form and matter are relevant as well in terms of reference to the subject. If we may be permitted the phrases, we must distinguish an "aesthetic form" and an "aesthetic matter" as properties of the representation-of-the-object. These may not simply be conflated with space and sensation. These aesthetic elements in or "bound up with" the representation could have *no* objective reference, Kant insisted.[74]

How does the "aesthetic form" of the representation connect with formal purposiveness? Earlier we operated with a fairly secure notion of what formal purposiveness signified in its figurative sense: likeness to purpose, the appearance of design. Now Kant seems confoundingly close to identifying the formality of purposiveness with the form of the representation as it refers to the subject—"aesthetic form."[75] But that is ostensibly only *feeling.* The element of objective reference that made the representation serviceable for empirical interpretation seems now to have evaporated utterly. In the empirical cognitive use, the whole empirical existence of a thing was occasion for the recourse to purposiveness. In this new, "aesthetical" instance, what matters is the mere form of the representation of the object, but that in only its subjective reference. It is held to be not merely for the subject but about the subject.

Kant suggests a very important phenomenological distinction in the *Anthropology:* "We should distinguish between inner sense, which is a mere power of perception (of empirical intuition), and the feeling of pleasure and displeasure—that is our susceptibility to be determined, by certain representations, either to hold onto them or to drive them away—which could be called *interior sense (sensus interior)*."[76] Sensation provokes not merely attention (consciousness) but subjective reference, "attention to our own state" or self-consciousness. Every sensation is in inner sense, or for the subject, and yet almost all can be interpreted in terms of outer sense, objective reference. From the latter, judgments both of perception and of experience can be construed. But there remains that which is not merely for the subject but also about or of the subject: the "state of mind" which Kant associates with the feeling (*Gefühl*) of pleasure and pain. Sensation remains the occasion, however, even of this reference. Kant gives a fitting illustration in §3, where the green of a meadow is considered both in terms of its objective reference and in terms of the pleasantness or satisfaction it occasions in the subject.[77] This latter is the sphere of the "aesthetic."

Kant is addressing himself to the subjective response to empirical sensation and focusing his attention exclusively upon that reference to the subject. Therefore he abstracts from the cognitive aspect of the representation of the object, its objective reference, to clarify the aesthetic side, subjective reference. He recognizes that pleasure or pain can be involved in empirical cognition, yet he insists that this pleasure or pain has no cognitive relevance.[78]

When he writes of a "purposiveness . . . which precedes the cognition of an object," the only sense in which that "*cannot be an ingredient of cognition,*" as he also insists, is if cognition is taken in the rigorous sense of a "judgment of experience," of a "determinant judgment." But what about a *reflective* judgment? Is the characterization of the subjective purposiveness of a "logical reflective judgment" (a teleological judgment) at all different from that of an "aesthetic reflective judgment?" That is, can there be any difference in what is present to consciousness? Is it not really a matter of how we attend that presence—the *use*, the intellectual interest taken in what is given? In short, does not subjective formal purposiveness, as Kant articulates it in this crucial passage, implicitly contain a reference to the object—not, to be sure, in the sense of the judgment of experience and its "valid" claim, but in terms of the judgment of perception, that "other kind of judging," and its "reflective" claim?

But in light of this parallelism between the discernment of purposiveness and the subjective reference of feeling, the full significance of "subjective purposiveness" in its formal sense, i.e., "purposiveness without purpose," emerges. That the same subjective reference can serve as the essential determination of the experience of beauty and as the basis for a cognitive use of purposiveness (teleology) suggests the power in Kant's notion. Here we have an indication of our capacity to "experience" prior to and separately from cognition. We see that the kind of "judging" which we have betokened by *kennen* and *erkennen*, by judgment of perception, by the synthesis of apprehension and imagination, by *beobachten* and *bemerken*, and finally by reflection, is identified with the aesthetic sense of purposiveness. It is what Kant would later call "reflective judgment."

But at this stage of his argument Kant was exclusively concerned with using his language of purposiveness to articulate the possibility of a subjective response which was not for the purposes of cognition and hence not explicitly determined by the rules of the understanding, but which was nevertheless grounded in the rational structures of the mind and consequently eligible for an a priori determination. In short, Kant had only a partial interest in the structure of purposiveness. He was concerned with one pure case within it, just as, in his consideration of the pure moral choice, he isolated one pure case within the general structure of purposiveness as willed action in general. There were two linked strategies to pursue in generating the pure case, in performing the transcendental deduction of taste. The first was to discriminate between a merely passive affect, material pleasure, and the pleasure which attended mental activity itself. The second was to discriminate between two judgments about pleasure, one claiming the object was "pleasant" and the other that it was "beautiful." As I will show, both strategies turn on the complex subjective phenomenology we have labored so hard to bring into clarity.

📚 Five

THE BEAUTIFUL AND THE PLEASANT: KANT'S TRANSCENDENTAL DEDUCTION OF TASTE

The pleasure in beauty is a singular event. It cannot be generalized. It is not a property of the object, but a subjective response without concept. Taste is always a subjective judgment in the essential sense that it must be made in the first person, of a specific instance, on the basis of that person's individual response.[1] Kant assures us that it cannot be a prescriptive rule, grounded in discursive concepts. What is consciousness aware of in the experience of beauty that it should make the judgment of taste? Are we cognizant "aesthetically by sensation and our mere internal sense? Or . . . intellectually by consciousness of our intentional activity in bringing these powers into play?"[2] Kant's answer is unequivocal: "There is . . . no way for the subjective unity of the relation in question to make itself known [other] than by sensation."[3] Since "it is absolutely out of the question to require that pleasure in [material] objects should be acknowleded by every one," it can only be the *form* of the representation of the object, but even this not so much in itself as in what it elicits in the subject, which is the basis of the judgment of taste.[4] Thus §9 crucially contends: "If the pleasure in the given object precedes . . . the judgment of taste about the representation of the object, . . . such pleasure would be nothing different from the mere pleasantness in sensation, and so . . . could have only private validity."[5] The true source of the validity of the judgment of taste cannot rest on the mere sensation, but can only derive from its determination by the mental function which attends it. Something distinctive about the subjective feeling involved in taste differentiates it from mere sensuous pleasure. Kant discriminated mere passive affect from the delight in mental activity itself. This led to a distinction of form and matter in the aesthetic representation of an object, the discrim-

106

ination of the beautiful from the pleasant in terms of the phenomenology of their respective experiences.

The Phenomenology of the Pleasant

Only in terms of this discrimination does Kant's notion of aesthetic *judgment* become clear. "Beautiful" and "agreeable" occur only as predicates in judgments. That is to say, these terms arise in consciousness only in the context of the observations "X is beautiful" or "X is pleasant." These observations are inept, because the predicates refer not to X but to the state of the subject in the presence of X. Insofar, however, as judgments can be made at all, the state of the subject must in some sense be amenable to conscious attention. Kant is acutely aware of the incongruity of the phrase "aesthetic judgment." To take it in any sense cognitively, he concedes, would be "blatantly contradictory."[6] If Kant will not have us call it cognition, it remains to ask what "reference" and "reflection" then mean, and why he stubbornly clings to the word "judgment" in characterizing these events. Kant wishes to hold out for the possibility that an "aesthetic judgment of reflection" should retain some status as a judgment, but why should he keep the term for the merely sensual experience of the agreeable? Can it have been because judgment *(Urteil)* was a traditional term in German treatment of aesthetic experience—even the "merely sensuous"—in the eighteenth century?[7] Was Kant merely following convention? Possibly, but we would not be wise to take that as a complete account of a philosophical procedure so self-consciously undertaken by so subtle a mind. Can it have been, then, Kant's notorious hankering after "architectonic"—a violence to the sense of the language for the sake of system? Some have been tempted to read it so.[8] Yet there is an alternative that would render matters more coherent and plausible: to have recourse to that other kind of judging, Kant's complex sense of "subjective reference" in terms of the state of mind of the subject. This is why we labored so long over the meaning of "subjective judgment" in Kant.

Kant characterizes the agreeable or pleasant *(das Angenehme)* in §§2ff. of the *Third Critique* by the following essential features: (1) it pleases in sensation, that is, it "rests entirely on sensation" or "represents the object simply in relation to sensation"; (2) in the agreeable "it is not merely the object that pleases, but also its existence"; and, consequently, (3) it is merely "private."[9] In the *First Introduction to the Critique of Judgment*, Kant characterizes observations about the agreeable as "aesthetic judgments of sense" and explains that such judgments are "completely independent of the faculty of knowledge, being directly related via sense to the feeling of pleasure."[10] By contrast, Kant ascribes to the beautiful the following features: (1) it pleases in reflection; (2) it is disinterested; and consequently, (3) it is universal. In the *First Introduction* Kant describes observations about the beautiful ("judgments of taste") as "aesthetic judgments of reflection," and claims that they are grounded in the "specific [*eigentümlichen*] principles of the faculty of judgment."[11] Thereupon Kant makes the following discrimination: "Aesthetic judgments of sense express material purposiveness; aesthetic judgments of reflection, on the other hand, formal purposiveness."[12]

Clearly, the significance of either term hinges on the juxtaposition with its alternate. The question that immediately arises is why Kant uses the term judgment at all for the experience of the agreeable. It would seem more a matter of physiological response to stimulus than a "judgment." Nevertheless, the term gets articulated in an observation that has the form of a judgment. It is, however remotely, an aspect of conscious articulation, of cognitive process, even if only of a physiological or subjective event.

That quasi-judgmental feature also helps explain how the agreeable can, as Kant insists, be bound up with "interest," i.e., how it can be "not merely the object that pleases, but also its existence." We are back with our familiar theme of usefulness. Yet our earlier account of it presumed the cognition of the object prior to its evaluation as available for use. Now, Kant implies that such subjective material purposiveness arises without any cognition.[13] It is necessary to reconsider the notion of interest in terms of what Kant claims about the agreeable resting entirely on sensation. That calls for a phenomenological account of this experience.

Kant holds the experience of the agreeable to be impossible to predict a priori. Before the first experience there can be no anticipation and therefore no interest, because the connection of pleasure with the experience can come only a posteriori. At the outset of this pristine initial encounter, then, there is the presence to consciousness of X, for example, one's first taste of kiwi. Let us assume that upon tasting kiwi for the first time there is a feeling of pleasure "immediately bound up with it." That experience is not yet a judgment. It is merely "physiological" or at best "psychological." But the experience does not terminate there. Instead, an inference is drawn. There is reflection of some sort after and on account of the pleasure. The first part of this inference is the judgment "X (in our case, the kiwi) is agreeable." It might be held that this initial judgment should have the more primitive form of *"This* is agreeable." Yet for the balance of the reflection precisely what is required is that somehow what occasioned the pleasure be "recognized" *(erkannt),* i.e., named, tagged, and marked sufficiently for further consideration culminating in an interest. On our first consideration this required cognition in the full sense of recourse to concepts. Here is where our understanding of the capacities associated with that other kind of judging now offers an alternative. What it permits is precisely the kind of recognition *(erkennen)* required. In consequence, however, two senses of "materiality" we encountered earlier—the givenness of matter in sensation ("actuality") and the availability for use attached to the existence of an object ("interest") —draw substantially closer to one another, and with that the plausibility of an "actuality without validity" as a sense of Kant's term "objectivity" increases.

How does the judgment of sense lead to interest? By the time I make the observation about the agreeable, an appetite has been aroused. I cannot say I find something pleasant without simultaneously confessing a desire for more. In Kant's own words: "Now that a judgment about an object by which I describe it as pleasant expresses an interest in it, is plain from the fact that by sensation it excites a desire for objects of that kind [*dergleichen Gegenständen*]; consequently the satisfaction presupposes not the mere judgment about it, but the relation of its existence to my state, so far as this is affected by such an object [*ein solches Objekt*]."[14] Note that the language implies a very important generalization. The judgment, "X is agreeable," changes into "X's are agreeable." But this promotion from singularity to generality does *not* occur, according to Kant, with the beautiful.[15] The initial judgment of sense is "aesthetical and singular" in a manner analogous to the judgment of taste, but the subsequent generalization is not. Kant characterizes this generalization as a "logical" or "cognitive" judgment.[16]

Two things succeed upon the original physiological experience of pleasure in the presence of X: a cognitive generalization and an awakening desire. The cognitive generalization is hasty. (One may turn out to be allergic to kiwi.) Yet it is essential to the genesis of the desire. The judgment takes the practical form: "I want things like X." That, precisely, is what interest means. Interest occasions an "inclination" *(Neigung)* in the faculty of desire; it "pathologically conditions" it. This motivates the will. *Willkür* takes an interest in, concerns itself with the availability of, things like X, for the purpose of maintaining its pleasurable state.

As this account indicates, insofar as Kant wishes to associate the agreeable with interest he must abandon his claim that it has nothing whatever to do with the faculty of knowledge. Kant's model of will completely obviates this, since it involves reason choosing the good—whether absolute or merely relative. Interest is connected strongly to the notion of the relative good, the useful. "The pleasant, which, as such, represents the object simply in relation to sense, must first be brought by the concept of a purpose under principles of reason, in order to call it good, as an object of the will."[17] The judgment of sense must be "elevated," though what is being judged has changed no more than that which is the "object" of a judgment of experience has changed from what was the "object" of a judgment of perception.

Kant claims both the judgment of sense and the subsequent interest associated with it are "private." They do not admit of any necessary generality, either for other subjects or even across instances for the same subject. (One can grow tired of kiwi.) The privacy of the judgments has to do not merely with the materiality of the object, but above all with that of the subject. One's empirical singularity, one's particular sensory apparatus, one's particular dispositions, create the possibility that one "depends or can depend on the existence of the thing," i.e., becomes existentially entangled with it.[18] One develops a craving that colors every subsequent encounter; preferences intrude throughout experience and ruin impartiality.

Now we can understand subjective material purposiveness. It is subjective not merely in reference to "interior sense," the subject's response, but also in the sense of partiality—limited generality. That, however, is bound up in turn with the subject's materiality, and helps explain why this purposiveness is material. Another sense of this materiality lies in the fact that the agreeable is occasioned not by the "aesthetic form" (as in the beautiful) but by the "aesthetic matter" in sensation. This is the significance of the Kantian term *Reiz* (charm).[19] In addition, this experience creates an "interest," i.e., a concern for the availability or material existence of the object or objects of that kind for the use of the subject.

The adventitiousness of the delight associated with the agreeable led Kant to try to distinguish the beautiful from it. The judgment of taste seemed too imperious, the claim of beauty too grand, to derive from the same experiential process that accounted for the agreeable. The judgment of taste could not be merely private. The judgment of taste could not be colored by any interest. The judgment of taste had to claim a universal validity. It could not if it were merely sensuous. The project, then, was to find a transcendental ground in the higher faculty of understanding. Kant wished to raise the judgment of taste to transcendental validity. Thus he drew a parallel between the judgment of taste and the empirical cognitive judgment, the judgment of experience: "like all empirical judgments, it can declare no objective necessity and lay claim to no a priori validity. But the judgment of taste also claims, as every other empirical judgment does, to be valid for all men."[20] Neither aesthetic judgments nor empirical cognitive judgments are in themselves a priori necessary in a logical-universal sense.[21] But the empirical cognitive judgment may claim intersubjective validity and objective truth because it is grounded in universal rules which are themselves a priori valid. Similarly, Kant wishes to ground the judgment of taste in a universal a priori structure of consciousness. Only, with the beautiful, he is in the sphere of feeling, not concept, and the logical rules as such cannot serve him.

Before inquiring into Kant's recourse under these circumstances, a second parallel between the judgment of taste and the judgment of experience deserves to be explored. As we have noted, the judgment of experience results from a reinterpretation, at a higher level, of a prior judgment of perception. The question now to consider is whether there might be a similar sequence of judgments involved in the genesis of the judgment of taste. Can there be a primordial experience of pleasure analogous (or identical) to that of the judgment of sense in the agreeable, out of which, at a higher level of authority, the final judgment of taste is formulated? Is it a simple or a complex phenomenological event?

Kant seems to deny emphatically that such a possibility of sequential judgments could arise in this case: "If the pleasure in the given object precedes . . . the judgment of taste about the representation of the object . . . such pleasure would be nothing different from the mere pleasantness [*Annehmlichkeit*] in sensation."[22] Kant devotes a very long section, which he calls the "key to the critique," to the contention that the reflection must precede and occasion the pleasure.[23] Otherwise, Kant fears, the judgment of taste would sink to the level of the merely private. Yet is he wise to conflate the manifestly empirical character of the experience with merely private validity? The beautiful, no less than the agreeable, is inextricably a posteriori: it cannot be anticipated. Indeed, given Kant's insistence upon its singularity, the beautiful is even less predictable than the agreeable. It would seem that if the beautiful is to have a more august claim, it cannot be by denying all this, but rather by transcending it.

Still, we must attend carefully to Kant's claims in §9. He wishes to suggest that his model of pleasure as "immediately bound up with" the representation-of-the-object as its "aesthetical character" should be revised to include the possibility that pleasure not immediately accompany the representation, but rather may result from an intervening reflective judgment. On the face of it, there is no reason to believe that pleasure cannot be occasioned by the mind's own activities.[24] Just that seems to be one sense of Kant's use of the term "spirit" *(Geist)* in §49.[25] But the problem is to see how this activity is occasioned by specific representations, and to account for their eliciting it. In addition, it is necessary to describe the activity itself and explain why it should occasion pleasure. All this calls for a much more complex phenomenology of the experience.

Kant's posture in §9 should be juxtaposed to that which he adopts in the "Deduction of Aesthetic Judgment" and especially in §37 of that part of the *Third Critique*. There it would appear that Kant favors the notion of a sequence of judgments. In §36, Kant begins to break out what in §9 he tried to read as a single judgment. He writes: "Although the predicate (of the *personal* pleasure bound up with the representation) is empirical, nevertheless, as concerns the required assent of *everyone* the judgments are *a priori*."[26] He continues along this line in §37, acknowledging that it is a "merely empirical judgment" that a "representation of an object is immediately bound up with pleasure." Yet this no longer keeps him from ascribing greater validity to the ensuing judgment of taste:

> And so it is not the pleasure, but the *universal validity of this pleasure*, perceived as mentally bound up with the mere judgment upon an object, which is represented *a priori* in a judgment of taste as a universal rule for the judgment and valid for

everyone. It is an empirical judgment (to say) that I perceive and judge an object with pleasure. But it is an *a priori* judgment (to say) that I find it beautiful, i.e. I attribute this satisfaction necessarily to everyone.[27]

Kant takes the same line in the crucial exposition of §vii of the Introduction, the most meticulous account of the phenomenology of this experience.[28]

Of the two stances, that of §§37 and vii seems the more apt.[29] To claim judgments of taste have a priori validity would not only be inconsistent with his statement in §vii, but would result in the incongruity that aesthetic judgments would enjoy higher validity than judgments of experience, a result that Kant can hardly have countenanced. Rather, as §vii more soundly holds, they remain empirical, but, sanctioned by transcendental grounds, have claim nevertheless to "intersubjective" validity. Kant expounds the difference between objective and intersubjective validity in §8.[30]

Other problems remain. One is that a sequential theory of the genesis of the judgment of taste must still give an account of the initial experience which incorporates Kant's distinctive marks of the beautiful, i.e., its singularity, and its basis in the aesthetic form, not the matter, of the representation. In so far as the agreeable derives from the "aesthetic matter," we cannot use it as the basis for our characterization of that initial experience. Moreover, there is something telling in Kant's proposition that in the case of the beautiful there is a mediation of reflection. This does not refute the sequence theory; it only complicates the phenomenology. The question, appropriately enough for transcendental philosophy, is: How passive is the subject in the experience of the beautiful?

While Kant stresses the degree to which the subject is affected (*afficiert*) in the experience, nevertheless it is striking how not merely the object but even the representation of the object shifts far into the background. Its form serves as the occasion, becomes at most a catalyst, for a complex subjective response. Kant stresses repeatedly the "act" of reflection, the "act" of judging, and above all, the freedom of the imagination: "the imagination must be considered in its freedom . . . as productive and spontaneous (as the author of arbitrary [*willkürlichen*] forms of possible intuition)."[31] On the one side, the imagination seems constrained by the givenness of the object. On the other, it appears constrained by the laws of the understanding. But we recall that the givenness of representations is primarily in their "matter," not their form. And we recall that imagination as that "other kind of judging" has the capacity to "be *free* and yet *of itself conformed to law.*" Kant acknowledges that this seems "contradictory" in the General Remark to §22, yet he insists it is nevertheless the case.[32] In the *Anthropology* he shows clearly how this is *not* a contradiction, but merely a difference in the level of phenomenological self-consciousness.[33] The imagination is operating in accordance with law without yet being aware of it and expressly observing it.

It remains to explain what this free act of the imagination can mean. Kant offers a very useful characterization in §67 of the *Anthropology:* "In taste (taste that chooses)—that is, in aesthetic judgment—what produces our pleasure in the object is not the *sensation* immediately (the material element in our representation of the object). It is rather the way in which free (productive) imagination arranges this matter inventively—that is, the *form;* for only form can lay claim to a universal rule for the feeling of pleasure."[34] If the higher faculty of understanding manifests its spontaneity and its transcendental authority in reinterpreting the merely given after its own rules, here too Kant seems to indicate a reinterpretation, a reconfiguration *(Umgestaltung)* of the merely apprehended, betokening once again spontaneity and transcendental authority. It is precisely the refusal to stay with the mere givenness, the willful *(willkürlichen)* play upon it in the activity of the imagination, which elevates taste above appetite. In §12 of the *Anthropology,* Kant writes of "Artificial Play with Sensory Semblance [*Sinnenschein*]" and contends that we know it for illusion, and yet we linger over it without rectifying it (objectifying it) through conceptualization. "This play with sensory semblance is very pleasant and entertaining for the mind."[35] Imagination takes the merely given and reconfigures it, taking joy in just this reconfigurative play. Obviously imagination is in no position to supply the matter in sensation, for that is simply given. What it can and does reconfigure is the form.

The most impressive account of this was offered by Rudolf Odebrecht in a work rarely cited, *Form und Geist,* which appeared in 1930. Odebrecht argues that aesthetic appreciation is an interruption of the normal cognitive experience. But more, he contends that it is a gesture of subjective liberation: a *"Zurückgewinnung der Gestaltung an sich"*—a retrieval of the (power of) configuration by the subject. Odebrecht elaborates:

There takes place, in the context of intense activity of my consciousness, a liberation [*Loslösung*] from the first stage of charm and emotion, a shattering of the form of appearance [*Scheinform*] and a spirited [*stimmungshaftes*] reconstruction of the in-itself meaningless rhythm of configuration in the material. In this configuration there awakens for me symbolically a new object [*Gegenständlichkeit*] which is entirely referred to the feeling of self of my ego [*Selbstgefühl meines Ich*] and constitutes it.[36]

This is the "experience of pure construction" as an *act* of consciousness. We redesign the given in aesthetic experience, and this, Odebrecht contends, is what Kant meant by the cryptic term *Zeichnung* (delineation) in §14 of the *Third Critique* when he wrote: "the delineation is the essential thing; and here it is not what gratifies in sensation but what pleases by means of its form that is fundamental for taste."[37]

What Odebrecht saw is that *Zeichnung* must be read as *act*, not object, and form, consequently, not as found but made, and finally that otherwise difficult phrase "how it is possible that a thing can please in the mere act of judging it (without sensation or concept)" as Kant's indication that *act* is the crucial thing.[38] Judging is act in that crucially "other kind" of significance belonging to imaginative configuration. It is without sensation in the sense that it liberates itself from the merely given, the charm and emotion that attend the "in-itself meaningless rhythm of configuration in the material." It is without concept because it does not propose to know the material, but only to play with it, to enjoy playing with it, for the sake of the feeling of self that play, and not simply matter, offers. Obviously we are now in a position to characterize what happens in the contrasting experience of the pleasant or agreeable. We do not liberate ourselves. We do not reconfigure. We do not play. We simply take up the given charm and emotion and enjoy that. We expend no mental effort, cognitive or imaginative.

Now that we grasp the first phase of the experience of the beautiful, we must return to the issue of the validity of the ultimate judgment of taste pronounced upon it. That is to seek its transcendental ground, and Kant insists "nothing can be universally communicated except cognition and representation, so far as it belongs to cognition."[39] The task of finding a transcendental ground, then, is to find the basis in the cognitive faculties for what has appeared a matter of mere feeling. But in discovering that this pleasure involves the spontaneous play of the imagination and the relish of its freedom, and in recognizing further that this freedom nevertheless anticipates and accords with the requirements that a fully self-conscious understanding would impose, we have the ingredients for the Kantian solution: "harmony of the faculties."

The phrases "harmony" or "free play" of the faculties are metaphorical and accordingly mysterious in themselves. Kant falls short of offering a clear discursive redemption of these phrases in the *Third Critique*. He never sorts out clearly the transcendental from the empirical in his formulation. He does not carefully enough distinguish what ordinary consciousness can think and assert in justifying a claim like "X is beautiful" from what the transcendental philosopher can adduce to explain the ultimate basis for such judgments. It is necessary to retrieve Kant's scattered accounts of what ordinary consciousness makes of its experience and thinks of its claims in the judgment of taste, and see how far that goes toward the ultimate transcendental grounding. If harmony of the faculties lies at the transcendental basis of the validity of judgments of taste, surely Kant cannot have meant ordinary consciousness to make the transcendental deduction before uttering the claim. Indeed, he explicitly asserts that ordinary consciousess is aware of this harmony only as a sensation of pleasure.[40]

How does ordinary consciousness come to make and justify the judgment of taste? Quite simply, it starts from the recognition that a particular pleasure is different from the merely pleasant. The subject investigates the source of his own pleasure. It is not that nothing agreeable may have been present. *Reiz* can, and usually does, accompany pleasure in the beautiful. But the subject recognizes that more than *Reiz* affects him. He did not start from appetite. He was not swayed by preference. He had no stake, no interest in the case. He did not need to know what the thing was for. He did not need to know whether it was right or wrong. He did not even need to know what it was. Just encountering it set him off, "since the person who judges feels himself quite *free* as regards the satisfaction which he attaches to the object [since it does not rest on any inclination of the subject, nor upon any other premeditated interest], he cannot find the ground of this satisfaction in any private conditions connected with his own subject, and hence it must be regarded as grounded on what he can presuppose in every other person."[41] In other words, the subject believes the way he responded is the way anyone else could, would, and should. If pressed to justify this last belief, the subject would have recourse to the notion of a "common sense" *(sensus communis)*, that is, that he is only expressing what all humans feel and judge, given only that they abstract from their preferences.[42] Beyond this conviction of speaking with a "universal voice," of claiming only what "we regard as the least to be expected from anyone claiming the name of man," ordinary consciousness *cannot* go.[43]

The balance of the argument falls to the transcendental philosopher. The situation is analogous to the case of judgments of experience. There, too, ordinary consciousness can carry the argument for particular claims only to such generalities as cause or substance. It remains for transcendental philosophy to demonstrate their binding universality. So here it is transcendental philosophy's task to demonstrate definitively that the claim of taste is grounded. Only the philosopher can formulate such propositions as: "Now a representation by which an object is given that is to become a cognition in general requires *imagination* for the gathering together the manifold of intuition, and *understanding* for the unity of the concept uniting the representations."[44] The interaction of these two faculties is the key to Kant's account of the experience of beauty.

What is necessary for knowledge in general occurs in the case of beauty without intent. As §vii puts it,

that apprehension of forms in the imagination can never take place without the reflective judgment, though undesignedly [*unabsichtlich*], at least comparing them with its faculty of referring intuitions to concepts. If, now, in this comparison the imagination (as the faculty of *a priori* intuitions) is placed by means of a given representation undesignedly [*unabsichtlich*] in agreement with the understanding, as the faculty of concepts, and thus a feeling of pleasure is aroused, the object must then be regarded as purposive for the reflective judgment.[45]

The conformity to law without intent is related to the process of "cognition in general," and the transcendental ground is shifted from the authority of universal rules of the understanding, which in the cognitive case promoted the mere apprehension of imagination to objective validity, to the necessity of these faculties themselves for the possibility of any cognition at all: "the subjective formal conditions of a judgment in general."[46] The universality and necessity of these faculties themselves ground the validity of the judgment of taste.

That imagination and understanding work together—can work together—is the foundation of the validity of the judgment. "The proportion between these cognitive faculties requisite for taste is also requisite for that ordinary sound understanding which we have to presuppose in everyone."[47] The proportion, the "harmony," that "state of mind, which is to be met with in the relation of our representative powers to each other, so far as they refer a given representation to *cognition in general,*" is just as necessary to the possibility of experience as any of the categories taken in isolation.[48] "For without this as the subjective condition of cognition, cognition as an effect could not arise."[49] Therefore, "if cognitions are to admit of communicability, so must also the state of mind—i.e. the accordance of the cognitive powers."[50] That is the gist of the transcendental deduction.[51] What the transcendental philosopher thus discursively establishes, the subject experiences as pleasure, or more precisely: "the more lively play of both mental powers (the imagination and the understanding) when animated by mutual agreement."[52] The play of the imagination is in itself pleasurable: "We *linger* over the contemplation of the beautiful because this contemplation strengthens and reproduces itself."[53] That is subjective formal purposiveness.

There is a paradoxical aspect even in Kant's pure solution of the problem of taste, namely, why only certain representations-of-the-object should occasion the experience.[54] Not *every* object of sense occasions the feeling of beauty.[55] Even if "beauty" refers to subjective response, it is only the catalytic presence of some given representation which makes its possible, and it is at least plausible to ask whether the trait which makes certain objects catalytic can be identified. If subjective proportionality of faculties is constant for all humans, and if, therefore, they ought all to recognize the same empirical intuitions as beautiful, then there should, in principle, be some—even if only empirical—traits which such intuitions must share, and some reason why those occasion beauty. Hence, in that measure, the nature of the object seems objectively involved. It may be difficult to establish the traits. They may only be empirical, but it would seem to be logically possible to find them.

While it is the case that some representations-of-objects occasion beauty, Kant argues it is not possible of anticipation, i.e., no rule can be made prescriptive for it, and any generalization descriptive of it, if possible at all, would be empirical, i.e., an empirical canon in that genre of beauty. Such canons of beauty are not to be found in discursive generalizations but exclusively in exemplary instances. The point is just that no discursive generalization can catch what makes the instances exemplary. If there are instances to which "all times and all peoples" ascribe beauty, they represent at most empirical *examples* in which there may lie an implicit canon ("deep-lying general grounds"), but not one which can be formulated in words.[56] Kant usually stressed that references to such a "classical" standard for taste was an empirical recourse, worthy and essential, but still merely empirical.

Backsliding: The Confusion of Aesthetic with Cognitive Reference

For the Kantian theory of beauty to work, it must be possible for aesthetic form to arise even from the mere matter in sensation. The characterization of color and tone cognitively as "secondary qualities," i.e., mere sensation or "intrinsic magnitude," must not deny them the possibility of occasioning a feeling of beauty and a judgment of taste, for then, indeed, Bach could not be beautiful, nor Delacroix. The same holds, of course, for color and tone in nature—the song of a bird, the color of a flower. Yet Kant allowed his concern for "purity" to mislead him. Purity for Kant is exclusively a matter of form. He was troubled by the seeming incongruity that several artistic media, especially music and painting, evoked beauty via sense experience which, on his theory of objective reference, could only be considered "mere sensation"—"matter," not "form." How could mere matter have aesthetic form? "A mere color, such as the green of a plot of grass, or a mere tone (as distinguished from sound or noise), like that of a violin, is described by most people as in itself beautiful, notwithstanding the fact that both seem to depend merely on the matter of the representation—in other words, simply on sensation, which only entitles them to be called agreeable."[57] Form was for Kant almost synonymous with transcendental potential. He had already exploited fully the transcendental potential of sensible form *(Sinn)* as the structure of a priori intuition in the "Transcendental Aesthetic" of the *First Critique*. Such form in representations-of-objects was eligible for cognitive use, for reference to the object.[58] In order to give a clear and compelling account of the judgment of taste, Kant had differentiated from that a notion of "aesthetic form," which referred exclusively to the subject, and which consequently was not to be confused with the other. It was not the form of the representation-of-the-object in its objective reference which occasioned beauty, but rather the aesthetic formality of that representation, its reference to the subject, the harmony of the faculties it occasioned.[59] If, as Kant persuaded himself in §14, only form as objective reference in a representation-of-an-object could elicit a feeling of beauty, then musical tones and the colors in painting—and therewith two of the greatest realms of art—would fall out of the conspectus of his aesthetic theory: a fatal flaw.

In his effort to promote them to objective formality, he had recourse to the theories of Leonhard Euler, who tried to established mathematical regularities in these phenomena in terms of wave frequencies. This, as mathematical and formal, struck Kant as a plausible solution. Color and tone would be rescued from their mere materiality. "The mind not alone perceives by sense their effect . . . but also, by reflection, the regular play of the impressions, (and consequently the form in which different representations are united,) . . . They would be nothing short of formal determinations of the unity of the manifold of sensations, and in that case could even be counted beauties in themselves."[60] What Kant believed he had done was to establish the "purity" of these sensations as a kind of form. "[S]ensations of color as well as of tone are only entitled to be immediately regarded as beautiful where, in either case, they are *pure*." Having found "purity" in this mathematical structure behind color and tone, he then compounded his error by asserting: "all simple colors are regarded as beautiful so far as pure . . . Composite colors have not this advantage." That violates Kant's principle that judgments of taste may never be universal judgments. It is also dubious experientially, with reference to painting or, for that matter, natural color.[61]

Kant was tempted to identify aesthetic form and objective form for two reasons. First, he believed that form always carried with it the potential for objective validity, and he certainly wished to believe that the judgment of taste entailed some form of validity. But he also had a second motive for this enterprise: his strong interest in discriminating "aesthetic form" from "aesthetic matter," the beautiful from the pleasant. "Charm" [*Reiz*], or aesthetic matter, could have no relevance to beauty, aesthetic form, which fell exclusively to the judgment of taste. The presence of *Reiz* could only ruin the "purity" of a judgment of taste. All of this is perfectly consistent with the theory of beauty we have already encountered. The problem arises when Kant proceeds to confuse "aesthetic matter" with "cognitive matter" in the representation-of-the-object, and asserts that "cognitive matter" is ineligible for a judgment of taste.

If Kant strove to extract objective form from the mere matter of sensation in color and sound, he also tried to identify aesthetic form in general with objective form. Kant's identification of *Gestalt* (figure) with "regularity" exposes the ambiguity of the whole proceeding: "Every form of objects of sense (both of external and also, mediately, of internal sense) is either *figure* or *play* [*entweder* Gestalt *oder* Spiel]. In the latter case it is either play of figures (in space: mimic and dance), or mere play of sensations (in time)."[62] The words *Gestalt* and *Spiel* have enormous potential for a theory of beauty along Kantian lines—if only Kant would leave them where they belong, in the realm of aesthetic form, namely, the playful reconfiguration [*Umgestaltung*] of sense input according to the fancy of the imagination, exclusively for its subjective gratification. That *is*, we must never forget, the true Kantian theory. What is an aesthetic whole may be a fragment of some cognitive object, or some congeries of such distinguishable objects, and just in that measure aesthetic form and its essential *Gestalt* must not be confused with objective form and its determinate contour. Boundedness cannot be a sufficient criterion for beauty, because all objects are bounded, but not all are beautiful.

Kant himself recognizes the limitations of his sense of the boundedness, the regularity and symmetry, of the beautiful "thing." In a crucial paragraph in the General Remark to §22, he states the issue and defends his authentic position against this "objective subreption" of symmetrical, logical form:

> Now geometrically regular figures, a circle, a square, a cube, and the like, are commonly brought forward by critics of taste as the most simple and unquestionable examples of beauty. And yet the very reason why they are called regular, is because the only way of representing them is by looking on them as mere presentations of a determinate concept by which the figure has its rule (according to which alone it is possible) prescribed for it. One or other of these two views must, therefore, be wrong: either the verdict of the critics that attributes beauty to such figures, or else our own, which makes purposiveness apart from any concept necessary for beauty.[63]

In the General Remark to §22 Kant rescues himself from his own confusion on the score of taking objective form—mere disposition in space (and time)—for beauty (aesthetic form).

The Scope of the "Critique of Taste"

Let us review our reconstruction of the "Critique of Taste" of 1787. It had a clear and careful "Analytic," in the exposition of the peculiarities of the judgment of taste. It obviously had a very precise

"Deduction," in the transcendental argument about the "harmony of the faculties" and "subjective formal purposiveness." But what is a "Critique" without a "Dialectic"? If we look to the "Dialectic of Aesthetic Judgment" as it stands in the finished *Critique of Judgment*, however, we find ourselves virtually in a different universe from the one we have been considering. It is very hard to believe that this was the "Dialectic" that Kant had in mind in his original version.

On the other hand, it offers us a clue as to what the more primordial "Dialectic" may have been. Consider §56, the "Representation of the Antinomy of Taste." It presents two positions which were both widely articulated in the eighteenth-century literature about taste and which seemed mutually inconsistent. On the one hand there was the proverb, old as the Romans, that there is no disputing about taste, that is, that the ground of aesthetic experience or taste is subjective, indeed private. On the other hand, the very nature of any judgment of taste was that one's claim as to beauty ought to be acknowledged as valid, that there should be universality of concurrence. But the consequence of this claim is obviously controversy, because that concurrence does not arise. Controversy, however, implies the possibility of discourse and resolution, but such discourse, if it were conducted rationally, would be dispute. Hence there would appear to be a necessary contradiction between two positions, each of which has a rational foundation. That is the stuff of dialectic. It is also composed entirely of the ingredients intrinsic to the original "Critique of Taste."[64] And the proof that such a structure was present in the original "Critique of Taste" is to be found in §7.

The odd thing is, §7 also solves the "Dialectic," for the key to the antinomy is that the thesis is true of aesthetic judgments of sense, while the antithesis is true of aesthetic judgments of taste. Yet we should not be put off by the simplicity. Kant originally believed that both the "Deduction," which he expressly acknowledged was "easy," and the "Dialectic" were simple, because this "department of philosophy," as he called it in his letter to Reinhold, was so "poor" in transcendental determinations, and hence in their potential conflicts.[65] It was only later, when he became aware of great potential latent in the material he had worked up to ground the faculty of feeling in an a priori principle, that he came upon a whole new idea for the "Dialectic."

On the conjecture that §56 and §7 may have been all the "Dialectic" there was in the original "Critique of Taste," let us compare that archaeological reconstruction with the ultimate "Critique of

Aesthetic Judgment" for the major differences. First, as we have just contended, the actual "Dialectic" of the final version was a later addition. Also, as we observed in the Introduction, the "Analytic of the Sublime" was not a part of the original "Critique of Taste." But note also that the material on art, §§43–54, played no part whatever in our reconstruction. Tonelli dates this material to the year 1788, i.e., he considers the treatment of art an extension of the project which had been undertaken in the "Critique of Taste" of 1787.[66]

Finally, there are certain sections in the "Analytic of the Beautiful" which did not have a place in our reconstruction of the original "Critique of Taste," in particular §§15–17 and portions of the General Remark to §22. Meredith, in assessing §§15–17, observes that they do not seem to fit naturally into the flow of the exposition before and after them.[67] Indeed, they represent a far more complex consideration of the problem of beauty. Not all these considerations were new to Kant, but all were added to his text later.

Six

KANT'S PHILOSOPHY OF ART IN THE YEAR 1788

K
ant's transcendental method was to distill from a complex mental process a pure a priori principle, and make that principle the warrant for the reconstruction of the more complex problem from which he initially regressed. In the *Third Critique,* Kant had to establish the implications of the solution for his "pure" judgment for the full complexity of aesthetic matters. Kant understood that there were great complexities in the critique of taste which remained, despite his transcendental grounding of the pure judgment of taste.[1] Any "critique of taste" which could account for the beauty only of foliage but not of da Vinci, of sea shells but not of Shakespeare, would not have had great standing in eighteenth-century culture. To prove the power of his new insight, Kant had to be able to clarify the questions of criticism that arose in the context of works of art.[2]

"Dependent" and "Ideal" Beauty

Kant had to acknowledge that the "pure" judgment of taste he had struggled so hard to isolate was so restrictive that the only phenomena which seemed to fall within it were relatively trivial—sea shells and flowers, arabesques and foliage—things perceived as gratuitously elegant without the least intrinsic meaning. Most of the things of any substantive importance to man—human beauty, the beauty of organisms, the beauty of artifice—do not seem to fall under the rubric of Kant's "pure judgment of taste." They are not so simple that their concept need not be involved in their recognition, making problematic the "purity" of their aesthetic reception. A theory of beauty which could find it in the bloom of narcissus or the swirl of a nautilus, but not in the Sistine ceiling or a sonnet of Shakespeare, could hardly have satisfied Kant.

This explains his distinction of "free" from "dependent" beauty (§16).[3] He required a transition from his "pure" case to the complex issues involved in the appraisal of beauty in complex forms of nature and above all in works of art. In developing his "pure judgment of taste," Kant denied the idea of "objective purposiveness" (intrinsic perfection) any place in his aesthetic theory. "What is formal in the representation of a thing, i.e. the agreement of its manifold with a unity (i.e. irrespective of what it is to be) does not, of itself, afford us any cognition whatsoever of objective purposiveness. For since [in a judgment of taste] abstraction is made from this unity as *purpose* (what the thing is to be) nothing is left but the subjective purposiveness of the representations in the mind." But that is entirely a subjective reference, namely, to a state of mind "in which the subject feels itself quite at home."[4]

"Free beauty" is the extreme case, from which the underlying principle can most obviously be deduced. Kant explains that "dependent beauty" is called such because it "does presuppose a concept and the perfection of the object in accordance therewith." It is therefore a "conditioned beauty" [*bedingte Schönheit*], which relies upon the "concept of a particular purpose" in its aesthetic assessment. "If now the judgment of taste in respect of the beauty of a thing is made dependent on the purpose in its manifold, like a judgment of reason, and thus limited, it is no longer a free and pure judgment of taste."[5] Kant is most explicit about "dependent beauty," or the connection of beauty with perfection, in §48, where he writes: "It is true that in forming an estimate, especially of animate objects of nature, e.g. of a man or a horse, objective purposiveness is also commonly taken into account with a view to judgment upon their beauty; but then the judgment also ceases to be purely aesthetic, i.e. a mere judgment of taste."[6] In *pulchritudo adhaerens*, the *aesthetic* judgment is contingent upon the idea of perfection: it is "a logically conditioned aesthetic judgment [*ein logisch-bedingtes ästhetisches Urtheil*]." Another kind of "interest" threatens to compromise the disinterestedness of the judgment of taste: the ethical interest in the good or the perfect.[7]

The idea of perfection, that is, "a concept of the purpose which determines what the thing is to be," asserts itself in the concept of "dependent beauty." But it involves an ethical judgment, not an aesthetical one. If an entity is recognized as intrinsically purposive, this can occasion delight.[8] But that delight is in the good, not in the beautiful. Beauty can never be a necessary, hence prescriptive and predictable, delight. It is singular and it is unanticipatable. It is, of course, possible that a feeling of beauty might be aroused; such an occurrence, however, would of necessity have to free itself from the sense of the objective purposiveness of the entity.

The problem is, in what sense is "dependent beauty" *(pulchritudo adhaerens)* still beauty? The judgment involved is unequivocally impure. What measure of aesthetic value does it retain? "A judgment of taste, then, in respect of an object with a definite internal purpose, can only be pure if either the person judging has no concept of this purpose or else abstracts from it in his judgment." Kant's solution is that two separate "judgments" can be discerned. "[W]hen we compare the representation by which an object is given to us with the object (as regards what it ought to be) by means of a concept, we cannot avoid considering along with it the sensation in the subject [*es [kann] nicht vermieden werden, wenn wir die Vorstellung, wodurch uns ein Gegenstand gegeben wird, mit dem Objecte (in Ansehung dessen, was es sein soll) durch einen Begriff vergleichen, sie zugleich mit der Empfindung im Subjecte zusammen zu halten].*"[9] That is, the representation-of-the-object, i.e., the empirical intuition, has in itself both reference to the object and reference to the subject.

Kant here considerably widens the possibilities of his theory of taste. It is possible both to misunderstand intrinsic purpose as inadvertent purposiveness and, even more interestingly, to abstract from it and judge solely aesthetically. This latter power to abstract from a cognitive or ethical appraisal in order to undertake an aesthetical one is a very significant addition to the Kantian arsenal. The capacity to abstract would seem to fit very nicely with a theory of aesthetic appraisal as reflective, and especially with the rendering of this notion as one which inserts reference to the subjective processes of mind prior to the appraisal of delight. But in that case, the *pulchritudo* in purposive objects is in fact no different from the *pulchritudo* in random phenomena, and the distinction of *vaga* from *adhaerens* has nothing to do with aesthetics at all. What Kant illustrated with reference to foliage should hold without amendment for a Bach sonata. Then why did Kant undertake the whole distinction? And can we be satisfied with the result?

In my view, §17 is an effort to reconsider the issues and perplexities of §§15–16 in a new light, in terms of the "ideal of beauty." Kant distinguishes two elements in his "ideal of beauty," an *aesthetic normal idea* and a *rational idea*. The "aesthetic normal idea," an "individual intuition (of the imagination)," would appear to be the aesthetic side of the complex, while the "rational idea" would encompass the "perfection" involved in a complex ("dependent") case of beauty.[10]

Kant explains the "aesthetic normal idea" in the following terms:

> The normal idea must draw from experience the constituents which it requires for the form of an animal of a particular kind. But the greatest purposiveness in the construction of this form—that which would serve as a universal norm for forming an estimate of each individual of the species in question—the image that, as it were, forms an intentional basis underlying the technic of nature, to which no separate individual, but only the race as a whole, is adequate, has its seat merely in the idea of the judging subject. Yet it is, with all its proportions, an aesthetic idea, and, as such, capable of being fully presented *in concreto* in a model image.[11]

The norm is prior to the instances, and cannot be determinately formulated from them. Rather it is by virtue of the norm that they can be recognized as instances: "This *normal idea* is not derived from proportions taken from experience *as definite rules:* rather is it according to this idea that rules for forming estimates first become possible."[12] Kant spells out the idea: "It is an intermediate between all singular intuitions of individuals, with their manifold variations—a floating image for the whole genus."[13] That is precisely what a schema is. This primordial "idea" in the judging subject, a schema of beauty, seems analogous to the imputed purpose in nature whereby she designs individuals according to a principle of the species as a whole, so that they each instantiate it, while remaining nevertheless distinguishable individuals. The difference between this schema and one which serves determinant judgment is that the latter is constituted and fixed by the understanding, whereas the one which serves the reflective aesthetic judgment is indefinite.[14]

Beauty has to do with that which preceeds conceptualization, i.e., that singular instance which incites imagination to playful reconfiguration. In that sense, beauty resides only in "what cannot be represented by concepts but only in an individual presentation [*in einzelner Darstellung*]." The "faculty of presentation" is imagination. Hence beauty can only be an ideal of the imagination. Imagination, Kant suggests, has the empirical capacity to generate what one might term an "ideal type."[15] The "aesthetic normal idea" distills from a series of experiences a standard for any particular instantiation (note that the issue has shifted to production rather than recognition) of a species. Kant offers a "psychological explanation" of this process which in fact turns out to be a more extended description. "The imagination, in a manner quite incomprehensible to us," is able to form an image, "a mean contour which serves as a common standard for all [*ein Mittleres [Bild]* . . . , *welches allen zum gemeinschaftlichen Maße dient*]."[16] This "mean contour" is like a statistical average of all the empirical instances, which we might construct mechanically, but that is not how imagination does it. It "does all this by means of a dynamical effect upon the organ of internal sense, arising from the frequent apprehension of such forms [*durch einen dynamischen Effect, der aus der vielfältigen Auffassung solcher Gestalten auf das Organ des innern Sinnes entspringt*]."[17]

This is very strange language from Kant. Is the "organ of internal sense" the intuition of time as form for "objective reference" or the receptivity of aesthetic form, namely, the "state of mind" or feeling of the subject? What exactly is a "dynamic effect?" The more Kant develops the ideas, the more questions arise, and the less clarity remains. Insofar as any ideal of beauty as latent criterion for judgments of taste can be ascribed to the judging subject, it can only be the schematic analog of that condition of harmony between the free play of the imagination and the lawfulness of the understanding as they relate to any empirical intuition, or, in Kant's words, to "cognition in general." Thus the "ideal of beauty" as the "highest model" would be the implicit schema to which judgment compares any singular instance to discern whether it is beautiful or not. Phenomenologically that comparison is via pleasure, transcendentally it is via harmony of the faculties, empirically it is the implicit unity in all the previous instances in which beauty has been discerned. But finding a tulip beautiful should be just as relevant to that implicit unity of the experience of beauty, and hence of any "ideal of beauty," as finding Beethoven's Pastoral Symphony beautiful.

The idea of an aesthetic normal idea, while interesting, only offers a different language to formulate what Kant had explicated more clearly in relating the judgment of taste to the harmony of the faculties. It does not at all advance our understanding of how the judgment of taste may be extended to more complex objects, particularly those which seem to entail intrinsic purpose, and therefore it does not advance our understanding of *pulchritudo adhaerens* as an aesthetic matter. In fact Kant could not resolve the issue at this point of his thinking. It would take what I call the "ethical turn" to lead him to a theory of symbolism which would clarify the issues.

Kant's further observations on the "aesthetic normal idea" in §17 try to offer a more fruitful sense of the term as related to *art*. He suggests that this notion represents the minimum aptness of a presentation: "the form that constitutes the indispensable condition of all beauty, and, consequently, only *correctness* in the presentation of the genus."[18] Thus he illustrates with two classical standards—the *Doryphorus* of Polycletus and Myron's *Cow*. Hence the aesthetic normal idea, instead of being a ground for beauty, is only a limiting condition, guaranteeing "the presentation is merely academically correct." Everything unique and distinctive, which characterizes a true singular instance, remains undetermined by this aesthetic normal idea.[19] Kant has demoted the whole notion to the "mechanical" character of art.

In the second paragraph of §17, Kant's discourse implicitly shifts from the question of finding beautiful things in nature to making beautiful objects (art). In discussing the "exemplary," Kant writes of "products of taste," and then proceeds to a very important assertion: "He who imitates [*nachahmt*] a model [*Muster*] shows, no doubt, in so far as he attains to it, skill [*Geschicklichkeit*]; but only shows taste in so far as he can judge of this model himself [*sofern als er dieses Muster selbst beurtheilen kann*]."[20] Taste here for the first time involves that which produces, not merely appreciates, beauty. Hence, art for the first time enters consideration in a serious manner. Indeed, the notions of imitation *(Nachahmung)*, of model *(Muster)*, and of skill *(Geschicklichkeit)* all play a crucial role in Kant's theory of art. Thus, §17 represents the transition to the consideration of art.

The Philosophy of Art

What is art? Kant presented a very orderly, precise, even brilliant exposition of it in the *Third Critique*. There is not the least hint of casualness or indifference in the analysis. Yet one cannot help but recognize how structurally negligent he was in the placement of his whole exposition of the topic within the work. The treatment of art (§§43–54) is run into the "Deduction of Aesthetic Judgments" via two transitional sections (§§41–42), though there is no apparent reason why it belongs there. To make matters even worse, the whole of the "Deduction" is left under the heading of "Book Two" of the "Critique of Aesthetic Judgment," which is called the "Analytic of the Sublime." Johann Gottfried Kiesewetter, Kant's proofreader, suggested that Kant introduce a new division of the book at that point to give due weight to the shift in attention. He suggested a "Book Three" to include the "Deduction" and the treatment of art.[21] But even that does not really address the discontinuity between the actual "Deduction" (§§31–40) and the exposition of art.

The structural neglect is puzzling, especially in a philosopher so architectonic. It raises the question: What function was the exposition of art to serve? Could it in some sense be part of the deduction of aesthetic judgments? Would it perhaps make sense to say that the point of this exposition was to demonstrate that the deduction which worked for the "pure" judgment of taste also held in the case of works of art? Possibly. Could one then make an even more extravagant leap and suppose that the whole matter belonged to the "Analytic of the Sublime" in some sense? There is a very strained sense in which the whole theory of symbolism, which is the culmination of the exposition of art and the basis for the final form of the "Dialectic," can be considered in terms of the most profound meaning of the sublime, namely, the aesthetic consciousness of subjective moral worth. Yet all of this is so tenuous that it seems more appropriate to find Kant unjustifiably lax in the organization of his book.

Suspending the question of its poor placement, let us consider the exposition of art starting in §43. What is immediately obvious is that this exposition has every aspect of a fresh beginning. It presumes nothing of the previous analysis. It defines each of its concepts as it proceeds, and it develops rigorously along the lines it itself sets up. While it is clearly related to the prior "Analytic of the Beautiful," especially to §§15–17, it stands autonomously. The elegance and conciseness of this exposition is very noteworthy, especially in view of the monumentality of the issues under consideration and the vast literature which Kant had to digest in making his discriminations. This last point needs to be underscored: the exposition of art is an analysis which takes for granted a massive body of interpretation, a "conventional wisdom," and is offered as a clarification and elevation of that discourse.

Kant sets about clarifying the concept of art in terms of three discriminations. He distinguishes between artifice and nature. He distinguishes between art and artifice. And he distinguishes between art and science. The power and implication of these discriminations are impressive. At the heart of the exposition of the first discrimination is what I will call the grounding paradox of art: its odd parallelism with nature. There has long been controversy over Kant's appreciation of the relative beauty in nature and in art. Some contend that Kant substantially underestimated the importance of artistic beauty, and that his treatment of it in the *Critique of Judgment* was subordinated to considerations deriving from his appreciation for natural beauty, and from his ulterior philosophical interests in natural beauty, i.e., its cognitive and ethical implications.[22] Kant's theory of aesthetics in general set out from the standpoint of the appreciation or reception of beauty, and not its creation. Even when he assessed the creative dimension of aesthetics, as he had to in considering art, he did so, as it were, from outside, disengaged from the immanent artistic process, and assessing it with "cold-blooded" detachment.[23]

All this may well be true, but before we adopt it as our hermeneutic vantage, it behooves us to consider another alternative, namely, that Kant may have come to treat art, as a complex issue in aesthetics, after he considered natural beauty, merely because in the latter he could more easily isolate the essential elements of a "pure" judgment of taste, and consequently that he always intended to bring his findings to bear upon the complex problem of art. That is, in my view, a very worthwhile consideration. But there is another, more subtle and more rewarding. While there is undoubtedly some ground for suspicion of Kant's attitude toward art, one can enter an immediate corrective whose implications might in fact be capable of reversing the whole line of criticism against Kant. The corrective is simply that natural beauty appears to be artifice, or, the idea of art is implicit in the appreciation of natural beauty. Kant's aesthetic emphasizes the active role of the mind in every aesthetic experience, not simply those of creation but those of reception as well. Indeed, one could go so far as to say that there can be no aesthetic experience at all which is not creative, in that every one involves harmony of the faculties, and harmony of the faculties, in its turn, the free play of the imagination which is, simply, creativity.

Perhaps one of the most famous lines in the *Third Critique,* and deservedly so, is from §45: "Nature proved beautiful when it wore the appearance of art; and art can only be termed beautiful, when we are conscious of its being art, while yet it has the appearance of nature."[24] This profound paradox is pregnant with the whole Idealist-Romantic vision. It is from this paradox that we must generate the entire theory of art which Kant presents in the *Third Cri-*

tique. But first, let us dwell a moment on the natural side of this paradox. Nature is considered beautiful when it looks like art, but we know it is not. It is inadvertent artifice: what seems to be designed, yet cannot be ascribed to any worldly artist. Hence Kant treats natural beauty "as if" it were art, and he calls this, frequently, the "technic of nature."

There is no question that this is a metaphor, yet it raises two matters for theoretical reflection. First, is what we appreciate as design in the object or only in our response? The whole question of "objective subreption" comes back into consideration, with this subreption now formulated in terms of the problematic conception "intrinsic objective purposiveness." But second, regarding nature as the sphere of relentless mechanical laws and efficient causality, how can any phenomenon in nature, no matter how apparently designed, possess intrinsic purpose ("perfection")? Must not these works of nature which approximate art be ascribed literally to an Artificer?[25] In short, the imputation of beauty to objects in nature raises questions which are fundamentally ontological and theological and find their expression precisely in an investigation of teleology. Thus, one side of Kant's aesthetic paradox pushes his thought decisively in the direction of the "cognitive turn."

But what of the other side? What does it mean that art must have the appearance of nature while still being recognized as art? Kant takes *Kunst* to signify, like the ancient Greek *techne,* all human intervention in the natural order, all artifice. He distinguishes between the verb *tun,* which he associates with the Latin *facere,* and the verbs *wirken* and (more problematically) *handeln,* which he associates with the Latin *agere. Tun* means to do, and it invariably refers to intentional action, to a "deed." *Facere,* in addition, has the sense of "making." *Wirken,* which Meredith translates lamely as "operating" and Bernard as "working," involves, in the German, the sense of *causing* or *effecting,* and it is this sense that Kant wishes to evoke. Kant calls the result of art *(Kunst, tun)* a "work" *(Werke; opus),* and the result of nature an "effect" *(Wirkung; effectus).* The sense of the whole is now clear. Nature refers to that construction of matters which involves cause and effect (in the efficient, mechanistic-deterministic sense) and art refers to that construction of matters which involves the intervention of purpose.

In that sense, *Kunst* is only approximately rendered by "art" and would be best conceived as "artifice," as in the adjectival contrast "artificial/natural." Artifice stands for the whole realm of human action in general, i.e., *techne.* It is the whole of human experience under the rubric of man's active stance in the world, what Heidegger called attending to the "ready-to-hand," as contrasted with the purely contemplative or cognitive stance toward the "present-to-hand." Moreover, it is important to recognize that in §43 Kant still considers the "technical" as part of the "practical" sphere, i.e., to be understood within the framework of rational will. After he takes the "cognitive turn," he will correct himself and assign all "technical practical purposiveness" to the theoretical or cognitive domain, as a matter, to be sure, of rationality, but of merely efficient rationality— what Max Weber would call *Zweckrationalität*—as contrasted with authentically practical action, which had to be grounded in value, i.e., moral choice—which, borrowing from Weber, we might term *Wertrationalität*.[26] That reassignment of *Technik*, with fundamental repercussions for the notion "*Technik der Natur,*" belongs to the period of the composition of the *First Introduction to the Critique of Judgment*.

Insofar as all human intervention is *Kunst*, or artifice, the contrast of this with nature, or the autonomous flow of natural events, is clear. Indeed, Kant made a great deal of the distinction between an action *(Handlung)* and an event *(Wirkung)* in his *Second Critique*. While it was always possible, he wrote, for the subject to present a cognitive account of his actions retrospectively as the result of a causal chain, and hence as an event, this belied the prospective character of each and every act undertaken by that subject as a free agent, including the decision to view prior acts as determined. As artifice or *Technik*, *Kunst* implied purpose, i.e., the causality of a representation in the actual existence of an object or state of affairs. But more, it entailed a consideration of that causality as effective, i.e., actually in the world of sense, hence a matter not only of intention *(Absicht* or *Zweckvorstellung)* but of actualization, and hence entailed the whole matter of skill and efficiency *(Geschicklichkeit)* which were irrelevant in the case of pure moral choice.

Artifice is simply too wide a category to help us with an aesthetic clarification of art. Hence Kant had to proceed to a distinction of art as such from artifice in general. That was his second distinction. It will come as no surprise that what Kant undertook was another search for "purity," and that the key to such a search would be the isolation of "form." Thus Kant made three discriminations in isolating the "pure" case of art within the complex field of artifice in general. The first is the discrimination of art from labor. The key to this distinction is that the motive of the latter is the return to be derived from the action, the payment. Hence, like a practical choice based on a material principle, or like a simple judgment of sense, the interest in the satisfaction ultimately to be expected is the basis for the action. The implication, further, is that the means—and labor is clearly for Kant merely a means—is unpleasant drudgery, and consequently the only reason one would subject oneself to it is for the payment. That cannot be the case for art. It can only be "purposive as play, i.e., as occupation that is pleasant in itself [*nur als Spiel, d. i. Beschäftigung, die für sich selbst angenehm ist, zweckmäßig ausfallen (gelingen)*]."[27] The word "pleasant" is a bit disconcerting in this sentence, but the idea of "play" is the main harvest: Kant identifies art with an activity which is the source of delight in itself, which needs no external recompense. He salvages the distinction of the beautiful from the pleasant in his next discrimination, which is between "fine [*schöne*] art" and "agreeable art." Kant develops that distinction in §44. The pleasant is, as we would expect, eliminated from the "pure" consideration of beauty.

That leaves one final distinction in the "purification" of art as such from artifice in general. It is the most problematic and the most important: the distinction between "aesthetical art" and "mechanical art." The idea of the mechanical first arose in consideration of the role of the "aesthetic normal idea" in the "ideal of beauty." There, Kant associated the mechanical with "academic correctness," though he implied that true art had something more about it. He explains this idea in §§43–44. In §43 he makes the following observation: "In all free arts, something of a compulsory character is still required, or, as it is called, a *mechanism*."[28] In §44, Kant explains that "mechanical arts" are those which are based on a clear and determinate concept of what is to be produced, i.e., they follow a rule. Thus "mechanical arts" signfies, precisely, artifice in general, as purposive action. But with respect to fine art it has a further implication, namely, that a rule must be followed. But we know that no prescriptive rule can be claimed for the *appreciation* of beauty. Can it be that one could apply in its *creation?* Kant clearly recognizes this cannot be. Once again, we must be attentive to his notion of "play" in this context: the action is undertaken for the intrinsic satisfaction—i.e., the delight—it provides. Somehow, the recognition that art falls within artifice, i.e., purposeful action, seems now to threaten its fundamental nature, namely, freedom. Rules are rational, cognitive, and determinant. Artifice in general falls under rules. Fine art falls under artifice in general, yet it must not subordinate itself to a prescriptive rule. Kant has landed himself squarely in a paradox. It is, indeed, the second half of his grounding paradox of art: that art must appear like nature (that which suffers no human intervention), and yet must be recognized as art (namely, a human act).

There are two sides to this issue. First, what can it mean that fine art appear like nature? And second, what sort of human act is fine art? Let us take each of them up in turn. When Kant writes that art must look like nature, what he means is that it should appear "as free from all constraint of arbitrary rules as if it were a product of mere nature [*von allem Zwange willkürlicher Regeln so frei scheinen, als ob es ein Product der bloßen Natur sei*]."[29] But since when is nature "free"? Kant's definition of nature is precisely the ensemble of laws, or the existence of phenomena under the constraint of those laws. Even in ordinary language, when we think of nature as "unconstrained," what sorts of events do we have in mind? Certainly not the "starry heavens." Even a "meandering brook" or a "vagrant breeze" follow, in fact, utterly fixed physical laws. If we respond to a spontaneity, a dynamism in nature, an effortlessness of order, we also know that that order is real, binding, and fixed. Perhaps it is in the phenomena of life in nature that we are most struck by its "freedom," in the luxuriant creativity which makes each leaf of an oak tree distinct, each instance of a species unique. Perhaps it is the lushness, this spendthrift vitality of nature, that we mean by that sense of "freedom" from the constraint of arbitrary rules. Certainly if man were to make an oak tree, each leaf would be produced to identical specifications of the most mechanical sort. Individuality is something our rational constructions seem to consider thoroughly dispensable.

There is a further point, however. In the sense that rules are arbitrary *(willkürlich)*, they are artificial. They are products of purpose or rational will. Reason is the only source of rule in the world. To be rule-bounded is to be subject to reason. But Kant locates the entire aesthetic sphere not in subordination to reason but in the free play of the imagination, in sensibility, the realm of the merely given, the domain of objective actuality, not validity. Hence what art must entail is a purposiveness without a purpose: as human act it falls under the rubric of artifice, of purpose, and hence of rule, but as free act it falls under the dispensation of the mere formality of purpose, *Zweckmäßigkeit ohne Zweck*. Yet the formality of purpose is still analogous to rule, to design. Some element of rule must remain.

If, then, there is a sense to the idea that art should be like nature in its freedom from the constraint of arbitrary rules, the stress must be on the two words "constraint" and "arbitrary," and not on the word "rules." This is the way in which Kant elaborates his point in §45:

> But the way in which a product of art seems like nature, is by the presence of perfect *exactness* [*Püncktlichkeit*] in the agreement with rules prescribing how alone the product can be what it is intended to be, but with an absence of *labored effect* [*Peinlichkeit*], (without academic form betraying itself,) i.e. without a trace appearing of the artist having always had the rule present to him and of its having fettered his mental powers.[30]

There are two key points to be extracted. First, there is a necessary place for rule in free or fine art, hence Kant's insistence on the mechanical as "academic form" or correctness. But the deeper point is that this "correctness" must be of a higher sort. The "exactness" Kant prescribes for art is not that of its conformity to mechanical canons of correctness, but rather the parallel it shows to the inevitability and ease of natural order, its aptness in a much grander sense. That is the other side of the analogy of art and nature: it is not just in its lack of constraint but in its precision, indeed, effortless precision, that art must seem natural. The distinction here is between ease and clumsiness, but even more is at stake, some primordial sense of rightness which is not only aesthetic but cognitive and ethical. And there is one final, Romantic fillip to the argument, which Kant deftly and ironically takes up: man is after all also a creature of nature. Nature, in its effortless creativity, can then be taken to act *through* man to generate works of fine art. And that is exactly what Kant takes "genius" to mean.

With "genius" all the contextual issues come to a head. The conflict between rule and genius was the essential issue between Neoclassicism and Romanticism. It was also the self-professed mission of the *Sturm und Drang* in Germany to free its culture from the constraint of arbitrary classical rules (Latin and French in derivation) by the articulation, the celebration, and the untrammeled pursuit of "genius." And all this was repugnant to Immanuel Kant. That explains the third key discrimination Kant introduced in his exposition of the concept of art: the distinction of art from science. Looking at the problem of genius in this light first will help contextualize the whole issue and serve us mightily at a later juncture.

Kant's hostility to the *Sturm und Drang* is the decisive context in which one must read not only his distinction of art from science in §43, but also his whole treatment of genius in §§46–47. Kant has a very definite target in mind, even within the *Sturm und Drang:* Johann Herder. His juxtaposition of science and art can be read— should be read—as a juxtaposition, as well, of his own *method* with Herder's *manner.*[31] Let us first examine Kant's exposition, then turn our sights to the context to which it unquestionably refers. The campaign begins in §43. Kant insists that there is an element of rule, of academic regimen, i.e., of mechanism, even in "free art." It is appropriate to make this point, he asseverates, because "not a few leaders of a newer school believe that the best way to promote a free art is to sweep away all restraint, and convert it from labor into mere play [*manche neuere Erzieher eine freie Kunst am besten zu befördern glauben, wenn sie allen Zwang von ihr wegnehmen und sie aus Arbeit in bloßes Spiel verwandeln*]."[32] The result of such a posture, however, is that though the "spirit" [*Geist*], which "alone gives life to the work [*allein das Werk belebt*]," would be free, it would be all-too-free, namely, "become bodyless and evanescent [*gar keinen Körper haben und gänzlich verdunsten würde*]."

There is no question that the reference here is to the *Sturm und Drang* theory of genius and its rebellion against Neoclassical canons of taste. The question is rather whether we can be more precise in determining who the target of Kant's criticism might have been. Without question, in the 1780s, and certainly by 1788, the leader of the *Sturm und Drang* and the most important theorist of aesthetic genius in Germany was Herder. Although Kant had had run-ins also with their mutual associate, Hamann, the latter died in 1788, and while it is highly likely that he was to be tarred with the same brush, he could hardly pose a further threat to the direction of German culture. On the strength of this alone, Herder seems the most obvious candidate. That conjecture receives great reinforcement in Kant's next section.

Kant argues at the outset of §44 that there can be no such thing as a "beautiful science," any more than there can be a "science of the beautiful." It is clear that by the latter he meant a logically prescriptive rule which determined the concept of the beautiful. What is interesting is the meaning of the other notion, a "beautiful science." "As for a beautiful science—a science which, as such, is to be beautiful, is a nonentity. For if, treating it as a science, we were to ask for reasons and proofs, we would be put off with elegant phrases *(bons mots).*"[33] Kant is saying that in such an instance, something purporting to be science, hence a matter of logical discourse, would, when challenged, reply that it was justified in its propositions not by proofs but by elegance or beauty. Beauty was an inept ground for truth, for Kant, and nothing irked him more than to raise a rational query of someone's ostensible science and be reproached for insensitivity to his target's lyrical sensibility. He had gone through just such an episode—in his review of Herder's *Ideen.*

The argument thrusts more deeply than this personal dimension, for Kant is questioning the justice in using the word "science" in the whole realm of the humanities as such. In other words, Kant is launching the campaign for the separation of the so-called "two cultures" by the demotion of the humanities from the rank of *Wissenschaft.* He writes that these "elegant sciences" [*schönen Wissenschaften*] constitute merely the preparation in scholarship requisite for the cultivation of taste:

> for fine art, in the fulness of its perfection, a large store of science [*Wissenschaft*—though it would be better, and catch the nature of Kant's distinction, were it translated as "scholarship"] is required, as, for example, knowledge of ancient languages, acquaintance with classical authors, history, antiquarian learning, etc. Hence these historical sciences [*historischen Wissenschaften*], owing to the fact that they form the necessary preparation and groundwork for fine art, and partly also owing to the fact that they are taken to comprise even the knowledge of the products of fine art (rhetoric and poetry), have by a confusion of words, actually got the name of elegant sciences.[34]

The *studia humanitatis* are all here carefully adumbrated, and all lumped together as failing of the full stature of science. While they are, to be sure, worthy studies, they do not have the same theoretical status, the same objective validity.

This stance must be placed in context. Romanticism is often taken, in general, as the rebellion against the primacy of theoretical reason and of science in the discernment of the essential meanings of human experience. It was the effort to replace the natural scientist or natural philosopher—the terms and often the figures were, in the eighteenth century, synonymous—with the artist as the true seer, the *vates.* The suggestion of richer potentials of meaning to which aesthetic sensibility opened the artist up, and of the actual *inspiration* of artists by these ultimate meanings, is what lent such power to the idea of genius in the eighteenth century, and surrounded it with a nimbus of mystery and even mysticism. As a good son of the Enlightenment, Kant found such notions revolting. Science should not endure such indignity. "Genius" had to be put in its place. And that was exactly what Kant proceeded to do.[35]

The only possible reconciliation of the paradox of art as at once "free" and limited by "mechanism," as at once "natural" and as "purposive/artificial," was to read the actual agent in artistic creativity not as the subject in his self-possession, but rather as nature working through the subject. Hence, all "free," all "beautiful" or "fine" art had to be the product of genius. But genius—and this is the ironic point—had to be conceived as something which the artist neither controlled nor understood.

Kant's exposition of genius takes its terms from the "conventional wisdom."[36] Kant started with the notion of "genius" as "the talent (natural endowment) which gives the rule to art." But that only meant, Kant elaborated, that genius was "the innate mental aptitude *(ingenium) through which* nature gives the rule to art." This was not yet his analysis, merely his reading of what others had said, but it gave him a very useful vantage on the whole issue. The point was that "fine art cannot of its own self excogitate the rule according to which it is to effectuate its product [*Also kann die schöne Kunst sich selbst nicht die Regel ausdenken, nach der sie ihr Product zu Stande bringen soll*]."[37] With this construction Kant could now explicate, from the vantage of his own aesthetic theory, why genius had to be taken to be "original," as the conventional wisdom had it, and why it also could produce only "exemplary" instantiations which could neither be presribed in logical rules nor described in discursive empirical canons, but which stood in themselves as the one source not only for the cultivation of taste as appreciation but for further exemplification of beauty through art. But the ironic point is reserved for last:

It cannot indicate scientifically how it brings about its product, but rather gives the rule as *nature*. Hence, where an author owes a product to his genius, he does not himself know how the *ideas* for it have entered into his head, nor has he it in his power to invent the like at pleasure, or methodically, and communicate the same to others in such precepts as would put them in a position to produce similar products.[38]

The artistic genius cannot explain his own achievement, cannot reproduce it at will, and cannot teach it to others. From the vantage point of rationality, he is impotent. How ironic then is the phrase "leaders of a newer school" [neuere Erzieher] in reference to the Stürmer, for in the measure that they were indeed geniuses, they could not teach their genius. They were merely the vehicles of a natural revelation. There has rarely been so ironic a reading of poetic inspiration as this, and Kant intends to use it for all it is worth. If this is what genius means, then obviously the word genius has nothing to do with science. All of Kant's threads come together in a tight knot, indeed, a noose, and in it he has Herder. In §47, Kant explicitly exempts science from the sphere of genius.

It all lies in the natural path of investigation and reflection according to rules, and so is not specifically distinguishable from what may be acquired as the result of industry backed up by imitation. So all that Newton has set forth in his immortal work . . . may well be learned, however great a mind it took to find it all out . . . [because] all the steps that Newton had to take from the first elements of geometry to his greatest and most profound discoveries were such as he could make intuitively evident and plain to follow [ganz anschaulich und zur Nachfolge bestimmt vormachen könnte], not only for himself but for everyone else.[39]

Science, Kant asseverates, is merely prosaic, unlike the inimitable flights of poetic fancy of a Homer. "In matters of science, therefore, the greatest inventor differs only in degree from the most laborious imitator and apprentice." Not only is science prosaic, it is egalitarian. Art, however, is altogether different: "we cannot learn to write in a poetic vein." Poeta nascitur non fit. Poets are born, not made.

The highest distinction to which the genius lays claim, the inspiration of his guardian "daimon," Kant, by acknowledging, demeans. To be sure they are "the elect of nature [die Günstlinge der Natur]," but when Kant writes "No disparagement . . . of those great men, to whom the human race is so deeply indebted, [i.e., the men of science] is involved in this comparison" with nature's darlings, who entertains any serious doubt where his loyalties lie? Science promises "continued advances of greater perfection in knowledge, with all its dependent practical advantages." It is progressive and it can also be taught. It is the very stuff of education. Therefore, Kant bluntly states, it possesses a "ground of considerable superiority" over art. Indeed—and here Kant makes a staggering point which anticipates the Hegelian theory of art—"art must make a halt [at some point], as there is a limit imposed upon it which it cannot transcend. This limit has in all probability been long since attained."[40]

How is art then carried forward? How is taste cultivated? The answer is: through the exemplary instantiation of prior works of genius, on which subsequent artists must practice their taste, and from which they must derive not a rule to imitate, but an example to follow: not the result but the activity which produced it is what the artistic genius must gather from another's masterpiece. It is to retrieve the *Zweckmäßigkeit ohne Zweck* whose outcome was an artistic masterpiece that one artist studies another's work. And to discern it, while vital to the appreciation, is nothing if it does not elicit in the artist a latent capacity in himself to emulate that process, to make a work of art of his own. Therefore, the only way the potential genius can be cultivated is to subject him or her to that rigorous exposure to exemplary instances of artistic genius which is just what is meant by "academic training." And hence that very "mechanical" element cannot be evaded in the cultivation of the artist. But Kant wishes to assert even more: the mechanical is not only indispensable in the cultivation of the artist, it is also indispensable in the artist's creation of a work.

That is why the *Sturm und Drang* version of genius is incoherent, Kant argues. "Originality" is not enough. Realization of a work requires technique, skill, discipline: rule.

[S]hallow minds fancy that the best evidence they can give of their being full-blown geniuses is by emancipating themselves from all academic constraint of rules, in the belief that one cuts a finer figure on the back of an ill-tempered than of a trained horse. Genius can do no more than furnish rich *material* for products of fine art; its elaboration and its *form* require a talent academically trained, so that it may be employed in such a way as to stand the test of judgment.[41]

Hence Kant argues that the production of a work of art is a complex process, in which genius supplies the "matter" but judgment (taste) provides the "form." Knowing Kant, much of what follows is predictable. What is not predictable is the interjection that Kant places at just this point:

But, for a person to hold forth and pass sentence like a genius in matters that fall to the province of the most patient rational investigations, is ridiculous in the extreme. One is at a loss to know whether to laugh more at the impostor who envelops himself in such a cloud—in which we are given fuller scope to our imagination at the expense of all use of our critical faculty,—or at the simple-minded public which imagines that its inability clearly to cognize and comprehend this masterpiece of penetration is due to its being invaded by new truths *en masse*, in comparison with which, detail, due to carefully weighed exposition and an academic examination of root-principles, seems to it only the work of a tyro.[42]

Kant is in fact back in his polemic of §44, regarding "beautiful science." It was argued in considering that section that Kant was referring to Herder. Now, with this passage, the evidence is overwhelming. The language of this passage has only to be compared to that in which there is no question that the reference is to Herder, Kant's letter to Friedrich Jacobi of August 30, 1789.[43] And that means that Herder is the target not only of the disparagement of "beautiful science" but of the untrammeled theory of genius as well. Indeed, the whole ironic treatment of genius is a result of Kant's hostility to Herder.

It is in this sense that we must see that Kant never enters into the perspective of the artist in creation, but always judges him from outside, from the standpoint of—science. The result is often very penetrating, as we will see, but the detachment also has an ironic, indeed, patronizing element which we must not miss.[44] The artistic genius does not know what he is doing. There is suddenly an odd aptness to our imputation of a work of art to the bees, though they accomplish it only by instinct.[45] Is the matter so different with an artistic genius? As genius, that is, in terms of the "material" that is brought into the synthesis, no. It is taste, it is judgment that provides "form," that provides "rule," that brings with it the dignity of reason.

Kant's Architectonic Redemption of Art

Kant had an ironic intention in his treatment of genius: he intended to rebuff the *Sturm und Drang* and in particular Johann Herder for the outlandish pretenses they had introduced into the German cultural scene, not only within the narrow bounds of poetry, but also in aesthetic criticism, in history, and even, most outrageously, in science and philosophy. That impulse is very strong in the exposition of art and genius in the *Third Critique,* and if it is not attended, the complexity of the intentions of the work seems to suggest a very high level of confusion. There was no confusion at all, just a variety of scores to settle. When Kant felt satisfied that his long-standing grudge against the *Sturm und Drang* had been adequately articulated, he could return to his systematic task of analyzing the problems of aesthetics. Accordingly, his architectonic intention rescued his theory of art from serving a merely polemical function in the work.

The architectonic intention was to read the production of beauty in art as structurally homologous with the appreciation of beauty. Beauty always involved *Zweckmäßigkeit ohne Zweck,* i.e., subjective formal purposiveness, which, transcendentally analyzed, meant harmony of the faculties. Not only was this harmony of the faculties to be discerned transcendentally as the basis of the appreciation of beauty in the judgment of taste, it was now to be shown as the basis for the production of beauty in the work of art. Consequently, what Kant now turned to accomplish was the elucidation of the production of the work of art in terms of the relations of the faculties of the mind. He already set forth the major contention of that analysis when he argued that "genius" could only provide the "material" for beautiful art, but that it was taste, mechanically achieved through discipline and academic training, which supplied the "form." It is the relation of genius to taste that becomes the center of Kant's attention now that his polemical energies have dissipated.

Kant's claim that genius only supplies the "material" in a work of art would suggest that genius cannot stand in very high stead in his theory of the beauty of art, since for Kant beauty, like reason, is always exclusively linked with "form." That would, however, represent such a radical break with the conventional wisdom and such a repudiation of the new sensibility as to leave Kant utterly isolated from his culture. Certainly Kant was a brave thinker, but he did not expose himself needlessly to such estrangement, and he felt that he had found a way both to put genius in its place and, to mix the metaphor, to give the devil his due.[46] Let us begin with the tension between genius and taste.

Kant returns to the issue of the title at the close of §48. He contends that the beauty in a work of art is the result of taste, since taste alone gives it form. Kant defends this claim with a very penetrating analysis of the labor of artistic production, relevant not only for his own approach, but also as evidence of a more apt appreciation of creative activity than the rival *Sturm und Drang* notion of effortless genius:

> To give this form . . . to the product of fine art, taste merely is required. By this the artist, having practised and corrected his taste by a variety of examples from nature or art, controls his work and, after many, and often laborious, attempts to satisfy taste, finds the form which commends itself to him. Hence this form is not, as it were, a matter of inspiration, or of a free swing of the mental powers, but rather of a slow and even painful process of improvement, directed to making the form adequate to his thought without prejudice to the freedom in the play of those powers.[47]

In this passage Kant goes very far toward reintegrating art within the general sphere of artifice, and raises the self-conscious pursuit of *technique* to prominence in the theory of art.[48] He clearly articulates some of the grounding principles upon which aesthetic modernism would break radically with the Romantic, and indeed even the classical tradition.[49] But not only does Kant, by emphasizing technique, blur the distinction between art and artifice and hence draw it closer to "mechanical art," he also, by emphasizing the laboriousness and pain of the process, draws it much closer to labor, to "industrial art." Yet, to be sure, the labor is intended and experienced as play.

In putting so much emphasis on taste, however, Kant begins to fear that he threatens his whole approach to genius, and that leads him to take back in the very next paragraph almost everything he just ascribed to taste. "Taste is, however, merely a critical, not a productive faculty; and what conforms to it is not, merely on that account, a work of fine art." Kant then reasserts in all their rigor the distinctions between "fine" and "mechanical" art. Mere learning, academicism, does not suffice for beauty. It may be correct, Kant argues, but it is "spiritless [*ohne Geist*]."[50] Let us look back to the closing paragraph of §43, where the tension between "mechanism" and "spirit" [*Geist*] was first introduced, and the former associated with "body" and the latter with "life" or liveliness.[51] The polarities are skewed. Spirit and life, in the normal Kantian order of things, should belong with form. Mechanism and "body" should, in the normal Kantian order of things, belong with "matter." But mechanism has been associated with taste, and taste with "form," while genius has been associated with "matter." Yet "spirit" and "life" clearly fall to the side of genius. How are we to make sense of all this?

That Kant can view taste as "productive" is evidenced in §17.[52] That he views it as not productive is clear from §48. That genius provides only the "material" is stated bluntly in §47. That it nevertheless supplies the "spirit" and the "life," that it is the *productive* element in the work of art, is the stress of the entire exposition of art. There is obviously a problem with consistency here. Kant's considered view, as expressed in §50, is that it is only the synthesis of the two which can produce fine art. Therefore, taking taste in isolation, it can only produce a "mechanical," academically correct but "lifeless" product. Conversely, by taking genius in isolation—and here we get at the essential point—what is produced runs the risk of being "nonsense."[53]

It is in the juxtaposition of "spiritless academic correctness" on the one hand and "original nonsense" on the other that we grasp what Kant is trying to articulate in §48. Art cannot be achieved without the discipline of a rule, even if only in the very indefinite form of exemplary instances critically attended through academic training. But it derives its impulse from nature, from a gratuitous givenness in the subject, an "actuality without validity," which expresses itself in the play of the imagination as freely productive. Genius is grounded in this. Since the sphere in which all this takes place is sensibility in the sense in which it is most remote from cognitive legitimacy, or "objective validity" in the Kantian sense, Kant assigns it to "nature." Genius is construed as a natural kind of freedom. Yet here again all the problems of what "nature" means in such a context, all the force of the grounding paradox, intervene. Can nature be the strict mechanical realm of phenomenal law in this context?

We must ask what sort of freedom the aesthetic sphere possesses, and what dangers lurk in that sort of freedom. Why does it have this dangerous propensity to nonsense, to mere caprice, in the extreme to sheer lunacy? That is the question. Aesthetic freedom is the "free play of the imagination," but what that means is that it is not necessarily subject to any rule. When successful it behaves in a way which is consistent with rule. But what if it is unsuccessful? Then what we have is that "blooming, buzzing confusion" which Kant discussed in the cognitive context of the *First Critique* and in the decisive exposition of imagination in the *Anthropology*.[54] Indeed, that is madness in the precise sense of the loss of reason. Genius, in its liberty, in its caprice, in its play, flirts with madness. If in aesthetic freedom man is at his most free, free even from obligation to reason, just in this measure he is most in peril for his ultimate dignity, which for Kant is exclusively grounded in reason.[55]

In the General Remark to §29, with which Kant surveys his entire exposition of aesthetic judgments, he makes a very telling analysis of the freedom involved in morality and the freedom involved in aesthetics.

> [T]hough . . . the immediate pleasure in the beautiful in nature presupposes and cultivates a certain *liberality* [*Liberalität*] of thought, i.e. makes our delight independent of any mere enjoyment of sense, still it represents freedom rather as in *play* than as exercising a law-ordained *function*, which is the genuine characteristic of human morality, where reason has to impose its dominion upon sensibility.[56]

Accordingly, Kant's description of beauty in §5 must be read with a new skepticism. When Kant writes that "taste in the beautiful . . . [is] the one and only disinterested and *free* delight," that "*favor* [*Gunst*] is the only free liking," he is reckoning in man a sort of freedom which is dangerously autonomous, close to caprice, and can only be rescued, ultimately, by the supervention of the more authentic sort of human freedom, which is ethical. Hence the drive within Kantian aesthetics to establish a bond with the ethical, via "dependent beauty," "perfection," and the "ideal of beauty."

The theory of art has brought us to the brink of metaphysics. The grounding paradox of art opens out on many metaphysical possibilities. Amid this wealth, Kant's thought first hits upon one: the idea of "perfection." It was, as we have noted, an idea with a history in aesthetics dating at least from Baumgarten. But Baumgarten had wished to use the idea in a cognitive vein. Kant's notion of perfection, by contrast, was practical. Or so it seemed.

In §48, Kant returned to his idea of "dependent beauty" and his thinking there carried him back still further toward "objective subreption" and the question, involved in the nature side of the grounding paradox of art, whether natural beauty was real, rather than imputed. He set off the issue with an excruciatingly contradictory assertion: "A beauty of nature is a *beautiful thing;* beauty of art is a *beautiful representation* of a thing."[57] First of all, to call the beauty of nature a beautiful *thing* is to commit objective subreption. But second, to call the beauty of art a beautiful representation *(Vorstellung)* is to use the latter term in an extraordinarily awkward sense.[58]

It usually refers to that which is merely present to consciousness, i.e., internal to consciousness. But that is precisely what art cannot be. Art must be a realization, an objectification. It must have a sensuous givenness separate from the particular subjective consciousness of its creator. It must *exist*. It must be a *thing*. How can Kant have so thoroughly muddled things?

While, clearly, there is a difference between the beauty of art and the beauty of nature, it is not simple, as the grounding paradox of art clearly demonstrates. Let us attempt first to salvage Kant's notion of art. Clearly he is using "representation" in a drastically different sense from that typical of his thought. In what sense, then? We can rescue the sense of his argument if we read *Vorstellung* as *Darstellung,* or presentation. At the end of his discussion of the muddling phrase, Kant writes: "So much for the beautiful representation of an object, which is properly only the form of the presentation [*Darstellung*] of a concept."[59] "Representation" in this one instance merely signifies that which is artificially made to serve as a representation, a physical sign, of some thing.[60] By his association of the term *Vorstellung* with *Darstellung,* I believe Kant saves himself from hopeless obscurity or folly in his construction of art.

It remains to be seen what Kant intended by the contention that a natural beauty was a beautiful thing. Kant immediately went on to claim that there was no need in a pure aesthetic judgment to have recourse to the idea of an immanent purpose, or to the idea of perfection. Insofar as this was the case, then a natural beauty was, aesthetically considered, merely a representation, and an utterly subjective one at that, of the pleasure experienced through harmony of the faculties, and Kant had no business calling it a "thing."

Yet both art and "dependent beauty" in nature, according to Kant, require some notion of immanent purpose, of perfection. At his clearest, Kant insists that beauty, i.e., the authentically aesthetic experience, is not a matter of the properties of an object, but rather of the mental activity of the subject, and hence, for beauty, no "objective purposiveness" is requisite. In his idea of "dependent beauty" and in his discrimination of the beauty of nature from the beauty of art, however, Kant discovered a very important "intellectual interest in natural beauty," and its first impulse was toward a "cognitive turn" in his whole approach to reflection: the idea of a teleological judgment.

Part Two

THE GENESIS OF THE "CRITIQUE OF TELEOLOGICAL JUDGMENT"

 *Seven*

THE COGNITIVE TURN: THE DISCOVERY OF REFLECTIVE JUDGMENT

That Kant should produce a *Critique* of biological and cosmological speculation makes sense in view of the salience of these issues in the epoch, especially in Germany. But why and how did this project insinuate itself into Kant's ongoing project in aesthetics? What was it about his work on the "Critique of Taste" which suddenly led Kant to consider it appropriate to take up all those other questions which he clearly had in mind, but which one would think deserved separate articulation?[1] The most important point for the unity of the *Third Critique* is to show how the problem of teleological judgment arises immanently out of the problem of aesthetic judgment, i.e., out of the "objective subreption" which particularly attends the discernment of beauty in nature.

"Objective subreption" is the tendency to ascribe to the object itself the property which entailed beauty, even though according to Kant beauty resides in the response of the subject, i.e., in subjective formal purposiveness. The tendency to "objective subreption" is a natural error of judgment, yet Kant believed it might—not within the aesthetic experience as such, but subsequently, as a matter for reflection—be the source of "profound inquiries."[2] The "purposiveness of nature" aroused an "intellectual interest" after, and on account of, a purely aesthetic discernment of beauty in nature.[3]

In §29, Kant wrote that there were "numberless beautiful things in nature," whose beauty must be something specific to them, part of the givenness of their representations. Natural beauty was "independent," Kant claimed in several places, e.g. §23, where he expressed the view that "we must seek a ground external to ourselves for the beautiful of nature." In §30, Kant wrote that "purposiveness has its ground in the object and in its figure [*Gestalt*]" and hence was a "*species finalis data, non accepta.*" While clearly falling into "objective subreption," this line of thought brought Kant to a key turning point. Having experienced it, one was drawn to wonder why it should have happened, Kant wrote in §30: "With regard to the beautiful in nature . . . we may start a number of questions touching the cause of this purposiveness of their forms: e.g. How are we to explain why nature has scattered beauty abroad with so lavish a hand, even in the depths of the ocean where it can but seldom be reached by the eye of man—for which alone it is purposive."[4] In §23 he wrote:

> Self-subsisting natural beauty reveals to us a technic of nature which shows it in the light of a system ordered in accordance with laws the principle of which is not to be found within the range of our entire faculty of understanding. This principle is that of a purposiveness relative to the employment of judgment in respect of phenomena which have thus to be assigned, not merely to nature regarded as aimless mechanism, but also to nature regarded after the analogy of art. Hence it gives a veritable extension, not, of course, to our knowledge of objects of nature, but to our conception of nature itself— nature as mere mechanism being enlarged to the conception of nature as art—an extension inviting profound inquiries as to the possibility of such a form.[5]

This passage makes the crucial transition between the aesthetics and the teleology by suggesting that, insofar as we reflect upon the beauty in nature as given ("objective"), we impute to nature a form of ordering utterly distinct from that of mechanistic causality. When nature manifested orderliness in the empirical sphere, as it were, gratuitously, it appeared as if it were an *artist*. That is, its result appeared purposive. Kant suggested in the aesthetics that when we came upon an object of natural beauty, we were prone to make this inference. But it was simply a subjective fancy, not valid judgment. Yet the very subjective formal purposiveness with which the judgment of taste was concerned "provoked inquiries."

In garnering the full significance of this "technic of nature," whereby nature is interpreted "after the analogy of art," Kant began the *First Introduction to the Critique of Judgment* and made his "cognitive turn." His key was precisely the notion of reflection, that "other kind of judging" which we have been at such great pains to disclose in Kant's thinking. In his "cognitive turn," Kant considered the possibility of revising the fundamental theory of cognition and of metaphysics which he had constructed in the *First Critique.* The *locus classicus* of that reconsideration was the *First Introduction to the Critique of Judgment.* The ultimate outcome was the "Critique of Teleological Judgment" as we now have it.

The "Technic of Nature"

The phrase "*Technik der Natur*" developed in Kant's aesthetics, in the context of objects of natural beauty. In the *First Introduction to the Critique of Judgment,* this notion underwent closer cognitive scrutiny. According to Kant, consciousness discerned in nature gratuitous design, that is, works of nature [*Wirkungen*] which appeared like works of artifice [*Werke*].[6] Nature could hardly be taken for an artist, and what was really at play in the notion of a *Technik der Natur* was simply *analogy.*[7] It was not nature to which, in fact, "technic" belonged, but the faculty of judgment.[8] The *First Introduction* stressed the parallel between "reflection" as a cognitive enterprise and "art." Kant wrote: "The reflective judgment thus works . . . not schematically, but *technically,* not just mechanically, like a tool controlled by the understanding and the senses, but *artistically,* according to the universal but at the same time undefined principle of a purposive, systematic ordering of nature." It is judgment which "posits a priori the *technic of nature* as the principle of its reflection."[9] "We will in the future also use the term 'technic' where natural objects are only *judged* [*beurtheilt*] *as if* their possibility rested on art . . . [N]ature is judged [*beurtheilt*] . . . only by analogy with an art and, more particularly, only in a subjective relation to our faculty of knowledge and not in an objective relation to the objects."[10] That, to be sure, is only a matter of "thinking," not "knowing," after the rigorous Kantian distinction, but the "Critique of Teleological Judgment" sets out from just this thought that natural beauty acted as a stimulus to scientific inquiry.[11] Just by virtue of that gratifying discernment of gratuitous order, reflective judgment was in a position to generalize a principle for nature as a whole: the purposiveness of nature in its empirical variety for human comprehension in empirical concepts. This was the transcendental principle of reflective judgment.

The key cognitive strategy of reflective judgment was the idea of artifice projected from the subject onto empirical nature: nature as art. Since it could find instances of a *Technik der Natur* it felt entitled to generalize to the idea that nature in all its empirical manifestations would so conform to the logical requirements of human awareness. It attributed to nature the same design it employed in its own functioning. The grounding paradox of art emerges as crucial yet again, but in the obverse direction: it is not art's conformity to nature, but nature's to art which now concerns us. We are no longer dealing with the exclusively formal and hence completely spontaneous judgment of beauty. Kant argued that it was not human "favor" that nature appeared so ordered. Man had to presume upon nature's favor. Nature could not be objectively compelled to show such order. While it was true that in general natural law was imposed by the necessary structure of transcendental consciousness, it was just as true that empirically what law there might be had to be found, not made, by man. It was, indeed, nature's favor to man when and if such order showed itself. Kant argued that it was impossible for man to deal with his empirical experience except on the assumption that nature did so favor him, that it did operate in conformity with the processes which alone guaranteed efficacy to his logical operations. What that meant, in practice, was that human understanding of the empirical world could only find uniformities or homogeneity—i.e., it could only *classify*—if nature had already actually *specified* in a logical order, i.e., in hierarchical structure.

The issue at hand is the cognitive status of the analogy of nature and art, the *Technik der Natur* or the "purposiveness of nature in its empirical variety." We must ascertain the limitations of its cognitive validity. What did Kant mean it to signify? Why should theoretical reason tolerate it? Indeed, is such an "objective subreption" any more consistent with pure theoretical reason than with pure aesthetic judgment?[12] Has Kant's complex case of beauty not simply rendered the viability of his pure forms of both cognition and aesthetic appreciation incoherent? Unless the gravity of this anomaly is recognized as essential to Kant's philosophizing in the *Third Critique,* the internal dynamism of its evolution and the ultimately revolutionary implications of the work will never be grasped.

As Kant elaborated his interpretation of "subjective formal purposiveness" specifically with reference to natural beauty, he came to realize at last the latent cognitive significance of *Zweckmäßigkeit* and of the process associated with it, reflection. Not only did "subjective formal purposiveness" have an aesthetical dimension—beauty—but it also had a cognitive dimension, that "figurative use" in the "other kind of judging." Not only did the idea of purposiveness offer cognitive possibilities, but so did the process of reflection; they were mutually constitutive. This is hardly part of the constitutive operation of the understanding. "Since this kind of classification is not ordinary experiential knowledge, but is rather an artistic knowledge, insofar as nature is thought in such a way that it can be rendered specific by this kind of principle, it [nature] is regarded as *art*."[13] And Kant reiterates the point in §7: "Thus it is the faculty of *judgment* that is essentially technical; nature is represented as technical only to the extent that it agrees with this procedure and makes it necessary."[14] Thus a "teleological judgment" has a very peculiar cognitive status, and so, too, does the idea of the "purposiveness of nature" upon which it is founded. "Experience does exhibit ends [*Zwecke*], but nothing can prove that these are also intents [*Absichten*]."[15] To take the purposiveness of nature literally as purpose was to impute to it such (rational) intents, and this could only be "sophistic."

> [W]e have no empirical knowledge of such a relationship. For only in *works of art* can we become conscious of reason as the cause of objects, which are therefore called purposive or ends, and in that case calling reason 'technical' conforms to our experience of the causality of our own powers. But nature represented as technical analogously with reason (thus imputing purposiveness and moreover purpose *to nature*) is a special concept which is never met with in experience, and which is only posited by the judgment in reflecting on things in order to organize experience.[16]

The first sense to be drawn from this, of course, is that the usage involved in the notion of nature-as-art is merely heuristic or "regulative" in Kant's language. But there is a deeper point, which becomes very significant later, namely, that our discursive form of thought can only function with the sort of experience represented by natural art or "technic," i.e., gratuitous order, by imputing to it an intentional artifice modeled after our own purposive action. It is only by this projection of our purposive activity, our art, upon such instances that they become in any way accessible to our comprehension, yet even so they remain outside the determinate boundaries of empirical knowledge. This suggests that there is an ultimate incongruity between the cognitive system Kant developed in the *First Critique* and the intractable fact of the existence of "objective purposiveness." He would only draw the full implications of this dilemma when he had fully worked through his "cognitive turn" in the "Critique of Teleological Judgment."

It is historically useful to consider the whole issue of Kant's later cognitive philosophy in terms of his revision of the *Critique of Pure Reason*. Kant undertook that revision starting in April 1786, when he received word from his publisher, Hartknoch, that the first printing of the *Critique of Pure Reason* had been sold out. In view both of the general neglect and of the specific misunderstanding which had plagued that first version, Kant was intent upon revising his great work to make more obvious just what he had been trying to say. Not that the *substance* would change: Kant felt certain that he had achieved the correct solution in 1781 and need never vary.[17] But the rhetoric of presentation certainly could stand improvement, as his critics had not hesitated to advise him, and as he himself recognized, with reservations.[18] Thus, the revisions he undertook in the second edition of the *Critique of Pure Reason* can, very roughly, be linked with two intentions: first, to answer specific misinterpretations, especially the charge of "idealism," and second, to improve the rhetoric of exposition and render as accessible as possible a work which Kant knew well enough could never be "popular."[19]

Kant's revisions were hampered by the responsibilities of university rectorship in 1786, and he only completed them in April 1787, when he composed the preface to the second edition. Actually, it would be more accurate to say that Kant stopped revising, rather than completed his revisions, for he made no changes in the work after the first chapter of book 2 of the "Dialectic." In the preface he gave two grounds for leaving the bulk of the "Dialectic" unchanged.[20] First, he argued that his critics had not had any serious problems in grasping what he presented there. That argument is specious, for there were few matters which drew such uniform question as Kant's resolution of the Third Antinomy and his whole distinction of phenomena and noumena upon which it rested. Second, Kant argued, more realistically, that the time was too short, i.e., that he could delay no longer the issuance of the second edition.

There is a third possibility, advanced here merely as a working hypothesis, but one which has intrinsic interest and would be very significant if confirmed, namely, that Kant broke off his revisions of the *First Critique* at that point because crucial issues in the balance of the "Dialectic" required such substantial revisions that he could not carry them off yet. If we reflect that the balance of the "Dialectic" considers, first, the problems of cosmology and specifically the transition from transcendental principles to an empirical physical science; second, the problems of practical philosophy and theology; and, third, the problems of immanent rational process in inductive synthesis, leading, in the section on method, to a consideration of the unity of pure reason as a system, we can take most of the work Kant published after 1787 to have been, almost literally, a sustained revision of the balance of the *First Critique*.

No concept played a bigger role in all these revisions than *Zweckmäßigkeit*. It was an idea which only appeared in the *First Critique* in the unrevised segment, which fits our hypothesis.[21] It proved crucial in the formulation of Kant's ethical philosophy, both in the *Grounding of the Metaphysics of Morals* and in the *Critique of Practical Reason*. Purposiveness *(Zweckmäßigkeit)* featured in all of Kant's ruminations not only about ethics, but also about aesthetics and even about systematic theoretical reason. It is an idea which would mushroom in Kant's mind over the years 1781–90 until it became the most important symbol and concept for the unity of reason. It became, as we have seen, the central idea in the *Third Critique*.[22] But the issue goes far deeper than we have yet had opportunity to pursue it, for *Zweckmäßigkeit* has hitherto only received consideration in its practical and in its aesthetic significances. The key point is that, having employed the concept extensively in these areas, Kant came at last to consider its *cognitive* implications. *Zweckmäßigkeit* in its cognitive sense Kant calls "teleology."[23]

The advance Kant made between the *First Critique* of 1781 and the *First Introduction* of 1789 lay precisely in his discovery and elaboration of the subjective functioning of the mind which only the aesthetic experience had made accessible to transcendental philosophy. Through the judgment of taste, Kant was brought finally to recognize the many impulses within his thought toward a theory of "reflection" as in some measure cognitive. The result was the fusion of three distinct notions, each with powerful ranges of implication: judgment, reflection, and purposiveness. Once Kant put these three ideas together, what opened up was the tremendous role which this faculty of judgment could play in the cognitive sphere.

The key to reflective judgment is its connection with beauty, both in its subjective ground—purposiveness without purpose— and in its "application" to objects of nature. Kant contended that, subjectively, it was the state of mind in which imagination and understanding freely harmonized, and the attentiveness to that harmony, "reflection." But as "application," it was an active principle. As reflection, the faculty of judgment had the whole arsenal of the idea of purposiveness to work with: purposiveness not only in its literal sense of human action (artifice), but also its figurative sense of recognition of design and its aesthetic sense of pleasure in the merely formal accommodation of natural forms with the structure of mental action. It could find in nature objects which gratified it because they appeared, by virtue of their form, as if they were designed to accord with human consciousness. Purposiveness in nature, like the very beauty which raised it to Kant's attention, could only be subjective and formal, yet it offered a remarkable cognitive potential which Kant could well utilize to resolve the nagging difficulty in his transcendental philosophy concerning empirical entailment.

The Problem of Empirical Entailment

Kant's *First Critique* did not completely constitute and validate empirical science or, indeed, any particular empirical cognition in its particularity, but only the *possibility* of a cognition in general, according to his *First Introduction to the Critique of Judgment.* What had been accomplished in the *First Critique* was to guarantee the unity of experience in general by grounding it in the necessary unity of consciousness itself, i.e., in the transcendental unity of apperception. Kant worked strictly with the idea of an object in general, and with "pure intuition"—space and time without any particular content. Hence what he proved was that the categories could apply to all objects of possible experience.

But just in the structure of that proof the problem manifests itself: what can hold for all objects cannot completely determine any one in particular. Thus in a very important footnote to §2 of the *First Introduction,* Kant distinguished "analytic unity" from "synthetic unity" on precisely this line: what all objects of possible experience possessed in common could not serve in the specification of any particular object, i.e., could not complete the synthetic construction of its empirical concept, since it only provided the wherewithal for any empirical concept.[24] Since cognition is not adequately served by a blanket guarantee, but must be able to proceed to specifics, the problem of the entailment of the empirical, which remained open in the *First Critique,* loomed as a major problem for the critical philosophy.[25] Kant's cognitive philosophy stands or falls upon the principle of discursiveness and the clear articulation of the distinction between the aesthetical and the logical, between intuition and concept, imagination and understanding. Yet even as Kant insisted upon discursiveness, he recognized that the only ground for a possible philosophy as, indeed, for a possible experience, lay in the *synthesis* which bridged the gap between intuition and concept, imagination and understanding. Not only was that the crucial issue of the *First Critique,* but it also became the crucial cognitive issue of the *Third Critique.*

While Kant argued against Hume that the concept of causality was necessary at the transcendental level, he acknowledged at the same time that Hume had every right to consider any empirical application of that principle to be contingent. The problem, then, was how to make the transition from the transcendental certainty to the empirical application. From the outset, Kant felt confident that such a transition was possible. He frequently observed, in the *First Critique,* that consequences could be drawn analytically from the transcendental principles he was unearthing. Thus, in the discussion of the categories, Kant declined to offer definitions or follow out all their implications, reserving that for the "systematic" articulation of doctrine which could follow, in his view quite easily, from transcendental foundations. He promised his readers a speedy execution of his *Metaphysics of Nature* and his *Metaphysics of Morals,* which would perform this labor.[26] Indeed, that is the essential positive meaning of the term "metaphysics" for Kant after 1781: the analytic (hence a priori) derivation of principles from transcendental truths, toward the specification of empirical knowledge both cognitive and practical. Kant's definition of a "transcendental exposition" was precisely the elaboration of a principle which could serve as the basis for further a priori knowledge.[27] This project of a metaphysical foundation for the domains of nature and morals based on his transcendental principles absorbed the bulk of Kant's philosophical energy from 1781 to his death.

In the present instance, it is not with the metaphysics of nature that we must concern ourselves, but with something still more primordial, indeed, transcendental. In the *First Critique* the possibility of a metaphysical foundation of *empirical* science had not in fact been secured. In his work entitled *Metaphysical Foundations of Natural Science* (written in the summer of 1785), Kant set about the transition to empirical science via "transcendental explanations" of matter and motion in order to ground a Newtonian, mathematical physics.[28] Yet that was in a very important sense premature, for the whole question of the coordination of empirical nature with rational concepts of law—even in mathematical physics—had not been guaranteed. It was this realization which more than anything led Kant to reconsider his cognitive theory and introduce major revisions.

Kant made the situation quite plain in his *First Introduction.* While, according to the transcendental deduction of the *First Critique,* "we are to regard experience in general as a system under transcendental laws of the understanding, and not as a mere aggregate," Kant wrote, "it does not follow from this that nature is a system *comprehensible* by human cognition through *empirical* laws also . . . For the variety and diversity of the empirical laws might be so great that, while it would be in part possible to unify perceptions into an experience by particular laws, . . . it would never be possible to unify these laws themselves under a common principle." Indeed, each experience could be such that it showed no similarity to any other, so that each would stand in total isolation and consciousness would be "confronted by a crude, chaotic aggregate totally devoid of system . . ."[29] Under such conditions, consciousness, though a formal unity, would be faced with a nightmare of particulars, of individual intuitions for which no classificatory empirical concepts could be found.

There are three levels to this empirical embarrassment. First, there is the problem of the individual entity. This is the problem of the "synthesis of recognition" through empirical concepts. So far as empirical concepts remain, as concepts, universal, they cannot entail the full individuality of the intuition.[30] That is a very important sense of the notion "contingency" [*Zufälligkeit*] in the *Third Critique.*[31] It is precisely in this area that our argument concerning "actuality without validity" and the "other kind of judging" bound up in "aesthetic" reflection proves so important. Kant's theory of empirical cognition involves a problem of individual intuition from which he abstracted in his pure case of transcendental a priori knowledge. Once again, the complex case is far thornier than the pure case, as the *Third Critique* maintained.

The level at which Kant is most comfortable formulating the issue is not at the level of the individual intuition. On the one hand, he chooses at times to believe that the particular object *is* secured by his transcendental deduction, while, on the other, he recognizes that even securing the coherence of any particular intuition as an object of consciousness will not avail if some higher order classifications are not possible. Hence the idea of general empirical concepts is more crucial to human knowledge than grasping an individual intuition. Only in so far as we can classify similarities and differences among experiences is there any hope for order in our consciousness, however full each of our intuitions might be. Thus the second level of concern is with the possibility of *laws*, i.e., concepts which express uniformities among experiences and thereby organize empirical knowledge.

Yet these laws themselves would be capricious and unavailing if there were not some prospect of coherence among them, some guarantee of "system" analogous to that provided transcendentally by the unity of apperception and the categories. That, in its turn, meant that nature as an empirical whole had to be a unity, indeed, a system of laws in strict conformity with the systematic structure of human reason, such that the unity was accessible to human consciousness. The only way that there could be a hope for system in empirical laws was if it were possible for consciousness to presume in empirical nature a propensity to organize itself according to the principles of logical articulation to which human beings were necessitated by discursive consciousness.

The claim that categorial understanding did not determine empirical judgments, the view that only the general concept of nature had been secured for certainty and that the empirical had no a priori coherence, resulted in a substantial circumscription of what had seemed the established realm of the understanding, and cleared a very large space for the expanded notion of judgment as a theoretical or cognitive instrument of human reason.[32] Where the *First Critique* had recognized problems of empirical entailment, Kant had resorted to the regulative faculty of reason and its "hypothetical" uses. Now, it seemed, the *First Introduction* transferred this function of reason to judgment (or at least made the two virtually indistinguishable).[33] Thus judgment's domain was enlarged at the expense of both understanding and reason. If we are to understand how Kant came to resolve the problem of empirical entailment through the idea of a faculty of judgment, we must go back to the *First Critique* and appreciate his theory of the logical process of thought and the specific role played in it by "regulative ideas of reason," on the one hand, and the "faculty of judgment," on the other, and trace how these ideas evolved, and indeed merged, into the idea of "reflective judgment."

In §2 of the *First Introduction*, Kant reviewed briefly his notion of the faculties of cognition as articulated in the *First Critique*.[34] He identified three such "faculties"—understanding, reason, and judgment. Understanding, as he had it there, represented "knowledge of the *universal* (of rules)," and reason "the capacity for the *determination* of the particular through the universal (deduction from principles)."[35] Judgment, in this scheme, served as the mediation. Where understanding provided the major premise, or rule, judgment supplied the particular case to be subsumed under it, or the minor premise, and reason was the capacity to draw the conclusion with logical necessity.

These definitions derive from the formal logical theory of the syllogism as it was taught in the late eighteenth century, by Kant among others.[36] This formal definition of the "logical use" of the various faculties is a very important starting point, and not to be dismissed as "thoroughly architectonic and riddled with faculty-talk."[37] It must rather be grasped as Kant's effort to present a clear and determinate account of the process of mind. According to the theory of logical syllogisms, reasoning functioned immanently by recognizing concepts of greater generality (scope) as hierarchically "higher" and placing concepts of greater specificity (content) "under" these. Thus reasoning proceeded either up the chain of concepts (abstraction) toward more and more universal concepts (genera), each embracing wider classes of subordinate concepts but itself with less and less content, or down the chain of concepts (concretion) toward more and more particular concepts (species), each richer in content but narrower in scope. This movement of reason had to be continuous: there could be no gaps in the reasoning or the whole structure would fail of its essential unity.

These immanent principles of rational process were articulated in the "Transcendental Dialectic" of the *First Critique* in a very important methodological appendix entitled "The Regulative Employment of the Ideas of Pure Reason."[38] Kant called them *homogeneity, specification,* and *continuity.* In the *First Introduction,* he returned to this idea, claiming that it was absolutely necessary for man's empirical knowledge that these logical processes be accommodated by nature in its empirical variety.[39] As formal logic this system of ascending (regressive) reasoning and descending (specifying) reasoning had long since been established by logicians. What Kant wished to argue was that this whole pattern of thinking could, and had to, apply to empirical experience. Hence it had to belong to transcendental logic, and have a "real" use. But that required a transcendental principle. Kant equivocated about a transcendental deduction of such a principle for the faculty of reason in the *First Critique*. Eventually, the *First Introduction* assigned that principle to the faculty of judgment. In the *First Critique* Kant considered the operation under the general rubric of the "regulative use of the ideas of reason," and when the problem involved synthetic induction, the "hypothetical use" of reason. What we must now establish is how and why Kant came to transfer this operation from the faculty of reason to the faculty of judgment in the *Third Critique*.

The faculty of reason has a peculiar status in the *First Critique*. On the one hand, it would appear to be the most important part of cognition, and yet on the other, Kant seems to view it as the sphere primarily of "dialectical illusion." Certainly the faculty of understanding enjoys a higher esteem in the bulk of the work than does reason. Yet Kant endeavors to find a positive as well as a critical place for reason in human consciousness. It is this problematic struggle which informs the bulk of the "Transcendental Dialectic."

The issue of reason has two sides, the methodological and the ontological. The methodological aspect concerns the "use" of reason. The ontological aspect concerns the objectivity of reason, and in that connection we must always bear in mind the ambiguity of the Kantian concept of objectivity, its conflicting senses of validity and of actuality. In the *First Critique* Kant is primarily concerned to debunk the ontological idea of reason. It is only in an "Appendix" that he directly addresses its methodological role. Yet an attentive reading of the entire "Transcendental Dialectic" shows that Kant has an extraordinarily high estimation of the power of reason in its reflexivity: no issue within it can remain obscure. Reason is the complete judge of its own power. It is reason which submits itself to critique. It is reason which recognizes its own limits. Reason: not understanding. Only reason can supply the rules for its own immanent process.

Hence there are two methodological dimensions to reason: first, a transcendental one, governing the immanent operation of reasoning itself, and second, an empirical one, governing the specific application of the understanding to empirical science.[40] The former undertakes the laborious task not only of the transcendental deduction to ground the possibility of understanding's grasp of sensible intuition within its rule, but also of the antinomies, testing its own limits by the employment of the principle of contradiction against its own immanent process.

Kant argues that reason is always movement, process, act, rather than fixity, concept, or object. Reason creates, rather, ideas.[41] Ideas are metaconcepts, in the sense of providing rules for the organization of concepts into systems of thought.[42] Understanding holds exclusive sway within any given judgment. It is precisely the set of rules whereby any given assertion (categorical proposition) can be formulated—especially any empirical judgment via the schematism, i.e., one which has an object of sensible intuition as its possible subject and the categories as predicate. Such synthetic judgments have their warrant exclusively in the principles of the understanding. But the combination of these categorical propositions into systems of thought, the building of syllogisms, falls under the purview of reason.

At the same time, two of the judgments of the understanding involve the relation of propositions (hypothetical and disjunctive judgments), and all the modal judgments refer to a higher order criterion of validity over and above the specific proposition. Hence certain of the categories have an ambivalent status: they fall both under the understanding and under reason. These categories are the categories of relation and the categories of modality. Kant calls them "dynamical" as opposed to "mathematical," and he also terms them "regulative." Those two terms, dynamical and regulative, lie at the heart of the notion of reason in Kant, and create ambiguities in his transcendental logic. Kant explains why he distinguishes between dynamical and mathematical categories in the "Transcendental Analytic." The mathematical categories are purely constitutive, in that they concern the appearance itself; "alike as regards their intuition and the real in their perception, they can be generated according to rules of mathematical synthesis."[43] The dynamical categories, however, "are not concerned with appearances and the synthesis of their empirical intuition, but only with the *existence* of such appearances and their *relation* to one another in respect of their existence."[44] But "since existence cannot be constructed, the principles can apply only to the relations of existence, and can yield only *regulative* principles."[45] Hence, the "analogies of experience" are not "*constitutive* of the objects, that is, of the appearances, but only *regulative*. The same can be asserted of the postulates of empirical thought in general."[46] The distinction between the mathematical and the dynamical categories has to do not with their "certainty—both have certainty a *priori*"—but rather "as regards the character of the intuitive (and consequently of the demonstrative) factors."[47]

Kant related this distinction of "constitutive" and "regulative" to the more familiar one whereby he distinguished the empirical role of understanding and reason as entire faculties in the "Transcendental Dialectic."[48] He writes there:

> The principle of reason is . . . properly only a *rule*, prescribing a regress in the series of the conditions of given appearances . . . It is not a principle of the possibility of experience . . . [i.e.] a principle of the understanding . . . Nor is it a *constitutive* principle of reason, enabling us to extend our concept of the sensible world beyond all possible experience . . . Accordingly I entitle it a *regulative* principle of reason . . .
>
> In order properly to determine the meaning of this rule of pure reason, we must observe . . . that it cannot tell us *what the object is,* but only *how the empirical regress is to be carried out* so as to arrive at the complete concept of the object.[49]

Reason functions to order concepts (in a series or a system).[50] To create or constitute concepts is the function of the understanding, but reason does have a use in relation to empirical problems. It is the rule for the "empirical regress" mentioned in the citation above. Kant calls this the "regulative employment [*Gebrauch,* use]" of reason, and defines it as "directing the understanding towards a certain goal upon which the routes marked out by all its rules converge . . . to give to these concepts the greatest [possible] unity combined with the greatest [possible] extension."[51]

Kant addresses himself directly to the relation between the "regulative" principles of the understanding and the "regulative" function of reason later in the same section. The principles of the understanding, Kant claims, are "constitutive in respect of *experience,* since they render the *concepts,* without which there can be no experience, possible *a priori.*" That is, these principles are necessary in the process of promotion of mere perception into experience, in the movement from a judgment of perception to a judgment of experience, so that they are instrumental in the conceptual definition of sensible intuition, and have a "schematic" function. The "regulative" principles of pure reason cannot, because "no schema of sensibility corresponding to them can ever be given, [and] they can never have an object *in concreto.*"[52] Accordingly, the principles of the understanding can have "objective validity" in the sense of "objective reference," whereas the principles of pure reason (in its cognitive sense) cannot. Once again, it is not the "certainty" but the relation to intuition, to "actuality," that distinguishes "constitutive" from "regulative."

Yet this argument leaves some questions unanswered. For one thing, once we have advanced beyond the "mathematical" constitutive categories, the entire process of thinking has to do with rationally immanent rules, and these, surely, belong to reason as such.[53] To deny them "validity" is absurd; to deny them "reality" is typical of the Kantian ambiguity concerning "objectivity." Kant's suspicion of reason's dialectical propensity comes to the forefront. Only what concrete experience can sanction does Kant feel secure in terming "real." But the whole question of the validity and even the reality of reason as such cannot be left at that.

In any event, it is not merely the general "regulative" function of pure reason which is here in question, but more specifically its "hypothetical" employment. In making the distinction between the "apodictic" and the "hypothetical" use of reason in judgments, Kant came closest to anticipating the key distinction of reflective from determinant judgment which he enunciated in the *First Introduction*. Kant wrote:

> If reason is a faculty of deducing the particular from the universal, and if the universal is already *certain of itself* and given, only *judgment* is required to execute the process of subsumption, and the particular is thereby determined in a necessary manner. This I shall entitle the apodeictic use of reason. If, however, the universal is admitted as *problematic* only, and is a mere idea, the particular is certain, but the universality of the rule of which it is a consequence is still a problem. Several particular instances, which are one and all certain, are scrutinized in view of the rule, to see whether they follow from it. If it then appears that all particular instances which can be cited follow from the rule, we argue to its universality, and from this again to all particular instances, even to those which are not themselves given. This I shall entitle the hypothetical employment of reason.[54]

This is Kant's most explicit consideration of the problem of induction in the whole *First Critique*.

What needs to be recognized in this germ of a theory, which is elaborated upon in the *First Introduction* and then treated definitively in the *Third Critique*, is the relation between the inductive process and the ultimate basis of validity. Proof is always deductive. In

Kant's language, we can have knowledge only through "determinant" judgments. There is a radical incongruity between the reasoning involved in discovery (or invention) and the reasoning involved in proof. Once we have made the induction successfully, we then turn around and present the proof deductively. Kant did not work out the principles of induction; he assumed them. He did not explain the incongruity; he simply asserted it.[55]

But might this not help explain his reformulation of the whole issue of induction in terms of "judgment," not reason? Judgment as a faculty has none of the prestige and dignity which Kant cannot help but invest in reason. Indeed, he finds the occasion to lay the blame for all error squarely at the door of the faculty of judgment: "All errors of subreption are to be ascribed to a defect of judgment [*Urtheilskraft*], never to understanding or to reason."[56] How did Kant conceive of the "faculty of judgment" in the *First Critique*, and how did that conception change over the 1780s?

The full-fledged language of judgment was a late innovation in Kant's critical philosophy. In particular, the notion of "reflective judgment" was not worked out in the *First Critique* of 1781, or even integrated into the revised version of 1787.[57] It was only in the mid-1780s that Kant began to write a great deal more about the "faculty of judgment." Crucially, one of the first explicit articulations of the new language came in his remarks concerning the so-called "Pantheism Controversy" in 1786, in his essay "Was heißt: sich im Denken orientieren?"[58] But even that essay, since it had other tasks, failed to develop the idea sufficiently. That development fell to the *Third Critique*, and especially to its *First Introduction*.

While in its "logical use," Kant assigned the "faculty of judgment" merely a mediating role between understanding and reason in the *First Critique*, when he came to treat of its transcendental or "real" use, he spoke of the faculty of judgment as the faculty of cognition in general, i.e., as the process of reasoning or making judgments, of which the more elaborate syllogistic structure of reason and also the specific categorical procedure of the understanding were simply instances.[59] This grand notion of judgment in the *First Critique* was, at the same time, complemented by two narrower ones. The first characterized judgment as a virtually mechanical subsumption under the faculty of understanding.[60] The second took judgment as a matter not of universal and necessary reason but rather of natural skill, an endowment or talent for discriminating when the rule could hold in a given instance and when it could not.[61]

Kant claimed that judgment as a faculty was distinct from the other faculties of cognition in that it was strictly a matter of (subjective) mental process. While understanding had objectivity both in the sense of the transcendental validity of its universal categories and in the sense of application to "objects of experience" in the full Kantian sense of the "judgment of experience," and reason similarly had objectivity both in the transcendental purity of the moral law and in the application of its imperative commands to acts of the will, judgment had no objectivity of application. There was no objective reference, in the rigorous Kantian sense, which belonged to judgment (though, as we have argued, there is a quasi-objective reference in "reflection"). Hence judgment could produce no "metaphysical principles" and ground no "science" or "doctrine."[62] Indeed, there is question whether in the *First Critique* the faculty of judgment had any specific transcendental ground. Only understanding possessed this ground, i.e., a legitimate transcendental deduction.[63] It could be ascribed, in the *First Critique,* neither to reason, because it transcended experience and could not have objects in sensible intuition, nor to judgment, because, on the basis of the "narrow" definition just given, judgment was invariably either an instrumentality of understanding ("schematism") or it was a natural, hence empirical, endowment. While Kant found the transcendental warrant for reason in the *Second Critique,* the question of the transcendental status of the faculty of judgment remained open. It was the *Third Critique* which settled the issue.

A transcendental principle did guarantee the validity of judgment (and hence its "subjective" universality and necessity), since without one, it could not stand as a faculty of cognition at all. The transcendental warrant for the whole faculty of judgment lay in the harmony of the faculties, or more precisely, in the efficacious functioning of rationality in its empirical extension, i.e., in the conformity of the intuition produced by the imagination with the rules legislated by the understanding. Kant had worked out the transcendental ground already—in his deduction of the judgment of taste. When he secured the transcendental validity of subjective formal purposiveness as aesthetic, he simultaneously did so for the cognitive faculty of judgment, because they are one and the same.

In other words, the complex notion of a faculty of judgment came to be integrated with the equally complex sense of "reflection" which we unearthed in our earlier analysis.[64] Together they constituted the remarkable idea of "reflective judgment," the most synthetic concept Kant ever achieved concerning the process of human mental activity, especially in its creative—i.e., inductive or synthetic—mode. Reflective judgment was the mental procedure of induction, of finding some concept which unified particulars according to an empirical principle of order or design.

System, Organic Form, and the Unity of Reason

The discovery of "reflective judgment," as Giorgio Tonelli and others have argued, was the decisive turn which engendered the *Critique of Judgment* as the whole we know.[65] Kant found that his concern had become more general than he initially believed. He was not simply investigating taste, but a whole and very complicated "faculty" of mind: judgment. From the aesthetic judgment of beauty in nature, via "objective subreption," Kant came to the prospect of a teleological judgment, and in the coherence of the two he discovered a new mental process, "reflective judgment," which transformed his cognitive theory. That breakthrough came some time before May 1789, when he sent a letter to Reinhold announcing his involvement in a larger project than he had hitherto acknowledged: a "Critique of the Faculty of Judgment" of which the "Critique of Taste" constituted only a part.[66] Kant worked out the new idea of a "faculty of judgment" in the *First Introduction to the Critique of Judgment.*

It was only through the articulation of the "system" wherein judgment was constituted as a faculty that it could be raised to full critical examination, Kant wrote in §iii of the final version of the Introduction.[67] That entailed the discrimination of other faculties (cognitive and human) and the delimitation of their function such that the faculty of judgment was left with a possible and a necessary function of its own within the system. As he labored over his newfound faculty of judgment, he came to express a bolder notion of systematicity than he generally felt possible, and than he would eventually permit to be presented to the public under the prestigious rubric of "critique." This is why the *First Introduction* is such a remarkable document. It offers a tantalizing glimpse into the possibilities Kant allowed himself speculatively at one time, only later to repress.[68]

The idea of "system" played a major role in Kant's initial breakthrough to the *Third Critique* and again at the crucial "cognitive turn" in early 1789. The "Critique of Taste" originated from Kant's belief that he had determined the entire scope of the system of human faculties, both at the level of pure cognition and at the level of general human experience. This led him to believe that the problem which inevitably attended such discriminations, namely, the question of an underlying systematic unity of reason, was also amenable to solution. The conviction of approaching a solution to that problem had been growing in Kant in the course of his ethical writings, and it carried through the phase of the "Critique of Taste," as attested in the letter to Reinhold of December 1787. It peaked in the *First Introduction to the Critique of Judgment.* That work attempted a unified and systematic articulation of Kant's whole philosophy; that is, it sought to express the "unity of reason."[69] He took the elements both of the cognitive faculties and of the general human capacities which he articulated there to be definitive. His project was to demonstrate their systematicity in the two senses of completeness and interdependency.

That Kant intended this emerges from a passage late in the *First Introduction* which distinguished an "encyclopedic" introduction from ordinary "propaedeutic" ones. Encyclopedic introductions set the work that followed within a systematic order, and brought that systematic order therewith to a close. An "encyclopedic" introduction is

> possible only when one is in a position to present exhaustively, through the formal concept of a whole which at the same time contains in itself *a priori* the principle of a complete articulation into parts, the subjective and objective sources of a certain kind of cognitions.[70]

Kant claimed his *First Introduction to the Critique of Judgment* was an instance of an "encyclopedic" introduction.[71]

The term "system" appeared everywhere in the *First Introduction;* its first four sections had "system" in their titles.[72] Indeed, Kant described a plethora of "systems," many of which remained, though less obtrusively, in the final version. There was the "system" of cognitive-logical powers—the *Erkenntniskräfte.* There was the "system" of human capacities in general—the *Gemütsvermögen.* There was the "system" of knowledge from a priori principles—philosophy. There was the "system" of transcendental possibilities of knowledge—*Kritik.* Some scholars find the *First Introduction* suspect just for this impulse in the work, dismissing it as "thoroughly architectonic and riddled with faculty-talk."[73] Conversely, there are those who find this a vantage from which to integrate the entire Kantian philosophy.[74] My objective will be to link the idea of "system" with the idea of the "unity of reason."

Kant's conception of systematic reason, as he developed it even in the *First Critique,* suggested that he recognized, however hesitantly, a kind of causal determination which was not serial, not transeunt, but simultaneous and immanent, and that he recognized this "entelechy" not only in the regimen of reason itself but in organisms as well. Such a mode escaped his categorical determination of experience in the transcendental logic of the *First Critique,* but it proved ineluctable both in any transcendental account of the immanent functioning of reason and in any empirical-scientific account of organisms. Kant imputed to reason an immanent dynamism, the capacity to set its own goals and to pursue them.[75] He also imputed to reason a concern with its own self-realization.[76] Kant meant by reason a process of systematization. "The unity of reason is the unity of system."[77]

This unity of reason always presupposes an idea, namely that of the form of a whole of knowledge—a whole which is prior to the determinate knowledge of the parts and which contains the conditions that determine a priori for every part its position and relation to the other parts. This idea accordingly postulates a complete unity . . . not a mere contingent aggregate, but a system connected according to necessary laws.[78]

In the Appendix to the "Regulative Use of the Ideas of Pure Reason," Kant disclaimed anything more than a formal-logical sense for his theory of the systematicity of reason. "The systematic unity (as a mere idea) is, however, only a *projected* unity, to be regarded not as given in itself, but as a problem only."[79] This end remained a mere "postulation," Kant claimed. While it could serve as "the *criterion of the truth*" of its operations, it could not be taken as actual. It was, Kant argued, "a *logical* principle."[80]

Yet there is a good deal to the presentation of the idea of systematicity and unity of reason which seems to go beyond such diffidence. In drawing the whole discussion of the "Transcendental Dialectic" to a conclusion, Kant returned to the question of pure reason and its unity.

[S]ince the systematic connection which reason can give to the empirical employment of the understanding not only furthers its extension, but also guarantees its correctness, the principle of such systematic unity is so far also objective, but in an indeterminate manner *(principium vagum)* . . .

But reason cannot think this systematic unity otherwise

than by giving to the idea of this unity an object; and since experience can never give an example of complete systematic unity, the object which we have to assign to the idea is not such as experience can ever supply. This object, as thus entertained by reason *(ens rationis ratiocinatae)*, is a mere idea; it is not assumed as a something that is real absolutely and *in itself*, but is postulated only problematically.[81]

To uphold the principle of system in reason as "objective" even if indeterminate was already to make a very important assertion about objective validity without actuality. Moreover, in upholding the notion of an *ens rationis ratiocinatae*, Kant acknowledged that some sort of grounding entity was required by reason in its self-conception, even if only "problematically." He could still claim that any dogmatic assertion of its "existence" was a "subreption." Yet the issue is really what ontological status to ascribe to "objective validity without actuality." The question might be put otherwise: Is the empirical subject an adequate "substance" to ground the sort of reason that Kant is describing?

Kant frequently writes of the logical and the real "use" of reason. The question that arises, of course, is: Use by whom? Common sense answers: the empirical subject. However, Kant, in his most precise articulation, can ascribe "use" neither to the empirical subject nor to an indeterminate noumenal subject, and hence resorts simply to ascribing it to reason itself. Reason as subject—not simply as form—is what is here at stake. If we assume, for the sake of argument, that reason "uses" itself logically but also in a real manner, what this use requires is that reason itself possess an intrinsic dynamism, a self-determination which is at once spontaneous and autonomous.[82]

Kant distinguished system from aggregate in terms of the idea of "totality," which provided an "exact classification" of elements and explicated "their *interconnection in a system*." Kant then went on to give a very important characterization of system as "a unity self-subsistent, self-sufficient, and not to be increased by any additions from without . . . comprehended and determined by one idea. The completeness and articulation of this system can at the same time yield a criterion of the correctness and genuineness of all its components."[83] The elements of this definition, strictly logical in formulation, are illuminating both as regards Kant's idea of the dynamism of reason, and as regards the self-legislation of science. Kant's idea of systematicity entails the notions of articulation (architectonic) and closure (unity).[84] The principle of the priority of the whole over the parts (totality) is clear in all his versions, and there is moreover the implication that this whole is a *ground,* not just a bond.[85] Finally, system entails a dynamic propensity toward both the complete determination of its parts and the equally exhaustive exposition of their interrelation.

Kant returned to his concept of system near the very end of the *First Critique* in the section of the "Transcendental Doctrine of Method" entitled the "Architectonic of Pure Reason." There he defined system (cognitively) as "the unity of the manifold modes of knowledge under one idea." He went on to identify this one idea—totality,

> the form of a whole—in so far as the concept determines *a priori* not only the scope of its manifold content, but also the positions which the parts occupy relatively to one another . . . The unity of the end to which all the parts relate and in the idea of which they all stand in relation to one another, makes it possible for us to determine from our knowledge of the other parts whether any part be missing, and to prevent any arbitrary addition . . . The whole is thus an organised unity *(articulatio),* and not an aggregate *(coacervatio).* It may grow from within *(per intussusceptionem),* but not by external addition *(per appositionem).* It is thus like an animal body.[86]

In developing his most extended characterization of the system of reason, Kant ended up drawing an analogy to organic form.

The key element in Kant's concept of reason is system, but his most fruitful insight is that the systematicity of reason demonstrates a profound and persistent analogy with the idea of organic form. Kant's parallelism between the structure of organisms and the nature of reason is widely recognized. McFarland, for example, observes that Kant had an "evident conviction that the highest form of systematic unity to which knowledge can be brought is *organic* in type. In fact his conception of a system of knowledge is such that it can be interpreted in either logical or organic terms."[87] And Thomas Weldon argued that "what [Kant] really understands by 'idea' is the concept of any kind of organic whole as contrasted with a mere aggregate or mechanism."[88] Düsing also points out the significant interconnection between organism and system, and between reason and organism by virtue of their systematicity.[89]

Kant most definitively articulated this analogy of reason to organism via "system" in the revised version of the *First Critique.* In the preface to the B-version Kant wrote: "[P]ure reason, so far as the principles of its knowledge are concerned, is a quite separate self-subsistent unity, in which, as in an organized body, every member exists for every other, and all for the sake of each, so that no principle can safely be taken in *any one* relation, unless it has been investigated in the *entirety* of its relations to the whole employment of pure reason."[90] Indeed, Kant pressed the analogy much further, drawing upon the competing biological theories of the day to illustrate the alternative possibilities of a theory of mind, and designating his own as the "epigenesis of pure reason."[91] In that connection, Kant wrote: "pure speculative reason has a structure wherein everything is an *organ,* the whole being for the sake of every part, and every part for the sake of all the others."[92] What is so significant about this connection with organic form is the nature of causality that applies in such forms: immanent, holistic, and simultaneous. Kant called such determination "intrinsic purposiveness" in the *Third Critique.* It is this critical notion that is, I wish to establish, the key to the idea of the "unity of reason."

Kant's crucial concern in the later *Critiques* was with the "unity of reason."[93] System and architectonic are the talismans of that unity. From the inception of his "critical period" at the very latest, Kant clearly laid stress upon the systematicity and the architectonic of reason. In the *First Critique,* when Kant first articulated his idea of a "transcendental logic," he put forward a startlingly Idealist formulation:

> When a science is an aggregate brought into existence in a merely experimental manner, such completeness can never be guaranteed by any kind of mere estimate. It is possible only by means of *an idea of the totality* of the *a priori* knowledge yielded by the understanding; such an idea can furnish an exact classification of the concepts which compose that totality, exhibiting their *interconnection in a system.*[94]

The issue of system became particularly acute when Kant realized that the critical project of the *First Critique,* which he had initially supposed to have grounded all transcendental philosophy, only covered theoretical or "speculative" reason and in fact left out important issues involved in practical reason.[95] This sense, as it grew on him after 1781, can be taken to be the decisive stimulus to his further speculations.[96] But not only did Kant need to distinguish the arguments, and with them the concept of the a priori principles grounding practical reason, he was also left with the inevitable systematic task of reconciling the two aspects under the one concept of reason. Hence system entailed the concern for the "unity of reason."

The *Grounding of the Metaphysics of Morals,* composed between 1783 and 1785 and published in the latter year, argued that any extension of the critical philosophy toward the inclusion of a pure a priori principle for practical reason would necessarily entail the establishment of a proof of the unity of reason. "[I]f a critical examination of pure practical reason is to be complete, then there must, in my view, be the possibility at the same time of showing the unity of practical and speculative reason in a common principle; for in the final analysis there can be only one and the same reason, which is to be differentiated solely in its application."[97] In the *Second Critique,* Kant's concern for the unity of reason had become the linchpin in his philosophical enterprise:

> Whoever has been able to convince himself of the truth of the propositions in the Analytic will get a certain enjoyment . . . for they correctly occasion the expectation of bringing some day into one view the unity of the entire pure rational faculty (both theoretical and practical) and of being able to derive everything from one principle. The latter is an unavoidable need of human reason, as it finds complete satisfaction only in a perfectly systematic unity of its cognitions.[98]

Note, first, Kant's commitment to the idea of a unity of reason; second, his conviction that it was philosophically attainable; and finally, his acknowledgment that the *Second Critique* had not yet accomplished this task of establishing it incontrovertibly, though it supplied the material for such a grounding. Here was the great stimulus to Fichte and all the other Idealists, and here, too, the acknowledgement of incompleteness which Kant would later deny in his repudiation of Fichte's approach.

The possibility remains that precisely in the *Third Critique* Kant did complete that system of the unity of reason. His letter to Reinhold in December 1787 describing his new project of a third critique has a tone of confidence in the definitive totality of his system.[99] The Introduction to the *Third Critique,* and especially the first version of that Introduction, though composed somewhat later than the letter, represents perhaps the high point in Kant's confidence in the closure of his system.

This closure is not merely epistemological. It is unequivocally metaphysical. There is a discernible if gradual propensity in Kant's writings over the 1780s toward the articulation of determinate beliefs about the reality and nature of noumena—God, soul, and world. The architectonic of his critical philosophy came more and more to rest on its tangency with a "supersensible substrate" until, in the *Third Critique,* that notion of a transcendent ground featured decisively in rounding his system to a close. Kant rescued all this from "dialectical" dogmatism only by repeated admonitions that such speculations had strictly "practical" validity, and, taken in a strict, cognitive-epistemological light, represented "mere thinking." Yet there can be no real doubt about the seriousness of his convictions on the score of theism or on the related issue of human moral freedom.

However scrupulous Kant may have been about the inadequacy of speculative proofs, he was a "theist" in the precise sense of his "Transcendental Dialectic" of the *Critique of Pure Reason.*[100] A large part of his "critical" philosophy can be interpreted as an effort to balance his recognition of the limitations of speculative rationalism or "dogmatic metaphysics" with his recognition of the essential human interest in metaphysics. In the *Prolegomena to any Future Metaphysics* he wrote that the demand for metaphysics would never disappear, "since the interests of human reason in general are intimately interwoven with it."[101] In his Introduction to the *First Critique* he went even further: "Indeed, we prefer to run every risk of error rather than desist from such urgent inquiries, on the ground of their dubious character, or from disdain and indifference. These unavoidable problems set by pure reason itself are God, freedom and immortality."[102] The decisive ideas of reason had their ground in its *immanent interests,* what Kant termed the *"requirements (Bedürfnisse) of reason"* in the essay "Was heißt: sich im Denken orientieren?"[103] In that essay, as well, Kant recognized a natural propensity to ontology ("physico-theology") as both the "dialectical" danger and the metaphysical charm of teleology. In the *Third Critique* Kant made explicit what he had intimated in the essay of 1786: "There is, then, indeed a certain presentiment of our reason or a hint, as it were, given us by nature, that, by means of this concept of final cause, we go beyond nature and could unite it to the highest point in a series of causes."[104] And again: "the natural things that we find possible only as purposes supply the best proof of the contingency of the world-whole." Indeed, Kant's personal metaphysical preferences come to clear expression immediately after this statement: "to the common understanding and to the philosopher alike they are the only valid ground of proof for its dependence on and origin from a Being existing outside the world—a Being who must also be intelligent on account of its purposive form. Teleology, then, finds the consummation of its investigations only in theology."[105] It was this "physico-theology," and not the scientific issue, which made organic forms as "natural purposes" so philosophically important for Kant.

Eight

THE CONTEXTUAL ORIGINS
OF KANT'S CRITIQUE
OF CONTEMPORARY SCIENCE

Whereas hen we attempted to reconstruct the concerns which brought Kant to the specific cognitive turn leading to the "Critique of Teleological Judgment," it proved useful to construe them heuristically as revisions of the "Transcendental Dialectic" of the *Critique of Pure Reason*. We can best grasp the intentions behind Kant's cognitive revisions of the late 1780s if we clearly appreciate his purposes in the original and the revised versions of that *First Critique,* as he articulated them especially in the second preface to that work (April 1787). First, we can establish quite clearly that Kant sought to secure the validity of science not only against the skepticism of Hume, but also against the speculation of the "aesthetic" sorts of scientists.[1] Second, we can establish that Kant sought to set severe limits on the transcendent or "metaphysical" flights of school rationalism, but also on the "mystical" dreams of the *Schwärmer,* the religious and poetic "geniuses" of the *Sturm und Drang.*

There were many critics of Kant in these years, both empiricists and rationalists. While they irritated Kant, he did not feel the need to respond to them.[2] But Kant had other foes, the "aestheticists" of science and the "mystics" of metaphysics. They had been active to a fault, from Kant's vantage. Indeed, their campaigns were uppermost in Kant's mind in his epistemological and methodological considerations of the mid to late 1780s. Not that the *Schwärmer* directly challenged Kant. They carried on in blissful oblivion of the stern Königsberger, and it was this impertinence which provoked him to assert the rights and rigors of true science and philosophy against their sophistries.

The war began in earnest with Kant's flurry of "popular essays" in the mid-1780s, on contemporary topics in history and especially science, all of which aimed at the pretensions of the "aestheticists" of science and Herder in particular.³ The first showdown came in Kant's reviews of Herder's *Ideen* in 1785. Then matters became even more controversial with the outbreak of the "Pantheism Controversy." It had two provocative outcomes from Kant's point of view: first, the intimation (by Jacobi) that Kant's *Critique* lent support to the materialist determinism of Spinoza; and, second, the overt claim by Mendelssohn, in *Morgenstunden*, that Kant's *Critique* had destroyed everything in metaphysics, but most particularly, all rational grounds for credence in God.

These were profoundly dangerous charges which could easily bring the authorities down upon Kant. Hence Kant became more belligerent in the late 1780s, though that polemical edge rarely rose directly to the surface in his philosophical works. The prefaces to each of his major works give indication of the campaign he saw himself waging, not only for the triumph of his own philosophy, but more broadly for the triumph of Aufklärung against the forces of repression and of irrationalism. All these impulses fueled Kant's reconsiderations of epistemology and science at the close of the decade, and gave shape to the "Critique of Teleological Judgment."

Kant's decision in 1784 to review Herder's *Ideen* only makes sense within a contextual interpretation. Kant's venture into popular essay writing on the subject of history starting in late 1784 should occasion some wonder, for he otherwise steadfastly refused to be distracted from the pressing urgency of his systematic project. To be sure, Kant had profound observations to make in such fields as history, anthropology, and geography, about which he had been teaching courses for many years. To be sure, such matters were not unrelated to his critical system. Nevertheless, the timing is striking. How many reviews did Kant ever write? How many after 1781? Why of the *Ideen*, and why at that particular moment? Not only the reviews of Herder's *Ideen*, but also the essays in the *Berlinische Monatsschrift*, starting with "Idea for a Universal History" in November 1784 and culminating with "Muthmaßlicher Anfang der Menschengeschichte" in January 1786, represented an open attack upon Herder. Herder's success was an offense to Kant in the 1780s. The popular enthusiasm for Herder's *Ideen* seemed an implicit insult in view of the neglect of the *Critique of Pure Reason*.⁴

When we examine the circumstances surrounding Kant's reviews of Herder's *Ideen*, we find an intimate connection with Kant's concerns over the popular reception of his philosophy. The key figure in this case is Christian Gottfried Schütz, professor of Rhetoric at the University of Jena, the prime locus for the future of German Idealism. As managing editor of a new intellectual journal, the *Allgemeine Literatur-Zeitung*, Schütz was seeking the collaboration of as many distinguished German authors as he could find. Naturally, he thought of Kant, whose work he respected profoundly and who had not yet received the recognition that he rightfully deserved. Who better than Kant, Schütz thought, to review that other most prominent figure in the "philosophy" of the day, Herder? With that proposal, Schütz opened his correspondence with Kant in July 1784.[5]

In his lost reply, Kant apparently waxed eloquent over Schütz's kindness in taking such an active interest in his work and complained of the misunderstanding that seemed to haunt it. Schütz's response of August 23, 1784, set out with sympathetic remarks which betokened such a content: "It saddened me that the coldness with which your sublime efforts have been met from several sides and the misunderstanding of some of your most important principles should really have caused you to doubt whether our epoch is worthy of you and the outstanding work of your spirit."[6] Thenceforth Schütz saw to it that his letters to Kant carried news of the progress in the reception of Kantian philosophy, and, indeed, he was strategically placed to tell a vital part of that tale.

The letter of August also revealed that Kant had accepted Schütz's invitation to review Herder. Kant suggested that his review be considered an experimental participation in the new journal, and he declared himself prepared to renouce his honorarium, especially should the editorial board be displeased with his comments. That suggests a certain bellicosity toward the subject of the envisioned review. In accepting the assignment to review Herder's *Ideen*, Kant launched his open campaign of rivalry against Herder. The issue is: What led Kant to this open attack? The answer is "aestheticism in science"—pantheist *Naturphilosophie*. To understand this, we must examine Herder's work and the approach behind it.

Herder's Ideen zur Philosophie der Geschichte der Menschheit

As a historian as well as a philosopher of history, Herder wished to integrate into his *Ideen* as much empirical evidence as was then available regarding not merely recorded history but also what we would call the ecology and the physical anthropology of the human species.[7] Hence the first volume of the *Ideen* was an effort to harvest from the natural sciences of the day all the insight they could provide into the formation of mankind. To be sure, science was in its utter infancy in those fields, and Herder sought prematurely to speculate, just as Descartes, at the analogous infancy of the mathematical science of physics, had speculated a premature and disastrous synthesis. And, certainly, Herder did indulge in a lyrical bent in his language. Yet he also steeped himself in the best scientific thought available to him, and these scientists read his work with noteworthy approval.[8] Kant's contempt and the subsequent developments in the natural sciences must not mislead us regarding the *historical* integrity of Herder's project.

Herder's grand project in the *Ideen* was to find how man as a creature of nature figured in man as an artifice of culture, to read these two dimensions of man in continuity. Kant, by contrast, wished to dissociate them to the highest degree possible without contradiction. Accordingly, Hamann was correct when he pointed out to Herder, irate at Kant's unprovoked attack, that "in your *Ideen* there are many places which appear to be like arrows aimed at him and his system, even if you may not have been thinking of him."[9] It seems, too, that Hamann was correct in his sense that Herder's provocation of Kant was unintended, or at least not self-conscious. Herder's alienation from Kantian philosophy by 1783 is well documented. But so is his belief that he had not publicly uttered his opposition.[10] That he sincerely believed this to be the case is indicated by the extent of his shock and sense of betrayal over Kant's reviews of his work.[11]

Herder's concrete procedure in volume 1 of the *Ideen* was to situate man, i.e., to construe his emergence in terms of his geophysical placement. Hence, famously, Herder began his grand work with the line, "Our earth is a star among stars."[12] Herder built from this astronomical situation a characterization of the geographical and climatic conditions of human emergence. Drawing extensively from the exploration of the analogy of botanical and zoological forms with those of humanity, Herder worked toward the conception of man as a "middling creature among animals," that is, as the instance in which all their properties found the consummate integration and expression.[13] From this physical character of man as the "concrete universal" (to borrow a Hegelianism) of the animal world, Herder then moved on to man's decisive physiological difference from the rest: erect posture. In what was the most imaginative—and for Kant most suspect as lyrical-speculative—

segment of the work, Herder sought to correlate all man's distinctive cultural attributes with this essential physical attribute of erect posture.[14]

Turning at last to those aspects of humanity which were most authentically spiritual, Herder sought a conceptual structure of transition. He sought a model of the formation of this sphere in man which went beyond what he had articulated in his earlier theory of the origin of language, one which, in accordance with his larger concept, developed a continuity between the forces of nature and the forces of spirit.[15] He found it precisely in that notion of "forces" *(Kräfte)* which they both shared.[16] In this Herder drew explicitly upon Leibniz and Ruggero Guiseppe Boscovich, and there are indications that he was aware, as well, of the important metaphysical conclusions which Joseph Priestley had drawn from these scientific notions.

The result was a theory of the world as composed primarily of forces organized hierarchically. This notion, especially tied to a sense of the conservation of force in the world (though hardly in its modern acceptance), led to a connection long since dear to Herder: metempsychosis as the only coherent doctrine of the immortality of the soul. Here the influence of Lessing's *Education of the Human Race* figured prominently.[17] Herder's theological development in the 1770s, which moved away from the pietistic fideism of his Bückeburg years and his association with Lavater and Hamann toward a clear repudiation of essential tenets of orthodox Christianity, occurred under the aegis of Lessing.[18] In articulating such ideas, Herder was indulging in those "metaphysical" speculations in natural science which the Germans called *Naturphilosophie.*

Herder's works of the 1780s represent the central effort to transform the mood of the *Sturm und Drang* into a position, to take a raw intuition and raise it into a conscious argument. Hermann Korff's magisterial *Geist der Goethezeit* identifies this transformation in the work of Herder (and Goethe) in the 1780s as the essence of what the Germans call *die Klassik,* namely, the mature artistic period of the *Goethezeit* when order, balance, and coherence displace the wild outbursts of the early formative years.[19] Korff argues that it was not the content of the *Sturm und Drang* mentality but rather its articulation which underwent the major transformation. He writes elegantly of the character of the grounding intuition of the *Sturm und Drang:*

The quintessential spirit of the *Sturm und Drang* movement was that feeling for nature in the light of which the world appeared as a living unity and an organic being, which realized itself in an eternal becoming and passing away, in ceaseless creation and metamorphosis. Living Nature! That was the grand idea which divided [their] new humanity as much from the soulless materialism of the French Enlightenment as from the supernaturalism of Christianity.[20]

The authors of the *Sturm und Drang* read nature in the figure of their own creativity and restless freedom, i.e., in analogy to genius. They felt in nature an irrepressible dynamism, process, development—life. And they gave themselves over to a celebration of this Dionysian vitality as they gave themselves over to the untrammeled articulation of their own.

Within and emergent from the *Sturm und Drang* enthusiasm for nature was a sense for coherence, for a more dynamic vision of order. In a beautiful piece from 1782, his "Fragment on Nature," Goethe articulated this emergent sense.[21] The tone was still rhapsodic and the intuition of structure remained inchoate, as Goethe felt no hesitancy to proclaim from a later, more mature vantage.[22] Yet within the extreme variety of nature's "play"—and nature was for Goethe a *Spielerin*, indeed, a *Schauspielerin* (actress) who put on roles—Goethe sensed the marvelous simplicity of law.[23]

To capture clearly this emergent sense of law: this was the project of Goethe and of Herder in the years of their most intimate and productive association, the 1780s. They strove to find for their sense of nature a philosophical-conceptual structure. Hardly philosophers, they nonetheless turned to philosophy for inspiration. Thus Herder, who in this turn to philosophy vastly outpaced his more diffident friend, found by the late 1770s the triad from whom to forge his own vision: Spinoza, Shaftesbury and Leibniz.[24] While we will have occasion to dwell on Spinoza at length later in this work, and Leibniz must remain an omnipresent backdrop too vast ever to bring into the foreground, Shaftesbury must be brought immediately into consideration.[25] In his important article on the German reception of Shaftesbury, Oskar Walzel made the crucial argument: Shaftesbury saw nature "not as a dead mass of atoms but a unified, spiritualized whole . . . [an] organic unity [which was] animated by one unifying [spiritual] principle."[26] In this new notion of nature, Shaftesbury proved the decisive stimulus to the later pantheism of Goethe and Herder.[27] That connection has been noted, as well, by Ernest Tuveson.[28] Shaftesbury welded a crucial argument linking this sense for nature as a living whole with a view of human nature as possessing innate attunement or "sensibility"

which was not simply cognitive but simultaneously ethical, emotional, and aesthetic.[29] Walzel emphasizes the concept of "inner
harmony" as the key to Shaftesbury's *Weltanschauung*. He notes that
"inner harmony is for [Shaftesbury] the counterpart of the universal coherence of nature; inner harmony is also the presupposition
for the recognition of this coherence in nature."[30] Jerome Stolnitz
has discerned a very similar configuration in Shaftesbury's conception of the "Promethean" virtuoso: "[T]he inner harmony of his life
[is] an 'imitation of nature.'"[31] As Tuveson put it, Shaftesbury advanced the "proposition that man's nature is an integral part of the
harmony of the universe."[32] His great idea was that there existed
a "unique human sense of value as resulting from the uniquely
human ability to appreciate the aesthetic wholeness of the universe."[33]

   Shaftesbury's unitary responsiveness had the capacity to discern beauty, but this beauty was a form of rightness about the world
which had its cognitive and ethical concomitants.[34] His famous
declaration that beauty and truth are one must be understood in
this light. "He does not mean by truth a sum total of theoretical
knowledge, of propositions and judgments . . . To him 'truth' signifies rather the inner intellectual structure of the universe . . .
which can only be immediately experienced and intuitively understood."[35] Shaftesbury believed we had such a capacity. Ernst Cassirer
termed it "an intuitive understanding *(intellectus archetypus)*" and associated it with Plotinus's doctrine of intelligible beauty.[36] Shaftesbury had a profound impact upon important poetic minds of
eighteenth-century Germany, among them Christoph Wieland,
Goethe, and especially Herder.[37] These were the ideas which animated the *Sturm und Drang* and which Herder introduced into his
Ideen zur Philosophie der Geschichte der Menschheit. But there was one
German whose taste proved distinctly more British than German
on the score of "pantheism," and who was quick to blast it as *Schwärmerei:* Immanuel Kant.

Kant's Disparagement of Herder from the Reviews of Ideen
to the Third Critique

Kant's review of volume 1 of Herder's *Ideen* appeared in the *Allege-
meine Literatur-Zeitung* in February 1795—anonymously.[38] It was
an open secret, however, as Schütz reported to him in a letter dated
February 18, 1785. Schütz was delighted with the stir the review
had created, and felt it did wonders for the new journal. He also

thought the review a "masterpiece of precision" and felt any author should be happier to have Kant's criticisms than the praise of the multitude. Alas, he reported, Herr Herder did not share his view. Herder had proven very sensitive about it, and one of his supporters planned a rebuttal of the review, to appear in the *Teutsche Merkur*.[39]

It is not hard to understand Herder's reaction. While emphasizing Herder's literary grace and imaginative boldness, Kant constantly found fault with his philosophical clarity and conceptual penetration. Herder claimed in his methodology to have set all metaphysics aside and to have devoted himself to physiology and experience. Obviously, he had not followed that principle, and it was here that Kant drove the first and most telling thrust of his review:

> [H]ow should we regard the design which aims to explain that which one does not comprehend by that which one comprehends even less? . . . What can the philosopher now invoke here to justify his allegations except simple despair of finding clarification in some kind of knowledge of nature and the attendant necessity to seek it in the fertile field of the poetic imagination? But this is still metaphysics, and what is more, very dogmatic metaphysics, even though our author renounces it, as fashion demands.[40]

Certainly Kant lavished praise on Herder's lyrical inventiveness, but much in the way Antony lavished praise on Caesar's assassins. Kant's review begins: "His is not a logical precision in the definition of concepts or careful adherence to principles, but rather a fleeting, sweeping view, an adroitness in unearthing analogies in the wielding of which he shows bold imagination. This is combined with cleverness in soliciting sympathy for his subject—kept in increasingly hazy remoteness—by means of sentiment and sensation."[41] Under the guise of compliment, Kant's review indulged in denigration. It is hard to credit the view that this was unintended.[42] Of course, Kant was "correct," but in that punctilious sense which by upholding the letter dooms a great deal of the spirit to death.[43] That spirit, though wounded in Herder, would spring alive again and triumph over Kant in the works of his own finest disciples, the Idealists.

Kant was thinking through his own transcendental grounding of natural science even as he was reading and critically dissecting the early volumes of Herder's *Ideen,* one of the most important sources of later German *Naturphilosophie.*[44] Kant's criticism of

Herder forcefully articulated his discrimination of rigorous science (philosophy) from speculative empiricism, however imaginative or lyrical. Even as he pursued his project of cutting Herder down to size, Kant worked breakneck at his own systematic writings. That project initially found expression in his *Metaphysical Foundations of Natural Science* (written 1785, published 1786), but it continued in several essays on the methodology of science in the late 1780s which culminated in the *Third Critique*.

There is a direct connection between Kant's critical reviews of Herder's *Naturphilosophie* in 1785 and the argument in the "Analytic" and "Dialectic" of the "Critique of Teleological Judgment" of the *Third Critique*. Herder's views on the philosophy of nature, as they found expression not only in volume 1 of his *Ideen zur Philosophie der Geschichte der Menschheit* (1784) but above all in his *Gott: einige Gespräche* (1787), served as the decisive formulation of that "hylozoism" and "pantheism" which Kant disparaged throughout the "Critique of Teleological Judgment." That constitutes the cement that binds Kant's so-called popular excursions to his critical and systematic concerns.

Herder had the temerity to respond to Kant's criticism in subsequent volumes of the *Ideen* with sharp and ad hominem attacks on Kant's philosophy of history and on Kant's critical rigor. Their hostility was now public, accentuating the polarization within German intellectual culture between the *Sturm und Drang* and the Aufklärung and occasioning in younger intellectuals a major problem in reintegrating their cultural heritage. That Kant's hostility toward Herder persisted even after his two reviews of Herder's great work is clear from belligerent if veiled references Kant introduced into each of his major works of the late 1780s. In 1785, Kant published his *Grounding of the Metaphysics of Morals,* on a topic somewhat removed from those over which he had publicly disputed with Herder, but he gave almost immediate vent to his pique with Herder:

> Whether or not pure philosophy in all its parts requires its own special man might well be in itself a subject worthy of consideration. Would not the whole of this learned industry be better off if those who are accustomed, as the public taste demands, to purvey a mixture of the empirical with the rational in all sorts of proportions unknown even to themselves and who style themselves independent thinkers, while giving the name of hair-splitters to those who apply themselves to

the purely rational part, were to be given warning about pursuing simultaneously two jobs which are quite different in their technique, and each of which perhaps requires a special talent that when combined with the other talent produces nothing but bungling?[45]

Kant saw himself as the beleaguered defender of rigor and method. This was stated in all clarity in a *Reflection* from the late 1780s:

To handle profoundly complicated questions of philosophy in the manner of a genius: I decline the honor altogether. I try only to conduct my inquiry in an academic manner. When the labor, the consistent application and caution which this requires has succeeded, there remains for the true genius (not the sort who try to make everything out of nothing) to provide it with a sublime turn of spirit and so to set in motion the use of the dry principles.[46]

The juxtaposition of driness and thoroughness to "genius" and charlatanry found reiteration in the preface to the B-version of the *First Critique*, composed in April 1787. He celebrated the "spirit of thoroughness" of Wolff and the school philosophy as the only prospect of a "secure progress of the science [of metaphysics, because it] is to be attained only through orderly establishment of principles, clear determination of concepts, insistence upon strictness of proof, and avoidance of venturesome, non-consecutive steps in our inferences."[47] This "spirit of thoroughness," Kant went on slightly later in the preface, "is not extinct in Germany, but has only been temporarily overshadowed by the prevalence of a pretentiously free manner of thinking."[48] The pretentiously free manner of thinking, with its venturesome speculations, raised the danger of "materialism, fatalism, atheism, free-thinking, fanaticism, and superstition," from whose universal injuriousness only criticism could protect culture. The context, by 1787, of Spinozism and pantheism, with Herder as their prime exponent, raised profound dangers for the Aufklärung, in Kant's view. That concern would stamp all his other projects.

In the *Second Critique,* Kant returned to the attack against Herder. "Consistency," he wrote, "is the highest obligation of a philosopher." But it was hardly to be found "in our syncretistic age, when a certain shallow and dishonest system of coalition between contradictory principles is devised because it is more acceptable to a public which is satisfied to know a little about everything and at bottom nothing, thus playing the jack-of-all-trades."[49] The discussion shortly thereafter of "syncretism" and "Spinozism" betrays the target of Kant's disdain: once again it is Herder.

Herder, too, must be the target of disparagement in Kant's important essay from late 1787, "Über den Gebrauch teleologischer Principien in der Philosophie." There Kant attacked "hasty sophists" *(rasche Vernünftler)* who "are so lacking in foresight as to carry their own ideas over into their observations." They were particularly to be found among those interested in the "origins of plants and animals," which, however, Kant claimed was a "science for gods, . . . not for men."[50] Such "hypermetaphysicians," he wrote, "are ignorant of elementary concepts and also profess to disdain them, and nevertheless venture forth heroically to make new conquests."[51] The essay culminated in an attack on the idea of a single fundamental force integrating nature and man, the very idea which Herder had speculatively embraced in his *Ideen* and reiterated in *Gott,* and which Joseph Priestley had also articulated, much to Kant's displeasure.[52]

Thus there is a continuous trail of hostile remarks about Herder up to the beginning of Kant's composition of the *Third Critique.* Within each phase of its composition, as well, Kant waged a direct and important polemic against Herder. In the "Critique of Taste," he attacked Herder's theory of genius and made a very harsh distinction between the "manner" of Herder's lyrical speculation and the "method" of science. In the "Critique of Teleological Judgment," he attacked Herder's theories of biological force and development as an "aestheticism of science" incongruous with its true rigor. And in the final form of the *Critique of Judgment,* he attacked the "Spinozism" and "syncretism" of Herder's moral-religious views. The rivalry with Herder is the most important contextual background to Kant's *Critique of Judgment.*

 *Nine*

KANT AGAINST
EIGHTEENTH-CENTURY
HYLOZOISM

Developments in eighteenth-century natural science provide the essential backdrop both for Kant's intentions in the 1780s, culminating in the *Third Critique,* and for the reception of that work by the generation of the 1790s who created German Idealism around a philosophy of nature. The strategy of our investigation will be first to set the context of late eighteenth-century scientific thought, then to trace Kant's own reflections on biology up to the decisive consideration of the problem of organic form in the "Critique of Teleological Judgment." On that basis we can proceed to the metaphysical issues that lay behind Kant's methodological conflict with "hylozoism."

In addition to Newtonian physics, Kant took a significant interest in biology. Indeed, Germans of the late nineteenth and early twentieth century considered him one of the forerunners of Darwin—a dubious idea.[1] Though hardly a proto-Darwinian, Kant did concern himself with issues in the Darwinian purview: geology, paleontology, ecology, and "natural history." Most of his work on biology investigated the methodology of "natural history" in terms of two overriding concerns. First, he wished to secure the distinction of life from the inorganic, affirming the uniqueness and mystery of organisms as phenomena of empirical nature, and upholding the utter inexplicability of the origins of life.[2] Second, Kant insisted upon a distinction of man from the rest of organic life.

There were few ideas Kant struggled to keep divided more than life and matter. He repeatedly claimed that there could never be a Newton of the blade of grass.[3] The radical removal of life from matter defined it into impossibility.[4] Organisms, as empirically given forms of nature, became simply impenetrable once the concept of life was removed. Kant defended an idea which Descartes first proposed for physics and which Newton ostensibly maintained in his great works, namely, *inert* matter.[5] In fact, however, eighteenth-century science, inspired by Newton, had advanced far beyond this notion, as many other intellectuals in Germany knew well, certainly by 1786.

Kant's attitudes impeded his recognition of these recent developments in eighteenth-century science and left him sharply estranged from its most creative and effective currents.[6] His refusal to consider these possibilities cannot be ascribed to a lack of intellectual capacity, or to a lack of study. It must be associated squarely with his views about *method* and about *metaphysics*. Kant's "paradigm" for science had been set by the Leibniz-Clarke controversy.[7] The issues with which he was comfortable, and toward which he applied himself assiduously, were those which arose between the Newtonians and the Leibnizians of the early eighteenth century. Thus Kant repeatedly investigated the objective status of space, disputing both the Newtonian view of "absolute" space and the Leibnizian view of an interstitial or "relative" space, to develop his own doctrine ultimately in the "Transcendental Aesthetic."[8] Similarly, Kant attacked the atomist theory, arguing for the infinite divisibility of matter and the completely nominal concept of a fundamental particle.[9] He upheld the Leibnizian argument that action at a distance involved an "occult quality" repugnant to science, and he tried to work out a theory of empirical physics which would incorporate Leibniz's theory of dynamism and force.[10] On the other hand, he upheld Newton's theory of causality as mechanical, Newton's rules for the scientific method, above all the repudiation of "hypotheses," and Newton's mathematical approach to science. Indeed, Kant made mathematical formulation the criterion of the efficacy of a science.[11]

These were all worthy and fundamental issues, but they were the issues of the generation of the first half of the eighteenth century. The history of science has recognized a very important generational break in this period which substantially changed the orientation of science around the middle of the century.[12] It started in Britain in the 1740s and reached France in the 1750s, where it spurred both the development of French materialism in Julien de La Mettrie and Étienne de Condillac, and the development of the more eclectic approach of the Encyclopedists, Jean D'Alembert and Denis Diderot. D'Alembert's *Preliminary Discourse to the Encyclopedia* is a particularly useful source for this, since it shows an acute awareness of the generational shift and its scientific and philosophical issues.[13] Diderot, who figured prominently in both the materialist and the Encyclopedist approaches (they were by no means mutually exclusive), gave literary expression to the impact of these ideas in his *D'Alembert's Dream*.[14] But perhaps the most important figures in this scientific ferment in France at mid-century were the biologists—men like Pierre Maupertuis, Georges Buffon, Théophile Bordeu, and Charles Bonnet.[15]

That same generational shift in science came to Germany a bit later in the eighteenth century. It simply arrived too late for Kant. His mind was set in the thought patterns, the paradigm, of the earlier period, and he never achieved any sympathy for the problems or the insights of the new approach.[16] Indeed, his concern to correct their deviations from the authentic scientific approach led him to take up the question of methodology in the nascent biological sciences, first in a series of popular essays, then more formally in his own systematic version of Newtonian physical science, *Metaphysical Foundations of Natural Science,* and finally in the "Critique of Teleological Judgment." Even as he in fact redefined Newton's atomic theory in terms of the decisive notion of "force," Kant wished to uphold the letter of the Newtonian law, to keep the maxim against "feigning hypotheses" at the heart of all true science.[17] Kant chose to adhere to a relentless sense of mechanical causality in the explication of physical phenomena, even though he realized it would not work in the case of organic life.[18]

But this methodological commitment cannot account alone, or even primarily, for Kant's posture. Kant had not only scientific but also metaphysical positions to defend: the traditional notion of a transcendent, intelligent Deity who created the world, and the notion of individual moral freedom and responsibility. As he saw it, the trends in science and cosmology, "materialist" and "pantheist," threatened these positions. Above all, the renaissance of the philosophy of Spinoza in Germany seemed to Kant to portend atheism in the form of materialistic determinism. Hence he ventured into the field of biology in the 1780s in a campaign against what he could only see as metaphysical sophistry within the new science.

This dread of atheism and determinism accounted for Kant's second guiding principle in approaching the biological sciences: to uphold the distinction of man from the balance of organic life. His insistence upon the uniqueness of reason and freedom necessitated the categorial separation of man from other animals. Kant had come to biology because of its role in the empirical anthropology evolving out of travelers' narratives of faraway places and "primitive" races. Kant determined to deliver lectures on this subject, which he associated with "Physical Geography," starting in 1757.[19] From the outset he showed his resolute opposition to any effort to develop a physiological account of human evolution, since it would in fact be an argument for man's continuity with other organisms.

The mid-1780s appear to be the period of Kant's most intense concern with biology. Since the issue of the differentiation of life from matter is central to Kant's biological considerations, the *Metaphysical Foundations of Natural Science* figures as part of this project. Indeed, there is evidence that Kant's biological preoccupations even intruded into the celebrated revisions of the "Transcendental Deduction" of the *Critique of Pure Reason* in 1786.[20]

Natural Science in the Eighteenth Century: Some Soundings

New elements in metaphysics were astir in the scientific discoveries and theories of the eighteenth century, especially in the nascent sciences of "electricity," chemistry, and biology. Without pretending to offer original research but only to synthesize from the current literature, this section will suggest, first, that the "Newtonianism" which prevailed in the eighteenth century did not carry the scientific revolution forward according to the conventional model of the "mechanization of the world picture."[21] Rather, it pursued the most speculative hypotheses Newton felt prepared to interject into later editions of his great works.[22] Second, it will articulate the "hypotheses" of the new Newtonianism of the eighteenth century in terms of its new language of "force," showing that this expanded physical language had clear and crucial metaphysical concommitants.[23] Finally, and crucially, it will argue that the shift in the sense of nature which took place in the mid-eighteenth century, in which matter and spirit collapsed toward unity, could be, and was, read in two radically different ways: as the materialization of spirit, and as the spiritualization of matter. A retrieval and historical vindication of the latter possibility ("hylozoism") is essential to a proper historical appreciation of German *Naturphilosophie*.

The notion of a "mechanization of the world picture" is appropriate for the developments in physical astronomy and in terrestrial mechanics over the course of the seventeenth century.[24] Descartes and Newton, despite their serious differences, shared a theoretical commitment to mechanical cause and a notion of the inertness of matter. Newton's notion of that inertness—i.e., his principle of inertia—was more subtle than Descartes's and, as a result, evaded the problem of explaining the sources of uniform rectilinear motion. Nevertheless, while Newton considered inertial velocity an inherent property of bodies, he did not feel prepared to recognize any other forces, like attraction or repulsion, as inherent. Hence his sense of matter retained a good part of the Cartesian notion of inert mass.

Newton did displace the plenum theory of matter of Descartes with atomism; consequently, space (extension) and matter had to be distinguished, and even seemingly solid bodies had to be construed as porous. All bodies could be analyzed into a series of fundamental particles uniform in their essential properties. The one difficulty in the triumph of Newton's atomist theory over the Cartesian plenum was the notorious problem of "action at a distance." Mechanical cause in terrestrial mechanics worked on the notion of the direct transmission of force through impact. It required contiguity, as in the instance of billiard balls colliding. Terrestrial mechanics posed few difficulties for the atomists. But there were other actions in the physical universe, as Newton was all too aware, which failed to establish the transmission of force through impact. The most important of these was gravity itself. The plausibility of the plenum theory of matter lay not insignificantly in its ability to account for the transmission of such forces through the material medium it claimed filled the space between ostensibly separate objects. It was on this very point that Leibniz made some of his most telling physical objections to Newtonian physics, and such objections kept Cartesian physics alive on the continent until the mid-eighteenth century.[25]

Action at a distance and the distinction of space from matter were not simply physical theories, but expressed metaphysical commitments in Newtonian natural philosophy. Newton was a man obsessed with theological and metaphysical concerns.[26] He could not have been otherwise, living in the seventeenth century. The point is not simply to note the "quaint" ideas he cultivated "alongside" his "valid" physical theories, but to recognize that metaphysics and physics interpenetrated utterly in that age, and that the one inspired and informed the other. Newton's theory of action at a distance had starkly theological elements.

Newton explained action at a distance by conceiving of God as the requisite "etherial medium" for the transmission of force.[27] Indeed, Newton believed space was divine, a notion which he inherited from decidedly metaphysical speculations developed by the

Cambridge Platonist Henry More and continued by that Christian virtuoso Robert Boyle.[28] That such metaphysical notions were not lost on his contemporaries is evidenced in the decidedly theological cast of the Leibniz-Clarke controversy.[29] At stake already in that debate was the suggestion that God and the world might be *one*, an idea repugnant to orthodox Christianity, and associated with "dangerous" and "atheistic" ideas—those of Hobbes and Spinoza. The possibilities for a "materialist" reading were obviously there, as certain trends in the eighteenth century and later demonstrated. But there were alternative possibilities for what we might call a "spiritual" reading, which must not be lost from sight.[30]

"Newtonianism" not only involved the large notion of God as space or as etherial force maintaining the world and imparting its accelerations, but also the more concrete physical notion of a fundamental and uniform atom of particulate matter. Newton's atomism led to extremely fruitful speculations ("queries" or, in fact, hypotheses) about the structure of the physical world which undercut the notion of inert matter. The series of speculations Newton inserted into later editions of his widely studied *Opticks* centered around the properties which could legitimately be considered inherent in particulate matter. Newton recognized the existence of forces, and their vital importance to physical science, but he found it impossible to recognize them as immanent properties of particulate matter. Instead he simply termed them "etherial" or "imponderable principles" of physical action. Obviously, the term "principle" is extremely vague as to the exact nature of these phenomena, i.e., as to their substantive reality and metaphysical implications. His successors would wrestle with this question intensely in the eighteenth century.

Newton's speculations about the ultimate nature of the particulate matter in the universe also raised the prospect that the actual mass of the universe might, in terms of its physical extension, constitute a vanishingly small volume as compared to the vast interstices of "imponderable" or "etherial" space.[31] In that measure the brute massiveness of the world could be theoretically transfigured into the play of energies upon an airy immaterial field, and the gap which the Cartesian and the Christian models set between nature and spirit (as "animating" or "energizing" principle) closed. Newton introduced a new and powerful impetus into both metaphysics and the physical sciences with these notions.

The Newtonian scientists of the eighteenth century pursued the leads Newton had offered in his queries in the *Opticks* by studying the numerous physical phenomena which did not fit neatly into an impact model of force. They dwelled upon attraction and repulsion, upon chemical and electrical phenomena, and as they did so, they began to redefine the properties of the physical world in such a way that the Cartesian notion of inert matter, and with it the Cartesian notion of mechanical cause as the impact model of force, came to seem entirely inadequate. In central Europe, Leibniz, and, following him, Boscovich pursued these lines aggressively, both in the metaphysical and in the physical vein, articulating a theory of physical "dynamism" which, in Boscovich, completely eliminated the idea of particulate matter (extended mass) and replaced it with a point center of force.

Such developments in particle theory proved central to the development of the emergent science of chemistry, and of the related physics of electricity and magnetism. The result was a recognition of the necessity of the physical postulation of such forces as *real* elements in the explanation of natural phenomena, and the consequent abandonment of any explanation of the world exclusively in terms of inert matter and the impact model of force, which together comprised the "mechanization of the world picture." This was particularly the case in the even less developed field of biological science, where the mechanical theory of science had both given a fruitful impetus to revisions of scientific interpretation and also run up against its clearest limitations in construing the empirical data.

Let us consider these developments in science as Robert Schofield chronicled them in his widely cited work, *Mechanism and Materialism*. While Schofield's general categories appear confusing, he nevertheless recognized a definite shift in scientific orientation around mid-century in Britain.[32] The new—and for Schofield obviously problematic—"speculative influence of Newtonian matter theory was felt in chemistry and physiology."[33] What transpired was a substantialization of the problematic forces which experiment had unearthed as operative in the physical world: light, heat, electricity, and magnetism. Schofield characterized these new forces in the following terms: "The materialized, substantial causes are almost all imponderable, highly tenuous fluids, and most of these are partially characterized by their possession of varying forces of attraction and repulsion."[34] Schofield found in his scientists a shift from logical, mathematical, abstract rationalism toward a more complex qualitative and metaphysical orientation. He claimed these new scientists shared Bacon's crude empiricism along with Linnaeus's "Aristotelian contentment with the creation and categorizing of different qualities."[35] Schofield blamed this more naturalistic and metaphysical approach on continental influences and "religious mysticism."[36] In terms of scientific influence, he emphasized Linnaeus in particular, but one might also include Leibniz and Boscovich. Schofield associated the more abstract and mechanistic approach of the earlier generation with "Augustan rationality" and with deism.[37] He lamented that in the new generation "that peculiar combination of classics, logic and mathematics which had tempered the mind to abstract studies was missing."

While Schofield chose to see metaphysics inspiring this shift in orientation, he did admit that there were some difficulties in carrying on scientifically in the mechanistic mode once the physical importance of forces had to be acknowledged.[38] The mechanists could not "assign magnitude or a determination of form to any of the various forces of attraction and repulsion which they used with such ingenuity in their speculations."[39] It had become impossible, scientifically or philosophically, to enforce a categorial distinction between matter and force, between "inert mass" and "active principles." And no satisfactory mechanistic account could be given for the origins or the nature of "force" as such.

It is not because I share Schofield's opinions about the relative worth of these two orientations, but rather precisely because I do not that I find his testimony so fruitful. The distinction between matter and spirit which had been the key to Cartesian thought and the interminable wrangle of philosophy in his wake (the so-called "mind-body" problem) came in the light of the new science to collapse toward a unity. Yet it was a collapse to unity which could be read in two lights. It could be read, as the deists and pantheists of the Radical Enlightenment read it, as the confirmation of materialism, tending in its extreme to atheism (as in Hume, Voltaire, and the French Materialists). But it could also be read, as the poets of sensibility in mid-eighteenth century Britain; their German counterparts, the *Empfindsamkeit* and later the *Sturm und Drang;* and, most importantly, the eighteenth-century scientists of chemistry and biology across Europe would read it, as a *spiritualization* of matter. The Newtonianism of the eighteenth century had a rich metaphysical content. Indeed, theology remained very close to the developments in natural philosophy in the eighteenth century, and while at the extremes the note of atheism and materialism came to be heard clearly, for the bulk of the century's scientific thinkers, such radicalism seemed clearly unattractive, and indeed even inconsistent with their own physical results. Consequently, they sought to suggest something quite different. They began to reconceive nature as a *living whole*.

Let us pursue this question a bit more concretely in terms of the biological sciences, in order to demonstrate the peculiar complexity but also coherence of the new mentality and its grounding not in "mystical excess" but in problems of concrete empirical science. The crisis of the so-called "iatromechanical" approach in the biological sciences, i.e., the approach which sought to explain all biological phenomena in terms of the inert-matter, impact-theory-of-force approach of mechanical cause, is crucial not only for its intrinsic importance in eighteenth-century science but because it is the field directly addressed in Kant's "Critique of Teleological Judgment" and, not coincidentally, in Herder's *Ideen zur Philosophie der Geschichte der Menshheit*. The new scientific rationalism, with its epoch-making success in mathematical physics, had profoundly influenced the sciences of medicine and biology in the seventeenth century. The effort to revise these sciences to accord with the new methodology of scientific rationalism led to a systematic pursuit of "iatromechanical" explanations for biological phenomena. That enthusiasm led many medical scientists, most prominently figures like Hermann Boerhaave, to become pioneering advocates of Newtonianism. But while such a posture was all the rage at the close of the seventeenth century, its impulse had exhausted itself by the mid-eighteenth century, and a new orientation became increasingly important—one which, forced by the materials under examination, reached out for more complex causal-explanatory theories.

In this search for new theories, antiquated terms frequently served to describe the most novel experiments, and scientists, embarrassed at the metaphysical baggage their borrowed terms carried with them, sought to find a clearer and more appropriate language without sacrificing the richness and determinacy of their experimental and theoretical results. When Kant wrote in the *Third Critique* that there could never be a Newton of the blade of grass, he meant a number of things, not all of which the biologists of the eighteenth century would have agreed with. But one thing they most assuredly did: namely, that no model of inert matter and mechanical cause would serve to account for the problems of biology. Kant wished to turn this result to a theological point, noumenal causality by a transcendent-personal God. The scientists, on the other hand, wanted to complicate their physical model of nature to incorporate those complex forces which they hypothesized to account for physical phenomena. Where Kant wished to build a wall between spirit and matter, the scientists were finding "vitalism" a necessary element in their *physical* theorizing. Kant segregated "life" from organisms. A biologist could not, at the peril of losing his field of inquiry.

Two central European scientists figured prominently in the biologists' development of an alternative stance: Georg Ernst Stahl and Albert von Haller. It was Stahl who proposed the antiquated language of "animism" to help characterize the elements in experimental phenomena for which the "iatromechanical" approach had no lexicon. Unquestionably Stahl wanted with this language to reintroduce into natural science a considerable amount of traditional metaphysics, which few of his younger contemporaries in the biological sciences felt enthusiastic about.[40] Yet they took up his language, *faute de mieux.* Similarly, the new generation of biologists learned a great deal from the pioneering work in comparative physiology done by von Haller, and in particular his characterization of "irritability." A great deal of controversy arose over the distinction of this property of organic life from "sensitivity."[41] But the whole movement was toward "vitalism." In the medical school of Montpellier these issues came to a theoretical crisis, and in the thought of Bordeu achieved as much clarification as the preliminary state of the science allowed.[42] In a brilliant essay, Sergio Moravia has documented the shift from the "iatromechanical" to the "vitalist" orientation. By focusing on Bordeu, Moravia demonstrated the perplexity and the resolution through which the school of Montpellier, and with it modern biology, passed during the course of the eighteenth century.[43]

More generally, Moravia structured his conceptualization around a very fecund pair of terms: *l'homme machine,* drawn, of course, from La Mettrie's provocative work of that title, and *l'homme sensible,* which, alas, has no such singular text to which to trace its parentage, but is by far the more interesting of the two. *L'homme sensible* gestures as a phrase to all those issues of spirituality that mechanism would deny. By placing *man* at the center of his treatment, Moravia stressed the direct and crucial sense in which the implications of biology bore upon the possibilities for anthropology. Man was at stake in all the experiments with regenerating hydra. Man was at issue in all the theories of animal and vegetable "spirits." Without that sense, the whole drama of eighteenth-century science is lost. And so, too, the motives behind Immanuel Kant's philosophy of science of the 1780s.

Kant's Writings on Biology

Kant's publications in biology began with his review, in 1771, of Peter Moscati's argument claiming that erect posture was not physiologically advantageous to man, but instead caused the species difficulties, hence, it could not be seen as a strictly biological adaptation. Moscati's claim that "the erect posture of man was forced and unnatural" sustained Kant's own conviction of a decisive difference between man and the animal kingdom: the intervention of reason. Kant concluded that man "had been led by reason and imitation to diverge from the original, animal arrangement." Since he could walk erect, reason enforced this shift in posture, despite all physiological hardship, for reasons of its own: "[In man] a germ of reason also lay, through which, if it was to develop, he was determined *for society*. Accordingly he assumed permanently the most appropriate posture [for such society], namely that of a biped. On the one hand, he gained infinitely much over the animals, but he also had to accept the consequent adversities of so proudly holding his head higher than his old comrades."[44] The issue of erect posture, and of a physiological transition from other animal forms to man, would arise again, in Kant's controversy with Herder in the 1780s. For Kant, any effort to think man in continuity with the rest of the animal kingdom threatened the dignity of the species, which rested in reason and freedom, elements which could have no physical ground.

Kant's next essay in the field of biology came four years later, appearing initially as an advertisement for his lectures in physical geography during the summer term of 1775, then in a slightly revised form in a popular science journal in 1777.[45] Many of the ideas Kant would uphold through the 1780s he first articulated in this essay, and it therefore merits close examination. The theme, the variety of human races, was central to the emergent field of physical and cultural anthropology in the eighteenth century and had momentous consequences for social and political relations.[46] Kant wished to clarify some methodological principles and offer some substantive hypotheses regarding race. Moreover, the topic drew Kant to larger questions in the philosophy of science.

First, he took sides with Buffon against Linnaeus in arguing that the principle of natural science had to do not with nominal classes but with real relations. "The divisions of the schools have to do with *classes* based on *similarities*, the divisions of nature, however, concern lineages [*Stämme*] which discriminate animals in terms of *consanguinity* [*Verwandtschaften*] in terms of their generation."[47] This distinction of "nominal" and "real" types would have not only a methodological but also a transcendental significance for Kant in the 1780s and consequently would play a major role in his disputations.

Second, Kant argued that the distinction between *Schulgattungen* and *Naturgattungen* could only be sustained if it were possible to establish the latter. That could only be done if one could discover, beyond the artificial typologies (Linnaeus), natural laws (Buffon). To find such laws required a new sense of the phrase "natural history," which in practice had only been a "natural description," and even then only in the sense of nominal typologies. Kant argued that a *science* had to take the idea of history seriously, i.e., recognize that even the best description of how the forms of nature stood at present did not explain how they got that way. Hence Kant proposed a new conception of "natural history" which

> would teach us about the changes in the form of the earth and at the same time about the [changes which] the creatures of the earth (plants and animals) suffered in the course of their natural wanderings, and the consequent variations [*Abartungen*] from the original form of their ancestral line [*Stammgattung*]. It would in all likelihood reinterpret a large number of apparently distinct types [*Arten*] into races of the same species [*Gattung*] and transform the currently so diffuse system of academic natural description into a physical system for the understanding [i.e, a science].[48]

Given Buffon's definition of species as that real consanguinity shown by organisms which when crossed produced offspring capable of reproduction, Kant asked how from any original form of the species one could derive "through a chain of alterations" the varieties or races encountered in present natural descriptions.

Kant argued that the potential for variation was built into the organism as part of its species-heritage. "The grounds of a particular development [*Auswickelung*] which lie in the nature of an organic body (of a plant or an animal) are called *germs* [*Keime*] if these developments affect particular parts, but if they affect only the size or the interrelation of the parts, then I term them *natural* endowments [*natürliche Anlagen*]."⁴⁹ Variation was part of the original germ-plasm, and it manifested itself when the environment placed the species under specific ecological constraints for a sustained period of time. Hence Kant maintained simultaneously the doctrines of the fixity of species and of the adaptation of varieties within species to ecological constraints.

Kant held to these doctrines because the alternative would be to allow that environmental factors could cause the strictly genetic nature of the species to alter, and Kant disbelieved utterly in such a possibility. "Chance or general mechanical laws can never bring about such adaptation. Therefore we must see such developments, which appear accidental according to them, as *predetermined* [*vorgebildet*]." External factors could be occasions, but not direct causes of changes which could be inherited through generation. "As little as chance or physical-mechanical causes can generate [*hervorbringen*] an organic body, so little will they be able to effect in them a modification of their reproductive powers which can be inherited."⁵⁰

Here Kant introduced the phrase *Zweckmäßigkeit*. There had to be purposive grounds for the modification or variation of organisms, and therefore it had to be possible to establish an account of their variation, a "natural history," which would indicate the original natural endowment of the species and explain its actualization in variety over time in different environments. Hence the method of "natural history" would be "to bring forward purposive causes [*zweckmäßige Ursachen*] where natural ones are not easily discerned, and natural ones where we cannot observe purposes."⁵¹ Hence teleology and mechanism were complementary modes of interpretation. This notion would receive minute attention in the *Third Critique*. Kant attempted to follow this methodology in accounting for the divergences of races within the single human species in terms of adaptation to different environments over long stretches of time.

Arthur Lovejoy has offered some useful historical indications of the sources of Kant's ideas in this essay. From the text itself it was obvious that Kant was familiar with the works of Linnaeus, Buffon, and Maupertuis, and Lovejoy argues that "Kant derived not only most of his zoological facts, but also some of his ideas of scientific method, from Buffon."⁵² But more, Lovejoy pointed to the influence of a contemporary German author whom Kant mentioned by name in the *Third Critique* and later praised publicly: Johann Friedrich Blumenbach. In 1775, the same year as Kant's essay, Blumenbach published a major study on similar themes: *De generis humani variatione nativa.*[53] Blumenbach derived his data from Buffon but his concepts from Leibniz. His two objectives in the work were to differentiate between man and animals and to explain the different races of man. Another key conception which drew Blumenbach and Kant together was the Leibnizian notion of "preformation." Clearly, Kant got the material for his reflections from this company—Linnaeus and Leibniz, Buffon and Blumenbach, and he knew, in addition, of Maupertuis's ideas of selective breeding.[54]

There was very little in the *Critique of Pure Reason* in its first version which related directly to biology. There are, however, a few points which deserve attention—all of them, incidentally, in the "Dialectic." Kant made reference to the uniqueness of organic form at several junctures.[55] He also made a very important distinction between the rational-mathematical principle of continuity and the fact that an object in nature was empirically always a *quantum discretum.*[56] In that context he addressed himself directly to "the widely discussed law of the *continuous gradation* of created beings, which was propounded by Leibniz, and admirably supported by Bonnet."[57] Kant argued that the maxim of continuity could not be taken as an objective principle of empirical nature:

> For observation and insight into the constitution of nature could never justify us in the objective assertion of the law. The steps of this ladder, as they are presented to us in experience, stand much too far apart; and what may seem to us small differences are usually in nature itself such wide gaps, that from any such observations we can come to no decision in regard to nature's ultimate design—especially if we bear in mind that in so great a multiplicity of things there can never be much difficulty in finding similarities and approximations.[58]

This argument, which aimed directly against any theory of continuity (and mutation) across species, figured prominently in Kant's later writings, and was fundamental to his resistance to "transformationism" and "hylozoism."

Kant felt that his *First Critique* had established the necessary parameters for the pursuit not only of philosophy but also of science. While, to be sure, the exposition of his "metaphysics of nature" was not complete, it could be derived virtually by analysis of the transcendental principles he had established in the *Critique.* He had not only clarified certain perplexities of reason but established the appropriate principles of scientific investigation into nature. Above

all he believed he had pronounced an interdict against "speculation" in science, and especially against two particular errors—
"materialism" and "spiritualism" in cosmology.[59] But in Germany,
the 1780s proved to be not a decade of "critical" restraint, but
rather the seedtime of *Naturphilosophie*, that highly speculative and
distinctive "Romanticism" in science. Its source was the *Sturm und
Drang*, and its prophet was Herder.

Hence, when Herder proceeded in his *Ideen* to overstep all the
limits that Kant had so laboriously postulated for philosophy and
natural science, Kant felt called upon to set his former pupil
straight. While we have already considered the tone of the reviews
of Herder's *Ideen*, here we will examine the concrete issues in science which were raised there. Kant took the thesis of the first volume of Herder's work to be as follows: "The spiritual nature of the
human soul, its persistence and progress to perfection, were to be
proven through analogy with the natural formations of matter primarily in its organic form, avoiding all metaphysical investigations."[60] Kant cited two extended passages from Herder which
expressed this thesis. The first deserves citation here, since it would
echo repeatedly in later writings:

> Before it was possible for our air, our water, our earth to be
> brought forth, many mutually displacing and destroying lin-
> eages [*Stamina*] were necessary; and the manifold species
> [*Gattungen*] of earth, of minerals, of crystalizations, even of
> the organization of mollusks, plants, animals, finally in man—
> how many dissolutions and revolutions of the one into the
> other were not presupposed? He, the son of all the elements
> and beings, their choicest totalization [*auserlesenster Inbegriff*]
> and at the same time the flower of earthly creation, could be
> nothing but the ultimate child of nature's womb [*letze Schooß-
> kind der Natur*], toward whose cultivation and reception many
> developments and revolutions must have served as prece-
> dents.[61]

Herder thus seemed prepared to see not only man in continuity
with organic form, but organic form itself in continuity with the inorganic, i.e., in his own words, "perhaps even in so-called *dead*
things one and the same endowment [*Anlage*] for organization,
only infinitely cruder and more muddled, might preside."

Indeed, this idea of one all-pervasive force [*Kraft*] was the essential idea which Herder entertained in his work, according to
Kant. He cited yet another passage from Herder which advanced

this speculation: "From rock to crystal, from these to metals, from these to plantlife, from there to animal, ultimately to man we have seen the form of organization ascend [*steigen*], and with it also the powers and drives of the creatures grown more various, until ultimately everything came to unity in the figure of man, so far as this could encompass them." In the course of this speculation, Herder denied the theory of preformation and epigenesis, advocated the thesis of erect posture as the physiological distinction of man, and tried to derive from it the rational and volitional aspects of his behavior, i.e., he claimed that the human soul emerged gradually out of the all-pervasive force of nature itself. Herder wrote: "Theoretically and practically reason is nothing but a derivative [*Vernommenes*], a proportion and direction of ideas and powers [*Kräfte*] which is learned and for which man was cultivated by his organic form and way of living." Moreover, Herder tried to use the doctrine of the "conservation of force" as the ground for a belief in the immortality of the soul, since the latter was simply the all-pervasive force of the world in its human instance. All of these notions were anathema to Kant.

He proceeded to reject each one. First, as to the continuity of species, he raised the issue of *quanta discreta*.

As regards the hierarchy of organisms, . . . its use with reference to the realm of nature here on earth leads nowhere . . . The minuteness of differences when one compares species according to their *similarity* is, in view of such a great multiplicity [of species], a necessary consequence of that multiplicity. But a *consanguinity* [*Verwandtschaft*] among them, according to which either one species springs from another and all of them out of one original species or as it were they originate from one single generative mother-womb, would lead to ideas which are so monstrous that reason shrinks back.[62]

Even more emphatically did Kant reject the idea of a single all-pervasive form of force as the principle of the organization of nature. "The unity of organic force . . . is an idea which is entirely outside the field of empirical natural science and belongs to merely speculative philosophy."[63] Moreover, in ascribing this as the basis of human reason and freedom, as an explanation of the human soul, Kant intimated, Herder "took the spiritual powers of man in a quite different sense from that of the human soul, and did not consider it a particular substance but merely an effect of general nature working upon matter in an invisible and animating manner"—i.e., Herder was very close to a doctrine of pantheism or "hylozoism."[64]

Kant also reviewed the second volume of Herder's *Ideen*, in which Herder discussed the issues of physical geography and the different races of man, issues which, as we have noted, were the subject of Kant's regular lectures at Königsberg and also of one of his essays. In other words, Herder was writing on matters about which Kant considered himself somewhat expert. Moreover, Herder took the opportunity of this second volume to respond to Kant's hostile criticism with some hostile criticism of his own, specifically of Kant's philosophy of history in "Idea for a Universal History with Cosmopolitan Intent." Those historical issues belong in a separate context, but the issue of race figures directly in our current considerations. After setting the context of the dispersal of the human race across the physical geography of the planet in book 6, Herder devoted himself to the specific issue of race and the explanation of its variations in book 7. Herder denied the theory of individual preformation [*das Evolutionssystem*—"transformationism"] and the theory of merely mechanical, external factors as sufficient explanations, and argued that there had to be an immanent force behind such variation. Herder called it a "genetic force" which modified itself according to environmental constraints. Kant had no quarrel with that, but insisted that this "genetic force" was not unlimited, and could not lead to a mutation of species, and that the proper terms for it should be "germs" [*Keime*] or "original endowments." Such an interpretation, Kant added, should not resort to the speculative theory of mechanisms and archetypes [*Knospen*] which were preformed and succeeded one another under certain circumstances, as in the "transformationist" system, but should simply accept this capacity for variation as a given incapable of further determinate elucidation.[65]

Kant's review of the second volume of Herder's *Ideen* appeared in the November 15, 1785 issue of *Allgemeine Literatur-Zeitung*. In that same month, in the *Berlinische Monatsschrift*, appeared another contribution by Kant to this very topic of the anthropology of race. That can hardly be a coincidence. In the new essay on race, Kant reiterated his fundamental principles, making even more explicit his commitment to the fixity of species. "Throughout organic nature, amid all changes of individual creatures, the species maintain themselves unaltered [*die Species derselben sich unverändert erhalten*]." Kant went on to argue that this was an essential principle of scientific investigation, without which every concept would dissolve:

[I]f some magical power of the imagination . . . were capable of modifying . . . the reproductive faculty itself, of transforming Nature's original model or of making additions to it, . . . we should no longer know from what original Nature had begun, nor how far the alteration of that original may proceed, nor . . . into what grotesqueries of form species might eventually be transmogrified [*in welche Fratzengestalt die Gattungen und Arten zuletzt noch verwildern dürften*] . . . I for my part adopt it as a fundamental principle to recognize no power . . . to meddle with the reproductive work of Nature . . . [to] effect changes in the ancient original of a species in any such way as to implant those changes in the reproductive process and make them hereditary.[66]

The reiteration of the principles of the essay of 1775 a decade later can only be grasped as a direct comment upon the disregard for these ideas by Herder in the *Ideen*.

Why should Kant have found the idea of the mutation of species so unbearable? That empirical science did not draw back from it is clear from the work of the eighteenth-century biologists we have considered. Why, then, did Kant balk? The answer lies in his philosophical commitments, not his scientific insight.[67] Kant feared for the dissolution of the two essential boundaries upon which his philosophy rested: that between matter and life, and that between organisms and man. That natural science should venture into such hypotheses was horrifying to Kant, and he felt driven to confirm the legal limits of scientific investigation according to the sound principles of "Newtonianism." The summer of 1785 was the time of the composition of the *Metaphysical Foundations of Natural Science,* and two of its essential objectives were to prove beyond doubt the distinction of life from matter and to give a more rational and critical theory of force [*Kraft*], as against the wildly speculative notions which, taking off from Leibniz and Boscovich, were inundating the new sciences of chemistry and biology.

The *Metaphysical Foundations of Natural Science* is a work which has not received a great deal of attention in the Kant literature. This is strange in view of Kant's promises in the *First Critique*. It is also unfortunate, because it leaves the important question of the *metaphysical* elaboration of Kant's system in that measure out of consideration. The most important point about the work, from our current vantage, is Kant's insistence upon grounding physical science upon matter and motion, i.e., on the seventeenth-century principles of physics, even as he revised that theory in crucial Leibnizian ways toward a theory of matter as force. This, combined with his unequivocal statement that "in every special doctrine of nature only so much science proper can be found as there is mathematics in it," tended to be extremely hostile to all of the recent work in chemistry and biology.[68] Indeed, in accordance with this criterion, Kant claimed that chemistry failed to qualify as a science and should be regarded merely as a "systematic art of analysis." That notion of a "systematic art" can be related rather directly to the "technic" of reflective judgment, especially as the latter would apply to biology in the *Third Critique*. It follows that biology could pretend even less than chemistry to science in Kant's sense of the word. Still worse was the situation for any "science" of empirical psychology, which could not even be a "systematic art."[69] The point is, Kant made his criterion for science so restrictive that almost all the new sciences were ineligible. There is something profoundly reactionary about such a stance.[70] But it was part and parcel of the commitments to which Kant felt bound by the mid-1780s.

Kant's biological preoccupations manifested themselves in the revisions of the *First Critique* in 1786, through his use of biological illustrations and metaphors for his cognitive theory.[71] But the next significant piece of writing really devoted to the questions of biology was an essay composed in the fall of 1787—the essay entitled "Über den Gebrauch teleologischer Principien in der Philosophie."[72] It is widely recognized to have been of crucial relevance to the genesis of the "Critique of Teleological Judgment."[73] The occasion for the composition of this essay is on the surface quite straightforward, but the implications turn out to be more intricate. Kant not only published his reviews of Herder and his second essay on race in 1785, but he also published an essay entitled "Muthmaßlicher Anfang der Menschengeschichte" in the *Berlinische Monatsschrift* in January, 1786. It, too, was composed in that busy year of 1785 in which Kant's central preoccupation appears to have been the methodology of science. In October and November of 1786, in the *Teutsche Merkur*, the journal which had carried Reinhold's spirited defense of Herder's *Ideen* against Kant's review and which Reinhold coedited with his distinguished father-in-law, Wieland, there appeared a two-part critique of Kant's writings on the anthropology of race and of human origins by an important German scientist, Georg Forster, later to become famous for his involvement in the French Revolution. Kant, ever sensitive to criticism and viewing this particular criticism as yet a further rejoinder from the camp of Herder and the "aestheticists" of science, felt a need to reply.[74]

The matter came even more forcefully to a head when Herder himself reasserted all those ideas which Kant found so irresponsible in an even more outrageous form, the unequivocally pantheist tract *Gott: einige Gespräche* in early summer 1787. Kant was furious about the "syncretist" and "pantheist" sophistries emanating from that quarter and anxious to debunk them. At the same time, Reinhold, and with him the journal *Teutsche Merkur,* had converted to Kantianism, and since August of 1786 Reinhold had been publishing serially his crucial *Briefe über die Kantische Philosophie,* which did so much to popularize Kantian thought in Germany. In October 1787, Reinhold wrote to Kant asking for a public acknowledgment of the accuracy of his representation of the latter's work, and Kant saw the opportunity to use the very *Teutsche Merkur* to rebutt his critics. The result was the essay on teleology.

Forster had published on the question of race theory himself, and his own views differed from Kant's, but they were respectably scientific for the most part, and Kant wished not so much to dispute Forster's scientific standing as to defend his own. Forster had impugned Kant's scientific objectivity and his methodology, not merely his hypotheses, and so Kant had a number of points to address in his essay. It is, indeed, a most complex and important piece of writing. The title has often been termed a bit misleading, for much of the essay concerns the same old issues of race with which we have become familiar. But that is to misapprehend the importance of the introductory and concluding sections of the essay, which operate on a much higher level of generality and in fact represent some of the most important writing Kant ever did on the methodology of science and also on questions of his own philosophy. Therefore it behooves us to address the issues of the essay in terms of their increasing scope, starting with the most concrete and familiar, the problem of race, and proceeding to the larger considerations in that context.

Forster had charged, with an eye as much to Kant's "Muthmaßlicher Anfang der Menschengeschichte" as to his essays on the anthropology of race, that Kant introduced theological considerations into matters of empirical science. Not only did Kant seem to ascribe to Providence a role in nature (teleology), but his account of the origins of the human species derived much from the scriptural account.[75] A particular instance of this, Forster claimed, was Kant's dogmatic assertion that the entire human race sprang from one set of parents, which Forster believed Kant took literally from Scripture.[76] Kant denied the charge, and argued that it was not biblical literalism but rather the facts of the case which led him to believe that the only way to advance the science of race was to work from a theory of *consanguinity* rather than mere *similarity,* and consanguinity simply meant common parentage.[77] Whether there was only one pair at the outset, or many pairs with identical genetic endowments, did not really matter, for it was the principle alone which Kant was trying to establish.

Forster questioned the whole distinction between natural description and natural history, arguing that Kant's approach to science was too metaphysical in that he began with principles, definitions, etc., instead of working empirically. Here Kant responded that science could not proceed without any orienting hypotheses.[78] Kant's concepts were not metaphysical, but simply hypothetical, designed to clarify the problem. Forster accused him further of advocating teleological explanation, whereas science ought to work only with natural explanation. Kant conceded that of course science always preferred efficient causes, when it could find them, but he insisted that in their absence, science was fully entitled to resort to teleology.[79] This was not capricious, it was necessary for the investigation itself.

Kant argued that it was simply impossible to conceive of organisms and above all of the process of generation and variation in heredity except in terms of purposiveness. Mechanical accounts simply were not adequate. In his preliminary draft for the essay, Kant wrote very clearly on this line: "The principle of purposiveness in the construction of organic and especially living creatures is as much bound up with reason as the principle of efficient causes in regard to all changes in the world. To take any part of a creature for useless [*zwecklos*] which is a permanent fixture of its species is the same thing as to take an occurrence in the world to have arisen without a cause."[80] Blind natural mechanism simply could not explain the complexity of the reciprocal relations of an organism.

Kant made the same point at the conclusion of the essay, in his most exacting definition of "organism" prior to the *Third Critique.* He wrote:

Because the concept of an organized being already implies that it is a material thing in which everything stands in relation to everything else reciprocally as end and means [*Zweck und Mittel*], and this can only be conceived as a *system of final causes,* and hence *human* reason at least is left certainly not with a physical-mechanical, but only with a teleological way to explain its possibility: for this reason one cannot ask of physics whence all such organization originally springs. The answer to this question would, if it were accessible at all, obviously lie *outside* natural science in *metaphysics.*[81]

And this was the point Kant wished most to stress to Forster: that the real dividing line was not between the two of them as scientists, but rather between authentic scientists and arrant speculators.

Kant struck out at such arrant speculators several times in the essay. The first such blast came early on, when he warned against overhasty inferences from empirical observations to general principles. He claimed that Linnaeus had fallen prey to error by taking the similarity of certain instances for a proof of the similarity of their fundamental principles. Such hasty generalization was not something a careful scientist permitted himself, but there were those "so indiscriminate as to read their ideas into their observations." Kant called such individuals "rash sophists [*rasche Vernünftler*]."[82] He went on a few pages later to castigate "the common, shallow way of thinking which takes all the differences in our species on the same footing, namely, that of mere chance, and sees them emerging and fading as external circumstances direct, and hence which considers all [scientific] inquiries superfluous and even the preservation of species in the same purposive form pointless."[83]

To whom Kant was referring might be unclear, out of context, but there can be little doubt after all we have considered, and there is more evidence to be brought to bear. Kant renewed his imprecation against sophistical science at the close of the essay, before his crucial definition of organisms, and there he explicitly attacked the theory of force which had been so widely bandied about. Such a theory, Kant charged, could never be proven by experience. But "where the latter stops and one must carry on with self-invented forces of matter [*selbst erdachten Kräften der Materie*] in accordance with unheard-of laws incapable of proof, one has passed beyond natural science."[84] That was what Herder had done.

Forster had used Kant's representation of the utter fluidity of species from the review of Herder as an instance of Kant's metaphysical approach to science, but Kant insisted that he was hardly upholding such a preposterous notion as the "relatedness [*Verwandtschaft*] of everything in an imperceptible gradient from man to the whale and on downward (conjecturally even to the lichens and mosses)—and not simply in a system of comparisons but in terms of a system of generation from common lineages [*Stämme*] in a natural chain of organic beings." It was not he who held that all life "sprang from the mother womb of earth fertilized by the sea-slime"—though there were plenty who did, and Kant gave the example of Bonnet.[85] Kant withdrew his own charge that such ideas were monstrous and that reason was horrified by them (though he only did so as if these were Forster's phrases, not his own). Rather, he said, any sound scholar would repudiate them because they abandoned "the fruitful soil of natural science" for the "wastelands of metaphysics." He acknowledged a "not unmanly fear" of whatever "led reason away from its first principles and made it permissible to rove about in boundless imaginations." Not Forster, but *Herder* was the target of all this.

At the core of Herder's sophistries, in Kant's view, was his unjustifiable notion of fundamental forces [*Grundkräfte*]. Hence Kant brought his essay to a close with an exposition of the problem of any conception of fundamental forces from the vantage of transcendental philosophy. Such a fundamental force by definition could not be discerned in any empirical experience. Hence it could only be a matter of knowledge if one could offer a transcendental account for it. But, Kant was adamant, human reason "absolutely cannot conceive such *fundamental forces* a priori."[86]

What were the implications for transcendental philosophy of such a stark assertion? We must reflect that "powers" [*Kräfte*] was a term which Kant had used to characterize the faculties of mind. What was the status of such concepts in light of Kant's claim? He addressed himself explicitly to this question in the same paragraph. It was not, he argued, as though reason should not deal with the problem posed by the question of fundamental forces. But there was a proper method which alone offered any prospect of results. First, in the bewildering variety of such forces, reason should, as always, aim to reduce them to the least possible number, though it was implausible to believe they could ever be reduced to unity. The only evidence of the existence of such forces was through the relation of cause and effect, and the only knowledge we had of them was in the effect, so that our conception could only draw from that evidence, and only express this causal relation. In a footnote, Kant gave as his example the faculty of imagination [*Einbildungskraft*]. He argued that we recognized it by its effects, and that we were in no position to explain it by some other force.

This led him to a much more general point, still in the footnote, with regard to the relation of substance to force. Here Kant addressed himself to one of the core doctrines of Wolffian philosophy, the contention that the soul was a substance with a single fundamental power, the power of representation. Wolff's error lay in the confusion of a *nominal* universal for a *real* one, Kant argued, demonstrating the philosophical potential implicit in all his thinking about the problem of race.[87] Kant illustrated his point with a reference to the theory of physical science. To say all the forces of material nature were forces of movement was true but useless, because from this we could not derive the specific forces of attraction and repulsion which were alone constitutive of material dynamics. The more abstract concept was certainly higher, but it did not *contain* the lower concepts, since the latter were richer in content and had many elements which fell outside of what was shared under the higher concept.

But Kant had an even more remarkable point to make. The thrust of the new ontologies of science was to try to identify the concept of substance with the concept of fundamental force, i.e., to dissolve matter into force. But that was a misapprehension of the meaning of the terms, Kant claimed. Force did not constitute the ground of the reality of properties. That was what substance signified. Force was merely the relation of substance to its properties insofar as it (substance) grounded their actuality. And substance could have as many relations as it has properties. Therefore there could be no homology of substance with fundamental force. The relevance of this argument will only emerge fully when we are dealing with the ultimate issues of ontology between Kant and the new metaphysics.

Kant brought these notions of substance and force at last to bear on the concept of an organism, and came directly to the threshold of the "Critique of Teleological Judgment." He wrote:

> Now, the concept of an organized being is this: that it is a material thing which is only possible through the interrelation of all that it contains reciprocally as end and means (in fact every anatomist and physiologist has presumed such a concept). A fundamental force through which organic form is achieved must consequently be thought as a causality working according to purposes, and indeed in such a manner that these purposes must be assumed as the basis for the very possibilty of its efficacy. We, however, are acquainted with such forces, in

terms of their *basis of determination*, only in *ourselves*, i.e. in our understanding and will, as cause of the possibility of certain products which are totally constructed according to purposes, that is, *works of art*.[88]

To try to conceive of a form of causality which, without intellect and will, could nevertheless organize itself, was something for which we had no model in ourselves and no basis in experience. It was, Kant concluded, "completely fanciful [*erdichtet*] and empty," and there was not the slightest reason to believe that any evidence could be found for it. Therefore, should organic form exist in the world, some intelligent cause for it would have to be conceived, either in the world or outside it. Kant's writings on biology through "Über den Gebrauch teleologischer Principien in der Philosophie" have brought us to the problem of organisms. Kant's manifold considerations of the decade fuse into this one crucial consideration.

Ten

THE PROBLEM OF ORGANIC
FORM IN THE *CRITIQUE*
OF TELEOLOGICAL JUDGMENT

While the *First Introduction* examined the purposiveness of nature as a whole, the "Critique of Teleological Judgment," which Kant worked on in the spring and summer of 1789, concerned itself with the issue of more specific organic forms.[1] Indeed, the "Critique" should be read as the culmination of Kant's biological reflections. Yet all that we have determined concerning the whole *Third Critique*—its problem formulation, its development, its languages—raises the discourse to a different plane, and thus, while the familiar issues arise in the "Critique," they take on a whole new significance and figure in a much grander philosophical project. The strategy of interpretation will begin with problems of biological interpretation familiar from Kant's earlier writings, proceed to his formulation of a theory of organic form, and culminate in the "Dialectic of Teleological Judgment," where Kant addressed the metaphysical problems his approach entailed.

Certain sections of the "Critique" directly restate themes in the teleology essay. Thus, §68 seems to be a reformulation of the methodological self-defense Kant offered against the criticisms of Georg Forster. And §80 can be seen as Kant's reiteration of his quarrel with the theorists of the mutability of species and the unity of force. Similarly, §81 can be seen as Kant's clearest position statement on late eighteenth-century biological theories of reproduction and "evolution," and hence his definitive stance on issues in biological science. Similarly, §§64–66 represent a more deliberate and sustained effort to formulate a definition of organic form, but depart in no significant manner from the conception offered at the close of the teleology essay. Let us take up these familiar issues briefly in turn.

The gist of Forster's criticism was that Kant had not conducted himself properly as a scientist, i.e., that Kant betrayed the methodology of science. In §68, Kant again defended his methodology. He emphasized its "systematic" character and also its use of conceptual hypotheses, though only heuristically, as guides for investigation. He argued that the very metaphorical character of his language should have signaled the metaphysical diffidence of the approach. "Design is ascribed to nature, i.e. to matter . . . [But] no design in the proper meaning of the word can possibly be ascribed to inanimate matter . . . Hence we speak quite correctly in teleology . . . without either making an intelligent being of [nature], for that would be preposterous, or even without presuming to place another intelligent Being above it as its Architect."[2] Kant was not advocating a theological approach to natural science. Physicoteleology simply pointed to the inescapable logical problem of some originating rational cause. Still, from that to a full-fledged notion of God was a considerable distance, and in any event, the originating cause was a regulative, i.e., heuristic notion, not an objective principle.[3]

Kant insisted that mechanical accounts failed to make sense of organic form, and that consequently, at some point in the most mechanical explanation of organic life some originating and nonmechanical cause would need to be invoked. Kant wished to bring this to bear even on the most extravagant hypotheses of generation offered in the biological sciences of his day, in §80. This was the section in which Kant appeared, especially to late nineteenth-century German students of his work, whose heads were full of Darwinism, to have anticipated much of the teaching of evolution. A careful consideration of the text shows that nothing could be further from the truth. Kant was not embracing the doctrine he articulated in §80 but rather holding it forward as the most extreme sort of hypothesis—one which, on any sound reading either of the clarifying footnote to that section or of §81, he then expressly repudiated.[4]

"If the naturalist would not waste his labor, he must, in judging of things the concept of any of which is indubitably established as a natural purpose (organized beings), always lay down as basis an original organization."[5] This is the starting point for the celebrated discussion of the fluidity of species in which Kant takes up the results of comparative anatomy as a possibility for a mechanical explanation of organic modification: "The agreement of so many genera of animals in a certain common schema, which appears to be fundamental not only in the structure of their bones but also in the disposition of their remaining parts . . . allows a ray of hope, however faint, . . . that here something may be accomplished by the aid of the principle of the mechanism of nature (without which there can be no natural science in general)."[6] Note that for Kant such a theory would be a theory of *mechanism*. Any immanent account of biological variation would be mechanistic in his view, and that is why for him there is no real difference between a strict mechanistic materialist and a hylozoist. They only differ in the properties they ascribe to matter, yet wish matter to suffice for the explanation of organic phenomena.

Kant struck immediately against the notion that any such insights yet qualified as objective knowledge. They were hints and hopes, not established facts, in his view—though not in that of the scientists of his day! At best, what they had was a fruitful *analogy*, Kant went on. "This analogy of forms, which with all their differences seem to have been produced according to a common original type, strengthens our suspicions of an actual relationship between them in their production from a common parent, through the gradual approximation of one animal genus to another."[7] The relationship biologists had uncovered was only analogy, only nominal. They had raised the question of an *actual* relationship, based on *Verwandtschaft*, but hardly confirmed it by their results, Kant insisted. There was, to be sure, a "gradual approximation" of genus to genus, but they remained *quanta discreta*. Hence it was an extravagant hypothesis indeed to try to link them all in an actual relationship which would extend "from man, down to the polyp, and again from this down to mosses and lichens, and finally to the lowest stage of nature noticeable by us, viz. to crude matter." Such a bold archaeologist of nature, reflecting on the "surviving traces of its oldest revolutions," might conjecture one "great family of creatures."

He can suppose the bosom of mother earth, as she passed out of her chaotic state (like a great animal), to have given birth in the beginning to creatures of less purposive form, that these again gave birth to others which formed themselves with greater adaptation to their place of birth and their relations to each other, until this womb becoming torpid and ossified, limited its births to definite species not further modifiable.[8]

Yet Kant's point about this "daring venture of reason" which "the most acute naturalists" might permit themselves was that such an archaeologist "must still in the end ascribe to this universal mother an organization purposive in respect of all these creatures." That is, at the origin, there must be some form of causality which is not material and which then persists and governs the whole process of reproduction and variation across time. "It would always remain *generatio univoca* in the most universal sense of the word, for it only considers one organic being as derived from another organic being, although from one which is specifically different."[9]

Moreover, Kant went on in the footnote, while such a hypothesis was not contrary to reason, and this distinguished it from the notion of spontaneous generation *(generatio aequivoca)*, it was nevertheless not to be found in experience that such fluidity between species *(generatio heteronyma)* had ever taken place. "Experience gives no example of it; according to experience, all generation that we know is *generatio homonyma*. This is not merely *univoca* in contrast to the generation out of unorganized material, but in the organization of the products is of like kind to that which produced it."[10] Hence Kant clearly denied the empirical plausibility of the "daring venture" of mutation of species. In §81 he took his own stand based on the necessity of a teleological principle in organic forms at some point. Either such rational (noumenal) causality intruded at every instance of such organic form, which was the metaphysical doctrine of "occasionalism," or it intruded only at the origin, which was the metaphysical doctrine of "preestablished harmony," or "preformation." The former was the utter abandonment of science, for it found miracle at every turn. "If we assume the occasionalism of the production of organized beings, all nature is quite lost."[11] That left "preformation." Kant distinguished two versions of the latter doctrine. One, "individual preformation," which Kant associated with the theory of *emboîtement* or "transformationism," commonly called the "evolution" theory in the eighteenth century, had serious drawbacks. First, in requiring a special providence in the creation of each specific organism, it made no great advance over "occasionalism," especially since placement at the origin (in time) was really not a significant difference when referring to noumenal (timeless) causality. But there were even empirical problems with the theory. It had great difficulty dealing with such problems as abortion and hybridization.

That left only the theory of "generic preformation" or "epigenesis." According to this theory, "the productive faculty of the generator, and consequently the specific form, would be *virtually* preformed according to the inner purposive capacities [*Anlagen*] which are part of its lineage [*Stamm*]." While the *species* were formed at the origin, the individuals within them varied, within the limits of their original endowments, according to the pressures of their environment. This was just the theory which Kant had advocated in his treatment of race. The advantage of such a theory was that it "regards nature as self-producing, not merely as self-evolving, and so with the least expenditure of the supernatural leaves to nature all that follows after the first beginning." The main advocate of such a theory of epigenesis, Kant wrote, was Blumenbach. It was he who demonstrated the validity and the limitations of the hypothesis by refuting the excesses of its materialist and hylozoist rivals.

> In all physical explanations of these formations he starts from organised matter. That crude matter should have originally formed itself according to mechanical laws, that life should have sprung from the nature of what is lifeless, that matter should have been able to dispose itself into the form of a self-maintaining purposiveness—this he rightly declares to be contradictory to reason.[12]

The ultimate enemies in the whole controversy over the boundary between the animate and the inanimate stand revealed: those who advocated an immanent account of organisms. Kant named them in the last segment of §80: Hume, the pantheists, and the Spinozists.[13] They were not *scientific* rivals; they were rivals in *metaphysics*.

Before we turn to that metaphysical rivalry, and the "Dialectic of Teleological Judgment" in which it was fought out, let us review briefly Kant's definition of organic form as he developed it in §§64–66. The essential definition Kant offered of such organic form, as we have seen from the essay "Über den Gebrauch teleologischer Principien inder Philosophie," was that of the reciprocal interrelation of parts as means and ends, and consequently, of the priority of the whole over the parts in the constitution of the entity. Structurally, that is, organisms appeared to be both cause and effect of themselves. Their parts were possible only through their reference to the whole. They were self-organizing beings. Kant made a much more painstaking presentation of these same points in the "Analytic of Teleological Judgment." In §64 Kant argued that such organic forms appeared "contingent" relative to all empirical laws, i.e., they could not be accounted for in judgments of experience based on mechanical causality. An organism was "cause and effect of itself." Kant pointed to three distinct processes which showed this trait: reproduction, internal growth and development, and reciprocal interdependence of parts. Hence, in §65 he associated with organisms a *"formative* power of a self-propagating kind."[14] In §66 he went on to characterize this reciprocal interdependence as that of ends and means and to argue that it was as inconceivable that there should be parts in an organism which had no purpose as that there could be events in nature without a cause.[15] But the really interesting question was not how Kant described organic forms. The question was how he reconciled their empirical actuality with his system of cognition and his philosophy as a whole. It is the metaphysical question which demands a hearing.

The Epistemological Problem of Empirical Organisms

Reflective judgment imputed purposiveness to nature as a whole merely heuristically, as a methodological recourse necessary for scientific insight into the empiricial diversity of nature. Its objective was to create a *system* of empirical science. One of the marks of a system is closure, i.e., the resolution of all the events that fall within its scope. The Newtonian physics in whose system Kant wished to set empirical science involved efficient mechanical cause. But within the empirical diversity it sought to organize, some objects presented anomalies which the mechanical framework could not explicate.

One might ask how it was even possible, according to Kant's model, to experience such entities, since experience was necessarily structured in terms of the categories of the understanding, and hence in a model which was already mechanical. Kant addressed himself to this question in the *First Introduction* in §7. As he put it, "the first question at this point is, how is the technic of nature *perceived* in its products?"[16] To explain how organisms could be recognized, Kant had to deploy his "other kind of judging," that involving "reflection" and "purposiveness," because the determinant form of judgment simply did not suffice. The judgment of experience presented consciousness with data which simply did not accord with the premises of that very judgment—it was anomalous, or, in his terms, "contingent"—and some crucial supplement became necessary to render the experience coherent. Purposiveness is never something we perceive directly in an experience. It is, rather, an inference, an imputation, which we make.[17] Kant put it well in a marginal note to his own copy of the *First Introduction:* "we read final causes into things and do not, so to speak, abstract them from perceptions."[18]

Yet we do so for good reasons. Kant made a very important observation in the *Second Critique* which is germane here: "all events in time according to natural law can be called the 'mechanism of nature,' even though it is not supposed that things which are subject to it must really be material machines."[19] This is the converse of the point he made so strenuously at the level of nature as a whole: just because nature appeared designed, that did not mean it could not have achieved this mechanically. Here the proposition is: just because nature appears under the categorical rules of mechanical law, that does not mean the real ground of its phenomenal appearances might not follow some other principle.

We can perceive, i.e., form a "judgment of perception" of, such entities. But how can we conceive of them? Is it possible to accommodate this anomaly without destroying the causal structure of the *First Critique*? How is it possible to explain determinately objects of experience which fall outside the structure of categories?[20] It must be remembered that while the reflective judgment served altogether well for the induction of new principles of scientific order in the empirical world, these principles could only be established as *valid* science through a proof structure which would work deductively in terms of the causal categories of the understanding. Thus, to illustrate, it was an act of imagination, of reflective judgment, which led Kepler to conceive of the orbits of the planets as elipses, but he only persuaded the scientific community of his insight when he was able to prove his claim mathematically and have it confirmed by empirical measurements. That is, he had to take his insight, his induction, and reformulate it as a "determinant judgment," in Kant's terminology. Only "judgments of experience," sanctioned by the rules of the understanding, constituted valid knowledge in his view.

The dilemma which organic forms presented was that such a mechanical mode of explanation did not, and as far as could be determined would not ever be able to, account for the phenomena to be construed, Kant argued. What were the characteristics of these empirical anomalies which rendered them so difficult to explicate mechanically? From the vantage of scientific explanation, the real problem with organisms was that their behavior was inconsistent with the human mode of causal explanation.[21] The intrinsic order of an organism was such that it was, in the full sense, systematic. Hence it was impossible to apply a serial model of causal construction to it. It fell not under the serial form of judgment (ground to consequence, cause to effect) but rather under the disjunctive form of judgment (whole to part).[22]

At the level of perception itself, however, it intractably remained that we encountered phenomena of which it was humanly impossible to make any sense apart from the ascription to the sequence of their behavior of a principle which was not mechanical. An organism was a self-constituting whole which transformed itself within its own systemic contours literally before our eyes in a manner which defied all our constitutive explanatory models. The only alternative principle we had at our rational disposal was the concept of purpose which we ourselves used to superimpose our will upon mechanical process, and so we had recourse to this in our conception of these empirical anomalies.

What was the usefulness of the analogy of purpose in the context of organic forms? Purpose signified that a representation in the mind served as the original cause of the existence of an entity or a state of affairs. Man could make sense of his own purposive activity as rational (even if noumenal) causality in terms of the temporal and logical precedence of an idea and willed act to the actuality he produced as an objective purpose, but how could such a self-determination be projected upon noncognitive entities? There was no ground to ascribe a mind capable of such willed action to the organic forms man observed in nature, Kant insisted. They appeared to be intrinsically self-regulating, but according to Kant it remained improper to ascribe to them, as phenomenal objects, an intelligent will. To view mere material phenomena in that manner was to fall into the contradiction of hylozoism.[23]

To ascribe to the phenomena of organic form the principle of purposiveness was not even very fruitful as analogy, because these objects exceeded utterly the most elaborate form of intrinsic purposiveness human beings could design, that is, works of art. Kant realized that the analogy had a gaping flaw. What an organism could do was "infinitely beyond the reach of art," he wrote in §64. And he developed this realization more extensively in §65. "We say of nature and its faculty in organized products far too little if we describe it as an *analogon of art,* for this suggests an artificer (a rational being) external to it." Kant recognized that organisms organized themselves. Such *"internal natural perfection . . .* is not even thinkable or explicable by means of any exactly fitting analogy to human art." Kant concluded: "To speak strictly, then, the organization of nature has in it nothing analogous to any causality we know."

Here Kant both acknowledged the limitation of his approach and set forth the intense philosophical difficulty of an alternative. It was the search for an alternative which led to the speculative recourse of hylozoism. On this score, Kant wrote:

We perhaps approach nearer to this inscrutable property if we describe it as an *analogon of life,* but then we must either endow matter, as mere matter, with a property which contradicts its very being (hylozoism) or associate therewith an alien principle *standing in communion* with it (a soul). But in the latter case we must, if such a product is to be a natural product, either presuppose organized matter as the instrument of that soul, which does not make the soul a whit more comprehensible, or regard the soul as artificer of this structure, and so remove the product from (corporeal) nature.[24]

Kant did not believe either of the two versions of hylozoism could stand up to rigorous analysis. He subjected them to it in the "Dialectic of Teleological Judgment." But if all these alternatives failed, was there any resolution of the dilemma? Kant believed there was one last out: "The concept of a thing as in itself a natural purpose is . . . no constitutive concept of understanding or of reason, but it can serve as a regulative concept for the reflective judgment, to guide our investigation about objects of this kind by a distant analogy with our own causality."[25] Driven to admit that it was impossible for man to see organisms other than as natural purposes, Kant held that this necessity lay in *our* projection, not *their* nature.[26]

The "Dialectic of Teleological Judgment": The Methodological Portion

The "Dialectic" turns on two distinctions, that between a subjective maxim and an objective principle, on the one hand, and that between a reflective and a determinant judgment, on the other. A reflective judgment is only a subjective recourse, and its warrant is consequently only a subjective maxim. A determinant judgment, a "judgment of experience" in Kant's earlier language, has the full warrant of an objective principle. Kant argued that reason fell into dialectical error when it took a subjective maxim as an objective principle, or a reflective judgment for a determinant one.[27] But the matter is not so simple.

The resolution of Kant's "Dialectic" hinged on conceiving of the *mechanistic* explanation of empirical events as just as much a subjective maxim as the teleological explanation, and this is a very problematic idea in light of the "Second Analogy" of the *First Critique*. How are we to understand this move? In his study of Kant's concept of teleology, McFarland offers an ingenious hypothesis.[28] He suggests that while mechanism has the full warrant of validity in its *transcendental* employment, constituting the object of possible experience or nature in general, its status alters when it is brought to bear upon problems in empirical nature, and it then stands merely as one possible maxim of interpretation among others. While it is constitutive at the transcendental level, it is only regulative at the empirical level.

Yet this ingenious theory runs into difficulty as to the meaning of a *determinant* judgment at the empirical level. Either McFarland must deny it occurs at this level, which goes against Kant's text, as McFarland realizes, or he faces the prospect that such a determinant judgment cannot in fact be discriminated from a *reflective* judgment in terms either of induction versus specification or of objective cognitive validity. Kant could not have meant this. He never surrendered the belief that even in the empirical, a mechanistic explanation in accordance with the categories resulted in valid knowledge, and hence it was not merely a subjective maxim. It had a claim to objectivity which was never accorded to reflection. It produced "real," not "nominal" concepts, though assertorically not apodictically.

At several junctures in the "Critique of Teleological Judgment" Kant insisted that, in terms of empirical knowledge, only the judgment of experience, i.e., only the explanation according to mechanical causality, could produce valid science. Thus in §70, Kant wrote: "unless this lies at the basis of investigation, there can be no proper knowledge of nature at all."[29] In §78, he made the same point: "It is infinitely important for reason not to let slip the mechanism of nature in its products, and in their explanation not to pass it by, because without it no insight into the nature of things can be attained."[30] And in §80, Kant, almost as an aside, observed that without the mechanism of nature "there can be no natural science in general."[31] He concluded the entire "Dialectic" on this note: "We should explain all products and occurrences in nature, even the most purposive, by mechanism as far as is in our power (the limits of which we cannot give an account of in this kind of investigation)."[32] This was the "privilege" which the principle of mechanism enjoyed in the study of nature.

Not only did Kant thus privilege empirical determinant judgments as truly scientific, but he also consistently denied to empirical reflective judgments any such title. This is most explicit in §79. In that section, Kant asked about the cognitive status of teleology: "Does it belong to natural science (properly so called) . . . ?" He replied: "natural science . . . needs determinant and not merely reflective principles in order to supply objective grounds for natural effects. In fact, nothing is gained for the theory of nature or the mechanical explanation of its phenomena by means of its effective causes by considering them as connected according to the relation of purposes . . . Teleology, therefore, as science, belongs to no doctrine but only to critique."[33] That is, it is purely subjective. Since it was impossible to think of organisms in any manner but as natural purposes, Kant claimed, "the question . . . can only be whether this fundamental proposition is merely subjectively valid, i.e. is a mere maxim of our judgment, or whether it is an objective principle of nature."[34] Kant clearly believed that to hold the latter was to "confuse a fundamental proposition of the reflective with one of the determinant judgment."[35]

Kant's "Dialectic of Teleological Judgment," considered methodologically, ends in precisely the same posture for nature as a whole as he ended the "Analytic" in the consideration of particular organic forms: with a "regulative" or "subjective" interpretation of reflective judgment in its cognitive application (teleology). The question that must be raised seriously is whether this suffices. Can Kant's cognitive system endure the *actuality* of the anomaly of organic forms within a presumably systematic empirical "science" and more fundamentally within a presumably systematic "transcendental logic"? Kant's presentation does not resolve the dilemma it uncovers, but only offers the unpleasant but ostensibly ineluctable expedient of "thinking" about actual problems of nature in terms which violate fundamentally the principle of his own science and epistemology. If, as he contended, the analogy with purpose was a weak projection, contingent upon our discursiveness, and one, moreover, which did not fully fit the case, and if, further, human experience with reason suggested a capacity for intrinsic self-determination as an actual force in the world, however "noumenal" its origins, the force of Kant's own argument thrusts us, willy-nilly, into considerations which must revise his notions of science and of epistemology toward a more inclusive frame of reference.

Kant wished to keep open the possibility of teleological judgments about nature in the "Dialectic of Teleological Judgment" not merely because the problem of organic form could find no other coherent resolution—since in fact even his own proposal offered only a lame resolution which exposed all the weaknesses of discursive reasoning—but because it offered, over and above its empirical assistance, a very important set of metaphysical concommitants. "[I]t is at least possible to consider the material world as mere phenomenon and to think as its substrate something like a thing in itself (which is not phenomenon), and to attach to this a corresponding intellectual intuition (even though it is not ours). Thus there would be, although incognizable by us, a supersensible real ground for nature, to which we ourselves belong."[36] That was the real point of the "Dialectic." Kant aimed not at the "conflict" of empirical research maxims but rather at the issue of plausible metaphysics of nature as a whole.

The issue of organic form renewed in an even more intense form the question of the objectivity of purposiveness in nature which reflective judgment had encountered in the idea of the technic of nature as a whole. The mere existence of *one* natural purpose, Kant argued, required a reconsideration of the entirety of nature as a system of laws: "if we once refer action of this sort *on the whole* to any supersensible ground of determination beyond the blind mechanism of nature, we must judge it altogether according to this principle," Kant wrote.[37] "But this concept leads necessarily to the idea of collective nature as a system in accordance with the rule of purposes, to which idea all the mechanism of nature must be subordinated."[38] Such a system would have its ground beyond nature, for only this would permit both a mechanical and a teleological principle of judgment to be viable in the conception of natural objects: "The principle which should render possible the compatibility of both in judging of nature must be placed in that which lies outside both (and consequently outside the possible empirical representation of nature), but yet contains their ground, i.e. in the supersensible."[39]

With these arguments about the supersensible, the ultimate consideration behind Kant's interest in biological science and in teleology at last comes to the forefront: his concern with theology, with the conception of an intelligent creator. "The natural things that we find possible only as purposes supply the best proof of the contingency of the world-whole."[40] Here is the grand temptation to *metaphysics*. "There is, then, indeed a certain presentiment of our reason or a hint, as it were, given us by nature, that, by means of this concept of final causes, we go beyond nature and could unite it to the highest point in the series of causes."[41] In a word, "teleology . . . finds the consummation of its investigations only in theology."[42] Of course this is "dialectical"—a natural error of reason which carries it beyond the bounds of its legitimate authority. And yet, as the "Dialectic of Teleological Judgment" reveals, it is for Kant an inescapable speculative urge whose very frustration should serve as a useful propaedeutic to man's reflection on his own being-in-the-world—moral considerations that lead once again, but, in Kant's view, with legitimacy, beyond the phenomenal world (i.e., "ethicotheology").[43]

Kant denied the notion of nature as living, as an active subject "in-and-for-itself," adamantly. First, he refused to believe we could know nature as a whole. Second, he argued we could barely "think" of nature as a whole as a purpose. If we did so, we could not think it an intrinsic or real purpose, i.e., he denied that we could even think of nature as alive: "the possibility of living matter cannot even be thought; its concept involves a contradiction, because lifelessness, *inertia,* constitutes the essential character of matter."[44] Kant insisted that "life means the capacity of a substance to determine itself to act from an internal principle, of a finite substance to determine itself to change, and of a material substance to determine itself to motion or rest as change of its state."[45] The only power capable of such self-determination, Kant went on, was intelligent will. Intelligent will could never be found in phenomena; it did not exist in nature. It belonged to noumena. Even man, a being of the natural order, only had "life" by virtue of his other, noumenal aspect.[46]

The philosophical problem of this "purposiveness of nature," Kant insisted, allowed only one solution: a transcendent creator. There were only two alternatives. Either consciousness had to admit that nature *was* capable of intrinsic purposiveness, or one had to assume a supernatural creator. Consequently, Kant believed man could only comprehend the purposiveness of nature through a projection of actual purpose beyond nature onto a transcendent and considerably superior intelligence. In §iv of the Introduction to the *Third Critique,* he wrote: "particular empirical laws, in respect of what is in them left undetermined by these universal laws, must be considered in accordance with such a unity as they would have if an understanding (although not our understanding) had furnished them to our cognitive faculties, so as to make possible a system of experience according to particular laws of nature."[47] To deal with the paradoxes which organic form posed for consciousness, Kant found profoundly attractive, even if merely conjectural, a notion we might term "nature-for-God." In Kant's words, "Nature is no longer estimated as it appears like art, but rather in so far as it actually *is* art, though superhuman art."[48] Such "physicotheology" was inevitable for man's discursive understanding, Kant claimed. This conjecture of a Nature-for-God came to formulation via the analogy of purposiveness. "Our reason has in its power for the judgment no other principle of the possibility of the object, which it inevitably judges teleologically, than that of subordinating the mechanism of nature to the architectonic of an intelligent Author of the world."[49]

Kant's willingness to articulate these speculative notions cannot be explained entirely in terms of the scientific or epistemological quandary into which the problem of organic form plunged discursive reason. Rather, it is crucial to bring into consideration some powerful contextual forces which were driving him toward the articulation and defense of a series of theological and moral commitments of a definitely metaphysical nature. The key to Kant's metaphysical adventure in the *Critique of Judgment* is the need to respond to a powerful new metaphysical vision which was catching the imagination of Germany in the second half of the 1780s: Spinozist pantheism. The issue that must be carried forward into that context is whether Kant had compellingly refuted hylozoism and whether his own position was coherent, either epistemologically or scientifically, i.e., in terms of the exhaustiveness of his concept of causality in transcendental logic, or in terms of the possibility of empirical-scientific accounts of organisms.

🐉 Eleven

THE PANTHEISM CONTROVERSY AND THE *THIRD CRITIQUE*

The Pantheism Controversy arose in August 1785, when Friedrich Jacobi published a slender volume intended to create a scandal over Lessing's alleged Spinozism and atheism.[1] At the end of September, Mendelssohn published *Morgenstunden*, with chapters devoted to the question of Lessing's attitude toward Spinoza.[2] The resulting controversy proved to be one of the most important events in German intellectual life.[3] It is only now beginning to receive the recognition it deserves. Frederick Beiser's recent history of German philosophy in the decade after the *First Critique* is a notable effort to do justice to the controversy.[4] Beiser conceives it as having three levels of significance.[5] The surface issue concerns Lessing's religious loyalties in the context of the rationalism of the Aufklärung. Beneath that is the question of the proper exegesis of Spinoza's philosophy. But Beiser argues correctly that the "inner core" of the controversy is the question of the "authority of reason," i.e., whether philosophy was capable of salvaging a meaningful cosmos.[6]

As a major moment in the struggle of Aufklärung against *Sturm und Drang*, the Pantheism Controversy inevitably affected Immanuel Kant. "Spinozism" was a *symbol* for two crucial issues of the age: "modern scientific naturalism" as "uncompromising mechanism," and criticism of traditional authority, both religious and civil, through "enlightened" examination of its bases. Spinozism appealed to elements in Germany insurgent against orthodoxy in religion and also against the ancien régime in politics.[7] That not only Spinoza's biblical and political criticism but also the "orthodox" reading of his metaphysics certainly had this "radical" potential has been established in a wider eighteenth-century European context by Margaret Jacob.[8] Lessing's Spinozism appeared to embrace both of these aspects, and that was why it provoked so many: "Spinozism" was so radical that it threatened to isolate the Aufklärung from the support of the establishment and bring down upon it the reprisals of orthodox religion. For Mendelssohn, Spinozism was a dangerous and extreme philosophical enterprise which compromised the security of the Aufklärung's progress, but for Jacobi Aufklärung progress itself was the danger, and Mendelssohn's version in particular needed to be overthrown.

Jacobi insisted that it was not merely the "radical" form of Spinozism but the entire enterprise of Aufklärung itself which had to be repudiated to rescue the Christian culture of Germany. In his challenge to the authority of reason and his argument for a "leap of faith" *(salto mortale)*, Jacobi used Spinozism as the exemplar of all consistent philosophy, which, in his view, had to drive its practitioners to a thoroughgoing nihilism.[9] That such nihilism discredited the authority of reason both Jacobi and Mendelssohn, bitter rivals though they were, agreed. The public dispute seemed on all sides deeply antipathetic to "Spinozism." Mendelssohn, and later Kant, accepted Jacobi's claim about Spinoza and argued only that while Spinozism did merit the criticism, other rational philosophy did not. Mendelssohn equivocated even about this.[10] Only Kant clearly defended the "authority of reason," but on the basis of his own peculiar system.

While Jacobi and Mendelssohn—and therefore Kant—saw Spinozism as a force (symbolic or actual) driving philosophy toward nihilism, Herder, Goethe and the generation of Idealism saw Spinozism as a decisive resource, once properly reformulated, for the rescue of philosophy from that debacle. What was it in Spinoza that the generation of the *Goethezeit* found so promising? Certainly not "uncompromising mechanism" or "atheism and fatalism." Instead, they saw in his idea of "intrinsic infinity" a kind of holism which provided a resolution to the conundrum of modern epistemology (in both its mind-body as well as its one-many forms).[11] The most spectacular outcome of the controversy was this formulation of a *heterodox* interpretation of Spinoza—a pantheism of an entirely different sort. What set it off was Lessing's notion of *hen kai pan*.[12] The idea caught the imagination of such figures as Goethe and Herder and was passed on as the decisive metaphysical impulse in the Idealist generation.[13] Of course, they believed Spinozism could only work when enlivened with the new ideas about nature which the poetry and also the science of the later eighteenth century had created.

Upon first learning of Jacobi's disclosures about Lessing, Herder had waxed ecstatic over the slogan *hen kai pan*. He wrote to Jacobi that he felt no one had yet developed that element in Spinoza's philosophy, and lamented that Lessing had not lived long enough to do so.[14] In that same letter, Herder disclosed a long-standing commitment to draw out the parallels among Spinoza, Shaftesbury, and Leibniz—a project which, provoked by this very controversy, resulted in his *Gott: einige Gespräche* of 1787. Then he put forth his main disagreement with Jacobi's view of Spinoza. They differed deeply, he wrote, over the character of the original Being, the *ens entium*. While Jacobi read it as empty, a propertyless ground, Herder read it as full, a positive infinity. Next, Herder questioned the sense of claiming the utter transcendence of God. God had to act in and through things to grant them force *(Kraft)* and order. While he had difficulties with the idea of a "world soul" as Jacobi ascribed it to Lessing, because it seemed to imply that the world was God's body, he claimed that seen properly, i.e., *sub specie aeternitatis*, the material world turned simply into the realized reason of God.

What is of interest for the genesis of the *Third Critique* (and also for the genesis of German Idealism) is how Kant followed out *Jacobi's* reading of Spinoza, and therefore struggled to demonstrate that while Spinoza did lead philosophy into the abyss of atheism and fatalism, his own transcendental idealism would not. He made that effort not only in his immediate comment on the Pantheism Controversy—"Was heißt: sich im Denken orientieren?"—but also in the *Second* and preeminently in the *Third Critique*. For the same reasons, it is just as important to see how Herder followed out *Lessing's* reading of Spinoza and struggled to demonstrate that Spinoza did not lead to atheism and fatalism, but rather to a new metaphysics of immanent reason, pantheism. Herder made this case in *Gott: einige Gespräche*. Kant, learning of this development, applied himself in the *Third Critique* vehemently to the rejection of Herder's vitalist pantheism as well as to the refutation of Spinozist "fatalism." That was the ontological dispute which Kant undertook in the "Dialectic of Teleological Judgment."

Kant's Involvement in the Pantheism Controversy

Embarked on a major controversy, Jacobi turned to his wider circle of intellectual contacts for confirmation and support. Jacobi, Herder, and Goethe met for a conference on Spinoza in Weimar in

September 1784, but they failed to come to an understanding.[15] Confronted with this refusal to see things his way, Jacobi turned elsewhere. In Weimar he, Goethe, and Herder had read with delight Hamann's *Golgotha und Scheblimini,* a polemic directed against Mendelssohn's *Jerusalem* and, more generally, against the secularizing culture of Berlin (and Berlin Jews).[16] Jacobi had already made contact with Hamann, with whom he shared a passionate, fideistic Christian pietism.[17] In November 1784 he sent the materials of the controversy to Hamann, and the Königsberger proved to be the stout support he had sought in vain in Goethe and Herder. Indeed, Hamann had long since been waging a private war with the Berliners. In Jacobi he saw a welcome ally for his own cause.[18]

Hamann and Kant encountered one another in Königsberg society from time to time and exchanged opinions on the contemporary cultural scene.[19] Hamann saw to it that a copy of Jacobi's book passed through Kant's hands. Kant held the *Büchlein* very briefly, but did read it.[20] When Jacobi pressed Hamann for details on Kant's response to the work, Hamann replied: "Kant was very pleased with your presentation and the contents of the whole edition. He had never been able to make sense of Spinoza's system, and he had a long and wide-ranging conversation about it with [Christian] Kraus [a future ally in the controversy], who had not yet read your piece, however."[21]

If Kant found the little book of interest, one suspects it was because it dealt with Lessing. Certainly there is no indication, apart from this ad hoc conversation reported by Hamann, that Kant found it important or that he felt called upon to take up a careful philosophical study of Spinoza.[22] Jacobi's revelations provoked radically different responses from other major German intellectuals of the period. Hamann himself turned to a thorough examination of Spinoza's philosophy in the winter of 1784–85.[23] A few months earlier, Goethe and Herder did as well. All of these figures, and with them Mendelssohn and Jacobi themselves, gave warrant of arduous effort at the study of Spinoza's work. We find the same ardor among the Idealists later. We do not find it in Kant. There is no evidence of any effort on Kant's part to study Spinoza.[24]

The specific circumstance that dragged Kant into the bitter dispute lies, most plausibly, in a line of argument which Mendelssohn first advanced against Jacobi, only to have him take it up in his turn: that Spinoza's metaphysics could be formulated in Kantian terms. Mendelssohn suggested that Jacobi's interpretation was "directly opposed to the system of Spinoza" as he understood it. "When you say the infinite unique substance of Spinoza has for itself alone and outside the particular things no determinate complete existence, you overthrow for me altogether the concept I had of Spinozism."[25] He went on:

If I understand you correctly, only the determinately particular entities are actually existent things [*so sind bloß die bestimmten einzelnen Wesen wirklich existierende Dinge*]; the infinite, on the other hand, as the principle of actuality, arises only in the *aggregate,* in the *totality* of all these particulars [*in dem* Zusammen, *in dem* Inbegriffe *aller dieser Einzelheiten*]. It is thus a mere collective entity which has no other substantiality than that of the parts of which it is composed.[26]

That view was incoherent, he charged. Where was the unity of the manifold? It could not be in the particular parts, which existed only in themselves. Hence it could not arise by their mere summation. There had to be a *prior* whole, "a truly transcendental unity." The notion of a transcendental whole as a prior unity has a clearly Kantian ring. By this point, Mendelssohn had encountered (though, by his own admission, not mastered) Kant's *First Critique.* Taking up Mendelssohn's hint, Jacobi linked Kant with Spinoza. For him all philosophy required tarring with the same brush. Jacobi's *Büchlein* claimed in a footnote that passages in Kant's *Critique of Pure Reason* "are completely in the spirit of Spinoza."[27] Such a claim drew down on Jacobi a bee swarm of protest from the Kantians.[28] Eventually it even forced Kant to take up the whole matter.

On October 16, 1785, Mendelssohn sent Kant a copy of *Morgenstunden* with a cover letter explaining his position in the controversy. Mendelssohn appealed to Kant as a supporter of the Aufklärung: "I fear that philosophy has its fanatics [*Schwärmer*] who persecute just as vehemently and seem even more intent upon proselytizing than the fanatics of positive religion."[29] While Mendelssohn's letter made an impression on Kant, the book with which it arrived made an even stronger one. *Morgenstunden,* as a major philosophical effort to restate the rationalist arguments in theology which Kant had refuted in the *First Critique,* did concern Kant directly in a way that Jacobi's *Spinoza-Büchlein* did not yet seem to do. He found the work, especially with its notorious prefatory remarks labeling him *alles-zermalmende*—"all-destroying"—a direct challenge, and for a time he entertained the notion of writing a response. Kant's new disciples, including the energetic Christian Schütz, protested that some people considered *Morgenstunden* a rebuttal to Kant's *First Critique,* and asked Kant to take Mendelssohn to task for his failure to comprehend the critical philosophy.[30] In the autumn of 1785 it appeared that Kant would do just that. Hamann was delighted with this prospect and spread the news vigorously.[31] He felt it could only help Jacobi's cause. But instead, at the end of November, Kant wrote a letter back to Schütz in which he presented a very gracious reading of Mendelssohn's work, urging the disciples of the critical philosophy to apply constructive criticism to it as "the last testament of dogmatic metaphysics and at the same time its most perfect product."[32] Schütz published Kant's letter along with his own review of *Morgenstunden* along the lines Kant had indicated.

Jacobi was disappointed to hear this, but his primary concern was still to ascertain Kant's response to his own work, to his interpretation of Spinoza. Writing to Hamann on November 18, Jacobi noted that the latter had never elaborated on Kant's impressions of the *Spinoza-Büchlein.* Jacobi wanted to know more about Kant's position.[33] Hamann answered on November 30: "Kant has admitted to me that he has never studied Spinoza and, being so taken up with his own system, that he has neither desire nor time to get involved with anyone else's."[34] Hamann reassured Jacobi that Kant liked his work, and left it at that. Kant simply had nothing more to say about it in 1785.

Things began to change in January 1786, when word of Mendelssohn's sudden death reached Königsberg. Simultaneously, the latter's last literary endeavor, *To the Friends of Lessing,* a brief but passionate repudiation of Jacobi's book, was published by his literary executors.[35] The controversy took on a far more personal and bitter tone as charges were aired that Jacobi's exposé had hastened the death of Mendelssohn. The Berlin circle took up Mendelssohn's cause with vehemence: Nicolai at the *Allgemeine Deutsche Bibliothek,* Johann Erich Biester at the *Berlinische Monatsschrift,* and the literary executors of the late philosopher, among them Marcus Herz, Kant's former student and good friend. Biester, too, was a close friend and the publisher of most of Kant's popular essays.[36] Both Biester and Herz turned to Kant asking him, as an ally of the Berlin Aufklärung, to take up Mendelssohn's cause against Jacobi.[37] In reponse to Herz's plea for his intervention, Kant gave vent to his maximal pique with Jacobi on April 7, 1785: "The Jacobian farce is no serious matter, but only affected geniuscultism [*Genieschwärmerei*], designed to make a name for himself and therefore hardly worthy of an earnest refutation. Maybe I might do something for the *Berlinische Monatsschrift* to expose this hocus-pocus [*Gaukelwerk*]."[38] Strong language: the Berliners seemed about to win him to their side. Hamann and Jacobi recognized the shift in the wind, and Jacobi began to press Hamann for information about Kant's attitude, fearing that he would now become the target of Kant's ire.[39]

On February 11, the Jena *Allgemeine Literatur-Zeitung* had carried an announcement of Jacobi's work, probably by Schütz, furious over Jacobi's cavalier association of Kant with Spinozism. Schütz directed a letter to Kant to the same effect in that month.[40] Jacobi realized he had erred badly, explaining to Hamann in a letter dated March 24 that he had referred to Kant in the *Büchlein* without sufficient discretion. But his anxiety took on tones of belligerence as well: "I would be very sorry if Kant joined the party of the Berlin mongrel-dogs [*Lumpenhunde*], and he would regret it pretty much in the end, for sure."[41] Jacobi worried about Kant's attitude not only to the work already published but also to the work he was about to publish: *Wider Mendelssohns Beschuldigungen* (April 1786). "In any case," Jacobi wrote, "this time he should not have any cause to complain about me."[42]

Indeed, no longer did Jacobi associate Kant with Spinozism or atheism; his new book invoked Kant's philosophy for its demonstration of the proper limits of speculative philosophy and its recognition of the rightful sphere of belief.[43] He sent Hamann a copy for Kant "if you think it good." On May 5, Jacobi added: "If Kant is not entirely happy with one or two places, point out to him that he should keep his disciples in Jena and Gotha in line. These epigoni really do not do him much credit."[44] Jacobi had a sharp eye for Kant's ongoing efforts to build up a following, complaining in an earlier letter, "his relations with the Berliners and the Jena people appear to me to betray something (wanting) petty in his character."[45]

Hamann passed on Jacobi's second pamphlet to Kant as he had been asked, and, on May 28, reported to Jacobi a conversation he had had with Kant about the book. Hamann had asked Kant if he was irked at Jacobi's references to him in the new work. "He assured me the opposite was the case and appeared to be perfectly content with your book."[46] Hamann concluded that Jacobi had nothing to fear; Kant would remain neutral. Certainly Hamann's assessment of Kant was correct. He did not want to enter into polemics on either side. He did not want to be involved at all. The question then arises: Why, in view of this, did Kant feel compelled to write "Was heißt: sich im Denken orientieren?" The answer is, simply, to defend his own philosophy. Letters from his closest supporters and friends convinced him over the late spring and summer of 1786 that not only Jacobi but also Mendelssohn were misleading the public about the critical philosophy. Christian Schütz became agitated at the liberties taken with Kantianism by Jacobi's latest defender, the still-anonymous author of *Resultate der Jacobischen und Mendelssohnschen Philosophie*, Thomas Wizenmann. Schütz wrote a harsh review of the work.[47] At the same time, Ludwig Heinrich Jakob alarmed Kant over the impact of Mendelssohn's work: "in some reviews the impression is quite clearly created that through this text [i.e., *Morgenstunden*] the Kantian *Critique* has received no slight blow, which in my opinion proves clearly that the *Critique* is still only being skimmed over, not studied thoroughly."[48]

But neither Schütz nor Jakob knew how to trigger Kant's fears the way his longtime associate and editor Biester did. It is Biester's letter of June 11, 1786 which proved the precipitating cause of Kant's intervention.[49] From Biester's letter it is clear that he had studied Kant's reply to Marcus Herz of April 1786. It is also fairly clear that Biester gave considerable thought to the presentation of his case. He knew what would seem vital to Kant, and where his ultimate solidarity with the Berlin point of view lay. Thus Biester distinguished two issues in the Pantheism Controversy: the first concerned Lessing's alleged atheism and Mendelssohn's culpability in covering it up; the second concerned the relation of reason to religion (i.e., what Beiser has termed the "authority of reason").

On the first issue Biester was prepared to make wholesale concessions. "I must acknowledge," he wrote, "that after what Herr Jacobi has presented in his latest piece on Lessing, it seems to me very probable that the latter did incline toward atheism."[50] As for Mendelssohn, to judge his intentions was more complex, and Biester claimed that Jacobi very likely withheld information about the precise unfolding of their discussions. But Biester was even willing to admit that Mendelssohn might have shown some personal weakness. Mendelssohn was not above flaws. One of the most outrageous claims of Jacobi and his ilk was that Berliners had turned Mendelssohn into an "idol." This was untrue; the very men who rose to his defense against the slurs of Jacobi had argued vigorously with him over his philosophy. Berlin was a context of free disagreement and debate, and all the talk of a "Berlin way of thinking" which implied the contrary was slander. Yet even this Biester, though now personally involved, declared himself prepared to set aside.

What he could not set aside, what led him to turn to Kant to fulfill what the latter had promised, was a concern for the proper esteem of philosophy and truth. For Biester, Jacobi and his clique represented at one and the same time the two great delusions of the epoch: religious fanaticism and atheism. It was, Biester claimed, "a miraculously strange occurrence that both confusions of the human understanding should be so unified in these new sophists [*Schwindelköpfen*]."⁵¹ Biester helps make clear the confusion Jacobi created by his simultaneous enthusiasm for Spinoza as philosophy and condemnation of that philosophy for the sake of religious faith. What Jacobi represented, according to Biester, was "the undermining and mockery of every rational theory of God, the celebration and virtual idolatry of Spinoza's incomprehensible chimeras, and the intolerant directive to take up a positive religion as the only necessary and at the same time the only available way out for any rational man."⁵² For Biester, this amounted to "affected genius-cultism." Jacobi was out "to make himself important."

The phrases are Kant's—from the Herz letter.⁵³ With those phrases echoing about, Biester became effusive about the salutary result of Kant's prospective intervention: "I wish that men who have hitherto held the helm in philosophy and to whom the entire public turns in grateful recognition as dependable and experienced leaders would publicly declare themselves against all this, so that readers will not be led astray by ungifted and unqualified navigators and dashed upon the reefs." That might have sufficed, but Biester had more. Now he turned to the scandalous use Jacobi had made of Kantian philosophy, which made it imperative "on principle and for the reassurance of your contemporaries" for Kant to disassociate himself from Jacobi.

> When readers find that a writer in every sphere defiant of truth and innocence has taken *you* as a supporting witness, they don't know what to think, and in the end come to believe his claims. I can assure you that this is already the case with many very respectable people, who have been misled in this manner. There is no more odious accusation that an enlightened philosopher can endure than that his principles foster *overt dogmatic atheism*, and thereby [religious] *fanaticism* [*Schwärmerei*]. *Fanaticism via atheism!* That is Jacobi's doctrine,

and he is not daunted from trying to delude the world into thinking *you* agree with him.[54]

Biester called upon his old friend and esteemed colleague to follow through on his pledge to address the matter, above all for the sake of the public, and to state firmly that he "has never been a member of the Christian society for the advancement of atheism and fanaticism." He recognized that Kant hated polemics, but insisted that this matter had to override such scruples. The last thing Kant would want, he added as a final touch, well aware of the change in tone toward Kant in Jacobi's latest work, was for the public to surmise that he withheld criticism because Jacobi had publicly praised him.

As a goad to Kant, that letter had to be a minor masterpiece. Kant felt himself constrained to address the issue. But in fact, he *had* been somewhat mollified by Jacobi's praise. And he *did* hate polemics. And Mendelssohn, too, seemed to be confusing the public about the true merits of the critical philosophy. When, in July 1786, Kant sat down to write "Was heißt: sich im Denken orientieren?" all these considerations intervened. Above all, Kant saw his purpose as the clarification of his own philosophy in contrast to both of the disputants. In that purpose there lay virtually no interest in the substantive issues of Spinoza's philosophy itself or of Lessing's religious stance. He was exclusively interested in the question of the "authority of reason."[55]

Kant's "Was heißt: sich im Denken orientieren?"

Kant set out in "Was heißt" from the standpoint of the discursive character of human consciousness, in which concepts without sense intuition could generate no objective validity.[56] To be sure, even abstracted from sense intuition, they could still have formal usefulness, Kant argued. He pointed not only to *logic,* whose preeminent domain this was, but also to maxims of methodology in interpretative science (i.e., "regulative" ideas of reason). At issue, he went on, was whether beyond these formal and heuristic uses, concepts abstracted from experience could yield valid insight. Traditional dogmatic metaphysics had upheld the view that they could, and Moses Mendelssohn had long aligned himself with this stance. Indeed, his own rational theology depended on it. But in his controversy with Jacobi, Kant noted, Mendelssohn had come to believe that this speculative reason needed the guidance of common sense to help "orient" it.[57] Alas, that move not only undercut the authority of speculative reason, but it also opened the way to "enthusiasm and the total dethroning of reason." To be sure, that was not Mendelssohn's intent, and Kant agreed with him in resisting the claim that reason should be abandoned in favor of immediate belief grounded in tradition or revelation. Reason remained the only recourse in judgment. Yet Kant added that reason had to be cognizant of its own limits. That was the sense of "orientation" that he himself wished to advocate.

This rational problem of orientation in the utterly obscure realm of the supersensible, where concepts had no experience to rely upon to establish objective validity, could only be resolved by a subjective recourse. But far from implying a *salto mortale* in this, Kant connected it rather to the "feeling of reason's own requirement [*das Gefühl des der Vernunft eigenen Bedürfnisses*]."[58] He characterized this process as one in which reason brought its judgments under determinate maxims "solely according to a subjective ground of discrimination of its own faculty of judgment [*lediglich nach einem subjektiven Unterscheidungsgrunde in der Bestimmung ihres eigenen Urtheilsvermögens*]."[59] These two passages are of decisive importance in discerning the distance Kant had come in his stance on transcendental faculties and transcendental deductions since the *First Critique*. In describing this domain, which in the *First Critique* found articulation in the language of reason and its "regulative" function, Kant now wrote of "judgment" and a "faculty of judgment," anticipating the vantage adopted in the *Third Critique*. The anticipatory relation looms even more strongly when we examine the two crucial terms "feeling" *(Gefühl)* and "requirement" *(Bedürfnis)* which Kant introduced in the article.

Kant clarified his formulation in a footnote somewhat later in the essay in the following terms: "Reason does not feel; it recognizes its shortcoming [*Mangel*] and incites [*wirkt*] via the *drive for knowledge* [*Erkenntnistrieb*] the feeling of a need [*Bedürfnis*—better rendered as *requirement*]."[60] Kant went on in the footnote to compare this to his notion of the "moral feeling" in the crucial sense that the feeling is the consequence, not the instigator, of reason.[61] We find ourselves in the innermost reaches of Kantian phenomenology of subjective consciousness: the relation among the subjective faculties. Reason engenders a feeling, but it does so for reasons of its own: that is why *Bedürfnis* must not be read too literally as itself a feeling or need. Reason has an immanent, transcendentally prior propensity to systematicity, to totality, to logical closure. This immanent principle regulates the entire function of the mind—feeling, understanding, and reason itself. It is this which makes knowledge a "drive." It is this which spurs imagination to visions of coherence in the world and in the self. The connection of this relentless law of reason with the proceedings of the other faculties, I submit, forms the systematic foundation for Kant's *Third Critique*.[62]

In the absence of any objective reference, reason tries to find the next closest approximation. If it cannot form a determinate insight into its supersensible object, it tries to reason about the *relation* of this object to the objects of experience, and to bring this relation under logical rules. Hence analogy is the rational form of orientation in the realm of the supersensible. Analogy cannot establish existence; only sense intuition can provide this. Nevertheless, there are representations in the mind to which no sense intuition corresponds. One such representation without correspondence in sense intuition must draw our attention: "the concept of an original being, as the highest intelligence and at the same time the highest good."[63] This notion of an *ens realissimum* or *ens perfectissimum*, Kant argues, is a necessary idea for our rational process. We can only grasp particulars in their concreteness within the conspectus of something all-encompassing. But what Kant insists is that this idea is "regulative," i.e., heuristic, not ontological. The error of all dogmatic metaphysics lay in moving from logical necessity to ontological necessity. Kant's point is just that there can be no analytic deduction of existence. Neither Descartes nor Mendelssohn could make the ontological proof of the existence of God work. Moreover, to believe reason capable of such feats was to throw open the gates to unrestricted speculation, the source of all kinds of *schwärmerisch* chimeras.

What sort of status does such an idea then have? It is cognitively indispensable and objectively indeterminate. For such a notion Kant offered the apt term *Vernunftglaube*, rational belief.[64] Kant argued that we had, for reason's sake, to believe in an original, rational creator. Only this assumption made sense of the purposiveness of nature. "Even if we cannot prove the impossibility of such purposiveness without an *intelligent* first *cause*," the problems of making sense of purposiveness in the world were so pressing that we would be justified in presuming it.[65] This is an anticipation of the argument of physico-theology as a propaedeutic to theism which played such a central role in the "Methodology" section of the "Critique of Teleological Judgment" in the *Third Critique*. Moreover, having established the theoretical plausibility of such an assumption, Kant went on to the question of its practical necessity in an anticipation of the ethico-theological argument for the existence of God which would find expression in the *Second Critique* (1788) and, again, feature importantly in the concluding sections of the *Third Critique*.

Kant devoted the balance of his essay to discriminating his notion of "rational belief" from Mendelssohn's notion that speculative reason could achieve real insight or objective knowledge, on the one hand, and from Jacobi's notion that reason should be thrown over entirely, on the other. Against the latter posture Kant devoted the concluding arguments of his text. The concept of God, he insisted, was a rational idea. It could be found in no intuition first. Indeed, all evidence of God had to be compared to this prior idea of God—not, to be sure, for adequacy, which would be impossible in view of the infinity of God and the incommensurable finitude of all possible experience, but for contradiction. To suspend this rational criterion in considerations of the divine, Kant argued, was the essence of *Schwärmerei,* and its consequences were superstition and atheism.

At that juncture, Kant apostrophized the fideists directly, calling upon them to recognize the danger inherent in their cult of genius, in their extreme claims for freedom. They demanded the freedom to believe whatever they wanted, freedom even from the constraints of reason. Thus the genius claimed to have richer insight than logic could provide. "The consequent assumption of the maxim that reason is not valid as the supreme arbiter we ordinary men call *Schwärmerei,* but those darlings of benevolent nature call it *illumination.*"[66] However prepossessed by this "illumination" the genius might be personally, Kant pointed out, he still had to convince others, and for this he had to have recourse to mere historical facts, to tradition, legend—foundations which could never bear the weight and which, in the end, boiled down to superstition, since reason could not interpose its criteria.

When geniuses took this recourse, they discredited themselves in the eyes of ordinary men, but worse, they provoked a more general skepticism about *any* kind of faith, even "rational belief," and encouraged an equally one-sided insistence that reason had no requirements for belief. That was "unbelief," the view that all faith was superstition—the stance of the radical Enlightenment, of Hume and of Voltaire. That "atheism" in its turn, Kant went on, had deleterious consequences beyond *its* intentions as well, for with the dissolution of the belief in God, the claims of morality upon the human heart were loosened and a "libertinism" *(Freigeisterei)* of conduct followed a free-thinking in matters theological.[67] That in its turn could only provoke the state to intervene to secure order in society. Consequently, the ultimate outcome of such radical claims of freedom against the legislation of reason could only be the ironic throttling of any freedom whatever under the tutelage of the state. That was why Kant argued so strenuously for reason as man's ultimate recourse in judgment. Reason as arbiter left man to his own self-determination; such rational freedom was the essence of "enlightenment." To forsake it was to run the risk of a repression which would affect not merely the extremists but everyone.

The Theological-Political Context of the Pantheism Controversy

One cannot stress too strongly Kant's attentiveness to the political context of religious disputes as it was expressed in this closing argument. In it one can find the key to Kant's frame of mind for the next nine years, up through the controversy surrounding his *Religion Within the Limits of Reason Alone.* Moreover, one can hardly find a clearer connection between this very lively contextual sensitivity and Kant's conception of "enlightenment" as both the principle and the project of his epoch.[68] Kant made perfectly clear in these lines the decisive connection between security and liberty offered by his notion of rational belief or enlightenment.[69]

After the publication of Karl Leonhard Reinhold's *Briefe über die Kantische Philosophie* starting in 1786, Kantianism had become all the rage in Germany.[70] In April of that year, the original printing of the *First Critique* had sold out. This allowed Kant to make important clarifying revisions and issue a second edition of the *Critique of Pure Reason* in 1787. It appeared that he had succeeded at last in taking command of the German philosophical scene, and he could afford now to devote himself entirely to the completion of his monumental systematic edifice. Hamann characterized Kant aptly in May 1787: he "carried on his work on his own system without caring much about anything else in the world, caring neither what takes place there nor what it thinks of him."[71] Kant no longer worried about the victory of his system. Indeed, he read Jacobi's preoccupation with his *First Critique* as yet another sign of the pervasive penetration of his critical philosophy. Of course he claimed that Jacobi had misunderstood him, but he claimed that about everyone.[72]

There were still political problems, however. The authorities had developed suspicions as to Kant's religious orthodoxy starting with the *First Critique*. Since it systematically demolished all rational arguments in theology, it was received by many in the theological community with dismay. Kant's *Grounding of the Metaphysics of Morals* (1785) did little to ease this suspicion in orthodox circles, and indeed contained material which might be construed as even more damaging to religious orthodoxy.[73] When Moses Mendelssohn called Kant the "all-destroyer" in his widely read preface to *Morgenstunden* (1785), he was referring to this theological impact. What Mendelssohn, Kant's friend, lamented without ire, others, less kindly disposed, were condemning in the halls of power.

At Marburg, a cabinet order had been issued banning the teaching of Kantian philosophy starting in the winter term of 1786.[74] The grounds were that Kant's thought led to total skepticism and jeopardized public morals! The source of such nonsense was Kant's old antagonist Feder at Göttingen. But others, like Christoff Meiners, in the preface to his *Psychology*, propagated these distortions.[75] Indeed, as Kantianism became more popular, official scrutiny increased. The death of Frederick II in 1787 and the succession of the far more conservative Frederick William II boded further state interventions in matters of faith and morals, and Kant, as the sequel showed, was far from exempt from suspicion.

Whether Kant himself wished to be so threatening to orthodox religion may be seriously questioned, but that his thought did inspire in others a radicalism in matters religious which could only occasion consternation among orthodox authorities can be proven easily. With *Schadenfreude* Hamann reported one particularly juicy instance of this to Herder as early as 1785. Some fifty theology students who declared themselves Kantians and disdainers of religion *(Religionsspöttern)* had risen up, arguing, in Hamann's words, that "there could be no moral philosophy [*Sittenlehre*] nor sound reason, nor public happiness under Christianity. Whether Kant has been informed about this equally outrageous and pathetic occurrence I don't know."[76]

Whatever Kant may have meant, there were Kantians who viewed his achievement as radically hostile to orthodoxy.[77] Official displeasure over Kantian extremism at Tübingen was communicated from Stuttgart to Berlin in the late 1780s, and the incident at Marburg was still fresh in Kant's memory.[78] Under the circumstances it is not hard to understand why he should have felt it necessary to stress the compatibility of his "theism" with religious orthodoxy and to distance it as much as possible from any form of "deism," in particular the Spinozan-Herderian sort.

Into this charged context in mid-1787, Herder threw his new work, *Gott: einige Gespräche*, raising once again all the issues of Spinozism and pantheism. This time things were even more appalling from Kant's vantage, for Herder was an unequivocal advocate of these new notions, celebrating Lessing, glorifying Spinoza, and perpetrating an unabashed pantheism with all the considerable power of his literary style and intellectual reputation. But there was also a personal element. Herder and Kant had become public antagonists over Kant's reviews of Herder's *Ideen zur Philosophie der Geschichte der Menschheit* (vol. 1, 1784), and Kantians could not help but see in Herder's new publication evidence of his bitterness toward their master.[79] Into his serenity Kant found once again that his rival had intruded.

Herder's Gott: einige Gespräche

What exactly did Herder argue in *Gott: einige Gespräche*? Quite simply, he elaborated on that coherence of the positions of Spinoza, Shaftesbury, and Leibniz which had already informed the *Ideen* and his correspondence with Jacobi of 1784–85. The publication of *Gott* in 1787 not only fulfilled Herder's personal commitment to write an essay on that theme, but it had three more immediate "inducements which the times themselves offered."[80] First, he wished to defend Spinoza from Jacobi's misinterpretation. Hence it was a work intended as part of the Pantheism Controversy. Second, he wished to *revise* Spinoza in the light of the new science, on the one hand, and of his own theological notions, on the other. In this light, it was part of those stirrings toward metaphysics that originated in the *Sturm und Drang* intuition of nature. But finally, he wished to attack Kantian philosophy and its inroads into theology. That this was a personal and bitter motive goes without saying. The complexity of these intentions resulted in a measure of obscurity in the work.

The first of the five dialogues of *Gott: einige Gespräche* sought to refute all the misrepresentations of Spinoza propagated by Pierre Bayle. This dialogue was the most effective in its argument. No less a critic than Schiller appreciated it, though the balance of the work left him cold.[81] The second dialogue located the core of Spinoza's philosophy in the notion of intrinsic infinity, in contrast to the merely indefinite extensiveness of a sum of finites.[82] Herder recognized "that few will understand this distinction between the infinite-in-itself and the endless conceived in the imagination in terms of time and space, a distinction which is yet true and necessary."[83] A correct understanding of this notion would dismiss the charge "of enclosing God within the world and identifying Him with it." Herder insisted that the notion of intrinsic infinity required a greatness of the whole beyond any mere sum of its parts, even as it required its logical priority. Hence, Herder interpreted Spinoza as pan*en*theism, not pantheism, though he lacked the terminology.[84]

The dilemma in Spinoza, Herder went on, lay not in this notion, but rather in his all-too-Cartesian identification of extension with matter. Spinoza identified God with extended matter. Herder accounted for this not simply by "pernicious Cartesian explanations" but also by "the childhood of natural science" in Spinoza's times, contending that more recent science offered the resolution of Spinoza's dilemma of finding a true unity between the disparate attributes of thought and matter in original Being.[85] The solution lay in the idea of "substantial forces," a theory of the dynamism of nature which had been articulated by Leibniz and extended by Boscovich. In that language it was possible to restate Spinoza's doctrine of the one substance as "absolutely infinite—that is, a substance consisting of infinite attributes, of which each expresses eternal and infinite essentiality" in a more plausible form: *"That the Deity reveals Himself in an infinite number of forces in an infinite number of ways."*[86]

Herder believed the innovations in the theory of the physical sciences had a direct bearing on the thorniest of metaphysical issues, claiming that his reworking of Spinozism along these lines provided a coherent interpretation which would bring

an end to all the objectionable expressions of how God, according to this or that system, may work on and through dead matter. It is not dead but lives. For in it and conforming to its outer and inner organs, a thousand living, manifold forces are at work. The more we learn about matter, the more forces we discover in it, so that the empty conception of a dead extension completely disappears. Just in recent times, what numerous and different forces have been discovered in the atmosphere! How many different forces of attraction, union, dissolution and repulsion, has not modern chemistry already found in bodies?[87]

Herder's "dynamic pantheism" thus invoked the most important recent innovations in the theories of the natural sciences, especially in the fields of electricity, chemistry, and biology.[88]

Herder used the fourth dialogue to express his distance from Jacobi in the strongest form: "I . . . took up Mendelssohn's *Morgenstunden,* and saw that we were more or less in agreement on the historical fact of what Spinoza's system really was."[89] Herder publicly sided with Mendelssohn, and even more with Lessing, against Jacobi. All the more astounding, then, the turn which Herder took when he came to Jacobi's doctrine of belief, toward which he had always been so cool. In *Gott* Herder picked up the idea and turned it against Kant. According to Herder, the truth of Jacobi's doctrine of belief lay in its insistence on the existential situatedness of thought.

Without existence, and a series of existences, man would not think as he does. Therefore, the purpose of his thought cannot be to dream fantasies and to play with illusory ideas and words as if with a self-made reality, but rather, as he says, "to disclose Existence" . . . Such knowledge, in union with the inner feeling for truth, is alone true. It alone illumines the spirit, nurtures the heart, brings order and regularity into all the spheres of our life.[90]

Against this holistic mode of coming to grips with reality, Herder found wanting all "over-subtle reasoning," all "metaphysical hairsplitting." Great philosophers, he went on, drawing up a list conspicuous for the absence of Kant, "loved precise ideas" but as "philosopher[s] deserving of the name," did not indulge "empty phantoms of an idly speculating imagination."[91]

Herder asserted—hardly *argued*—the validity of rational theology along the lines of Spinoza's ontological argument against "the transcendental philosopher, that is, one who overreaches himself."[92] Irony, alas, here showed its impotence against discursive logic. Herder went on as if a turn of phrase had settled the accounts. His character, Theophron, protested: "I, at least, . . . feel so enervated by every philosophy which plays with that type of symbolical words without ideas and without objects, that I cannot soon enough return to nature, to existence, just to become aware again that I am alive."[93] Then he went on far too long and far too obscurely to articulate a metaphysics of his own, trying to identify Spinoza's austere Divinity with Christian Providence and—of course—metempsychosis. While Herder recognized that Spinoza had an authentic notion of God as thinking substance—"I com-

pletely deny that Spinoza turned God into an unthinking being"—
he could not articulate that recognition without falling back toward
some of the anthropomorphic projections which Spinoza strove to
eliminate, and which Herder knew should not be countenanced, as
he indicated in his critical remarks about Leibniz.[94] Persisting
nonetheless, Herder laid himself wide open to the attack for "syncretism" which Jacobi and Kant immediately and effectively
launched.[95]

The Kantians' Response

Herder's work stirred a great deal of concern among the new Kantians at Jena by its open hostility toward Kant. Friedrich Schiller, a
recent convert, wrote to his friend, Körner, a more adept Kantian,
of his impressions of the new work, and Körner supplied him with a
detailed critique from the standpoint of orthodox Kantianism.[96] In
addition it is very likely that Schiller discussed the work with the two
most prominent Kantians in Jena, Schütz and Reinhold.

With all that, it is impossible that Kant would not have heard of
Herder's work very shortly after its publication, and indeed, if we
consider the text of the *Second Critique*, composed over that summer, we can find clear evidence of Kant's irritation with Herder and
his preoccupation with Spinozism. Certainly we know that Kant
had read the work by August of 1789, for he wrote a letter to Jacobi
which indicated his reading. But we can establish that the circle
around Kant was already very hot about Herder's *Gott* in 1787,
from the letter of one of Kant's Königsberg cronies, Christian
Kraus, to Christian Schütz, dated December 1787. Kraus wrote:
"It is appropriate to expose the pantheistic *Schwärmerei* which
dominates so many, particularly young minds, and the aesthetic-
metaphysical bombast with which Herder as a clever rogue calcu-
latedly nurtures his public."[97] The most alarming thing was that
many of these young enthusiasts for pantheism were at the same
time enthusiasts for Kantianism! That, Kant's circle believed, could
only result in political mischief. Thus, Kraus began working upon a
refutation of pantheism.[98]

Mindful of Kant's hostility to Herder, Jacobi sent him a copy of
the new edition of his work on Spinoza, full of criticisms of Herder
and praise for Kant. Kant's response was everything he could have
desired. In his letter to Jacobi of August 30, 1789, acknowledging
the gift, Kant praised the work for its "demonstration of the difficulties that beset the teleological path to theology."[99] It had been

this, Kant suggested, that had set Spinoza on his misguided course of denying teleology altogether. Kant went on to claim that it was merely a secondary matter *(Nebensache)* whether one came to a commitment to theism from reason or from revelation, for the point was to defend it, and freedom with it, against the "syncretism of Spinoza" and the "deism of Herder's *Gott.*"[100]

What characterizes all forms of syncretism generally is their foundation in a lack of uprightness [*Mangel an Aufrichtigkeit*]: a trait of mind which is particularly typical of this great artist in illusions (which, as through a magic lantern, make miraculous things momentarily manifest, only thereafter swiftly to vanish, leaving behind still among the naive a sense of wonderment and the impression that something extraordinary must be behind it all, which they just didn't catch).[101]

With this extremely caustic characterization of Herder, Kant declared Jacobi his ally, and explained that he meant him no harm in the essay "Was heißt," which he had written only under extreme pressure to dissociate himself from Spinozism. It behooves us to step back and juxtapose for a moment this letter of August 1789 *to* Jacobi with the letter of April 1786 *about* Jacobi. How things have changed! In 1786 Jacobi was the *Schwärmer,* but in 1789 he is shoulder to shoulder with Kant *against* the *Schwärmer.* In 1786 Jacobi was part of the genius-cult, ranged alongside Herder. In 1789, all this is forgotten. *Herder* is Kant's overweening concern.

Indeed, Kant and his circle had been agitated over Herder and pantheism from the moment of his publication of *Gott* in mid-1787. Kant's worries about political backlash had come too true with Wöllner's Edict of 1788. With some of his own followers lured toward pantheism, Kant decided to debunk it himself in the *Third Critique.* Kant's attacks on the "analogon of life" and on "hylozoism" in the *Third Critique* resonate in their very language with the attacks on Herder of five years earlier.[102] What provoked their reassertion was Herder's *Gott.* Kant's project in the "Dialectic of Teleological Judgment" was to refute such dangerous "syncretism."

Twelve

KANT'S ATTACK ON SPINOZA IN THE "DIALECTIC OF TELEOLOGICAL JUDGMENT"

aving explored the Pantheism Controversy in detail from the Kantian vantage, it has become clear why the issue of Spinozism should have become so central to the "Dialectic of Teleological Judgment." Kant's struggle with Spinoza, as Allison has noted, was "central, not peripheral, to the overall argument of the *Critique of Judgment*."[1] Indeed, I wish to argue that it is precisely as he composed these sections in late summer 1789 that Kant made his "ethical turn." Therefore, §§72–77 of the "Critique of Teleological Judgment" represent the heart of the whole work. Their concern is explicitly with (dogmatic) systems of ontology and their plausibility in accounting for the complexities of objective purposiveness within a lawfully coherent nature.

In §72 of the *Third Critique* Kant laid out a typology of "dogmatic metaphysical" ontologies. At the outset of §73 Kant asked: "What do all these systems desire? They desire to explain our teleological judgments about nature."[2] Kant formulated all the ontologies in terms of his concept of "objective purposiveness." He discriminated between "realism" and "idealism" of this purposiveness and between "physical" and "hyperphysical" accounts of causality. This occasioned a fourfold schema, which he set out in §72:

1. *idealist-physical:* "lifeless matter," the mechanistic materialism of *causality,* which Kant associated with Epicurus and Democritus among the ancients;

2. *idealist-hyperphysical:* a "lifeless God," or *fatality,* which Kant associated with Spinoza among the moderns;

3. *realist-physical:* "living matter," the doctrine of *hylozoism,* which Kant did not *explicitly* link to any thinker or school; and

4. *realist-hyperphysical:* a "living God," the doctrine of *theism,* which "certainly is superior to all other grounds of explanation" because it ascribed intelligent will to a transcendent Creator and thereby "rescues in the best way the purposiveness of nature."[3]

By the realism and idealism of objective purposiveness Kant meant the validity and illusion of natural purpose. Hence all "idealist" ontologies rejected teleology. Kant's setting of all metaphysics in a teleological framework seems for that reason forced. These metaphysics address themselves with equal plausibility to the ancient question of the One and the Many, or, in a more recent but apposite formulation, of the relation of Being *(Sein)* to entities *(Seienden),* in terms of the classical language of substance.[4] By thrusting discourse on ontology which rejected teleology into that alien language, Kant did it fundamental violence. By setting the problem of entities in terms of the language of purposiveness, he generated an absurdity: "If all things must be thought of as purposes, then to be a thing is the same as to be a purpose."[5] That was, as he claimed, preposterous. But he was wrong to castigate Spinoza or the "schoolmen" for this folly: it was his own shift of language which had precipitated it.[6]

These schoolmen had something else in mind: what Kant termed their doctrine of the "transcendental perfection of things (in reference to their proper being), according to which everything has in itself that which is requisite to make it one thing and not another."[7] This was simply what the schoolmen meant by the concept substance. In their language system, substance signified entity, i.e., a determinate grammatical-logical subject which was eligible for predications. A substance was simply that about which something could be said. Discourse could illuminate sufficient of its properties—achieve a degree of completeness ("perfection") in their listing—that its individuality became clear and distinct. But the question of entities as substances became clouded when the concept of "perfection" was lifted out of its scholastic sense of quantitative completeness and transposed into Kant's language system as qualitative perfection or purpose.[8] Such a notion of perfection entailed intrinsic self-determination, Kant argued. While this made sense of some entities—organic forms and intelligent life—it added to the ordinary sense of entity a complexity too heavy for it to sustain. Not all things were purposes. Kant's tactic makes sense only in the context of a new urgency about the prospect of a metaphysic grounded in teleology which could claim validity. That was exactly what the pantheist reading of Spinozism seemed to entail.[9]

Kant's transcendental criticism entitled him, on the most favorable reading, to reject all metaphysics, not to privilege some.[10] The moment he moved from the level of epistemological scruple to a disputation of particular conceptions, he became but one metaphysician more. That Kant preferred the fourth of the dogmatic options he described is perfectly clear, even though he acknowledged that it could not be proven theoretically. He criticized the others not merely for their dogmatism but for their dogma. And the two which drew the most sustained criticism were "fatality" and "hylozoism," or in other terms, Spinozism and pantheism.

In §73 Kant offered more extensive criticism of each of the metaphysical views he had schematized in §72. Conspicuously, his argument against Spinozism was by far the most protracted. In that section, Kant gave his most elaborate characterization of Spinoza's doctrine of original Being:

> to this Being, as substrate of those natural things, he ascribes in regard to them, not causality, but mere subsistence. On account of its unconditioned necessity, and also that of all natural things as accidents inhering in it, he secures, it is true, to the forms of nature that unity of ground which is requisite for all purposiveness, but at the same time he tears away their contingence, without which no *unity of purpose* can be thought, and with it all design, inasmuch as he takes away all intelligence from the original ground of natural things.[11]

Kant distinguished "causality" from "subsistence," and though he conceded that Spinoza established the "unity of ground" *(Einheit des Grundes)* which was necessary for a comprehension of the "forms of nature" *(Naturformen)*, he argued that Spinoza's view robbed them of "contingence" *(Zufälligkeit)*, and hence of "unity of purpose." Spinoza's original Being *(Urwesen)*, in which "accidents inhere," constituted a mere "substrate of things in nature." This in turn meant that Spinoza denied all design *(alles Absichtliche)* and even understanding *(Verstand)* to the "original ground."

Kant's whole sense of Spinoza centered around the doctrine of a "lifeless God." "So much is clear," he wrote, "that on this theory the purposive combination in the world must be taken as undesigned; for although derived from an original Being, it is not derived from His understanding or from any design of His, but rather from the necessity of His nature and of the world unity which emanates from Him."[12] Kant elaborated on the meaning of "fatality" in §73 by offering the following characterization of Spinozism: "as it appeals to something supersensible to which our insight does not extend, [it] is not so easy to controvert, but that is because its concept of the original Being is not possible to understand."[13]

Kant was not merely claiming "dialectical excess" in Spinoza's notion of God; he was claiming it was determinately *wrong*. When he argued that it was not possible to understand Spinoza's concept of the original Being he meant that the notion was logically incoherent. That was a much more radical claim, and one that Kant could not sustain. In essence, what Kant, following Jacobi, claimed was that Spinoza denied intellect or thought to the original Being.[14] Yet this representation of Spinoza's original Being as "lifeless" is more than a little problematic.[15]

To summarize Kant's key charges against Spinoza's notion of original Being *(Sein)*, Kant believed Spinoza's God was *lifeless* since:

1. Spinoza denied God *intelligence;*
2. Spinoza denied God *purposiveness;*
3. Spinoza denied God *freedom;* and
4. Spinoza denied God *causality.*

Consequently, Spinoza made God over into a mere *Urstoff*— primordial matter, "blind necessity"—i.e., his concept of God as substance was "lifeless." As I will show, however, Kant's own conjectures about the *intellectus archetypus* in §§76–77 of the *Third Critique* demonstrate the internal coherence of a model of intellect very close to what Spinoza ascribed to his original Being.[16]

1. *The Question of God's Intelligence.* Kant claimed that Spinoza "takes away all intelligence from the original ground of natural things" for the things of the world are "not derived from His understanding or from any design of His . . ." But that is widely at variance with what Spinoza actually claimed in the *Ethics.* There is a profuse and profound ascription of intelligence to God in that work.[17] One is at a loss to see how Kant can have made his assertion. Can it be that Spinoza should have used the terms "thought" and "intellect" but not understood them, or not meant them?[18] Is it that elsewhere Spinoza made arguments or assertions which contradicted these—consciously or unwittingly? That seems a more likely alternative. Yet we must at the very least recognize that Spinoza affirmed the consciousness, the self-consciousness and indeed the infinite consciousness of God, for which all possibility is actual. However contradictory his philosophy might ultimately be proven

to be, Spinoza cannot be charged with having altogether denied these things, and in this measure Kant was just plain wrong. But the point needs to be sharpened. *Was* Spinoza contradictory?

There is a notorious passage, the "Note to Proposition 17" of book 1 of the *Ethics,* in which Spinoza proposed to show "that neither intellect nor will appertain to God's nature."[19] There stands our contradiction, apparently. It is shocking, but it was meant to be. A serious interpreter, bearing all the other passages in mind, would seek to reconcile the apparent discord. A hostile reader, seeking to be scandalized by offense to his religious sensibilities, would latch onto these words with a vengeance. Kant was certainly not that kind of a reader, but *Jacobi* was.

What did Spinoza mean by his shocking line? For Spinoza the terms "intellect" and "will" were distinctly human attributes and he envisioned those of more conventional piety saying "they know of nothing more perfect, which they can attribute to God, than that which is the highest perfection in ourselves."[20] The hubris of that projection provoked Spinoza's assertion, as he made vividly clear in a remarkable and conclusive passage:

> if intellect and will appertain to the eternal essence of God, we must take these words in some signification quite different from those they usually bear. For intellect and will, which should constitute the essence of God, would perforce be as far apart as the poles from the human intellect and will, in fact, would have nothing in common with them but the name; there would be about as much correspondence between the two as there is between the Dog, the heavenly constellation, and a dog, an animal that barks.[21]

Spinoza hardly denied intellect to God; he wished to alert his reader to the idea that divine intellect was not simply some multiple analogue of ours. Let Spinoza make his own point: "Now the intellect of God is the cause of both the essence and the existence of our intellect; therefore, the intellect of God so far as it is conceived to constitute the divine essence, differs from our intellect both in respect to essence and in respect to existence, nor can it in anywise agree therewith save in name, as we have said before."[22] To believe that because Spinoza denied God's intellect corresponded to ours, Spinoza denied him intellect altogether is to believe there can only be one *kind* of intellect, with differences of degree. Jacobi might hold such a view. Kant could not. One of his crucial philosophical strategies was to distinguish our *discursive* intellect from a conjectural alternative form: the *intuitive* intellect. This *intellectus archetypus*, I contend, tallies altogether well with the intellect of Spinoza's God.

2. *The Question of God's Purposiveness.* Kant contended that Spinoza's original Being did not act by design, intention, or purpose; there was in it no causality through ideas. To evaluate the significance of this claim, we must recall that Kant meant by purpose the relation whereby an "idea" (technically, a representation, or *Vorstellung*) served as the ground or cause of the "existence" of an object.[23] Now, in man, merely thinking, even knowing the representation does not generate the thing.[24] What is required is an intervening *praxis*, actualization. Men labor to bring forth, and they have projected this back upon their "creator." In religious language, God "labored" seven days to create the world. Kant's model, too, read divine causality on the model of human practical purposiveness. This anthropomorphism was pervasive and basic to the entire Kantian system. The kind of God Kant required in his ethico-theology was the "living" God of the Christian tradition, with a providential and personal character, who "created" the world.

Yet this whole distinction of mental from material, intended from actual, only makes sense in the context of human discursive nature. To project these quandaries of mortal man back upon the original Being is problematic. Spinoza could not accept this: "this doctrine does away with the perfection of God: for, if God acts for an object, he necessarily desires some thing which he lacks." The notion of final cause, the language of purposiveness, when applied to God, "makes that which is by nature first to be last, and that which is highest and most perfect to be most imperfect."[25] The notion of God as a purposive creator, a creator from intention and design who had to realize the world in an act, was profoundly foreign to Spinoza.

Hence Kant was correct in his claim that Spinoza denied purposiveness to his original Being. What is incorrect is the implication Kant drew, namely, that God could not any longer be regarded as a cause. Spinoza still felt entitled to view the intellect of God as the cause of all entities. That causality was not transeunt and sequential, however, but immanent and eternal. Nevertheless, as cause, it remained logically prior.

If intellect belongs to the Divine nature, it cannot be in nature, as ours is generally thought to be, posterior to, or simultaneous with the things understood, inasmuch as God is prior to all things by reason of his causality. On the contrary, the truth and formal essence of things is as it is, because it exists by representation as such in the intellect of God. Wherefore the intellect of God, in so far as it is conceived to constitute God's essence, is, in reality, the cause of things, both of their essence and of their existence.[26]

This notion of causation, and especially of *divine* causation, will concern us further below.

    3. *The Question of God's Freedom.* With the rubric of "fatality" and with his frequent suggestion that it was "mere necessity" and "blind necessity" that was operative in the relation between Spinoza's original Being and the world, Kant made the claim that Spinoza's God had no freedom. Spinoza had a very clear notion of what freedom signified within his system: "That thing is called free, which exists solely by the necessity of its own nature, and of which the action is determined by itself alone. On the other hand, that thing is necessary, or rather constrained, which is determined by something external to itself to a fixed and definite method of existence or action."[27] The implications for God were drawn quite clearly: "God acts solely by the laws of his own nature, and is not constrained by anyone." Hence, "God is the sole free cause. For God alone exists by the sole necessity of his nature, and acts by the sole necessity of his nature."[28] Spinoza's doctrine quite unequivocally asserted the freedom of God—and equally denied it to every other entity. It was precisely Spinoza's doctrine of a substance that its existence should be determined solely by its own essence. By that very definition he could conceive of only a single substance, God, as existent. God as this one substance possessed an intrinsic, self-determining necessity which was freedom. Entities, which owed both their essence and their existence to the original substance, necessarily could not enjoy such freedom.

    What did freedom mean to Kant, then, that he should have found it denied in Spinoza? Manifestly he did not mean caprice. Freedom for Kant was precisely the capacity to conform to a self-legislated principle. Rationality was the ground of freedom. Only because that rationality was the intrinsic essence of man as noumenon did he have freedom. So much more, then, should this reasoning apply to Kant's notion of God. But then it would appear difficult, apart from the imagistic wrappings, to see what was so different about the two stances. Indeed, I submit Kant's doctrine of "life" and of freedom at the level of an original Being do not significantly differ from Spinoza, properly understood. The real locus of conflict between Kant and Spinoza on the question of freedom lay not at the level of the original Being or God, but rather at the level of the individual existent human being. Kant insisted upon, and Spinoza rejected utterly, the freedom of existent man. This situation is at the heart of the conflict between the two great philosophers. Kant's entire philosophical energy radiates from his concern for the efficacious practical freedom of man, i.e., his moral duty in the world of things. That was the origin of his language of purposiveness. It was the heart of Kantianism. But Spinoza utterly denied it.[29]

4. *The Question of God's Causality.* Kant argued that Spinoza confused causality with inherence or subsistence.[30] Kant agreed with his contemporary, Crusius, in maintaining that the logical relation of ground to consequence was not the same as, and could not serve as the basis for, the actual relation of cause to effect. Logical relations were "analytic"; actual relations were "synthetic."[31] Precisely what the latter entailed was the separateness of the *relata*. That separateness, for Kant, was only conceivable in terms of existential— i.e., material—separateness. All causality, therefore, required materiality and was transeunt. Such a posture creates enormous difficulties for purposiveness as a mode of causality, for purposiveness posits an immaterial (noumenal) cause as materially (phenomenally) efficacious. This Kant admitted to be flagrantly incongruent with categorial understanding of causality, but he held out that it was not in itself contradictory.[32]

The essential issue lies elsewhere, however. Kant has formulated the entire problem in terms of a *discursive* rational being, but Spinoza was conceiving of something quite other. What may be true of the cognitive problem of man in view of his discursive situation, and of the practical problem of man, in view of the difference between an intention and an object, between ought and is, simply may not be projected back upon the original Being. As a consequence, Kant's distinction of ground and consequence from cause and effect, of logical from actual, simply does not apply. To demonstrate this we have only to consider Kant's own brilliant juxtaposition of discursive and intuitive intelligence in §§76–77 of the *Third Critique.*

In those sections, Kant's purpose was to explain the problem of human consciousness in terms of the conflict between reason's aspiration to totality and understanding's requirements for validity—

in short, the discursive dilemma that objective knowledge required, in humans, sensible intuition in addition to pure reason. To make clear the implications of discursiveness in man, Kant argued, "the idea of a possible understanding different from the human must be fundamental."[33] That idea was the notion of an "intuitive" understanding. Kant used this thought experiment throughout his critical period, and in the *Third Critique* he spelled out the essential elements of the juxtaposition.

For the discursive intellect, the distinction of the possible from the actual was decisive. Human beings were caught in the disjunction of representation *(Vorstellung)* and object, of intention and realization, of ought and is. Cognitively this expressed itself in the empty liberty of thought, which could think possible all that was noncontradictory, but could not entail its actuality. *But* "if our understanding were intuitive, it would have no objects but those which are actual. Concepts (which merely extend to the possibility of an object) and sensible intuitions (which give us something without allowing us to cognize it thus as an object) would both disappear."[34] Concepts, as designations of the merely possible, would disappear because all possibility in an intuitive understanding would entail actuality. Similarly the dilemma of the discursive intellect over ought and is would fall away "were reason considered as in its causality independent of sensibility . . . and so as cause in an intelligible world entirely in agreement with the moral law . . . [I]n such a world there would be no distinction between 'ought to do' and 'does,' between a practical law of that which is possible through us and the theoretical law of that which is actual through us."[35]

Most pertinent to the question of theism versus deism and of the place of teleology in their conflict, Kant wrote that for the discursive intellect the whole could only be achieved by the mechanical summation of its parts. Discursive understanding had to proceed from analytic-universals to particulars in the construction of any concept of an object. But Kant claimed we could "think an *intuitive* understanding, which does not proceed from the universal to the particular, and so to the individual (through concepts)" but would instead proceed "from the *synthetic-universal* (the intuition of a whole as such), to the particular, i.e. from the whole to the parts."[36]

The closest approximation discursive understanding could make to the notion of a systemic whole, an organic entity, was via the language of purposiveness. In that language, a representation of the whole stood prior to the existence of that whole, and formed, as it were, the causal security that subordinated the parts pending its constitution.[37] Manifestly this language did not really capture the relation of whole to parts which Kant characterized as accessible to the hypothetical intuitive intellect and as alone adequate to the notion of a true whole prior to and higher than its parts.[38] Hence purposiveness as a model was a discursive approximation, and a weak one. It was hardly consistent with an intuitive intellect. For that intellect, to think *was* to actualize. Furthermore, the whole notion of the contingency of particulars, as in the problem of empirical nature's lawfulness for a discursive understanding, becomes irrelevant for the intuitive intellect. Kant's strictures against Spinoza's characterization of the causal relation of his original Being to natural things are palpably out of place. One final point: Kant explicitly stated that the idea of such an *intellectus archetypus* "contains no contradiction."[39] With that he destroyed his own claim that there was a logical incoherence in Spinoza's notion of the original Being. In sum, Kant's interpretation of Spinoza's original Being as a "lifeless God" fails utterly.

Still, if terming Spinoza's God "lifeless" in Kant's technical sense of the term has been shown inappropriate, that does not signify that it was anything approaching the orthodox theistic version of a *personal* God. Having devoted so much energy to revindicating God in his attribute of "thinking thing" or thought in Spinoza, we run the risk of understating the inevitably scandalous concommitant position of that philosophy, namely, that God was also an "extended thing" or matter. Whatever may have been the merits of the first position, the mere claim that God was matter remained outrageous beyond redemption to orthodox religious sensibility. God as substance in Spinoza's sense blurred with God as substance in the vulgar sense, and the result seemed indiscernible from atheistic materialism. Just by that measure had the doctrine of pantheism served the radical Enlightenment of the eighteenth century against orthodox religion, and it was no coincidence that Spinoza was dear to the hearts of these deist free-thinkers.[40] This association with matter was the source of that suspicion of the inertness of Spinoza's original Being which so possessed Jacobi and provoked Kant. It would lead the Idealists to believe that they had to show that Being as Spinoza conceived it needed to be reconceived in a more spiritualized form.[41] Yet, if my reconstruction has any merit, there was already a lot of this in Spinoza himself, awaiting Idealist discovery.

First and most importantly, as a good essentialist, Spinoza insisted upon the reality of intellectual intuition and on its epistemological preeminence.[42] Another powerful implication of his thought was that "the true is the whole"—that one had to start from the idea of the intrinsic infinite and think in terms of perfection *sub specie aeternitatis*. Another essential principle he endowed them with was that all negation was limitation. This created the logical prospect that within the infinite whole there might be an immanent articulation to particularity. The elements of *dialectics* as a logical process of differentiation and limitation compatible with ontological unity glimmered in his formulations.

In one way, Kant worked sharply to divide Spinoza from the "pantheist" standpoint of the radical Enlightenment. He insisted upon reading Spinoza's original Being as "hyperphysical," as supersensible or transcendent. This, too, was an inadequate grasp of Spinoza's stance; just as Spinoza's idea of the original Being did not fit comfortably with the orthodox notion of a personal divinity, it did not fit the orthodox notion of a transcendent one either. On the other hand, the radical Enlightenment's materialist reading did not really grasp his position either, for Spinoza's affirmation of immanence, as against conventional transcendence, signified the immanence of entities in Being, of the world in God, and not the converse. Spinoza offered a third possibility, which would be taken up and developed brilliantly in German Idealism. Spinoza created the possibility of a "panentheism," though only the full development of German Idealist thought would bring sufficient clarity to these issues that the term itself would be invented.[43]

Lessing had built his interpretation of Spinoza on a panentheist reading.[44] Herder developed the same line of thought in his *Gott: einige Gespräche*. The young Idealists would take up and transfigure these beginnings by bringing Spinoza's idea of the original Being into a much more intimate penetration of the world of entities, fusing a far from "lifeless" Absolute with an equally *animated* Nature. They sought a way to renew Spinoza's metaphysical synthesis via what Lessing dubbed the *hen kai pan*.

Lessing's phrase captured the essential magic of Spinozism for the Idealists. What it betokened was synthesis, totality, holism—that closure lusted after by reason and by feeling: the bridge of subject to object, sign to signified, ought to is, desire to fulfillment, man to nature. It is in those most famous phrases from Spinoza—*Deus sive Natura* and *Natura naturans*—that we pick up an additional and crucial element in the appeal of Spinozism, in the affinity between what Kant disparaged as "fatalism" and "hylozoism." Spinoza's idea allowed the German Idealists to give way to their overweening intuition of nature as dynamic, active, creative—alive. That seemed to resolve the immanence-transcendence problem. Nature as a living force was both in the world and its higher principle. It was *immanent Reason*.

Nature was *more* than matter, and it was *Nature* that lived. The very protest Kant made on behalf of God, his objection to "lifelessness," the Idealists would make on behalf of the world. And, paradoxically in the spirit of Kant, for the sake of the freedom of that most inextricably worldly spirit, man himself. With his arguments in the *Third Critique*, Kant set the issues of the metaphysical vision which would inform German Idealism. Kant failed in his mission to reverse the tide of Spinozism and pantheism in Germany. The treatment he gave these topics in the *Third Critique* served to rally just those who were most adept and interested in his philosophy to the defense of Spinoza and pantheism, and thus provoked the new metaphysics of German Idealism. The latter could no more abide the denial of life to the Absolute than it could to the existent, and as a result made *Life,* properly construed, out to be the *hen kai pan.* If one accepted both Spinoza's claim that utterly disparate substances could not interact and Kant's claim that empirical man must be seen as free, the only possible recourse was to read what Kant termed the noumenal, transcendent, or intelligible order as in fact the immanent principle of the real, natural, existential order. Spinoza's Being, indwelling in Nature and in man, became Reason and Freedom in one: the distinctive metaphysical principle of German Idealism, *Geist.*

From the "Cognitive" to the "Ethical" Turn

We have come a vast distance in our consideration of Kant's "cognitive turn," and it may be well to sum up, provisionally, the key points of our itinerary. The cognitive turn took place in the spring of 1789, as a result of Kant's discovery of the cognitive potential in "subjective formal purposiveness" or the "technic of nature." In the wake of this, he came to formulate his theory of "reflective judgment" and to reconceive his notion of the "faculty of judgment." Accordingly, he envisioned his work thenceforth no longer as a "Critique of Taste" but as the *Critique of Judgment.*

Kant's works of 1787–90 may plausibly be read as a sustained revision of the "Transcendental Dialectic" of the *First Critique* of 1781. From at least 1785 forward, Kant had felt obliged to offer a theory of the "unity of reason" which went beyond his restrictive considerations in the *First Critique*'s "Transcendental Dialectic." As he made the "cognitive turn" in 1789, he came as close to offering that unified vision of human consciousness as he was ever to come, and what he attempted, despite his reservations, inspired his followers to even grander adventures in synthesis. If that perhaps exceeded Kant's avowed project, it was certainly the case that elements emerged in the *Third Critique* which seemed to offer support for such a systematic revision, especially on the vexed questions of the "unity of reason" and the possibility of valid self-awareness. His confidence in the closure of his cognitive system with the discovery of a transcendental principle grounding taste, and then with his discovery of the cognitive power of this same principle, reached a maximum, perhaps for his whole philosophical career. In particular, he believed he could now resolve the nagging problem of his epistemology, the failure in the *First Critique* to entail the objective validity of empirical judgments. To flesh out these notions, he plunged into the *First Introduction to the Critique of Judgment*.

But Kant also had an eye toward the contemporary context, especially in natural science. There were those who wished to push some of the ideas with which Kant was working too far, who fell into "dialectical" excess and perpetrated "aestheticism of science." Against them he had already been conducting an extended campaign during the late 1780s, and he saw that it would need to be buttressed in the new *Critique of Judgment*. He directed himself to that task in the "Analytic of Teleological Judgment" in the late spring and early summer of 1789. In the process, he saw that the "aestheticists of science" could all too frequently be identified with the pantheists and materialists who threatened the orthodox theistic peace of German religious culture. The receipt of Jacobi's second edition of the *Spinoza-Büchlein* in late summer of 1789 triggered a far more polemical turn in his argument against hylozoism both in the "Analytic" and above all in the "Dialectic." His campaign sought not only to rectify the methodological excess of "speculation" in the new science of biology, but at the same time to demolish the metaphysical excess of Spinozism and hylozoism. The result was the climactic argument with Spinoza in the "Dialectic of Teleological Judgment" over the question of plausible ontologies—not only of nature but of self. Kant made his transcendental argument against metaphysical speculation, but he went on to insinuate clearly his own metaphysical position, identified with theism and the free will of individual human actors. That is what I call the "ethical turn."

Part Three

THE FINAL FORM OF THE
CRITIQUE OF JUDGMENT

⚜️ *Thirteen*

THE ETHICAL TURN IN KANT'S *CRITIQUE OF JUDGMENT*

n §12 of the *First Introduction* Kant presented a plan for the organization of his newly conceived *Critique of Judgment* which sheds a great deal of light upon the coherence of the ultimate work. In keeping with his notion of an "encyclopedic introduction," Kant proposed that the body of his book provide a systematic articulation of the faculty of judgment, i.e., one which would be complete and internally consistent.[1] He proceeded to lay down a framework for this through three distinctions. First he distinguished between determinant and reflective judgments. Determinant judgment needed no consideration within the faculty of judgment itself since it was completely governed by the faculty of understanding. Therefore the systematic articulation of the faculty of judgment in terms of its own intrinsic principle would focus exclusively upon reflective judgment. Kant proceeded then to a second discrimination, between aesthetic and logical reflective judgments. This required that a critique of judgment should have two parts, one considering aesthetic judgments (judgments of taste), and one considering logical judgments (teleology).

At first glance, these would seem to be sufficient divisions. But in fact Kant went on to a third, decisive distinction, between intrinsic and relative purposiveness.[2] Accordingly, the simple twofold division turned into a fourfold division. In the sphere of the aesthetic reflective judgment, Kant identified the consideration of intrinsic purposiveness with beauty, and then he linked the consideration of relative purposiveness with the *sublime*. In the sphere of the logical reflective judgment, he discriminated the consideration of intrinsic purposiveness, i.e., natural purposes or organic forms, from consideration of relative purposiveness, i.e., the purpose of nature (as a whole) in its relation to man.[3]

This organization, while not acknowledged in the final structure of the work, nevertheless informed its ultimate design. The whole "ethical turn" would be an elaboration of the problems entailed by the third discrimination. It is the basis for the consideration of the sublime in the *Third Critique,* and it helps clarify the importance of the elaborate "Methodology of Teleological Judgment," which is really the consideration of the final problem.

Starting in late summer of 1789, Kant's *Critique of Judgment* went through a third, major metamorphosis centered above all in three places in the *Third Critique:* the "Dialectic of Aesthetic Judgment," the "Analytic of the Sublime," and §49 (the analysis of genius).[4] He continued along this line in early 1790, elaborating his "Methodology of Teleological Judgment" and then revising substantially the Introduction to the whole work in the last months before delivering his manuscript to the publisher. It is this final turn in the composition of his work that I will call Kant's "ethical turn."

He made it for contextual as well as for immanent reasons. The new "practical-metaphysical" emphasis of the final version can be explained contextually in terms of Kant's struggle against Spinozism and pantheism. Kant's "ethical turn" must be seen as part of a strategy to defend his crucial metaphysical commitments: to the free will and moral duty of individual human beings, and to the idea of a transcendent-personal Divinity on Christian lines. The immanent reason had to do with his desire to reconcile his phenomena-noumena theory of freedom with the problem of actualizing the moral good. He needed, or felt he needed, to reformulate and strengthen the analogue to schematism which he had developed in the *Second Critique.*

That was the thrust of the crucial §ii of the Introduction to the *Critique of Judgment,* entitled "Of the Realm of Philosophy in General." Kant argued there that

> understanding and reason exercise . . . two distinct legislations on one and the same territory of experience, without prejudice to each other . . . That they do not constitute *one* realm arises from this that the natural concept represents its objects in intuition, not as things in themselves, but as mere phenomena; the concept of freedom, on the other hand, represents in its object a thing in itself, but not in intuition.[5]

In terms of his phenomena-noumena distinction, this seemed perfectly adequate. Unfortunately, though these two different realms "do not limit each other in their legislation . . . they perpetually do so in the world of sense." This is because even if philosophy may be divided into theoretical and practical, "the territory to which its realm extends and in which its legislation is *exercised* is always only the complex of objects of all possible experience, so long as they are taken for nothing more than mere phenomena."[6] Reason in its moral legislation must legislate to phenomena as though they were noumena. But that meant that both laws must obtain simultaneously. Therefore, practical laws *did* and had to infringe upon natural order. The question was how they could do so without violating the legislation of cognitive laws. The answer, for Kant, was of course the resort to teleology. But the force behind the whole strategy was his committed belief in the reality of noumena.

The best way to illuminate the nature of the "ethical turn" is to contrast the final version of the Introduction, composed in March 1790, with the *First Introduction*, composed by May 1789. Kant's interest in the heuristic utility of teleological judgments for cognition appears to have fallen off substantially between the composition of the two versions. It is not so much that Kant abandoned the position of the *First Introduction* as that it simply did not seem so important to him. Rather, he felt a strong need to underscore the merely subjective character of teleological thinking about objects of nature. His disparagement of "natural purpose" centered on his rejection of any possible immanence in nature in connection with his struggle against Spinozism and pantheism.

By far the most important difference between the two versions comes at their very outset: the mention of will as a "natural cause" in §1 of the final version is new. That novelty becomes salient in §ii of the final version, a section which had no precedent in the *First Introduction* and which explored in detail the problem of will as a natural cause raised at the conclusion of §i. Kant stated the definitive concern of the *Third Critique* in the final paragraph of the section. It may well be one of the clearest statements Kant ever made regarding the point of his entire philosophical enterprise. Kant sought to reconcile nature and freedom, the laws of causality with the law of morality, within his system. He wrote:

> Now even if an immeasurable gulf is fixed between the sensible realm of the concept of nature and the supersensible realm of the concept of freedom, so that no transition is possible from the first to the second (by means of the theoretical use of reason), just as if they were two different worlds of

which the first could have no influence upon the second, yet the second is *meant* to have an influence upon the first.[7]

Man's free will had to try to actualize its purposes in the world of sense, hence this had to be at least possible. Kant's moral philosophy required not success, but an attempt to actualize the individual's moral will in the world. That required the translation of a transcendental, rational determination of the will into an actual, efficacious act: free will as a "natural cause."

Kant chose to resolve the dilemma in the following manner: "nature must be so thought that the conformity to law of its form at least harmonizes with the possibility of the purposes to be effected in it according to laws of freedom." Kant went on to explicate this sentence with one even more problematic: "There must, therefore, be a ground of the *unity* of the supersensible, which lies at the basis of nature, with that which the concept of freedom practically contains."[8] Kant recognized that "the concept of this ground" could yield no knowledge; the "supersensible" was obviously beyond sense, and hence ineligible for categorial determination.[9] Nevertheless Kant maintained it made possible the "transition" from the principles of freedom to the principles of nature. What Kant appears to have meant is that the reconciliation of the laws of nature and the law of freedom could be thought only in terms of the idea of a "supersensible ground," the transcendent unity of nature and man: a metaphysical idea if ever there was one!

The whole tenor of the consideration was metaphysical in that Kant addressed himself to the intervention of the supersensible in the world of sense. Kant upheld his distinction of phenomena and noumena but he validated the latter not only as indispensable to human *thought* (theoretical reason as "regulative"), but much more importantly as essential to human *action* (practical reason as autonomous freedom).

Since Kant's critical philosophy did not permit any cognitive ascription of objective reality to noumena, he had to demonstrate that the concept of a unifying supersensible "ground" was a transcendentally necessary structure for consciousness in general. The concept he required had to recognize the lawfulness of nature in terms analogous to the lawfulness of will. It could be neither theoretical, i.e., constitutive of the objects of cognition, nor practical, i.e., legislative of moral imperatives, but only a manner of thinking: subjective, but nevertheless indispensable. What fit the bill was the concept of "purposiveness" *(Zweckmäßigkeit)*. Kant had seen in teleology the key to his a priori principle determining the faculty of feeling in his original breakthrough to the "Critique of Taste" in late 1787. Purposiveness provided the link in aesthetics between judgment and feeling, though only in its formal, not actual significance. Similarly, purposiveness found its way into Kant's cognitive philosophy as a way to resolve the problem of induction and to secure the possibility of empirical science. At the final stage of his composition, this vastly expanded notion proved decisive for his metaphysical adventure with the "supersensible substrate." Purposiveness, by virtue of its multiple linguistic links, provided the integument binding the supersensible substrate of nature with the supersensible freedom of the moral subject. The language of purposiveness set the tone on which all the harmonics of the *Third Critique* were built.

It had its original and literal place, however, in the theory of human action, especially practical or moral action. This moral dimension of teleology reasserted itself as Kant worked out his position in the *Third Critique*. This new concern intruded powerfully into the "Critique of Teleological Judgment" and the revised Introduction. Just as teleology had found its way into the problem of cognition in terms of empirical investigations, so now teleology found its way into problems of morality in terms of the natural, material aspect of human experience. It was essential for man to find a solution whereby he could both recognize the order (lawfulness) of nature and yet confirm his own freedom not merely noumenally but practically. As the "Third Antinomy" of the *First Critique* had it, freedom and necessity were compatible, but only so long as each remained in its own realm. Nevertheless, Kant was quite aware that human moral obligation entailed the penetration of moral choices into the world of things. But was there any place for them there? While man took himself for a real purpose, he was a natural phenomenon nevertheless. Man found himself a mere object of nature's processes: "nature has not in the least excepted him from its destructive or its productive powers, but has subjected everything to a mechanism of its own without any purpose."[10]

Man as purposive had been at stake all along in the *Third Critique*. For Kant the one ultimate and persistent problem for man was how to reconcile his self-conception as noumenally free with his knowledge of his own natural materiality. The cognitive conception of nature operated within a framework of relentless causal necessity. As phenomenon, man was "always only a link in the chain of natural purposes."[11] Kant hammered away at this point. And yet, he insisted, only in man himself could a final purpose be found in nature. "He is the ultimate purpose of creation here on earth, because he is the only being upon it who can form a concept of purposes and who can, by his reason, make out of an aggregate of purposively formed things a system of purposes."[12] He was unique in the world for having noumenal freedom "to determine purposes . . . as unconditioned and independent of natural conditions."[13]

Man's task, according to Kant, was to realize his stature as a free agent. "The concept of freedom is meant to actualize in the world of sense the purpose proposed by its laws, and consequently nature must be so thought that the conformity to law of its form at least harmonizes with the possibility of the purposes to be effected in it according to laws of freedom."[14] Man had to evaluate his own purpose under the double tension between his material determinacy and the ultimate transcendence of his *freedom* (the problem of the *unity of man* as a finite-rational subject), and between his individual subjectivity and the ultimate destiny of his *kind* (the problem of the *unity of mankind* as a spiritual force transfiguring nature into history). It is this metaphysical question of human purpose that the *Critique of Judgment* ultimately takes up: the crucial relation between man's duty and his destiny in the world.

The ethical turn entailed the effort to come to grips with man's being-in-the-world. It had both an aesthetic and a practical dimension. In the aesthetic sphere, the ethical turn invoked beauty as the symbol of morality. In the practical sphere, it had to do with duty and destiny, i.e., history, religion and the concept of the "highest good." The theory of the sublime and the symbolic only clarified the aesthetic dimension of the relation of the sensible to the supersensible, and Kant turned to the final question of its practical dimension, the problem of the "highest good," in the very last stages of the composition of the text. Indeed, he elaborated it substantially in the first months of 1790 after he had already informed his publisher that the work was finished. The "Methodology of Teleological Judgment," as we now have it, must be dated to this last period.[15] It incorporated the metaphysical progress Kant had made via his theory of the sublime and the symbolic and extended it into a general theory of man's being-in-the-world.

Fourteen

THE SUBLIME, THE SYMBOLIC, AND MAN'S "SUPERSENSIBLE DESTINATION"

I n the "Dialectic of Aesthetic Judgment," the "Analytic of the Sublime," and §49 (the analysis of genius) Kant developed a new theory of symbolism. Along with a renewed interest in the sublime, two other terms assumed salience in his work: the "supersensible" and "indeterminate concepts." The intimate relation of these three notions constitutes the theory of symbolism. This new interest in symbolism originated in Kant's elaboration of his theory of noumenal human freedom in the complex case of human being-in-the-world. The key to the theory of symbolism lies in Kant's revision of the antinomy in the "Dialectic of Aesthetic Judgment."

In revising and deepening the "simple" antinomy of his "Critique of Taste," Kant moved from a negative to a positive notion of the antinomy: from "discipline" (critique) to speculation (metaphysics).[1] The positive sense urges us to "think" the unity of reason the ground of our own subjectivity.[2] To be sure, as in the *First Critique*, Kant continued to deny strict "objective reality" (i.e., cognitive validity) to such thought. But he also, and much more emphatically than in the *First Critique*, emphasized the meaningfulness of the antinomy in grounding noumena for reason. Such a grounding was of course not theoretically objective. It was only "practical." But in Remark II to §57, Kant argued that the point of all the antinomies was to "force" us to recognize "an intelligible substrate (something supersensible of which the concept is only an idea and supplies no proper knowledge)."[3] This he articulated with even more eloquence and importance in §57 itself: "And thus here, as also in the *Critique of Practical Reason*, the antinomies force us against our will to look beyond the sensible and to seek in the supersensible the point of union for all our a priori faculties, because no other expedient is left to make our reason harmonious with itself."[4] That Kant used the word "force" in both contexts is striking. He suggested with it that the mind resisted the notion that there is a supersensible realm over and above the sensible one. Such resistance derived from two quarters: the natural dialectical impetus to subreption, regarding the sensible world as the only world (common sense), and the sophisticated philosophical suspicion of such a transcendent world (skepticism). Kant claimed that the first resistance could be overcome once it was demonstrated that nothing fundamental to the actual needs of ordinary men was lost by such a distinction, but rather a great deal gained for their ultimate meaning.[5] Against the second resistance, Kant argued that reason, upon which skeptics rely for critical efficacy, could not itself remain coherent without resort to such a distinction.

If an antinomy exists, there must be a conflict at the level of transcendental principle, i.e., some question of necessary validity must be at stake, and this inevitably implies that pure reason (the faculty of cognition in general) must exercise its critical function. The faculty of reason (in general) operates exclusively with thoughts, i.e., via the function of concepts. Hence any antinomy must involve concepts. The problem in the specific case of the faculty of judgment is that apparently reflective judgment, at least in its aesthetic employment, does not involve concepts. Kant therefore argues that either judgment has no claim to necessary validity, which destroys the legitimacy of the judgment of taste, or else judgment must have some connection with concepts after all.[6]

This was the new form of the antinomy in the "Dialectic of Aesthetic Judgment" which Kant introduced in the late summer or fall of 1789. In this antinomy, only the second possibility was acceptable for Kant. His solution was to associate the sorts of concepts excluded from judgments of taste with "determinate" concepts (of the understanding), and to conceive of another sort of "concept"—namely, one which did not belong to the understanding and which was consequently not determinate: ideas of reason now described as "indeterminate" or "undeterminable" concepts.[7] Concepts of the understanding were determinate because they could be applied concretely, via the schematism, to objects of sensible intuition. Ideas of reason were indeterminate because they could never be presented completely by an object of sensible intuition. Hence, Kant now argued that the judgment of taste possessed an a priori warrant for its claim to universal consent by virtue of its reference not to any determinate concept, but rather to indeterminate ideas of reason.

Kant went on to articulate in general what such rational concepts contained. He argued that the indeterminate concept of reason referred to the supersensible "which lies at the basis of all sensible intuition." In a reflective judgment, "the mere pure rational concept of the supersensible which underlies the object (and also the subject judging it) [is] regarded as an object of sense and thus phenomenal."[8] Kant suggested, then, that the judgment of taste ultimately entailed the assertion of the reality of "the concept of the general ground of the subjective purposiveness of nature for the judgment" as a "determining ground" and as the "supersensible substrate of humanity." That is clearly "dialectical" subreption in terms of the *First Critique*. As determining, rather than determined, the "supersensible" could never be a true object of cognition.[9] Kant now stressed, however, that it could be thought, and it could also be attended via reflection, i.e., aesthetically. What understanding could not prove, reason could think, reflection could feel. What they both pointed to was the supersensible, conceived of not only as the "substrate of phenomena" but also as a "subjective principle," i.e., "the indefinite idea of the supersensible in us."

Kant articulated three aspects of this idea in his Remark II to §57. There was the idea of the supersensible in general, as the substrate of nature, which corresponded to the idea of the thing-in-itself or transcendental object in the "Transcendental Analytic," and also, perhaps, to the idea of nature as a whole in the "Transcendental Dialectic" of the *First Critique*. There was the principle of subjective purposiveness of nature for our cognition, or the imputed "technic of nature" involved in the transcendental principle of logical reflective judgment. And finally there was the principle of the purposes of freedom and its conformity to moral law, or the idea of transcendental or noumenal freedom as developed in the *Second Critique*. Hence each of the three *Critiques* explored an idea of the supersensible. The question implied by this articulation was whether there was some *unity* to the idea of the supersensible which was more than nominal, and which could then stand as a universal ground for both nature and freedom. Kant asserted in the *First Critique* that unity was methodologically indispensable for the function of reason, but remained merely a formal or heuristic principle, hence objectively nominal. The new antinomy seemed to raise again the question of whether there were grounds for considering the supersensible objectively real.

Unless reflective judgment could refer to this indeterminate concept of the supersensible, Kant decided, it could not lay claim to transcendental grounding and would fall out of the realm of the faculty of cognition into that of mere sense.[10] But if it did make such a reference, and drew upon it as its ultimate ground, then what appeared to be a merely aesthetic judgment from the vantage of the understanding could be construed as a "disguised judgment of reason."[11] This "disguised judgment of reason" would concern "the perfection discovered in a thing and the reference of the manifold in it to a purpose." Accordingly, it would be a "confusion" to consider it an aesthetic reflection, since "it is at bottom teleological." Kant had systematically rejected such an approach to the problem of beauty throughout the "Critique of Aesthetic Judgment." He sustained that rejection in the Remark to §57. Yet he formulated it as the possibility that would obtain were we endowed with intellectual intuition of noumena, i.e., were it possible to "know," not merely "think" the supersensible. While such overt metaphysics remained proscribed in the "critical philosophy," Kant was now working toward a new access to these crucial ideas. The natural continuation of the argument came in §59.

It is important to draw attention first, however, to a strange passage in §22, at the conclusion of the exposition of the "Analytic of the Beautiful," where Kant discussed his notion of a *sensus communis*. He wrote:

This indeterminate norm of a common sense is actually presupposed by us, as is shown by our claim to lay down judgments of taste. Whether there is in fact such a common sense, as a constitutive principle of the possibility of experience, or whether a yet higher principle of reason makes it only into a regulative principle for producing in us a common sense for higher purposes; whether, therefore, taste is an original and natural faculty or only the idea of an artificial one yet to be acquired, so that a judgment of taste with its assumption of a universal assent in fact is only a requirement of reason for producing such harmony of sentiment; whether the ought, i.e. the objective necessity of the confluence of the feeling of any one man with that of every other, only signifies the possibility of arriving at this accord, and the judgment of taste only affords an example of the application of this principle—these questions we have neither the wish nor the power to investigate as yet.[12]

The placement of this passage is extremely awkward in the context of the argument which was being developed at that point in the "Analytic of the Beautiful." The reference to an "indeterminate" norm is evidence of this, for the distinction is not at all employed in the "Analytic of the Beautiful" up to that point. Since the passage involves considerations to which nothing in the preceding sections would point, it appears to be a later addition. The notion that the judgment of taste might be a "disguised judgment of reason," which was clearly intimated as a possibility in the passage, had been rejected out of hand in terms of the idea of perfection in §15, and would hardly merit reassertion. Yet Kant here intruded some intimations that the notion of "common sense" and the claim to universality and necessity in the judgment of taste betokened some far vaster and more metaphysical possibilities than his straightforward articulation would seem to require. As a consequence, we should not be too hasty to conclude in Remark II of §57 that Kant wished altogether to dismiss the prospect that the judgment of taste might be a disguised judgment of reason. Indeed, if we turn to §59, we discover he asserted rather than denied this prospect, though in a new and remarkable form: the theory of symbolism.

Perhaps the most striking phrase in the *Third Critique* occurs in the title of §59: "Of Beauty as the Symbol of Morality." Eighteenth-century aesthetics fundamentally sought to liberate the realm of aesthetics from its submission to ethics, or, in another formulation, to distinguish a kind of feeling in which no desire was implicated, but with this phrase Kant dramatically reintroduced the bond between the aesthetic and the ethical. Yet he wished to restore the linkage not discursively, not cognitively, but only symbolically.

§59 begins not with an exposition of its dramatic title but rather with the clearest articulation of Kant's notion of "presentation" [*Darstellung*] of concepts in general, *hypotyposis*. Presentation means simply "sensible illustration." Empirically, it is an example. It is what a mathematician or a scientist means by a "demonstration."[13] Some concepts can be demonstrated determinately, either through construction in pure intuition (as in geometry, and mathematics generally), or through schematism. Schematism is that procedure of presentation in which for a pure concept of the understanding an intuitive determination is constituted directly and adequately. Schematism *is* determinant judgment. But there are concepts available to consciousness—indeterminate ideas of reason—"to which no sensible intuition can be adequate."

Kant developed his theory of symbolism with reference to these indeterminate concepts. Kant described the procedure of symbolism as follows: "an intuition is supplied with which accords a procedure of the judgment analogous to what it observes in schematism, i.e. merely analogous to the rule of this procedure, not to the intuition itself, consequently to the form of reflection merely and not to its content."[14] First, it is important to note that some intuitive correlative—however inadequate—is sought or supplied by the imagination. We will have to ask why. Second, the principle of the procedure is analogy.

Symbolism works by analogy to the procedure of schematism in determinant judgment, the constitution of sensible intuition by the understanding. This principle of analogy Kant made the basis for "orientation of thinking" in reference to the supersensible in his crucial article on the Pantheism Controversy, "Was heißt: sich im Denken orientieren?"[15] Let us retrieve two points from that discussion: what the principle of analogy can achieve, and why it is invoked. The latter idea deserves first consideration, for that article linked it unequivocally with the "requirements of reason."[16] Reason *must* think about the supersensible. Given this, the only question it will consider is how most contructively to do so. The answer is: by analogy. Kant explained what philosophical analogy could achieve in the *First Critique* in discussing his "Analogies of Experience."[17] That notion of analogy was reiterated in the article "Was heißt" and again in the *Third Critique.*[18] The principle of analogy allows the rational confirmation of a relation, but not of its determinate content. The analogy of symbol to schema allows the rational validity of a relation between an indeterminate idea of reason and a sensible intuition, even though that relation cannot establish the identity of the content. Thus, while schematism achieves a direct presentation of concepts, symbolism achieves an indirect presentation.

That brings us to the third key point to take from the cited passage, namely, that in symbolism the mind is set in motion in a procedure which is strictly analogous to that of the understanding in its determinant or constitutive procedure. That is, a thought seeks presentation in the form of intuition. The movement of the mind is from thought to sensibility. The source of the impulse lies in reason, not sense. It is "expressionist," not "impressionist." That is to say, the problem is not one of recognition but of creation. The symbol is invented, not discovered, though, of course, once the procedure has been established, it is easy to see how it becomes possible that a natural occurrence might be taken for a symbol: we are in the familiar grip of the grounding paradox of art once more.

Let us sum up what we have established. First, symbolism is an enterprise aimed at finding intuitive expression for an indeterminate, i.e., supersensible idea of reason. It involves a procedure of analogy, which is able only to secure the relation between the supersensible and the intuitive object, but not the identity of their contents. Hence the primary concern is with this relation, with the sense of affinity, with the evocation of the supersensible in reason by the sensible object. And precisely what the symbol is to evoke is that supersensible subjectivity which for Kant is distinctly moral. All of these elements converge in a single concept: *Geistesgefühl*. *Geistesgefühl* was what Kant "provisionally term[ed] the faculty of representing a sublimity in objects."[19] Hence our examination of Kant's theory of symbolism leads us directly to the sublime. It is only by considering the idea of the sublime that we can make sense of the relation of "aesthetic ideas" to "rational ideas" in such a way as to do full justice to Kant's claim that "beauty is the symbol of the morally good."

The Analytic of the Sublime

The placement of the "Analytic of the Sublime" (§§23–30) in the composition of the *Third Critique* is problematic. Meredith, at one extreme, considered the material on the sublime to be among the oldest writing in the *Third Critique,* and hence "almost certainly included" in the original version of the "Critique of Taste."[20] Souriau, at the other extreme, claimed that the treatment of the sublime was "the very latest exposition of Kant's aesthetic thought," and dated it to the very last days prior to publication of the book in spring 1790.[21] Tonelli argues that the treatment of the sublime, as it stands in the *Third Critique,* is informed by the full conception of reflective judgment, hence had to follow the "cognitive turn" of spring 1789.[22] His case is persuasive. But Meredith's observation is not without point, nor, despite its obvious chronological impossibility, can we dismiss Souriau's claim, for it contains a very important, though still unclarified insight.

When Kant turned to the sublime, he had before him a considerable body of material, long since dissected and formulated, including not merely the view published in his *Observations* of 1764—of which at least one significant idea, the moral relevance of the sublime, proved essential for the *Third Critique*—but his unpublished *Reflections,* his lecture formulations, his critical annotations from Burke's treatise, and so on.[23] Meredith is correct, for the most part, about the vintage of the "Analytic of the Sublime." But he misses the crucial difference between the bulk of the exposition (§§25–29) and the sections which, on Tonelli's reading, were inserted to ease the transitions into and out of this new segment of the "Analytic." Precisely there—in §§23–24, 30, and above all in the first part of the General Remark to §29—the more sophisticated idea of reflective judgment intrudes. That suggests—as Souriau and Tonelli both believe—that the sublime was *not* "almost certainly included" in the original "Critique of Taste," contra Meredith.

Why did Kant introduce it, and why, in spite of the new sophistication of his theory of judgment, did he find his older formulations of the sublime appropriate? Here is where Souriau's sense that the sublime represented something more mature in Kant's thought in the *Third Critique* can be rescued. While Tonelli is correct that it was not possible that the "Analytic of the Sublime" could be dated as late as 1790, as Souriau wished, he does not recognize, as Souriau did, the profound affinity between the changes which without question Kant *did* introduce in 1790 and the point behind the "Analytic of the Sublime." Both of these reflect another turn in Kant's thinking, beyond the "cognitive turn" of spring 1789. The new turn was an *ethical* turn. That made the sublime relevant for inclusion in the *Third Critique,* because it had been connected with Kant's ethical thought from as early as 1764. Since the ethical turn came after the composition of the *First Introduction,* Tonelli is correct in dating the insertion of the sublime after spring 1789, but it was old material (as Meredith claimed) used for the most mature purposes of the work as a whole (as Souriau claimed).

The sublime did not figure at all in the original "Critique of Taste." It was added only late in the composition of the *Critique of Judgment* as a result of Kant's elaboration of the theory of reflective judgment, and even more as a result of his "ethical turn." In the text as we now have it, the concept first appears in §14 in what is clearly a tacked-on final paragraph inserted, long after the composition of the original section, to prepare the reader for the new segment on the sublime that Kant decided to append to his treatment of the beautiful.[24]

Kant took up the idea of the sublime, as he took up so many of the terms in the *Critique of Judgment,* from his context, redefining and elevating such notions by incorporating them within his system of transcendental philosophy. In the *Third Critique,* Kant drew certain features and illustrations from the conventional wisdom. He accepted the association, starting with Longinus, of the sublime with the grand—indeed, even the infinite—and within that framework, with such ideas as formlessness and unboundedness. He also accepted the complex psychological account of the experience of the sublime which had been articulated first for the eighteenth century by Addison, then taken up and refined in subsequent accounts to achieve its definitive form in Burke, i.e., that the sublime commenced in a feeling of sensual discomfort or pain, only later succeeded by a feeling of gratification. But Kant, in transferring these notions into his own aesthetic philosophy, and especially in linking the sublime with the moral and rational, completely transfigured the significance of these conventional connections.

In considering the significance of the idea of the sublime in eighteenth-century aesthetics in general and in the genesis of the German *Sturm und Drang,* we noted that Kant had transformed that general notion already in his essay of 1764 by advancing the conception of the sublime as grounded in the notion of human moral worth.[25] That was not a line pursued by the British aestheticians, nor a tack taken by the Germans of the *Sturm und Drang.* While they stressed wonder and awe, and even developed complex psychological accounts of the experience, they first of all found the ground for such an experience in the objects of nature, and second, if they related it to subjectivity, found the relation not in human moral grandeur but rather in human genius and creativity. Indeed, one might call theirs a posture of the primacy of the aesthetic. That was anathema to Kant. He endeavored, consequently, to assert the primacy of the practical (ethical). His first move was to capture the sublime for his purpose. His next, as we shall see, was to capture the notion of genius. With those two bastions fallen, he could advance in triumph to claim beauty itself as a symbol, indeed "pendant," of morality.

The first serious articulation of the problem of the sublime in terms of the genesis of the *Third Critique* came in the final section of the *First Introduction to the Critique of Judgment,* hence in early spring

1789. Kant conceived of the sublime there as the issue of "relative purposiveness" in the aesthetic reflective judgment. That formulation already signals the ultimate significance of Kant's theory. Beauty betokened the recognition of a purposiveness in the form of the object as given, Kant argued, and hence the imputation of that purposiveness to the object of nature, and hence to nature, in itself.[26] With the sublime, however, the phenomena were not purposive in themselves, and just that fact occasioned their significance. Such representations of the "formless," the "boundless," the unpurposive, aroused "a feeling of purposiveness lying *a priori* in the subject (perhaps the supersensible determination of the subject's mental powers)."[27] In the sublime a phenomenal experience occasioned a reflection in the subject not regarding the object but regarding itself. Hence no "intrinsic purposiveness" in the object need be involved in this experience, "because it depends only on the contingent [*zufälligen*] use of the representation . . . [for] a different feeling, namely, that of the inner purposiveness in the constitution of the powers of the mind."[28] In short, the sublime is an experience which occasions self-consciousness through aesthetic reflection.

A correct estimation of the role of the "Analytic of the Sublime" in the *Third Critique* must find its function not simply in completing the architectonic articulation of aesthetic judgments but much more in demonstrating a connection between aesthetic experience in general and the ultimate nature of the self. Kant confirmed this point by terming his consideration of the sublime a *Kritik des Geistesgefühls*, a critique of spiritual feeling.[29] What will emerge from an exposition of the concept of the sublime is that the aspect of the subject to which the experience points is precisely the moral dimension of transcendental freedom, and hence the supersensible ground of subjectivity.

In §23, where Kant commenced the "Analytic of the Sublime," his objective was to compare and contrast the sublime with the beautiful, which had hitherto been the exclusive focus of his consideration. In the General Remark to §29, at the end of that discussion, Kant compared the sublime not only with the beautiful but with the pleasant and the good, making all the more palpable its absence from the detailed examination of these experiences in §§1–5 of the "Analytic of the Beautiful." The sublime was added late, and it was added precisely to establish a much more substantive relation between the aesthetic experience and the ethical one. While the analogy of the *form* of the judgment of taste with the moral judgment provided the original insight leading to the transcendental grounding of the judgment of taste, Kant did not initially feel prepared to press the analogy from form to substance. He had not yet seen the full potential of the idea of symbol. But with his elaboration of the theory of symbolism, the sublime came to play a crucial mediating role in connecting the aesthetic with the ethical. The sublime was the aesthetic experience which par excellence symbolized the moral dimension of human existence.

The discussion of the sublime in §23 begins with a discussion of "indeterminate concepts." In that section, indeed, Kant suggested that there were indeterminate concepts not only of reason but also of the understanding, and that while the sublime had to do with the former, beauty involved the latter.[30] What it can mean that there should be indeterminate concepts of the understanding will be a question which can only be clarified in the context of the notion of "aesthetic ideas," and we will have a better purchase on that when we understand how the procedure works in the realm of the sublime, for which all our previous discussion prepares us. The question is: why does the experience of the sublime arise? What is the place of this aesthetic experience in human life?

In the General Remark to §29, in what appears to be a classic instance of his penchant for architectonic, Kant proceeded to associate each of the four sorts of feeling he had identified—the pleasant, the beautiful, the sublime, and the good—with one of the four moments of logical judgment—quantity, quality, relation, and modality.[31] The exercise might appear trivial, but some very important implications derive from it. By associating the pleasant with quantity, Kant reasserted that strictly sensual gratification was homogeneous and could be conceived only in terms of its quantity (either positive or negative). The association of beauty with quality can be connected with the unanticipatable uniqueness of each event, comparable to the unanticipatable qualities of empirical judgment. The association of the good with modality had to do with Kant's view that the only feeling which could be established a priori was the moral feeling which attended the imperative necessity of moral law. This idea of "respect" will preoccupy us shortly, but for the moment we must focus on the association of the sublime with relation.

In §12 of the *First Introduction*, Kant argued that, as distinct from the experience of beauty, which ascribed "intrinsic" purposiveness to its object, the sublime involved only a "relative" purposiveness in the sense of serving as the occasion for a subjective reflection. Kant's whole theory of the sublime revolved around "subreption"—viewing an object of nature as though it were the ground of a feeling which in fact had its source in the self. As Kant put it, "We must seek a ground external to ourselves for the beautiful of nature, but seek it for the sublime merely in ourselves and in our attitude of thought, which introduces sublimity into the representation of nature."[32] More concretely, Kant wrote: "the feeling of the sublime in nature is respect for our own destination, which, by a certain subreption, we attribute to an object of nature (conversion of respect for the idea of humanity in our own subject into respect for the object)."[33]

As an experience of nature, the sublime was an erroneous projection, Kant believed, and hence he found the sublime generally fruitless for our understanding of nature, as compared with the rich stimulation the experience of beauty provided for our study and grasp of nature.[34] What the sublime illuminated rather was *metaphysics*.[35] It might appear that such metaphysics should entail only a subjective reference, and consequently at most, a subjective idealism. But that is precisely where the idea of relation becomes most interesting. Having this experience of the sublime with an object of intuition in fact demonstrated our capacity to symbolize, i.e., to take an actual object, however inadequate, as an illustration, a metaphor, for a supersensible idea. The sublime is, in that measure, the warrant for the possibility of art. But in just that measure it brings the supersensible subjectivity of our moral sense together with the ostensibly merely sensible experience of beauty, and demonstrates that aesthetic feeling in general is grounded far more deeply than any merely sensual experience. Thus Kant could offer a whole new theory of the transcendental grounding of beauty and of genius, a whole new, far more metaphysical theory of taste, once he had worked out the idea of the sublime.

Kant's idea of the sublime is that it constitutes the harmony of imagination with reason, as contrasted with beauty's harmonizing of imagination with understanding. But the notion of harmony, as we have noted earlier, is itself a metaphor, and we are now far advanced toward a more discursive formulation of the unity of reason. Starting from the relation of imagination and reason via the sublime, we can procede to the relation between aesthetical ideas and rational ideas (symbolism), and on to the ultimate outcome whereby beauty becomes the symbol of morality.

According to Kant, the sublime could be divided into two moments, the mathematical and the dynamical, because it referred imagination to the faculty of reason in its two aspects: theoretical reason, the principle of "totality," i.e., finding the unconditioned for every given condition; and practical reason, the principle of "autonomy," i.e., the categorical imperative supervening over every interest of sense. In the mathematical moment, the sublime experience arises when imagination attempts to offer an intuitive whole for an idea of reason so grand that it defeats imagination's effort. Imagination, Kant informs us, involves two projects, "apprehension" and "comprehension."[36] It is able to apprehend *ad infinitum,* that is, it meets no bound or limit, since the forms of intuition, space and time, are mathematically indefinite or "extensively infinite," as Kant had demonstrated in the first antinomy of the *First Critique.*[37] But it is not able to achieve the same in its comprehension. According to Kant "in comprehension there is a maximum beyond which it [the imagination] cannot go."[38] As he puts it, some of the "partial representations of sensuous intuition" which it tries to hold together are lost as new ones are added. It is on this ground that we can have, for instance, no intuition of nature as a whole, though conceptually we can carry the limits of the sensible world beyond the comprehension of imagination.[39] "The logical estimation of magnitude goes on without hindrance to infinity."[40] The easiest illustrations of this are mathematical. While it is possible to form an image of three and perhaps four dimensions, it is impossible to carry forward into additional dimensions in images, but it is no problem at all to do so in algebraic formulas.

Kant contended that imagination tried to keep pace with the demands of reason, tried to encompass in one individual intuition something "absolutely great" according to reason's requirement, and by its failure both humiliated the subject and filled him with respect. Kant formulated it as follows: "But because there is in our imagination a striving toward infinite progress and in our reason a claim for absolute totality, regarded as a real idea, therefore this very inadequateness for that idea in our faculty for estimating the magnitude of things of sense excites in us the feeling of a supersensible faculty."[41] That reason can think of such absolute greatness as a whole, that it "renders it unavoidable to think the infinite (in the judgment of common reason) as *entirely given* (according to its totality)" establishes that this faculty is itself beyond sensibility, i.e., "surpasses every standard of sensibility," or is, itself, noumenal. "*The bare capability of thinking* this infinite without contradiction requires in the human mind a faculty itself supersensible."[42] It is capable, in other words, of what we have called the idea of "intrinsic infinity," the infinite *"completely* comprehended *under* one concept." This completeness or closure was not possible in the extensive infinitity involved in "the mathematical estimation of magnitude by means of *concepts of number."*[43]

The confrontation with the problem of infinity, then, forms the basis of the mathematical sublime. Imagination is overwhelmed, and in awe of reason's capacity for such synthesis, the subject feels respect, which is a feeling of satisfaction. That is to say, in relation to theoretical reason, imagination finds itself faced with a task, the initial imposition of which is unpleasant, but the ultimate consequence of which is a feeling of satisfaction. Hence the sublime is a complex experience, one which involves mental "movement," shifting feeling: *Rührung* or emotion. Kant claims that the sublime can be contrasted with the beautiful in this regard, for the latter is, he claims, "restful." This is hard to reconcile with his notion of the enlivening play associated with beauty, and it can perhaps be explained by his effort to approximate his psychological accounts to those of Burke, whom he took as the exemplary psychologist of aesthetic states.[44] Kant would have been better off discriminating the simplicity of the lingering play of the mind involved in the experience of beauty, its mere pleasure, from the complexity of the changing state of the mind in the experience of the sublime, which begins in pain and only eventually achieves satisfaction. In any event, the sublime is grounded in the initial disappointment, frustration, or even humiliation of the imagination, followed by a realization of higher purpose and a feeling of pleasure. There is to it, consequently, nothing of play, nothing of charm, but rather the earnestness of labor and the strain of deprivation.

The whole drama takes place within and between the faculties. The particular objects of nature—indeed, even nature itself as an object—are really not intrinsically relevant. "And it is not the object of sense, but the use which the judgment naturally makes of certain objects on behalf of this latter feeling that is absolutely great . . . Consequently it is the state of mind produced by a certain representation with which the reflective judgment is occupied, and not the object, that is to be called sublime."[45] Yet objects in nature which press imagination beyond its capacity for comprehension instill this idea of infinity, create the situation in which we discover "the inadequacy of the greatest effort of our imagination."

The feeling which attends this discovery is "respect," because reason set down a law for imagination which it cannot fulfill. Kant defines respect precisely as "the feeling of our incapacity to attain to an idea *which is a law for us.*"[46] The moral resonance of that definition is unmistakable. But reason imposes laws, "regulates" the faculties of the mind, and imposes "requirements" not simply in its practical form, but also in its theoretical form. In the humiliation of failing to achieve what reason commanded, the subject experiences a pain, but by the realization that it is its own reason which not only commanded but comprehended that which sensible intuition via imagination could not achieve, satisfaction overcomes the pain. The experience "arouses in us the feeling of this supersensible destination" inherent in our rationality. "Thus that very violence which is done to the subject through the imagination is judged as purposive *in reference to the whole determination* of the mind."[47] The evidence for the supersensible destination of the subject, it must be reemphasized, takes the form of a feeling. Reflection can attain the sense of the supersensible destination of the subject through the experience of the sublime.

The treatment of the "dynamical sublime" simply carries the same line of argument forward in reference directly to the practical laws of reason, i.e., the superiority of moral law to all considerations of material gratification, even that of life itself. This recognition of our moral grandeur is most vivid in confrontation with material forces of such might as to dwarf our natural strength and imperil (though only by implication, not immediately) our natural satisfactions "(goods, health, and life)."[48] The experience of such awe-inspiring phenomena in nature—and Kant can list them as readily as the most romantic author of his day—evokes in the mind of man a sense of the superiority of his moral destiny. "Reason exerts a dominion over sensibility in order to extend it in conformity with its proper realm (the practical) and to make it look out into the infinite."[49] The experience of the sublime is inherently one which points to the moral ground of man, "the feeling for (practical) ideas, i.e., to what is moral."

The Spiritual Interpretation of Genius

Now we can fully appreciate how profoundly Kant intended his claim that the essence of the sublime was its aspect of "relation," i.e., the relation of the sensible to the supersensible. This theory of the sublime explains Kant's metaphysical theory of genius, i.e., the notion of *Geist* as the faculty for "aesthetic ideas," and explains how the full-fledged theory of symbolism can at last incorporate not only the idea of genius but also of beauty into Kant's notion of expressive reason.[50]

In §49, Kant reevaluates the faculty of imagination, recognizing what had long been latent in his thought and which we have brought out in our consideration of that "other kind of judging," namely, that it belongs on the side of spontaneity and has an intimate and crucial connection with reason. "The imagination (as a productive faculty of cognition) is a powerful agent for creating, as it were, a second nature out of the material supplied to it by actual nature," Kant writes.[51] Not only does it entertain us when experience is boring, but "we even use it to remodel experience [*wir . . . bilden diese [die Erfahrung] auch wohl um*]"—i.e., we reconfigure [*umgestalten*], in Odebrecht's decisive sense. To be sure, reproductive imagination functions according to the "laws of association," i.e., in a "psychological" manner, as Burke and Hartley argued. But Kant now articulates clearly that "productive" imagination is not restricted, not limited to such a merely sensationalist pattern, and instead can be seen as "also following principles which have a higher seat in reason (and which are every whit as natural to us as those followed by the understanding in laying hold of empirical nature)."[52]

Here Kant has said it: there are principles of reason which are "natural" to us. What "nature" is that? Not the sensible one. "By this means we get a sense of our freedom from the law of association (which attaches to the empirical employment of the imagination), with the result that the material can be borrowed by us from nature in accordance with that law, but be worked up by us into something else—namely, what surpasses nature."[53] Kant is unquestionably talking about the noumenal freedom of the subject in this passage. That is, he presses a metaphysical interpretation of genius, instead of the natural one. Spirit [*Geist*], as the "animating principle of the mind, . . . is no other than the faculty of presenting *aesthetical ideas*." Genius presents "aesthetic ideas," i.e., imaginative representations through which ideas of reason find symbolic expression and therewith cultural articulation ("universal communicability").[54]

The concept of aesthetical ideas was first broached in §17, but it only achieved real clarity in the exposition of §49. In the earlier section, Kant was still entangled in some distinctions from the *First Critique* which required modification to accommodate his new theory of symbolism. Kant distinguished an idea of reason from an ideal: "Properly speaking, an *idea* signifies a concept of reason, and an *ideal* the representation of an individual entity [*eines einzelnen . . . Wesens*] as adequate to an idea." He distinguished further between two kinds of *ideals:* those of reason and those of imagination. The archetype of taste was "merely an ideal of the imagination [*bloß ein Ideal der Einbildungskraft*]."[55]

In the *First Critique* Kant had gone to some length to distinguish an "ideal of reason" from an "ideal of imagination." Ideals of reason, conceptual totalities which served as regulative goals for reason's process of seeking the unconditioned for every condition, "must always rest on determinate concepts and serve as a rule and archetype, alike in our actions and in our critical judgments." Such ideals—God, humanity, or virtue, for example—though "we cannot concede to [them] objective reality (existence), . . . are not therefore to be regarded as figments of the brain; they supply reason with a standard which is indispensable to it."[56] As contrasted with these rational ideals, Kant wrote,

the products of imagination are of an entirely different nature; no one can explain or give an intelligible concept of them; each is a kind of *monogram,* a mere set of particular qualities, determined by no assignable rule, and forming rather a blurred sketch drawn from diverse experiences than a determinate image—a representation such as painters and physiognomists profess to carry in their heads and which they treat as being an incommunicable image [*Schattenbild*] of their creations or even of their critical judgments . . . Such representations . . . furnish no rules that allow of being explained and examined.[57]

Not only was there no conceptual redemption of an "ideal of imagination," because no determinate rule could ever be found for it, but similarly there was no way that an ideal of reason could find suitable illustration in experience, Kant claimed in the same argument. "To attempt to realize the ideal in an example, that is, in the [field of] appearance, as, for instance, to depict the [character of the perfectly] wise man in a romance, is impracticable . . . absurd and far from edifying . . . in as much as the natural limitations . . . are constantly doing violence to the completeness of the idea . . . and so cast suspicion on the good itself . . . by giving it the air of being a mere fiction."[58]

This attitude toward symbolic and artistic expression of rational ideas had changed dramatically by the fall of 1789. Kant had achieved a far more meaningful theory of art and symbolism. Accordingly, in §49, Kant gave a new definition of aesthetical ideas:

> by an aesthetical idea I understand that representation of the imagination which occasions much thought, without however any definite thought, i.e. any *concept,* being capable of being adequate to it; it consequently cannot be completely compassed and made intelligible by language. We easily see that it is the counterpart (pendant) of a *rational idea,* which conversely is a concept to which no *intuition* (or representation of the imagination) can be adequate.[59]

The representation is a whole, an individual which, though perhaps determinate as an empirical object of the understanding, stands metaphorically (symbolically) for much more than that determinacy. For example, Napoleon or Macbeth—one actual, and one fictive—constitute intuitive wholes for which we also have empirical concepts. We can explicate them in terms of determinate concepts. Napoleon lived for so many years and did such and such; Macbeth was a figure in Shakespeare's play of the same name; and so on. But the point about these two empirical individuals is that they occasion thoughts which vastly exceed their mere determinate objectivity. They symbolize a great field of conflict between power and right, talent and virtue, and occasion meditations which can scarcely reach a simple resolution. What they involve is the "enlargement" of the determinate concept into indeterminacy.[60]

The aesthetic idea initiates a movement of the mind; it "occasions in itself more thought than can ever be comprehended in a definite concept and which consequently aesthetically enlarges the concept itself in an unbounded fashion."[61] That is to say, understanding strives to offer a determinate concept for such an intuition. It seeks a "discursive redemption," in the language of modern criticism. But it fails. Such an aesthetic whole "cannot be completely compassed and made intelligible by language." We cannot explain all the significances which flow out of such a symbol.[62] In Freud's terms it is "overdetermined." By exhausting understanding's capacity to determine the concept, the imagination presents a reflective judgment which cannot be converted into a determinant one, which cannot be explained definitively, i.e., cognitively, but only reflected upon at a higher level, and hence what occurs is that reason, the faculty of intellectual ideas, intervenes. Such an aesthetic idea "brings the faculty of intellectual ideas (the reason) into movement."[63]

At this point we must reconsider the relation between aesthetic ideas and rational ideas. Kant called the aesthetic idea "the counterpart (pendant) of a *rational idea.*"[64] He claimed it was easy to recognize this, because such a rational idea was conversely a concept to which no intuition was adequate. Now, it is indeed easy to see the formal symmetry of these two notions, their converse relation. But it is quite another matter when one presses the idea further, and it *is* pressed further by Kant's parenthetical insertion of the word "pendant." "Counterpart," taken as "pendant," suggests that Kant does not wish to develop simply the formal symmetry of converse propositions, but a substantive relation between the two. This entire discussion is not couched in terms of the passivity of the subject in aesthetic contemplation, but in terms of an articulation of the elements in the subject which make genius, that is, artistic creativity, possible. Counterpart as pendant signifies precisely an *expressive* potential, i.e., a symbolical relation between aesthetic ideas and rational ideas. Not only is the faculty of reason mobilized by the inadequacy of the understanding, it was in fact the origin of the very enterprise, and the aesthetic idea is its own symbolic project. If we wish to view this proceeding merely from the vantage of aesthetic reception, however, the point only turns out to be the same, for what we will be describing is simply the experience of the sublime.

Kant developed the conception of aesthetic ideas directly out of the notion of indeterminate concepts in Remark I to §57 of the "Dialectic of Aesthetic Judgment."[65] He worked out many of the implications of §49 explicitly in that Remark, especially the idea of a symbolical, not simply formal connection between rational ideas and aesthetical ideas, and the assignment of the origins of such a connection to the dynamism of reason itself. In that light Kant redefined *genius.* The "nature" with which genius had been identified in the original interpretation of art (§§46ff.) had been the material, sensual, "natural" element in human subjectivity. But now Kant seized this notion from such "irrational" grounds and transferred genius to a radically different "nature" in man: "It can only be that in the subject which is nature and cannot be brought under rules of concepts, i.e. the supersensible substrate of all his faculties (to which no concept of the understanding extends), and consequently that with respect to which it is the final purpose given by the intelligible [part] of our nature to harmonize all our cognitive faculties."[66] The dynamic requirement of reason as the supersensible unity of the subject now emerges as the real ground of genius, as the source of its quest for metaphorical expressions of its own immediate but indeterminate essence. The drive toward "harmony" of the faculties is now to be recognized as the immanent requirement of the unity of reason. But its grounding is not merely methodological; it is transcendent ("supersensible"). And because this transcendent grounding is beyond the extent of understanding, i.e., beyond determinant judgment and its schematism, the only recourse available to it is *symbolical* expression.

In this light, all the efforts toward a connection of aesthetics with ethics—"perfection" and "dependent beauty," the "aesthetic normal idea" and the "ideal of beauty"—which seemed so problematic from the vantage of a merely aesthetic intepretation, make perfect sense within a breathtakingly metaphysical revision of the whole project: art offers symbolic access to the ultimate. But there is a further point, which Kant articulates as the essence of this notion of "aesthetic ideas," namely, that there would be no recourse to *metaphor* unless there was an ineluctable incapacity of discursive reasoning to secure *metaphysics.* Art therewith assumes a central place in culture. Art is the vehicle through which the supersensible gives token of its real presence. And it is just for this reason that the aesthetic experience is transcendentally grounded.

> Now I say the beautiful is the symbol of the morally good, and that it is only in this respect (a reference which is natural to every man and which every man postulates in others as a duty) that it gives pleasure with a claim for the agreement of everyone else. By this the mind is made conscious of a certain ennoblement and elevation above the mere sensibility to pleasure received through sense, and the worth of others is estimated in accordance with a like maxim of their judgment. That is the *intelligible* to which . . . taste looks, with which our higher cognitive faculties are in accord, and without which a downright contradiction would arise between their nature and the claims made by taste.[67]

Kant put it much more simply in §60: "Taste is at bottom a faculty for judging the sensible illustration of moral ideas."[68]

In the aesthetic experience, i.e., via feeling, reflection is pointed toward the ultimate meaning of subjectivity which no exertion of the understanding in determinant judgments could ever attain, an insight into the unity not only of reason, but of being, in the supersensible ground. Kant wrote:

Hence, both on account of this inner possibility in the subject and of the external possibility of a nature that agrees with it, it finds itself to be referred to something within the subject as well as without him, something which is neither nature nor freedom, but which is yet connected with the supersensible ground of the latter. In this supersensible ground, therefore, the theoretical faculty is bound together in unity with the practical in a way which, though common, is yet unknown.[69]

The unity of reason in the supersensible substrate: this was the point to which all the antinomies "forced" us, in Kant's view. It was the peculiar achievement of the antinomy of aesthetic judgment, of the whole faculty of reflective judgment, to throw open to our attention, and to make accessible to our consciousness, that which was at one and the same time not determined by concepts or directly objectified in a specific intuition.

Beauty as the Symbol of Morality

Kant insisted upon the reservation of objectivity to that coincidence of actuality and validity which occurs in a determinant judgment.[70] But that obviously made inadmissible what he took to be the essential aspect of human experience: the primacy of the practical and its openness toward the supersensible. Hence, to make these latter concerns accessible to ordinary consciousness he turned to symbolism. Through metaphor Kant could permit the articulation of the metaphysical concerns which he prohited within the sphere of cognition proper. Not only had he limited reason to make room for faith, but he also had elevated art to the medium of the expression of reason's interests and insights in the supersensible realm. Imagination functioned not only according to the (mechanically) natural laws of association but also "in accordance with principles which occupy a higher place in reason (laws, too, which are just as natural to us as those by which understanding comprehends empirical nature)."[71] This connection with reason gave art, via genius, the power to work up "the material supplied to us by nature . . . into something different which surpasses nature."[72]

Consequently, for Kant art could not be simply *mimetic*. Its primary purpose was to *express* the supersensible. Art was a vehicle for the expression of religious and rational ideas. Philosophy itself had need of such rhetorical recourses to illustrate its metaphysical arguments. Kant several times acknowledged this in his presentation of his theory of ethics.[73] Accordingly, formalism and play are insufficient to explain Kant's theory of art. There is a seriousness, an "earnest" about it, which suggests a *discipline:* taste, precisely, requiring some higher significance in the work. This point bears directly upon the aesthetics of modernism. If Kant was profoundly suspicious of mere "inspiration," it would be wrong to take him to advocate the dominion of mere technique. One of Kant's most potent insights into the problem of formalism is his recognition that aesthetic freedom can generate mere *nonsense.*[74] Once one abandons a mimetic aesthetic, it becomes necessary to find some ground for an expressive one. The point of a symbol is to mean. Without reference, expression is empty. In one of the most penetrating essays ever written on the paradox and pretension of aesthetic modernism, José Ortega y Gasset put this with characteristic precision: "There is no difficulty in painting or saying things which make no sense whatever, which are unintelligible and therefore nothing. One only needs to assemble unconnected words or to draw random lines. But to construct something that is not a copy of 'nature' and yet possesses substance of its own is a feat which presupposes nothing less than genius."[75] As Kant put the same thought, the poet "tries . . . to go beyond the limits of experience and to present [ideas] to sense with a completeness of which there is no example in nature."[76] An expressionist theory of art, then, involves more than technique, more than form. The message is more than the medium, and a strictly formalist "autonomy of art" can only be purchased at the cost of its utter triviality.[77]

Beauty was the symbol of morality.[78] What Kant would not permit theoretical reason to assert, he now demonstrated to be essential to moral conduct and accessible both in the pure *thought* of reason, and even more tangibly in the rich *symbolism* of aesthetic experience, both in its receptive and in its creative dimensions. And that, at last, resolves the nagging problem of the idea of "dependent beauty." As Kant formulated the matter in §§16–17, it was impossible to understand how the pure judgment of taste could be complicated into a judgment of dependent beauty without losing everything aesthetic about it. Kant's treatment of perfection in that context seemed in fact to preempt the aesthetic. Now we are in a position to appraise the situation more judiciously. Let us consider the crucial paragraph of §16 in the light of the theory of beauty as the symbol of morality. Kant's text reads:

It is true that taste gains nothing by this combination of aesthetical with intellectual satisfaction, inasmuch as it becomes fixed; and though it is not universal, yet in respect to certain purposively determined objects it becomes possible to prescribe rules for it. These, however, are not rules of taste, but merely rules for the unification of taste with reason, i.e. of the beautiful with the good, by which the former becomes available as an instrument of design of the latter. Thus the tone of mind which is self-maintaining and of subjective universal validity is subordinated to the way of thinking which can be maintained only by painful resolve, but is of objective universal validity.[79]

On a strictly formalist reading of art, the loss of autonomy involved in this proceeding is undeniable. Beauty "becomes available as an instrument," it is "subordinated," rules are "prescribed for it." The liveliness and play which are essential to it are now harnessed to the "painful resolve" of duty. Kant is clear that "properly speaking, . . . perfection gains nothing from beauty, or beauty by perfection . . ." Morality's claim is valid without the sweetening of beauty. Beauty in its pure formality can function without reference to perfection (though only with *pulchritudo vaga*). It only achieves it true purpose, however—which is not pleasure but the "harmony of the faculties"—when it does in fact serve for the expression of perfection. "And thus when both states of mind are in harmony our *whole faculty* of representative power gains."[80] The "whole faculty" is reason in its unity—its supersensible unity, which is transcendental freedom. The philosophical significance of beauty, then, is that it symbolizes morality. Kant's whole discourse regarding aesthetics culminates in the primacy of practical reason.

✦ Fifteen

AESTHETICS AS THE KEY TO ANTHROPOLOGY: *LEBENSGEFÜHL* AND *GEISTESGEFÜHL*

The spontaneous conformity to the rules of the understanding by the imagination in its free play reveals the intrinsic organization and orientation of human consciousness. That is, the human mind has certain ends or purposes in its functioning, which an event like the experience of beauty exposes to conscious scrutiny, much as an empirical judgment exposes to conscious scrutiny the problem of cognitive validity. But the experience of the beautiful involves a good deal more complexity than the empirical cognitive judgment, because *all* the aspects of human responsiveness turn out to be involved—even the understanding, though not for its own purposes. Thus, the beautiful can serve as a peculiarly illuminating field for the consideration of human life as a whole. This was articulated in §5 of the *Third Critique,* when the beautiful was identified as a distinctively *human* experience, because it involved man both as rational and as animal.[1] This simultaneous animality and rationality is the core both of the theory of feeling and of the theory of morality which Kant developed in his philosophy generally and in the *Third Critique* specifically. Beauty allowed Kant a scope in which to work out the full complexities of the mixed form which was man. Aesthetics was the key to anthropology.

Kant's position is that aesthetics can only be placed properly within a scheme of philosophical anthropology which stresses the primacy of the practical and the groundedness of human meaning in a supersensible order of value. Art can serve, in that context, as a vehicle for moral education. Kant developed this idea, via the mediation of the sublime, as the basis of his connection of beauty with morality in the General Remark to §29. Both aesthetic feelings, the beautiful and the sublime, insofar as they had their origins not in

292

mere sense but in reflection, were "purposive in reference to the moral feeling."[2] That is, they contributed to the awareness and acceptance of the moral principle in complex human beings (animal as well as spiritual).

Kant drew a parallel between the purity of the form of these aesthetic judgments and the purity of the form of moral judgment in terms of the resultant feeling. In each case, the feeling derived from a purely immanent rational process. As a result, Kant wrote, "the moral feeling . . . is . . . so far cognate to the aesthetical judgment and its formal conditions that it can serve to represent the conformity to law of action from duty as aesthetical, i.e. as sublime or even as beautiful, without losing purity."[3] That is to say, one can *symbolize* moral considerations via the aesthetic feelings, because the feeling evoked by moral law in the subject is "cognate" with these feelings.

The sublime showed a much closer fit than the beautiful, hence Kant's qualifier "even." Kant made the point about the closer proximity of the sublime to the moral feeling a bit later in the General Remark:

> The object of a pure and unconditioned intellectual satisfaction is the moral law in that might which it exercises in us over all mental motives *that precede it*. This might makes itself aesthetically known to us through sacrifices (which causing a feeling of deprivation, though on behalf of internal freedom, in return discloses in us an unfathomable depth of this supersensible faculty, with consequences extending beyond our ken) . . . Hence it follows that the intellectual, in itself purposive, (moral) good, aesthetically judged, must be presented as sublime rather than beautiful, so that it rather awakens the feeling of respect (which disdains charm) than that of love and familiar inclination; for human nature does not attach itself to this good spontaneously, but only by the authority which reason exercises over sensibility.[4]

As complex, animal and spirit, man experiences this supersensible not as play but as obligation. While the essence of man's supersensible ground is transcendental freedom, the nature of that freedom as experienced concretely is duty. Consequently, once again, there is a closer approximation between the experience of the sublime and the moral than between the experience of the beautiful and the moral:

although the immediate pleasure in the beautiful of nature likewise presupposes and cultivates a certain *liberality* in our mental attitude, i.e. a satisfaction independent of mere sensible enjoyment, yet freedom is thus represented as in *play* rather than in law-directed *occupation* which is the genuine characteristic of human morality, in which reason must exercise dominion over sensibility. But in aesthetical judgments upon the sublime this dominion is represented as exercised by the imagination, regarded as an instrument of reason.[5]

Yet despite the closer proximity of the sublime to the moral, by demonstrating the fittingness of aesthetic feeling in general for the experience (and the expression) of our rational ground in moral obligation, the sublime also makes the relation between the beautiful and the moral accessible.

What makes the beautiful in itself purposive for morality is that it "prepares us to love disinterestedly something, even nature itself." More generally, "it cultivates us, in that it teaches us to attend to the purposiveness in the feeling of pleasure."[6] In the reflection about beauty, the subject not only recognizes pleasure but reflects upon its sources and its worth. It is this capacity to rise above appetite which is precisely taste, or cultivation. Consequently, as Kant argued in §59: "taste makes possible the transition, without any violent leap, from the charm of sense to habitual moral interest."[7]

The Transcendental Relevance of Feeling

For Kant there is a very important transcendental relation between feeling and reason. Feelings turn out to have great value in the subjective reckoning of consciousness regarding its states and its purposes.[8] In addition to the pure rational self-appraisal called "apperception," there is another dimension of self-awareness upon which we can count for evidence of mental states and mental functions: the sphere of feelings and the reflective judgment about them. Reflection arrives at the same result that pure rational apperception achieves. Feeling can be the mark of the existence of a relation of reason. As a mark of existence, it is empirical. But it refers, subjectively to be sure, to an a priori rational principle. Feeling is possible because man is sensible, but not all feelings are caused by sense. The peculiar feeling of respect is the crucial instance of this. "Sensuous feeling . . . is the condition of the particular feeling we call respect, but the cause that determines this feeling lies in the pure practical reason."⁹ This transcendental potential of feeling is most striking in the later *Critiques*. The relation between imagination and understanding is marked by the distinctive feeling of beauty. The relation between imagination and reason is marked by the distinctive feeling of the sublime. And the relation between will and reason is marked by the distinctive feeling of respect.

How is self-consciousness, immediately via the feelings of one's internal state, possible? In §1 of the *Third Critique* Kant wrote of "a quite separate faculty of distinction and judgment . . . comparing the given representation in the subject with the whole faculty of representations, of which the mind is conscious in the feeling of its state [*das ganze Vermögen der Vorstellungen . . . , dessen sich das Gemüt im Gefühl seines Zustandes bewußt wird*] . . . Here the representation is altogether referred to the subject and its feeling of life [*Lebensgefühl*], under the name of the feeling of pleasure or pain."¹⁰ Kant argues that we can infer from a feeling to the rational structure which determines it by reflection. When the mind attends its "feeling," it attends its subjective processes. Pleasure and pain are not the final terms of that consciousness, but only the data, the matter for interpretation, for judgment. *Lebensgefühl* is grounded in Kant's theory of subjective self-consciousness under the rubric of reflection, or what we have identified with that "other kind of judging." Kant is loath to call this cognition, yet it is self-consciousness of the subject not as merely passive but as active. The mind has the power to respond to its appraisals of its states, and to alter them. And it has at least one criterion by which this data—pleasure or pain—is to be evaluated: the feeling of life.

What does *Lebensgefühl* point to, what does it mark by its data of pleasure? Life, for Kant, is the property of an intelligent will, the capacity to choose, to act.¹¹ It is freedom of will in its actuality: *Willkür*, in Kant's precise sense. The *feeling* of life, therefore, is the awareness of our empirical freedom, our status as practically purposive in the world of sense. Pleasure, in that context, is either what fosters our consciousness of this freedom, or what accompanies and underscores its efficaciousness. In either case, pleasure is bound up with the *materiality* of man, his capacity to sense, his bodily existence. Kant referred to Epicurus in this connection:

> [A]s Epicurus maintained, all *gratification* or *grief* may ultimately be corporeal . . . because life without a feeling of bodily organs would be merely a consciousness of existence, without any feeling of well-being or the reverse . . . For the

mind is by itself alone life (the principle of life), and hindrances or furtherances must be sought outside it and yet in the man, consequently in union with his body.[12]

Similarly, in §54, Kant connects gratification with a "feeling of the furtherance of the whole life of the man, and consequently also of his bodily well-being, i.e. his health."[13] Thus *Lebensgefühl*, like *Willkür*, is involved in that complex dualism of human experience as between pure reason and mere matter. It can be read simply physiologically, and then assuredly we are in the realm of empirical psychology, not only with *Lebensgefühl*, but also with *Willkür*. But it can also be read mentally, in accordance with the technical sense of Kant's term life. In the latter sense, both *Lebensgefühl* and *Willkür* offer the possibility of a transcendental significance: they point to a pure rational determination. While transcendental self-consciousness ("apperception") attends principles of pure reason a priori in "transcendental reflection," reflective self-consciousness *(Lebensgefühl)* attends feelings as keys to its state *(Gemütszustand)*, and thus undertakes aesthetic reflection.[14]

Kant believed that there is (or ought to be) a difference between "sensuous" and "intellectual" pleasure, not so much in terms of psycho-physical response as in terms of rational significance.[15] "Sensuous" pleasure is occasioned by the senses or the imagination; "intellectual" pleasure by concepts or ideas. For Kant not all feelings were homogeneous quantities (such that, opposed, they would cancel one another), for both in the *Anthropology* and in the *Third Critique* he identified circumstances in which it makes sense to find pain justified and joy bitter. As Kant put it in the *Anthropology,* "a *higher* satisfaction or dissatisfaction with ourselves (namely, a moral one) [serves to] judge enjoyment and pain."[16] In the *Third Critique* Kant explained: "The satisfaction or dissatisfaction here depends on reason and is the same as *approbation* or *disapprobation;* but gratification and grief can only rest on the feeling or prospect of a possible . . . *well-being* or its opposite."[17]

If all that mattered were quantitative gratification, Kant argued in §3 of the *Third Critique,* "the impressions of sense which determine the inclination, fundamental propositions of reason which determine the will, mere reflective forms of intuition which determine the judgment, are quite the same as regards the effect upon the feeling of pleasure."[18] If our goal were simply happiness, we would not scruple over the source of pleasure, but simply maximize it; indeed, there would be no moral issue at all, only a question of efficiency. But obviously for Kant there was a moral issue here. And that profoundly colored his view of mere gratification. Thus Kant introduced a crucial complication: there were conflicting criteria for the evaluation of states of mind and for actions taken to alter them. He discriminated between a feeling of life *(Lebensgefühl)* and a feeling of autonomous spirituality *(Geistesgefühl)*.[19]

"'Spirit *[Geist]*' in an aesthetical sense, signifies the animating principle *[das belebende Princip]* in the mind," Kant writes in §49.[20] "Animating," "enlivening," "life"—a whole series of words which previously arose in connection with Kant's characterization of the "harmony of the faculties"—here achieve renewed prominence. Kant elaborates in the following terms:

> But that whereby this principle animates the soul—the material which it employs for that purpose—is that which sets the mental powers into a swing that is purposive, i.e. into a play which is self-maintaining and which strengthens those powers for such activity *[Dasjenige aber, wodurch dieses Princip die Seele belebt, der Stoff, den es dazu anwendet, ist das, was die Gemüthskräfte zweckmäßig in Schwung versetzt, d.i. in ein solches Spiel, welches sich von selbst erhält und selbst die Kräfte dazu stärkt]*.[21]

While beauty operates in the realm primarily of *Lebensgefühl*, it has within it, as its only source of transcendental value, a reference as well to *Geistesgefühl*. The harmony and conflict between these two subjective states parallels the relation of subjective and objective will-determinations. In §54 Kant connected gratification with a "feeling of the furtherance of the whole life of the man, and consequently also of his bodily well-being, i.e. his health."[22] But he then made what was for him the key distinction: between gratification which was merely "animal *[animalische]*, i.e. bodily sensation," and that which was a "*spiritual* feeling *[geistigen Gefühl]* of respect for moral ideas."[23]

For Kant, health (physical well-being) was a particularly indicative aspect of the feeling of life, but duty was the ultimate ground of the feeling of spirituality. With health (as a physiological as well as psychical quality) he associated the general idea of human happiness. With the feeling of spirituality (as a satisfaction, respect, which involved subordination of physical desires) he connected the majesty of moral law. While *Lebensgefühl* operated on the natural assumption that health and well-being were good, *Geistesgefühl* introduced the question of worth, of value in an ultimate sense, which threw this natural assumption into suspicion. Kant's ethical rigor-

ism thrust at the very heart of subjective purposiveness as enhance-
ment of liveliness by asking: What is the purpose of life itself, and is
enjoyment man's purpose? In §4 he made his position clear:

> Even in the judging of health we may notice this distinction. It
> is immediately pleasant to everyone possessing it . . . But in
> order to say that it is good, it must be considered by reason
> with reference to purpose, viz. that it is a state that makes us fit
> for all our business . . . reason can never be persuaded that
> the existence of a man who merely lives for *enjoyment* (however
> busy he may be in this point of view) has a worth in itself . . .
> Only what he does, without reference to enjoyment, in full
> freedom and independently of what nature can procure for
> him passively, gives an (absolute) worth to his presence (in the
> world) as the existence of a person.[24]

Man must evaluate all in terms of his spiritual estate, his moral purpose, and consequently life itself, empirical freedom, and the
capacity to enjoy it must come under a sterner criterion. In that
light, "life as such . . . has no intrinsic value at all . . . it has value
only as regards the use to which we put it, the ends to which we direct it."[25] "The value of life for us, if it is estimated by that *which we
enjoy*, . . . sinks to zero . . . There remains then nothing but the
value which we ourselves give our life."[26]

The full significance of the tension between *Lebensgefühl* and
Geistesgefühl lies in man's recognition of his supersensible destiny.
In the sphere of feeling, that recognition is called "respect." The
distinctiveness of respect lies not only in its necessity and a priori
derivation, but also in the difference it manifests as feeling from
other feelings.[27] Kant writes of it as "a positive feeling not of empirical origin . . . which can be known a priori . . . a feeling produced by an intellectual cause."[28] "Respect is properly the representation of a worth that thwarts my self-love," but one which as a
feeling is "not received through any outside influence . . . hence it
is specifically different from all feelings of the first kind."[29] It is not
a feeling of sense, though it is sensible. It is a feeling which refers to
the supersensible. It is not *Lebensgefühl* but *Geistesgefühl*.

The primary practical role of sensibility, of course, is in generating "inclinations" oriented toward "happiness" or "self-love."
Consequently, "whatever checks all inclination of self-love necessarily has, by that fact, an influence on feeling."[30] From the side of
reason, it can be established a priori from the nature of moral law,

and from the actual condition of man as a natural-material subject, a finite rational being necessarily determined by the moral law, that he must experience this determination subjectively in feeling as compulsion and pain: "[W]e can see a priori that the moral law as a ground of determination of the will, by thwarting all our inclinations, must produce a feeling which can be called pain. Here we have the first and perhaps the only case wherein we can determine from a priori concepts the relation of a cognition (here a cognition of pure practical reason) to the feeling of pleasure or displeasure."[31] Since "respect" is for law, for the necessity of duty, it is a necessary, not a voluntary feeling: "a tribute we cannot refuse to pay to merit whether we will or not."[32] It is also an ultimately affirmative one, despite the initial displeasure. The subject experiences a pain, but reflection upon this pain, i.e., judgment about the state of mind via *Lebensgefühl*, leads to the recognition that the rejection of desire was commanded by reason within the subject. Reflection, through *Lebensgefühl*, becomes aware of a relation to its own immanent rationality, and of the authority of that rationality in the subject. But this produces a feeling of "intellectual pleasure," or, more precisely, approbation. That is *Geistesgefühl*.

The concept of *Geistesgefühl* has already arisen in our consideration of the feeling of the sublime, and the parallelisms between the feeling of respect and the feeling of the sublime are obvious. The first parallel is in the psychology of the experience. Both respect and sublimity are "mixed feelings" or complex states of mind involving change. Both start out with a feeling of displeasure or pain. But this feeling in the sensible subject is discerned to be caused by the subject's own rational determination, and this induces a new feeling of approbation, which is pleasant but in a different manner. Thus the subjective experience of both respect and sublimity is a movement in mental states, a *Rührung*, a stirring of emotions. But the connection is not merely one of similar subjective process. In both cases, the experience is no longer merely a feeling of life [*Lebensgefühl*], i.e., the actual efficacy of the will. It is a feeling of spirit [*Geistesgefühl*], i.e., the rational authority in the will.

Kant argues that in the experience of respect for the law, "contemplating the majesty of this law, . . . the soul believes itself to be elevated in proportion as it sees the holy law as elevated over it and its frail nature [*die Seele sich in dem Maße zu erheben glaubt, als sie das heilige Gesetz über sich und ihre gebrechliche Natur erhaben sieht*]."[33] The verb Kant used is in its nominal form the term for the sublime.

Again, in describing duty, Kant writes that it is "something which elevates man above himself as part of the world of sense, something which connects him with an order of things which only the understanding can think [*was den Menschen über sich selbst (als einen Theil der Sinnenwelt) erhebt, was ihn an eine Ordnung der Dinge knüpft, die nur der Verstand denken kann*]."[34] And Kant uses the nominal form of sublimity as well: "the sublimity of our own supersensuous existence . . . subjectively effects respect for their higher vocation in men."[35] Thus the connection is extremely close between the feeling of respect and the feeling of the sublime. Yet they can and should be distinguished. Kant writes that respect "applies to persons only, never to things."[36] A bit later he clarifies himself still further: "respect can never have other than a moral ground."[37] This accords with the argument he made in the *Grounding:* "All respect for a person is properly only respect for the law . . . of which the person provides an example."[38] Thus Kant comes back to his basic assertion: "only the law itself can be an object of respect."[39] In others and in oneself, what causes respect is the law. Subjectively it is duty. Objectively it is the moral law and, behind it, the autonomy of the will in rational freedom.

Precisely what distinguishes the moral feeling from the sublime is that the moral feeling attends the subjective supersensible directly, while the sublime involves a "subreption," whereby it seeks it in an object of nature.[40] Yet the sublime is the experience whereby that subreption reveals the limitations of the merely phenomenal presence of nature. Thus Kant defined the feeling of the sublime as "an object (of nature) *the representation of which determines the mind to think the unattainability of nature regarded as a presentation of ideas.*"[41] The experience of seeking such an "objective correlative," such a "sensible illustration" in nature demonstrates not perhaps the idea, but the process of reason itself, "as the faculty expressing the independence of absolute totality [*als Vermögen der Independenz der absoluten Totalität*]," that is, what really gets presented is "the subjective purposiveness of our mind in the employment of the imagination for its supersensible destination."[42] While Kant is merely restating the theory of the sublime in this passage, it is even more clear how decisively the notion of aesthetic ideas, the theory of symbolism, represents the culmination of his whole vision of aesthetics, and how that fits profoundly into his conception of man as a being grounded in the supersensible.

What the *Third Critique* sought to establish is that this awe when projected upon nature was a "subreption," a misplacement of the actual ground of the feeling, which authentically betokened the supersensible destination in the subject. This "subreption" distinguished the feeling of the sublime from the feeling of respect. Respect was inevitably aware of its proper and true ground, while the sublime feeling was characteristically misguided about its source. Yet this subreption was fruitful precisely for the metaphysical openness it occasioned, namely, for the harmony of nature with *Geist,* and hence the possible ontological unity of the supersensible ground of nature with the supersensible ground of man.

Kant's Speculations about Geist

Kant's discussion of *Geist* in §49 is one of the most difficult and rewarding sections in the whole *Third Critique.* For the intellectual historian, the treatment of *Geist* is fascinating simply for its relation to the articulation of that crucial concept in subsequent Idealism. But even when our attention remains strictly with Kant, this section opens up astonishing depths of Kantian metaphysics. All of Kant's metaphysical intimations culminated in the idea of *Geist.* But Kant proved extremely reticent about acknowledging the metaphysical potential latent in that concept.

In his criticism of rational psychology in the *First Critique,* he had intimated (negatively) the potential in the notion. He observed: "Neither the transcendental object which underlies outer appearances nor that which underlies inner intuition, is in itself either matter or a thinking being, but a ground (to us unknown) of the appearances which supply to us the empirical concept of the former as well as of the latter mode of existence."[43] The inaccessibility of the transcendental subject and the universality of its impositions upon the empirical ego's experience of inner sense are such that it can in no way be established whether it is something specific to each individual or something which in fact encompasses all such empirical individuals—indeed, all reality, i.e., not merely the transcendental subject but the transcendental object as well— within the totality of its own noumenal nature. "If . . . we compare the thinking 'I' not with matter but with the intelligible that lies at the basis of the outer appearance which we call matter, we have no knowledge whatsoever of the intelligible, and therefore are in no position to say that the soul is in any inward respect different from it."[44] Thus the entertainment of such speculations as the ground for a subjective idealism could not preclude their extension to an even vaster objective idealism.

While Kant used such arguments in the "Paralogisms" in a negative mode, to demonstrate the emptiness of these speculations, he was nevertheless conceiving possibilities which had doctrinal significance in both the school-rationalist tradition and the religious tradition in Germany, and possibilities which he would himself take up, in the context of the *Third Critique,* in defense of these orthodoxies against the threat of an alternative, pantheist ontology. What rational psychology tried to establish from the transcendental subjectivity of the "I think" was quite grandiose:

> The substance, merely as object of inner sense, gives the concept of *immateriality;* as simple substance, that of *incorruptibility;* its identity, as intellectual substance, *personality;* all these three together, *spirituality;* while the relation to objects in space gives *commercium* with bodies, and so leads us to represent the thinking substance as the principle of life in matter, that is, as soul *(anima),* and as the ground of *animality.* This last, in turn, as limited by spirituality, gives the concept of *immortality.*[45]

Kant proceeded in his "Transcendental Dialectic" to deny that rational psychology could attain any of these crucial conceptions through a cognitive procedure, and yet, via "practical reason" and "rational faith" *(Vernunftglaube)* Kant rescued each and every one of the conceptions for his own philosophy. The ideas of "life" and "animality" play a crucial—though heuristic—role in his theory of organic form. The idea of "spirituality" figured not only in his moral and religious teaching, but also in his analysis of the subjective foundations of aesthetic experience. And of course, the notions of "personality" and "immortality" were essential to his specific moral teachings. Yet Kant, despite his belief in each and every one of these notions, denied their cognitive certainty.

The question that remains is how much of a turn Kant made in his attitude toward *Geist,* as the noumenal ground or substrate of human freedom, by the time of the *Third Critique.* The whole thrust of his reformulation of the antinomy in the "Dialectic of Aesthetic Judgment" was to "force" us to consider the "supersensible substrate" of human nature and reason as a "unity."[46] But this line of speculation carried beyond a subjective to an objective idealism. In

§ii of the Introduction, Kant wrote: "There must, therefore, be a ground of the *unity* of the supersensible, which lies at the basis of nature, with that which the concept of freedom practically contains."[47] In Remark II to §57, Kant made the same metaphysical argument, and he took it up again in the culminating section of that whole "Dialectic," §59, in the following terms:

> Hence, both on account of this inner possibility in the subject and of the external possibility of a nature that agrees with it, it finds itself to be referred to something within the subject as well as without him, something which is neither nature nor freedom, but which yet is connected with the supersensible ground of the latter. In this supersensible ground, therefore, the theoretical faculty is bound together in unity with the practical in a way which, though common, is yet unknown.[48]

Despite his epistemological scruples, Kant insisted on the legitimacy of rational belief in this unity of the supersensible. "We have therefore in us a principle capable of determining the idea of the supersensible within us, and thus also that of the supersensible without us, for knowledge, although only in a practical point of view . . . Consequently the concept of freedom (as fundamental concept of all unconditioned practical laws) can extend reason beyond those bounds within which every natural (theoretical) concept must remain hopelessly limited."[49] In this context it would appear that Kant's notion of practical reason did entail a "knowledge" which extended reason beyond the theoretical parameters of "understanding." This was a kind of "knowledge" which had a higher validity than mere "belief," and which also had clearly *metaphysical* implications. As we turn to Kant's ethics, we will press this point toward a teleological and metaphysical interpretation of his notion of man and of his relation to the order of the world. Those notions would be taken up by his successors under the rubric *Geist* along the very lines which Kant was implying.

The richest insight into the metaphysical potential in Kant's concept of *Geist* is to be found in his *Reflections* of the late 1770s. These private speculations, which proved more daring than his published writings, set out from the definition of *Geist* which Kant would enunciate in §49 of the *Third Critique*, namely, the "animating principle of the mind."[50] He had formulated this definition already in 1771.[51] Yet in the *Reflections* Kant was more candid about the latent metaphysical potential of the notion. In *Reflection* 782 Kant wrote of the *geistige Gefühl* as a sense of "participation in an ideal whole." He identified this ideal whole with the "fundamental idea of reason."[52] In another *Reflection* he wrote: "the feeling of spiritual life [*das Gefühl des geistigen Lebens*] has to do with understanding and freedom, for man has within himself the bases of knowledge and well-being."[53] For Kant, *Geist* was this "secret spring of life." It was not subject to volition, but arose spontaneously, "from nature." That was what it meant to say that what arises from spirit is "original" [*ursprünglich*].[54] *Geist*, Kant wrote, was the "inner principle of activity." It required the "sustained exertion of the mind."[55]

In some linked *Reflections* from the late 1770s, Kant developed the idea in its most remarkable form. He first noted that the term itself was novel, and that "a new term does not find immediate acceptance if it is not very apt."

> In us there are delightful and compelling, but also enlivening causes of mental power; this last principle has its own quite unique nature and laws. Nothing is enlivened but a certain universality which the mind fastens upon prior to all particulars, and from which it fashions its viewpoint and its products. That is why genius resides in this capacity to create the universal and the ideal.[56]

Geist is the "generative ground [*Erzeugungsgrund*] of ideas."[57] The "expression of the idea through manifold and unified sensibility is proof of spirit." It is the source of "system" as contrasted with mere aggregation. It is no particular talent, but the "animating principle of all talents."[58] *Geist* is the active principle; "soul" is what is animated. *Geist* is the source of all animation, and can be derived from nothing prior.[59] This line of thought brought Kant to his ultimate consideration regarding the concept:

> Because spirit involves the universal, it is so to speak *divinae particula aurae* [a particular emanation of the divine] and it is created out of the universal spirit. That is why spirit has no specific properties; rather, according to the different talents and sensibilities it affects, it animates in varying ways, and, because these are so manifold, every spirit has something unique. One ought to say not that it belongs to the genius. It is the unity of the world soul.[60]

The metaphysical potential of the Idealist concept of *Geist* was already fully latent in the repressed speculations of Immanuel Kant, and it filtered through, above all in the *Third Critique,* to stimulate his successors to its outright articulation.[61]

Sixteen

THE UNITY OF MAN: MAN AS AN "END-IN-HIMSELF"

Kant began his critical philosophy by acknowledging nature as causal necessity, but conceiving of morality as free will adhering only to its own law. His problem was to reconcile these two commitments. The *First Critique* developed the antinomian argument that freedom and necessity need not be logically contradictory, but it could only succeed in this by distinguishing phenomena from noumena, and assigning freedom to the noumenal. This produced, in the *Second Critique,* a new antinomy which asserted the "practical necessity" of regarding oneself as morally responsible and hence free. But, once again, freedom had its locus exclusively in the noumenal. To be moral was a matter of motive, not efficacy. Acting from duty sufficed both to evidence the freedom of the will and to satisfy moral obligation. Yet moral duty and free will, while they were strictly noumenal in their origin, exercised authority over an *actual* being. Concern for the efficaciousness of morality in the world of sense motivated Kant's "ethical turn" in the *Third Critique.*

The practical, as the active character of the whole person, inevitably raised two distinct but related issues for Kant: the problem of the real "unity of reason," since he identified reason both with its theoretical and with its practical uses; and also the problem of the unity of the *person,* for the practical entailed not merely a disembodied ratiocination but a human act in the world of sense. Metaphysically, Kant required an intrinsic (self-determining) dynamism of reason, freedom as autonomy, man as an "end-in-himself," for his notion of morality to be possible. The problem he faced was that it was epistemologically impossible to prove such a thing. Yet he insisted it was more than merely a "belief," even a *rational* belief (*Vernunftglaube*). It was a "fact of pure reason."[1] Even vaster metaphysical ideas intrude in the second line, for Kant had to establish transcendentally how it was possible that noumenal freedom could be an efficacious cause in the phenomenal world. In a decisive passage in the Introduction to the *Third Critique*, Kant argued that it was a "metaphysical principle *a priori*" that the empirical elective will (*Willkür*) was free and efficacious as "natural cause."[2] Ultimately, Kant's ethical turn involved two issues of "metaphysics"— first, the question of the "objective reality" of freedom, and second, the question of the efficacy of noumenal causality in the world of sense. Kant committed himself to a determinate claim about each of these. The first involved his idea of man as an "end-in-himself" in a "kingdom of ends." The second involved his idea of the "highest good." The historical Kant was in fact committed to each of these notions: the "primacy of practical reason" within the "unity of reason," the idea of man as an "end-in-himself" in a "kingdom of ends," and the "highest good" as the "ideal" pursued by efficacious human freedom in the actual world. This chapter traces the argument concerning free will from the *Grounding of the Metaphysics of Morals* through the *Second* and *Third Critiques,* to demonstrate how the "primacy of practical reason" in the "unity of reason" culminated in the idea of "autonomy," the notion of man as an "end-in-himself." The next chapter will concern itself with the "highest good."

The Unity of Reason

Kant's transcendental philosophy explains the involuntary spontaneity of consciousness by recognizing it as the act not of the empirical, but of the transcendental subject. Kant's attempt to conceive human consciousness in terms of two subjects—one empirical and one transcendental, one phenomenal and one noumenal— while at the same time insisting upon the identity of the human person and the unity of reason, threatened a grave incoherence.[3] On the one side, Kant was so adamant about the pure formalism of the transcendental subject that it became very difficult to recognize it as a "being" [*Wesen*].[4] On the other side, Kant was so adamant about the mere phenomenality of the empirical ego that it became very difficult to recognize it as a subject.

If it was impossible, according to Kant's teachings in the "Paralogisms," and more generally according to his doctrine of "inner sense," to move beyond the mere formality of the "I" of transcendental apperception, it was just as impossible to demonstrate any foundation for ascribing spontaneity to the empirical ego. The transcendental subject could never be known objectively because the process or act which constituted consciousness could never be an object of cognition.[5] The transcendental subject did have knowledge *that* it existed, but not *how*, in what determinate form it did so.[6] The determinations of experience which it could discern were not properties of primordial active intelligence, but merely its effects upon a passive sensible intuition—"inner sense." That upon which it acted was a *"passive* subject."[7] It was at best a "me." Kant claimed that empirical consciousness could never achieve the kind of unity which he posited for the transcendental and also for the practical subject. He wrote: "the empirical consciousness, which accompanies different representations, is in itself diverse and without relation to the identity of the subject."[8] Kant assigned empirical experience of the self merely to the sphere of the "analytic unity of consciousness" which derived from and depended upon a prior "synthetic unity of consciousness" in the transcendental subject.[9] "The empirical unity of consciousness, through association of representations, itself concerns an appearance, and is wholly contingent."[10]

Kant insisted that these two notions of subject, active and passive, could not be collapsed into one, and yet at the same time he considered both to be elements in an identical human person. Kant indeed strove to keep the two subjects distinct, insisting "the least object of perception (for example, even pleasure or displeasure), if added to the universal representation of self-consciousness, would at once transform rational psychology into empirical psychology."[11] But empirical psychology, which encompassed everything about the ego except the empty formality of the "I think," could in its own right achieve virtually nothing in the way of concrete knowledge of the self.[12] Consequently he cast the notion of self-consciousness into considerable obscurity.[13]

While Kant denied valid cognition of the transcendental subject, it is clear he also ascribed some form of presence or reality to it. It is the "intellectual representation of spontaneity," the consciousness of self as intelligence and act. A mode of awareness (not "cognition" in the strict sense) and a mode of existence (not "intuition" in the strict sense) are indicated. Obviously they do not fall clearly within the framework of Kant's synthetic judgments, empirical or a priori.[14] Kant refused to admit that any ontological judgment was possible here, despite an overwhelming "natural dialectical" propensity to make just such a judgment. "[T]here is nothing more natural and more misleading than the illusion which leads us to regard the unity in the synthesis of thoughts as a perceived unity in the subject of these thoughts. We might call it the subreption of the hypostatised consciousness (*apperceptionis substantiae*)."[15]

Kant insists upon the irreducible mystery of the origins of the transcendental subject.[16] Space and time, the number and nature of the categories, indeed, the transcendental unity of apperception itself: all of these are given. Without them, experience as we know it would not be possible at all. This givenness cannot be explained empirically because it is logically prior to experience. It exerts necessity not only upon the subject but upon the appearance, such that this appearance can be conceived of as an object. It is this givenness which is the "synthetic" unity upon which all subsequent analysis and exposition are grounded. Hence it is unconditionally valid. If it is both universal and necessary, if it is a priori valid, it is objective. It would seem to follow, then, that it is *real*. Yet Kant wished to reserve the notion of reality exclusively to empirical reference, to possible experience or "actuality." In themselves, apart from such experience, space, time, and the categories remained merely "formal."

Kant's restriction of transcendental apperception to impotence in self-consciousness derived from his hostility to the notion of "intellectual intuition" and the dialectical license which traditional rationalism allowed itself on the premise of the candor of self-awareness. Kant was certainly correct in challenging the view, typical of Descartes among the moderns, that everything subjective was transparent to self-consciousness. That was perniciously false, both cognitively and morally. Cognitively, it gave license to all sorts of dialectical fantasies. Morally, it deluded the subject as to his grasp of his own motives. Kant's problem was to articulate this insight, and to discriminate between two sources of that internal obscurity— the involuntary spontaneity of the transcendental structures of consciousness and the involuntary passivity of man's physical actuality—yet to do so in a way that did not annul utterly what cognitive insight and moral conscience did in fact exist in man's complex experience.

It is not altogether clear that he could do the latter without some recognition of the objective reality of reason, at the very least as *practical*. Consequently, it is important to reconsider Kant's objections to the idea of an "intellectual intuition." The best account of what Kant meant by intellectual intuition came, as we have seen, in §§76–77 of the *Third Critique*. But the idea was used extensively in the *First Critique,* precisely in order to establish the discursiveness of human understanding. In that context, Kant associated his notion of intuition in general with unquestionable givenness, with immediacy, and with wholeness. Kant held "intellectual intuition" inaccessible to man in that, first, only the sensible is indubitably actual for consciousness and second, that the principles of the activity of the human subject can only be logically disembedded through an analysis of consciousness, hence that act is not cognitively immediate in itself. Finally, the unity of the transcendental subject, while logically indispensable, can never be known—at least not in terms of a determinant judgment.

Yet Kant seemed to wish to distinguish "intellectual intuition" not merely negatively as against these limitations of the discursive (sensible) intuition of man, but positively in terms of its originary or creative capacity to transcend the distinction of actuality and possibility so that anything conceived by the intellectual intuition is made actual by that very conception. Most assuredly that is a capacity beyond the human mind. Yet if this capacity, which Kant prudently restricts to a primordial Creator, is only a most extravagant form of intellectual intuition, and if, considering the other properties, an argument might be made that the presence to consciousness of the transcendental subject does in fact have the elements of individuality, givenness and immediacy which characterize intuition, then it might be possible to claim that an inferior but crucial sense of intellectual intuition can be ascribed to humans, and most vividly so in the self-consciousness of the subject as morally active.

That presence to consciousness would be precisely the "fact of pure reason." Against Kant, but in strict conformity with his own definitions, the "fact of pure reason" would signify non-sensible intuition.[17] Moreover, the involuntary spontaneity which organizes and structures consciouness with transcendentally necessary validity might be regarded as yet another instance of this "fact of pure reason." The phrase "fact of pure reason" in the *Second Critique* signified inescapable and ubiquitous necessity, prior to and constitutive of human consciousness of moral obligation. Such compelling force was real for Kant. If we conjecture a theoretical "fact of pure reason" it is because it exerts a similarly compelling force upon human consciousness. Both "facts of pure reason" are grounded within the subject, and yet command also in reference to objects. Both gesture to the ontological presence of something without which the empirical experience would be impossible.

Kant did occasionally, even in the *First Critique,* acknowledge the prospect of an apperception of the rational subject.

> Man, . . . who knows all the rest of nature solely through the senses, knows himself also through pure [*bloße*] apperception; and this, indeed, in acts and inner determinations which he cannot regard as impressions of the senses. He is thus to himself . . . in respect of certain faculties the action of which cannot be ascribed to the receptivity of sensibility, a purely [*bloß*] intelligible object. We entitle these faculties understanding and reason. The latter, in particular, . . . views its objects exclusively [*bloß*] in the light of ideas.[18]

Kant here seems to argue that there is real knowledge of the noumenal self not only practically (as the faculty of reason) but also cognitively (as the faculty of understanding). This passage lends support to the notions of spontaneity as the immanent principle of reason and of reason as an objective reality.[19]

The heart of Kantian philosophy is the idea of consciousness— of reason—as *act.* Kant defined "spontaneity" as the power to produce concepts or to think when he first introduced it at the outset of the "Transcendental Logic," in contradistinction to the receptivity of intuition.[20] Spontaneity is the decisive characteristic of reason as such. It is identified with an "act."[21] Spontaneity is responsible for all acts of combination, of synthesis.[22] It is, as act, pure apperception.[23] Moreover, it is identifed as "the ground of the threefold synthesis which must necessarily be found in all knowledge."[24]

In the "Third Antinomy," Kant developed the conception of "transcendental freedom" and equated it with "*absolute spontaneity.*"[25] He returned to this notion in explicating the cosmological antinomy: "reason creates for itself the idea of a spontaneity which can begin to act of itself, without requiring to be determined to action by an antecedent cause."[26] Kant was only able fully to explicate the meaning of spontaneity and of reason, insofar as it had as its essence this immanent dynamism, by incorporating the notion of transcendental freedom. Kant suggested that reason could not be read simply in the light of the cognitive aspect of human experience, but that it had its ground rather in the *practical.*

Practical reason, Kant believed, offered the best prospect of a "correct employment of pure reason," i.e., a positive or "real" use. In the "Paralogisms" of the B-version, Kant allowed the possibility that reason's spontaneity might be determinately known—by practical reason. He wrote:

Should it be granted that we may in due course discover not in experience but in certain laws of the pure employment of reason—laws which are not merely logical rules, but which while holding *a priori* also concern our existence—ground for regarding ourselves as *legislating* completely *a priori* in regard to our own *existence,* and as determining this existence, there would thereby be revealed a spontaneity through which our reality would be determinable, independently of the conditions of empirical intuition. And we should also become aware that in the consciousness of our existence there is contained a something *a priori,* which can serve to determine our existence—the complete determination of which is possible only in sensible terms—as being related, in respect of a certain inner faculty, to a non-sensible intelligible world.[27]

In the crucial section of the *First Critique* called the "Canon of Pure Reason," Kant wrote: "Reason is impelled by a tendency of its nature to go out beyond the field of its empirical employment, and to venture in a pure employment, by means of ideas alone, to the utmost limits of all knowledge, and not to be satisfied save through the completion of its course in a self-subsistent systematic whole."[28] In all his phrases regarding the immanent propensities of reason— "needs," "interests," "vocations," "ends"—Kant implied, whether he wished to defend it or not, a conception of reason not as a mere "logical" form for empirical agents, but as a real force determining them as it determined the "nature" of their subjective experience.[29]

The Primacy of Practical Reason

Human consciousness is not exclusively, indeed not even primarily cognitive. It is active or practical.[30] In Kant's own words, "in the end all the operations of our faculties must issue in the practical and unite in it as their goal."[31] This principle Kant termed the "primacy of practical reason." By "primacy" he meant "the prerogative of one [thing] by virtue of which it is the prime ground of determination of the combination with the others."[32] It was in terms of the unity of reason that the practical had primacy. "It is only one and the same reason which judges a priori by principles, whether for theoretical or for practical purposes."[33] Kant argued that reason had its own "interests," and that within reason each of its preeminent uses—cognition and volition—had interests. The question of primacy had to do with the relation of those interests. The very concept of interest, Kant realized, was practical in its ultimate sense, and therefore "every interest is ultimately practical, even that of speculative reason."[34]

The problem was whether theoretical reason should tolerate the postulation of the reality of ideas of reason which practical reason required for the pursuit of its interests. If reason could not recognize anything beyond what cognition could establish as valid knowledge, then crucial interests of practical reason would be thwarted. But Kant had already demonstrated that theoretical reason was free to think anything noncontradictory, and therefore could recognize the possibility of the ideas which practical reason required. Further, the antinomies had shown that the positing of these ideas, however indeterminate for cognition, was absolutely necessary for the internal functioning of cognitive reason itself. Thus, subjectively, these ideas were necessary. Practical reason claimed an objective, i.e., ontological status for one of these ideas, that of freedom, and a postulated reality of others for the sake of this freedom. The "primacy of practical reason," for Kant, meant the authority of the interest of practical reason in demanding that theoretical reason abide by this in their unity.

This idea of the primacy of practical reason is controversial. Its critics are certainly correct in pointing out that Kant could not mean by it that cognitive reason should accept something clearly incongruous with its own principles.[35] Practical reason could not require cognition to accept the validity of two contradictory assertions, for example. The "methodological" primacy of practical reason is a myth.[36] But, as Beck points out, practical reason does not make such demands.[37] It proposes to take possession of a realm for which cognitive reason has already established itself incapable of prescribing constitutive rules, but which it has *also* designated as a territory of vital interest to its own intrinsic functioning.[38]

This discreet formulation is not yet clear enough. What the primacy of practical reason means is the claim to objective reality, i.e., to ontological status, for reason itself. Reason's ultimate concept for itself is freedom, which is the metaphysical principle which integrates spontaneity and autonomy. It was only when Kant advanced from the concept of freedom as spontaneity—what Beck terms "negative freedom" and Kant "transcendental freedom"—to the concept of freedom as autonomy, a step he took around 1785, that Kant could make any advance on the metaphysical conundrum of the reality of reason from the vantage of a finite rational being.[39]

Kant came to recognize that in one crucial sphere the subject participated voluntarily in his spontaneity and was thus raised into the sphere of pure reason: autonomy, "practical self-legislation." With autonomy Kant had a concept of freedom adequate to the dignity of a rational subject. While the finite rational subject participated in pure reason, at the constitutive level that participation had seemed to Kant purely automatic and mechanical, hence from the individual-empirical vantage, passive. Cognitively, pure reason acted as an involuntary spontaneity constituting sensible intuition into empirical knowledge. Morally, pure reason acted as compulsory obligation making constitutive rules for practical action in the world of sense. Insofar as spontaneity was involuntary, it could never be the empirical subject's own. But Kant recognized that mere passivity was neither an accurate depiction of empirical man's moral (or even cognitive) experience nor—far more crucially—consistent with the model of reason's actualization. Hence he stressed man's cognitive capacity to learn—to discover and to invent—but even more, man's practical self-legislation: autonomy.

There were two sides to this innovation in his thought. On the one hand, Kant had to loosen the determinacy of the understanding in cognition of the empirical to make possible the active pursuit of knowledge through judgment. On the other, Kant had to acknowledge the moral freedom of the empirical will in order to vindicate the autonomy of the rational will as accessible even to a finite rational being. As rational, human nature could ascribe to itself a freedom of self-determination and a capacity to modify reality in accordance with that freedom. Thus concrete man could participate in the reason which determined the laws of his action and in the constitution of those laws.

Kant ultimately found a way to assert the "objective reality" of freedom through his ethical philosophy, his "*metaphysics* of morals." Kant claimed that man was an "end-in-himself." Autonomy posited quite unequivocally a rational *being*. Kant required a concept through which to articulate this problematic ontological character of reason. He found it in the idea of "objective end [purpose]." The essential connection was between practical reason and "intrinsic purposiveness." All along this study has argued for the centrality of the language of purposiveness. While the language of system is reason's language of self-consciousness as formal or logical, reason's self-consciousness as effective or real finds articulation in the language of purposiveness. These notions were at the outermost extreme of Kant's consideration in the *First Critique*, but, as our whole study has established, they became central for the *Third*

Critique. Objective purposiveness betokened the single most crucial metaphysical idea of Immanuel Kant: reason as autonomy, as freedom.

Purpose is a language of reason. It is in fact a language exclusively and natively rational: not for the determinate judgment of phenomena, but for reason's internal process, most importantly its practical requirements. Thus the decisive element Kant introduced into his discussion of the "unity of reason" was the idea of purposiveness. "This highest formal unity, which rests solely on concepts of reason, is the *purposive* unity of things."[40] A few pages later Kant added: "Complete purposive unity constitutes what is, in the absolute sense, perfection."[41] *Absicht*, or intention, is a matter exclusively of rational beings. Objects of desire, however, are actual for all animal life forms. This desire can be imputed to them as a necessary trait or drive [*Trieb*], but its operation is merely instinctual, not rational, i.e., not purposeful but purposive. That was the whole thrust of Kant's argument concerning so-called "natural purposes." Their "intrinsic purposiveness" was imputed to them on analogy to rational purpose. But with man himself we are no longer in the domain of analogy. Man *is* intentional *(absichtlich)*. He is purposeful, i.e., an intelligent cause.[42] He is an end-in-himself.

Kant believed that the involuntary spontaneity behind cognition and the transcendental freedom behind choice were identical: they were the noumenal human soul. But he questioned whether it was possible to prove this, and he also questioned whether it was wise to do so.[43] The first scruple was epistemological. The second was religious. To disregard the first scruple would threaten the principle of the discursiveness of the understanding. To disregard the second scruple would threaten the idea of moral freedom. Only the preservation of his distinction between the phenomenal and the noumenal could avoid these threats, he argued.[44]

This tension between belief and proof was of the essence of his notion of *Vernunftglaube*, rational belief. He held that by limiting the scope of reason he made room for faith, and in that measure took nothing away from common humanity but only demolished the monopoly of the schools.[45] At the same time, he was anxious to demonstrate that belief in God, freedom, and immortality could be shown to be rational according to the critical philosophy. Religion within the limits of reason is but one half of Kant's guiding principle, for it would appear that prudence required reason within the limits of religion as well.[46]

The idealism of purposiveness in nature as a whole tallied well with Kant's critical project of clearing a space for faith by denying determinate capacities to reason in the sphere of the supersensible. Kant wished only to establish the *possibility* of immanent purpose, the subjective necessity of its presumption, but no more. If it were possible to promote this subjective possibility into an objective actuality, the consequences would be very serious for his whole system. The possibility of purpose in the world of nature was necessary to accommodate human ethical action, but it was not necessary to secure the validity of aesthetic experience. Conversely, the actuality of purpose in nature would destroy aesthetic freedom, and hence the whole possibility of beauty, by making it contingent upon nature. Even more profoundly, it would threaten human moral freedom, by making nature as a noumenal force immediately real to our consciousness. Such immediacy before the might of God, Kant believed, would destroy the independence human beings needed to be authentically moral.[47] Thus, crucially, the metaphysical survival of both beauty and morality hinged upon the denial of the objectivity of purposiveness in nature.

Man As an End-in-Himself

The fundamental principle of Kant's metaphysics of morals is the idea of man as an end-in-himself, i.e., the objective reality of freedom.[48] But Kant remains epistemologically scrupulous to claim that we cannot know such a reality, because it is noumenal. We can—indeed we must—think it, and practically we can infer its objective reality from our experience of necessary law. Still, Kant warns against the "mysticism of practical reason" which "makes into a schema that which should serve only as a symbol."[49] Kant's own usage of "objective reality" for practical reason, however, is not too far removed from the very practice he chastises, but for a bit more discretion, and it is clear that he is not too hostile to such "mysticism." Still, he cloaks himself in the full rigor of "criticism" and consequently, in his most extensive discussion of man as an end-in-himself, in the *Grounding of the Metaphysics of Morals,* Kant introduces the notion rather circumspectly, in a hypothetical vein: "Suppose that there were something whose existence has in itself an absolute worth, something which as an end in itself could be a ground of determinate law."[50] This sentence requires the most careful analysis. For Kant the only thing whose existence can have an absolute worth is an end-in-itself. That is the fundamental principle of the apposition. Each clause contributes distinctive elements to Kant's conception which only come clear on the basis of subsequent comments.

Only an intrinsic purpose can ground all external purposes, and therefore all purposiveness is grounded in this capacity and derives its possibility and value from it. An end-in-itself, Kant tells us, is an "objective end [purpose]"—that is, it exists as the capacity to assign worth, and, as the only such capacity in the world, it possesses "absolute" worth.[51] The capacity to assign worth is the capacity to have intentions, *Absichten*. That capacity is *autonomy:* the power, which is exclusively reason's, of legislating for itself ("grounding determinate law"). A "person" (an objective end in the moral context) has "dignity" (absolute worth in the moral context) by virtue strictly of the rationality which is the ground and also the principle of one's capacity for choice, one's nature as a purpose-maker, an end-in-itself.[52] Reason alone has absolute worth. Reason alone provides the "representation of law" according to which purpose is possible. But most importantly, reason alone is the real ground for worth, purpose, and principle.

"The ground of all practical legislation lies objectively in the rules and in the form of universality, which . . . makes the rule capable of being a law . . . Subjectively, however, the ground of all practical legislation lies in the end [purpose]; but . . . the subject of all ends [purposes] is every rational being as an end in himself."[53] Kant is making the usual moves with the terms "objective" and "subjective" here. By "objective" he refers to validity and form, but the issue is whether Kant is entitled to call the reality in this situation merely subjective. It is not the sensible subject which is at stake here but "every rational being as an end in himself."

Kant's metaphysics of morals requires that there be rational, essential being. "Rational nature is distinguished from the rest of nature by the fact that it sets itself an end . . . the end must here be conceived, not as an end to be effected, but as an independently existing end."[54] That is, it is possible for rationality to determine the will as a formal principle only if it is real as a prior ground. Autonomy grounds rational choice. Reason is at one and the same time real and legislative. "Rational nature exists as an end in itself." Moreover, the reason which grounds and determines legislatively the purposive action of any rational being is the same for every rational being. Self-recognition of the "objective principle of the will" or the "moral law" must lead one to recognize at the same time "what is necessarily an end for everyone," the "ground of such a principle," i.e., shared reason.[55] If there are rational beings, and my own self-conception as an end-in-myself could have no other basis, then not only I but every rational being, simply by virtue of rationality, must also be an end in itself.[56]

That is why the recognition of oneself as an end-in-itself, i.e., the recognition of one's own capacity to have intentions, in and of itself binds one to the community of all ends-in-themselves. Man, as a finite rational being, recognizes the capacity to choose in himself, i.e., recognizes his own rationality "as legislating for itself and only on this account as being subject to the law."[57] But that immediately entails his recognition that should any other rational beings exist, they too would necessarily enjoy the same status. Hence Kant's notion of "a world of rational beings *(mundus intelligibilis)* as a kingdom of ends"—i.e., a community not of objects of will but of wills: "a systematic union of rational beings through common objective laws."[58] The law is common not only "because [it is] legislation belonging to all persons as members" but also because one and the same reason is involved, as ground and as principle.[59] The membership in a "kingdom of ends" which derives from shared rationality is the key point we must harvest at once. "A rational being must always regard himself as legislator in a kingdom of ends rendered possible by freedom of the will."[60] Autonomy and spontaneity, as the essential elements of reason, constitute freedom of the will.

In the "Dialectic of Teleological Judgment," Kant went at length into the hypothetical character of an *intellectus archetypus* as a cognitive model of pure rationality. In the *Grounding of the Metaphysics of Morals* Kant developed the notion of a "holy will" to characterize a practical model of pure rationality. In a holy will, the immanent requirements of reason are automatically, spontaneously actualized.[61] There is no gap between is and ought, no labor to be undertaken, no *external* purpose as means or as end (result) to be distinguished from the immanent self-sufficiency of the holy will itself. Such a holy will Kant also termed a "sovereign" in the "kingdom of ends." Now this sovereignty could not involve the domination over any other members of the kingdom, for to treat them as means and not ends is forbidden even to a holy will, though it would never be tempted to violate this principle. Hence the idea of sovereignty suggests a new conception of the "kingdom of ends." Sovereignty lies not in the relation of the holy will to other rational wills, whom it may not command, but in relation to the objects of all wills. A "sovereign" will immediately actualizes all its objects. All nonintuitive, nonholy intelligences need to labor to realize or actualize the specific ends (results) they have chosen according to their intentions (motives). This set of results, when included with the "independently existing ends," results in a *second,* expanded notion of the "kingdom of ends." Kant wrote that it was "possible to think of a whole of all ends in systematic connection (a whole of both rational beings as ends in themselves and also of the particular ends which each may set for himself)."[62]

Let us be clear about our result so far. Man as a rational being possesses *autonomy,* the capacity to legislate his own freedom. As such he belongs to the community of all such legislators, the "kingdom of ends" in its first, clear and unequivocal sense of a community of wills, in which all, by virtue of their common reason, stand as ends-in-themselves in relation to one another. But since not all rational wills are *pure* rational wills, i.e., not every intelligence is an *intellectus archetypus* and not every will is a holy will, the intentions which these imperfect, finite legislators require must be actualized by exertion in the world of sense. That occasions uncertainty. Moreover, as finite, these legislators also find themselves saddled—"burdened" is Kant's prefered term—with actual needs. Since membership in the kingdom of ends precludes exploiting others as means merely and since the prospect of actualizing one's legislations must be contingent upon their toleration and may be contingent on their assistance, that occasions some risk. But if any goal can be actualized, any result achieved within these binding constraints, that result belongs, as well, within the "kingdom of ends." The latter now becomes an expanded concept: not merely a community of wills but this community together with all its legitimate achievements.

This expanded concept of a "kingdom of ends" was an "intelligible world," a "moral world" which Kant called the "highest good."[63] As such, Kant maintained in the *Grounding of the Metaphysics of Morals,* it was "certainly only an ideal."[64] The point is, this *would be* the world were the rational agents in the "kingdom of ends" capable of the powers of actualization of an *intellectus archetypus.* The issue that remains is: given the limitations of human nature ("finitude"), what becomes of the notion of this expanded "kingdom of ends"? But that is no longer a question of pure rationality. That is a question of man in his full complexity as sensual as well as rational. That is a question of being-in-the-world.

The crucial question for a finite rational being is how to conceive it possible to act as a legislator in the "kingdom of ends," which is its rational right, when it finds itself, as its natural condition, in a world of sense governed by natural laws. The problem is one of the transcendental applicability of the pure law of practical reason in the concrete case of a finite rational being. "A kingdom of ends is possible only on the analogy of a kingdom of nature," Kant wrote.[65] That is the problem of "practical judgment." In analogy to the *First Critique*, we may term it the problem of "schematism"—Kant's discussion of the "kingdom of ends" in the *Grounding of the Metaphysics of Morals* becomes a discussion of the "typic of practical judgment" in the *Critique of Practical Reason.*

That transition is made more intelligible by his discussion of "ectypal nature" earlier in the "Analytic." Kant introduced the notion of "ectypal nature" in a discussion of the possibility of a transcendental deduction of pure practical reason.[66] The question, in analogy to that of the *First Critique,* is what warrant pure reason may have to legislate over given actuality. But the situation is by no means so strained as in the *First Critique,* for while there the radical alienness of matter given in sensation ("actuality without validity") confronted pure reason, here it is instead "nature" as phenomena ordered and constituted by reason cognitively according to law. While a "kingdom of ends" requires the law of freedom, the kingdom of nature is bound by mechanical laws of causality; nevertheless, the feature they share is precisely lawfulness, the authority of reason. It is, then, simply a matter of finding a mode of reading the lawfulness of one sort into the lawfulness of the other.

Already in the *Grounding,* Kant recognized the striking convergence of moral judgment and teleological judgment in this context: "Teleology considers nature as a kingdom of ends; morals regards a possible kingdom of ends as a kingdom of nature. In the former the kingdom of ends is a theoretical idea for explaining what exists. In the latter it is a practical idea for bringing about what does not exist but can be made actual by our conduct, i.e., what can be actualized in accordance with this very idea."[67] We have considered the question of teleology as an examination of natural purpose. What we must now see is how it serves as a vehicle for conceptualizing the complex "schematization" of practical reason.

Morality conceives of a world that does not yet exist in nature and seeks to actualize it by acting in the given world according to the laws of the possible one. "This [moral] law gives to the sensible world, as sensuous nature (as this concerns rational beings), the form of an intelligible world, i.e., the form of supersensuous nature, without interfering with the mechanism of the former."[68] The presumption is that the natural world can accommodate this at least in some measure. That is just what is at stake in the discussion of "ectypal nature." The idea of a "supersensuous nature" refers back to the *mundus intelligibilis* of the *First Critique* and to the "moral world" as a "kingdom of ends" in the expanded sense in the *Grounding*. It is the world as noumenal, which is not accessible to human cognition. But it is also conceivable in terms of a shift in optics from what is to what ought to be. Reason, even finite human reason, can readily enough conceive of a just world, even in its absence. For Kant, such a just world would draw its material from the natural world, but it would be formed by the ideal, moral world: "supersensuous nature, so far as we can form a concept of it, is nothing else than nature under the autonomy of pure practical reason. The law of this autonomy is the moral law, and it, therefore, is the fundamental law of supersensible nature and of a pure world of the understanding."[69] This is *natura archetypa*, the world we can know only by reason, an intelligible world. But its "counterpart must exist in the world of sense without interfering with the laws of the latter . . . [this] could be called the ectypal world *(natura ectypa),* because it contains the possible effects of the idea of the former [*natural archetypa*] as the determining ground of the will."[70] In the "Typic," Kant picks up this very argument: "we are therefore allowed to use the nature of the sensuous world as the type of an intelligible nature."[71]

In the "Typic" Kant offered a careful transcendental justification of this proceeding. The problem of the "Typic" was part of the general problem of "hypotyposis"—of finding in the world of sensible intuition correlates for the concepts of reason.[72] In the sphere of understanding and sensible intuition, the hypotyposis occurred through schematism in a determinant judgment, and the result was natural law and nature as existence (actuality) under this law. In the case of the pure ideas of reason, the problem of their presentation *(Darstellung)* was extreme, and Kant clarified it only in his theory of symbolism in the *Third Critique.* But in the case of *applied* ideas of reason, i.e., moral judgments as imperatives, the hypotyposis was accomplished by the mediation of a postulated law of nature. As Kant put it, "natural law serves only as the *type* of a law of freedom."[73] Because nature is lawful cognitively (for the understanding), "reason has a right, and is even compelled, to use nature (in its pure intellible form) as the type of judgment."[74] The warrant or right lies in lawfulness as such, the mark of reason in general: "laws as such are all equivalent [as rational], regardless of whence [which faculty] they derive their determining grounds."[75]

But having established how it was possible did not of itself establish that it was completely actual or even that it would be completely actualized. To the extent that there was an obligation to actualize this ideal world, some serious problems arose, in Kant's view. Kant's "kingdom of ends," in its expanded sense, entailed the actualization of the "highest good." "For, in fact, the moral law ideally transfers us into a nature in which reason would bring forth the highest good were it accompanied by sufficient physical capacities; and it determines our will to impart to the sensuous world the form of a system of rational beings."[76] We must plunge, at last, into the controversy over the nature and necessity of Kant's notion of the "highest good."

 *Seventeen*

THE UNITY OF MANKIND:
THE HIGHEST GOOD,
HISTORY, AND RELIGION

The viability of man's moral purpose in the world of sense is, as I have argued, the most salient theme of Kant's *Third Critique* in its final form. He enunciated this theme in §ii of the Introduction. He closed the work with it in the "Methodology of Teleological Judgment" in the discussion of "moral teleology."[1] The issue for "moral teleology" is the reconciliation of nature as it is with nature as it ought to be if we are to be effective free agents: "[M]oral teleology concerns us as beings of the world, and therefore as beings bound up with other things in the world . . . [and] has to do with the reference of our own causality to purposes and even to a final purpose that we must aim at in the world . . . and the external possibility of its accomplishment."[2] The moral law which is the ground of our freedom commands that freedom act in the world to realize justice. "Moral teleology" involves the problem of that realization, the highly controversial idea of the "highest good" in Kant's ethics.[3] In the preface to *Religion Within the Limits of Reason Alone* he stated it with great clarity:

> It cannot be a matter of unconcern to morality as to whether or not it forms for itself the concept of a final end of all things (harmony with which, while not multiplying men's duties, yet provides them with a special point of focus for the unification of all ends); for only thereby can objective, practical reality be given to the union of the purposiveness arising from freedom with the purposiveness of nature, a union with which we cannot possibly dispense.[4]

As John Silber notes, Kant claimed reason's task was to achieve the unity of the good.[5] To do so Kant needed to extend his analysis of ethics from man as a merely rational being to man as a rational and a sensible being at once. Granted the heterogeneity of the good, i.e., two forms of the good which man must recognize and integrate into his practice as a finite rational being, then the idea of the "highest good" as "immanent" becomes intelligible within Kant's moral philosophy.[6] The "schematization" of the moral law in actuality can be rationally recognized by the subject as the project of promoting the highest good in the world.[7] In this way Kant in *Religion*, for example, writes of "the synthetic enlargement of the concept of the law taking place through [reference to] the natural character of man as a being of needs who cannot be indifferent to the results of his actions."[8]

On a coherent reading, Kant never intended to claim that the highest good *constituted* the duty imposed by the moral law, but only that it *specified* it in actuality, and that as a moral ideal it could be known a priori. Kant requires the "schematization," i.e., actual application of pure moral law in the world of sense by a finite rational being with objective needs. Therefore he conceives of "ends (results) which are duties," and further of the entire set of such ends— for each individual and for mankind as a whole—as a "kingdom of ends" and as a "highest good." Beck writes that "the moral will must have an object as well as a form, and, because of the finite and sensible nature of man, the concept of the possiblity of the highest good is necessary to the moral disposition, but not to the definition of duty."[9] Still, Beck rejects this argument as "heteronomy," the sullying of pure moral will with "all-too-human" ends. It is hard to see how Beck can uphold his position without arrogating the good entirely to the pure will. That reduces Kant to Stoicism, which he could never have accepted. Moreover, the heterogeneity of the good is grounded in the heterogeneity of human nature. Man's mixed nature intrudes equally in the discursiveness of cognition. Beck does not by that token deny the efficacy of pure reason in actual human cognition. That man is not an *intellectus archetypus* is indeed a pity, but it does not prevent him from making actual cognitive judgments in which pure reason constitutes (legislatively determines) nature without losing any of its rational character. Schematism is certainly involved in this synthetic (ampliative) judgment. That man is not a holy will is also a pity, for such a holy will, presumably because it is an *intellectus archetypus,* would automatically actualize all its moral intentions and there would arise for it no gap between is and ought. But that does not entail that the same pure moral determination could not be applied to actuality, that this application by its very nature would be synthetic (or ampliative), or that it would constitute thereby a morally legitimate object rather than sully pure moral will itself. Beck's "purism," while it has some warrant in Kant's texts, has serious limitations.

Mary Zeldin devotes a careful article to the defense of Kant's notion of the highest good against Beck's criticisms.[10] She contends that the highest good is more complex than the categorical imperative, since it is an ampliative synthetic judgment which applies that imperative to the concrete conditions of actuality. "Just as the schematized categories contain more than the 'empty' pure categories," she writes, so does the highest good as a synthetic practical judgment contain more than the pure moral law as stated in the categorical imperative. The highest good, she claims, is in fact a "moral ideal" or goal of purposive action in the world of sense. It conceives the synthetic totality of all the achievements in the actual world which are compatible with the moral law and conducive to the welfare of mankind. It represents that ampliative, second sense of the "kingdom of ends" which includes not only all rational wills but all their legitimate achievements.[11]

Allen Wood makes the same argument in *Kant's Moral Religion.* He argues that "there must be a systematic unity in which natural ends, the ends given by man's finite needs, can be included within the ends of morality, the objects of pure practical reason."[12] In his argument, Wood distinguishes between the unconditioned (pure) good and the conditioned (schematized) good, associating the first with the moral law and the categorical imperative and the second with the completed actualization of that imperative in the world of sense. Wood argues that Kant's moral philosophy aims at more than an analysis of particular moral choices. It carries forward to larger totalities: a concern for the person and his virtue, not just right action in a given instance. A person is a coherent rational being with a character and disposition, a being of intrinsic worth. The degree of that worth is virtue. Virtue is not a single right action but a whole pattern of choice and the grounding disposition behind it. Finally, Wood argues, morality involves not simply motives but consequences. Men have actual obligations in the world. There are, as Kant would insist in *Metaphysics of Morals* (1797), "ends which are duties." Even to oneself as a natural being such duties obtained, Wood points out, and Kant accepted that position as the key to his rejection of Stoicism.[13]

Perhaps the most extended effort to formulate this moral interpretation of the idea of the highest good is to be found in Thomas Auxter's works on "ectypal nature." Particularly fruitful is the distinction Auxter introduces between an ethic of inclusive ends and an ethic of ultimate end.[14] While a formalist reading (and a fortiori a rigorist one) would take Kant to uphold an ethic of ultimate end, i.e., the execution of duty for duty's sake, there is sufficient textual evidence, in Auxter's view, to suggest that Kant also wished to uphold the idea of an ethic of inclusive ends, an ethic which had as its supreme principle the idea of a maximal integration of all the specific purposes of rational agents into wholes. Within the individual this signified unity of personality, character, disposition, virtue. But this "harmonious order of human purposes" extended beyond any single individual and involved a social and historical, a species dimension.[15] The highest good was, Auxter argues, a "regulative principle" for the expression of this idea of moral progress: "The final good is an inclusive end—a life in which we harmonize the exercise of all natural abilities through the influence of reason."[16] Auxter tries to develop a theory of Kant's "highest good" in this sense according to the idea of a "teleological convergence" in which a "progressive harmonization and realization of human values" (morality as an inclusive end) substantiates or actualizes the pure moral law (morality as an ultimate end).[17]

The objectification of the moral law in the world of sense involves the actualization of man's latent capacities, and above all the question of man's effort to achieve a just world. This is a matter not so much of individual conduct as of interaction among moral agents. It is a universal, not a particular mandate, to be sought not simply individually but collectively. Therefore it raises the issues of the meaning of history and of political-religious community, as well.[18] Kant put this in terms of the "kingdom of ends" in the *Grounding of the Metaphysics of Morals* and in terms of a "just civil community" in "Idea for a Universal History with Cosmopolitan Intent," then reformulated it in terms of "ectypal nature" in the *Second Critique* and "man under moral laws" as the "final purpose of creation" in the *Third Critique*. What is most exciting for modern thinkers is the strictly moral reading of the "highest good" as the extension of noumenally grounded moral law into the actual world beyond the subject: justice, community, history, cosmology, and religion. These issues came to formulation in the very last phase of composition of the *Third Critique,* in early 1790, above all in the "Methodology of Teleological Judgment."[19]

In terms of the architectonic of the work, the "Methodology of Teleological Judgment" set out to explore the problem of relative purposiveness in theoretical reflective judgment.[20] A "relative" purpose is that which serves some other, active and hence "intrinsic" purpose.[21] It is therefore "external"; its purposiveness is not something inherent in its own essential principle, but only serves the intention of some other entity. It is not inherent in the nature of cork bark, for instance, that it stop wine bottles. It takes the external intervention of man to make the cork bark purposive in this way. It is then relative to man's purpose. It is not the purpose of man to provide blood for mosquitos. But they use him anyway. Man is a relative purpose for them. Purposiveness in this external and relative sense is natural in a world which is populated by organic forms, i.e., intrinsic purposes. More problematic, of course, is the nature of an intrinsic purpose itself, and without this, relative purposiveness becomes impossible. An intrinsic purpose, on Kant's reading, sets its own purposes, or is self-organizing. Whatever the difficulties this notion poses for the categorial determination of nature, Kant finds it necessary in order to make sense of certain things in the world.

All of this is quite familiar. The new issue Kant raises is the relative purposiveness not of particular things in nature to others, but of nature as a whole. If nature as a whole is to be a relative purpose, what intrinsic purpose is it serving? In order to be "ultimate," i.e., serve as the purpose for nature as a whole, such an intrinsic purpose would need to be "final," not only "organized" but of value in itself (i.e., capable of moral freedom).[22] There are two logical candidates for this status. The first is man, taken not as natural but as noumenal. The second is God, taken not as immanent but as transcendent. In short, to think of nature in terms of its "ultimate purpose" we must think of man or of God as "final purposes," i.e., as ends-in-themselves, autonomous rational wills. They are, as such, unquestionably noumenal. They are beyond categorial determination. But they are not beyond thought. Kant proposes that they be thought through quite rigorously.

If we seek within nature itself for an "ultimate purpose," the only candidate is man. To see man as nature's ultimate purpose is to think him "privileged" by nature. While he is intrinsically purposive even as a natural organic form, he is by no means "nature's darling," for he is as much the victim of nature as her beneficiary.[23] While there are certainly occasions in which it appears to him as though the entire world is there for his sake, there are others in which, as with the mosquitos, it seems the other way around. As natural purpose, man seeks to maximize his "happiness." Unfortunately for him, "happiness" is a chimera.[24] It is a nominal, not a real universal. It cannot be specified concretely, because it is indeterminate, shifting not only between human subjects but even for each human subject. It is nevertheless an inevitable result of our material subjectivity. Not only will it necessarily exist; it will necessarily exact practical acknowledgment.[25] The claim of "happiness" cannot be extirpated any more than it can be satiated. But if that were not bad enough, nature hardly seems driven to accommodate him anyway.

What does nature do for man, then, if not provide him "happiness"? Kant answers this question in three distinct veins. First, most notoriously, nature challenges his skill, and therewith forces him to develop his talents in order to survive and prosper in the world.[26] Nature proves purposive for man in just the measure that she resists his ease and comfort, forcing him to exert himself to dominate her and extract from her that quotient of "happiness" he restlessly and vainly pursues. This is put most bluntly in Kant's essay of 1784, "Idea for a Universal History with Cosmopolitan Intent":

> Thanks are due to nature for [man's] quarrelsomeness, his enviously competitive vanity, and for his insatiable desire to possess or to rule, for without them all the excellent natural faculties of mankind would forever remain undeveloped. Man wants concord but nature knows better what is good for his kind; nature wants discord. Man wants to live comfortably and pleasurably but nature intends that he should raise himself out of lethargy and inactive contentment into work and trouble and then he should find means of extricating himself adroitly from these latter.[27]

This is the foundation of Kant's philosophy of history and politics— a very stark, Hobbesian foundation, however Rousseauist the solution he believes will eventually supervene.

The second provision of nature is to cultivate his taste. In this disciplining of taste, schooling man's gratification away from coarse appetite and elevating it to more urbane and dispassionate delights, Kant finds the connection between beauty and morality, the principle of "aesthetic education," as Schiller would soon put it.[28]

Once again, however, this strictly natural cultivation, while it is less strenuous and privative than the first, does not satisfy man's natural craving for happiness. It merely sublimates it a bit. Desire is deflected from its original objects.[29] That is progress, to be sure, but not on the standard of man's natural impulse. Nature is inadvertently at the service of something unnatural. It is satisfying to man's rationality, both cognitive and practical. The beautiful and the sublime reinforce man's awareness of these "noumenal" elements in his "nature."

And that awareness, or rather the stimulation to such reflection, is the third distinct and important purpose nature serves for man. Nature occasions reflection, through its order, about its ultimate purpose and hence man's own intrinsic purpose, and helps bring man to the crucial recognition of his freedom.[30] An ultimate purpose would have to be a final (intrinsic) purpose. But man is a final purpose, according to Kant, not as natural, but as moral. Thus nature is purposive for man precisely in making man ask after his own final purpose. In all three of these services, nature makes man better able to be what he already is: a free will.[31]

The discussion in §83 of the *Third Critique* reformulates the philosophy of history which Kant had first sketched in "Idea for a Universal History."[32] Kant raised the issue there: Did history make sense? What a historian had to do, he asserted, was "attempt to discover an end of nature in this senseless march of human events."[33] Accordingly, the philosopher of history had to posit "teleology" in nature, since conjectures about historical coherence required a determinate "natural purpose of man." Kant asserted as his first principle: "All natural faculties of a creature are destined to unfold completely and according to their end [*Zweck*]."

The incongruous and dogmatic character of Kant's use of "nature" in this work has occasioned a great deal of comment.[34] Nature in these phrases can only have signified God's providential design for the world. That Kant did not write "Providence" may be simply a question of stylistic grace and common usage. This was a popular essay. But there are two other possibilities. First, Kant may not have felt comfortable publishing his work on history "with cosmopolitan intent" in such unequivocally religious garb, especially as it was to appear in the *Berlinische Monatsschrift,* one of the most aggressive of the secularizing-rationalist journals of the period. But second, and more plausibly, Kant may have meant his readers to be struck by the extravagance of the personification of nature. A deeper literary trope may have underlain the more obvious one: irony directed at proponents of an immanent natural destiny of man—a view very popular in intellectual circles in Germany associated with Herder, the first volume of whose *Ideen zur Philosophie der Geschichte der Menschheit* was appearing almost simultaneously with the essay, and whom Kant was about to attack in a series of harsh reviews.[35]

In short, here again the controversy with Herder proves essential to the *Third Critique*.[36] The dispute between Kant and Herder over the meaning of history and the proper relation between nature and culture was one of the most important events in the literary life of Germany in the last years of the eighteenth century. It brought to a climax the whole extensive discussion of the philosophy of history which was one of the most lively aspects of Aufklärung.[37] It would bring forward even more important speculation about the meaning of history, that of the German Idealists and Karl Marx. Yet there is interesting evidence that as he composed the *Third Critique,* Kant began a shift in his historical thinking, perhaps influenced by the events taking place simultaneously in France, which moved him away from his harshly Hobbesian orientation and closer, if not to Herder, then to that generation which inherited Herder's agenda.[38]

In any event, with the premise of Providence in hand, the essay of 1784 proceeded to claim a crucial second principle: the natural purpose of man could not be realized by the individual but only by the species. "Every man would have to live excessively long in order to learn how to make full use of all his faculties." This was because those faculties were grounded in reason, which had to progress by learning—through "trials, experience and information"—and which recognized no boundary or limit in its "capacity to enlarge the rules and purposes of the use of his resources." Not only did this result in the discomfiture of particular individuals, but all those transitional generations which slowly wove the rich fabric of human realization would themselves be denied the full fruits of their labor. Kant acknowledged that "it remains perplexing that earlier generations seem to do their laborious work for the sake of later generations . . . [but, he concluded] however mysterious this may be, it is nevertheless necessary."[39] Kant conceded that at the level of the individual—and perhaps even for the whole of the transition— "Rousseau was not so very wrong when he preferred the condition of savages."[40] But Kant insisted that Rousseau *was* nevertheless wrong, for it was not the individual but the species, and indeed, the ultimate destiny of the species, that had to serve as criterion.[41]

How did nature see to it that the human species progressed?

Kant's third principle replied that it was by throwing man upon his own devices: "Nature seems to have delighted in the greatest parsimony; she seems to have barely provided man's animal equipment and limited it to the most urgent needs of a beginning existence, as if nature intended that man should owe all to himself."[42] By denying him a determinate physical advantage in the struggle for survival, nature consigned man to his latent faculties—reason and free will. This deviousness of natural purpose, this "invisible hand" or "cunning of nature," did not halt at the physical endowments of man.[43] Kant's fourth principle took up Rousseau's gravest strictures and read them in an ironically constructive light. Kant saw in Rousseau's *amour propre* not merely moral viciousness but social productivity. Nature used "the antagonism of men in society," their "asocial sociability," as the device for species progress. Man, "impelled by vainglory, ambition and avarice, . . . seeks to achieve a standing among his fellows."[44]

"Private vice conduces to public virtue." Here was the great relief that political economy offered the anxious moralists of the eighteenth century. Competition, with its enforcement not only of labor but of prudence under the rubric of "interest," offered not only an order, but a prospect of "improvement."[45] To be sure, no appeal was made to virtue, which seemed, in any event, too weak to weld society together. It was inappropriate in a hardheaded, naturalistic interpretation of human behavior.[46] In the 1780s, Kant read the history at least of the past on such a strictly mechanistic, naturalistic, indeed Hobbesian line.[47] Kant was willing to countenance not merely the loss of happiness, but even that amoral—indeed immoral—aggression, for the sake of the progress it had achieved. Through competition, relentless pursuit of personal interest, "all man's talents are gradually unfolded, taste is developed . . . the basis is laid for a frame of mind which, in the course of time, transforms the raw natural faculty of moral discrimination into definite practical principles." Kant found the justification for these "unlovely" means in the end: "a *pathologically* enforced coordination of society finally transforms it into a *moral* whole."[48] The difficulty of such a project was not lost on him. "Man is an animal who, if he lives among others of his kind, *needs a master,* for man certainly misuses his freedom in regard to others of his kind . . . Man therefore *needs* a master who can break man's will and compel him to obey a general will under which every man could be free."[49] The final terms are Rousseau's, but without Rousseau's humans with a natural endowment of good. Indeed, Kant articulates far more clearly the staunch Lutheran conviction of man's baser nature and the need for an authoritarian state to control it.[50] Kant's dim view of "brute nature" in man lies at the core of his philosophy of history. Animals indeed, men were schooled by their very "asocial sociability" to an attitude altogether inconsistent with a *moral whole.*" Kant commented: "The task involved is therefore most difficult; indeed, a complete solution is impossible. One cannot fashion something absolutely straight from wood which is as crooked as that of which man is made."[51] No, and still less if one's whole conception of "progress" is a warping of that wood on an altogether different line!

Kant characterized man's "final purpose" *(Endzweck),* "the highest task nature has set mankind," as a "moral whole," "a completely *just civic constitution.*" This was the most difficult problem mankind had to solve; nevertheless Kant believed it was also the current problem, or, in short, that "the achievement of a civil society which administers law generally" was the task to which the "age of enlightenment" had turned.[52] Yet it is not at all to be seen how a "*pathologically* enforced coordination of society finally transforms it into a *moral* whole."[53] Kant wrote: "*great experience* in many activities and a *good will* which is prepared to accept such a constitution are all required." Whence would they have come? How should they prevail?

It was to evade the embarrassment of this problem that Kant reformulated the question in §83 of the *Third Critique.* Kant shifted from a view of history as progressing according to some mechanical natural law, to one of history as a voluntary project of human moral realization. Nature still had a tutelary role to play, but Kant, in the context of his pervasive purposiveness in the *Third Critique,* clearly assigned to voluntarism and purpose a good deal more responsibility in the fabric of history. There were still enormous problems of transition and mediation, but Kant proposed a whole new principle for history with this shift. History became a realm between nature and freedom: the record of the interventions of freedom in the world of mechanical causality and the string of their consequences (intended and unintended). Moreover, reason's intervention did not come only at the end (or at the present, "Enlightened" turning point, though that continued to have a decisive role to play in Kant's philosophy of history). Reason intervened from the origin of the species. In "Muthmaßlicher Anfang der Menschengeschichte," Kant had taken up this issue, drawing on Rousseau (and disputing Herder's use of Genesis). He traced the natural ("pragmatic" or "technical") interventions of reason in human fate prior to the *moral* intervention.[54] At the same time he elaborated on nature's intervention in human affairs, thwarting, tempting, cajoling, structuring. The dialectic of history, in this new formulation, proved far more intricate.

Kant's model of history started from the premise that nature was not spontaneously moral but could be changed by human praxis. At the same time, nature did act in ways that stimulated the emergence of human praxis as this moral transfiguration. It schooled man in his own freedom.[55] Through discipline and cultivation, nature primed man's natural capacities and evoked rational reflection and the realization of man's fundamental power to seize control of his own fate. This decisive turning point in universal history Kant identified with Enlightenment.[56] That was the moment when nature surrendered control of the human project and left the balance of history in the hands of freedom. Prospective history would, in a Kantian frame, proceed under the self-conscious and voluntary ideal of a perfection of the world according to moral laws: the pursuit of the "highest good." The vehicles for this pursuit in history would be the political community or state on the level of legality—the "civil community" to which Kant devoted a great deal of attention in his writings on history and especially on the philosophy of right—and the "ethical community" which found its institutional embodiment in religion, but its philosophical essence in the "kingdom of ends."[57]

These ideas, intimated in §83 of the *Third Critique,* became the major focus of Kant's attention in the subsequent decade, stimulated no doubt by the French Revolution.[58] Human action transfiguring the world from the determinism which characterized the natural order into an order of freedom, Yirmiahu Yovel argues, is Kant's richest sense of the highest good. It is nothing less than "the regulative idea of history," according to Yovel.[59] For him, Kant's concept of the highest good only comes fully into its own at this communal-collective level. It is as a species interest that the highest good makes sense in Kant's system of philosophy. It is the ideal according to which rational, i.e., voluntary history as a work of human freedom, proceeds. "The work of moral history is to overcome the alienness of nature by imprinting human patterns and ends upon it."[60] The language Yovel uses is strikingly—and appropriately—Hegelo-Marxian. But it is also Kantian: "we have to create a 'second nature' which exhibits moral ideas."[61] The task of moral history is to transform the empirically given into a human purpose, to objectify morality. "Kant makes this idea of subduing nature and reshaping it in accordance with human reason the principle of critical history."[62] This "can only be created by a cumulative and cooperative effort of humanity."[63] In religious language, what Kant saw as the project of moral history was the creation of the "kingdom of God on earth."[64]

Kant wished to use this dimension of the concept also as a transition to theology. G. E. Michaelson notes that there was a shift, in the *Religion*, from a political to a religious conception of the "ethical community" to be associated with the "highest good" in the world.[65] Wood, too, argues that the ultimate sense of Kant's "kingdom of ends" must be that of the "Kingdom of God on earth."[66] This position is reinforced by Michel Despland, who argues for the centrality of a Christian eschatology in Kant's philosophy of history.[67] Yet Kant's philosophy of history ended in failure, even his most careful expositors tend to conclude.[68] Rather, his thought has seemed to be more coherent as political theory, because essentially it is through his timeless moral theory that he most richly and powerfully endows social theory with a point of departure.[69] Thus, critics of his approach to history and teleology nevertheless find in his theory of political right strong stimulus to thought. Still, in essaying the integration of morality with teleology in historical time, Kant came to grips with great questions of the human state, and accorded them dignity as part of the realm of philosophy.

The *Third Critique* is recognized as the crucial text for the foundation of this historical, political, and religious philosophy in Kant, yet he offers there a remarkably compressed account of these areas, with the exception of the theological aspect of religion. It is more the case that the *Third Critique* clears the ground for the work in these fields which would occupy Kant extensively in the 1790s than that it actually accomplishes much of that work. It is the vehicle for accessing such questions, a threshold before the rich fields of social and cultural philosophy. The simultaneous impact of the French Revolution could only have accentuated this reorientation. Yet the very fact of this massive contextual impact, to say nothing of the emergence of the rival Idealist school within Germany in that same decade, suggests that a contextual reading of Kant's thought on history and politics in the light of the *Third Critique* would need to be quite ambitious and extensive. That is clearly beyond the scope of this study.

There is, however, a contextual point that is germane, namely, the strong religious interest that animates the *Third Critique*, growing out of Kant's struggle with Spinozism, pantheism, and materialism. The insistence upon theism which is so central to the "ethical turn" of the *Third Critique*, and indeed, an even more determinately Christian reading of that theism, finds strong expression in the final pages of the work. Kant elaborated extensively upon the religious dimension of the "highest good" in the "Methodology of Teleological Judgment" in order to buttress his case against the Spinozists. While the extraordinarily important discussion of history occupied only §83, the discussion of ethico-theology took up almost the entire segment, §§84–91.

"Ethico-theology" in the "Methodology of Teleological Judgment"

The historical issue distracted us from the ongoing argument of the "Methodology" about the relative purposiveness of nature as a whole, and the relation betwen "ultimate" and "final" purposes. Kant continues that discussion in §84. Only as a morally intrinsic purpose is man a "final purpose"—one which "needs no other as condition of its possibility."[70] Because man is certain via the "fact of pure reason" of his status as moral and hence final purpose, he can see himself, as a moral entity ("under moral laws"), eligible to be the "ultimate purpose" of nature.

> Now we have in the world only one kind of beings whose causality is teleological, i.e. is directed to purposes, and is at the same time so constituted that the law according to which they have to determine purposes for themselves is represented as unconditioned and independent of natural conditions, and yet as in itself necessary. The being of this kind is man, but man considered as noumenon, the only natural being in which we can recognize, on the side of its peculiar constitution, a supersensible faculty *(freedom)* and also the law of causality, together with the object, which this faculty may propose to itself as highest purpose (the highest good in the world).[71]

He needs no further ground for his own freedom or for the possibility of his relation to nature as ultimate purpose.[72] The problem lies not with the *possibility* of this relation, but with its full actualization. Man is eligible to be nature's ultimate purpose. But does nature even have a purpose?

While man's freedom is a fact, its efficacy in the actual world is entirely contingent upon the laws of the natural order, and those laws need not necessarily accord with his design, however final. In that measure, nature may not be a consistent or even a frequent "relative purpose" for man. We might reformulate Kant's argument as follows. While man "under moral laws" was indubitably a "final purpose" and hence he could see himself as a *possible* "ultimate purpose" for nature, he could not establish himself as its *actual* "ultimate purpose," much less its necessary one. He required, therefore, a warrant which would secure this actuality. That is, he needed a guarantee that the "highest good" was possible, for this would make man "under moral laws" the actual ultimate purpose of nature.[73] The only way this actuality could be warranted, Kant argued, was for another "final purpose" to establish with necessity the ultimate purpose of nature as man under moral laws. That other final purpose, of course, was God, and that ultimate purpose he would have for nature would be Providence, creating the possibility for man's realization of freedom. The existence of God would guarantee man's actual chance to realize the "highest good," through the transfiguration of the natural order into a "kingdom of ends," i.e., "man under moral laws." God did not guarantee the necessity of success, for it was man's task to see to it. God simply made nature amenable to the project.

By the time of the *Third Critique,* the highest good for Kant was a step in an argument which was from the outset intentionally theological, not merely moral.[74] If we consider the manner in which Kant constructed his argument from "moral teleology" to the "highest good" in the "Methodology of Teleological Judgment," we can see that his interest lies quite unequivocally in justifying belief in the existence of a transcendent-personal God. His classic refutation of all rational proofs of God in the *First Critique* had included a refutation of the so-called "physico-theological" proof.[75] Nevertheless he expressed respect for this argument.[76] The *Third Critique* advanced the argument that it was at least subjectively necessary to think of an intelligent will as the original cause of the world.[77] But there "physico-theology" reached its outer limit. It could not proceed from this to the full notion of a God.[78] That step was possible only in and through moral experience and "ethico-theology."

Kant tried in the "Methodology" to establish a necessary connection between "moral teleology" and "theology." This argument moved from the practical reality of freedom through the obligation to realize the "highest good," to the requirement for a warrant of the possibility of that realization. Kant claimed we need a theology precisely for the sake of the "highest good"—not, to be sure, for our obligation to pursue it, but for the hope that this obligation is not Sisyphean. In seeking a warrant for the achievement of justice in this world man first conceives the rational need for God. There are two crucial points which must be clarified in this connection. First, man's moral obligation is not grounded in the existence of God. As Kant argues concerning the "highest good" itself, the existence of God is not "necessary for morals," but rather "necessitated by morality."[79] It is because we are morally obliged to secure justice in the world that we must believe in a God to make this possible. In other words, it is not what one knows of God that makes him moral, but what is moral which tells one what he knows about God. The idea of God is the principle necessary to secure the possibility of the full realization of the "highest good." Nothing more is needed in that concept, and nothing less. Second, "theology" arises out of an immanent practical concern, out of "moral teleology," and hence the nature and the validity of theology derive from that context. One need have no concern with what God may be as a speculative entity, but only with knowing that God provides certain essential requirements for man's practical destiny in the world. With that the warrant for the reality of God shifts from a cognitive principle to a practical requirement. Kant wrote extensively in the balance of the "Methodology" to square the circle of his commitment to determinate beliefs about the nature of God with the "critical" restrictions of knowledge of the transcendent. His protracted discussion reaffirmed all the positions of the "critical philosophy," including the doctrine of "rational belief." Though it was to serve a metaphysical function, the highest good as a warrant for postulating God could not appeal to theoretical reason, because it originated in practical reason.

At the level of the individual human being, Kant argued, the only kind of justice which man can find consistent with his principle of morality and his condition as a natural being is one in which happiness, as the inevitable aspiration of his natural existence, is legitimated by worthiness. As a natural, not merely rational being, man has objective needs which reason associates with happiness. As a free being, man can act purely for the sake of the moral law. Such an act, according to Kant, is virtuous and adds to the worth of the agent who performs it. This "merit" should, in a perfect world, find recompense in a proportionate happiness. For an individual human being, the highest good involves the relation of his virtue to its reward. The problem for man is that his empirical experience suggests that neither in his own particular case nor in the universal case of his species are the prospects of such a just world encouraging. It remains, however, that it is altogether human to ask—over and above "What should I do?"—the question "What may I hope?" That question must not determine the will, but it is certainly a rational question that the subject may ask about the disposition of affairs in the cosmos. Kant believed the question "What may I hope?" was legitimate and indeed inevitable in man as a finite rational being. Such a question, however, was at least as speculative as it was practical.[80] Ultimately, it involved a religious, not merely a moral dimension. Hence, in the highest good as the problem of individual reward, the link between morality and religion is at its most salient.

Kant argued that "speculative reason" would not find the plausibility of the "highest good" confirmed by an inspection of the real world, and it would therefore either think it "an ungrounded and vain, though well-meant, expectation" or have to satisfy itself that there was a God to make it right. If it could not convince itself of God, "it would regard the moral law itself as the mere deception of our reason in a practical aspect."[81] Kant claimed that despair could induce man not to strive to live up to his duty. "[A]lthough the necessity of duty is very plain for practical reason, yet the attainment of its final purpose, so far as it is not altogether in our power, is only assumed on behalf of the practical use of reason, and therefore is not so practically necessary as duty itself."[82] Kant therefore argued that man had to expect some success in his endeavors or he would succumb to despair. The notion of the highest good served as a security that such success would attend man's project of moral virtue. Kant sought to defend his view by demonstrating the plight of a putative "righteous atheist" (such as Spinoza):

[H]is effort is bounded; and from nature, although he may expect here and there a contingent accordance, he can never expect a regular harmony agreeing according to constant rules . . . with the purpose that he yet feels himself obliged and impelled to accomplish. Deceit, violence, and envy will always surround him, although he himself be honest, peaceable, and kindly; and the righteous men with whom he meets will, notwithstanding all their worthiness of happiness, be yet subjected by nature, which regards not this, to all the evils of want, disease, and untimely death, just like the beasts of the earth. So it will be until one wide grave engulfs them together (honest or not, it makes no difference) . . . The purpose, then, which this well-intentioned person had and ought to have before him in his pursuit of moral laws, he must certainly give up as impossible.[83]

Kant believed that without God this "tragic" dilemma would occasion cynicism and the abandonment of moral righteousness. It need not.[84] It should not.[85] It certainly does not abolish the duty entailed by the moral law, for that is a priori and ineluctable.[86] But Kant's profession of despair of such tragic endurance is consistent with his religious background and culture. The Christian origin of this whole constellation of considerations is not to be overlooked.[87] Kant clearly relates the ethical life to the problem of radical evil and the Christian notions of atonement and salvation.[88]

What is Kant really concerned about in this treatment of the "highest good"? While it would appear that he is concerned with the problem of psychological despair that results when morality commands things which are too hard for the natural subject, one must wonder about this. Kant is rigoristic in his moral theory.[89] At the same time, he clearly has no sympathy for man's natural needs.[90] He barely makes room for them within his scheme of morality. That he should nevertheless make such an issue of psychological discomfort suggest that he must have an ulterior motive to secure rational access to two very high desiderata of his culture and his religion: the immortality of the soul and the existence of a transcendent-personal God. These were principles which his theoretical philosophy could not secure as objectively real. They existed at best as "ideas of reason" with a regulative and subjective value for reason. That did not suffice for Kant or for the culture to which he was committed. Hence he needed to find a way to provide them objective reality in the critical philosophy. Kant sought a path to that reintegration via the "problem of the highest good."

In the *Third Critique,* Kant is really concerned with the kind of world which would exist were everyone to be fully moral. In a world of full worthiness, everyone should also be proportionately happy. What is required to compel the natural order to make happiness for man as a species a real possibility is nothing less than God. It might then take all man's strivings to actualize that possibility, and hence his skill and his merit would be entailed, but God must provide the crucial metaphysical security for the whole project. The realization of the "highest good" would accordingly become the realization of the "Kingdom of God in this world." Kant's philosophy culminates, it would appear, in the affirmation of some crucial tenets of the

Christian religion, though ostensibly "within the limits of reason alone." Rational belief in God and the immortality of the soul finds justification in the requirements of practical reason to realize the highest good. The objective reality of these spiritual noumena is to be "postulated."

The ultimate question of the "highest good" can be taken to be the coherence of the cosmos itself and its absolute worth. The question then becomes one of the unity of nature and freedom, that real unity of the supersensible at the ground of nature with that at the ground of freedom. The ideal of the highest good represents in this light not only the idea of an ultimate wholeness about the cosmos, but of a prior, grounding wholeness at its origin. This wholeness, the *ens perfectissimum* of classical metaphysics and the transcendent-personal God of orthodox Christianity, was obviously, again, beyond the pale of a rigorous epistemology, once again "dogmatic metaphysics."[91] But that did not keep Kant from pursuing these questions, not only in the *Third Critique* but also in the work which took up where it left off, *Religion Within the Limits of Reason Alone*. There Kant used the idea of the "highest good" to articulate an eschatological sense of the consummate wholeness of the cosmos, the coming of utopia, the "Kingdom of God on Earth." In this context, religion merged with a notion of a freely chosen future. Secular and sacred history converged.

The core of Kant's argument is the suggestion that man needed Divine Providence in order psychologically to motivate the actual will to persist in the course of virtue. The obvious objection is, of course, that psychological need is not a logical argument. This objection was made by Wizenmann against the Kantians in the context of the Pantheism Controversy.[92] Beck is correct to invoke it against this particular form of the Kantian argument for the highest good.[93] Wood tries to defend this argument by urging that it is not psychological but moral, an "absurdum practicum" which results the moment one accepts moral duty in the context of a recalcitrant world.[94] But the ulterior, religious-dogmatic commitment clearly intrudes into Kant's moral argument. Beck is quite correct to argue that at the very least the religious sense of the highest good (reward for merit) was not necessary to ground moral obligation, but part of a "practical-dogmatic metaphysics" which sought to bring theoretical and practical reason together into a unity. For Beck, this unity is merely a "dialectical Ideal of reason."[95] Upholding Beck's interpretation, Jeffrie Murphy calls it an "aesthetic ideal."[96] That is, the motive behind the idea of the highest good was not ethical but speculative, and the sense of "rightness" sought was not moral or even theoretical but "aesthetic."[97] Moreover, the doctrinal commitment and its contextual motive are particularly clear.

According to Auxter, in the *Second Critique* "the distinction between the moral ideal of the 'Analytic' and the religious ideal of the 'Dialectic' cannot be too strongly insisted upon."[98] While he denies the highest good conceived in the latter, he reformulates the notion of the objectification of moral principle in terms of Kant's idea of "ectypal nature." The "moral ideal" was indispensable for Kant's "moral teleology," i.e., for the actualization of moral purposes in the world of sense, and hence warranted a notion of the "highest good" as the ideal expressing the goal in actuality. But the "religious ideal" pointed in directions which were not strictly necessary to Kant's moral philosophy and had, for Auxter, a blatantly dogmatic metaphysical character.[99] It is very difficult, in light of all this, to resist the view that Kant's *Third Critique,* and above all its "ethical turn," intensely highlighted all the metaphysical issues in the "critical philosophy." Kant's contextual struggles and his personal commitments to a "theistic" if not outright Christian posture strongly colored the ultimate shape of the work.

THE ULTIMATE MEANING
OF THE *THIRD CRITIQUE*

The *Third Critique* finds its decisive concerns neither in questions of beauty nor in questions of empirical biology, but rather in the ultimate questions of the place of man in the order of the world—his freedom and his destiny. The evidence amassed in that endeavor ranges from the impromptu beauty of nature to the intractable purposiveness of organisms to the mysterious natural gift of genius. Across it all, however, nature serves only as a mirror: its purposiveness as a sign of our purpose, its beauty as the symbol of morality. The design of nature and even its very chaos give occasion for reflection upon the sublime power of freedom and for a stern consideration of its proper uses. The *Third Critique* thus stands as Kant's master work on man's complex being-in-the-world.

If this reading of the ethical turn and consequently of the ultimate purpose of the *Critique of Judgment* is valid, it goes a long way toward establishing that the occasion for Idealism lay *within* the philosophy of Kant himself. Despite contemporary inclinations to distinguish Kant from his Idealist successors, the continuity from the later Kant to the Idealists is very clear. The "sage of Königsberg" had definite ontological and theological preferences, which became increasingly explicit over the 1780s and took on exceptional prominence in the *Third Critique* (1790).

Kant's *Third Critique* was a work of great importance not only in its influence on the succeeding generation of German Idealism and Romanticism but also in its revision of the Kantian philosophy. There are strong grounds for the view that Kant's thinking evolved beyond the posture of the *First Critique,* and that a historical appreciation of his philosophizing must take into account a tendency in his later thought to try to resolve certain dilemmas of dualism which haunted that first great effort.[1] That tendency, under the aegis of such terms as the "unity of reason," the "primacy of practical reason," and "intrinsic purposiveness," drew Kant close to the kinds of speculations in metaphysics which his "Transcendental Dialectic" of the *First Critique* had proscribed. It is well to understand that Kant maintained into the *Third Critique* his distinction of "thought" from "knowledge," and hence adhered to the essential critical posture about the indeterminacy of reason beyond sensible intuition. Nevertheless, the degree of determinacy to which his thinking edged in the discussion of the "supersensible"—both within man and as a ground without which the coherence of knowledge even of the sensible world would be impossible—suggests that his critical stance had to it an element of transparency, beneath which a profoundly metaphysical Kantianism lay clear for any who wished to see it.

There were two aspects of metaphysics in Kant's philosophy. First, metaphysics was involved in the *entailment of the empirical:* in the actualization of reason, whether theoretical or practical.[2] This was the front on which Kant met Hume and sought to rescue the possibility of valid knowledge. Second, metaphysics involved *access to the transcendent:* grasping those fundamental ideas indispensable for human meaning but inaccessible to material measurement. Here Kant confronted the dogmatic metaphysicians of "school philosophy" and the whole heritage of traditional Western metaphysics. In the *First Critique* he had salvaged the first kind of metaphysics and scuttled the second. Nevertheless, he acknowledged even in the *First Critique* that human beings could not renounce the questions raised in the second vein, and he made provision that we might "think" about these, though such thought would be vain of all knowledge. Such a conclusion, he assured his readers, made room for *faith.* That this faith should also be *rational* was perhaps a piety even exceeding the notion that faith could serve at all. Too much that was vital to human experience had been sealed off from rational consideration by the *First Critique,* and we can only make sense of the next twenty years of Kant's thinking when we realize that he had to rebuild rational structures to access these domains and that his later works were devoted to this task.

Epistemologically, grave reservations can be raised against the posture of the *First Critique.* In this study, three such problems have surfaced repeatedly: the problem of a singular intuition, the problem of transcendental deduction (the utter disjunction of reason and sense), and the problem of self-consciousness (the unity of the subject). Kant had modified his stance on each of these questions, in my view, by the *Third Critique*. On the first, his theory of reflective judgment represented a major effort to revise his understanding of the phenomenology of perception. On the second, his notion of "transcendental explanations" allowed him to take into the critical philosophy crucial new aspects of human experience and relate them to a much more dynamic and integral theory of reason in which the two key terms were system and purpose. Out of this emerged the crucial idea of "intrinsic purpose," which expressed a view of holism and immanent causality distinctly incongruous with his theory of categorial determination of knowledge but which proved indispensable both for a transcendental account of reason and for an empirical account of organisms. Finally, on the third issue, Kant elaborated substantially on his idea of practical reason over the decade of the 1780s, and the glimmer of belief in "practical apperception" which surfaced in the *First Critique* took on more intensity and transcendental warrant in the *Second*. The *Third Critique* supplemented this "practical apperception" with a theory of self-consciousness via reflection on subjective states *(Geistesgefühl)*, enriching and confirming Kant's central conviction of man's moral essence as an end-in-himself. With his idea of *Geist* all these metaphysical impulses came to their consummation, for it was the idea of the "unity of the supersensible ground" of which he spoke in the Introduction to the *Third Critique* and in the "Dialectic of Aesthetic Judgment" as that to which reason "forced" thought about the fundamental structure of knowledge and being.

As Michaelson has put it, "For Kant to have posited such a common ground would have involved him in the creation of a higher metaphysical unity more characteristic of Hegel than of the author of the *Critique of Pure Reason*."[3] In the *Third Critique* Kant at times did come very close to sounding like a Hegelian Idealist. Patrick Riley recognizes, too, that in the *Third Critique*, and especially in §57, the discussion of the supersensible in the "Dialectic of Aesthetic Judgment," Kant came closest to Hegel in recognizing the reality of reason.[4] Yovel articulates throughout his study of Kant's philosophy of history that impetus in his work which found expression in Hegelian philosophy.[5] With the *Third Critique* Kant signaled to his heirs the vision they were to try to realize. Kantianism itself made Idealism inevitable. Reading the *Third Critique* created an urgent and specific philosophical problem for Kant's successors.[6] By demonstrating at the very least the intensity and urgency with which Kant took up these questions in his work, this study has shown that Kant—in addition to, and perhaps even in conscious supersession of, his epistemological scruples—carried within his system the germs of that metaphysics which his immediate disciples created largely in his name: German Idealism.

The most profound way to express this from within Kantianism would be to say that Kant recognized that the most important matters about the ultimate reality of the universe and about man himself were beyond the limits of mere cognitive judgment, but that not only the urgency of practical life but the most rigorous pursuit of this strictly cognitive function compelled man to recognize his membership in that ultimate reality and hence to transcend the limitations of his understanding. For Kant that realization took on a religious dimension. For his successors it remained a philosophical one. What Kant believed, they sought rationally to defend. His successors wished to reestablish those beliefs at the center of philosophy in terms of reason's own reality. What Kant had locked away in an inaccessible transcendence, they retrieved as a transfiguring immanence.

Kant's commitment to the idea of a "unity of reason" is not questioned even by so epistemologically stringent an interpreter as Beck. He simply says that Kant could never achieve it.[7] That it was a very serious philosophical and "systemic" preoccupation of Kant from at least the time of the *Grounding of the Metaphysics of Morals* forward is clear. There Kant asserted the necessity for the critical elucidation of the unity of reason.[8] The *Second Critique* reaffirmed his commitment.[9] But the ambition was not completely realized there. Beck believes the ambition was misguided in the first place, and hence incapable of realization. Yet in the *Third Critique* Kant made his most strenuous effort to achieve the unity of reason.[10] Those very elements of epistemological scruple that Beck praises, the generation of young Idealists after 1790 would see as Kant's reneging on his own deepest insights.[11]

"The rational is real"—that is one half of Hegel's objective idealism, the subjective half. Kant had in fact gone very far toward grounding that subjective idealism, and it is this impetus in his thinking which I have tried to recover in as much systematic detail as Kant allowed to escape his own self-censorship. The reality of reason is the key issue in the problem of self-consciousness in Kant. Indeed, it is exactly here that the most authentic challenge to Kant must be made: what is the ontological status of pure reason itself? Kant vacillated between a merely logical and an ontological conception of the transcendental unity of apperception. That vacillation proved unacceptable to his successors in Idealism. They opted for the ontological conception as the only one capable of sustaining the entire architectonic of systematic philosophy, and as the only one which recognized the full rights of reason. If, as Kant in fact believed, it constituted a spiritual being with the power to change the world (of experience), then it was utterly prejudicial to its dignity, its autonomy, and its ultimate significance to deny it reality and reckon it merely a formal structure latent in empirical experience. Kant offered remarkable insights into the nature and power of reason, but his fear of dialectical hypostasis held him back from a full ontological commitment to the reality of reason, at least cognitively. But what Kant believed, and the vivid formulation of those beliefs in his works, seemed to his followers to cry out for a more wholehearted articulation and defense. In Kant's own work they believed they could see the basis for such a stance. They came to believe that the involuntary spontaneity Kant associated with the active, transcendental subject should be understood, together with the essential, ontological ground of human nature, as *Geist*. That is, they identified generative ("spontaneous") and systemic reason with the metaphysical ground of being.

 *Notes*

Abbreviation and Citation Format

Sources are cited in abbreviated form in the notes and given with full details in the bibliography. German titles for Kant's works indicate that I am translating from the original; English titles indicate that the reference is to a translation. The following particular conventions are used:

Critique of Judgment, §[no]:[page][GR = General Remark] = Bernard translation
Critique of Judgment, §[no]:M[page][GR = General Remark] = Meredith translation. All citations from this translation amend "judgement" to "judgment" for uniformity.
A.A. [vol]:[page] = *Kants Gesammelte Schriften Herausgegeben von der Preußischen Akademie der Wissenschaften zu Berlin. (Akademie Ausgabe).*
Hauptschriften = *Die Hauptschriften zum Pantheismus Streit zwischen Jacobi und Mendelssohn.* Ed. Heinrich Scholz.

Introduction

1. In English, N. Kemp-Smith's *Commentary on Kant's Critique of Pure Reason* is the most obvious instance; he derived his approach from German scholars of the close of the nineteenth century like E. Adickes and H. Vaihinger.

2. For example: T. Cohen and P. Guyer, eds., *Essays in Kant's Aesthetics,* esp. "Introduction," 1–13; P. Guyer, *Kant and the Claims of Taste;* and E. Schaper, *Studies in Kant's Aesthetics.*

3. In addition to the works cited above, see F. Coleman, *The Harmony of Reason;* D. Crawford, *Kant's Aesthetic Theory;* K. Rogerson, *Kant's Aesthetics;* and M. McCloskey, *Kant's Aesthetic.*

4. See especially K. Düsing, *Die Teleologie in Kants Weltbegriff;* P. Heintel, *Die Bedeutung;* W. Bartuschat, *Zum Systematischen Ort;* H. Mertens, *Kommentar zur Ersten Einleitung;* F. Kaulbach, *Ästhetische Welterkenntnis bei Kant;* A. Model, *Metaphysik und reflektierende Urteilskraft;* and the exchange

between in R. Horstmann and R. Brandt in E. Förster, ed., *Kant's Transcendental Deductions*, 157–190.

5. The Germans have been attentive to this systematic importance of teleology and the *Third Critique* since the late nineteenth century: see A. Stadler, *Kants Teleologie*.

6. Among the older German works the following are most important: R. Odebrecht, *Form und Geist;* K. Marc-Wogau, *Vier Studien;* and G. Lehmann, *Kants Nachlaßwerk* and his collected essays, *Beiträge*.

7. Writing of the young Friedrich Nietzsche, M. Silk and J. Stern have noted: "'Aesthetics'. . . is not confined to art, not even to 'art as a whole.' It runs into history, psychology and moral philosophy, into life itself . . . the most significant of German 'aesthetic' enquiries have invariably moved beyond 'aesthetic' in the narrow sense, and often into a quest for the 'whole man.'" M. Silk and J. Stern, *Nietzsche on Tragedy*, 35. It is just this sense of 'aesthetic' that the young Idealists drew out of Kant, especially out of his *Third Critique*, to create Idealism. See E. Cassirer, *Philosophy of the Enlightenment*, 332, for a similar contention.

8. See especially P. Riley, *Kant's Political Philosophy;* Y. Yovel, *Kant and the Philosophy of History;* H. Arendt, *Lectures on Kant's Political Philosophy;* W. Booth, *Interpreting the World: Kant's Philosophy of History and Politics;* A. Wood, *Kant's Moral Religion;* T. Auxter, *Kant's Moral Teleology;* and M. Despland *Kant on History and Religion*.

9. J. McFarland, *Kant's Concept of Teleology*.

10. See G. Schrader, "The Status of Teleological Judgment."

11. See, for example, J. McFarland, "The Bogus Unity."

12. A new and very important effort to draw out the implications of Kant's teleology for hermeneutics, based on the *Third Critique*, is R. Makkreel, *Imagination and Interpretation in Kant*.

13. M. Souriau, *Le jugement réfléchissant;* F. van de Pitte, *Kant as Philosophical Anthropologist;* F. Williams, "Philosophical Anthropology"; E. Cassirer, "Critical Idealism."

14. Kant, letter to K. L. Reinhold, December 28–31, 1787, in *Briefwechsel, A.A.* 10:513–15.

15. Windelband, "Einleitung in Kants *Kritik der Urteilskraft*"; G. Lehmann, "Einleitung zur *Ersten Einleitung*."

16. J. Meredith, "Last Stages," xxxvii–l.

17. G. Tonelli, "La formazione."

18. See Kant's letters to K. L. Reinhold, May 12, 1789 (*A.A.* 11:39) and M. Herz, May 26, 1789 (*A.A.* 11:48).

19. Kant was also embroiled in his controversy with Eberhard at this time, which helps to account for the substantial delay, from October 1789 to January 1790, in Kant's dispatch of the manuscript of the *Third Critique*.

20. Tonelli, "La formazione," 444.

21. E. Schulz, "Kant und die Berliner Aufklärung." On Lessing's role in the Aufklärung, see H. Allison, *Lessing and the Enlightenment*. On the whole Aufklärung see H. Wolff, *Die Weltanschauung*, and J. Schober, *Die deutsche Spätaufklärung (1770–1790)*. F. Beiser, *Fate of Reason*, sees the period as one in which Aufklärung, despite Kant, suffered defeat, but

Kant certainly did not see it that way, and it is certainly arguable that the generation of the Idealists did not either.

22. In his observations about the genesis of the *Third Critique,* J. Meredith wrote: "an attack on the leaders of the *Sturm und Drang* movement was almost certainly meditated from the start" ("Last Stages," xli). See R. Pascal, *The German Sturm und Drang.* See also H. Korff, *Geist der Goethezeit,* vol. 1.

23. See especially K. Vorländer, *Immanuel Kant;* E. Cassirer, *Kant's Life and Thought;* and W. Ritzel, *Kant, eine Biographie.* For an overview of Kant biographies see R. George, "The Lives of Kant." But George, like the biographers themselves, concludes: "Not much can be said about Kant's personal development in [the 1780s] that would aid us in understanding his work; there are no external influences to be recounted and, indeed, devotion to the work itself left little room for other matters" (493). I strongly disagree.

24. For a similar position, see G. Lehmann, "Kants Lebenskrise," in *Beiträge,* 411–21. Lehmann argues that Kant's biography takes on great relevance after the publication of the *First Critique* in 1781.

25. The best account of the early reaction to Kant's philosophy is B. Erdmann, *Kants Kriticismus,* esp. 98–128. See also K. Vorländer, *Immanuel Kant,* 406–30.

26. In addition to Erdmann, see H. de Vleeschauwer, *La déduction transcendentale,* 497–535.

27. Kant to Mendelssohn, Aug. 16, 1783, in *Briefwechsel, A.A.* 10:346.

28. See Kant's correspondence, esp. with Johann Schulz about a popularization of the *First Critique,* in *Briefwechsel, A.A.* 10:348–54.

29. K. Vorländer, *Immanuel Kant,* 317n. Some Kant scholars have minimized the reliability of this report (e.g., A. Tumarkin, *Herder und Kant,* 23). But there is too much intensity about Kant's preoccupation with Herder. It has a long and important history which we must unearth.

30. See L. Beck, *Commentary,* 56–57; and esp. F. Beiser, *Fate of Reason,* 165–225, for discussion of Kant's critics and his attitude toward them.

31. Kant, *Critique of Pure Reason,* preface to A-version, Ax.

32. Kant, *Prolegomena,* 6–8 (*A.A.* 4:261–62).

33. A brilliant pursuit of that connection is G. Kelly, *Idealism, Politics and History,* 92–178.

34. For a similar conclusion, see Beiser, *Fate of Reason,* 153–64.

35. On Lessing I have relied upon W. Dilthey, *Das Erlebnis und die Dichtung,* 18–123; H. Allison, *Lessing and the Enlightenment;* K. Aner, *Die Theologie der Lessingzeit;* and E. Zeller, "Lessing als Theolog."

36. For a recent study of the Spinoza controversy see H. Timm, *Gott und die Freiheit,* vol. 1, and on its role in the philosophy of the period, Beiser, *Fate of Reason.*

37. See H. Brunschwig, *La crise de l'État prussien* and R. Koselleck, *Preussen zwischen Reform und Revolution.*

38. See T. Greene, "Historical Context."

39. Kant, "Was heißt: sich im Denken orientieren?" *A.A.* 8:143n.

40. The Pantheism Controversy did contribute to Kant's popularity,

because K. L. Reinhold used that dispute to highlight the strengths of the Kantian position in his *Briefe über die kantische Philosophie.* See Beiser, *Fate of Reason,* 45, 233.

41. By the time Mme. de Stael made her historic survey of Germany, this cultural identity was not only available but prominent. See de Stael's classic account, *Of Germany.*

42. See W. Dilthey, "Die dichterische und philosophische Bewegung," 11–27; W. Windelband, *Die Geschichte der neueren Philosophie;* E. Troeltsch, "Der deutsche Idealismus"; F. Meinecke, *Cosmopolitanism and the National State;* E. Cassirer, *Freiheit und Form;* K. Vorländer, *Kant-Schiller-Goethe.*

43. For the social context see M. Walker, *German Home Towns* and W. Bruford, *Germany in the Eighteenth Century.* For the social character of the intellectuals, see esp. H. Gerth, *Die sozialgeschichtliche Lage* and H. Holborn, "German Idealism," 1–32; and on Weimar "classicism," see W. Bruford, *Culture and Society in Classical Weimar, 1775–1806.*

44. E. Aron, *Die deutsche Erweckung;* J. Taminiaux, *La nostalgie de la Grèce;* and H. Hatfield, *Winckelmann and his German Critics.*

45. This key term, *Bildung,* is at the heart of German Idealism. See the classic accounts of its significance: F. Paulsen, "Bildung"; see also E. Troeltsch, *Deutsche Bildung,* and H. Weil, *Die Entstehung des deutschen Bildungsprinzips.* For a recent bibliographical essay on this concept, see R. Vierhaus, "Bildung."

46. See part 2 of Meinecke's *Entstehung des Historismus,* for the most extended statement of this. For a recent and penetrating assessment of these matters, see P. Reill, *The German Enlightenment.* Unsympathetic is the account by G. Iggers, *The German Conception of History.*

47. The literature on Schiller and Kant is vast. Some views which have clarified the issues for me are: K. Vorländer, "Ethischer Rigorismus und sittlicher Schönheit"; E. Cassirer, "Die Methodik des Idealismus in Schillers Philosophischen Schriften"; P. Menzer, "Schiller und Kant"; E. Schaper, "Schiller's Kant: A Chapter in the History of Creative Misunderstanding," in Schaper, *Studies in Kant's Aesthetics,* 99–117; and D. Henrich, "Beauty and Freedom."

48. J. W. von Goethe, "Einwirkung der neueren Philosophie." The historiography of the *deutsche Bewegung* and of Idealism places enormous stress on the link between Kant's *Third Critique* and Goethe. A. Bäumler wrote: "The *Critique of Judgment* and Goethe—that means the thought and its existential expression. In their division as in their unity with equal significance Kant and Goethe come before us as symbols of our historical existence . . . One could never fathom Kant from the vantage of Goethe. On the other hand it is easy enough to grasp Goethe from Kant's vantage. Kant knew nothing personally or actually about Goethe, but he *thought* him. Goethe's having been thought by Kant is perhaps the greatest and most significant occurrence of German intellectual history" (*Kants Kritik der Urteilskraft,* vi–vii). Windelband, in his history of philosophy, also made this connection, as E. Cassirer has noted: "Kant's *Critique of Judgment* . . . constructs, as it were, *a priori* the concept of Goethe's poetry, and . . . what the latter presents as achievement and act is founded and demanded in the former by the pure necessity of philosophical thought" (*Philosophy of the*

Enlightenment, 278). See also E. Cassirer, "Goethe and the Kantian Philoso-phy"; K. Vorländer, "Goethe und Kant"; and F. J. v. Rintelen, "Kant and Goethe."

49. See R. Bubner, ed., *Das älteste Systemprogramm.*

50. F. Beiser notes: "If one were a Kantian in the early 1790s, the main question was no longer how to defend Kant against his enemies, but how to rebuild the critical philosophy from within upon a new foundation. The center of interest thus shifted from external defense toward inner reform. Reinhold's demand for a new foundation was indeed the starting point for Fichte, Schelling, and Hegel. Although they disagreed with Reinhold con-cerning the nature of that foundation, they accepted his contention that it was a necessity" (*Fate of Reason,* 227).

51. See Kant's public letter against Fichte, Aug. 7, 1799, in *Brief-wechsel, A.A.* 12:396–97 (*Philosophical Correspondence,* 253–54).

52. On the idea of an "aesthetic solution" see G. Rohrmoser, "Zum Problem der ästhetischen Versöhnung"; and F. Strack, *Ästhetik und Freiheit.*

53. The classic locus is, of course, Schelling's *System of Transcendental Idealism* [1800], but perhaps just as crucial and not so well known is his *Phi-losophy of Art* [1802–3].

One: Kant and the Pursuit of Aufklärung

1. As P. Gay proposed in his important study, *The Enlightenment.* Gay acknowledged a great debt to E. Cassirer's classic *Philosophy of the Enlighten-ment* but dissented from him on this question (see Gay, 1:544). Cassirer's assessments are nevertheless far more apt on this point.

2. See the classic essay by E. Troeltsch, "The Ideas of Natural Law and Humanity in World Politics." See also the important effort to establish a history of specifically German philosophy: L. Beck, *Early German Philoso-phy,* upon which I have drawn heavily, though occasionally in dissent.

3. On the Pietist movement, see F. Stoeffler, *The Rise of Evangelical Pie-tism* and *German Pietism During the Eighteenth Century.* On university culture, see the classic work by F. Paulsen, *Geschichte des gelehrten Unterrichts,* and the recent study, C. McClelland, *State, Society and University in Germany, 1700–1914.*

4. On the religious orientation of the German Aufklärung see K. Aner, *Die Theologie der Lessingzeit;* W. Philipp, *Das Werden der Aufklärung in theologiegeschichtlicher Sicht;* K. Barth, *Protestant Thought from Rousseau to Ritschl;* and W. Lütgert, *Die Religion des deutschen Idealismus und ihr Ende.*

5. W. Dilthey, "Friedrich der Große," esp. 134ff.

6. On the conflict between Wolff and Thomasius, see esp. Hans Wolff, *Die Weltanschauung,* 109–71.

7. L. Beck, *Early German Philosophy,* 394–402.

8. Tonelli mentions A. Reinhard in particular in his article "Crusius, Christian August."

9. L. Beck has pointed to Crusius's importance in distinguishing the formal logical relation between ground and consequence from the "syn-thetic" or ontological relation between cause and effect. Kant would follow out this distinction all the way to the key notion of "synthetic a priori judg-ment" (*Early German Philosophy,* 396–99).

10. See R. Popkin, *History of Scepticism*, for a penetrating account of the connection between skepticism and fideism in the early modern period.

11. G. Tonelli, "Crusius," 269.

12. L. Beck, *Early German Philosophy*, 439.

13. "Kant, educated in the Pietistic, eclectic, and anti-Wolffian milieu of Königsberg University, was mainly trying . . . to counteract Wolffian philosophy . . . [He] appealed both to recent anti-Wolffian trends—Maupertuis and his Berlin circle and through Maupertuis to Newton—and to Crusius, the new leader of Pietist philosophy . . . whose reputation grew tremendously from 1744 on" (G. Tonelli, "Crusius," 270). See also G. Tonelli, "Die Umwälzung von 1769 bei Kant." (Both brief articles present the results of his monograph, *Kant, dall' estetica metafisica all'estetica psicoempirica, Memorie della Academia delle scienze di Torino*, series 3, vol. 3, part 2 [1955]. Unfortunately, the Italian text is inaccessible to me.) That Kant should conceive the philosophical battle-line in any measure to lie between Pietism and Wolffianism is very important for our future construction of his works, especially his response to the Pantheism Controversy. It would be misguided to take Kant for a Pietist. On the other hand, he was steeped in the Pietist background; Pietism shaped his character and moral sense, and it was an issue in the public controversies of his day from which he could not remove himself had he even wished to. See P. Schlipp, *Kant's Pre-Critical Ethics*, 50ff. for some telling remarks on this score.

14. Beck, *Early German Philosophy*, 431; see also G. Buchdahl, "Gravity and Intelligibility" and "The Conception of Lawlikeness in Kant's Philosophy of Science."

15. L. Beck makes much of the issue of space as the major concern of the early Kant, *Early German Philosophy*, 446–51.

16. A. Bäumler, *Kants Kritik der Urteilskraft*.

17. See also M. Wundt, *Die deutsche Schulphilosophie im Zeitalter der Aufklärung*, and E. Cassirer, *Freiheit und Form*.

18. On this inauguration of modern aesthetics, see P. Kristeller, "The Modern System in the Arts (II)," 34ff.; on Baumgarten see esp. M. Gregor, "Baumgarten's *Aesthetica*."

19. A. Bäumler, *Kants Kritik der Urteilskraft*, 200.

20. P. Menzer, *Kants Ästhetik*, 28.

21. *Reflection* 2387, dated 1755–56 by Menzer, ibid., 26.

22. See Voltaire, *Letters on England*, 57–86.

23. R. Wolff, "Kant's Debt to Hume via Beattie."

24. For the importance of cosmopolitanism and cultural nationalism in the German context of the later eighteenth century, F. Meinecke's *Cosmopolitanism and the National State* is indispensable. R. George, "The Lives of Kant," 490, 495–96, stresses the importance of this in Kant's life especially in the 1760s in his review of the recent biographical literature.

25. See L. Beck, "Philosophers on the Spree," in *Early German Philosophy*, esp. 324ff.

26. G. Tonelli, "Conditions in Königsberg and the Making of Kant's Philosophy."

27. He wished to assess the wide variety of travelogues and histories dealing with people and places remote in space (and time) which the Euro-

pean Enlightenment was amassing to develop what we would now call cultural anthropology, and through this, evolve a theory of human nature, or philosophical anthropology. For reflections on these questions see F. van Pitte, *Kant as Philosophical Anthropologist*, 7–29.

28. P. Menzer, *Kants Ästhetik*, 37.

29. L. Beck, *Early German Philosophy*, 431.

30. Herder, *Werke* 18:324–25, cited in Kant, *Critique of Practical Reason*, xxii.

31. R. Pascal, *The German Sturm und Drang*, 13, 31.

32. On the popularity of English trends, see Bäumler, *Kants Kritik der Urteilskraft*, 117, 261.

33. L. Goldstein, *Moses Mendelssohn und die deutsche Ästhetik*.

34. F. Will, "Cognition through Beauty," 100.

35. Ibid., 97–105, and the chapter on Mendelssohn in Will's monograph, *Intelligible Beauty;* E. Cassirer, *Freiheit und Form*, 99–221.

36. L. Beck, *Commentary*, 105.

37. Mendelssohn, "Über die Mischung" (*Gesammelte Schriften*, 1:254), cited in Menzer, *Kants Ästhetik*, 44.

38. On this, the German historians of aesthetics are all of one voice. Thus Bäumler, *Kants Kritik der Urteilskraft*, 39ff.; Menzer, *Kants Ästhetik*, 54; and R. Sommer, *Grundzüge einer Geschichte*, 120.

39. For a mercifully brief summary of their views see E. Cassirer, *Philosophy of the Enlightenment*, 331ff.

40. H. Wolf, *Versuch einer Geschichte*, 115.

41. Mendelssohn reviewed each of these works in his *Briefe, die neueste Literatur betreffend*, in letters 92–93, reprinted in Mendelssohn, *Gesammelte Schriften*, 4:2, 46–54.

42. The wording of the essay competition was as follows: "Whether metaphysical truths generally, and in particular the fundamental principles of natural theology and morals, are not capable of proofs as distinct as those of geometry; and if they are not, what is the true nature of their certainty, to what degree can this certainty be developed, and is this degree sufficient for conviction [of their truth]?" (cited in L. Beck, *Early German Philosophy*, 441–42).

43. His effort, part of the overall strategy of the Berlin Academy, in this particular instance had the good fortune to encounter among the French themselves a new attunement to the spiritual element in genius, particularly in Diderot. See H. Dieckmann, "Diderot's Conception of Genius," esp. 13ff. See also H. Wolf, *Versuch einer Geschichte*, 63ff.

44. H. Wolf, *Versuch einer Geschichte*, 146; see also P. Menzer, *Kants Ästhetik*, 85. Sulzer's major work only appeared in 1771, when it was too late to have much impact on Kant (though not too late to have some, however ill received, on Goethe and the *Sturm und Drang*—see R. Pascal, *The German Sturm und Drang*, 297).

45. It made a very big impression in Germany when it was translated, less than a year later, as well. See M. Steinke, *Edward Young's "Conjectures on Original Composition" in England and Germany*, who tries to minimize this impact, but still documents its importance in the epoch.

46. H. Wolf, *Versuch einer Geschichte*, 30n. The title of this collection of

publications is in itself a marvelous documentation of the project of the Berlin Aufklärung.

47. E. Hooker, "The Discussion of Taste"; W. Bate, *From Classic to Romantic;* and G. McKenzie, *Critical Responsiveness.*

48. A. Lovejoy, "'Nature' as Aesthetic Norm," "The First Gothic Revival and the Return to Nature," and "The Chinese Origins of a Romanticism," in *Essays in the History of Ideas;* C. Thacker, *The Wildness Pleases.*

49. D. Morris, *The Religious Sublime,* 4.

50. Hence the subtitle of M. Nicolson, *Mountain Gloom and Mountain Glory: The Development of the Aesthetics of the Infinite.* The phrase "aesthetics of the infinite" she acknowledges as Ernest Tuveson's creation.

51. Nicolson, *Mountain Gloom;* E. Tuveson, *The Imagination as a Means of Grace,* and especially his earlier article, "Space, Deity, and the 'Natural Sublime,'" the basis for chap. 3 of his monograph.

52. "Eighteenth-century man experienced the sublime in two main contexts—literature and nature—but while the context changed, the experience remained much the same. And perhaps the single most important point of continuity is the basic association between sublimity and religion" (Morris, *The Religious Sublime,* 8).

53. "[T]he scientists and popularizers of science . . . were lyrical on the subject of the fullness and diversity of the universe. Their 'Prefaces' and 'Conclusions' are often paeans of praise to the Infinite God of an infinitely full universe" (M. Nicolson, *Mountain Gloom,* 142n.).

54. See M. Nicolson, *Newton Commands the Muse.*

55. F. Staver, "'Sublime' as Applied to Nature."

56. See H. Thüme, *Beiträge;* H. Wolf, *Versuch einer Geschichte;* and J. Engell, *The Creative Imagination.*

57. E. Cassirer, *Philosophy of the Enlightenment,* 322–25.

58. Ibid., 316.

59. H. Thüme, *Beiträge,* 68ff.; H. Wolf, *Versuch einer Geschichte,* 16ff.

60. "In England, . . . Shaftesbury has been largely ignored," J. Stolnitz has noted, since "among his countrymen . . . his writings seem . . . a mere *Schwärmerei.*" Yet Stolnitz recognizes that Shaftesbury "exercised a profound influence on the continental, particularly the German thinkers of his century" (Stolnitz, "On the Significance of Lord Shaftesbury in Modern Aesthetic Theory"). See also H. Thüme, *Beiträge,* 74–75; W. Alderman, "The Significance of Shaftesbury in English Speculation"; and D. Townsend, "From Shaftesbury to Kant."

61. J. Addison, "Genius"; see H. Thüme, *Beiträge,* 78ff.; H. Wolf, *Versuch einer Geschichte,* 26ff.; J. Engell, *The Creative Imagination,* 37.

62. Even earlier, M. Akenside, in *Pleasures of Imagination,* had insisted upon the element of frenzy and ecstasy, i.e., great emotion, as essential to genius, and had equated genius with divinity in its creative power. These elements did not sit lightly within a neoclassical frame. While Addison, Akenside's avowed mentor, had been clear about the connection between passion and imagination, he had tried to keep it circumscribed by taste and reason. The upshot, as far as the new generation felt, was a body of deadening rule.

63. The Germans have traced the Prometheus motif from Shaftes-

bury to Goethe and beyond. See O. Walzel, *Das Prometheussymbol*, and H. Wolf, *Versuch einer Geschichte*, 20ff.

64. E. Young, *Conjectures on Original Composition*, 45. What is important about Young is the religious and spiritualist element in his celebration of original genius. There was a strong connection between his faith in imaginative creativity and his faith in human spirituality, and indeed, in a transcendent divinity. That was what Tuveson was getting at with his title, "The Imagination as a Means of Grace." And see H. Wolf, *Versuch einer Geschichte*, 36, who stresses "the deep religiosity and 'irrationality' in Young's concept of genius." Wolf thinks it very important that Young was a Theist, for in that measure he could not accept fully the Shaftesburian pantheist interpretation of genius. He substituted a version of Milton's divine inspiration. A similar line would be taken up by Klopstock in Germany, defended by such critics as Resewitz and Hamann, and feed into the *Sturm und Drang*.

65. J. Benziger, "Organic Unity."

66. H. Thüme suggests that these "naturalistic" theorists of genius fell into as one-sided an error as the neoclassicists they rejected. For in their theory there was no place for "conscious artistry" (*Beiträge*, 94).

67. A. Gerard, *An Essay on Genius*.

68. M. Nahm makes this the crux of his many disquisitions on genius. He distinguishes, along these lines, between Addison, Kames, Duff (and Herder), who succumb—in Nahm's view—to the "mystagoguery of inspiration" or the "cult of genius," and the sober and rational approach which sees the artist as a mere artisan, remaking the naturally given through his craft, which he associates with Gerard (and Kant) (Nahm, "Imagination as the Productive Faculty for 'Creating Another Nature . . .'"). See also Nahm's other works: *Genius and Creativity* and "Genius and the Aesthetic Relation of the Arts."

69. Cassirer, *Philosophy of the Enlightenment*, 319n. But see a more recent effort to trace Kant's evolving aesthetic exclusively to Baumgarten: H. Juchem, *Die Entwicklung des Begriffs des Schönen bei Kant*.

70. E. Carritt, "Sources and Effects in England of Kant's Philosophy of Beauty," 315.

71. T. Gracyk, "Kant's Shifting Debt to British Aesthetics."

72. L. Beck, *Early German Philosophy*, 332.

73. L. Beck argues that in terms of elegance and clarity, Mendelssohn's essay was certainly more impressive than Kant's admitted uncertainty. But Kant was on the verge of crucial innovations across the board, while Mendelssohn was telling the German philosophical community only its own conventional wisdom. See L. Beck, *Early German Philosophy*, 332.

74. Cited in ibid., 443n.

75. Lessing, for example, translated Hutcheson's *System of Moral Philosophy* in 1756.

76. See D. Henrich, "Hutcheson und Kant."

77. B. Erdmann, "Kant und Hume um 1762." One important connection is Johann Hamann. He went to England in 1757, and he returned to Königsberg shortly thereafter with a lively awareness of British intellectual life, in particular with a very enthusiastic if eccentric appreciation for

David Hume. (See his important letter to Kant, July 27, 1759, in *Brief-wechsel, A.A.* 10:7–16 *(Philosophical Correspondence,* 35–43.) The experience was undoubtedly complex and Hamann's assimilation partial, but we can be very confident that all of it, in Hamann's inimitable fashion, got communicated to Kant. See P. Merlan, "From Hume to Hamann" and "Kant, Hamann-Jacobi and Schelling on Hume"; I. Berlin, "Hume and the Sources of German Anti-Rationalism"; and F. Beiser, *Fate of Reason,* 24ff.

78. His great early work, the *Treatise on Human Nature,* on the other hand, did not get translated during the period of Kant's decisive philosophical work. See R. Wolff, "Kant's Debt to Hume via Beattie."

79. In Germany and especially in Kant, this took the form of a distinction between a priori and a posteriori judgments.

80. In addition to Wolff, see W. Piper, "Kant's Contact with British Empiricism."

81. L. Shaw, "Henry Home of Kames."

82. Kant, *Logic, A.A.* 9:15, my translation.

83. Kant, *Reflection* 1588, *A.A.* 16:27.

84. Most notably 622, 623, 624, and 626: Kant, *A.A.* 15:269–72.

85. Kant's connection of history with learning, discipline, and discipleship, and science with system, autonomy, and mastery forms much of the argument in such works as *Logic,* and is not without relevance to the great *Critiques.*

86. Kant, *Reflection* 626, *A.A.* 15:272, and see the equivalent stance in the *First Critique,* A21.

87. Kant, *Observations,* 72.

88. Kant, *Reflection* 622 (1760s), *A.A.* 15:269.

89. Kant, *Reflection* 623 (1769 or earlier), *A.A.* 15:270.

90. Kant, *Reflections* 648, 653, 686, 721, *A.A.* 15:284, 289, 306, 319. See P. Guyer, "Pleasure and Society in Kant's Theory of Taste," esp. 41ff.

91. Kant, *Nachricht, A.A.* 2:311.

92. Gracyk, "Kant's Shifting Debt to British Aesthetics," 207.

93. Kant, *Observations,* 58.

94. See G. Tonelli, "Kant's Early Theory of Genius (1770–1779)."

95. Kant, *Reflection* 621 (1769 or perhaps the mid-1760s), *A.A.* 15:268.

96. Kant, *Reflection* 622 (1760s), *A.A.* 15:269. Genius and aesthetic judgment or "taste" could not be learned, but only exercised *(geübt).* The notion of *Übung* preceded the use of the specific word.

97. Baumgarten's *Psychologia empirica,* with Kant's annotations, is reprinted in *A.A.* 15:3–54; for §648, p. 39.

98. It was with Addison that imagination began its great surge to the throne of human capacities in the course of the eighteenth century (see J. Engell, *The Creative Imagination,* passim). But behind Addison's enthusiasm were some Lockian reservations, and these came to stark restatement in the philosophical writings of David Hume. Hume's discontent with imagination goes back to Locke, even as his rigorous affirmation of the "association of ideas" goes back to Hobbes. He was also the first to formulate the idea of imagination as the function of synthesizing new images (see M. Kallich, "Association of Ideas and Critical Theory," 303n., 314). In the British tradition a distinction arose accordingly between constructive "imagination"

and wild "fancy" (see J. Bullitt and W. Bate, "Distinction of Fancy and Imagination in Eighteenth-Century English Criticism").

99. Kant's early observations on the negative potential of imagination suggest the influence of foreign thought, most likely Hume.

100. Kant, *Reflection* 313, *A.A.* 15:122.

101. In one *Reflection* he connects it explicitly with the Herrenhuter and Pietists in Germany. In another with Mme. Guyon.

102. Shaftesbury, "A Letter Concerning Enthusiasm to My Lord *****," 3–39.

103. Dieckmann, "Diderot's Concept of Genius," 21.

104. R. Unger, *Hamann und die Aufklärung;* W. Alexander, *Johann Georg Hamann;* J. O'Flaherty, *Hamann's Socratic Memorabilia;* L. Beck, *Early German Philosophy,* 374ff; F. Beiser, *Fate of Reason,* 16ff.; and the proceedings of the last two Hamann colloquia: B. Gajek, ed., *Hamann—Kant—Herder* and B. Gajek and A. Meier, eds., *Johann Georg Hamann und die Krise der Aufklärung.*

105. Kant, *Träume eines Geistersehers, A.A.* 2:315–73. The editor's notes suggest that the work was completed in the year 1765, though it only appeared in the subsequent year. That it was provoked by the opinions of friends was stated in the text itself, as the editor noted, *A.A.* 2:500–1.

106. Kant to Herder, May 9, 1768, in *Briefwechsel, A.A.* 10:73–74.

107. That Kant was not wrong in seeing there the origins of the *Sturm und Drang* cult of genius has long been recognized. See J. Ernst, *Der Geniebegriff der Stürmer und Dränger und der Frühromantiker,* 17ff. See also M. Steinke, *Edward Young's 'Conjectures on Original Composition' in England and Germany.* Hamann is considered by many to be the real founder of the movement. See F. Beiser, *Fate of Reason,* 34, for a recent statement of this view.

108. G. Tonelli, "Die Umwälzung von 1769 bei Kant."

109. Kant to Mendelssohn, April 8, 1766, in *Briefwechsel, A.A.* 10:69–73.

110. J. Hamann, *Sokratische Denkwürdigkeiten/Aesthetica in nuce;* F. Beiser, *Fate of Reason,* 35–37. Contrasting Hamann's approach to Kant's, Beiser underestimates the measure to which even Kant—precisely in the *Third Critique—does* develop a symbolic theory of art.

111. Kant to Herder, May 9, 1768, in *Briefwechsel, A.A.* 10:73–74.

112. R. Pascal, *The German Sturm und Drang,* 5ff.

113. These essays were accompanied by an essay on local history by the older historian Justus Möser. Möser was sympathetic to their efforts to establish an indigenous literary culture, steeped in locality. Möser had the courage to respond publicly to Frederick II's denigration of German as a literary language and to celebrate the literary renaissance in Germany.

114. On Lavater, see R. Pascal, *The German Sturm und Drang,* 2.

115. E. Flajole, "Lessing's Attitude in the Lavater-Mendelssohn Controversy," and H. Allison, *Lessing and the Enlightenment,* 198.

116. E. Flajole, "Lessing's Attitude"; E. Schoonhoven, "Hamann in der Kontroverse mit Moses Mendelssohn"; and Z. Levy, "Hamanns Kontroverse mit Moses Mendelssohn."

117. Evidence of this can be found in his letter to Mendelssohn of Au-

gust 1783, in which Kant praised Mendelssohn's *Jerusalem,* the ultimate formulation of Mendelssohn's position in the controversy. See E. Schulz, "Kant und die Berlin Aufklärung."

118. In the *Observations,* Kant had treated both ideas in a rather positive light, particularly *Rührung.*

119. Kant, *Reflection* 767 (1772–73), *A.A.* 15:334. The parenthetical remark was lined out later by Kant, but it is the most revealing passage in the *Reflection.*

120. See Menzer on this, *Kants Ästhetik,* 15ff., esp. 20–21; and L. Beck, *Early German Philosophy,* 427, who, in the context of sketching Kant's *"Weltanschauung"* observed that it was hostile to the sort of *Schwärmerei* that the *Stürmer* engaged in.

121. Kant, *Reflection* 767, *A.A.* 15:334. See also *Reflection* 762 (1772–73): "In order to appear a genius, nowadays one abandons rules. It is all well and good to go beyond the rules where they arise out of a constriction of the spirit; but where they merely have to do with the familiar and coincidental, one should have the modesty to accept them, because otherwise, since others will also demand their freedom, in the end everything will become unruly" (*A.A.* 15:332).

122. R. Pascal, *The German Strum und Drang,* 95ff.

123. R. Lowth, *Lectures on the Sacred Poetry of the Hebrews* (Latin, 1753; German tr. 1758). This was a favorite work of Hamann's and the basis of many of his arguments with Kant about the superiority of his approach to that of the Enlightenment.

124. See H. Wolf, "Die Genielehre des jungen Herder."

125. R. Pascal, *The German Sturm und Drang,* 18.

126. Kant, *Reflection* 771 (1774–75), *A.A.* 15:337.

127. Kant, *Reflection* 775 (1774–75), *A.A.* 15:339.

128. R. Pascal, *The German Sturm und Drang,* 97, makes this point.

129. Kant, *Reflection* 765 (1772–73), *A.A.* 15:333.

130. Kant, *Reflection* 789 (1774–75), *A.A.* 15:345.

131. Kant, *A.A.* 15:344–45n. The anthropology lectures are cited from a manuscript in the Royal Berlin Library (see the bibliographical note, *A.A.* 15:vii) and from *Immanuel Kants Menschenkunde oder philosophische Anthropologie,* ed. Fr. Ch. Starke (1838), 152.

132. Kant to Hamann, Apr. 6, 1774, in *Briefwechsel, A.A.* 10:156.

133. Hamann to Kant, Apr. 7, 1774, in *Briefwechsel, A.A.* 10:156–58.

134. Kant to Hamann, Apr. 8, 1774, in *Briefwechsel, A.A.* 10:160.

135. Lavater to Kant, Apr. 8, 1774, in *Briefwechsel, A.A.* 10:165–66.

136. Allison, *Lessing and the Enlightenment,* passim.

137. M. Mendelssohn, *Jerusalem, or On Religious Power and Judaism,* tr. A. Arkush (University Press of New England, 1983).

138. J. Engell, *Creative Imagination,* 102–3.

139. P. Menzer noted (*Kants Ästhetik,* 87) that Kant was unusual in his day for rejecting the idea of genius in science. None of the others who wrote on the subject made such distinctions, and especially those who shared his "cold-blooded" view tended to write about Newton as frequently as about Homer in elaborating their theories of genius. Menzer was mystified by Kant's choice to depart from the others, and pointed out that he

had not always thought that way. His earliest *Reflections* accept the idea of genius in science. What Menzer missed was Kant's outrage at the excesses of the *Sturm und Drang* cult of genius, and hence the polemical slant behind the theory of genius Kant constructed.

140. K. Vorländer, *Immanuel Kant,* 243n.

141. Ibid. and W. Dilthey, "Friedrich der Große," 136. Dilthey dates the prize to the year it was awarded, not the year it was announced. Eberhard would later, in the time Kant was finishing the *Third Critique,* open the school-philosophical onslaught against Kant's critical philosophy.

142. W. Dilthey, "Friedrich der Große," 137.

143. Ironically, both Goethe and Herder had begun to disengage themselves from the excesses of the *Sturm und Drang* as soon as they moved to Weimar, and their enterprise was to achieve a classical balance. See R. Pascal, *The German Sturm und Drang,* 31; H. Korff, *Geist der Goethezeit,* 2:16. Kant never recognized this, not even in the 1780s when it was apparent to the rest of Germany.

144. R. Pascal, *The German Sturm und Drang,* 134ff.; Beiser, *Fate of Reason,* 127ff., 145–49.

145. Kant, *Reflection* 911 (late 1770s), *A.A.* 15:398.

146. Kant, *Reflection* 912 (late 1770s), *A.A.* 15:399.

147. Kant, *Reflection* 896 (late 1770s), *A.A.* 15:391.

148. Kant, *Reflection* 897 (late 1770s), *A.A.* 15:392.

149. Kant, *Reflection* 898 (late 1770s), *A.A.* 15:393.

150. Kant, *Reflection* 899 (late 1770s), *A.A.* 15:393.

151. Kant, *Reflection* 914 (late 1770s), *A.A.* 15:399.

152. Kant, *Reflection* 921 (late 1770s), *A.A.* 15:406.

153. Kant, *Reflection* 921a (late 1770s), *A.A.* 15:407.

154. Kant, *Reflection* 335 (mid to late 1770s), *A.A.* 15:132.

155. Kant, additions from the late 1770s to *Reflection* 364, *A.A.* 15:142.

156. See Kant, *Reflections* 369 and 499, *A.A.* 15:144, 217.

Two: Kant's Return to Aesthetics

1. M. Gregor, "Aesthetic Form and Sensory Content in the *Critique of Judgment,*" 194n.

2. Although M. Liedtke wished to establish that the idea of reflective judgment was already *latent* in the *First Critique,* his work demonstrates the degree to which it is not fully worked out there. See Liedtke, *Der Begriff.* Similarly, G. Prauss makes the point quite compellingly that Kant had not really conceived clearly of the problem of subjective consciousness in the first edition of the *Critique of Pure Reason,* and that this led to his revisions in the *Prolegomena* culminating in the idea of "judgments of perception" (Prauss, *Erscheinung bei Kant,* 102). This will all be taken up in detail in the next chapter.

3. Kant, *Critique of Pure Reason,* A21.

4. Kant to K. L. Reinhold, Dec. 28–31, 1787, in *Briefwechsel, A.A.* 10:513–15 (*Philosophical Correspondence,* 127–28).

5. See K. Ameriks, "Recent Work," for an excellent overview.

6. D. Henrich, "Proof-Structure," 640.

7. K. Ameriks, "Recent Work."

8. This demand to recognize the historical Kant's frame of reference is the strength of J. Hintikka's essay "Transcendental Arguments," esp. 274; this principle may be generalized from an extremely perceptive statement found in H. Seigfried, "Kant's 'Spanish Bank Account'": "[T]he troubles of Anglo-American philosophers with Kant's [philosophy] . . . are due not so much to a lack of solid knowledge of German as to a lack of familiarity with Kant's philosophical environment and, even more so, to our strong absorption in contemporary philosophical discussions" (126). He insists that we must "grasp Kant's explanation in its own historical context first" (123), indeed "*entwicklungsgeschichtlich*" (115). That is the methodological commitment of this study.

9. See Kant, *Logic*, 17, 39ff., esp. 40–41 (*A.A.* 9:15, 35ff., esp. 35–37).

10. In a *Reflection* which is impossible to date precisely, but which seems to fall just at this logical juncture in his thinking, Kant jotted: "Extensive clarity through external characteristics [*Merkmale*], intensive through inner, the former through coordinated, the latter through subordinated [characteristics]. In the former, a broad, in the latter a deep clarity. The flaw of the one: dryness; of the second, flatness. The advantage of the former: aesthetic; of the latter: logical" (*Reflection* 2368, cited in P. Menzer, *Kants Ästhetik*, 29).

11. Kant, *Reflection* 204, *A.A.* 15:79.

12. Kant, *Reflection* 643 (1769–70), *A.A.* 15:283.

13. Kant, *Reflection* 179, 182, *A.A.* 15:67–68.

14. Kant, *Reflection* 619, *A.A.* 15:268.

15. Ibid.

16. Kant, *Reflections* 619, 620, 622; *A.A.* 15:268–69.

17. "Sensation has in it feeling [*Gefühl*] and perception [*Wahrnehmen*]; the first is subjective, the second is objective" (*Reflection* 279 [1770], *A.A.* 15:105).

18. Kant, *Reflections* 177 (1769) and 681 (1769), *A.A.* 15:65, 303; and, from a later period, 408 (1770s), *A.A.* 15:165.

19. Ibid., most particularly 408.

20. Kant, *Reflection* 680 (1769), *A.A.* 15:302. In another such reflection, Kant writes: "Sensible representations are either sensations and require sense, or appearances and are grounded upon the power of intuition; the former are changes in the condition of the subject through the presence of the object; the latter are representations of the object itself insofar as it is open to the senses" (*Reflection* 650, *A.A.* 15:287).

21. Kant, *Reflection* 287 (1770s), *A.A.* 15:107. The notion of *Einbildung* as a spontaneous power was not entirely clear to Kant in the period 1769–70. It only emerged over the 1770s. For detailed discussion of Kant's precritical theory of imagination, see R. Makkreel, *Imagination and Interpretation*, 9–25; and H. Mörchen, "Die Einbildungskraft bei Kant," esp. 386ff. (reprint, 76ff.).

22. Kant, *Reflection* 643 (1769–70), *A.A.* 15:283.

23. On Tetens, see J. Barnouw, "The Philosophical Achievement and

Historical Significance of Johann Nicolas Tetens," 301–35, and L. Beck, *Early German Philosophy*, 412–25.

24. Kant, *Reflection* 624, *A.A.* 15:270
25. Kant, *Reflection* 638, *A.A.* 15:276.
26. Kant, *Reflection* 209, *A.A.* 15:80; and *Reflection* 681, *A.A.* 15:303.
27. Kant, *Reflection* 625, *A.A.* 15:271.
28. Kant, *Reflection* 683, *A.A.* 15:304.
29. Ibid.
30. See Kant's discussion of the "threefold synthesis" in the *First Critique*, A97.
31. See *Reflection* 213 (1770), *A.A.* 15:82, where Kant begins to sense the difficulty.
32. This crucial insight into the holism of space and time constituted Kant's great breakthrough of this period, leading to the theory of pure (sensible) intuition (see *Reflection* 662, *A.A.* 15:293). Space is a prior whole, unitary and interpersonally valid, according to Kant. It is the form of sensible intuition. The perfection which sensibility has, compared with reason, is the prior unity of the whole form itself. Such a prior whole is only a conceptual goal ("totality") for rationality. On the other hand, the imperfection of intuition is sensibility itself, namely, dependence upon the matter of sensation, and the limitation of the sensible forms to space and time. Reason is not limited in these ways.
33. Kant, *Critique of Pure Reason*, A11/B25. See T. Pinder, "Kants Begriff der transzendentalen Erkenntnis." Pinder stresses the antidogmatic thrust of this phrasing and insists on Kant's departure from his predecessors' usage. See, in this connection, the debate between I. Angelelli and N. Hinske: Angelelli, "On the Origins of Kant's 'Transcendental'"; Hinske, "Kants Begriff des Transcendentalen und die Problematik seiner Begriffsgeschichte."
34. Kant, *Prolegomena*, 37 (*A.A.* 4:294).
35. See *Critique of Pure Reason* A56: "not all cognition a priori must be called transcendental, but instead only that by means of which we recognize that and how certain ideas (perceptions and concepts) are a priori applied and possible."
36. D. Henrich, "Proof-Structure," 646; J. Hintikka, "Transcendental Arguments," 274–76.
37. That the mind works by processes which need not be self-conscious in their functioning is a fundamental and necessary element in the "transcendental" philosophy. That Kant thought along these lines is clear if nowhere else at the very least in the *Logic:* "The exercise of our own powers also takes place according to certain rules which we first follow without being conscious of them" (13 [*A.A.* 9:11]).
38. This is why Hegel insisted that a phenomenology of spirit entail a bifurcation of perspective as between the consciousness appropriating its own experience and that of the philosopher already conversant with the essentials of that experience. Hegel argued that consciousness was not, for a substantial segment of its itinerary of self-discovery, aware of what it was or what it was about.

39. Kant, *Critique of Pure Reason*, A367–74, A490–97/B518–25.

40. Ibid., B145.

41. The difference between *Objekt* and *Gegenstand* is essential. In traditional school philosophy, it was the difference between *res* and *ens*, i.e., between a matter of formal judgment and a matter entailing an existent entity. See H. Seigfried, "Kant's 'Spanish Bank Account.'" On the distinction in Kant himself, see esp. H. Allison, *Transcendental Idealism*, 27–28, 135–36.

42. D. Kolb, "Thought and Intuition in Kant's Critical System." And see H. Seigfried, "Kant's 'Spanish Bank Account'": "in order for the conceptual reality of a thing to be the reality of a *possible* object of experience, the thing has to be posited also in accordance 'with the formal conditions of experience, that is, with the conditions of intuitions and concepts.' [B265] And in order for it to be the reality of an *actual* object of experience, it has to be posited as 'bound up with the material conditions of experience, that is, with sensation,' [B266] as well" (122).

43. I take this to parallel Allison's argument in *Transcendental Idealism* that the two parts of the proof in the "Transcendental Deduction" involved first the "metaphysical deduction," i.e., the theoretical constitution of a "real use" for the categories, and then the "transcendental synthesis" which established that this "real use" did apply to "pure intuition" and could be articulated as a "transcendental synthesis of the imagination" in the "Schematism" chapter.

44. On this notion of pure or originary synthesis see H. Allison, "Transcendental Schematism"; and R. Aquila, "The Relationship between Pure and Empirical Intuition in Kant" and *Matter in Mind*, 49ff.; skeptical of this notion is P. Guyer, "Apperception and *A Priori* Synthesis."

45. See H. Allison, "Transcendental Schematism," 64–65.

46. It was against this that S. Korner protested, albeit too drastically, in "The Impossibility of Transcendental Deductions." Schaper's response, "Arguing Transcendentally," presupposes the regressive Kantian formulation and so defends Kant's sense of "deduction," but fails to confute Korner's logical point, as Bubner, "Kant, Transcendental Arguments," esp. 460n., observed. The point is that Korner and a fortiori P. Strawson *(The Bounds of Sense),* B. Stroud ("Transcendental Arguments," 54–69), and R. Wolff *(Kant's Theory of Mental Activity)* are seeking in Kant a kind of deduction he never intended.

47. D. Henrich, "Kant's Notion"; see also J. Rosenberg, "Transcendental Arguments Revisited," 612.

48. J. Rosenberg, "Transcendental Arguments Revisited," 612–13; Stroud, "Transcendental Arguments," 54; and Bubner, "Kant, Transcendental Arguments," 461.

49. P. Guyer, "Psychology and the Transcendental Deduction." See also G. Bird, "Logik und Psychologie in der Transzendentalen Deduktion," and W. Walsh, "Philosophy and Psychology in Kant's Critique."

50. D. Henrich, "Kant's Notion," 34–35.

51. K. Ameriks, "Kant's Transcendental Deduction as a Regressive Argument," 273–87, esp. 282n. See also N. Rescher, "Kant and the 'Special Constitution' of Man's Mind."

52. Frustration with this phantom form of logical argumentation is the driving impetus of M. Gram's several refutations of transcendental arguments: "Transcendental Arguments" and "Must Transcendental Arguments be Spurious?" See also G. Bird, "Recent Interpretations of Kant's Transcendental Deduction," for a criticism of the antiskeptical concept of transcendental argument in Strawson, Stroud etc. Gram, in his turn, provoked J. Hintikka to protest that the argument had been transposed entirely out of the Kantian key (Hintikka, "Transcendental Arguments," 274–81). He was right. Gram set aside at the very outset of his remarks the only fruitful content for considering transcendental arguments: "his theory of the synthetic *a priori* and his doctrine of the categories" (15).

53. "That Kant not only sets out from this fact of empirical judgment but actually must and also has a right to do so is immediately apparent. He *has* to set out from this because otherwise his philosophy as a theory of experience would be literally lacking an object." Prauss, *Erscheinung bei Kant,* 62.

54. For a thorough consideration of this notion, see R. Pippin, *Kant's Theory of Form,* passim and esp. 15.

55. Kant, "Über den Gebrauch," *A.A.* 8:183–84.

56. Kant, *Critique of Practical Reason,* 29 (*A.A.* 5:30).

57. The modality of necessity in the intentional act in general signaled to Kant the presence of his sought-after pure a priori principle of practical reason: the moral law with its "categorical"—and more essentially *apodictic*—imperative. See L. Beck, "Apodictic Imperatives."

58. This interpretation I take to be congruent with that of L. Beck in "The Putative Apriority of Judgments of Taste," in *Essays on Kant and Hume,* 167–70; and also of G. Prauss, *Erscheinung bei Kant,* 86.

59. Kant, *Critique of Pure Reason,* A56/B81. Beck puts this clearly in terms of analytic versus synthetic judgments: "the distinction between analytic and synthetic judgments is not one of formal logic, for formal logic abstracts from the meaning of all terms" ("Can Kant's Synthetic Judgments Be Made Analytic?" 10–11). See also F. Grayeff, "The Relationship of the Transcendental and Formal Logic," and T. Swing, *Kant's Transcendental Logic,* 28–46.

60. This sense can be expressed in terms of the *logical* versus the *real* use of reason, a distinction Kant makes throughout his work. Beck explains: "A real definition not only puts the word in place of others, but the *definiens* contains a clear mark by which the object can be recognized and by virtue of which the defined concept is shown to have 'objective reality' . . . Kant is saying that in a real definition we do not mainly equate a word with a logical product of arbitrarily chosen logical predicates, but we make at least a problematical existential judgment and state the conditions under which this judgment could be justified" ("Kant's Theory of Definition," 26–27). This line of thought has been developed by H. Allison in his debate with M. S. Gram on syntheticity with specific reference to the Kant-Eberhard controversy, but with direct relevance to the whole "critical philosophy": M. Gram, *Kant, Ontology and the A Priori;* H. Allison, *The Kant-Eberhard Controversy,* esp. 54ff.; Gram, "The Crisis of Syntheticity"; and

Allison, "The Originality of Kant's Distinction between Analytic and Synthetic Judgments."

61. That was why, among other things, the ontological proof of God fell apart, as Kant argued so forcefully in the *Critique of Pure Reason* (A592–602/B620–31). That was also why Leibniz's great speculative system failed, as Kant argued there as well in a crucial appendix entitled "The Amphiboly of Concepts of Reflection" (A260–92/B316–49). This appendix is the seedbed of many of Kant's later epistemological and ontological considerations.

62. Ibid., A260/B316.

63. See M. Liedke, "Kants Begriff der Reflektion."

64. Kant to Reinhold, Dec. 28–31, 1787, *Briefwechsel, A.A.* 10:513–15 (*Philosophical Correspondence,* 127–28).

65. See, e.g.: D. Henrich, "The Proof-Structure," *Identität und Objektivität,* and "Kant's Notion of a Deduction." For evaluations of Henrich, see P. Guyer, Review of *Identität und Objektivität,* and K. Ameriks, "Recent Work," 15–16.

66. This point is all too frequently neglected by contemporary philosophers, but it was essential to Kant. See *Critique of Pure Reason* A3/B7; *Prolegomena,* 2–3 (*A.A.* 4:257). It is time to return to a *discriminating* metaphysical interpretation of his work. (Ameriks suggested this prospect in his review, "Recent Work," 1.)

67. Scholars have maintained that most of the revisions of the B-version worked to eliminate the "psychologism" and to suppress the "faculty-talk." While there can be no doubt that Kant reformulated his argument in the B-version, it did not imply at all a repudiation of what he had written in the A-version, and certainly not of the "subjective deduction." It remained implicit in the B-version, and its elements figured explicitly throughout the unrevised "Analytic of Principles." (See esp. *Critique of Pure Reason,* A180/B223.) Moreover, a concern for an account of subjective mental process stayed with Kant in his later critical work and played a major role in the genesis of the *Third Critique.* (See esp. *First Introduction to the Critique of Judgment,* 24 [*A.A.* 20:220].)

68. On this concern for a "gap" which haunted Kant to the end of his years, see E. Förster, "Is There a 'Gap' in Kant's Critical System?"

69. "[T]hat there should be a second or even a third *Critique* with an 'Analytic' and a 'Dialectic' was a completely foreign thought for Kant in 1781": Brandt, "The Deductions in the *Critique of Judgment,*" 183.

70. In the *Third Critique* he would attempt his most comprehensive characterization not merely of each aspect of consciousness in itself but also of the systematic interrelations among them. See W. Bartuschat, *Zum Systematischen Ort,* for the most thorough statement of this interpretation.

71. This takes the "critical philosophy" to be essentially a philosophical anthropology, as E. Cassirer has argued in "Critical Idealism as a Philosophy of Culture."

72. Kant to Reinhold, Dec. 28–31, 1787, *Briefwechsel, A.A.* 10:513–15 (*Philosophical Correspondence,* 127–28).

73. Kant, *Critique of Judgment,* §10:54.

74. Kant, *Critique of Practical Reason,* 9n. (*A.A.* 5, 9n.).

75. Kant gave several examples of such "transcendental explanations" in this footnote: "*Life* is the faculty of a being by which it acts according to the laws of the faculty of desire. The *faculty of desire* is the faculty such a being has of causing, through its [representations], the reality of the objects of these [representations]. *Pleasure* is the [representation] of the agreement of an object or an action with the *subjective* conditions of life, i.e., with the faculty through which [a representation] causes the reality of its object (or the direction of the energies of a subject to such an action as will produce the object)" (ibid.). The analysis of the concrete nature of each of these transcendental explanations will concern us later in this study.

76. Kant, *Critique of Pure Reason*, A260–92/B316–49.

77. My historical interest in finding continuities between Kant's *Third Critique* and the later Idealists will be apparent. On transcendental arguments in the later *Critiques* I have learned a great deal from R. Benton, *Kant's Second Critique and the Problem of Transcendental Arguments*, 24 and passim.

78. Originally this allowed the extension of transcendental analysis to volition and feeling, but eventually it would double back on the transcendental analysis of cognition itself, i.e., the categorial determination of objects of experience would come under reexamination in terms of the structure of purpose of a dynamic rationality. This was the "cognitive turn" which led to the highly systematic *First Introduction to the Critique of Judgment*.

79. Kant to Reinhold, Dec. 28–31, 1787, *Briefwechsel*, A.A. 10:513–15 (*Philosophical Correspondence*, 127–28).

Three: Validity and Actuality

1. R. Meerbote raises this question, but in an entirely different light. See "Kant's Use of the Notions of 'Objective Reality' and 'Objective Validity.'" More to the point are H. Seigfried, "Kant's 'Spanish Bank Account,'" and H. Allison, "Objective Validity and Objective Reality," chap. 7 of *Transcendental Idealism*.

2. Is there a "real use" of reason with reference to its own immanent process? See R. Pippin, *Kant's Theory of Form*, 90 and esp. 102: "[A] claim that we possess concepts a priori is a transcendental claim; it is a claim about a kind of *knowledge*."

3. According to Prauss, Kant only came to recognize a problem in his theory of subjective consciousness *after* he published the A-version of the *First Critique*, and his response to that lacuna was the theory of a "judgment of perception" in the *Prolegomena to Any Future Metaphysics* of 1783 (Prauss, *Erscheinung bei Kant*, 102).

4. See Kant, *Critique of Pure Reason*, B161. In making this interpretation I believe I find myself in the company of Aquila, *Matter in Mind*, 126; and Young, "Kant's View of Imagination." Also emphatic on this point is G. Prauss, *Erscheinung bei Kant*: "The theory of judgments of perception which was evolved in the *Prolegomena*, of which the first edition of the *Critique [of Pure Reason]* had not even a trace, was not only not surrendered by Kant in the second edition, but only actually *introduced* into the *Critique* for

the first time [cf. B139f.]. This [mis]perception fails to take cognizance, further, that also in the *Critique of Judgment* the distinction between judgments of perception and judgments of experience serves as a necessary and, for Kant, self-evident presupposition" (141n.).

5. Kant, *Logic,* 69ff. (*A.A.* 9:63). The idea of concept *formation* in relation to empirical judgments and the constitution of objects is richly examined in Bäumler, *Kants Kritik der Urteilskraft,* and deserves more consideration as a link between the projects of Leibniz and Baumgarten *before,* and Hegel *after* Kant. See A. Model, *Metaphysik und reflektierende Urteilskraft,* on these issues.

6. An empirical concept, Kant makes quite clear, differs little from a mere name: "an *empirical* concept cannot be defined at all, but only *made explicit.* For since we find in it only a few characteristics of a certain species of sensible object, it is never certain that we are not using the word, in denoting one and the same object, sometimes so as to stand for more, and sometimes so as to stand for fewer characteristics . . . The word, with the few characteristics which attach to it, is more properly to be regarded as merely a *designation* than as a *concept* of the thing" (*Critique of Pure Reason* A727–28/B755–56). See R. Pippin, "The Schematism and Empirical Concepts" and "Kant on Empirical Concepts"; and G. Schrader, "Kant's Theory of Concepts."

7. Synthesis is the crucial concept in Kant's epistemology. This has been recognized by many scholars. See R. Bubner, "Kant, Transcendental Arguments," 466; R. Aquila, chap. 3 of *Matter in Mind,* 49ff.; and H. Allison, *Transcendental Idealism,* passim and esp. 141–44, 159–64. R. Makkreel (*Imagination and Interpretation,* 25ff.) construes synthesis narrowly in terms of transcendental constitution, but it may well be that the term is Kant's most general for the spontaneous activity of mind in many aspects, including those Makkreel sees as "formative" rather than "synthetic." In any event, it is crucial to reconstruct this constitutive process and to recognize that since it is sequential, in some sense, parts of it can be carried out without always necessarily completing the whole constitutive procedure. That will prove the key to those peculiar sorts of judgment that Kant calls subjective.

8. Kant, *Prolegomena,* §26:52 (*A.A.* 4:309).

9. Kant, *Critique of Judgment,* §vii:29. See R. Aquila, "Is Sensation the Matter of Appearances?" 14.

10. See Kant, *Critique of Judgment,* §14. These are of course synonyms for *Bildung,* formation, the most important such concept, as we shall see.

11. For this sense of "besides" see Kant, *Prolegomena,* §26:52 (*A.A.* 4:309), and *Critique of Pure Reason* A166/B207.

12. Kant, *Prolegomena,* §26:52.

13. On primary and secondary qualities see: R. Jackson, "Locke's Distinction"; R. Popkin, "Berkeley and Pyrrhonism"; E. Curley, "Locke, Boyle,"; J. Bennett, "Substance, Reality"; and M. Ayers, "Substance, Reality."

14. See Bennett's discussion of phenol as a secondary quality, "Substance, Reality," 8.

15. On Kant's "transcendental idealism" and the continuing controversy over its precise meaning, see Ameriks, "Recent Work," 1–11, for a careful overview. While there are elements of the "two view" approach which seem attractive from the contemporary vantage, it remains that there is probably a good deal to the "two world" view, with its attendant metaphysics, as a *historical* gloss of Kant's doctrines. That will be considered further at a later point in this study.

16. Kant, *Critique of Pure Reason,* A189–90/B234–35.

17. Ibid., A191/B236.

18. Ibid., A178/B220. The centrality of the categories of relation in the establishment of objective reference has become central to the discrimination of "subjective" from "objective" judgments, as will appear below.

19. Ibid., A180/B223.

20. Ibid., A191/B236.

21. Ibid.

22. Kant, *Critique of Judgment,* §iv:15.

23. Kant, *Critique of Pure Reason,* A195/B240.

24. Kant, *Critique of Judgment,* §76, makes this point vividly in terms of the discursiveness of human consciousness.

25. I take this interpretation to be roughly congruent with L. Beck's analysis in "The Putative Apriority of Judgments of Taste," in *Essays on Kant and Hume,* 167ff.

26. Intuition is perhaps the most problematic notion in Kant's epistemology. It has been interpreted in terms of three distinct properties in the scholarly literature: "singularity" or "individuality," in the sense of completeness of a manifold in a whole; "givenness," in the sense of indubitable actuality for consciousness (hence, for Kant, there is no certainty equal to intuitive certainty); and finally, "immediacy" to consciousness, that which needs and can have no rational mediation to assure its presence to consciousness. See J. Hintikka, "On Kant's Notion of Intuition *(Anschauung)*"; M. Thompson, "Singular Terms and Intuitions in Kant's Epistemology"; K. Wilson, "Kant on Intuition"; M. Gram, "The Sense of a Kantian Intuition"; K. Robson, "Kant's Concept of Intuition"; and R. Smyth, *Forms of Intuition,* 134–69.

27. As E. Schaper does in "Imagination and Knowledge," in *Studies in Kant's Aesthetics,* 1–17.

28. Strawson, "Imagination and Perception."

29. R. Makkreel, *Imagination and Interpretation,* 29, notes Kant's text-emendation in his personal copy of the B-version of the *First Critique* substituting "understanding" for "imagination" as the source of all synthesis; nevertheless Young ("Kant's View of Imagination," 148) claims that the A-version is more authentic to the critical philosophy taken as a whole. I concur.

30. Schaper, "Imagination and Knowledge" and "Kant und das Problem der Einbildungskraft." More moderate is M. Warnock, "Imagination and Perception."

31. M. Heidegger, *Kant and the Problem of Metaphysics;* H. Mörchen, "Die Einbildungskraft in Kant." For a criticism of Heidegger's metaphysi-

cal project with imagination, see D. Henrich, "Über die Einheit der Subjektivität."

32. On some readings of the *First Critique,* one might question whether "matter," the manifold in sensation, can even be registered by consciousness apart from judgment's synthesis of recognition. One passage where Kant raises the possibility of incoherence, only later to repudiate it, is *Critique of Pure Reason* A90/B123. See R. Wolff, *Kant's Theory of Mental Activity,* 156ff.; and E. Schaper, *Studies in Kant's Aesthetics,* 18–75.

33. For a recent statement of this view, see D. Kolb, "Thought and Intuition," 229.

34. Not only will the *Third Critique* offer this evidence; there is also a letter from Kant, written to Herz during the time of that *Critique's* composition, which bears decisively on this question. See below.

35. G. Prauss, *Erscheinung bei Kant,* is surely the most important work on the phenomenology of subjective consciousness in Kant in recent times. K. Ameriks ("Recent Work," 18) clearly assigns Prauss this stature; see also W. Marx, Review of Prauss. But Prauss has not been without his critics. See H. Seigfried, "Zum Problem des Wahrnehmungsurteil bei Kant," and R. Pippin, Review of Prauss and *Kant's Theory of Form,* 180–81. Prauss has rescued the distinction between judgments of perception and judgments of experience from centuries of disdain and neglect and brought it to the center of attention. For other considerations of this distinction see T. Uehling's survey, "*Wahrnehmungsurteile* and *Erfahrungsurteile* Reconsidered."

36. L. Beck, "Did the Sage of Königsberg Have No Dreams?" in *Essays on Kant and Hume,* 38–60.

37. See W. Sellars, *Science and Metaphysics,* 1–59; R. Aquila, "Is Sensation the Matter of Apearance?" 11–29; and Aquila's other studies: *Matter in Mind,* "The Relationship between Pure and Empirical Intuition in Kant," and "Matter, Forms, and Imaginative Association in Sensory Intuition." See also J. Baumgartner, "On Kant's 'Matter of the Appearance.'"

38. Gram, "Must Transcendental Arguments Be Spurious?" 311–12.

39. Kant, *Critique of Pure Reason,* B122.

40. G. Bird, "Recent Work in Kant's Transcendental Deduction," 8–9.

41. D. Henrich, "Proof-Structure," 654.

42. P. Guyer, "Apperception and *A Priori* Synthesis," 210.

43. D. Kolb, "Thought and Intuition," 229.

44. P. Guyer, Review of *Identität und Objektivität,* 160. For appreciation of this formulation, see K. Ameriks, "Recent Work," 16.

45. K. Ameriks, "Recent Work," 16.

46. Ibid., 17.

47. Ibid., 18.

48. Prauss generically encompasses with *Erscheinung* all the other Kantian terms for givenness-in-sensation like *Empfindung* and *Wahrnehmung (Erscheinung bei Kant,* 148). My own purpose is to associate Kant's usage of *Erscheinung* with *Vorstellung eines Objekts* and to reserve *Empfindung* or *Wahrnehmung* for a more primordial—unreferred *(unbezogene)*—representation in consciousness.

49. A very clear formulation of this, without explicit reference to Prauss, is in R. Aquila, "Matter, Forms," 87.

50. Even such terms as "whiffs" and "hues" are in fact conceptual-objective, as R. Pippin points out, *Kant's Theory of Form*, 33.

51. Prauss, *Erscheinungen bei Kant*, passim.

52. Pippin, *Kant's Theory of Form*, 39.

53. Prauss, *Erscheinungen bei Kant*, 237.

54. K. Ameriks makes this quite clear in his review: "[T]he realm of subjective objects is thought of as tied not to a peculiar stratum of pre- or suprajudgmental items (such as mere association, dreams or commands) but rather to a kind of consciousness that is present precisely in the most ordinary acts of objective perception; it is the purely subjective side of such acts" ("Recent Work," 17).

55. Prauss, *Erscheinungen bei Kant*, 163.

56. Ibid., 145–46.

57. R. Aquila, *Matter in Mind*, 121 and note (234).

58. Ibid., 54, citing *A.A.* 24:907.

59. Ibid., 55.

60. Aquila, "Matter, Forms," 74.

61. Ibid., 80.

62. Ibid., 92.

63. Ibid., 94.

64. Aquila, *Matter in Mind*, 138.

65. Aquila writes: "the 'application' of concepts to objects (or appearances) can in its own turn be nothing other than an 'application' *of the very faculty of understanding itself*. For nothing else is given to the understanding to 'apply' to objects—not even concepts" (*Matter in Mind*, 134).

66. H. Allison, "The Originality of Kant's Distinction between Analytic and Synthetic Judgments," 20; Kant, note to J. S. Beck letter of Nov. 11, 1791, in *Briefwechsel*, *A.A.* 11:298n. (*Philosophical Correspondence*, 181).

67. Allison, "The Originality of Kant's Distinction between Analytic and Synthetic Judgments," 18.

68. Prauss, *Erscheinungen bei Kant*, 105.

69. Ibid., 117.

70. Ibid., 164.

71. Ibid., 171. All of these insights bear with great consequence upon aesthetic judgments, as I will demonstrate. The crucial connection lies in the concept of imagination.

72. L. Beck, "Did the Sage of Königsberg Have No Dreams?" in *Essays on Kant and Hume*, 45.

73. Ibid., 47–48n.

74. L. Beck acknowledges in a note the influence of Prauss in this realization, ibid., 52n.

75. Ibid., 56.

76. Ibid., 58.

77. R. Aquila, *Matter in Mind*, 127ff., takes a very strong stance that accords with my own, as does Prauss, *Erscheinungen bei Kant*, 141n.

78. M. Gregor, "Aesthetic Form," 195.

79. J. M. Young, "Kant's View of Imagination," 150.

80. Ibid., 158.

81. This qualifier will be elaborated below.

82. Kant, *Critique of Pure Reason*, A51/B75.

83. Kant, *Logic*, §11:103 (*A.A.* 9:97).

84. Meerbote, "'Objective Validity' and 'Objective Reality,'" 53ff.

85. The notion of a "subjective principle a priori" is, of course, essential to the argument of the *Third Critique*.

86. Kant, *Critique of Judgment*, §vii:25.

87. Kant, *Critique of Pure Reason*, A44/B61.

88. Mathematical constructions take place in "pure" intuition, according to Kant. Pure intuition is not empirical. The space of mathematical construction is ideal, and therefore any "object" which is "realized" in a mathematical construction is not a real object. It is merely formal, not actual. What it lacks is precisely material existence. In his preface to *Metaphysical Foundations of Natural Science*, Kant explained this distinction in terms of a contrast of "nature" with "essence." Nature, he wrote, "signifies the primal, internal principle of everything that belongs to the existence of a thing," whereas "essence is the primal, internal principle of everything that belongs to the possibility of a thing." Kant continued: "Therefore, one can attribute to geometrical figures only an essence and not a nature (since there is thought in their concept nothing which expresses an existence)" (*Metaphysical Foundations*, 3). The heart of the distinction between nature and essence is the contrast between existence (actuality) and possibility. Kant makes the same distinction in the *Third Critique*, arguing that the ground of this distinction "lies in the subject and in the nature of our cognitive faculties." He elaborates: "if the understanding *thinks* . . . a thing (which it may do at pleasure), the thing is merely represented as possible. If it is conscious of it as given in intuition, then it is actual" (*Critique of Judgment*, §76:249–50).

89. Kant, *Critique of Pure Reason*, A320/B376–77.

90. Kant, *Logic*, 71n.

91. "In man (and so in beasts too) there is an immense field of sensuous intuitions and sensations we are not conscious of, though we can conclude with certainty that we have them. In other words, the field of our *obscure* [representations] is immeasurable, while our clear [representations] are only the infinitesimally few points on this map that lie open to consciousness: our mind is like an immense map with only a few places illuminated." (*Anthropology*, §5:16. Here and in all citations from this translation, I replace Gregor's "idea" with the standard "representation" for the German term *Vorstellung* in order to avoid confusion.)

92. Kant, Letter to Herz, May 26, 1789, in *Briefwechsel, A.A.* 11:51–52 (*Philosophical Correspondence*, 153–54).

93. G. Prauss, *Erscheinung bei Kant*, 75, notes Kant's revealing use of "*metamorphosis (Verwandlung)*" of [subjective] appearance [*Erscheinung*] into cognition [*Erkenntnis*]" in such works as *Metaphysical Foundations* (*A.A.* 4:555) and the *Prolegomena* (*A.A.* 4:297).

94. Kant, *Logic*, 71 (*A.A.* 9:65).

95. J. M. Young holds that his cat is capable of this sort of discrimina-

tion: "What the cat has, if my suggestion is correct, is the capacity to interpret his sensible states in accordance with certain rules and to discriminate sensible things of one sort from those of other sorts" ("Kant's View of Imagination," 149–50). Aquila writes: "Kant himself is prepared to grant that animals are in fact capable of a kind of judgment . . . a kind of 'reflective' judgment . . . the notion of a certain sort of suitability or affinity between the work of the mere imagination and that of an at least potential understanding" (*Matter in Mind*, 69).

96. Animals can "recognize" in the sense of comparing likeness and difference; they are manifestly acquainted with such things as scents, tracks, salt licks, and water holes without having to subsume these "objects" to conceptual universals. Indeed, they don't articulate an experience like "That is George," but they certainly have it. The animal would not be perplexed by the emptiness of "that" or "this" in these propositions, for it would never have come to propositions. It is humans who articulate, who name. Yet *erkennen* in this sense would still have the sense of acquaintance *(kennen, not wissen)*. "That is George" remains a matter of attaching arbitrary signs to the signified, not yet a matter of logical understanding. Yet humans worry over sentences and their referents. Having named, they wish to "understand" *(verstehen)* and therefore have to reflect upon propositions, elevating them to logical scrutiny and universal validation. See Sellars and Gram, cited in notes 37 and 26 above, for divergent notions about the status of "thises" and "thats" in judgments of recognition like "That is George."

97. Kant, *Prolegomena* §18:41–42 (*A.A.* 4:298).

98. Ibid., §20:43 (*A.A.* 4:300). The repeated reference to "consciousness of my state" and "state of my mind" should be connected with the argument in the "Amphiboly" of the *First Critique*. We will return to this notion.

99. Ibid., §22:48 (*A.A.* 4:305).

100. See *Critique of Judgment* §iv:15–16. This would apppear to be the predominant sense of judgment in the *First Critique*. See A132–34/B171–73. On the implicit distinction from reflective judgment in the *First Critique* see M. Liedtke, *Der Begriff.*

101. This issue resurfaces in Kant's own epistemology as the problem of "empirical entailment" in the *Third Critique*, and especially in its *First Introduction.*

102. See Kant's note on the letter from Jacob Sigismund Beck, Nov. 11, 1791, *A.A.* 11:298n. (*Philosophical Correspondence*, 181).

103. Kant, *Critique of Pure Reason*, A120.

104. Ibid., A78/B103.

105. Kant called imagination "a blind but indispensable function of the soul, without which we should have no knowledge whatsoever, but of which we are scarcely ever conscious" (*Critique of Pure Reason*, A78/B103).

106. Kant, *Anthropology*, §6:19.

107. Ibid., §31:50.

108. Ibid., 52. In connection with this see the controversial text in the *First Critique*, A90/B123.

109. Ibid. Note the symmetry with conduct in the practical sphere that

is "in accordance with" but not done "for the sake of" duty, i.e., in explicit acknowledgement of its rule.

110. Ibid., §25:40. The use of "concept" here may seem a bit misleading, yet by its placement in the text and by the term "attention" associated with it, we must recognize that the only sense of concept here is that of an empirical concept, and Kant is clear that it differs little from a mere name.

111. Ibid., §44:73.

112. Ibid., §54:89. On this see the extensive discussion in A. Bäumler, *Kants Kritik der Urteilskraft*, 142ff.; O. Schlapp, *Kants Lehre vom Genie*, 268; and G. Tonelli, "Kant's Early Theory of Genius." See also that remarkable passage about judgment in the *First Critique* (A132–36/B171–75), which obviously takes judgment in a different sense from the standard determinant judgment under the authority of the categories. See M. Liedtke, *Der Begriff*, for details.

113. Kant, *Anthropology*, §55:90.

114. J. M. Young, "Kant's View of Imagination," 141–42.

115. This draws close to Makkreel's project to construe imagination in Kant's *Third Critique* as a source for hermeneutics as a mode of "interpretation."

116. J. M. Young, Kant's View of Imagination," 147.

117. E. Schaper, *Studies in Kant's Aesthetics*, 1–17.

118. J. M. Young, "Kant's View of Imagination," 149.

119. Ibid., 151. We will return to these issues in our discussion of *hypotyposis* or *Darstellung* in connection with Kant's theory of symbolism in part 3 of this study.

120. This sense of a faculty of judgment with distinctive features parallels closely the remarkable passage concerning judgment in the *First Critique:* A133–34/B172–73.

121. Makkreel conceives of imagination in this determined sense as "synthetic," while he calls undetermined (or indeterminate) imagination "formative." The terms are certainly distinguishable, but what seems to differentiate the so-called "synthetic" from the "formative" is the explicit acknowledgement of rule in the judgment, a distinction Kant formulates most clearly as that between determinant and reflective judgment.

122. J. M. Young, "Kant's View of Imagination," 154.

123. Kant, *Anthropology*, §40:69.

124. In §26 of the *Third Critique*, Kant will term this capacity of imagination "comprehension."

125. Kant, *Anthropology*, §28:45.

126. Kant, *Critique of Judgment*, §10:55–56.

127. Kant, *Critique of Pure Reason*, A260–61/B316–17. See also M. Liedtke, *Der Begriff*.

128. Kant, *Critique of Pure Reason*, A260–61/B316–17.

129. Ibid., A261/B317.

130. Ibid., A269/B325.

Four: The Transcendental Grounding of Taste

1. See Kant, *Critique of Practical Reason* 29 (*A.A.* 5, 30).

2. See Meredith, "Last Stages," xxxvii–l.

3. Kant, *Critique of Judgment,* §9.

4. Kant to K. L. Reinhold, Dec. 28–31, 1787, in *Briefwechsel, A.A.* 10:513–15 (*Philosophical Correspondence* 127–28).

5. Kant, *Critique of Judgment,* §10:55.

6. On Kant's language of purpose see esp. K. Marc-Wogau, *Vier Studien,* part 2: *Wesen und Arten der Zweckmäßigkeit.* My view is heavily indebted to his work. For other recent contributions, see G. Tonelli, "Von den verschiedenen Bedeutungen"; and W. Pluhar, "How to Render 'Zweckmäßigkeit.'" For the older literature, see, e.g., R. Eisler, *Der Zweck.* On the superiority of "purpose" and "purposiveness" as renderings of *Zweck* and *Zweckmäßigkeit* over Meredith's "end" and "finality," I find myself in complete agreement with Pluhar.

7. Kant, *Critique of Judgment,* §10:55.

8. Ibid.

9. N. Rescher, "Noumenal Causality"; R. Wolff, "Remarks."

10. Kant, *Critique of Practical Reason,* 164 (*A.A.* 5:160).

11. Kant, *Critique of Pure Reason,* A23/B38.

12. Kant, *Critique of Judgment,* §31:M135, §33:M140, §8:M53–55.

13. Ibid., §33:M140. A second passage contrasted identical propositions, substituting rose for tulip (ibid., §8:M55).

14. Ibid., §3.

15. Ibid., §12:M63, §35:M142–43, §36:M144, §37:M145.

16. Ibid., §vii:25–26.

17. Ibid., §8. See L. Beck, "On the Putative Apriority of Judgments of Taste," in *Essays on Kant and Hume,* 167–70; E. Schaper, "Epistemological Claims and Judgments of Taste," in *Studies in Kant's Aesthetics,* 18ff.; P. Guyer, *Kant and the Claims of Taste,* 310–26; K. Ameriks, "Kant and the Objectivity of Taste."

18. Kant defined "exemplary necessity" as "a necessity of the assent of *all* to a judgment which is regarded as the example of a universal rule that we cannot state." *Critique of Judgment,* §18:74.

19. Ibid., §29:M117.

20. Ibid., §8:M53.

21. Ibid., §13:M64.

22. Ibid., §14:M65.

23. Ibid., §31:M135–36.

24. Ibid., §32:124.

25. Ibid., §5.

26. Ibid., §36:M144–45.

27. Ibid., §40:M151.

28. Ibid., §40, §8, §6, §22.

29. Ibid., §34.

30. Ibid., §34:M141.

31. These ideas have been explored extensively in the article literature on Kant's *Third Critique.* For some important contributions, see T. Greene, "A Reassessment of Kant's Aesthetic Theory"; R. Zimmermann, "Kant: The Aesthetic Judgment"; H. Blocker, "Kant's Theory of the Relation of Imagination and Understanding in Aesthetic Judgments of Taste"; B. Lang, "Kant and the Subjective Objects of Taste"; S. Petock, "Kant,

Beauty, and the Object of Taste"; W. Henckmann, "Das Problem der ästhetischen Wahrnehmung in Kants Ästhetik"; M. Neville, "Kant's Characterization of Aesthetic Experience"; and J. Fisher and J. Maitland, "The Subjectivist Turn in Aesthetics."

32. Kant, *Critique of Judgment,* §32:M137.

33. Ibid., §9:M58.

34. Ibid., §9:M60.

35. Ibid., §12:M63.

36. Ibid., §10.

37. Ibid., §10:55.

38. Ibid., §iv:17.

39. Ibid., §10:55.

40. Kant, *Critique of Pure Reason* A686–94/B714–22.

41. See Kant, *Critique of Judgment* §15:64, and K. Marc-Wogau, *Vier Studien,* 70–71.

42. Kant, *Critique of Judgment,* §62:210.

43. Ibid., §vii:26.

44. We will have to correct this impression ultimately and claim that precisely because of the "animality" in man, his susceptibility to "subjective material purposiveness" operates even prior to any empirical cognitive judgment, through a mere "judgment of sense."

45. Kant, *Critique of Judgment,* §64:216. See also §43:M163: "if, as sometimes happens, in a search through a bog, we light on a piece of hewn wood, we do not say it is a product of nature but of art [artifice]. Its producing cause had an end in view to which the object owes its form." Though we can ascribe such artifice to nature figuratively, as in the case of bee's work, on analogy to art, it is because it is only conceivable to us "in such a way that its actuality must have been preceded by a representation of the thing in its cause . . . although its effect could not have been *thought* by the cause." And see, finally, §64:216–17: "If in a seemingly uninhabited country a man perceived a geometrical figure, say a regular hexagon, inscribed on the sand, his reflection busied with such a concept would attribute, although obscurely, the unity in the principle of its genesis to reason, and consequently would not regard as a ground of the possibility of such a shape the sand, or the neighboring sea, or the winds, or beasts with familiar footprints, or any other irrational cause. For the chance against meeting with such a concept, which is only possible through reason, would seem so infinitely great that it would be just as if there were no natural law, no cause in the mere mechanical working of nature capable of producing it . . . This, then, would be regarded as a purpose."

46. Of course, even there we have difficulty with the *unintended* consequences of our purposes—both in recognizing and in acknowledging them. But that is a Hegelian insight, not a Kantian one. See Hegel, *Phenomenology of Spirit,* 211–52.

47. For a sense of the richness of this particular illustration for the mentality of the age see A. Lovejoy on changes in styles of gardening in the eighteenth century ("The Chinese Origins of a Romanticism" and "The First Gothic Revival and the Return to Nature," in *Essays in the History of Ideas*).

48. Kant, *Critique of Judgment* §45:149, §48:154. A great deal more needs to be said about these notions, but this is not the place. See below.

49. This is Kant's essential point about organisms.

50. Kant, *Critique of Judgment*, §10:55.

51. See L. Beck, *Commentary*, 90–108, on the role "interest" plays in Kant's theory of action. See P. Guyer, "Interest, Nature and Art," "Disinterestedness and Desire in Kant's Aesthetics," and *Kant and the Claims of Taste*, 174ff., for a considered view of the role of this notion in Kant's aesthetics.

52. It is a notion with which the *Third Critique* will wrestle ever after, and never completely resolve. Kant's notion of "objective purposiveness" is problematic because it fails of *both* the two senses in which "objective" works in the Kantian philosophy. It cannot be primordially *given*, because purposiveness is always an *inference*, not an inherent property of the object (*Third Critique*, Introduction, §vii:26). And it cannot be objectively *valid* because it cannot be brought under determinant judgments.

53. Kant, *Grounding*, 42. There are two key attributes of such an "end-in-itself." First, it is a rational agent, an "independently existing end"—a will, not an object of will. Second, as such, it is "final." By "final" Kant meant two things: ultimacy, that which can never be taken as a means for any other purpose; and autonomy, having the capacity independently to determine its own purposes (Kant, *Critique of Judgment*, §82:276). It is in the concept of "final purpose" that Kant supplies the crucial clarification of "objective purpose" which specifies it within the general category of "intrinsic purposiveness" and allows the essential claim that man is an end-in-himself. But this clarification was only achieved in the *Third Critique*. It was the fruit of Kant's "ethical turn."

54. Kant, *Critique of Judgment*, §15:63.

55. Kant, *Reflection* 696 (1769–71), *A.A.* 15:309.

56. Kant, *Reflection* 403 (1750s), *A.A.* 15:161.

57. Kant, *Reflection* 622, *A.A.* 15:269.

58. Kant, *Reflection* 628 (1769), *A.A.* 15:273.

59. Ibid., 267.

60. That, and even the example which first comes to his mind, the beauty of flowers, anticipates what became the crux of Kant's theory of "free beauty" in the *Third Critique*.

61. Kant, *Reflection* 628 (1769), *A.A.* 15:267.

62. Kant, *Reflection* 656 (1769), *A.A.* 15:290.

63. Kant, *Reflection* 643 (1769–79), *A.A.* 15:283.

64. Kant, *Reflection* 694, *A.A.* 15:308. Kant added a further comment: "the form of synthesis for any purpose in general [*die Form der Zusammenstimmung zum Belieben überhaupt*] is absolute perfection." This definition should be related to Kant's later formulations of objective purposiveness as organism and system, i.e., as a self-determining whole.

65. Kant, *Reflection* 279 (1770), *A.A.* 15:105. A little later, in 1771, Kant comes even to distinguish between the cognitive and the evaluative approach to the object. A cognitive representation of the object is distinct from the evaluation [*Beurteilung*] of the object, which has to do with its worth (*Reflection* 714 [1771], *A.A.* 15:316).

66. Kant, *Reflection* 676 (1769), *A.A.* 15:299–300.
67. Kant, *Reflection* 630 (1769), *A.A.* 15:274.
68. Kant, *Reflection* 618 (mid-1760s), *A.A.* 15:266. There were the germs of his own later theory.
69. Kant, *Reflection* 638 (1769), *A.A.* 15:276.
70. Kant, *Critique of Judgment,* §vii:26.
71. Ibid.
72. Ibid., §10:55.
73. Ibid., §vii:26.
74. It might seem that I have unduly complicated matters by introducing the notion of aesthetic *matter,* when only form was alluded to in the passage. But the Kantian distinction of the agreeable from the beautiful will be seen to turn on just this discrimination.
75. Compare Guyer's discussion of "form of finality" and "finality of form," *Kant and the Claims of Taste,* 211ff.
76. Kant, *Anthropology,* §15:32.
77. Kant, *Critique of Judgment,* §3:40.
78. "It is also not to be denied that all representations in us, whether, objectively viewed, they are merely sensible or are quite intellectual, may yet subjectively be united to gratification or grief, however imperceptible either may be, because they all affect the feeling of life, and none of them, so far as it is a modification of the subject, can be indifferent" (*Critique of Judgment* §29:119). See also §1, where Kant considers it possible that rational representations can have mere subjective reference and be, then, aesthetical. In his discussion of the cognitive use of the language of purposiveness, Kant suggested that satisfaction could accompany even an empirical judgment about nature. He was speaking of the thrill of discovery, as he made clear in §vi of the Introduction. He wrote there: "The discovery that two or more empirical heterogeneous laws of nature may be combined under one principle comprehending them both is the ground of a very marked pleasure" (*Critique of Judgment,* §1:24). Nevertheless, Kant did not believe there was any *necessary* role for pleasure in a logical reflective judgment. See the preface to the *Third Critique* (5). A determinant judgment, presumably, would be altogether *abstracted* from any possible "aesthetic character" in the representation.

Five: The Beautiful and the Pleasant

1. Kant, *Critique of Judgment,* §34:127.
2. Ibid., §9:M59.
3. Ibid., §9:M60.
4. Ibid., §39:M149.
5. Ibid., §9:51.
6. Ibid., 26.
7. A. Bäumler, *Kants Kritik der Urteilskraft,* 84ff.
8. See, for example, T. Cohen and P. Guyer, introduction to *Essays in Kant's Aesthetics,* 4; and P. Guyer, *Kant and the Claims of Taste,* 10–11.
9. Kant, *Critique of Judgment,* §4:41–42, §5:43, §7:46–47.
10. Kant, *First Introduction,* 28.

11. Ibid., 28–29. Translation slightly amended.

12. Ibid., 28. Translation slightly amended.

13. See Kant's letter to M. Herz, May 26, 1789, *A.A.* 11:51–52.

14. Kant, *Critique of Judgment,* §3:41.

15. Ibid., §8:49–50.

16. Ibid., §8:50, §33:127.

17. Ibid., §4:42.

18. Ibid., §2:38.

19. Ibid., §13:58.

20. Ibid., §vii:27.

21. L. Beck, "On the Putative Apriority of Judgments of Taste," in *Essays on Kant and Hume,* 167–70; and E. Schaper, "Epistemological Claims and Judgments of Taste," in *Studies in Kant's Aesthetics,* 18ff. On this question Guyer, *Kant and the Claims of Taste,* is the most rigorous extended study; see esp. 310–26.

22. Kant, *Critique of Judgment,* §9:51.

23. Ibid., §9:51ff.

24. Ibid., §1:38.

25. Ibid., §49:157.

26. Ibid., §36:131.

27. Ibid., §37:131–32.

28. Ibid., §vii:27.

29. The sequential or stage theory is at the heart of Guyer's interpretation in *Kant and the Claims of Taste,* esp. 110ff., whose analysis of §§9 and 37 makes a very compelling case for the superiority of the second argument. For an earlier formulation of this view, which Guyer drew upon, see A. Tumarkin, "Zur transscendentalen [sic] Methode der Kantischen Ästhetik."

30. Kant, *Critique of Judgment,* §8:49–50.

31. Ibid., §22GR:77–78.

32. Ibid., §22GR:78.

33. Kant, *Anthropology,* §31:52.

34. Ibid., §67:108.

35. Ibid., §12:29.

36. R. Odebrecht, *Form und Geist,* 97.

37. Kant, *Critique of Judgment,* §14:61.

38. Ibid., §31:122.

39. Ibid., §9:51.

40. Ibid., §9:53.

41. Ibid., §6:46. Note the centrality of disinterestedness in this approach.

42. Ibid., §40:136.

43. Ibid., §8:50–51, §40:135.

44. Ibid., §9:52.

45. Ibid., §vii:26.

46. Ibid., §35:129.

47. Ibid., §39:135.

48. Ibid., §9:52.

49. Ibid., §21:75.

50. Ibid.

51. See Guyer, *Kant and the Claims of Taste*, passim; A. Tumarkin, "Zur transscendentalen Methode"; and A. Genova, "Kant's Transcendental Deduction of Aesthetical Judgments" for critical examinations of this deduction in detail.

52. Kant, *Critique of Judgment*, §9:54.

53. Ibid., §12:58.

54. On the face of it, if the process is entirely subjective in its grounding, and presumably the faculties work in harmony freely, it should be entirely at the subject's disposition which representations should occasion beauty. If it isn't, then something about the object must be necessary to the experience. It is not the case that a parallel with empirical cognitive judgment resolves the issue, because *all* sensible intuition is constituted the moment *any* ground for the applicability of categories of understanding has been established. That only *some* empirical intuitions occasion the feeling of beauty, however, poses an altogether different problem.

55. There are some who argue that on Kant's theory, every object *should* occasion this feeling, and that this decisively weakens Kant's approach. The criticism has been formulated by R. Meerbote, "Reflection on Beauty." An attempt to answer the criticism, by accepting but reinterpreting its key assertion, was made in T. Gracyk, "Sublimity, Ugliness, and Formlessness." Both essays recognize in Kant's aesthetics a notion of a preconceptual ordering with aesthetic value. For a very effective treatment of this issue, see M. Gregor, "Aesthetic Form."

56. Kant, *Critique of Judgment*, §17:68.

57. Ibid., §14:M66 amended.

58. To say that representations-of-objects are eligible for objective reference is simply to say that they necessarily occur in space and time, i.e., they have the form of sensible intuition.

59. P. Guyer has analyzed this confusion in terms of the convergence of the "finality of form" with the "form of finality." See P. Guyer, *Kant and the Claims of Taste*, 211ff.

60. Kant, *Critique of Judgment*, §14:M66 amended.

61. The distortion finds echoes later in the text. In §42 Kant gave another go at distilling "form" from the *Reiz* of color and tone. "The charms [*Reize*] in natural beauty, which are to be found blended, as it were, so frequently with beauty of form, belong either to the modifications of light (in coloring) or of sound (in tones). For these are the only sensations which permit not merely of a feeling of the senses, but also of reflection upon the form of these modifications of sense" (ibid., §42:M161).

62. Ibid., §14:61.

63. Ibid., §22GR:M86–87, substituting "purposiveness" for "finality."

64. See Kant's *Reflection* 706 (1771–72), *A.A.* 15:313, for an anticipation of this conception of the dialectic.

65. For the "ease" of the "Deduction," see §38, Remark; for the poverty in transcendental determinations, see the letter to Reinhold, Dec. 28–31, 1787, in *Briefwechsel A.A.* 10:513–15 (*Philosophical Correspondence*, 127–

28); for further reflections on this question, see §55, the introduction to the final version of the "Dialectic."

66. Tonelli, "La formazione," 447.

67. Meredith, "Last Stages," 253–54.

Six: Kant's Philosophy of Art in the Year 1788

1. M. Johnson, "Kant's Unified Theory of Beauty."

2. R. Burch, "Kant's Theory of Beauty as Ideal Art."

3. It is useful to look to the Latin for these terms. "Free beauty" is termed *pulchritudo vaga*. "Dependent beauty" is *pulchritudo adhaerens*. To render *vaga* as "free," as Kant did, is indicative of the peculiar character of the freedom he wished to assign to taste.

4. Kant, *Critique of Judgment*, §15:M70.

5. Ibid., §16:67. See E. Schaper, "Free and Dependent Beauty," in *Studies in Kant's Aesthetics*, 78–95; and P. Guyer, *Kant and the Claims of Taste*, 242–52.

6. Kant, *Critique of Judgment*, §48:M173, substituting "purposiveness" for "finality."

7. Kant goes to great lengths to distinguish among merely sensual pleasure, *das Angenehme*, beauty, *das Schöne*, and the good, *das Gute*, in §§1–5 of the *Third Critique*. These ideas had been distinguished in his thinking since the 1760s.

8. Ibid., §15:M70. And see *Reflection* 656 (1769), A.A. 15:290.

9. Ibid., §16:67.

10. It is, in other words, an "*ideal*" in the terminology of the *First Critique*. Why Kant insists on calling it an "aesthetic idea" will only be fully clear after we have incorporated his theory of symbolism. For the moment, let us suspend that question.

11. Kant, *Critique of Judgment*, §17:M77, with emendations.

12. Ibid., §17:M78–79.

13. Ibid.; Kant discusses the ideal of the imagination along similar lines in the *First Critique* at B384–85.

14. Or, alternatively, has its source in something less determinately applicable to sensible intuition, namely, ideas of reason. This last possibility is the one Kant will eventually opt for.

15. The phrase, which is so utterly apt, is from Max Weber, who uses it in an entirely different context. Kant's sense accords more with an idea which one of Weber's students developed: Georg Lukács's idea of the *typical* as a Hegelian "concrete universal." See, e.g., Lukács, *Realism in Our Time*, 122.

16. Kant, *Critique of Judgment*, §17:M77.

17. Ibid., §17:M78.

18. Ibid., §17:M79.

19. What could be an image of anyone cannot very well serve as a portrait of someone. A. Malraux makes a very interesting analysis of this idea in juxtaposing a head sculpted in antiquity with one sculpted in the Middle Ages. The Roman head is in just the relevant sense impersonal. The medieval head is utterly personal. See Malraux, *Voices of Silence*, 218–19.

20. Kant, *Critique of Judgment*, §17:68.
21. Kiesewetter to Kant, Jan. 29, 1790, *A.A.* 11:126ff.
22. Hegel was one who criticized Kant along these lines. See *Hegel's Introduction to Aesthetics*, esp. 56ff.
23. Nietzsche has a great deal to say about the difference this introduces into the aesthetic theory one composes. See "The Will to Power as Art" in Nietzsche, *The Will to Power*, 419–53, and the discussion in M. Heidegger, *Nietzsche*, 1:107ff.
24. Kant, *Critique of Judgment*, §45:M167.
25. Ibid., §48:M173.
26. See Kant, *First Introduction*, §1. For these two senses of rationality in Weber, see "Politics as a Vocation," 120–22. I wish only to use his terms to help illuminate Kant.
27. Kant, *Critique of Judgment*, §43:146.
28. Ibid., §43:M164.
29. Ibid., §45:149.
30. Ibid., §45:M167.
31. Ibid., §49:M181.
32. Ibid., §43:M164.
33. Ibid., §44:M165.
34. Ibid. Kant frequently distinguished merely historical learning from rational or philosophical science. See his *First Critique*, A836/B864, and his announcement of his lectures, *A.A.* 2:305–313.
35. In all this one can see the enormous appeal of Kant to the Positivists of the late nineteenth century, whose phrase "back to Kant" was a rebellion largely against all the "Romantic excesses." In their acceptance of Kant's ironic handling of genius, they mislaid the very powerful Romantic stress on creativity, however. It is the great philosophical contribution of Michael Polanyi in all sobriety to reintroduce these questions with explicit reference to the philosophy of Kant, in *Personal Knowledge*.
36. Meredith cites Alexander Gerard, William Duff and Edward Young as the most likely sources of Kant's theory of genius. O. Schlapp, *Kants Lehre vom Genie*, offers a host of English sources. G. Tonelli, "Kant's Early Theory of Genius (1770–1779)," tries to sort out the early sources. What is clear, in any event, is that Kant had closely read the existing literature, and had taken Gerard, in particular, as the most important theorist before himself, and the one he had therefore to improve upon.
37. Kant, *Critique of Judgment*, §46:M168.
38. Ibid., 169.
39. Ibid., §47:M169–70.
40. The notions of the limitation of art, that this limitation in human culture had already been reached, and the consequent demotion of art in terms of its rank among elements in human culture constitute the decisive starting point for Hegel's philosophy of art, and also the basis of his criticism of Romanticism. It is remarkable that Kant should have made these assertions. Yet Kant never pursued or developed them. Indeed, he did not even justify them. They remained bald assertions in his work. All the real labor was left to Hegel.
41. Kant, *Critique of Judgment*, §47:M171–72.

42. Ibid., 172.

43. Kant to F. H. Jacobi, Aug. 30, 1789, in *Briefwechsel, A.A.* 11:73f.

44. What we have here, in short, is yet another chapter in that "ancient quarrel between the philosophers and the poets," as Plato put it long ago.

45. Kant, *Critique of Judgment*, §43:M163.

46. Indeed, he had an even more profound trick in mind: to steal genius away from the *Schwärmer* and make it a vehicle for *reason*. Kant's philosophy of art contains *two* theories of genius. The first, consistent with all that has gone before, regards genius as "natural" in the sense of belonging to sensibility, givenness, and imagination, and it articulates the phenomenology of genius in terms of the subjective conditions of the faculties of the mind. It is this "naturalistic" theory of genius that concerns us here. But in §49 Kant also articulates for the first time publicly a much more radical possibility, namely, that genius emanates not simply from "nature" in that sense of "actuality," but rather from "nature" in its noumenal sense, i.e., from reason as supersensible but real being. The latter notion, which is the foundation of Kant's theory of symbolism, only came to full articulation, however, in the wake of his "ethical turn," and we will reserve analysis of it for that later context.

47. Kant, *Critique of Judgment*, §48:M174.

48. Kantian theory of art sees *play* as a form of abstraction from the binding character of rule through the use of such rules for other purposes, as in setting up rules in a game through which to make play possible, but not out of any earnestness about the rules as such. There is a good deal of literature picking up on Kant's use of play in this context, starting with Schiller and carrying forward to some of the most recent scholarly efforts to make sense of Kant's theory of art. See, e.g., H. Gadamer, *Truth and Method*, 91ff., and A. Trebels, *Einbildungskraft und Spiel.*

49. See J. Barzun, *Classic, Romantic and Modern*, and I. Howe, ed., *The Idea of the Modern.*

50. Kant, *Critique of Judgment*, §49:M175.

51. Ibid., §43:M164.

52. Ibid., §17:M75.

53. Kant uses the contrast *geistreich* and *schön* in §50 to make his point. A work may be *geistreich*, full of spirit, when the imaginative genius supplies a good deal of its distinctive "material," but it may not be beautiful. Indeed, like those English gardens, it might verge on the grotesque. Conversely, that which has only taste, but no spark of genius, is, to be sure, in the measure that it conforms to the rules, "correct" and, Kant even seems to suggest, beautiful *(schön)*, yet unequivocally lifeless.

54. Kant, *Critique of Pure Reason*, A90/B123; *Anthropology*, §31, 52.

55. See Kant, *Critique of Judgment*, §5.

56. Ibid., §29GR:M120.

57. Ibid., §48:M172.

58. Thus Meredith notes, in his commentary: "Of course, 'representation' is not here used in the technical sense with which readers of the *Critique of Pure Reason* will be familiar. At the same time it is somewhat difficult to fix its meaning . . . Kant's distinction raises more difficulties than it solves" (*Kant's Critique of Aesthetical Judgement,* editor's note, 285).

59. Kant, *Critique of Judgment*, §48:M174.

60. In fact, the meaning of this essentially expressive theory of art will only become clear when we address ourselves to Kant's theory of symbolism.

Seven: The Cognitive Turn

1. R. Horstmann recognizes the problem of the process of development: "The two years during which Kant wrote the book must have witnessed a remarkable process of adjusting the initial idea of a *Critique of Taste* to needs originating from sources not directly related to the theory of taste." Yet he declines to "investigate the details of the historical development of the *Critique of Judgment*" ("Why Must There Be a Transcendental Deduction in Kant's *Critique of Judgment?*" 160–61).

2. Kant, *Critique of Judgment*, §23:M92.

3. In these considerations the cognitive and the practical senses of "intellectual" were peculiarly fused, because the matter which was at issue was the "purposiveness of nature." Insofar as it was "purposive," it referred to a judgment of reason rather than understanding, but insofar as it had to do with "nature," it seemed at least in some sense cognitive. In §42, Kant wrote: "it . . . interests reason that the ideas (for which in the moral feeling it arouses an immediate interest) should have objective reality, i.e that nature should at least show a trace or give an indication that it contains in itself a ground for assuming a regular agreement of its products with our entirely disinterested satisfaction" (143). What Kant is intimating is that, in fact, there are two interests involved in the rational consideration of beauty, first a cognitive one in finding empirical order, but second an ethical one in finding our moral purposes compatible with nature's laws. The first interest would lead him to his "cognitive turn" and the second to his "ethical turn."

4. Kant, *Critique of Judgment*, §30:M133 (replacing "finality" with "purposiveness").

5. Ibid., §23:M92 (replacing "finality" with "purposiveness"). In his Remark to §38, Kant elaborated on the "profound inquiries" he meant in the following terms: "But if the question were: How is it possible to assume *a priori* that nature is a complex of objects of taste? the problem would then have reference to teleology, because it would have to be regarded as an end of nature belonging essentially to its concept that it should exhibit forms that are final for our judgment" (ibid., §38:M148). Kant insists that two considerations be kept clearly in mind: first, this *speculation* about the intrinsic purposiveness of nature cannot be proven, and hence remains subject to doubt. And second, it is unnecessary to his theory of beauty in nature.

6. Ibid., §43:145.

7. In the *First Critique,* Kant explained that analogy could not, in philosophy, achieve the specificity of result that it could in mathematics. It could not give the fourth element, when the other three were given in analogical relation, but it could only validate the *relation.* Yet analogies were extremely important in human cognition. They functioned especially in

the sphere where determinate concepts failed, i.e., where understanding was not legislative. In this context, it is worthwhile to point out that Kant used the term "Analogies of Experience" for the crucial categories of relation in the "Transcendental Analytic," and distinguished them as "regulative" and "dynamical" in contrast to the more mathematical categories (*Critique of Pure Reason*, A179–80/B222). This suggests that the dividing line between analogy and indicative assertion in Kant's theory of knowledge may not be as simple as he would have wished.

8. Kant, *First Introduction*, §7:24 (*A.A.* 20:220).

9. Ibid., §5:18 (*A.A.* 20:213–14).

10. Ibid., §1:8 (*A.A.* 20:200–1). *Beurtheilen* is less rigorous than *urtheilen;* it does not have the same cognitive validity as *erklären* and seems closer to *kennen* than to *wissen.*

11. Kant, *Critique of Judgment*, §23, paragraphs 4 and 5. This was Kant's point about the beneficial impact of natural beauty upon scientific inquiry. It was also his point about the affective accompaniment of discovery, and the more sustained (transcendental) gratification at the conformity of empirical nature with human reason, which occasioned Kant's memorable apostrophe to the starry heavens. Compare §iv of the Introduction, on the delight associated with discovery in science, which attends the cognition of gratuitous order.

12. See the crucial line in the *Transcendental Dialectic*, A643/B671: "All errors of subreption are to be ascribed to a defect of judgment [*Urtheilskraft*], never to understanding or to reason." This is a matter to which we must return.

13. *First Introduction*, §5:20 (*A.A.* 20:215).

14. Ibid., §7:24 (*A.A.* 20:220).

15. Ibid., §9:38 (*A.A.* 20:234).

16. Ibid., §9:38–39 (*A.A.* 20:234–35).

17. Kant makes this assertion in his preface to the B-version. It is also implicit in his letter to Reinhold of 1787, of which we have made so much use.

18. The question of "popularity" was a sore point for Kant. He seemed to have had a rather sound attitude about it in the preface to the first edition of the *Critique of Pure Reason*, but its reception clearly annoyed him, and he was far more irascible about the issue in his prefaces both to the *Prolegomena* and to the second edition of the *First Critique*.

19. For a more detailed analysis of this question, see H. de Vleeschauwer, *La déduction*, 2:552ff. and vol. 3, passim. See also B. Erdmann, *Kants Kriticismus*, 163ff.; and M. Washburn, "The Second Edition of the Critique."

20. Kant, *Critique of Pure Reason*, preface to B-version, Bxl–xli.

21. Kant discusses "purposiveness" in a very important manner in the "Transcendental Dialectic," A625/B653; A686–87/B714–15; A743/B771; A815/B843. We will take this up below.

22. H. Allison, "Kant's Critique of Spinoza," 211.

23. Horstmann, "Why Must There Be a Transcendental Deduction in Kant's *Critique of Judgment?*" 166–69 and 259n., discusses the perplexity of

the status of *Zweckmäßigkeit* in the *First Critique* in terms of methodological versus transcendental principles of subjective consciousness.

24. Kant, *First Introduction*, §4 (*A.A.* 20:203n). See K. Düsing, *Die Teleologie in Kants Weltbegriff*, 57, for a very clear exposition of this.

25. The best statement of this insight, and one which has deeply influenced my study, is G. Schrader, "The Status of Teleological Judgment in the Critical Philosophy." But see also H. Allison, "Kant's Critique of Spinoza," 211, who argues that the "conformity [of particulars to empirical laws] was not guaranteed by the *Transcendental Analytic*." And, too, Horstmann, "Why Must There Be a Transcendental Deduction in Kant's *Critique of Judgment*?" 163: the transcendental principles established in the *First Critique* "do not account for the contingent or empirical fact that nature consists of very many individual objects [with] . . . special contingent characteristics."

26. See the preface to the first edition of the *Critique of Pure Reason*, where Kant promised a *Metaphysics of Nature* "not half as large, yet incomparably richer in content than this present *Critique*" (A:xxi). While the *Critique* offered an exhaustive *synthesis* of transcendental principles a priori, Kant argued that the concepts so constituted contained a great deal more, and consequently "there will remain the further work of making their *analysis* similarly complete" (ibid.).

27. Ibid., "Transcendental Aesthetic," B:40. The contrast of "transcendental" and "metaphysical" expositions was an innovation of the B-version, in which Kant was working toward the conception of a mediating role for metaphysical principles as analytic corollaries of his transcendental principles which would provide the transition to their empirical employment.

28. Kant's physics was only partly Newtonian, as commentators have noted in evaluating his *Metaphysical Foundations of Natural Science*. See G. Brittan, Jr., *Kant's Theory of Science*, 131–40; and M. Jammer, *Concepts of Force*, 82ff.

29. Kant, *First Introduction*, §4:14 (*A.A.* 20:209).

30. G. Schrader, "The Status of Teleological Judgment in the Kantian Philosophy."

31. K. Düsing, *Die Teleogie in Kants Weltbegriff*, 65; I. Bauer-Drevermann, "Zufälligkeit in Kants *Kritik der Urteilskraft*"; Allison, "Kant's Critique of Spinoza," 218: "the concept of contingency is central to the entire Third Critique."

32. One of the important shifts that transpires over the course of the "Critical" decade of Kant's works is that whereas in the *First Critique* "understanding" clearly dominates over all other faculties and seems to be the driving force of the mind altogether, in the later works, reason and judgment come to the fore. It is particularly important to note that already in the *First Critique* there were grounds for ascribing dynamism to "reason" within the whole operation of the mind. See the apt arguments for this offered by R. Brandt, "The Deductions in the *Critique of Judgment*." Most modern, and a fortiori most Anglo-American, philosophers routinely privilege "understanding" in their reading of Kant's theory of mental activity. See G. Buchdahl, "The Relation between 'Understanding' and 'Reason' in

the Architectonic of Kant's Philosophy." Though Kant began with that posture, by the later critical writings, reason and judgment had become far more important—and they were consistently complementary, one in the "pure," and one in the complex sphere of human rational activity. The parallelism of reason in pure operations with judgment in empirical applications is the striking counterpart of the *restriction* of the understanding. See the preface to the *Third Critique* for a very clear statement of this. The close parallel between judgment in its "technical" function (teleological judgment) and judgment in its "practical" function (moral judgment) is a systematic principle which deserves far more philosophical attention than it has hitherto received.

33. See A. Stadler, *Kants Teleologie und ihre erkenntnistheoretische Bedeutung,* for the first sustained analysis of this relation between the "Transcendental Dialectic" of the *First Critique* and the *Third Critique.* For more nuanced readings, see W. Bartuschat, *Zum systematischen Ort;* H. Mertens, *Kommentar zur Ersten Einleitung in Kants Kritik der Urteilskraft;* and the exchange between Horstmann and Brandt, in E. Förster, ed., *Kant's Transcendental Deductions.*

34. Kant, *Critique of Pure Reason,* A304/B360.

35. Kant, *First Introduction,* §2:8 (*A.A.* 20:201).

36. See Kant, *Logic,* 125–30; *Critique of Pure Reason* A303–5/B359–61.

37. See J. McFarland, *Kant's Concept of Teleology,* 70.

38. Kant, *Critique of Pure Reason,* A642–68/B670–96, esp. A657–58/B685–86.

39. Kant, *First Introduction,* §4:14 (*A.A.* 20:209).

40. See: J. Dister, "Kant's Regulative Ideas and the 'Objectivity' of Reason"; R. Zocher, "Der Doppelsinn der kantischen Ideenlehre"; and J. Evans, "The Empirical Employment of Pure Reason."

41. Kant used the term "idea" in a very specific sense, which he worked out at the outset of the "Transcendental Dialectic," A310–38/B366–96. He saw fit to make no changes in this section of the "Dialectic" in the B-version.

42. At several junctures, Kant wrote of reason as governing the understanding in a way strictly analogous to understanding's legislation, through the schematism, for experience. On the importance Kant attached to this parallelism, see McFarland, *Kant's Concept of Teleology,* 27.

43. Kant, *Critique of Pure Reason,* A178/B221.

44. Ibid., A178/B220.

45. Ibid., A179/B222.

46. Ibid., A180/B222–23.

47. Ibid., A180/B223. Even within the mathematical categories there is a difference between quantity and quality. All that can be "anticipated" as regards the "real" in appearances is that it will have *degree,* but *which* properties and *what* degree—i.e., all that is essential to the specification of an empirical object of experience—*cannot* be anticipated or "constructed" a priori.

48. See S. French, "Kant's Constitutive-Regulative Distinction."

49. Kant, *Critique of Pure Reason,* A508–10/B536–38.

50. Ibid., A643/B671.

51. Ibid., A644/B672.

52. Ibid., A664/B692.

53. That is the point of Kant's distinction of *philosophy* from *mathematics*. Philosophy is the exclusive affair of reason. It works with concepts, not constructions in intuition. See *Critique of Pure Reason,* A713–27/B741–55.

54. Ibid., A646–47/B674–75.

55. Michael Polanyi has explored these matters in a rigorous and insightful manner from a "post-critical" vantage in *Personal Knowledge.*

56. Kant, *Critique of Pure Reason,* A643/B671.

57. Compare M. Liedtke, *Der Begriff.*

58. *A.A.* 8:133–47.

59. See, e.g., *Critique of Pure Reason,* A69/B94, where the faculty of judgment is the set of "all acts of the understanding," or A81/B106, where the faculty of judgment is held to be "the same as the faculty of thought."

60. See ibid., A132/B171, where the faculty of judgment is contrasted with understanding: "understanding in general is to be viewed as the faculty of rules, judgment will be the faculty of subsuming under rules" and similarly at A247/B304: "the employment of a concept involves a function of judgment [*Urtheilskraft*] whereby an object is subsumed under the concept." And especially see A646/B674 of the "Transcendental Dialectic," where Kant comes closest to the sense of a "determinant judgment": "If reason is a faculty of deducing the particular from the universal, and if the universal is already *certain in itself* and given, only *judgment* [*Urtheilskraft*] is required to execute the process of subsumption, and the particular is thereby determined in a necessary manner."

61. This is the most striking, indeed even incongruous usage of *Urtheilskraft* in the *First Critique,* and smacks of Kant's style in the *Anthropology* or in the *Third Critique.* Kant wrote: "judgment [*Urtheilskraft*] is a peculiar talent which can be practiced only, and cannot be taught. It is the specific quality of so-called mother-wit; and its lack no school can make good . . . [I]n the absence of such a natural gift no rule that may be prescribed to [a learner] for this purpose can ensure against misuse . . . He may comprehend the universal *in abstracto,* and yet not be able to distinguish whether a case *in concreto* comes under it" (A133–34/B172–73). This is, so far as I can establish, the only place in the *First Critique* where Kant treats the faculty of judgment autonomously of understanding in the largest sense. Hence here Kant approached the "other kind of judging" which he only came fully to acknowledge in the *Third Critique.*

62. Kant explains all this in his "architectonic" first section of the *First Introduction,* §1:3–8 (*A.A.* 20:195–201).

63. See Horstmann's discussion of the distinction in the *First Critique* between methodological and transcendental principles, "Why Must There Be a Transcendental Deduction in Kant's *Critique of Judgment?*" 164–76. Kant did not yet recognize in the *First Critique* the idea of a *subjective* transcendental principle a priori, but he was forced to in the *Third Critique* in terms of the faculty of judgment.

64. Kant, *First Introduction,* §5:20 (*A.A.* 20:215).

65. See, above all, G. Tonelli, "La formazione," and M. Souriau, *Le jugement refléchissant*.

66. Kant to Reinhold, May 12, 1789, in *Briefwechsel, A.A.* 11:39.

67. Kant, *Critique of Judgment*, §iii:13–14. Kant made the claim of the systematic closure of the faculties in his letter to Reinhold of December 1787 as well.

68. Kant did allow the text to be published, unedited, later, and he also claimed that it was not in any philosophical way different from the final version of the Introduction, only longer. The latter claim is clearly inaccurate, and the significance of the later publication—as a fragment—is unclear. What is clear, however, is that Kant was never before or after so caught up with the idea of system.

69. P. Riley, *Kant's Political Philosophy*, 8.

70. Kant, *Erste Einleitung in die Kritik der Urteilskraft*, §11, *A.A.* 20:241–42 (my translation).

71. Ibid., 242.

72. It appears in *none* of the section titles in the final version. In its place, the language of "purpose" increases in prominence.

73. J. McFarland, *Kant's Concept of Teleology*, 70.

74. See H. Mertens, *Kommentar zur Ersten Einleitung*, and A. Genova, "Kant's Complex Problem of Reflective Judgment."

75. "What is peculiarly distinctive of reason . . . is that it prescribes and seeks to achieve its *systematisation*, that is, to exhibit the connection of its parts in conformity with a single principle" (*Critique of Pure Reason*, A645/B673). See G. Buchdahl, "The Kantian 'Dynamic of Reason.'"

76. "Pure reason is in fact occupied with nothing but itself. It can have no other vocation" (ibid., A680/B708).

77. Ibid., A680/B708.

78. Ibid., A645/B673.

79. Ibid., A647/B675.

80. Ibid.

81. Ibid., A680–81/B708–9.

82. These issues assume ineluctable saliency in the sphere of *practical reason*, as we shall see when we return to them in the context of the "ethical turn."

83. Kant, *Critique of Pure Reason*, A65/B89–90.

84. For this distinction of architectonic from system, see H. Mertens, *Kommentar zur Ersten Einleitung*, 71.

85. In terms of Kant's theory of space, it is not Leibnizian, i.e., merely the result of the interrelation of things, that which is "between" them, linking them, but more Newtonian, i.e., that within which they are deployed. But the fundamental question which obviously arises is whether Kant, like Newton, takes this ground to have objective reality (space as Divine substance) and hence considers reason as being (the soul, in rational psychology), or only takes it to be merely transcendentally ideal, i.e., a necessary structure of consciousness but not by that alone warranted as objectively real.

86. Kant, *Critique of Pure Reason*, A832–33/B860–61.

87. McFarland, *Kant's Concept of Teleology*, 38.

88. Weldon, *Introduction to Kant's Critique of Pure Reason*, 239.

89. K. Düsing, *Die Teleologie in Kants Weltbegriff*, 89.

90. Kant, *Critique of Pure Reason*, Bxxiii.

91. See J. Wubnig, "The Epigenesis of Pure Reason."

92. Kant, *Critique of Pure Reason*, Bxxxvii–xxxviii.

93. See K. Konhardt, *Die Einheit der Vernunft*.

94. Kant, *Critique of Pure Reason*, A64–65/B89.

95. Hence Kant's revision of the title of his *First Critique* in his famous letter to K. L. Reinhold of Dec. 28–31, 1787, in *Briefwechsel, A.A.* 10:513–15 (*Philosophical Correspondence*, 127–28), and in many other texts of this and later periods to read "Critique of Pure Theoretical (or Speculative) Reason."

96. Kant's letter to Reinhold gave clear notice of a change in his position. While he wrote as though the change only made possible a *Third* critique, the change was involved in creating the possibility of the *Second*. See R. Benton, *Kant's Second Critique and the Problem of Transcendental Arguments*, 24 and passim.

97. Kant, *Grounding*, 4.

98. Kant, *Critique of Practical Reason*, 94.

99. Kant to Reinhold, Dec. 28–31, 1787, in *Briefwechsel, A.A.* 10:513–15 (*Philosophical Correspondence*, 127–28).

100. Kant makes an explicit distinction between *theism* and *deism* in the *First Critique:* "Since we are wont to understand by the concept of God not merely an eternal nature that works blindly, as the root-source of all things, but a supreme being who through understanding and freedom is the Author of all things; and since it is in this sense only that the concept interests us, we could, strictly speaking, deny to the *deist* any belief in God, allowing him only the assertion of an original being or supreme cause. However . . . it is less harsh and more just to say that the *deist* believes in a *God*, the *theist* in a *living God (summa intelligentia)*" (A632–33/B660–61).

101. Kant, *Prolegomena*, 2–3 (*A.A.* 4:257).

102. Kant, *Critique of Pure Reason*, A3/B7.

103. Kant, "Was heißt: sich im Denken orientieren?" *A.A.* 8:136.

104. Kant, *Critique of Judgment*, §72:237.

105. Ibid., §75:246.

Eight: Kant's Critique of Science

1. Thus Kant's remarks about the German spirit of thoroughness and those who had tried to dissolve it, in the second preface, e.g., Bxlii–xliii.

2. See F. Beiser, *Fate of Reason*, 165–225, for a current discussion of Kant and his critics in the early to mid-1780s. He notes that it was only in 1788 that the intensity of criticism from empiricists and Wolffians alike assumed such proportions that Kant felt compelled to defend himself publicly.

3. These were the essays with which Kant assumed leardership of the Aufklärung movement. Most of them appeared in the *Berlinische Monatsschrift*, one of the flagship journals of the movement. For bold statements of

Aufklärung ideology from Kant, see the preface to the A-version of the *First Critique,* Axi, note; the entire section entitled "The Discipline of Pure Reason in Respect of its Polemical Employment" in the *First Critique,* A737–57/B766–86; and the preface to the B-version, Bxxxii–xxxv. The *locus classicus* is, of course, his essay "What Is Enlightenment?" (1784).

4. For a similar conclusion, see F. Beiser, *Fate of Reason,* 149–50.

5. C. Schütz to Kant, July 10, 1784, in *Briefwechsel, A.A.* 10:371.

6. C. Schütz to Kant, Aug. 23, 1784, in *Briefwechsel, A.A.* 10:373.

7. When he took up the project of his *Ideen zur Philosophie der Geschichte der Menschheit,* Herder was at the prime of his powers, and in that project he addressed his most important concern. The result, without question, was his greatest work. (For the finest study of Herder to this day see R. Haym, *Herder;* on this specific point, 2:193.) It remains one of the greatest works of the German 1780s. Yet, because of Kant, Goethe, and Hegel, Herder's bright star is dimmed as by glaring suns. It was his peculiar historical lot to be a grand figure dwarfed by titans. Yet he deserves better than the condescension or even contempt to which he has been so frequently subjected by literary and historical scholars. Even so major an effort as I. Berlin's "Herder and Enlightenment" fails to do him full justice. More just, if briefer, is L. Beck in *Early German Philosophy,* 382–92.

8. Haym, *Herder,* makes this important point, 2:262–63.

9. Hamann to Herder, May 8, 1785, in *Hamanns Briefwechsel,* 5:432.

10. See his remark to Hartknoch in 1783, cited by K. Vorländer, *Immanuel Kant,* 317n.: "Kant's works were certainly not enjoyable for him and against his way of thinking, but at the same time he had neither written nor occasioned to be written anything against them." Of course, Kant would disagree: *Von Erkennen und Empfinden* ssemed a direct attack on his philosophy.

11. Those reviews, intervening in the middle of his great synthetic project, adversely affected the balance of Herder's work, and the bitter hostility to Kant they engendered worked like a cancer to corrode his thinking thereafter, until it resulted in those last bilious and futile outbursts—the *Metakritik der reinen Vernunft* and the *Kalligone*—of the close of the century. See Haym, *Herder,* 2:251, for the question of Kant's immediate and destructive impact on the composition of the *Ideen.*

12. Herder, *Ideen,* vol. 1, 13:13.

13. Ibid., 65.

14. Ibid., 109ff. The issue of erect posture had drawn Kant's attention in an earlier review, "Recension von Moscatis Schrift" (*A.A.* 2:423–25).

15. See J. Herder, *Essay on the Origin of Language.*

16. Herder, *Ideen,* book 5. See R. Clarke, "Herder's Concept of '*Kraft.*'"

17. Haym, *Herder,* 2:212ff.

18. H. Korff, *Geist der Goethezeit* 2:22.

19. Ibid., esp. 2:11ff.

20. Ibid., 2:14.

21. Goethe, "Natur-Fragment."

22. Goethe, letter to Kanzler von Müller, May 24, 1828, cited in Pascal, *German Sturm und Drang,* 210.

23. Korff, *Geist der Goethezeit,* 2:18–19; but see the very negative as-

sessment of Goethe as scientist despite praise for his poetry of nature, illustrated by this fragment, in C. Sherrington, *Goethe on Nature and Science*. For a monumental rebuttal of this utter severance of poetic from scientific insight, see E. Sewell, *The Orphic Voice*, esp. part 3, "Erasmus Darwin and Goethe," 169–276. On the impact of Goethe's thinking see J. Hoffmeister, *Goethe und der deutsche Idealismus*.

24. See Herder's letter to F. Jacobi, Feb. 6, 1784, *Herders Briefe*, 227, and the preface to *God: Some Conversations*, 67.

25. See esp. E. Cassirer, *The Platonic Renaissance in England*, chap. 6. Cassirer has throughout his works shown a sound appreciation for the importance of the Earl of Shaftesbury for eighteenth-century thought.

26. O. Walzel developed this idea explicitly: "Shaftesbury prophetically anticipated the later recognition that the cosmos and every particular organism is a system, in which the parts are coordinated into a whole by the unity of purpose" ("Shaftesbury"). On the relation of the idea of organic unity to pantheist metaphysics in the eighteenth century, see J. Benziger, "Organic Unity," esp. 29.

27. W. Dilthey, "Aus der Zeit des Spinozastudien Goethes." See also Cassirer, *Philosophy of the Enlightenment*, 85.

28. Shaftesbury's "metaphor of the world as a living body anticipates the later conception, held by such Romantics as Diderot and Goethe, that the universe is a complex of active processes rather than a mechanism composed of dead matter" (Tuveson, "Shaftesbury and the Age of Sensibility," 87).

29. A. Cooper, Earl of Shaftesbury, *Characteristics of Men, Manners, Opinions, Times*, esp. "The Moralists" (1709), 2:1–156.

30. Walzel, "Shaftesbury," 428.

31. "The highest good for man is to imbue the microcosm, his life, with the 'vital principle' which animates [Nature as a work of God]." J. Stolnitz, "On the Significance of Lord Shaftesbury," 102.

32. E. Tuveson, "Shaftesbury and the Age of Sensibility," 83.

33. Ibid., 82.

34. On the whole notion of aesthetic attunement as implicating cognitive or ethical validity, see the first part of H. Gadamer, *Truth and Method*, 5–90.

35. Cassirer, *Philosophy of the Enlightenment*, 314. And: "Nature itself in its deeper sense is not the sum total of created things but the creative power from which the form and order of the universe are derived" (ibid., 328). "The deeper truth of this world . . . consists in the fact that an operative principle obtains in it, which is embodied in and reflected by all its creatures in varying degrees and force" (ibid., 314). The beautiful "is independent and original, and innate and necessary, in the sense that it is no mere accident but belongs to the substance of the spirit and expresses this substance in an entirely original way" (ibid., 322).

36. Ibid., 317.

37. "Shaftesbury's doctrine of 'enthusiasm,' of 'disinterested passion,' of genius in man which is akin to and not inferior to the 'Genius of the World,' contain the first seeds of this new fundamental conception whose development and systematic justification took place at the hands of Less-

ing, Herder, and Kant." Cassirer, *Philosophy of the Englightenment*, 319–20n. See also: O. Walzel, "Shaftesbury"; and W. Bruford, *Culture and Society in Classical Weimar 1775–1806*, 26–37. See also C. Weiser, *Shaftesbury und das deutsche Geistesleben;* and I. Hatch, *Der Einfluß Shaftesburys auf Herder.*

38. The text is in *A.A.* 8:44–55. The scientific substance of the review will be treated in a later chapter.

39. C. Schütz to Kant, Feb. 18, 1785, in *Briefwechsel, A.A.* 10:375. Ironically, this defender of Herder, whom Kant demolished in short order in a response printed in the March issue of *Allgemeine Literatur-Zeitung*, proved to be none other than K. L. Reinhold, who would, a year later, use the same *Teutsche Merkur* as the forum for his *Briefe über die Kantische Philosophie* (1786–90), the decisive popularization of Kantianism in Germany.

40. Kant, "Recension von Herders *Ideen*," *A.A.* 8:53–54.

41. Ibid., 27.

42. Haym, *Herder*, 2:247–48, and K. Vorländer, *Immanuel Kant*, 319, blame Kant. Even L. Beck writes that "Kant deserved all the blame" for the falling out (*Early German Philosophy*, 384) but he also insists that Kant was correct (ibid., 390–91).

43. Haym wrote aptly: "Kant uncovered with victorious sharpness and clarity the halftruths and confusions of his opponent, but he passed over without recognition the legitimate motives of the latter, indeed, he did him an injustice" (*Herder*, 2:256). And see Hamann to Herder, Feb. 4, 1785: "Kant is too full of his own system to be able to judge you objectively—and no one is in a position yet to see the whole scope of your project" (*Hamanns Briefwechsel*, 5:352).

44. The first volume of Herder's *Ideen* is preponderantly *Naturphilosophie*. The second volume, which Kant also reviewed, dealt with physical anthropology and race theory, scientific topics of direct relevance to Kant's teleology essay. For background on these questions in the eighteenth century, see C. Glacken, *Traces on the Rhodian Shore*, 508ff.

45. Kant, *Grounding*, 2.

46. Kant, *Reflection* 990 (later 1780s), *A.A.* 15:435.

47. Kant, *Critique of Pure Reason*, B:xxxvi.

48. Ibid., Bxlii–xliii.

49. Kant, *Critique of Practical Reason*, 23.

50. Kant, "Über den Gebrauch," *A.A.* 8:161.

51. Ibid., 180.

52. Kant, *Critique of Practical Reason*, 102. On Priestley's "syncretism" see J. McEvoy and J. McGuire, "God and Nature."

Nine: Kant Against Eighteenth-Century Hylozoism

1. See P. Menzer, *Kants Lehre von der Entwicklung*. For correction see A. Lovejoy, "Kant and Evolution," and G. Lehmann, "Kant und der Evolutionismus: Zur Thematik der Kantforschung Paul Menzers," in Lehmann, *Beiträge*, 219–243.

2. K. Roretz, *Zur Analyse von Kants Philosophie des Organischen*, 112–50; E. Ungerer, *Die Teleologie Kants und ihre Bedeutung für die Logik der Biologie*, 64–132; P. Bommersheim, "Der vierfache Sinn der inneren Zweckmäßig-

keit in Kants Philosophie des Organischen"; and H. Lieber, "Kants Philosophie des Organischen und die Biologie seiner Zeit." For a recent study of Kant's theory of organic form see R. Löw, *Philosophie des Lebendigen,* esp. 138ff.

3. Kant, *Critique of Judgment,* §75:248, §77:254.

4. On Kant's concept of life see Löw, *Philosophie des Lebendigen,* 153–67. And see R. Makkreel, *Imagination and Interpretation,* 91ff.

5. Hence Kant situated himself squarely in the tradition of the new scientific rationalism. For an old but still trenchant assessment of this view see E. Burtt, *Metaphysical Foundations of Modern Physical Science.* For a recent and penetrating analysis, see G. Buchdahl, *Metaphysics and the Philosophy of Science.*

6. That did not escape younger intellectuals in Germany who did keep abreast of the latest developments in natural science, and who could sense in Kant's work, even of the later 1780s, a position which did not quite incorporate the then current level of scholarship. In the aftermath of the publication of the *Third Critique,* young philosophers, steeped in the latest science, came to find his posture insupportable. Hence here was one of the impulses which led to German Idealism.

7. For this notion of "paradigm" see T. Kuhn, *The Structure of Scientific Revolutions.*

8. Kant, *Critique of Pure Reason,* A39–40/B56–57. See L. Beck, *Early German Philosophy,* 446–51, for a consideration of this. For more detail, see G. Martin, *Kant's Metaphysic and Theory of Science,* which stresses the Leibnizian origins, and Buchdahl, *Metaphysics and the Philosophy of Science.*

9. This is the thrust of the "Second Antinomy" of the *Critique of Pure Reason,* A434–45/B462–73, A523–27/B551–55. See J. Ellington, "The Unity of Kant's Thought" and "Translator's Introduction," esp. vi–x; 205–13.

10. Kant, *Metaphysical Foundations of Natural Science,* chap. 2, "Metaphysical Foundations of Dynamics," 40–94 (*A.A.* 4:496–535).

11. Ibid., 60 (*A.A.* 4:470).

12. See, for example, R. Schofield, *Mechanism and Materialism.*

13. J. D'Alembert, *Preliminary Discourse to the Encyclopédie;* see also Cassirer's use of D'Alembert's work in *Philosophy of the Enlightenment,* 8ff.

14. See L. Crocker, "Diderot and Eighteenth-Century French Transformationism."

15. See B. Glass, ed., *Forerunners of Darwin: 1745–1859,* esp. 51–83.

16. Or perhaps he did, but only in the *Opus posthumum,* where it was too late to salvage the relationship between the elder Kant and his Idealist heirs. See G. Lehmann, *Kants Nachlaßwerk,* and K. Düsing, *Die Teleologie in Kants Weltbegriff,* 143.

17. In the "Transcendental Dialectic" of the *First Critique* Kant made quite clear the extent of his commitment to this principle: "Order and purposiveness in nature must themselves be explained from natural grounds and according to natural laws; . . . the wildest hypotheses, if only they are physical, are here more tolerable than a hyperphysical hypothesis" (A772–73/B800–1).

18. Indeed, Kant never relented from his stance that valid scientific knowledge was possible only through mechanical explanations—not even in the "Critique of Teleological Judgment."

19. For a clear statement of his objective in the course, see his *Nachricht* (*A.A.* 2:305–13, esp. 312).

20. J. Wubnig, "The Epigenesis of Pure Reason."

21. See, e.g., E. Dijkterhuis, *The Mechanization of the World Picture,* and J. Heilbron, *Elements of Early Modern Physics.*

22. H. Guerlac, "Newton's Changing Reputation in the Eighteenth Century"; M. and A. Hall, "Newton's Electric Spirit"; I. Cohen and A. Koyré, "Newton's Electric and Elastic Spirit"; J. McGuire, "Force, Active Principles, and Newton's Invisible Realm," 187–208, "Transmutation and Immutability," "The Origins of Newton's Doctrine of Essential Qualities," and "Atoms and the 'Analogy of Nature'"; M. Jammer, *Concepts of Force,* 158–87; M. Hesse, *Forces and Fields,* 157–88.

23. P. Heimann and J. McGuire, "Newtonian Forces and Lockean Powers"; P. Heimann, "Voluntarism and Immanence" and "'Nature is a perpetual worker'"; P. Harman, *Metaphysics and Natural Philosophy;* A. Thackray, *Atoms and Powers;* J. Yolton, *Thinking Matter;* M. Jacob, *The Radical Enlightenment,* esp. 1–64.

24. I by no means wish to suggest anything but respect for E. Dijkterhuis's masterful study of these developments, *The Mechanization of the World Picture,* but only to suggest that the same model on which he so acutely interpreted the seventeenth century does not hold for the eighteenth.

25. See Voltaire's amusing comments in his *Letters on England* (1734) that upon crossing the channel the language for describing the physical world suddenly underwent a radical transformation. This persistence of Cartesianism in France cannot be written off to any cultural chauvinism, for the same resistance was to be found in the low countries among the eminent disciples of Huygens and in Germany of Leibniz himself.

26. J. Keynes, "Newton, the Man."

27. J. McGuire, "Force, Active Principles, and Newton's Invisible Realm," 187–208.

28. The finest treatment of these questions is without doubt Alexandre Koyré's *From the Closed World,* esp. 125–235. Koyré's influence upon my interpretation of the history of science in this period has been decisive.

29. On the Leibniz-Clarke controversy, the work of Koyré is again definitive. See not only *From the Closed World,* 235–76, but also his article with I. Cohen, "Newton and the Leibniz-Clarke Correspondence."

30. This is my only reservation about the otherwise so powerfully wrought and original work of M. Jacob, *The Radical Enlightenment.* Within the limits she has sketched out, her thesis is compelling and provocative, but it leaves us a bit at a loss to account for figures like Joseph Priestley in the second half of the British eighteenth century. See J. Yolton, *Thinking Matter,* for a more encompassing perspective.

31. A. Thackray, *Atoms and Powers,* 56, and "Matter in a Nut-Shell."

32. That Schofield's categories are confusing has been recognized nu-

merous times in the literature. See the pointed criticisms in P. Heimann and J. McGuire, "Newtonian Forces and Lockian Powers," 234–35 and passim.

33. R. Schofield, *Mechanism and Materialism*, 68.

34. Ibid., 95.

35. Ibid.

36. Ibid., 99.

37. The parallels between these two positions were worked out long ago by A. Lovejoy: "The Parallels of Deism and Classicism," in *Essays in the History of Ideas*.

38. Schofield, *Mechanism and Materialism*, 94.

39. Ibid., 100.

40. H. Metzger, *Newton, Stahl, Boerhaave et la Doctrine Chimique;* L. King, "Stahl and Hoffmann" and "Basic Concepts of Eighteenth-Century Animism"; L. Rather, "G. E. Stahl's Psychological Physiology"; and L. Rather and J. Frerichs, "The Leibniz-Stahl Controversy."

41. G. Rudolph, "Hallers Lehre von der Irritabilität und Sensibilität"; S. Roe, *Matter, Life and Generation;* A. Vartanian, "Trembley's Polyp, La Mettrie and Eighteenth-Century French Materialism"; T. Hall, *Ideas of Life and Matter,* 1:351–407 and vol. 2, passim, and "On Biological Analogs of Newtonian Paradigms"; J. Schiller, "Queries, Answers and Unsolved Problems in Eighteenth-century Biology"; and P. Ritterbush, *Overtures to Biology*.

42. Bordeu appeared in fiction as the attending physician in Diderot's provocative little essay on the perplexities in implication of the new science, *D'Alembert's Dream.* Diderot represents a remarkable figure in this whole matter, for he seemed at once at home with the utter materialists, and yet attuned to aspects which one would normally associate with the more *vitalist* currents of the age. His insertion of the redoubtable Dr. Bordeu into his text suggests he was quite aware of the importance of Bordeu's conjectures. See H. Dieckmann, "Théophile Bordeu und Diderots *Rêve de D'Alembert.*"

43. S. Moravia, "From *Homme Machine* to *Homme Sensible.*"

44. Kant, "Recension von Moscatis Schrift," *A.A.* 2:425.

45. Kant, "Von den verschiedenen Racen der Menschen," *A.A.* 2:429–43; editor's note, 518.

46. See C. Glacken, *Traces on the Rhodian Shore,* 512ff.

47. Kant, "Von den verschiedenen Racen," *A.A.* 2:429.

48. Ibid., 434n.

49. Ibid., 434.

50. Ibid., 435.

51. Ibid.

52. A. Lovejoy, "Kant and Evolution," 179. See also the essay on Buffon in that volume, where Buffon's theory of species and principles of method in natural science are given a sympathetic exposition.

53. J. Larson, "Vital Forces"; T. Lenoir, "Kant, Blumenbach and Vital Materialism in Germany Biology" and "Teleology without Regrets."

54. Kant offered a very interesting observation on Maupertuis's suggestion for selective breeding of men to segregate virtuous and productive

people from the less worthy. Kant conceded this might be possible, but it would not be wise. Nature was "wiser" in using the "mingling of the good and the bad" as the great driving force [*Triebfeder*] which "sets the sleeping powers of humanity into motion and requires it to develop all its talents and thus approach the perfection of their destiny [*Bestimmung*]" ("Von den verschiedenen Racen," *A.A.* 2:431). The anticipation of his arguments in "Idea for a Universal History" (1784) is striking.

55. E.g., A317–18/B374, A384, A526–27/B554–55.

56. Ibid., A526/B554, A661/B689.

57. Ibid., A668/B696. Hence Kant was familiar with Bonnet's work at least by 1781, and presumably earlier.

58. Ibid. On the whole theme of the law of continuity, see Lovejoy's classic, *The Great Chain of Being.*

59. Kant, *Critique of Pure Reason,* Bxxxiv–xxxv.

60. Kant, "Recension von J. G. Herders *Ideen zur Philosophie der Geschichte der Menschheit,* Theil I" (1784), *A.A.* 8:52.

61. Cited in ibid., 46.

62. Ibid., 54.

63. Ibid.

64. Ibid., 53.

65. Kant, "Recension von J. G. Herders *Ideen zur Philosophie der Geschichte der Menschheit,* Theil II" (1785), *A.A.* 8:62.

66. Kant, "Bestimmung des Begriffs einer Menschenrace" (1785), *A.A.* 8:97; tr. in A. Lovejoy, "Kant and Evolution," 184.

67. A. Lovejoy has some interesting things to say about this in his essay. According to Lovejoy, Kant "recoils in horror before the idea of admitting that real species are capable of transformation . . . because of certain temperamental peculiarities of his mind—a mind with a deep scholastic strain . . . one that could not quite endure the notion of a nature all fluent and promiscuous and confused, in which series of organisms are to an indefinite degree capable of losing one set of characters and assuming another set. He craved, above all, a universe sharply categorized and classified and tied up in orderly parcels . . . [T]his scholastic side of his mind prevented him from making any thorough application of the principle to biology" (*Kant and Evolution,* 185). Lovejoy is often intemperate in his criticism of Kant (see L. Beck, "Lovejoy as a Critic of Kant," in *Essays on Kant and Hume,* 61–79), but there is at least a germ of truth in this passage which we will try to cultivate in the balance of the exposition.

68. Kant, *Metaphysical Foundations,* 6 (*A.A.* 4:470).

69. Ibid., 8 (*A.A.* 4:471).

70. As A. Lovejoy put it, "Kant was, of course, by no means abreast of the latest chemistry of his time" ("Kant and Evolution," 186n.). But the point is that even if Kant had been perfectly well informed, he would not have able to accept the new ideas. That, and not Kant's familiarity with the literature, is the real consideration. Kant had certainly read much of the pioneering literature in biology, and one suspects that he was also familiar with chemistry from his frequent use of chemical analogies in his writing. But he could not accept the new theories emerging in those fields.

71. J. Wubnig, "The Epigenesis of Pure Reason." These analogies

work in the inverse direction, as well, toward a conceptualization of human reason.

72. Kant, "Über den Gebrauch" (1787), A.A. 8:159–84, editor's notes, 487–89; and "Vorarbeit zu *Über den Gebrauch teleologischer Principien in der Philosophie,*" A.A. 23:75–76.

73. For example by G. Tonelli, "Von den verschiedenen Bedeutungen," 156; J. McFarland, *Kant's Concept of Teleology,* 50ff.

74. See M. Riedel, "Historizismus und Kritizismus."

75. Kant certainly used the language of providence liberally in his writings on nature, but he clarified the methodological significance of this language in the "Transcendental Dialectic" of the *First Critique,* A698–702/B726–30. That he could be quite extravagant in exploiting this metaphorical license was clear in the essay "Idea for a Universal History," and it was this, with its ironical cut at figures like Herder who did believe in a form of immanent purpose, which roused the ire of the hylozoist camp, and perhaps led to Forster's counterthrust.

76. Forster, "Noch etwas über die Menschenraßen." A. Lovejoy's assessment of "Muthmaßlicher Anfang der Menschengeschichte" would seem to support Forster's complaints (see "Kant and Evolution," 196n.). But they are both being too literal-minded. Kant's method in the essay only makes sense as a rejoinder to Herder's work on the same subject, toward which Kant had always been very negative.

77. Kant, "Über den Gebrauch," A.A. 8:163n., 178.

78. Ibid., 161, 178.

79. Ibid., 159, 169.

80. Kant, "Vorarbeit zu *Über den Gebrauch,*" A.A. 23:75.

81. Kant, "Über den Gebrauch," A.A. 8:179.

82. Ibid., 161.

83. Ibid., 168.

84. Ibid., 179.

85. Ibid., 179–80; reference to Bonnet in note, 180; Kant also mentioned in this note that Blumenbach had made some very fine criticisms of such a stance in his work on natural history.

86. Ibid., 180.

87. Kant did not believe that all the capacities or powers *(Kräfte)* of the mind could be reduced to a single, all-comprehensive fundamental force *(Grundkraft).* Some effort at conceiving such "forces" was necessary, he conceded, and reason did make the effort. It strove "to bring them nearer to a radical, that is, absolutely fundamental power."

> Though logic is not capable of deciding whether a *fundamental power* actually exists, the idea of such a power is the problem involved in a systematic representation of the multiplicity of powers. The logical principle of reason calls upon us to bring about such unity as completely as possible; and the more the appearances of this or that power are found to be identical with one another, the more probable it becomes that they are simply different manifestations of one and the same power. (*First Critique,* A649/B677)

But, Kant went on, such "relatively fundamental powers" could not themselves be brought to unity. "This unity of reason is purely hypothetical" (ibid.). It was only an operating maxim, not an ultimate reality, Kant insisted. Thus the idea of an all-encompassing *Vorstellungsvermögen* such as Wolff had placed at the foundation of his theory of mind was, in Kant's view, merely nominal, not real. No real concept of a fundamental power, from which all the others could be derived, was possible. See D. Henrich, "Über die Einheit der Subjektivität," for a penetrating discussion of these issues. Henrich disputes the metaphysical attempts of Heidegger (and Hegel) to develop such a unity, and upholds Kant's disclaimer of such a possibility.

88. Kant, "Über den Gebrauch," *A.A.* 8:181.

Ten: The Problem of Organic Form

1. K. Roretz. *Zur Analyse,* 12–74; E. Ungerer, *Die Teleologie Kants,* 64–119; Bommersheim, "Der Begriff"; H. Driesch, "Kant und das Ganze"; and R. Löw, *Philosophie des Lebendigen,* 138ff.

2. Kant, *Critique of Judgment,* §68:230.

3. Ibid., §75:246–47, esp. §85:286–92.

4. A. Lovejoy puts this correctly: "No contemporary of Kant's, reading this passage in the *Critique of Judgment* as a whole, was likely to find in it encouragement to risk that 'bold adventure of the reason' of which it speaks" ("Kant and Evolution," 199). Even so careful a Kantian as Cassirer occasionally succumbs to the temptation to misread Kant, as in "Goethe and the Kantian Philosophy," 71–72.

5. Kant, *Critique of Judgment,* §80:267.

6. Ibid.

7. Ibid., 267–68.

8. Ibid.

9. Ibid., 268n.

10. Ibid.

11. Ibid., §81:272.

12. Ibid., 274.

13. Ibid., §80:269–70.

14. Ibid., §65:221.

15. Ibid., 223. The parallelism with the language of the "Vorarbeit zu *Über den Gebrauch*" cited earlier is striking, and confirms the close relationship between that essay and the shape of the final *Critique.*

16. Kant, *First Introduction,* 24 (*A.A.* 20:219).

17. "For since we do not, properly speaking, *observe* the purposes in nature as designed, but only in our reflection upon its products *think* this concept as a guiding thread for our judgment, they are not given to us through the object" (Kant, *Critique of Judgment,* §75:247).

18. Kant, *First Introduction,* 24n.

19. Kant, *Critique of Practical Reason,* 100 (*A.A.* 5:97).

20. For other considerations of this particular conundrum see: P. Baumanns, *Das Problem der organischen Zweckmäßigkeit,* 99–131; E. Heintel, "Naturzweck und Wesenbegriff"; N. Rotenstreich, *Experience and Its Systematization,* 88–110; M. Kraft, "Kant's Theory of Teleology"; J. Simon,

"Teleologisches Reflektieren und kausales Bestimmen"; D. Siewert, "Kant's Dialectic of Teleological Judgment"; and F. van de Pitte, "Is Kant's Distinction between Reflective and Determinant Judgement Valid?"

21. See *Critique of Judgment*, §65:220, §77:255–56.

22. Ibid., §76:251–52. The kind of individual an organism represents as an empirical problem is more intractable of solution than the individual constituted by space, which we can be satisfied to render as the indefinitely vast frame of reference for the vastest set of motions and relations we wish to consider (see ibid., §77:257).

23. Ibid., §65:221–22; §73:242. One wonders how *other human beings* as phenomenal objects should be construed under this rubric: as phenomena, presumably, *lifeless* and determined. How does one square that with one's ethical obligation to regard them as ends, i.e., as *real purposes*? Presumably we infer from their merely phenomenal presence a *noumenal* being within them. But how is that different from the case with organisms, apart from a religious bias about a human spirit or soul?

24. Ibid., §65:221.

25. Ibid., 222.

26. Ibid., §75:247, and, most vividly, §65:221–22.

27. Ibid., §§69–71, 232–36.

28. J. McFarland, *Kant's Concept of Teleology*, 30–32, 70–74.

29. Kant, *Critique of Judgment*, §70:234.

30. Ibid., §78:258–59.

31. Ibid., §80:267.

32. Ibid., §78:264.

33. Ibid., §79:265–66.

34. Ibid., §72:237.

35. Ibid., §71:236. K. Marc-Wogau, *Vier Studien*, 275, observes that Kant's dialectic is resolved in the very course of stating it in §70, and that the remaining sections appear redundant. They do indeed if *all* that Kant cared to do was resolve the scientific, and not the metaphysical issues at stake. He is willing to allow the speculative inferences to run their course because he has *metaphysical* concerns. H. Allison notes that the "Dialectic of Teleological Judgment" has two moves—a preliminary (methodological) one—"the assertion of the merely regulative status of the maxims" (which is all that McFarland, *Kant's Concept of Teleology*, 120–21, finds significant)— and an ultimate, *metaphysical* one: "an appeal to the supersensible (noumenal) ground of phenomenal nature" ("Kant's Critique of Spinoza," 213). Allison observes: "the second move (the appeal to the supersensible) . . . seems to constitute the actual solution" (ibid., 214). The notion of the "supersensible" is the keyword of the "ethical turn," as I will argue in part 3. Its centrality in the "Dialectic of Teleological Judgment" signals the moment of crisis at which Kant's work would begin its third and final metamorphosis.

36. Ibid., §77:257.

37. Ibid., §66:223.

38. Ibid., §67:225.

39. Ibid., §78:260.

40. Ibid., §75:246.

41. Ibid., §72:237.
42. Ibid., §75:246.
43. Even in the context of the *First Critique*'s rigorous assault on the dialectical errors of reason, this physico-theological approach to a proof of God's existence was treated with great respect. See A623–24/B651–52.
44. Kant, *Critique of Judgment*, §73:242.
45. Kant, *Metaphysical Foundations*, 105.
46. Kant, *Critique of Judgment*, §84:285.
47. Ibid., §iv:16.
48. Ibid., §48:M173.
49. Ibid. While our reason is driven that far, it cannot make the final step and establish "the determinate concept of that supreme intelligence." Kant concluded: "the concept of a deity, which would be adequate for our teleological judging of nature, can never be derived according to mere teleological principles of the use of reason (on which physico-theology alone is based)" (ibid., §85:290). The notion of a transcendent, intelligent cause can only be promoted from its heuristic, theoretical use to the full-fledged notion of God through "ethico-theology," Kant argued in the closing segments of the *Third Critique*. Yet the kind of being physico-theology required to make the world coherent for discursive understanding tallied with the kind of being practical reason required in terms of the indubitability of the moral law and all the consequences it brought in its train. This, in turn, allowed Kant to translate his "theist" notion—merely conjecturally, of course—from the one sphere to the other. The resultant notion of "Providence" tallied well with traditional religion.

Eleven: The Pantheism Controversy

1. Jacobi, *Über die Lehre*, in *Hauptschriften*, 92–93, 102. [Unless specified, all citations are from the original, 1785 edition.] The best analysis of Jacobi's conversations with Lessing is in A. Altmann, "Lessing und Jacobi." On Jacobi and Spinoza, see: T. van Stockum, *Spinoza-Jacobi-Lessing;* A. Hebeisen, *Friedrich Heinrich Jacobi;* and H. Nicolai, *Goethe und Jacobi,* esp. 156–77.
2. Mendelssohn argued that even if Lessing appreciated Spinoza, he remained a conventional theist. Lessing advocated at most a "refined Spinozism" *(geläuterte Spinozismus)* consistent with orthodox theism. See Mendelssohn, *Morgenstunden*, in *Hauptschriften*, 1–44.
3. The vitriolic pamphlets which the two antagonists exchanged thereafter, Mendelssohn's *An die Freunde Lessings* and Jacobi's *Wider Mendelssohns Beschuldigungen,* are reprinted in *Hauptschriften*.
4. Beiser, *Fate of Reason,* 47ff.
5. For a similar conception of the issues in the controversy, see H. Allison, "Kant's Critique of Spinoza," 201.
6. Beiser, *Fate of Reason,* 47. "What is at stake for Jacobi and Mendelssohn is not the specific question whether *Spinoza's* metaphysics ends in atheism and fatalism, but the more general question of whether all metaphysics ends in it" (80). For Beiser, the essential development of this epoch in philosophy was to discredit the authority of reason. A much more radi-

cal skepticism and relativism asserted itself under the sponsorship of such maverick critics as Hamann and Jacobi, but with powerful connections backwards to Hume and forwards to Nietzsche. Beiser goes so far as to argue that, in this sense, the Pantheism Controversy was more important for the history of philosophy in the next century than was Kant's *First Critique* itself (44). While this long-term view is insightful, and while it raises the historical stature of such figures as Hamann and Jacobi, it nevertheless underestimates the immediate outcome of the controversy, which was *not* the triumph of skepticism and relativism but rather one of the most remarkable outbursts of metaphysical rationalism in the history of philosophy, German Idealism. As Beiser himself recognizes, Fichte, Schelling, and Hegel were striving to "preserve the authority of reason" (48). In this, they were self-consciously striving to carry out a *Kantian* project.

7. Beiser, *Fate of Reason*, 56–60.

8. M. Jacob, *The Radical Enlightenment*, traces Spinozism in the rise of English deism and in the Masonic forms of free-thinking and radical republicanism. This movement read Spinozism and "pantheism" (coined, adjectivally, by the Deist John Toland in 1705 in reference to Spinoza and "Socinianism"), interchangeably to signify *materialism*. She points to a significant body of literature tracing a similar outcome in France: P. Vernière, *Spinoza et la pensée française avant la révolution* and H. El Noussy, "Le panthéisme dans les lettres françaises au XIIIe siècle."

9. Jacobi, *Über die Lehre*, in *Hauptschriften*, 81.

10. Thomas Wizenmann made this painfully obvious in his powerful intervention into the dispute. On Wizenmann, see Beiser, *Fate of Reason*, 109–13.

11. On this, see Spinoza's "Letter on the Infinite" (= Letter to Lewis Meyer, Apr. 20, 1663) in B. Spinoza, *On the Improvement of the Understanding*, 317–23. The doctrine of *intrinsic* infinity does not derive the notion from a contrast with or endless expansion of a prior finite magnitude, as in the conventional mathematical notion of infinity, but rather reckons the infinite as a complete whole in itself. Such a concept of infinity has always characterized the religious notion of God as infinite. Spinoza reckoned that the concept should be taken as the first and primordial concept, upon which substance itself could find a metaphysical ground, and a coherent ontology find foundation. One might even claim that Spinoza's philosophical greatness resides precisely in striving to grasp intrinsic infinity first and in itself, *sub specie aeternitatis*. The centrality of this notion of infinity in Spinoza's metaphysic was recognized by the Wolffian school in Germany, esp. in Wolff's *Theologia naturalis* (1737), §§671–716, and in M. Mendelssohn's *An die Freunde Lessings* (1786), though they did not do full justice to Spinoza's position.

12. Lessing used this phrase in his conversation with Jacobi: *Über die Lehre*, in *Hauptschriften*, 77. *Hen kai pan* (the one is the all), a Greek slogan of murky origins but unquestionably pantheistic or monistic implications, took on a very prominent role in the evolution of German Idealism. Lessing introduced the phrase *hen kai pan*—at least for the German audience of the late eighteenth century. See R. Knoll, *Johann G. Hamann und Friedrich H. Jacobi*, 52–53 on the novelty and impact of the phrase. Jacobi

did manage to find an earlier usage—in Giordano Bruno's *Of the Cause, Principle and One,* which he quoted at some length in an appendix to the second edition of his book. See *Hauptschriften,* 205–23. For the importance of the phrase to one of the Idealists, see M. Bäumler, "Hölderlin und das Hen Kai Pan."

13. Goethe and Herder were thrilled with the news about Lessing. (Goethe to Herder, mid-Dec. 1784, in F. Düntzer and F. v. Herder, eds., *Aus Herders Nachlaß,* 1:84.) Lessing's praise for Spinoza galvanized their latent enthusiasm for the Jewish philosopher, and stimulated their own deviations from religious orthodoxy. In his autobiography, *Dichtung und Wahrheit,* Goethe made the most perspicacious assessment of the Pantheism Controversy and its disclosure about Lessing's attitudes in religion. He compared the revelation to "an explosion which suddenly uncovered the most hidden conditions of men of the first rank, conditions which, unknown even to themselves, lay dormant in the midst of an otherwise extremely enlightened society." (Cited in H. Korff, *Geist der Goethezeit* 2:23–24. See also B. Suphan, "Goethe und Spinoza, 1783–86," 164.) Certainly he and others felt a monumental affirmation of their deepest intuitions in what they were surprised to learn their great compatriot had believed. It gave them a courage of conviction which played no small part in the incomparable intellectual boldness of the epoch of German Idealism. The involvement of Goethe and Herder is crucial not only to the history of the Pantheism Controversy itself, but to Kant's response as well, since ultimately it was Herder's views of Lessing and Spinoza which provoked Kant's arguments in the *Third Critique.*

14. Herder to Jacobi, Feb. 6, 1784, *Herders Briefe,* 227.

15. B. Suphan, "Goethe und Spinoza, 1783–86," 174–75.

16. Herder to Hamann, end Oct. 1784. in *Hamanns Briefwechsel* 5:248–49. This was part of the controversy which had been launched by Lavater's attack on Mendelssohn. See E. Schoonhoven, "Hamann in der Kontroverse mit Moses Mendelssohn"; and Z. Levy, "Hamanns Kontroverse mit Moses Mendelssohn."

17. On the mentality which Hamann and Jacobi shared, see I. Berlin, "Hume and the Sources of German Anti-Rationalism"; and L. Beck, *Early German Philosophy,* 361ff.: "The Counter-Enlightenment." For an effort to distinguish Hamann from Jacobi's "irrationalism," see Beiser, *Fate of Reason,* 29, 47.

18. R. Knoll, *Johann G. Hamann und Friedrich H. Jacobi,* 33ff. The volume of their correspondence swelled to flood proportions from late 1784 to Hamann's death in 1788. See *Hamanns Briefwechsel,* vols. 5–7.

19. K. Vorländer, *Immanuel Kant,* 90ff., 231ff.

20. Hamann to Jacobi, Sept. 28, 1785, *Hamanns Briefwechsel* 6:74.

21. Hamann to Jacobi, Oct. 3, 1785, ibid., 77. Hamann's correspondence, despite its gargantuan self-indulgence, proves to be a most instructive source for the assessment of Kant's connection with the Pantheism Controversy.

22. Indeed, one wonders how closely Kant read the *Büchlein.* It seems unlikely that Kant would have been pleased if he had read the text closely enough to note certain footnotes linking the *First Critique* with Spinozism.

23. See *Hamanns Briefwechsel,* 5:264, 271, 317, 326.

24. Indeed, there is evidence to the contrary, not only inferentially from his writings, but directly in his testimony to Hamann.

25. Mendelssohn, "Erinnerungen an Hrn. Jacobi," in *Hauptschriften,* 120.

26. Ibid., 119.

27. Jacobi, *Über die Lehre,* in *Hauptschriften,* 146n. The passages in question are from the "Transcendental Aesthetic" and have to do with the unique and all-inclusive totality of space and time as forms of sensibility. Jacobi cited Kant again in his footnote to point twenty-one, this time refering to A107 of the *First Critique,* where Kant articulated the notion of the transcendental unity of apperception (156–57n). See H. Allison, "Kant's Critique of Spinoza," 203 and n.

28. See the *Anzeige* of Jacobi's work which appeared in the Jena *Allgemeine Literatur-Zeitung,* Feb. 11, 1786, in all likelihood by Christian Schütz. The key points of that text are reprinted in *Hauptschriften,* lxxviii–lxxix.

29. Mendelssohn to Kant, Oct. 16, 1785, in *Briefwechsel, A.A.* 10:390.

30. C. Schütz to Kant, Nov. 13, 1785, in *Briefwechsel, A.A.* 10:400.

31. Hamann to Jacobi, Oct. 28, 1785, *Hamanns Briefwechsel,* 6:107; Hamann to Jacobi, Nov. 10, 1785, ibid., 127.

32. Kant to Schütz, end of Nov. 1785, in *Briefwechsel, A.A.* 10:406.

33. Jacobi to Hamann, Nov. 18, 1785, *Hamanns Briefwechsel,* 6:146.

34. Hamann to Jacobi, Nov. 30, 1785, ibid., 161. There is no reason to question this statement's authenticity. As I will argue in detail in the next chapter, there is no evidence that Kant ever thoroughly studied Spinoza. I am not convinced by H. Allison, "Kant's Critique of Spinoza," who offers references in Kant's lectures as evidence of a more careful assessment. Even Allison acknowledges that Kant's conception of Spinoza's philosophy was "not particularly well-informed" (201). Indeed, I will contend that it was based all too heavily on secondary materials—Wolff, Mendelssohn, and above all Jacobi.

35. Reprinted in *Hauptschriften,* 283–325.

36. On Biester and Kant, see Vorländer, *Immanuel Kant* 310–11.

37. Biester to Kant, Nov. 8, 1785, in *Briefwechsel, A.A.* 10:394; Biester to Kant, Mar. 6, 1786, ibid., 410; Herz to Kant, Feb. 27, 1786, ibid., 408–9.

38. Kant to Herz, Apr. 7, 1786, ibid., 419.

39. Jacobi to Hamann, Mar. 21, 1786 (323), Mar. 24, 1786 (325), May 12, 1786 (385) in *Hamanns Briefwechsel,* vol. 6.

40. C. Schütz to Kant, Feb. 1787, in *Briefwechsel, A.A.* 10:407.

41. Jacobi to Hamann, Mar. 24, 1786, *Hamanns Briefwechsel* 6:324–25.

42. Ibid.

43. Jacobi, *Wider Mendelssohns Beschuldigungen,* reprinted in *Hauptschriften,* 327–64. For the reference to Kant see 351–52.

44. Jacobi to Hamann, May 5, 1786, *Hamanns Briefwechsel,* 6:384.

45. Jacobi to Hamann, Apr. 9, 1786, *ibid.,* 325.

46. Hamann to Jacobi, May 28, 1786, *ibid.,* 408.

47. It was this review by Schütz which provoked Jacobi's ire at the Jena Kantians.

48. L. Jakob to Kant, Mar. 26, 1786, in *Briefwechsel, A.A.* 10:413.
49. For a similar assessment of Biester's importance, see Beiser, *Fate of Reason*, 115. H. Allison, "Kant's Critique of Spinoza," misses this connection.
50. Biester to Kant, June 11, 1786, in *Briefwechsel, A.A.* 10:430.
51. Ibid.
52. Ibid.
53. Kant to Herz, Apr. 7, 1786, in *Briefwechsel, A.A.* 10:419.
54. Biester, in *Briefwechsel, A.A.* 10:432.
55. Beiser writes that Kant's essay "reveals the motivation and justification behind his allegiance to reason" (*Fate of Reason*, 115). Kant said *nothing* in his essay on the question of Lessing, and *virtually nothing* on the question of the meaning of Spinoza. He had taken Biester's lead very skillfully. While Biester was charmed that Kant had "conquered the hydra" of *Genieschwärmerei* and expressed his contentment with Kant's essay, Jacobi was not charmed at all. (Biester to Kant, Aug. 8, 1786, in *Briefwechsel, A.A.* 10:439; Jacobi to Hamann, Oct. 31, 1786, *Hamanns Briefwechsel*, 7:37. Biester read Kant's essay in manuscript, since it was submitted to his journal. Jacobi only saw it once it was in print, in October 1786.) He felt wronged by Kant's characterization of belief. "About Kant's essay I don't know what to tell you," he wrote to Hamann. "The man is trying with all his might to found a sect. I'm going to try to see if I can make clear to people what he is really saying." Accordingly, Jacobi set himself to buttressing his own position regarding belief by a lengthy recourse to David Hume. The result, *David Hume über den Glauben*, a work if anything even more important for the emergence of German Idealism than his *Büchlein*, appeared in 1787, together with a short appendix aimed directly at Kant in which his famous and fruitful objection was entered that without the thing-in-itself it was impossible to enter the Kantian system, and with it it became impossible to remain inside (Jacobi, "Zur transcendentalen Idealismus," 289ff.; the famous line is on 304). That objection inspired much of the Idealist reconstruction of Kant's metaphysics, from Reinhold and Fichte to Schelling and Hegel. But for Jacobi the Hume book was a continuation of the Pantheism Controversy at its deepest level, with *Kant's* philosophy now the target of the charge of nihilism.
56. Kant, "Was heißt," *A.A.* 8:133.
57. Mendelssohn had expressed sympathy for Jacobi's turn to the *salto mortale* in the face of the difficulties encountered in speculative philosophy. It was sometimes necessary, he agreed, to descend out of the speculative clouds and seek orientation by common sense. This was a phrase Kant would seize upon in the article "Was heißt: sich im Denken orientieren?" (See Mendelssohn, "Erinnerungen," *Hauptschriften*, 114.)
58. Kant, "Was heißt," 136.
59. Ibid.
60. Ibid., 139n.
61. On Kant's notion of moral feeling see: A. MacBeath, "Kant on Moral Feeling"; A. Broadie and E. Pybus, "Kant's Concept of Respect."
62. It drives him from his conjectures about formal beauty through

the perplexities of sublimity and art to his grand metaphysical insight of the link between beauty and morality in term of his conception of aesthetic ideas. See part 3, below.

63. Kant, "Was heißt," 137.

64. The term *Vernunftglaube* was articulated in the *Kanon* of the *First Critique*, A820–30/B848–58. The question that will be explored in the third part of this study is the degree to which Kant's philosophy *changed* in its orientation toward this concept, and whether, in the later *Critiques*, more of an effort was made toward establishing the transcendental validity of such beliefs.

65. Kant, "Was heißt," *A.A.* 8:138.

66. Ibid., 145.

67. This premonitory construction of the consequences of religious extremism is, I think, read too literally as Kant's interpretation of history by M. Despland, *Kant on History and Religion*, 35ff.

68. See "What Is Enlightenment?" (*Berlinische Monatsscrift*, Dec. 1784). Kant was acutely aware that his Aufklärung was still in the process of being born and that the existing state could still *abort* it. For the context, see J. Schober, *Die deutsche Spätaufklärung (1770–1790)*, 241–72; and L. Beck, *Early German Philosophy*, 434–35.

69. That still leaves open the question of the profundity of Kant's own Christian religious feelings. No less hostile a figure than Jacobi reckoned Kant an authentic Christian in his personal life, but he did not believe that carried through to Kant's thought. M. Despland, *Kant on History and Religion*, has marshalled a very interesting case than even this *thought* must be grasped from the Christian Pietist vantage. At the very least, Kant was committed theoretically to a "theism" consistent, in his mind, with Christian tradition.

70. See N. Hartmann, *Die Philosophie des deutschen Idealismus*, 8–15; Beiser, *Fate of Reason*, 226ff.

71. Hamann to Jacobi, May 10, 1787, *Hamanns Briefwechsel*, 7:194.

72. There were *many* challengers, but few he took seriously. Among the latter was, however, Thomas Wizenmann, whose response to Kant's "Was heißt" drew substantial attention in the *Second Critique*.

73. Kant, *Grounding*, 47.

74. J. Bering to Kant, Sep. 21, 1786, in *Briefwechsel, A.A.* 10:442.

75. Beiser, *Fate of Reason*, 165–92.

76. Hamann to Herder, Aug. 18, 1785, *Hamanns Briefwechsel*, 6:55. Just this sort of thing was what alarmed the officials at the Tübingen seminary and also provoked the cabinet order at Marburg.

77. R. Malter, "Zeitgenössische Reaktionen auf Kants Religionsphilosophie," 145–67.

78. Tübingen was the seat of one of the most important seminaries in Germany. The fact that Kant felt anxious about criticism emanating from there *already in 1786* (see the remarks ascribed to him about criticism in the press of Tübingen and Göttigen in Hamann's letter to Jacobi of May 28, 1786, in *Hamanns Briefwechsel*, 6:409) adds weight to the contextualist interpretation of Kant's philosophy in this period. That orthodox sentiment at Tübingen did become suspicious of Kantianism is now well established.

See D. Henrich and J. Döderlein, "Carl Immanuel Diez." That the whole question of Kantianism at Tübingen is of course crucial follows simply from the fact that the great young generation of Idealists, Schelling, Hölderlin, and Hegel studied there and became exposed to the entire ferment in that context. On the Württemberg context of Hegel and his classmates, see L. Dickey, *Hegel.*

79. See G. Körner's interpretation of Herder's *Gott* in his letter to Schiller, Aug. 19, 1787, in *Schillers Briefwechsel mit Körner,* 92–96.

80. Herder, *God,* 67.

81. Schiller to Körner, Aug. 8, 1787, *Schillers Briefwechsel mit Körner,* 84.

82. See note 11 above.

83. Herder, *God,* 107.

84. H. Korff, *Geist der Goethezeit,* 2:28, gets this exactly.

85. Herder, *God,* 102, 119.

86. The first phrase is from Spinoza's *Ethics,* Book 1, def. 6, p. 45; the second phrase is Herder's, from *God,* 103.

87. Herder, *God,* 105.

88. On the notion of Herder's "dynamic pantheism" see F. Schmidt, *Herders pantheistische Weltanschauung;* E. Hoffart, *Herders 'Gott';* W. Vollrath, *Die Auseinandersetzung Herders mit Spinoza;* J. Dieterle, "Die Grundgedanken in Herders Schrift 'Gott' und ihr Verhältnis zu Spinozas Philosophie."

89. Herder, *God,* 145. That is, they agreed that Spinoza argued for an *intrinsic infinity.* Otherwise there were substantial differences in their respective interpretations of Spinoza's metaphysics. Mendelssohn was very critical of such pantheism. See Mendelssohn, *Morgenstunden,* 38, and Beiser, *Fate of Reason,* 104–5.

90. Herder, *God,* 146.

91. Ibid.

92. Ibid.

93. Ibid., 147.

94. Ibid., 119 for the statement on Spinoza, and 126 for the comment on Leibniz and anthropomorphism.

95. See Jacobi's Appendices 4 and 5 to the second edition of *Über die Lehre,* in *Hauptschriften,* 236–47. For Kant, see his letter to Jacobi of Aug. 30, 1787, *A.A.* 10:73f. and §85 of the *Third Critique,* 290: "Others who wished to be theologians as well as physicists . . ."

96. See notes 79, 81.

97. C. Kraus to C. Schütz, Dec. 11, 1787, cited in Vorländer, *Immanuel Kant,* 323n.

98. See Jacobi's reference to this essay in his notes to the third and final edition of his *Spinoza-Büchlein,* in *Hauptschriften,* 176–77n.

99. Kant to Jacobi, Aug. 30, 1789, in *Briefwechsel, A.A.* 11:73f. Jacobi must have been astounded to learn this was what he had been doing. The line shows how deeply enmeshed Kant had become in his own problems and system, and how outside impulses tended to be incorporated into his own project and even his own language.

100. That it was *not* a *Nebensache* for either of them (as they each well

knew) gives us a sign of just how threatened Kant must have felt that he should welcome such an alliance.

101. Kant to Jacobi, Aug. 30, 1789, in *Briefwechsel, A.A.* 11:73f.

102. See Kant, *Critique of Judgment,* §65:221.

Twelve: Kant's Attack on Spinoza

1. H. Allison, "Kant's Critique of Spinoza," 219.

2. Kant, *Critique of Judgment,* §73:239.

3. Ibid., §73:242.

4. This language I take from M. Heidegger, *Introduction to Metaphysics* and *What is a Thing?*

5. Kant, *Critique of Judgment,* §73:241.

6. Here I find myself in disagreement with Allison's analysis, "Kant's Critique of Spinoza," 205–6.

7. Kant, *Critique of Judgment,* §73:241.

8. Ibid., §15:63, and note the translator's reference there to Kant's elaboration of these notions in the preface to his *Metaphysical Elements of Justice.*

9. Beiser, *Fate of Reason,* 13, 15, 128, 147, and esp. 154 recognizes the issue, but does not pursue it.

10. H. Allison writes of a "broad brush [which] covers all pre-critical metaphysics," "Kant's Critique of Spinoza," 204.

11. Kant, *Critique of Judgment,* §73:240.

12. Ibid., §72:239.

13. Ibid. Since Kant makes rather extensive appeals to the supersensible himself throughout the *Third Critique,* the query that immediately presents itself is what difference Kant saw between his recourse and Spinoza's. To suggest that Spinoza offered *determinations* of the supersensible object which were "dialectical," i.e., incapable of objective validation, is of course true. But so did Kant in conjecturing *theism.*

14. Kant associated just these traits with his notion of *life.* See above all his statement in *Metaphysical Foundations,* 105.

15. Kant's interpretation strongly suggests his reliance upon Jacobi's gloss of Spinoza. There is reason to doubt whether Kant ever closely studied the *Ethics.* Spinoza is not mentioned once in the *Critique of Pure Reason.* (K. Vorländer noted this in *Immanuel Kant,* 331.) The names of his decisive precessors somehow manage to intrude, however marginally, into his great work. Plato and Aristotle, Galileo and Newton, Locke and Leibniz, Berkeley and Hume, Wolff and Baumgarten—even Lambert and Mendelssohn—find their way to mention in the *First Critique.* But not Spinoza. Kant regarded Spinozism philosophically as old business. He might never have troubled himself with Spinoza had not the pantheistic revival of his ideas threatened Kant's own rise to philosophical ascendancy in the Germany of the late 1780s.

16. For a different fourfold explication of Kant's quarrel with Spinoza, see Allison, "Kant's Critique of Spinoza," 204–9.

17. "By God, I mean a being absolutely infinite—that is, a substance consisting in infinite attributes" (Spinoza, *Ethics,* book 1, def 6, p. 45);

"Thought is an attribute of God, or God is a thinking thing" (book 2, prop. 1, p. 83); "God's intellect is entirely actual, and not at all potential" (book 1, prop. 33, note 2, p. 73); "God's power of thinking is equal to his realized power of action" (book 2, prop. 7, corollary, p. 86); "In God there is necessarily the idea not only of his essence, but also of all things which necessarily follow from his essence" (book 2, prop. 7, corollary, p. 86); "God understands himself," (book 2, prop. 3, p. 84; book 22, prop. 3, note, p. 84).

18. This is precisely what the eighteenth-century materialists took him to have meant, and what Jacobi insisted he had to have meant.

19. Spinoza, *Ethics,* 60.

20. Ibid.

21. Ibid., 61.

22. Ibid., book 1, prop. 17, note, p. 62.

23. Kant, *Critique of Judgment,* §10:54–55, §iv:17.

24. See ibid., §10:55: "Where then not merely the cognition of an object but the object itself (its form and existence) is thought as an effect only possible by means of the concept of this latter, there we think a purpose."

25. Spinoza, *Ethics,* 77. Allison aptly stresses the *theocentric* commitment of Spinoza's philosophy and its methodological expression: *sub specie aeternitatis,* "Kant's Critique of Spinoza," 225–26.

26. Ibid., book 1, prop. 17, note, p. 61.

27. Ibid., book 1, def. 7, p. 46.

28. Ibid., book 1, prop. 17, p. 59–60.

29. Spinoza expressed himself very bluntly to this effect: "men think themselves free inasmuch as they are conscious of their volitions and desires, and never even dream, in their ignorance, of the causes which have disposed them so to wish and desire . . . [M]en do all things for an end, namely, for that which is useful to them, and which they seek. Thus it comes to pass that they only look for a knowledge of the final causes of events, and when these are learned, they are content, as having no cause for further doubt. If they cannot learn such causes from external sources, they are compelled to turn to considering themselves, and reflecting what end would have induced them personally to bring about the given event, and thus they necessarily judge other natures by their own" (*Ethics,* book 1, Appendix, 75).

30. Allison develops this Kantian criticism extensively, "Kant's Critique of Spinoza," 205–6, 210ff.

31. L. Beck, *Early German Philosophy,* 452.

32. Kant, *Critique of Judgment,* §ii:12.

33. Ibid., §77:253.

34. Ibid., §76:250. The parenthetical remarks are Kant's.

35. Ibid., 252.

36. Ibid., §77:254–55.

37. Ibid., and also §74:243.

38. Ibid., §65:222.

39. Ibid., §77:256–57.

40. M. Jacob, *The Radical Enlightenment.*

41. See Schelling's letter to Hegel of Feb. 4, 1795 in J. Hoffmeister, ed., *Briefe von und an Hegel,* 20–23. See also Hegel's famous remarks in the

preface to the *Phenomenology of Spirit*, 10: "everything turns on grasping and expressing the True, not only as *Substance*, but equally as *Subject* . . . If the conception of God as the one Substance shocked the age in which it was proclaimed, the reason for this was . . . an instinctive awareness that, in this definition, self-consciousness was only submerged and not preserved."

42. On Spinoza's notion of intellectual intuition and his epistemology generally, see G. Floistad, "Spinoza's Theory of Knowledge in the *Ethics*."

43. The term *panentheism* was invented by Karl Christian Krause (1781–1832), a disciple of Schelling. Its philosophical *meaning* had been implicit in many earlier metaphysical speculations. See esp. H. Schwarz, "Die Entwicklung des Pantheismus in der neueren Zeit"; and W. Dilthey, "Der entwicklungsgeschichtliche Pantheismus nach seinem geschichtlichen Zusammenhang mit den älteren pantheistischen Systemen."

44. See K. Rehorn, *G. E. Lessings Stellung zur Philosophie des Spinoza* and the excellent discussion in A. Altmann, "Lessing und Jacobi," 45–57.

Thirteen: The Ethical Turn

1. Kant, *First Introduction*, §12:51–55 (*A.A.* 20:247–51).

2. Ibid., §12:53 (*A.A.* 20:249); Kant explicated that distinction three times in the body of the *Third Critique*, in §15, §63, and §82.

3. Ibid., 55 (*A.A.* 20:251).

4. A related earlier discussion, §§16–17 of the "Analytic of the Beautiful," on "dependent beauty" and the "ideal of the beautiful," was probably revised to accord with the new conception achieved in 1789.

5. Kant, *Critique of Judgment*, §ii:11.

6. Ibid., 10.

7. Ibid., 12.

8. Ibid.

9. It should be noted that the term "supersensible" appears already in §1 of the final version of the Introduction and goes on to quite extensive usage there, whereas it is mentioned only rarely and without obtrusiveness of any kind in the *First Introduction*. The notion of the "supersensible" in §ii should be compared especially with its usage in the final sections of the main body of the work, the "Dialectic" and the "Methodology of Teleological Judgment." It is discernibly absent in the sections originally belonging to the "Critique of Taste."

10. Kant, *Critique of Judgment*, §82:277.

11. Ibid., §83:280.

12. Ibid., §82:276.

13. Ibid., §84:285.

14. Ibid., §ii:12.

15. G. Tonelli, "La formazione," 444, notes that it tripled in length in the period from February to March 1790, just before Kant committed the whole work to press.

Fourteen: The Sublime, the Symbolic, and Man's Destination

1. On the idea of "discipline" as the defense against dogmatists (atheistic and otherwise) see *First Critique*, A738–94/B766–822. The same point

is articulated in the *Third Critique* (§90:312). On the positive aspect of the antinomy see *Critique of Judgment*, §57, Remark II. See also G. Schrader, "The Status of Teleological Judgment in Kant's Transcendental Philosophy."

2. Kant, *Critique of Judgment*, §57, Remark I.

3. Ibid., §57, Remark II, 190.

4. Ibid., §57:186–87.

5. This argument for transcendental idealism was made especially in the Preface to the B-version of the *First Critique*, and then reiterated in the *Third*.

6. Kant, *Critique of Judgment*, §57:184–85.

7. Ibid., §57:186.

8. Ibid., §57, Remark II, 184–85.

9. Ibid. This is parallel to the argument regarding transcendental apperception in the "Paralogisms" of the *First Critique*.

10. P. Guyer, *Kant and the Claims of Taste*, 331ff. argues that Kant need not have drawn this conclusion, and that in doing so he clearly abandoned the transcendental for a "metaphysical" treatment of beauty. Guyer finds this misguided. R. Makkreel, *Imagination and Interpretation in Kant*, 79, 81ff., also sees a metaphysical drift in these portions of the work, and likewise seeks to minimize it. I would argue, however, that this metaphysical turn is significant and needs to be taken seriously.

11. Kant, *Critique of Judgment*, §57, Remark II, 191.

12. Ibid., §22:77.

13. Ibid., §57, Remark I, 188.

14. Ibid., §59:197.

15. *A.A.* 8:137.

16. Note that the phrase "requirement of reason" appears in the passage from §22 cited above. This notion represents Kant's most explicit acknowledgement of the *intrinsic dynamism* of reason, or as the ontological, not simply methodological, sense of the *spontaneity of reason*.

17. Kant, *Critique of Pure Reason*, A179–80/B222.

18. Kant, "Was heißt," *A.A.* 8:137; *Critique of Judgment*, §90:315n.

19. Kant, *First Introduction*, §12:54 (*A.A.* 20:250).

20. Meredith, "Last Stages," xli.

21. Souriau, *Le jugement refléchissant*, 85–86.

22. Tonelli, "La formazione," 442ff. Much of Tonelli's essay focuses on his dispute with Souriau over the placement of this section.

23. Lehmann ("Einleitung") had the most clearminded approach to these questions in recognizing that Kant would hardly have had to start from scratch in composing most of the material that went into the "Critique of Aesthetic Judgment," especially the "Analytic" and the "Deduction." He had been reading and writing and lecturing about these ideas for thirty years.

24. Kant, *Critique of Judgment*, §14:62.

25. Kant, *Observations* (1764).

26. Especially in his distinction of the beautiful from the sublime, Kant indulged in what we have termed "objective subreption."

27. Kant, *First Introduction*, §12:53–54 (*A.A.* 20:250–51). The tenta-

tiveness of the term "perhaps" and the parenthetical formulation of the whole idea suggest the diffidence with which at the point of composing the *First Introduction* Kant still regarded discussion of the supersensible. That tentativeness vanished in the full "ethical turn" of late 1789 and early 1790.

28. Ibid., 54 (*A.A.* 20:250).

29. Ibid. For other conceptions—many starkly disparaging—of Kant's treatment of the sublime in the *Third Critique*, see: R. Bretall, "Kant's Theory of the Sublime"; M. Nahm, "'Sublimity' and the 'Moral Law' in Kant's Philosophy"; A. Lazaroff, "The Kantian Sublime"; J. Barnouw, "The Morality of the Sublime"; P. Guyer, "Kant's Distinction between the Sublime and the Beautiful"; W. Hund, "The Sublime and God in Kant's *Critique of Judgment*"; R. Makkreel, "Imagination and Temporality in Kant's Theory of the Sublime"; D. Crawford, "The Place of the Sublime in Kant's Aesthetic Theory"; and T. Gracyk, "Sublimity, Ugliness, and Formlessness in Kant's Aesthetic Theory," 49–56.

30. Kant, *Critique of Judgment*, §23:82.

31. Ibid., §29GR:106–7.

32. Ibid., §23:84.

33. Ibid., §27:96.

34. Ibid., §23:84.

35. Ibid., §29GR:115–16.

36. Ibid., §26:90.

37. Kant, *First Critique*, especially exposition of the first antinomy, A510–23/B538–51.

38. Kant, *Critique of Judgment*, §26:90.

39. Again, this whole line of thought is grounded in the "First Antinomy" of the *Critique of Pure Reason*.

40. Kant, *Critique of Judgment*, §26:93.

41. Ibid., §26:88–89. The phrase "striving toward infinite progress" is redolent with the metaphysics of Fichte and the sensibility of Romanticism.

42. Ibid., §26:93.

43. Ibid.

44. Kant claimed Burke gave the best psychological account of these states (§29GR:118). Yet the idea is still inappropriate except in that qua *pleasure,* the impetus is to remain *in* the state rather than to *change* it.

45. Ibid., §26:88–89.

46. Ibid., §27:96.

47. Ibid., §27:98.

48. Ibid., §28:101.

49. Ibid., §29:105.

50. M. Nahm, "Imagination as the Productive Faculty for 'Creating Another Nature . . .'" and "Productive Imagination, Tragedy and Ugliness"; and M. Zeldin, "The Role of Art and Genius in the 'Vocation of Man'" and "Kant's Theory of Art and Genius."

51. Kant, *Critique of Judgment*, §49:M176. See also Kant's discussion of imagination in GR§22.

52. Ibid.

53. Ibid.

54. Ibid.

55. Ibid., §17:M76.

56. Kant, *Critique of Pure Reason*, A569–70/B597–98.

57. Ibid., A570–71/B598–99. This anticipates Kant's formulation of the "aesthetic normal idea" in §17 as a *schema*.

58. Ibid., A570/B598.

59. Kant, *Critique of Judgment*, §49:157.

60. We might make the same point about the Grand Canyon or Van Gogh's *Starry Night*. That is, the empirical objects need not be intrinsic purposes, and they can be both objects of nature and objects of art. What they require, however, and what distinguishes them from the sorts of things which belong to *pulchritudo vaga*, is just some higher significance for the subject, which Kant associates with purposiveness, and hence with perfection.

61. Kant, *Critique of Judgment*, §49:158.

62. This is the only sense to be made of Kant's notion of indeterminate concepts of the understanding associated with beauty.

63. Kant, *Critique of Judgment*, §49:158.

64. Ibid., §49:157.

65. Ibid., §57, Remark I, 187.

66. Ibid., 189.

67. Ibid., §59:198–99.

68. Ibid., §60:202.

69. Ibid., §59:199.

70. "Nothing can be universally communicated except cognition and representation, so far as it belongs to cognition. For it is only thus that this latter can be objective, and only through this has it a universal point of reference, with which the representative power of everyone is compelled to harmonize" (Kant, *Critique of Judgment*, §9:51).

71. Ibid., §49:157.

72. Ibid.

73. See Kant, *Grounding*, 41.

74. Kant, *Critique of Judgment*, §50:163.

75. J. Ortega y Gasset, *The Dehumanization of Art*, 23.

76. Kant, *Critique of Judgment*, §49:158.

77. See H. Gadamer, *Truth and Method*, 73–90, for a similar position.

78. For other readings of the notion of beauty as the symbol of morality in Kant, see: J. Glenn, "Kant's Theory of Symbolism"; T. Cohen, "Why Beauty is a Symbol of Morality"; D. White, "On Bridging the Gulf between Nature and Morality in the *Critique of Judgment*"; and R. Kuhns, "That Kant Did Not Complete His Argument Concerning the Relation of Art to Morality and How It Might be Completed."

79. Kant, *Critique of Judgment*, §16:67.

80. Ibid.

Fifteen: Aesthetics As the Key to Anthropology

1. It "concerns men, i.e. animal, but still rational, beings—not merely *quâ* rational (e.g. spirits), but *quâ* animal also" (Kant, *Critique of Judgment*,

§5:44). See O. Larère, "Sentiment esthétique et unité de la nature humaine," and J. Möller, "Die anthropologische Relevanz der Ästhetik."

2. Kant, *Critique of Judgment*, §29GR:108.
3. Ibid., §29GR:107.
4. Ibid., §29GR:111–12.
5. Ibid., 109.
6. Ibid., 107–8.
7. Ibid., §59:200.
8. G. Schrader, "The Status of Feeling in Kant's Philosophy."
9. Kant, *Critique of Practical Reason*, 78.
10. Kant, *Critique of Judgment*, §1:38.
11. Kant, *Metaphysical Foundations*, 105.
12. Kant, *Critique of Judgment*, §29GR:119.
13. Ibid., §54:175.
14. See R. Makkreel, *Imagination and Interpretation*, chap. 5, "The Life of the Imagination," 88–107, a reworking of his earlier article, "The Feeling of Life: Some Kantian Sources of Life-Philosophy," *Dilthey-Jahrbuch für Philosophie und Geschichte der Geisteswissenschaften* 3 (1985), 83–104.
15. Kant, *Anthropology*, book 2: "Of Pleasure and Pain," opening remarks, 99. And see *Critique of Practical Reason*, 122.
16. Ibid., §64:105.
17. Kant, *Critique of Judgment*, §54:175–76. This disjunction expressed Kant's key ethical insight into the "heterogeneity of the good." See J. Silber, "The Moral Good and the Natural Good in Kant's Ethics."
18. Kant, *Critique of Judgment*, §3:40.
19. *Geistesgefühl* points to two key elements: first, to the tension between natural inclination and "supersensible destination," i.e., *moral* self-consciousness; and, second, to the metaphysical potential in the idea of *Geist*, especially as Kant articulated it in §49.
20. Kant, *Critique of Judgment*, §49:157.
21. Ibid., §49:M175.
22. Ibid., §54:175.
23. Ibid., §54:180.
24. Ibid., §4:42–43.
25. Kant, *Anthropology*, §66:107.
26. Kant, *Critique of Judgment*, §83:284n.
27. A. Broadie and E. Pybus, "Kant's Concept of Respect"; A. MacBeath, "Kant on Moral Feeling."
28. Kant, *Critique of Practical Reason*, 76.
29. Kant, *Grounding*, 14n.
30. Kant, *Critique of Practical Reason*, 77.
31. Ibid., 75.
32. Ibid., 80.
33. Ibid., 80.
34. Ibid., 89.
35. Ibid., 91.
36. Ibid., 79.
37. Ibid., 84n.

38. Kant, *Grounding*, 14n.

39. Ibid., 13.

40. What Kant is referring to by admiration and astonishment for such things as "lofty mountains, the magnitude, number, and distance of the heavenly bodies, the strength and swiftness of many animals, etc." (Kant, *Critique of Practical Reason*, 79) is what is called the "natural sublime." Kant also discusses admiration, astonishment, awe and their distinctions in *Anthropology from a Pragmatic Point of View*, and in the *Third Critique* these distinctions are revived in connection with the sublime. That it could move even Kant was betokened not only in the magnificent apostrophe which ended the *Second Critique*—"Two things fill the mind with ever new and increasing admiration and awe . . . the starry heavens above me and the moral law within me." (ibid., 166)—but by his earlier writings and concern with natural science. (P. Menzer, *Kants Ästhetik in ihrer Entwicklung*, 3–7.)

41. Kant, *Critique of Judgment*, §29GR:108.

42. Ibid.

43. Kant, *Critique of Pure Reason*, A379–80.

44. Ibid., A360.

45. Ibid., A345/B403.

46. Kant, *Critique of Judgment*, §57:187.

47. Ibid., §ii:12.

48. Ibid., §59:199.

49. Ibid., §91:327.

50. Ibid., §49:157.

51. Kant, *Reflection* 740 (1771, perhaps earlier), *A.A.* 15:326.

52. Kant, *Reflection* 782 (1772–75), ibid., 342.

53. Kant, *Reflection* 824 (1776–78), ibid., 367.

54. The insistent wordplay with "spring" is certainly not inadvertent. Kant, *Reflection* 831 (1776–78), ibid., 371.

55. Kant, *Reflection* 844 (1776–78), ibid., 375.

56. Kant, *Reflection* 932 (1776–78), ibid., 413.

57. Kant, *Reflection* 933 (1776–78), ibid., 414.

58. Ibid.

59. Kant, *Reflection* 934 (1776–78), ibid., 415.

60. Kant, *Reflection* 938 (1776–78), ibid., 416. The notion of *Weltseele* is extraordinarily important. Not only does it gesture to pantheism as advocated by Herder in the 1780s, but it obviously found its great articulation also in Schelling's Idealism of the 1790s. See G. di Giovanni, "Kant's Metaphysics of Nature and Schelling's *Ideas for a Philosophy of Nature*." That the notion of *Weltseele* was of profound significance within Kantianism in the 1790s is clear not only from Kant's own *opus posthumum*, but in the speculations along those lines by that remarkable Kantian Solomon Maimon in the early 1790s, which he published ("Über die Weltseele") and to which he sought to draw Kant's attention. (Maimon to Kant, May 15, 1790, in *Briefwechsel*, *A.A.* 11:174ff.). See K. Düsing, *Die Teleologie in Kants Weltbegriff*, 164, 174ff. See also G. Lehmann, *Kants Nachlaßwerk*, 19–40.

61. H. Dreyer, *Der Begriff Geist in der deutschen Philosophie von Kant bis Hegel;* R. Solomon, "Hegel's Concept of Geist."

Sixteen: The Unity of Man

1. More precisely, freedom was an a priori metaphysical corollary of the fact of pure reason, which was itself the apodictic imperative of the moral law. It remains that *both* had unconditional validity in Kant's view, hence represented something significantly higher than mere belief.

2. Kant, *Critique of Judgment*, §v:18.

3. In the "Transcendental Aesthetic" of the *First Critique*, Kant acknowledged the paradoxical nature of his theory of subjectivity (*Critique of Pure Reason*, B68 and B152–53.) He claimed that the problem of self-consciousness was inevitably difficult in any philosophical approach:

> How the "I" that thinks can be distinct from the "I" that intuits itself (for I can represent still other modes of intuition as at least possible), and yet, as being the same subject, can be identical with the latter; and how, therefore, I can say: "I, as intelligence and *thinking* subject, know myself as an object that is *thought*, in so far as I am given to myself [as something other or] beyond that [I] which is [given to myself] in intuition, and yet know myself, like other phenomena, only as I appear to myself, not as I am to the understanding"—these are questions that raise no greater nor less difficulty than how I can be an object to myself at all, and, more particularly, an object of intuition and of inner perceptions. (Ibid., B155–56.)

This is surely one of the most daunting sentences in Kant's entire *First Critique*.

4. That Kant nevertheless thought of it in such a manner, at least in terms of *practical* reason, is apparent in the transcendental definitions he offered for the notions of "life," the "faculty of desire," and "pleasure" in the crucial footnote to the preface to the *Critique of Practical Reason*, 9 (*A.A.* 5, 8–9n.).

5. Pure reason is determining *(ratiocinans)*, hence it cannot catch itself as such, but only in its determinations *(ratiocinatae)*. Kant wrote: "since I do not have another self-intuition which gives the *determining* in me (I am conscious only of the spontaneity of it) prior to the act of *determination*, . . . I cannot determine my existence as that of a self-active being; all that I can do is to represent to myself the spontaneity of my thought, that is, of the determination; and my existence is still only determinable sensibly, that is, as the existence of an appearance. But it is owing to this spontaneity that I entitle myself an *intelligence*" (*Critique of Pure Reason*, B156–58n.). In the "Paralogisms," Kant wrote: "this identity of the subject . . . cannot . . . signify the identity of the person, if by that is understood the consciousness of the identity of one's own substance, as a thinking being, in all change of its states" (ibid., B408). It was too empty. Hence, "I have no *knowledge* of myself as I am but merely as I appear to myself. The consciousness of self is thus very far from being a knowledge of the self . . . I exist as an intelligence which is conscious solely of its power of combination" (ibid., B158). See K. Ameriks, "Kant's Deduction of Freedom and Morality" and *Kant's Theory of Mind*.

6. "In the synthetic original unity of apperception, I am conscious of

myself, not as I appear to myself, nor as I am in myself, but only that I am" (*Critique of Pure Reason*, B157). While the "I think" as transcendental subject was utterly certain, it was not even a concept but rather "a bare consciousness which accompanies all concepts. Through this I or he or it (the thing) which thinks, nothing further is represented than a transcendental subject of the thoughts = X" (ibid., A346/B404). Such bare consciousness is merely form and process, not thing.

7. Ibid., B153.

8. Ibid., B133.

9. Kant, *First Introduction*, 10n. (*A.A.* 20:204n.); K. Düsing, *Die Teleologie in Kants Weltbegriff*, 57.

10. Kant, *Critique of Pure Reason*, B140.

11. Ibid., A343/B401.

12. Kant, *Metaphysical Foundations*, 8; T. Mischel, "Kant and the Possibility of a Science of Psychology"; M. Washburn, "Did Kant Have a Theory of Self-Knowledge?" In the *First Introduction*, Kant argued that there could be no empirical psychology as a science because time "does not furnish enough material for an entire science, unlike the pure theory of space (geometry)" (*First Introduction*, 41 [*A.A.* 20:237]).

13. P. Kitcher, "Kant's Real Self."

14. In a footnote to the B-version of the "Paralogisms," Kant introduced some new ideas on this subject:

> The "I think" expresses an indeterminate empirical intuition, i.e. perception (and thus shows that sensation, which as such belongs to sensibility, lies at the basis of this existential proposition) . . . An indeterminate perception here signifies only something real that is given, given indeed to thought in general, and so not as appearance, nor as thing in itself *(noumenon)*, but as something which actually [*in der Tat*] exists, and which in the proposition, "I think," is denoted as such. (*First Critique*, B422–23n.)

This language of an "indeterminate perception" seems to suggest the transcendental subject is experienced neither as appearance (phenomenon) nor as thing in itself (noumenon), but rather as a bare "fact." But that "fact" is of the essence of reason. It is not simply empirical. It is grounded in a necessary transcendental structure. It is—or rather, it ought to be—a "metaphysical principle," in Kant's precise sense, namely, that which can be analytically inferred from transcendental principles and thereby form the basis for valid knowledge. Kant suggests this possibility not only in his explanation of transcendental and metaphysical expositions in the B-version of the *First Critique* (B38–40) but also in the Introduction to the *Critique of Judgment* in a crucial passage concerning our certainty of the freedom of the empirical will (§v:17).

15. Kant, *Critique of Pure Reason*, A402.

16. D. Henrich, "Über die Einheit der Subjektivität."

17. Its "factuality" is an unresolved matter in Kantian epistemology. Beck notes this in passing in a footnote in his *Commentary*, 273n.; see also P. Riley, *Kant's Political Philosophy*, 56.

18. Kant, *Critique of Pure Reason*, A546–47/B574–75.

19. Heimsoeth stresses the importance of this passage in his classic essay, "Persönlichkeitsbewußtsein und Ding an sich in der Kantischen Philosophie." While D. Henrich adopts a more guarded approach, he too notes a definite cognitive element to at least *practical* apperception: "Der Begriff der sittlichen Einsicht und Kants Lehre vom Faktum der Vernunft" and "Das Problem der Grundlegung der Ethik bei Kant und im spekulativen Idealismus." Benton, *Kant's Second Critique*, 147–48, also stresses this passage as the strongest evidence of a "practical apperception" in Kant's *First Critique*. For a critical analytic stand on these questions, see L. Beck, "The Fact of Reason" and "Towards a Meta-Critique of Pure Reason."

20. Kant, *Critique of Pure Reason*, A50–51/B74–75.

21. Ibid., A68/B93. See R. Pippin, "Kant on the Spontaneity of Mind."

22. Ibid., B130. And see B152: "[S]ynthesis is an expression of spontaneity."

23. Ibid., B132.

24. Ibid., A97.

25. Ibid., A446/B474.

26. Ibid., A533/B561.

27. Ibid., B430–31. This passage seems to point to Kant's notion of a "fact of pure reason" as it would be developed in the *Second Critique*, probably only a few months after Kant composed these revisions of the "Paralogisms." For evidence that Kant developed the notion of the "fact of pure reason" while revising the *First Critique*, see preface to B-version, B:xxxviii: "a priori data of reason."

28. Ibid., A797/B825, following Silber in dropping Kemp-Smith's interpolation. See J. Silber, "The Metaphysical Importance of the Highest Good as the Canon of Pure Reason," 233.

29. Yovel writes, in *Kant's Philosophy of History*, "the Kantian texts are studded with expressions that amount to a virtual *erotic glossary* of reason. Reason is not only endowed with 'ends,' 'tasks,' and 'interests'; it also has 'needs,' 'satisfactions,' 'aspirations,' 'strivings,' and 'affection'; it has a 'vocation,' a 'destiny,' a 'calling,' and an 'appellation'; and needless to say, it has 'requirements,' 'claims,' and 'pretenses'—which Kant portrays as concrete attitudes. Many of these expressions should certainly be understood as metaphors; but metaphors for what? For . . . certain aspects of the *interest* of reason which, in itself, is no longer a metaphor in the same sense, but rather a systematic concept" (16). Nowhere before have I encountered so clear a recognition of the language Kant employs with reference to reason or of its metaphysical, not just metaphorical significance. See his development of these ideas: Yovel, "The Interests of Reason." See also M. Renault, "Le principe d'auto-conservation de la raison est le fondement de la croyance rationnelle"; P. Vignola, "'Seele' et 'Gemut' selon Kant"; and M. Westphal, "In Defense of the Thing in Itself."

30. The "practical" itself had two components: there was the praxis of cognitive-technical thinking—"judgment" in its teleological sense—and there was the praxis of moral evaluations—"practical judgments" and "practical purposes"—i.e., concrete projects grounded in a rational choice.

Spontaneity expressed these two dimensions of praxis as a freedom to inaugurate cognition or action. While it was subjectively possible to feel these aspects of praxis, Kant also insisted that it was cognitively possible to think them and even barely possible to know that they functioned via direct apperception. In 1789, Kant would shift the notion of technical praxis from the realm of moral philosophy to that of theoretical philosophy. *Zweckrationalität* was, Kant's *First Introduction to the Critique of Judgment* now proclaimed, merely theoretical. Spontaneity had its ground exclusively in *moral* purposiveness: in the "law of freedom."

31. Kant, *Critique of Judgment*, §3:40.

32. Kant, *Critique of Practical Reason*, 124.

33. Ibid., 125.

34. Ibid., 126.

35. See, e.g., N. Rotenstreich, *Experience and Its Systematization*, 111–31.

36. Y. Yovel, *Kant's Philosophy of History*, 288–89; and M. Casula, "Der Mythos des Primats der praktischen Vernunft."

37. L. Beck, *Commentary*, 249–50. See also N. McKenzie, "The Primacy of Practical Reason in Kant's System."

38. On "realm" and "territory" see Kant, *Critique of Judgment*, §ii:10–11.

39. Kant, *Critique of Pure Reason*, B476, B560ff., B830–31; L. Beck, *Commentary*, 177.

40. Kant, *Critique of Pure Reason*, A686/B714. Kant identified the principle of totality in systems with the idea of a purpose also in his crucial discussion in the "Architectonic of Pure Reason," A832–33/B860–61.

41. Ibid., A694/B722.

42. "Whatever in an object of the senses is not itself appearance, I entitle *intelligible*. If, therefore, that which in the sensible world must be regarded as appearance has in itself a faculty which is not an object of sensible intuition, but through which it can be the cause of appearances, the *causality* of this being can be regarded from two points of view. Regarded as the causality of a thing in itself, it is *intelligible* in its *action;* regarded as the causality of an appearance in the world of sense, it is *sensible* in its *effects*" (*Critique of Pure Reason*, A538/B566). "The idea of a moral world has, therefore, objective reality, not as referring to an object of an intelligible intuition (we are quite unable to think any such object), but as referring to the sensible world, viewed, however, as being an object of pure reason in its practical employment, that is, as a *corpus mysticum* of the rational beings in it" (ibid., A808/B836).

43. Kant, *Critique of Judgment*, §90:310–12.

44. Kant, *Critique of Practical Reason*, 105–6.

45. Kant, *Critique of Pure Reason*, preface to B-version, B:xxxii–xxxv.

46. The Wöllner Edict of 1788 made the question of censorship and orthodoxy very vivid in Prussia, and Kant suffered from it soon enough. But one might go so far as to argue that Kant had not only a prudent but also a positive ground for his campaign to "limit reason to make room for faith," namely, a genuinely religious commitment. See Despland, *Kant on History and Religion*, and A. Wood, *Kant's Moral Religion*.

47. J. Silber, "The Ethical Significance of Kant's *Religion*," lxxx.

48. P. Riley, *Kant's Political Philosophy*, 6. For alternative views, see J. Marshall, "Man as an End in Himself"; and P. Haezrahi, "The Concept of Man as an End-in-Himself," 291ff.

49. Kant, *Critique of Practical Reason*, 73.

50. Kant, *Grounding*, 35 (*A.A.* 4:428).

51. Ibid., 35–36 (*A.A.* 4:428).

52. "Autonomy is the ground of the dignity of human nature and of every rational nature." Ibid., 41 (*A.A.* 4:436).

53. Ibid., 38 (*A.A.* 4:431).

54. Ibid., 42 (*A.A.* 4:437).

55. Ibid., 36 (*A.A.* 4:428–29).

56. Kant was not very explicit about how we would be certain of the existence of other rational beings. He went to such lengths about the validity of finding reason in oneself that he left undeveloped the problem of the recognition of other rational beings. For him that was so obvious that it did not occasion practical concern. It is, however, neither obvious nor effortless to make these linkages. The point would be worse if we could attain the idea of the validity of the concept of an end-in-itself only via its universality among rational beings. But since it is in fact grounded immanently upon the necessary rationality of any, then it can be unhesitatingly ascribed to all rational beings. That includes even, should they exist, extraterrestrial or supernatural intelligences. Reason, not universality, but as reality, not merely as form, is the key here.

Here we must invoke the distinction between intersubjectivity and universality, and even more that between universality and validity. Validity grounds universality, not the converse. The essence of a priori validity is necessity, not universality. (Here I differ sharply with L. Beck, *Commentary*, 22, 67.) The latter follows inevitably, and may therefore be taken as an indicator, but it is not itself a modality which is apodictic. What is merely imputed to everyone is not as such objectively valid, as Kant made clear in a crucial argument in the *Critique of Judgment*, §8:49. Objective validity is a matter of necessary rationality; reason's intrinsic determination is decisive in this context. All rational beings share in taking themselves as ends in themselves, but it is not that they so share which makes them rational, but rather that they are rational which makes it possible for them to share. Reason is primary. It is the ground.

57. Kant, *Grounding*, 38 (*A.A.* 4:432).

58. Ibid., 39 (*A.A.* 4:433).

59. Ibid., 43 (*A.A.* 4:438).

60. Ibid., 40 (*A.A.* 4:434).

61. A purely rational being would necessarily actualize all the immanent interests of reason. In the *First Critique*, Kant wrote: "Now in an intelligible world, that is, in the moral world, in the concept of which we leave out of account all the hindrances to morality (the desires), such a system, in which happiness is bound up with and proportioned to morality, can be conceived as necessary, inasmuch as freedom, partly inspired and partly restricted by moral laws, would itself be the cause of general happiness, since rational beings, under the guidance of such principles, would them-

selves be the authors of both their own enduring well-being and of that of others" (Kant, *Critique of Pure Reason*, A809/B837). Similarly, Kant wrote extensively in the *Grounding* of the "holy will" for which there would be no impediments to perfect morality, and hence no need for the compulsion of duty. It was not that such a being would have no moral principle, but rather that this moral principle would not be experienced as constraint. Kant argued in the *Second Critique* that reason had the capacity to determine the moral intention entirely without reference to any intuition outside reason itself. The pure immanence of reason's autonomous self-determination in the practical domain betokened the objective reality of reason. This was a crucial result, at once the linchpin of the critical philosophy and the stumbling block for all empiricist philosophies.

62. Kant, *Grounding*, 39 (*A.A.* 4:433).

63. Kant, *First Critique*, A809/B837. The use of the concept of the "highest good" in the "Analytic" of the *Second Critique* hearkens back to the treatment of the term in the "Canon of Pure Reason" of the *First Critique* and to the discussion of the "kingdom of ends" in the *Grounding*. The question is: Is it the same concept as the one which Kant develops in the "Dialectic" of the *Second Critique* and takes up again in the "Methodology of Teleological Judgment" in the *Third Critique*? Is there only one concept of the "highest good" in Kant?

64. Kant, *Grounding* (39, *A.A.* 4:433).

65. Ibid., 43 (*A.A.* 4:438).

66. See the works of T. Auxter on this idea and its implications: "The Teleology of Kant's Ectypal World," "The Unimportance of the Highest Good," and *Kant's Moral Teleology*.

67. Kant, *Grounding*, 42n. (*A.A.* 4:436n.).

68. Kant, *Critique of Practical Reason*, 44.

69. Ibid.

70. Ibid.

71. Ibid., 72.

72. Kant explained the notion of "hypotyposis" in *Critique of Judgment*, §59:197–98. See chap. 13 above.

73. Kant, *Critique of Practical Reason*, 73.

74. Ibid.

75. Ibid., 73.

76. Ibid., 45.

Seventeen: The Unity of Mankind

1. T. Auxter, *Kant's Moral Teleology*, passim. See also F. van de Pitte, "The Importance of Moral Teleology for Kant's Critical Philosophy."

2. Kant, *Critique of Judgment*, §87:298.

3. Kant entertained more than one notion of the highest good. As Y. Yovel has put it, the "Kantian concept of the highest good is ambiguous; its meaning varies not only from one work to the next, but occasionally even in the same chapter. In fact there is no single text in which Kant discusses it exhaustively, and all his treatments of the notion must be taken as fragmentary and as calling for reciprocal supplementation and illumination"

(*Kant's Philosophy of History*, 81). The core definition Kant offered of the idea of the "highest good" was a proportionality of happiness to worthiness. This formula, or a close variant, appeared in a very large number of Kant's published works over a considerable span of time. But it frequently did so in the company of other definitions which at the very least amplified and often obscured the core meaning: the "Kingdom of God," *Critique of Practical Reason*, 128; the "intelligible world," ibid., 132; "natural beings under moral law," *Critique of Judgment*, §86; "moral vocation of man," *Critique of Pure Reason*, A840/B868. See Beck, *Commentary*, 242, for discussion.

The most important distinction to make in approaching the issue of the highest good in Kant is that between the problem of the objectification of moral laws in the actual world and the problem of the reward for worthiness and its transcendent requirements. Kant merged these two ideas together, perhaps for a motive ulterior to the strict question of morality. The result has been a monumental controversy over the meaning and even the legitimacy of this notion in his philosophy.

4. Kant, *Religion*, 5.

5. J. Silber, "The Importance of the Highest Good in Kant's Ethics," 179ff.

6. J. Silber, "Kant's Concept of the Highest Good as Immanent and Transcendent," 469ff.

7. J. Silber, "Der Schematismus der praktischen Vernunft," 253ff.

8. Kant, *Religion*, 6n.

9. Beck, *Commentary*, 243.

10. M. Zeldin, "The *Summum Bonum*, the Moral Law, and the Existence of God." See also R. Friedman, "The Importance and Function of Kant's Highest Good"; A. Reath, "Two Conceptions of the Highest Good in Kant"; S. Smith, "Worthiness to Be Happy and Kant's Concept of the Highest Good"; M. Packer, "The Highest Good in Kant's Psychology of Motivation"; R. Friedman, "Hypocrisy and the Highest Good"; and W. Brugger, "Kant und das Höchste Gut."

11. J. Atwell argues that if objects of the will derive their value other than from the law, then their achievement cannot be a duty. He denies that "objective ends" as results can be taken up by reason as moral ("Objective Ends in Kant's Ethics," 169–71). Yet the morally responsible agent is a sensual entity with already built-in propensities to seek certain natural goods. While duty could override them, it could not extirpate them entirely, and, more, it *should* not. The question Atwell's intepretation of Kant can never clarify adequately is the reason behind this "should."

12. A. Wood, *Kant's Moral Religion*, 55.

13. Ibid., 117n.

14. T. Auxter, *Kant's Moral Teleology*, 60.

15. T. Auxter, "Ectypal Nature," 488.

16. T. Auxter, *Kant's Moral Teleology*, 24.

17. Ibid., 150.

18. G. Barnes, "In Defense of Kant's Doctrine of the Highest Good," esp. 453; G. Krämling, "Das höchste Gut als mögliche Welt"; S. Anderson-Gold, "Kant's Ethical Commonwealth"; and T. Godlove, Jr., "Moral Actions, Moral Lives."

19. They would also lead from the *Third Critique* into Kant's next projects, both his *Religion Within the Limits of Reason Alone,* which pursued the religious dimension, and his *On the Old Saw: That Might Be Right in Theory but It Won't Work in Practice,* which carried on the historical-political analysis. See R. Makkreel, *Imagination and Interpretation,* chap. 7, for a discussion of the connection of the *Third Critique* to this output of the 1790s.

20. Kant, *First Introduction,* §12:53 (*A.A.* 20:249).

21. In §82 of the "Methodology of Teleological Judgment" Kant restated the distinction between relative and intrinsic purposiveness which he had formulated earlier in §15 of the "Critique of Aesthetic Judgment" and §63 of the "Critique of Teleological Judgment."

22. Kant makes this distinction in ibid., §82:276.

23. Ibid., §83:280.

24. Kant discusses the concept of happiness in ibid. §83:280, 284n. and §84:286n.

25. In the *Second Critique* Kant observed that no one needs to be commanded to pursue happiness. A human being cannot help but do that (*Critique of Practical Reason,* 38). This is a notion that has not received sufficient attention in some interpretations of Kant's ethics, especially as regards the controversial issue of the "highest good."

26. Kant, *Critique of Judgment,* §83:281ff.

27. Kant, "Idea for a Universal History," 121.

28. Ibid., 283–84. See Schiller, *On the Aesthetic Education of Man in a Series of Letters.*

29. The connection with Freud's theory of sublimation has not escaped some interpreters, e.g., N. Hertz, "The Notion of Blockage in the Literature of the Sublime."

30. This is what Kant means about the propaedeutic function of physical teleology in theology. See *Critique of Judgment,* §85.

31. This is Kant's definition of "culture." See ibid., §83:281.

32. The most thorough and in many ways provocative study of this is G. Kelly, *Idealism, Politics and History,* 89–178.

33. Kant, "Idea for a Universal History," 126.

34. G. Kelly, *Idealism, Politics and History,* 139–40.

35. Ibid., 100, 121. Also, E. Fackenheim, "Kant's Concept of History"; and K. Weyand, *Kants Geschichtsphilosophie,* 49–136.

36. On the Kant-Herder dispute in history see H. Irmscher, "Die geschichtsphilosophische Kontroverse zwischen Kant und Herder"; J. Simon, "Herder und Kant"; and M. Sakabe, "Freedom as a Regulative Principle."

37. P. Reill, *The German Enlightenment and the Rise of Historicism,* passim.

38. L. Krieger, *The German Idea of Freedom,* 105–6.

39. Kant, "Idea for a Universal History," 119–20.

40. Ibid.

41. The *asceticism* of this posture was extreme. It provoked Herder in the 1780s, and later it even roused the Kantian Schiller to protest. Schiller had absorbed enough of the social theory of the Enlightenment to "concede that, little as individuals might benefit from this fragmentation of their being, there was no other way in which the species as a whole could

have progressed" (*On the Aesthetic Education of Man*, 11). Yet Schiller was far more attentive to the loss involved. "Thus, however much the world as a whole may benefit through this fragmentary specialization of human powers, it cannot be denied that the individuals affected by it suffer under the curse of this cosmic purpose" (ibid., 14). Kant could claim that man deserved no more, since in terms of his own "natural dispositions . . . he himself, as far as in him lies, works for the destruction of his own race" (*Critique of Judgment*, §83:280). Schiller would not accept this: "But can Man really be destined to miss himself for the sake of any purpose whatsoever? Should Nature, for the sake of her own purposes, be able to rob us of a completeness which Reason, for the sake of hers, enjoins upon us? It must, therefore, be wrong if the cultivation of individual powers involves the sacrifice of wholeness. Or rather, however much the law of Nature tends in that direction, it must be open to us to restore by means of a higher Art the totality of our nature which the arts themselves have destroyed" (*On the Aesthetic Education of Man*, 15). That is the essence of the "aesthetic solution" of German Idealism.

42. Kant, "Idea for a Universal History," 119.

43. Relating Kant's idea of nature to the "invisible hand" suggests the enormous importance that the Scottish Enlightenment idea of a "civil society," as the impersonal order imposed by the market economy, had on German social thought, starting at least with Kant. The idea of a "cunning of nature"—a take-off on Hegel's full "cunning of reason"—was invented by Eric Weil and employed extensively by Y. Yovel to refer to the purely mechanical role nature plays in fostering man's capacity for freedom prior to his rational self-assertion.

44. Kant, "Idea for a Universal History," 120; Kelly, *Idealism, Politics and History*, 120.

45. See A. Hirschman, *The Passions and the Interests*, for a full articulation of this essential argument about the culture of the eighteenth century and the modern West, which found expression above all in the writings of the Scottish Enlightenment.

46. On this naturalistic line see Kelly, *Idealism, Politics and History*, 120–21, 135, 143; Krieger, *The German Idea of Freedom*, 93–94; and W. Booth, *Interpreting the World*, 96, 109.

47. In the 1790s he became more critical of such Hobbesianism, e.g., in *On the Old Saw* (1793), 57–65. See L. Krieger, *The German Idea of Freedom*, 93–95; P. Riley, *Kant's Political Philosophy*, 73–80; and Y. Yovel, *Kant's Philosophy of History*, 139ff., 161.

48. Kant, "Idea for a Universal History," 120.

49. Ibid., 122. The incongruity between the idea of "general will" and man needing a master is even starker than the well-cited contradictions in Rousseau himself. See, e.g., the tension in Kant's exposition of "constitutional law" in *On the Old Saw*, 57–74.

50. On Lutheran notions of the inevitability of sin in the world, and consequently of the need for a powerful secular authority, see: C. Trinkaus, "The Religious Foundations of Luther's Social Views," and E. Troeltsch's classic account *The Social Teachings of the Christian Churches*, esp. 518–31.

51. Kant, "Idea for a Universal History," 123. This reflects Kant's idea of "radical evil." See Wood, *Kant's Moral Religion*, 208ff., for a careful defense of Kant's notion. See also J. Silber, "Ethical Significance of Kant's Religion," passim; and E. Fackenheim, "Kant and Radical Evil."

52. This was the thrust of the second key essay of 1784, "What is Enlightenment?"

53. P. Riley, *Kant's Political Philosophy*, 95; L. Krieger, *The German Idea of Freedom*, 104.

54. Kant, "Muthmaßlicher Anfang der Menschengeschichte," *A.A.* 8:107–23; E. Fackenheim, *Kant's Concept of History*, 384–89; Y. Yovel, *Kant's Philosophy of History*, 125–41, 164–69; and G. Kelly, *Idealism, Politics and History*, 140–70.

55. Kant, *Critique of Judgment*, §83:281–82.

56. "Kant always emphasizes that the Enlightenment is not just a form of consciousness but a real historical force that can be institutionalized through praxis and become embodied in historical reality" (Yovel, *Kant's Philosophy of History*, 175).

57. This is the sphere of Kant to which Wood, Despland, Auxter, and Yovel have all devoted such innovative attention. That Kant was interested in the history of the future and in what philosophy could say about it, and that this interest had strong religious and political dimensions which were anchored firmly in his context all suggest the degree of continuity between Kant and his Idealist successors. It is the basis for a possible ultimate unity. "If one stresses reason and reason's ends as the known substrate of morality and as the estimated substrate of nature and art, then a (Godless) synthesis remains possible" (P. Riley, *Kant's Political Philosophy*, 92). Riley uses this argument to refute McFarland's claim in "The Bogus Unity" that the only unity the system could have would be God and Kant cannot be proven to have really believed in a God.

58. L. Krieger, *The German Idea of Freedom*, 112ff.; G. Kelly, *Idealism, Politics and History*, 153f.

59. Y. Yovel, *Kant's Philosophy of History*, 31.

60. Ibid., 73n.

61. Ibid., 84.

62. Ibid., 135.

63. Ibid., 75.

64. Ibid., 72.

65. G. Michaelson, Jr., *The Historical Dimension of a Rational Faith*, 133–83.

66. A. Wood, *Kant's Moral Religion*, passim.

67. M. Despland, *Kant on History and Religion*, 203ff., 263ff.

68. Thus Fackenheim, "Kant's Concept of History," 398; Y. Yovel, *Kant's Philosophy of History*, 300ff. See also P. Stern, "The Problem of History and Temporality in Kantian Ethics."

69. W. Booth, *Interpreting the World*, 125ff.; E. Vollrath, "Kants Kritik der Urteilskraft als Grundlegung einer Theorie des Politischen"; D. Pasini, "Das 'Reich der Zwecke' und der politisch-rechtliche Kantianische Gedanke"; and R. Pippin, "On the Moral Foundations of Kant's *Rechts-*

lehre." The influence of Kant on contemporary political theory, especially in view of the reconstruction of J. Rawls, is substantial.

70. Kant, *Critique of Judgment,* §84:284.
71. Ibid., §84:285.
72. Ibid., §91:320–21.
73. Ibid., §87:299n.
74. K. Düsing, "Das Problem des höchsten Gutes in Kants praktischer Philosophie."
75. Kant, *Critique of Pure Reason,* A590–642/B618–70, esp. A620–30/B648–58.
76. Ibid., A623/B651.
77. Kant, *Critique of Judgment,* §85:287.
78. Ibid., 290–91.
79. Ibid., §87:301n.
80. Kant, *First Critique,* A805–19/B833–47; L. Beck, *Commentary,* 241.
81. Kant, *Critique of Judgment,* §91:323n.
82. Ibid., §91:323.
83. Ibid., §87:303.
84. The "tragic worldview" takes this position. See Auxter, *Kant's Moral Teleology,* 97ff., 123, 183; A. Wood, *Kant's Moral Religion,* 179. Kant's treatment of the tragic position is not adequate. But see W. Booth, *Interpreting the World,* 114ff., for an effort to define Kant's position as "tragic" via the category of the sublime.
85. This is the Stoic position. On Kant's ambivalent relation to the Stoics, see Wood, *Kant's Moral Religion,* 117n., and esp. Booth, *Interpreting the World,* 43–47, who argues that Kant is ultimately quite close to Stoicism.
86. Kant says so much himself, in *Religion Within the Limits of Reason Alone,* 4.
87. Kant, *Critique of Practical Reason,* 128n., 132ff. There are those who question the sincerity of this belief and its consequence, Kant's "theism." See Y. Yovel, *Kant's Philosophy of History,* 94ff., 109; and J. McFarland, "The Bogus Unity," 280. That position seems to me irreconcilable with historical evidence. Here, Wood, Despland, and Silber have the stronger case by far. Yet there is a world of difference between the sincerity of this belief and its validity. With that at stake, the stance of Yovel and McFarland takes on a new importance. But see Riley, *Kant's Political Philosophy,* 91–93, for a response.
88. Silber, "The Ethical Significance of Kant's *Religion,"* cxxi–cxxxiii.
89. "Rigorism" is the suspicion of worthiness raised to a principle. Kant's rigorism is at times quite stark. While his defenders protest against the "caricature" of Kant as a rigorist, there is too much textual evidence for this caricature not to have caught (and admittedly exaggerated) some prominent features. The strongest articulation of this rigorism is in the first part of Kant's *Religion Within the Limits of Reason Alone,* where, in keeping with traditional Christian theology, though on the basis of his own critical philosophy, Kant argued for a radical disposition to evil in human nature. In another of his most rigoristic passages Kant argues that "when

we pay attention to our experience of the way human beings act, we meet frequent and—as we ourselves admit—justified complaints that there cannot be cited a single certain example of the disposition to act from pure duty" (Kant, *Grounding*, 19). This is an anthropological observation, and hence empirical, as Kant certainly recognized, but it makes a very strong negative claim, namely, that every action of a human being can be suspected, and that this suspicion is in itself sufficient warrant to deny worthiness. One can be very severe with oneself on that score. One's worthiness may be easily disproved, even if it is hard to prove. Still, only the most "rigoristic" posture would deny *any* worthiness. For a rigorist, mankind is guilty until proven innocent, and the proof is impossible. This kind of thinking, the "hermeneutic of suspicion," has its ground in the Pauline-Christian notion of sin as a condition, not an act, and finds its later expression in Freudian theories of unconscious (and unsavory) motivation. This idea of the "hermeneutic of suspicion" is developed by P. Ricoeur in reference to Freud and his predeccesors, Marx and Nietzsche. But, as he certainly knows, its origins lie far deeper in the religious tradition of the West. See Ricoeur, *Freud and Philosophy*, 32–35.

90. That is the *ascetic* element in Kant. The "rigorism" and the "asceticism" of Kant should be carefully distinguished, though there is an intimate association between them. Kant had a strong personal disposition toward asceticism, and this influenced his writings on ethics. For Kant, it was hard ever to regard "inclinations" of man's sensual nature otherwise than as a "burden." (See *Critique of Judgment*, §83:284n.) This dour attitude, which comes to clear expression in his ethics and in his anthropology, provoked sharp opposition from Herder, and later from the Idealists. It was the point over which Schiller publicly quarreled with Kant. Kant admitted philosophically that such asceticism was unjustified, but his personal preferences continued to color his treatment. Kant's ambivalence toward the "natural good" is one of the most pervasive and problematic features of his ethics.

91. For rigorous epistemologists, the only sphere left to consign this kind of thinking to is the aesthetic. It goes without saying that it could claim no objective validity.

92. See Kant's acknowledgement of the argument in *Second Critique*, 149n.

93. Beck, *Commentary*, 253f.

94. Wood, *Kant's Moral Religion*, 28–29.

95. Beck, *Commentary*, 245.

96. J. Murphy, "The Highest Good as Content for Kant's Ethical Formalism," 109.

97. For "rigorists" of their school, no more damning conclusion could be reached. But for those seeking to find in Kant's *Third Critique* the sources of the metaphysics of German Idealism, this result has quite another meaning. This whole realm of thought is decisive for the "aesthetic solution" of the Idealists.

98. Auxter, "Ectypal World," 493.

99. Auxter, "The Unimportance of the Highest Good."

Conclusion: The Meaning of the Third Critique

1. As E. Fackenheim put it, the *Third Critique* was the effort "to join together what the first two *Critiques* have put asunder" ("Kant's Concept of History," 389). This same point is made by L. Krieger in *The German Idea of Freedom*, 106, and by E. Cassirer in *Kant's Life and Thought*, 360. Kant sought to do so under the rubric of purposiveness or teleology. As G. Michaelson puts it, "Kant turns to teleology when he wants to bridge the gap between the worlds of nature and freedom" (*Historical Dimension of a Rational Faith*, 141).

2. Hence such titles for Kant's works after 1781 as "Metaphysics of Nature" and "Metaphysics of Morals." Those titles persisted for two decades after he ostensibly "preempted" metaphysics, according to the formalist reading.

3. Michaelson, *Historical Dimension of a Rational Faith*, 181; see P. Riley, *Kant's Political Philosophy*, 3, for a similar observation.

4. P. Riley, *Kant's Political Philosophy*, 71.

5. Y. Yovel, *Kant's Philosophy of History*, passim, esp. 302.

6. F. Beiser, *Fate of Reason*, 227.

7. L. Beck, *Commentary* 54; and see J. McFarland, "The Bogus Unity."

8. "If a critical examination of pure practical reason is to be complete, then there must, in my view, be the possibility at the same time of showing the unity of practical and speculative reason in a common principle; for in the final analysis there can be only one and the same reason, which is to be differentiated solely in its application" (Kant, *Grounding*, 4).

9. Kant wrote of the "expectation of bringing some day into one view the unity of the entire pure rational faculty (both theoretical and practical) and of being able to derive everything from one principle." This, he went on, was "an unavoidable need of human reason, as it finds complete satisfaction only in a perfectly systematic unity of its cognitions" (Kant, *Critique of Practical Reason*, 94).

10. For a similar conclusion, see P. Riley, *Kant's Political Philosophy*, 67–68.

11. Hegel, *Faith and Knowledge*, 92.

❧ Bibliography

Kant's Works

The standard German edition of Kant's work is *Kants Gesammelte Schriften Herausgegeben von der Preußischen Akademie der Wissenschaften zu Berlin* (Berlin: de Gruyter, 1902–83), usually called the *Akademie-Ausgabe* (*A.A.*).

Anthropology from a Pragmatic Point of View. Tr. Mary J. Gregor. The Hague: Nijhoff, 1974.
"Bestimmung des Begriffs einer Menschenrace." *A.A.* 8.
Briefwechsel. A.A. 10–11. Selections tr. in Arnulf Zweig, ed. *Kant's Philosophical Correspondence, 1759–1799.* Chicago: University of Chicago Press, 1967.
Critique of Judgement. Tr. James Meredith. Oxford: Clarendon, 1964.
Critique of Judgment. Tr. J. H. Bernard. New York: Haffner, 1968.
Critique of Practical Reason. Tr. Lewis W. Beck. Indianapolis: Bobbs, Merrill, 1956 (*A.A.* 5).
Critique of Pure Reason. Tr. Norman Kemp-Smith. New York: St. Martin's Press, 1965.
First Introduction to the Critique of Judgment. Tr. James Haden. Indianapolis: Bobbs, Merrill, 1965 (*A.A.* 20).
Grounding of the Metaphysics of Morals. Tr. James Ellington. Part 1 of *Kant's Ethical Philosophy.* Indianapolis and Cambridge: Hackett, 1983 (*A.A.* 4).
"Idea for a Universal History with Cosmopolitan Intent." Tr. Carl Friedrich. In Carl Friedrich, ed. *The Philosophy of Immanuel Kant.* New York: Modern Library, 1949.
Logic: A Manual for Lectures. Tr. Robert S. Hartman and Wolfgang Schwarz. Indianapolis: Bobbs, Merrill, 1974 (*A.A.* 9).
Metaphysical Foundations of Natural Science. Tr. James Ellington. Indianapolis: Bobbs, Merrill, 1970.
Metaphysics of Morals (introduction and part 2, "Metaphysical Principles of Virtue"). Tr. James Ellington. Part 2 of *Kant's Ethical Philosophy.* Indianapolis and Cambridge: Hackett, 1983.

"Muthmaßlicher Anfang der Menschengeschichte." *A.A.* 8.

Nachricht von der Einrichtung seiner Vorlesungen in dem Winterhalbjahre von 1765–1766. A.A. 2.

Observations on the Feelings of the Beautiful and the Sublime. Tr. John T. Goldthwait. Berkeley: University of California Press, 1960.

On the Old Saw: That May Be Right in Theory but It Won't Work in Practice. Tr. E. B. Ashton. Philadelphia: University of Pennsylvania Press, 1974.

Prolegomena to Any Future Metaphysics. Tr. James Ellington. Book 1 of *Philosophy of Material Nature.* Indianapolis: Hackett, 1985 (*A.A.* 4).

"Recension von J. G. Herders *Ideen zur Philosophie der Geschichte der Menschheit,* Theil I," (1784) and "Recension von J. G. Herders *Ideen zur Philosophie der Geschichte der Menschheit,* Theil II" (1785). *A.A.* 8. Tr. as "Review of Herder's *Ideas for a Philosophy of History of Mankind.*" In Lewis W. Beck, ed. *Kant on History.* Indianapolis: Bobbs, Merrill, 1963.

"Recension von Moscatis Schrift *Von den körperlichen wesentlichen Unterschiede zwischen der Structur der Thiere und Menschen.*" *A.A.* 2.

Reflexionen zur Anthropologie. A.A. 15.

Religion Within the Limits of Reason Alone. Tr. Theodore M. Greene and H. H. Hudson. La Salle, Ill.: Open Court, 1960.

Träume eines Geistersehers erläutert durch Träume der Metaphysik. A.A. 2.

"Über den Gebrauch teleologischer Principien in der Philosophie." *A.A.* 8.

"Von den verschiedenen Racen der Menschen." *A.A.* 2.

"Vorarbeit zu *Über den Gebrauch teleologischer Principien in der Philosophie.*" *A.A.* 23.

"Was heißt: sich im Denken orientieren?" *A.A.* 8.

"What Is Enlightenment?" Tr. Lewis W. Beck. In Lewis W. Beck, ed. *Kant on History.* Indianapolis: Bobbs, Merrill, 1963.

Other Primary Sources

Addison, Joseph. "Genius." *Spectator,* no. 160 (Sep. 1711). Reprinted in Scott Elledge, ed. *Eighteenth-Century Critical Essays,* vol. 1. Ithaca: Cornell University Press, 1961, 27–30.

Akenside, Mark. *Pleasures of Imagination.* London: Dodsley, 1744.

Cooper, Anthony Ashley, Earl of Shaftesbury. "A Letter Concerning Enthusiasm to My Lord *****," and "The Moralists." In John M. Robertson, ed. *Characteristics of Men, Manners, Opinions, Times.* Indianapolis: Bobbs, Merrill, 1964.

D'Alembert, Jean. *Preliminary Discourse to the Encyclopédie.* Indianapolis: Bobbs, Merrill, 1963.

Forster, Georg. "Noch etwas über die Menschenraßen." *Teutsche Merkur,* Oct. 1786, 57–86; Nov., 1786, 150–66.

Gerard, Alexander. *An Essay on Genius.* Reprint. Munich: Fink, 1966.

Goethe, Johann Wolfgang von. "Einwirkung der neueren Philosophie." In Jens Kulenkampf, ed. *Materialien zu Kants Kritik der Urteilskraft.* Frankfurt: Suhrkamp, 1974, 129–31.

———. "Natur-Fragment." In Wilhelm Dilthey, "Aus der Zeit der Spinozastudiens Goethes." *Gesammelte Schriften,* vol. 2. Leipzig and Berlin: Teubner, 1914, 400–7.

Hamann, Johann. *Hamanns Briefwechsel*, vols. 5–7. Ed. Arthur Henkel. Wiesbaden: Insel, 1955–79.

———. *Sokratische Denkwürdigkeiten/Aesthetica in nuce*. Stuttgart: Reclam, 1968.

Die Hauptschriften zum Pantheismus Streit zwischen Jacobi und Mendelssohn. Ed. Heinrich Scholz. Berlin: Reuther and Reichard, 1916.

Hegel, Georg Wilhelm Friedrich. *Faith and Knowledge*. Tr. Walter Cerf and H. S. Harris. Albany: State University of New York Press, 1977.

———. *Hegel's Introduction to Aesthetics*. Tr. T. M. Knox. Oxford: Clarendon, 1979.

———. *Phenomenology of Spirit*. Tr. A. V. Miller. Oxford: Oxford University Press, 1979.

[Hegel, Georg Wilhelm Friedrich.] *Briefe von und an Hegel*. Ed. Johannes Hoffmeister. Hamburg: Meiner, 1952.

Herder, Johann. *Essay on the Origin of Language*. Tr. Alexander Gode. In Alexander Gode, ed. *On the Origin of Language*. New York: Ungar, 1966.

———. *God: Some Conversations*. Tr. Frederick H. Burkhardt. New York: Veritas, 1943.

———. *Ideen zur Philosophie der Geschichte der Menschheit*. In Bernhard Suphan, ed. *Herders Sämmtliche Werke*, vol. 13. Berlin: Weidmann, 1887.

[Herder, Johann.] *Aus Herders Nachlaß*, vol. 1. Ed. Heinrich Duntzer and Ferdinand G. v. Herder. Frankfurt: Meilinger, 1856.

[Herder, Johann.] *Herders Briefe*. Ed. Wilhelm Dobbek. Weimar: Volksverlag, 1959.

Jacobi, Friedrich. *Über die Lehre des Spinoza in Briefe an den Hrn. Moses Mendelssohn*. (1785). Reprinted in Heinrich Scholz, ed. *Die Hauptschriften zum Pantheismus Streit zwischen Jacobi und Mendelssohn*. Berlin: Reuther and Reichard, 1916.

———. "Zur transcendentalen Idealismus." In *David Hume über den Glauben, oder Idealismus und Realismus* (1787). Reprinted in Friedrich Jacobi, *Werke*, vol. 2. Leipzig: G. Fleischer, 1815.

Lowth, Robert. *Lectures on the Sacred Poetry of the Hebrews*. London: Johnson, 1787.

Maimon, Solomon. "Über die Weltseele." *Berliner Journal für Aufklärung* 8 (1790), 47ff.

Mendelssohn, Moses. "Briefe, die neueste Literatur betreffend." In *Gesammelte Schriften*, vol 4. Leipzig: Brockhaus, 1844. Part 1, 497–599; part 2, 1–460.

———. *Morgenstunden* and *An die Freunde Lessings*. In H. Scholz, ed. *Die Hauptschriften zum Pantheismus Streit zwischen Jacobi und Mendelssohn*. Berlin: Reuther and Reichard, 1916.

Reinhold, Karl L. *Briefe über die Kantische Philosophie*. Leipzig: Goschen, 1790–92.

Schelling, Friedrich. *The Philosophy of Art*. Tr. Douglas W. Stott. Minneapolis: University of Minnesota Press, 1989.

———. *System of Transcendental Idealism*. Tr. Peter Heath. Charlottesville: University of Virginia Press, 1978.

Schiller, Friedrich. *On the Aesthetic Education of Man in a Series of Letters.* Tr. Elizabeth M. Wilkinson and L. A. Willoughby. Oxford: Clarendon, 1967.

[Schiller, Friedrich.] *Schillers Briefwechsel mit Körner.* Ed. Karl Gödecke. Leipzig: Veit, 1878.

Spinoza, Benedict. *On the Improvement of the Understanding. The Ethics. Correspondence.* New York: Dover, 1955.

Stael, Mme. de. *Of Germany.* 3 vols. London: Murray, 1814.

Voltaire. *Letters on England.* Harmondsworth: Penguin, 1982.

Young, Edward. *Conjectures on Original Composition.* Reprinted in Martin Steinke, *Edward Young's Conjectures on Original Composition in England and Germany.* New York: Stechert, 1917.

Secondary Sources

Akten des 4. Internationalen Kant-Kongresses, Mainz, 1974. Berlin: de Gruyter, 1974.

Alderman, William E. "The Significance of Shaftesbury in English Speculation." *Publications of the Modern Language Association* 38 (1923), 175–95.

Alexander, W. M. *Johann Georg Hamann: Philosophy and Faith.* The Hague: Nijhoff, 1966.

Allison, Henry. *The Kant-Eberhard Controversy.* Baltimore: Johns Hopkins University Press, 1973.

———. "Kant's Critique of Spinoza." In Richard Kennington, ed., *The Philosophy of Baruch Spinoza.* Washington, D.C.: Catholic University of America Press, 1980, 199–227.

———. *Lessing and the Enlightenment.* Ann Arbor: University of Michigan Press, 1966.

———. "The Originality of Kant's Distinction between Analytic and Synthetic Judgments." In Richard Kennington, ed. *The Philosophy of Immanuel Kant.* Washington, D.C.: Catholic University of America Press, 1985, 15–38.

———. "Things in Themselves, Noumena, and the Transcendental Object." *Dialectica* 32 (1978), 41–76.

———. *Transcendental Idealism.* New Haven: Yale University Press, 1983.

———. "Transcendental Idealism: The Two Aspect View." In Bernard den Ouden and Maria Moen, eds., *New Essays on Kant.* New York, Bern, Frankfurt: Peter Lang, 1987, 155–78.

———. "Transcendental Schematism and the Problem of the Synthetic *A Priori.*" *Dialectica* 35 (1981), 57–83.

Altmann, Alexander. "Lessing und Jacobi: Das Gespräch über den Spinozismus." *Lessing Yearbook* 3 (1971), 27–70.

Ameriks, Karl. "Kant and the Objectivity of Taste." *British Journal of Aesthetics* 23 (1978), 3–17.

———. "Kant's Deduction of Freedom and Morality." *Journal of the History of Philosophy* 19 (1981), 53–79.

———. *Kant's Theory of Mind.* Oxford: Clarendon, 1982.

———. "Kant's Transcendental Deduction as a Regressive Argument." *Kant-Studien* 69 (1978), 273–87.

———. "Recent Work on Kant's Theoretical Philosophy." *American Philosophical Quarterly* 19 (1982), 1–24.

Anderson-Gold, Sharon. "Kant's Ethical Commonwealth: The Highest Good as a Social Goal." *International Philosophical Quarterly* 26 (1986), 23–32.

Aner, Karl. *Die Theologie der Lessingzeit*. Halle: Niemeyer, 1929.

Angelelli, Ignacio. "On the Origins of Kant's 'Transcendental.'" *Kant-Studien* 63 (1972), 117–22.

Aquila, Richard. "Is Sensation the Matter of Appearances?" In Moltke S. Gram, ed. *Interpreting Kant*. Iowa City: University of Iowa Press, 1982, 11–29.

———. "Matter, Forms, and Imaginative Association in Sensory Intuition." In Bernard den Ouden and Maria Moen, eds. *New Essays on Kant*. New York: Peter Lang, 1987, 73–109.

———. *Matter in Mind*. Bloomington: Indiana University Press, 1989.

———. "The Relationship between Pure and Empirical Intuition in Kant." *Kant-Studien* 68 (1977), 275–89.

Arendt, Hannah. *Lectures on Kant's Political Philosophy*. Chicago: University of Chicago Press, 1982.

Aron, Erich. *Die deutsche Erweckung des Griechentums durch Winckelmann und Herder*. Heidelberg: Kampmann, 1929.

Atwell, John. "Objective Ends in Kant's Ethics." *Archiv für Geschichte der Philosophie* 56 (1974), 156–71.

Auxter, Thomas. *Kant's Moral Teleology*. Macon, GA: Mercer University Press, 1982.

———. "The Teleology of Kant's Ectypal World." In *Proceedings of the Ottawa Congress on Kant, 1974*. Ottawa: University of Ottawa Press, 1976, 488–493.

———. "The Unimportance of the Highest Good." *Journal of the History of Philosophy* 17 (1979), 121–34.

Ayers, Michael R. "Substance, Reality and the Great, Dead Philosophers." *American Philosophical Quarterly* 7 (1970), 38–49.

Barnes, Gerald. "In Defense of Kant's Doctrine of the Highest Good." *Philosophical Forum* 2 (1971), 446–58.

Barnouw, Jeffrey. "The Morality of the Sublime: Kant and Schiller." *Studies in Romanticism* 19 (1980), 497–514.

———. "The Philosophical Achievement and Historical Significance of Johann Nicolas Tetens." *Studies in Eighteenth-Century Culture* 9 (1979), 300–35.

Barth, Karl. *Protestant Thought from Rousseau to Ritschl*. New York: Harper, 1969.

Bartuschat, Wolfgang. *Zum Systematischen Ort von Kants Kritik der Urteilskraft*. Frankfurt am Main: Klostermann, 1972.

Barzun, Jacques. *Classic, Romantic and Modern*. Garden City, N.Y.: Anchor, 1961.

Bate, Walter J. *From Classic to Romantic: Premises of Taste in Eighteenth-Century England*. New York: Harper and Row, 1946.

Bauer-Drevermann, Ingrid. "Zufälligkeit in Kants *Kritik der Urteilskraft*." *Kant-Studien* 56 (1965–66), 497–504.

Baumanns, Peter. *Das Problem der organischen Zweckmäßigkeit.* Bonn: Bouvier, 1965.

Baumgartner, Jorg. "On Kant's 'Matter of the Appearance.'" In *Akten des 4. Internationalen Kant-Kongreses, Mainz 1974*, vol. 2:1. Berlin: de Gruyter, 1974, 265–69.

Bäumler, Alfred. *Kants Kritik der Urteilskraft. Bd. I. Das Irrationalitätsproblem in der Ästhetik des 18. Jahrhunderts.* Halle: Niemeyer, 1923.

Bäumler, Max. "Hölderlin und das Hen Kai Pan." *Monatshefte für deutsche Unterrichts* 59 (1967), 131–47.

Beck, Lewis W. "Apodictic Imperatives." *Kant-Studien* 49 (1957), 7–24.

———. "Can Kant's Synthetic Judgments Be Made Analytic?" In Robert P. Wolff, ed. *Kant: A Collection of Critical Essays.* Notre Dame and London: University of Notre Dame Press, 1968, 3–22.

———. *Commentary on Kant's Critique of Practical Reason.* Chicago: University of Chicago Press, 1960.

———. *Early German Philosophy.* Cambridge: Harvard University Press, 1969.

———. *Essays on Kant and Hume.* New Haven: Yale University Press, 1978.

———. "The Fact of Reason: An Essay on Justification in Ethics." In *Studies in the Philosophy of Kant.* Westport, Conn.: Greenwood, 1965, 200–29.

———. "Kant's Theory of Definition." In Robert P. Wolff, ed. *Kant: A Collection of Critical Essays.* Notre Dame and London: University of Notre Dame Press, 1968, 23–36.

———. "Towards a Meta-Critique of Pure Reason." In *Proceedings of the Ottawa Congress on Kant, 1974.* Ottawa: University of Ottawa Press, 1976, 182–96.

———, ed. *Kant Studies Today.* La Salle, Ill.: Open Court, 1969.

———, ed. *Proceedings of the Third International Kant Congress.* Dordrecht, Holland: Reidel, 1972.

Beiser, Frederick. *The Fate of Reason: German Philosophy from Kant to Fichte.* Cambridge: Harvard University Press, 1987.

Bennett, Jonathan. "Substance, Reality and Primary Qualities." *American Philosophical Quarterly* 2 (1965), 1–17.

Benton, Robert. *Kant's Second Critique and the Problem of Transcendental Arguments.* The Hague: Nijhoff, 1977.

Benziger, James. "Organic Unity: Leibniz to Coleridge." *Publications of the Modern Language Association* 66 (1951), 21–48.

Berlin, Isaiah. "Herder and Enlightenment." In *Vico and Herder.* London: Hogarth, 1966, 143–216.

———. "Hume and the Sources of German Anti-Rationalism." In *Against the Current.* New York: Viking, 1980, 162–87.

Biemel, Walter. *Die Bedeutung von Kants Begründung der Ästhetik für die Philosophie der Kunst.* Cologne: *Kant-Studien: Ergänzungshefte* 77, 1959.

Bird, Graham. "Logik und Psychologie in der Transzendentalen Deduktion." *Kant-Studien* 56 (1965–66), 373–84.

———. "Recent Interpretations of Kant's Transcendental Deduction," *Akten des 4. Internationalen Kant-Kongresses, Mainz, 1974*, 1:1–13.

Blocker, Harry. "Kant's Theory of the Relation of Imagination and Understanding in Aesthetic Judgments of Taste." *British Journal of Aesthetics* 5 (1965), 37–45.

Bommersheim, Paul. "Der Begriff der organischen Selbstregulation in Kants Kritik der Urteilskraft." *Kant-Studien* 23 (1919), 209–20.

———. "Der vierfache Sinn der inneren Zweckmäßigkeit in Kants Philosophie des Organischen." *Kant-Studien* 32 (1927), 290–309.

Booth, William J. *Interpreting the World: Kant's Philosophy of History and Politics.* Toronto: University of Toronto Press, 1986.

Brandt, Reinhard. "The Deductions in the *Critique of Judgment:* Comments on Hampshire and Horstmann." In Eckart Förster, ed. *Kant's Transcendental Deductions.* Stanford: Stanford University Press, 1989, 177–79.

Bretall, R. W. "Kant's Theory of the Sublime." In George T. Whitney and David F. Bowers, eds. *The Heritage of Kant.* Princeton: Princeton University Press, 1939, 377–402.

Brittan, Gordon G. Jr. *Kant's Theory of Science.* Princeton: Princeton University Press, 1978.

Broadie, Alexander and Elizabeth M. Pybus. "Kant's Concept of Respect." *Kant-Studien* 66 (1975), 58–64.

Bruford, Walter H. *Culture and Society in Classical Weimar, 1775–1806.* Cambridge: Cambridge University Press, 1962.

———. *Germany in the Eighteenth Century.* Cambridge: Cambridge University Press, 1965.

Brugger, Walter. "Kant und das Höchste Gut." *Zeitschrift für philosophische Forschung* 18 (1964), 50–61.

Brunschwig, Henri. *La crise de l'État prussien à la fin du XVIIIe siècle et la genèse de la mentalité romantique.* Paris: Presses Universitaires, 1947.

Bubner, Rüdiger. "Kant, Transcendental Arguments and the Problem of Deduction." *Review of Metaphysics* 28 (1975), 453–67.

———, ed. *Das älteste Systemprogramm: Studien zur Frühgeschichte des deutschen Idealismus.* Bonn: Bouvier, 1973.

Buchdahl, Gerd. "The Conception of Lawlikeness in Kant's Philosophy of Science." *Synthese* 23 (1971), 24–46.

———. "Gravity and Intelligibility: Newton to Kant." In R. E. Butts and J. W. Davis, eds. *The Methodological Heritage of Newton.* Oxford: Oxford University Press, 1970, 74–102.

———. "The Kantian 'Dynamic of Reason,' with Special Reference to the Place of Causality in Kant's System." In Lewis W. Beck, ed., *Kant Studies Today.* La Salle, Ill.: Open Court, 1969, 341–74.

———. *Metaphysics and the Philosophy of Science; The Classical Origins: Descartes to Kant.* Cambridge: MIT Press, 1969.

———. "The Relation between 'Understanding' and 'Reason' in the Architectonic of Kant's Philosophy." *Proceedings of the Aristotelian Society* 67 (1967), 209–26.

Bullitt, John and Walter J. Bate. "Distinction of Fancy and Imagination in

Eighteenth-Century English Criticism." *Modern Language Notes* 60 (1945), 8–15.

Burch, Robert. "Kant's Theory of Beauty as Ideal Art." In George Dickie and R. J. Sclafani, eds. *Aesthetics: A Critical Anthology.* New York: St. Martin's Press, 1977, 688–703.

Burtt, Edwin A. *Metaphysical Foundations of Modern Physical Science.* Garden City: Doubleday, 1954.

Carritt, Edgar F. "Sources and Effects in England of Kant's Philosophy of Beauty," *The Monist* 35 (1925), 315–28.

Cassirer, Ernst. "Critical Idealism as a Philosophy of Culture." In *Symbol, Myth and Culture.* New Haven: Yale University Press, 1979, 64–91.

————. *Freiheit und Form.* Berlin: B. Cassirer, 1916.

————. "Goethe and the Kantian Philosophy." In *Rousseau, Kant, Goethe.* Princeton: Princeton University Press, 1945, 61–98.

————. *Kant's Life and Thought.* New Haven: Yale University Press, 1981.

————. "Die Methodik des Idealismus in Schillers Philosophischen Schriften." In *Idee und Gestalt.* Berlin: B. Cassirer, 1921, 79–108.

————. *Philosophy of the Enlightenment.* Princeton: Princeton University Press, 1951.

————. *The Platonic Renaissance in England.* Austin: University of Texas Press, 1953.

Casula, Mario. "Der Mythos des Primats der praktischen Vernunft." In *Akten des 4. Internationalen Kant-Kongresses,* Mainz, 1974, vol. 2:1. Berlin: de Gruyter, 1976, 362–71.

Clarke, Robert T. "Herder's Concept of 'Kraft,'" *Publications of the Modern Language Association* 57 (1942), 737–52.

Cohen, I. Bernard and Alexandre Koyré. "Newton's Electric and Elastic Spirit." *Isis* 51 (1960), 337.

Cohen, Ted. "Why Beauty is a Symbol of Morality." In Ted Cohen and Paul Guyer, eds. *Essays in Kant's Aesthetics.* Chicago: University of Chicago Press, 1982, 221–36.

Cohen, Ted and Paul Guyer, eds. *Essays in Kant's Aesthetics.* Chicago: University of Chicago Press, 1982.

Coleman, Francis. *The Harmony of Reason: A Study in Kant's Aesthetics* Pittsburgh: University of Pittsburgh Press, 1974.

Crawford, Donald. *Kant's Aesthetic Theory.* Madison: University of Wisconsin Press, 1974.

————. "The Place of the Sublime in Kant's Aesthetic Theory." In Richard Kennington, ed. *The Philosophy of Immanuel Kant.* Washington, D.C.: Catholic University of America Press, 1985, 161–83.

Crocker, Lester. "Diderot and Eighteenth-Century French Transformationism." In Bentley Glass et al. *Forerunners of Darwin: 1745–1859.* Baltimore: Johns Hopkins University Press, 1959, 114–43.

Cummins, Phillip. "Kant on Outer and Inner Intuition." *Nous* 2 (1968), 271–92.

Curley, E. M. "Locke, Boyle and the Distinction between Primary and Secondary Qualities." *Philosophical Review* 81 (1972), 438–64.

Despland, Michel. *Kant on History and Religion.* Montreal: McGill University Press, 1973.

Dickey, Laurence. *Hegel: Religion, Economics and the Politics of Spirit, 1770–1804*. Cambridge: Cambridge University Press, 1987.

Dieckmann, Herbert. "Diderot's Conception of Genius." In *Studien zur europäischen Aufklärung*. Munich: Fink, 1974, 7–33.

———. "Théophile Bordeu und Diderots *Rêve de D'Alembert*." *Romanische Forschungen* 52 (1938), 55–122.

Dieterle, J. A. "Die Grundgedanken in Herders Schrift 'Gott' und ihr Verhältnis zu Spinozas Philosophie." *Theologische Studien und Kritiken* 87 (1914).

Dijkterhuis, Eduard J. *The Mechanization of the World Picture*. Oxford: Clarendon, 1961.

Dilthey, Wilhelm. "Aus der Zeit der Spinozastudiens Goethes." In *Gesammelte Schriften*, vol. 2. Leipzig and Berlin: Teubner, 1914, 400–407.

———. "Die dichterische und philosophische Bewegung in Deutschland 1770–1800." In *Gesammelte Schriften*, vol. 5. Stuttgart and Göttingen: Vandenhoeck and Rupprecht, 1957, 11–27.

———. "Der entwicklungsgeschichtliche Pantheismus nach seinem geschichtlichen Zusammenhang mit den älteren pantheistischen Systemen." In *Gesammelte Schriften*, vol. 2. Leipzig and Berlin: Teubner, 1914, 312–90.

———. *Das Erlebnis und die Dichtung*. Göttingen: Vandenhoeck and Rupprecht, 1970.

———. "Friedrich der Große und die deutsche Aufklärung." In *Gesammelte Schriften*, vol. 3. Leipzig and Berlin: Teubner, 1927, 83–209.

Dister, John E. "Kant's Regulative Ideas and the 'Objectivity' of Reason." In Lewis W. Beck, ed. *Proceedings of Third International Kant Congress*. Dordrecht, Holland: Reidel, 1972, 262–69.

Dreyer, Hans. *Der Begriff Geist in der deutschen Philosophie von Kant bis Hegel*. Berlin: Reuther and Reichard, 1907.

Driesch, Hans. "Kant und das Ganze." *Kant-Studien* 29 (1924), 365–76.

Düsing, Klaus. "Das Problem des höchsten Gutes in Kants praktischer Philosophie." *Kant-Studien* 62 (1971), 5–42.

———. *Die Teleologie in Kants Weltbegriff*. Bonn: Bouvier, 1968.

Eisler, Rudolf. *Der Zweck: Seine Bedeutung für Natur und Geist*. Berlin: Mittler and Sohn, 1914.

Ellington, James. "The Unity of Kant's Thought in His Philosophy of Corporeal Nature" and "Translator's Introduction." In Kant, *Metaphysical Foundations of Natural Science*. Indianapolis: Bobbs, Merrill, 1970.

Engell, James. *The Creative Imagination: Enlightenment to Romanticism*. Cambridge: Harvard University Press, 1981.

Erdmann, Benno. *Kants Kriticismus in der ersten und in der zweiten Auflage der Kritik der reinen Vernunft*. Leipzig: Voss, 1878.

———. "Kant und Hume um 1762." *Archiv für Geschichte der Philosophie* 1 (1887–88), 62–77, 216–30.

Ernst, Julius. *Der Geniebegriff der Stürmer und Dränger und der Frühromantiker*. Ph.D. Diss. Zürich, 1916.

Evans, J. J. "The Empirical Employment of Pure Reason." In *Proceedings of the Ottawa Congress on Kant, 1974*. Ottawa: University of Ottawa Press, 1976, 480–86.

Fackenheim, Emil. "Kant and Radical Evil." *University of Toronto Quarterly* 23 (1954), 439–53.

———. "Kant's Concept of History." *Kant-Studien* 48 (1956–57), 381–98.

Fisher, John and Jeffrey Maitland. "The Subjectivist Turn in Aesthetics: A Critical Analysis of Kant's Theory of Appreciation." *Review of Metaphysics* 27 (1974), 726–51.

Flajole, Edward, S.J. "Lessing's Attitude in the Lavater-Mendelssohn Controversy." *Publications of the Modern Language Association* 73 (1958), 201–14.

Floistad, Guttorm. "Spinoza's Theory of Knowledge in the *Ethics.*" In Marjorie Grene, ed. *Spinoza: A Collection of Critical Essays.* Notre Dame: University of Notre Dame Press, 1979, 101–27.

Förster, Eckart. "Is There a 'Gap' in Kant's Critical System?" *Journal of the History of Philosophy* 25 (1987), 533–55.

———, ed. *Kant's Transcendental Deductions: The Three Critiques and the Opus Postumum.* Stanford: Stanford University Press, 1989.

French, Stanley. "Kant's Constitutive-Regulative Distinction." In Lewis W. Beck, ed. *Kant Studies Today.* LaSalle, Ill.: Open Court, 1969, 375–91.

Friedman, R. Z. "Hypocrisy and the Highest Good: Hegel on Kant's Transition from Morality to Religion." *Journal of the History of Philosophy* 24 (1986), 503–22.

———. "The Importance and Function of Kant's Highest Good." *Journal of the History of Philosophy* 22 (1984), 325–42.

Gadamer, Hans-Georg. *Truth and Method.* New York: Continuum, 1975.

Gajek, Bernhard, ed. *Hamann—Kant—Herder. Acta des 4. Internationalen Hamann-Kolloqiums im Herder-Institut zu Marburg/Lahn 1985.* Frankfurt am Main: Peter Lang, 1987.

Gajek, Bernhard and Albert Meier, eds. *Johann Georg Hamann und die Krise der Aufklärung. Acta des 5. Internationalen Hamann-Kolloqiums im Münster i. W. 1988.* Frankfurt am Main: Peter Lang, 1990.

Gay, Peter. *The Enlightenment.* 2 vols. New York: Norton, 1967–69.

Genova, Anthony. "Kant's Complex Problem of Reflective Judgment." *Review of Metaphysics* 23 (1970), 452–80.

———. "Kant's Transcendental Deduction of Aesthetical Judgments." *Journal of Aesthetics and Art Criticism* 30 (1972), 459–75.

George, Rolf. "The Lives of Kant." *Philosophy and Phenomenological Research* 47 (1987), 485–500.

Gerth, Hans. *Die sozialgeschichtliche Lage der bürgerlichen Intelligenz um die Wende des 18. Jahrhunderts.* Ph.D. Diss. Frankfurt am Main, 1935.

Giovanni, George di. "Kant's Metaphysics of Nature and Schelling's *Ideas for a Philosophy of Nature.*" *Journal of the History of Philosophy* 17 (1979), 197–215.

Glacken, Clarence. *Traces on the Rhodian Shore: Nature and Culture in Western Thought from Ancient Times to the End of the 18th Century.* Berkeley and Los Angeles: University of California Press, 1967.

Glass, Bentley, ed. *Forerunners of Darwin: 1745–1859.* Baltimore: Johns Hopkins University Press, 1959.

Glenn, John D. "Kant's Theory of Symbolism." *Tulane Studies in Philosophy* 21 (1972), 13–21.

Godlove, Terry Jr. "Moral Actions, Moral Lives: Kant on Intending the Highest Good." *Southern Journal of Philosophy* 25 (1987), 49–64.

Goldstein, Ludwig. *Moses Mendelssohn und die deutsche Ästhetik.* Königsberg: Grafe and Unzer, 1904.

Gracyk, Theodore. "Kant's Shifting Debt to British Aesthetics." *British Journal of Aesthetics* 26 (1986), 204–17.

———. "Sublimity, Ugliness, and Formlessness in Kant's Aesthetic Theory." *Journal of Aesthetics and Art Criticism* 96 (1986), 49–56.

Gram, Moltke S. "The Crisis of Syntheticity: The Kant-Eberhard Controversy." *Kant-Studien* 71 (1980), 155–80.

———. *Kant, Ontology and the A Priori.* Evanston: Northwestern University Press, 1968.

———. "Must Transcendental Arguments Be Spurious?" *Kant-Studien* 65 (1974), 304–17.

———. "The Sense of a Kantian Intuition." In Moltke S. Gram, ed. *Interpreting Kant.* Iowa City: University of Iowa Press, 1982, 41–67.

———. "Transcendental Arguments," *Nous* 5 (1972), 15–28.

———, ed. *Interpreting Kant.* Iowa City: University of Iowa Press, 1982.

Grayeff, Felix. "The Relationship of the Transcendental and Formal Logic." *Kant-Studien* 51 (1959), 349–52.

Greene, Theodore M. "The Historical Context and Religious Significance of Kant's *Religion.*" In Theodore M. Greene and H. H. Hudson, trs. *Religion Within the Limits of Reason Alone.* La Salle, Ill.: Open Court, 1960, ix–lxxvii.

———. "A Reassessment of Kant's Aesthetic Theory." In George T. Whitney and David F. Bowers, eds. *The Heritage of Kant.* Princeton: Princeton University Press, 1939, 323–56.

Gregor, Mary. "Aesthetic Form and Sensory Content in the *Critique of Judgment.*" In Richard Kennington, ed. *The Philosophy of Immanuel Kant.* Washington, D.C.: Catholic University of America Press, 1985, 185–99.

———. "Baumgarten's *Aesthetica.*" *Review of Metaphysics* 37 (1983), 357–85.

Guerlac, Henri. "Newton's Changing Reputation in the Eighteenth Century." In Raymond O. Rockwood, ed. *Carl Becker's Heavenly City Revisited.* Cornell: Archon, 1969, 3–26.

Gueroult, Martial, "Vom Kanon der Kritik der reinen Vernunft zur Kritik der praktischen Vernunft." *Kant-Studien* 54 (1963), 432–44.

Guyer, Paul. "Apperception and *A Priori* Synthesis." *American Philosophical Quarterly* 17 (1980), 205–12.

———. "Disinterestedness and Desire in Kant's Aesthetics." *Journal of Aesthetics and Art Criticism* 36 (1978), 449–60.

———. "Interest, Nature and Art: A Problem in Kant's Aesthetics." *Review of Metaphysics* 31 (1978), 580–603.

———. *Kant and the Claims of Taste.* Cambridge: Harvard University Press, 1979.

———. "Kant's Distinction between the Sublime and the Beautiful." *Review of Metaphysics* 35 (1982), 753–83.

———. "Pleasure and Society in Kant's Theory of Taste." In Ted Cohen and Paul Guyer, eds. *Essays in Kant's Aesthetics.* Chicago: University of Chicago Press, 1982, 21–54.

———. "Psychology and the Transcendental Deduction." In Eckart Förster, ed. *Kant's Transcendental Deductions: The Three Critiques and the Opus Postumum.* Stanford: Stanford University Press, 1989, 48–56.

———. Review of *Identität und Objektivität. Journal of Philosophy* 76 (1979), 151–167.

Haezrahi, Pepita. "The Concept of Man as an End-in-Himself." In Robert P. Wolff, ed. *Kant: A Collection of Critical Essays.* Notre Dame and London: University of Notre Dame Press, 1967, 291–313.

Hall, Marie B. and A. Rupert Hall. "Newton's Electric Spirit: Four Oddities." *Isis* 50 (1959), 473–76.

Hall, Thomas S. *Ideas of Life and Matter: Studies in the History of General Physiology 600 B.C.–1900 A.D.* 2 vols. Chicago: University of Chicago Press, 1969.

———. "On Biological Analogs of Newtonian Paradigms." *Philosophy of Science* 35 (1968), 6–27.

Harman, P. M. *Metaphysics and Natural Philosophy: The Problem of Substance in Classical Physics.* Totowa, N.J.: Barnes and Noble, 1982.

Hartmann, Klaus. "On Taking the Transcendental Turn." *Review of Metaphysics* 20 (1966), 223–49.

Hartmann, Nicolai. *Die Philosophie des deutschen Idealismus.* Berlin: de Gruyter, 1960.

Hatch, Irvin C. *Der Einfluß Shaftesburys auf Herder.* Berlin: Duncker, 1901.

Hatfield, Henry. *Winckelmann and his German Critics.* New York: King's Crown, 1943.

Haym, Rudolf. *Herder, nach seinem Leben und seinem Werk.* 2 vols. Berlin: Gärtners, 1885.

Hebeisen, Alfred. *Friedrich Heinrich Jacobi: Seine Auseinandersetzung mit Spinoza.* Bern: Paul Haupt, 1960.

Heidegger, Martin. *Introduction to Metaphysics.* New Haven: Yale University Press, 1959.

———. *Kant and the Problem of Metaphysics.* Bloomington: Indiana University Press, 1962.

———. *Nietzsche.* Vol. 1, *The Will to Power as Art.* Tr. D. Krell. New York: Harper and Row, 1979.

———. *What is a Thing?* Chicago: Regnery, 1967.

Heilbron, John L. *Elements of Early Modern Physics.* Berkeley and Los Angeles: University of California Press, 1982.

Heimann, P. M. "'Nature is a perpetual worker': Newton's Aether and Eighteenth-Century Natural Philosophy." *Ambix* 20 (1973), 1–25.

———. "Voluntarism and Immanence: Conceptions of Nature in Eighteenth-Century Thought." *Journal of the History of Ideas* 39 (1978), 271–83.

Heimann, P. M. and J. E. McGuire. "Newtonian Forces and Lockean Powers: Concepts of Matter in Eighteenth-Century Thought." *Historical Studies in the Physical Sciences* 3 (1971), 233–306.

Heimsoeth, Heinz. "Metaphysische Motive in der Ausbildung der kritischen Idealismus." *Kant-Studien* 29 (1924), 121–59.

————. "Persönlichkeitsbewußtsein und Ding an sich in der Kantischen Philosophie." In *Studien zur Philosophie Immanuel Kants.* Cologne: *Kant-Studien: Ergänzungshefte* 71 (1956), 229–57.

Heintel, Erich. "Naturzweck und Wesenbegriff." In Dieter Henrich and H. Wagner, eds. *Subjektivität und Metaphysik: FS für W. Cramer.* Frankfurt am Main: Klostermann, 1966, 163–87.

Heintel, Peter. *Die Bedeutung der Kritik der ästhetischen Urteilskraft für die transcendentale Systematik.* Bonn: Bouvier, 1970.

Henckmann, Wolfhart. "Das Problem der ästhetischen Wahrnehmung in Kants Ästhetik." *Philosophisches Jahrbuch* 78 (1971), 323–59.

Henrich, Dieter. "Beauty and Freedom: Schiller's Struggle with Kant's Aesthetics." In Ted Cohen and Paul Guyer, eds. *Essays in Kant's Aesthetics.* Chicago: University of Chicago Press, 1982, 237–57.

————. "Der Begriff der sittlichen Einsicht und Kants Lehre vom Faktum der Vernunft." In Henrich et al., *Die Gegenwart der Griechen im neueren Denken. FS Gadamer.* Tübingen: J. C. B. Mohr, 1960, 77–115.

————. "Hutcheson und Kant." *Kant-Studien* 49 (1957), 49–69.

————. *Identität und Objektivität.* Heidelberg: C. Winter, 1976.

————. "Kant's Notion of a Deduction and the Methodological Background of the First *Critique.*" In Eckart Förster, ed. *Kant's Transcendental Deductions: The Three Critiques and the Opus Postumum.* Stanford: Stanford University Press, 1989, 30–40.

————. "Das Problem der Grundlegung der Ethik bei Kant und im spekulativen Idealismus." In Paulus Engelhardt, ed. *Sein und Ethos: Untersuchungen zur Grundlegung der Ethik.* Mainz: Grünewald, 1963, 350–86.

————. "The Proof-Structure of Kant's Transcendental Deduction." *Review of Metaphysics* 22 (1969), 640–59.

————. "Über die Einheit der Subjektivität." *Philosophische Rundschau* 3 (1955), 28–69.

Henrich, D. and Johann L. Döderlein. "Carl Immanuel Diez." *Hegel-Studien* 3 (1965), 276–87.

Hertz, Neil. "The Notion of Blockage in the Literature of the Sublime." In Geoffrey Hartman, ed. *Psychoanalysis and the Question of the Text.* Baltimore: Johns Hopkins University Press, 1976, 71–76.

Hesse, Mary B. *Forces and Fields: The Concept of Action at a Distance in the History of Physics.* New York: Philosophical Library, 1962.

Hinske, Norbert. "Kants Begriff des Transcendentalen und die Problematik seiner Begriffsgeschichte." *Kant-Studien* 64 (1973), 56–62.

Hintikka, Jaako. "On Kant's Notion of Intuition (*Anschauung*)." In Terence Penelhum and J. J. MacIntosh, eds. *The First Critique: Reflections on Kant's Critique of Pure Reason.* Belmont, Calif.: Wadsworth, 1969, 38–52.

————. "Transcendental Arguments: Genuine and Spurious." *Nous* 6 (1972), 274–81.

Hirschman, Albert O. *The Passions and the Interests.* Princeton: Princeton University Press, 1977.

Hoffart, Elizabeth. *Herders 'Gott.'* Halle: Niemeyer, 1918.

Hoffmeister, Johannes. *Goethe und der deutsche Idealismus*. Leipzig: Meiner, 1932.

Holborn, Hajo. "German Idealism in the Light of Social History." In *Germany and Europe*. New York: Doubleday, 1970, 1–32.

Hooker, Edward N. "The Discussion of Taste, from 1750 to 1770, and the New Trends in Literary Criticism," *Publications of the Modern Language Assocation* 49 (1934), 577–92.

Horstmann, Rolf-Peter. "Why Must There Be a Transcendental Deduction in Kant's *Critique of Judgment?*" In Eckart Förster, ed. *Kant's Transcendental Deductions: The Three Critiques and the Opus Postumum*. Stanford: Stanford University Press, 1989, 157–76.

Howe, Irwin, ed. *The Idea of the Modern in Literature and the Arts*. New York: Horizon, 1967.

Hund, William B. "The Sublime and God in Kant's *Critique of Judgment*." *New Scholasticism* 57 (1983), 42–70.

Iggers, George. *The German Conception of History: The National Tradition of Historical Thought from Herder to the Present*. Middletown, Conn.: Wesleyan University Press, 1968.

Irmscher, Hans D. "Die geschichtsphilosophische Kontroverse zwischen Kant und Herder." In Bernhard Gajek, ed. *Hamann—Kant—Herder. Acta des 4. Internationalen Hamann-Kolloqiums im Herder-Institut zu Marburg/Lahn 1985*. Frankfurt am Main: Peter Lang, 1987, 111–92.

Jackson, Reginald. "Locke's Distinction Between Primary and Secondary Qualities." In Charles Martin and D. Armstrong, eds. *Locke and Berkeley: A Collection of Critical Essays*. New York: Harper, 1968, 53–77.

Jacob, Margaret. *The Radical Enlightenment: Pantheists, Freemasons and Republicans*. London: Allen and Unwin, 1981.

Jammer, Max. *Concepts of Force: A Study in the Foundations of Dynamics*. Cambridge: Harvard University Press, 1957.

Johnson, Mark L. "Kant's Unified Theory of Beauty." *Journal of Aesthetics and Art Criticism* 38 (1979), 167–78.

Juchem, Hans-Georg. *Die Entwicklung des Begriffs des Schönen bei Kant*. Bonn: Bouvier, 1970.

Kallich, Martin. "Association of Ideas and Critical Theory: Hobbes, Locke, and Addison." *English Literary History* 12 (1945), 290–315.

Kaulbach, Friedrich. *Ästhetische Welterkenntnis bei Kant*. Würzburg: Königshausen and Neumann, 1984.

Kelly, George A. *Idealism, Politics and History: Sources of Hegelian Thought*. Cambridge: Cambridge University Press, 1969.

Kemp-Smith, Norman. *Commentary on Kant's Critique of Pure Reason*. London: Macmillan, 1923.

Kennington, Richard, ed. *The Philosophy of Immanuel Kant*. Washington, D.C.: Catholic University of America Press, 1985.

Keynes, John M. "Newton, the Man." In *Essays in Biography*. New York: Norton, 1963, 310–23.

King, Lester S. "Basic Concepts of Eighteenth-Century Animism." *American Journal of Psychiatry* 124 (1967), 797–802.

————. "Stahl and Hoffmann: A Study in Eighteenth-Century Animism." *Journal of the History of Medicine* 19 (1964), 118–30.

Kitcher, Patricia. "Kant's Real Self." In Allen Wood, ed. *Self and Nature in Kant's Philosophy*. Ithaca and London: Cornell University Press, 1984, 113–47.

Knoll, Renate. *Johann G. Hamann und Friedrich H. Jacobi*. Heidelberg: Winter, 1963.

Kolb, Daniel. "Thought and Intuition in Kant's Critical System." *Journal of the History of Philosophy* 24 (1986), 223–41.

Konhardt, Klaus. *Die Einheit der Vernunft*. Ph.D. Diss. Munich, 1977.

Korff, Hermann A. *Geist der Goethezeit*. Vol. 1, *Sturm und Drang;* vol. 2. *Die Klassik*. Leipzig: Weber, 1927.

Korner, Stephan. "The Impossibility of Transcendental Deductions." *The Monist* 51 (1967), 317–31.

Koselleck, Reinhard. *Preussen zwischen Reform und Revolution*. Stuttgart: Klett, 1967.

Koyré, Alexandre. *From the Closed World to the Infinite Universe*. Baltimore: Johns Hopkins University Press, 1957.

Koyré, Alexandre and I. Bernard Cohen, "Newton and the Leibniz-Clarke Correspondence." *Archives internationales d'Histoire des Sciences* 15 (1962), 63–126.

Kraft, Michael. "Kant's Theory of Teleology." *International Philosophical Quarterly* 22 (1982), 41–49.

Krämling, Gerhard. "Das höchste Gut als mögliche Welt." *Kant-Studien* 77 (1986), 273–88.

Krieger, Leonard. *The German Idea of Freedom*. Chicago: University of Chicago Press, 1957.

Kristeller, Paul. "The Modern System in the Arts (II)." *Journal of the History of Ideas* 13 (1952), 17–46.

Kuhn, Thomas S. *The Structure of Scientific Revolutions*. 2d ed. Chicago: University of Chicago Press, 1970.

Kuhns, Richard. "That Kant Did Not Complete His Argument Concerning the Relation of Art to Morality and How It Might Be Completed." *Idealistic Studies* 5 (1975), 190–206.

Kulenkampf, Jens, ed. *Materialien zu Kants Kritik der Urteilskraft*. Frankfurt am Main: Suhrkamp, 1974.

Lang, Berel. "Kant and the Subjective Objects of Taste." *Journal of Aesthetics and Art Criticism* 25 (1967), 247–53.

Larère, Odile. "Sentiment esthétique et unité de la nature humaine." *Revue des sciences philosophiques et théologiques* 55 (1971), 432–64.

Larson, James L. "Vital Forces: Regulative Principles or Constitutive Agents? A Strategy in German Physiology 1786–1802." *Isis* 70 (1979), 235–49.

Lazaroff, Allan. "The Kantian Sublime: Aesthetic Judgment and Religious Feeling." *Kant-Studien* 71 (1980), 202–20.

Lebrun, Gérard. "Le trosième 'Critique' ou la théologie retrouvée." *Proceedings of the Ottawa Congress on Kant, 1974*. Ottawa: University of Ottawa Press, 1976, 297–317.

Lehmann, Gerhard. *Beiträge zur Geschichte und Interpretation der Philosophie Kants.* Berlin: de Gruyter, 1969.

———. "Einleitung zur *Ersten Einleitung in die Kritik der Urteilskraft.*" *A.A.* 20:471–79.

———. *Kants Nachlaßwerk und die Kritik der Urteilskraft.* Berlin: Junker and Dunnhaupt, 1939.

Lenoir, Timothy. "Kant, Blumenbach and Vital Materialism in Germany Biology." *Isis* 71 (1980), 77–108.

———. "Teleology without Regrets: The Transformation of Physiology in Germany." *Studies in the History and Philosophy of Science* 12 (1981), 293–354.

Levy, Ze'ev. "Hamanns Kontroverse mit Moses Mendelssohn." In Bernhard Gajek and Albert Maier, eds. *Johann George Hamann und die Krise der Aufklärung. Acta des 5. Internationalen Hamann-Kolloqiums im Münster i. W. 1988.* Frankfurt am Main: Peter Lang, 1990, 327–44.

Lieber, Hans J. "Kants Philosophie des Organischen und die Biologie seiner Zeit." *Philosophia Naturalis* 1 (1950), 553–70.

Liedtke, Max. *Der Begriff der reflektierenden Urteilskraft in der Kritik der reinen Vernunft.* Ph.D. Diss. Hamburg, 1964.

———. "Kants Begriff der Reflektion," *Archiv für Geschichte der Philosophie* 48 (1966), 207–16.

Lovejoy, Arthur O. *Essays in the History of Ideas.* Baltimore: Johns Hopkins University Press, 1948.

———. *The Great Chain of Being.* New York: Harper, 1936.

———. "Herder: Progressionism without Transformationism." In Bentley Glass, et al. *Forerunners of Darwin 1745–1859.* Baltimore: Johns Hopkins University Press, 1959, 207–21.

———. "Kant and Evolution," in Bentley Glass et al. *Forerunners of Darwin 1745–1859.* Baltimore: Johns Hopkins University Press, 1959, 173–206.

Löw, Reinhard. *Philosophie des Lebendigen: Der Begriff des Organischen bei Kant, sein Grund und seine Aktualität.* Frankfurt: Suhrkamp, 1980.

Lukács, Georg. *Realism in Our Time.* New York: Harper and Row, 1971.

Lütgert, Wilhelm. *Die Religion des deutschen Idealismus und ihr Ende.* 3 vols. Gütersloh: Bertelsmann, 1923.

MacBeath, A. Murray. "Kant on Moral Feeling." *Kant-Studien* 64 (1973), 283–314.

McClelland, Charles. *State, Society and University in Germany, 1700–1914.* Cambridge: Cambridge University Press, 1980.

McCloskey, Mary. *Kant's Aesthetic.* Albany: State University of New York Press, 1987.

McEvoy, J. G. and J. E. McGuire. "God and Nature: Priestley's Way of Rational Dissent." *Historical Studies in the Physical Sciences* 6 (1975), 325–404.

McFarland, John. "The Bogus Unity of the Kantian Philosophy." In *Proceedings of the Ottawa Congress on Kant, 1974.* Ottawa: University of Ottawa Press, 1976, 280–96.

———. *Kant's Concept of Teleology.* Edinburgh: University of Edinburgh Press, 1970.

McGuire, J. E. "Atoms and the 'Analogy of Nature': Newton's Third Rule of Philosophizing." *Studies in History and Philosophy of Science* 1 (1970), 3–58.

———. "Force, Active Principles, and Newton's Invisible Realm." *Ambix* 15 (1968), 154–208.

———. "The Origins of Newton's Doctrine of Essential Qualities." *Centaurus* 12 (1968), 233–60.

———. "Transmutation and Immutability: Newton's Doctrine of Physical Qualities." *Ambix* 14 (1967), 69–95.

McKenzie, Gordon. *Critical Responsiveness: A Study of the Psychological Current in Later Eighteenth-Century Criticism.* University of California Publications in English, vol. 20, 1949.

McKenzie, Nancy. "The Primacy of Practical Reason in Kant's System." *Idealistic Studies* 15 (1985), 199–215.

Makkreel, Rudolf. *Imagination and Interpretation in Kant.* Chicago: University of Chicago Press, 1990.

———. "Imagination and Temporality in Kant's Theory of the Sublime." *Journal of Aesthetics and Art Criticism* 42 (1984), 303–15.

Malraux, André. *Voices of Silence.* Princeton: Bollingen, 1978.

Malter, Rudolf. "Zeitgenössische Reaktionen auf Kants Religionsphilosophie. Eine Skizze zur Wirkungsgeschichte des Kantischen und des reformatorischen Denkens." In A. Bucher, H. Drüe, and T. Seebohm, eds. *Bewußt Sein: Gerhard Funke zu eigen.* Bonn: Bouvier, 1975, 145–67.

Marc-Wogau, Konrad. *Vier Studien zu Kants Kritik der Urteilskraft.* Uppsala: Uppsala University Press, 1938.

Marshall, John. "Man as an End in Himself." In *Proceedings of the Ottawa Congress on Kant, 1974.* Ottawa: University of Ottawa Press, 1976, 467–73.

Martin, Gottfried. *Kant's Metaphysic and Theory of Science.* Manchester: Manchester University Press, 1961.

Marx, Werner. Review of G. Prauss, *Erscheinung bei Kant. Philosophisches Jahrbuch* 84 (1975), 422–26.

Meerbote, Ralf. "Kant's Use of the Notions of 'Objective Reality' and 'Objective Validity.'" *Kant-Studien* 63 (1972), 51–58.

———. "Reflection on Beauty." In Ted Cohen and Paul Guyer, eds. *Essays in Kant's Aesthetics.* Chicago: University of Chicago Press, 1982, 55–86.

———. "*Wille* and *Willkür* in Kant's Theory of Action." In Moltke S. Gram, ed. *Interpreting Kant.* Iowa City: University of Iowa Press, 1982, 69–83.

Meinecke, Friedrich. *Cosmopolitanism and the National State.* Princeton, Princeton University Press, 1970.

———. *Entstehung des Historismus.* In *Werke,* vol. 2. Munich: Oldenburg, 1936.

Menzer, Paul. *Kants Ästhetik in ihrer Entwicklung.* Berlin: Akademie, 1952.

———. *Kants Lehre von der Entwicklung.* Berlin: Reimer, 1911.

———. "Schiller und Kant." *Kant-Studien* 47 (1955–56), 113–47, 234–72.

Meredith, James. *Kants Critique of Aesthetic Judgement: Translated, with Seven Introductory Essays, Notes, and Analytical Index.* Oxford: Clarendon, 1911.

————. "Last Stages of the Development of Kant's Critique of Taste." In James Meredith, *Kant's Critique of Aesthetic Judgement: Translated, with Seven Introductory Essays, Notes, and Analytical Index*, Oxford: Clarendon, 1911.

Merlan, Philip. "From Hume to Hamann." *The Personalist* 32 (1951), 11–18.

————. "Kant, Hamann-Jacobi and Schelling on Hume." *Rivista Critica di Storia della Philosophia* 22 (1967), 481–94.

Mertens, Helga. *Kommentar zur Ersten Einleitung in Kants Kritik der Urteilskraft*. Munich: Berchtmanns, 1975.

Metzger, Hélène. *Newton, Stahl, Boerhaave et la Doctrine Chimique*. Paris: Alcan, 1930.

Michaelson, G. E. Jr. *The Historical Dimension of a Rational Faith*. Washington, D.C.: University Press of America, 1979.

Mischel, Theodore. "Kant and the Possibility of a Science of Psychology." In Lewis W. Beck, ed. *Kant Studies Today*. La Salle, Ill.: Open Court, 1969, 432–49.

Model, Anselm. *Metaphysik und reflektierende Urteilskraft bei Kant*. Frankfurt am Main: Athenäum, 1987.

Möller, Joseph. "Die anthropologische Relevanz der Ästhetik." In A. Bucher, H. Drüe, and T. Seebohm, eds. *Bewußt sein. Gerhard Funke zu eigen*. Bonn: Bouvier, 1975, 349–68.

Monk, Samuel. *The Sublime*. Ann Arbor: University of Michigan Press, 1960.

Moravia, Sergio. "From *Homme Machine* to *Homme Sensible:* Changing Eighteenth-Century Models of Man's Image." *Journal of the History of Ideas* 39 (1978), 45–60.

Mörchen, Hermann. "Die Einbildungskraft bei Kant." *Jahrbuch für Philosophie und phänomenologische Forschung* 11 (1930), 312–495. Reprint, Tübingen: Niemeyer, 1970.

Morris, David. *The Religious Sublime: Christian Poetry and Christian Tradition in Eighteenth-Century England*. Lexington: Kentucky University Press, 1972.

Murphy, Jeffrie. "The Highest Good as Content for Kant's Ethical Formalism: Beck versus Silber," *Kant-Studien* 56 (1965–66), 102–10.

Nahm, Milton C. *Genius and Creativity*. New York: Harper and Row, 1965.

————. "Genius and the Aesthetic Relation of the Arts." *Journal of Aesthetics and Art Criticism* 9 (1950), 1–12.

————. "Imagination as the Productive Faculty for 'Creating Another Nature . . .'" In Lewis W. Beck, ed. *Proceedings of the Third International Kant Congress*. Dordrecht, Holland: Reidel, 1972, 442–50.

————. "Productive Imagination, Tragedy and Ugliness." In *Proceedings of the Ottawa Congress on Kant, 1974*. Ottawa: University of Ottawa Press, 1976, 268–79.

————. "'Sublimity' and the 'Moral Law' in Kant's Philosophy." *Kant-Studien* 48 (1956–57), 502–24.

Neville, Michael. "Kant's Characterization of Aesthetic Experience." *Journal of Aesthetics and Art Criticism* 33 (1974), 193–202.

Nicolai, Heinz. *Goethe und Jacobi, Studien zur Geschichte ihrer Freundschaft.* Stuttgart: Metzler, 1965.

Nicolson, Marjorie. *Mountain Gloom and Mountain Glory: The Development of the Aesthetics of the Infinite.* Ithaca: Cornell University Press, 1959.

———. *Newton Commands the Muse.* Princeton: Princeton University Press, 1946.

Nietzsche, Friedrich. *The Will to Power.* Tr. W. Kaufmann. New York: Vintage, 1968.

Nivelle, Armand. *Kunst- und Dichtungstheorie zwischen Aufklärung und Klassik.* Berlin: de Gruyter, 1960.

Noussy, Hassan El. "Le panthéisme dans les lettres françaises au XIIIe siècle." *Revue des sciences humaines* 27 (1960), 435–57.

Odebrecht, Rudolf. *Form und Geist: Der Aufstieg des dialektischen Gedankens in Kants Ästhetik.* Berlin: Junker and Dunnhaupt, 1930.

O'Flaherty, James C. *Hamann's Socratic Memorabilia: A Translation and Commentary.* Baltimore: Johns Hopkins University Press, 1967.

O'Neil, Onora. "Agency and Anthropology in Kant's *Groundwork.*" In Yirmiahu Yovel, ed. *Kant's Practical Philosophy Reconsidered.* Dordrecht, Boston, and London: Kluwer, 1989, 63–82.

Ortega y Gasset, José. *The Dehumanization of Art.* Princeton: Princeton University Press, 1968.

Ouden, Bernard den and Maria Moen, eds. *New Essays on Kant.* New York: Peter Lang, 1987.

Packer, Mark. "The Highest Good in Kant's Psychology of Motivation." *Idealistic Studies* 13 (1988), 110–19.

Pascal, Roy. *The German Sturm und Drang.* Manchester: Manchester University Press, 1953.

Pasini, Dino. "Das 'Reich der Zwecke' und der politisch-rechtliche Kantianische Gedanke." In *Akten des 4. Internationalen Kant-Kongresses, Mainz 1974*, vol. 2:2. Berlin: de Gruyter, 1974, 675–691.

Paulsen, Friedrich. "Bildung." in *Gesammelte pädagogische Abhandlungen.* Stuttgart: Cotta, 1912, 127–50.

———. *Geschichte des gelehrten Unterrichts.* 2 vols. Berlin: de Gruyter, 1919–21.

Penelhum, Terence and J. J. MacIntosh, eds. *The First Critique: Reflections on Kant's Critique of Pure Reason.* Belmont, Calif.: Wadsworth, 1969.

Petock, Stuart J. "Kant, Beauty, and the Object of Taste." *Journal of Aesthetics and Art Criticism* 32 (1973), 183–86.

Philipp, Wolfgang. *Das Werden der Aufklärung in theologiegeschichtlicher Sicht,* vol. 3. Göttingen: Vandenhoeck and Rupprecht, 1957.

Pinder, Tillmann. "Kants Begriff der transzendentalen Erkenntnis." *Kant-Studien* 77 (1986), 1–40.

Piper, William B. "Kant's Contact with British Empiricism." *Eighteenth-Century Studies* 12 (1978–79), 174–89.

Pippin, Robert. "Kant on Empirical Concepts." *Studies in History and Philosophy of Science* 10 (1979) 1–19.

———. "Kant on the Spontaneity of Mind." *Canadian Journal of Philosophy* 17 (1987), 449–76.

———. *Kant's Theory of Form.* New Haven: Yale University Press, 1982.
———. "On the Moral Foundations of Kant's *Rechtslehre.*" In Richard Kennington, ed. *The Philosophy of Immanuel Kant.* Washington, D.C.: Catholic University of America Press, 1985, 107–42.
———. Review of G. Prauss, *Erscheinung bei Kant. Journal of the History of Philosophy* 12 (1974), 403–5.
———. "The Schematism and Empirical Concepts." *Kant-Studien* 67 (1976), 156–71.
Pitte, Frederich van de. "The Importance of Moral Teleology for Kant's Critical Philosophy." In *Proceedings of the Ottowa Congress on Kant, 1974.* Ottawa: University of Ottawa Press, 1976, 494–97.
———. "Is Kant's Distinction between Reflective and Determinant Judgement Valid?" In *Akten des 4. Internationalen Kant-Kongresses,* Mainz, 1974, vol. 2:1. Berlin: de Gruyter, 1974, 445–51.
———. *Kant as Philosophical Anthropologist.* The Hague: Nijhoff, 1971.
Pluhar, Werner. "How to Render 'Zweckmäßigkeit' in Kant's *Third Critique.*" In Moltke S. Gram, ed. *Interpreting Kant.* Iowa City: University of Iowa Press, 1982, 85–98.
Polanyi, Michael. *Personal Knowledge.* New York: Harper and Row, 1964.
Popkin, Richard. "Berkeley and Pyrrhonism." In Popkin, *The High Road to Pyrrhonism.* San Diego: Austin Hill, 1980, 297–318.
———. *History of Scepticism.* New York: Harper and Row, 1964.
Posy, Carl. "Autonomy, Omniscience and the Ethical Imagination: From Theoretical to Practical Philosophy." In Yirmiahu Yovel, ed. *Kant's Practical Philosophy Reconsidered.* Dordrecht, Boston, London: Kluwer, 1989, 106–34.
Prauss, Gerold. *Erscheinung bei Kant.* Berlin: de Gruyter, 1971.
Proceedings of the Ottawa Congress on Kant, 1974. Ottawa: University of Ottawa Press, 1976.
Rather, L. J. "G. E. Stahl's Psychological Physiology." *Bulletin of the History of Medicine* 35 (1961), 37–49.
Rather, L. J. and J. B. Frerichs. "The Leibniz-Stahl Controversy." *Clio Medica* 3 (1968), 21–40; 5 (1970), 53–67.
Reath, Andrews. "Two Conceptions of the Highest Good in Kant." *Journal of the History of Philosophy* 26 (1988), 593–619.
Rehorn, Karl. *G. E. Lessings Stellung zur Philosophie des Spinoza.* Frankfurt am Main: Diesterweg, 1877.
Reill, Peter. *The German Enlightenment and the Rise of Historicism.* Berkeley and Los Angeles: University of California Press, 1975.
Renault, Marc. "Le principe d'auto-conservation de la raison est le fondement de la croyance rationelle." In *Proceedings of the Ottawa Congress on Kant, 1974.* Ottawa: University of Ottawa Press, 1976, 474–79.
Rescher, Nicholas. "Kant and the 'Special Constitution' of Man's Mind." In *Akten des 4. Internationalen Kant-Kongresses, Mainz 1974,* vol 2:1. Berlin: de Gruyter, 1974, 318–28.
———. "Noumenal Causality." In Lewis W. Beck, ed. *Proceedings of the Third International Kant Congress.* Dordrecht: Reidel, 1972, 462–70.
Ricoeur, Paul. *Freud and Philosophy.* New Haven: Yale University Press, 1970.

Riedel, Manfred. "Historizismus und Kritizismus: Kants Streit mit G. Forster und J. G. Herder." *Kant-Studien* 72 (1981), 41–57.

Riley, Patrick. *Kant's Political Philosophy.* Totowa, N.J.: Rowman and Little, 1983.

Rintelen, Fritz J. v. "Kant and Goethe." In Lewis W. Beck, ed. *Proceedings of the Third International Kant Congress.* Dordrecht, Holland: Reidel, 1972, 471–79.

Ritterbush, Philip. *Overtures to Biology: The Speculations of Eighteenth-Century Naturalists.* New Haven: Yale University Press, 1964.

Ritzel, Wolfgang. *Kant, eine Biographie.* Berlin: de Gruyter, 1985.

Robson, Kent E. "Kant's Concept of Intuition." *Akten des 4. Internationalen Kant-Kongresses, Mainz, 1974,* vol. 2:1. Berlin: de Gruyter, 240–46.

Roe, Shirley A. *Matter, Life and Generation: Eighteenth-Century Embryology and the Haller-Wolff Debate.* New York: Cambridge University Press, 1981.

Rogerson, Kenneth. *Kant's Aesthetics: The Roles of Form and Expression.* Lanham, Md.: University Press of America, 1986.

Rohrmoser, Günter. "Zum Problem der ästhetischen Versöhnung: Schiller und Hegel." *Euphorion* 53 (1959), 351–66.

Roretz, Karl. *Zur Analyse von Kants Philosophie des Organischen.* Vienna: Akademie der Wissenschafter in Wien, 1922.

Rosenberg, Jay. "Transcendental Arguments Revisited." *Journal of Philosophy* 72 (1975), 611–26.

Rotenstreich, Nathan. *Experience and Its Systematization.* The Hague: Nijhoff, 1972.

Rudolph, G. A. "Hallers Lehre von der Irritabilität und Sensibilität." In Karl E. Rothschuh, ed. *Von Boerhaave bis Berger.* Stuttgart: G. Fischer, 1964.

Sakabe, Megumi. "Freedom as a Regulative Principle: On Some Aspects of the Kant-Herder Controversy on the Philosophy of History." In Yirmiahu Yovel, ed. *Kant's Practical Philosophy Reconsidered.* Dordrecht, Boston, London: Kluwer, 1989, 183–95.

Sauder, Gerhard, ed. *Johann Gottfried Herder 1744–1803.* Hamburg: Meiner, 1984.

Schaper, Eva. "Arguing Transcendentally." *Kant-Studien* 63 (1972), 101–16.

———. "Kant und das Problem der Einbildungskraft." In A. Bucher, H. Drüe, and T. Seebohm, eds. *Bewußt Sein: Gerhard Funke zu eigen.* Bonn: Bouvier, 1975, 373–92.

———. *Studies in Kant's Aesthetics.* Edinburgh: Edinburgh University Press, 1979.

Schiller, Joseph. "Queries, Answers and Unsolved Problems in Eighteenth-Century Biology." *History of Science* 12 (1974), 184–99.

Schlapp, Otto. *Kants Lehre vom Genie.* Göttingen: Vandenhoeck and Rupprecht, 1898.

Schlipp, Paul. *Kant's Pre-Critical Ethics.* Evanston: Northwestern University Press, 1938.

Schmidt, Ferdinand J. *Herders pantheistische Weltanschauung.* Ph.D. Diss. Berlin, 1888.

Schober, Joyce. *Die deutsche Spätaufklärung (1770–1790).* Bern: Lang, 1975.

Schofield, Robert. *Mechanism and Materialism: British Natural Philosophy in an Age of Reason.* Princeton: Princeton University Press, 1970.

Schoonhoven, Evert J. "Hamann in der Kontroverse mit Moses Mendelssohn." In Bernhard Gajek and Albert Maier, eds. *Johann Georg Hamann und die Krise der Aufklärung. Acta des 5. Internationalen Hamann-Kollegiums im Münster i. W. 1988.* Frankfurt am Main: Peter Lang, 1990, 307–26.

Schrader, George. "Kant's Theory of Concepts." In Robert P. Wolff, ed. *Kant: A Collection of Critical Essays.* Notre Dame and London: University of Notre Dame Press, 1967, 134–55.

———. "The Status of Feeling in Kant's Philosophy." *Proceedings of the Ottawa Congress on Kant, 1974,* 143–64.

———. "The Status of Teleological Judgment in the Critical Philosophy." *Kant-Studien* 45 (1953–54), 204–35.

Schulz, Eberhard G. "Kant und die Berliner Aufklärung." In *Akten des 4. Internationalen Kant-Kongresses, Mainz, 1974,* vol. 2.1. Berlin: de Gruyter, 1974, 60–80.

Schwarz, Hermann. "Die Entwicklung des Pantheismus in der neueren Zeit," *Zeitschrift für Philosophie und philosophische Kritik,* vol. 157, no. 1 (Leipzig, 1915), 20–80.

Seigfried, Hans. "Kant's 'Spanish Bank Account': *Realität* and *Wirklichkeit.*" In Moltke S. Gram, ed. *Interpreting Kant.* Iowa City: University of Iowa Press, 1982, 115–32.

———. "Zum Problem des Wahrnehmungsurteil bei Kant." In *Akten des 4. Internationalen Kant-Kongresses, Mainz, 1974,* vol. 2:1. Berlin: de Gruyter, 1974, 254–61.

Sellars, Wilfred. *Science and Metaphysics.* New York: Humanities Press, 1968.

Sewell, Elizabeth. *The Orphic Voice: Poetry and Natural History.* New Haven: Yale University Press, 1960.

Shaw, Leroy R. "Henry Home of Kames: Precursor of Herder." *Germanic Review* 35 (1960), 16–27.

Sherrington, Charles S. *Goethe on Nature and Science.* Cambridge: Cambridge University Press, 1949.

Siewert, Donald J. "Kant's Dialectic of Teleological Judgment." In *Akten des 4. Internationalen Kant-Kongresses, Mainz, 1974,* vol. 2:1. Berlin: de Gruyter, 1974, 452–60.

Silber, John R. "The Ethical Significance of Kant's *Religion.*" In Theodore M. Greene and H. H. Hudson, trs. *Religion Within the Limits of Reason Alone.* La Salle, Ill.: Open Court, 1960, lxxix–cxxxiv.

———. "The Importance of the Highest Good in Kant's Ethics." *Ethics* 73 (1962–63), 179–97.

———. "Kant's Concept of the Highest Good as Immanent and Transcendent." *Philosophical Review* 68 (1959), 469–92.

———. "The Metaphysical Importance of the Highest Good as the Canon of Pure Reason." *Texas Studies in Literature and Language* 1 (1959), 233–44.

————. "The Moral Good and the Natural Good in Kant's Ethics." *Review of Metaphysics* 36 (1982), 397–437.

————. "Der Schematismus der praktischen Vernunft." *Kant-Studien* 56 (1966), 252–73.

Silk, M. S. and J. P. Stern. *Nietzsche on Tragedy*. Cambridge: Cambridge University Press, 1982.

Simon, Josef. "Herder und Kant. Sprache und 'historischer Sinn.'" In Gerhard Sauder, ed. *Johann Gottfried Herder 1744–1803*. Hamburg: Meiner, 1984, 3–13.

————. "Teleologisches Reflektieren und kausales Bestimmen." *Zeitschrift für philosophische Forschung* 30 (1976), 369–88.

Smith, Steven G. "Worthiness to Be Happy and Kant's Concept of the Highest Good." *Kant-Studien* 75 (1984), 168–90.

Smyth, Richard A. *Forms of Intuition: An Historical Introduction to the Transcendental Aesthetic*. The Hague: Nijhoff, 1978.

Solomon, Robert. "Hegel's Concept of Geist." In Alasdair MacIntyre, ed. *Hegel: A Collection of Critical Essays*. Notre Dame and London: University of Notre Dame Press, 1976, 125–49.

Sommer, Robert. *Grundzüge einer Geschichte der deutschen Psychologie und Aesthetik von Wolff-Baumgarten bis Kant-Schiller*. Würzburg: Staehl, 1892.

Souriau, Michel. *Le jugement réfléchissant dans la philosophie critique de Kant*. Paris: Alcan, 1926.

Stadler, August. *Kants Teleologie und ihre erkenntnistheoretische Bedeutung*. Berlin: Dümmler, 1874.

Stadler, Ingrid. "Perception and Perfection in Kant's Aesthetics." In Robert P. Wolf, ed. *Kant: A Collection of Critical Essays*. Notre Dame: University of Notre Dame Press, 1968, 339–84.

Staver, Frederick. "'Sublime' as Applied to Nature." *Modern Language Notes* 70 (1955), 485–87.

Steinke, Martin W. *Edward Young's "Conjectures on Original Composition" in England and Germany*. New York: F. C. Stechert, 1917.

Stern, Paul. "The Problem of History and Temporality in Kantian Ethics." *Review of Metaphysics* 39 (1986), 505–45.

Stockum, Theodorus van. *Spinoza-Jacobi-Lessing*. Groningen: Noordhoff, 1916.

Stoeffler, F. Ernest. *German Pietism During the Eighteenth Century*. Leiden: Brill, 1973.

————. *The Rise of Evangelical Pietism*. Leiden: Brill, 1965.

Stolnitz, Jerome. "On the Origins of 'Aesthetic Disinterestedness.'" *Journal of Aesthetics and Art Criticism* 20 (1961), 131–43.

————. "On the Significance of Lord Shaftesbury in Modern Aesthetic Theory." *Philosophical Quarterly* 11 (1961), 96–112.

Strack, Friedrich. *Ästhetik und Freiheit: Hölderlins Idee von Schönheit, Sittlichkeit und Geschichte in der Frühzeit*. Tübingen: Niemeyer, 1976.

Strawson, P. F. *The Bounds of Sense*. London: Methuen, 1966.

————. "Imagination and Perception." In Laurence Foster and J. W. Swanson, eds. *Experience and Theory*. Amherst: University of Massachusetts Press, 1970, 31–54.

Stroud, Barry. "Transcendental Arguments." In Terence Penelhum and J. J. MacIntosh, eds. *The First Critique: Reflections on Kant's Critique of Pure Reason*. Belmont, Calif.: Wadsworth, 1969, 54–69.

Suphan, Bernhard. "Goethe und Spinoza, 1783–86." *Festschrift zum zweiten Säkularfeier des Friedrichs-Werderschen Gymnasiums zu Berlin* (1881), 159–93.

Swing, Thomas K. *Kant's Transcendental Logic*. New Haven: Yale University Press, 1969.

Taminiaux, Jacques. *La nostalgie de la Grèce à l'aube de l'idéalisme allemand*. The Hague: Nijhoff, 1967.

Thacker, Christopher. *The Wildness Pleases: The Origins of Romanticism*. New York: St. Martin's Press, 1983.

Thackray, Arnold. *Atoms and Powers: An Essay on Newtonian Matter-Theory and the Development of Chemistry*. Cambridge: Harvard University Press, 1970.

———. "Matter in a Nut-Shell." *Ambix* 15 (1968), 29–53.

Thompson, Manley. "Singular Terms and Intuitions in Kant's Epistemology." *Review of Metaphysics* 26 (1972), 314–43.

Thüme, Hans. *Beiträge zur Geschichte des Geniebegriffs in England*. Halle: Niemeyer, 1927.

Timm, Hermann. *Gott und die Freiheit: Studien zur Religionsphilosophie*. Vol. 1, *Die Spinozarenaissance*. Frankfurt: Klostermann, 1974.

Tonelli, Giorgio. "Conditions in Königsberg and the Making of Kant's Philosophy." In A. Bucher, H. Drüe, amd T. Seebohm, eds. *Bewußt Sein: Gerhard Funke zu eigen*. Bonn: Bouvier, 1975, 142-44.

———. "Crusius, Christian August." *Encyclopedia of Philosophy*, 1:270.

———. "La formazione del testo della *Kritik der Urteilskraft*." *Revue internationale de philosophie* 30 (Brussels, 1954), 423–48.

———. "Kant's Early Theory of Genius (1770–1779)," *Journal of the History of Philosophy* 4 (1966), 109–31; 209–24.

———. "Die Umwälzung von 1769 bei Kant," *Kant-Studien* 54 (1963), 369–73.

———. "Von den verschiedenen Bedeutungen des Wortes Zweckmäßigkeit in der Kritik der Urteilskraft," *Kant-Studien* 49 (1957–58), 154–66.

Townsend, Dabney. "From Shaftesbury to Kant: The Development of the Concept of Aesthetic Experience." *Journal of the History of Ideas* 48 (1987), 287–305.

Trebels, Andreas H. *Einbildungskraft und Spiel*. Bonn: Bouvier, 1967.

Trinkaus, Charles. "The Religious Foundations of Luther's Social Views." In John H. Mundy, Richard W. Emery, and Benjamin N. Nelson, eds. *Essays in Medieval Life and Thought*. New York: Biblo and Tannen, 1955, 71–87.

Troeltsch, Ernst. *Deutsche Bildung*. Darmstadt: Reichsdeutsche Schriften 12, 1919.

———. "Der deutsche Idealismus" [1900]. In *Gesammelte Schriften*, vol. 4. Tübingen: J. C. B. Mohr, 1925, 532–587.

———. "The Ideas of Natural Law and Humanity in World Politics." In

Otto Gierke, *Natural Law and the Theory of Society, 1500–1800*. Cambridge: Cambridge University Press, 1934, 201–22.

———. *The Social Teachings of the Christian Churches*, vol. 2. New York: Macmillan, 1931.

Tumarkin, Anna. *Herder und Kant*. Berlin: Siebert, 1896.

———. "Zur transscendentalen Methode der Kantischen Ästhetik." *Kant-Studien* 11 (1906), 348–78.

Tuveson, Ernest. *The Imagination as a Means of Grace: Locke and the Aesthetics of Romanticism*. Berkeley and Los Angeles: University of California Press, 1960.

———. "The Importance of Shaftesbury." *English Literary History* 20 (1953), 267–99.

———. "Shaftesbury and the Age of Sensibility." In Howard Anderson and John Shea, eds. *Studies in Criticism and Aesthetics, 1660–1800*. Minneapolis: University of Minnesota Press, 1967, 73–93.

———. "Space, Deity, and the 'Natural Sublime.'" *Modern Language Quarterly* 12 (1951), 20–38.

Uehling, Theodore. *The Notion of Form in Kant's Critique of Judgment*. The Hague: Nijhoff, 1971.

———. "*Wahrnehmungsurteile* and *Erfahrungsurteile* Reconsidered." *Kant-Studien* 69 (1978), 341–51.

Unger, Rudolf. *Hamann und die Aufklärung* 2 vols. Jena: Diederichs, 1911.

Ungerer, Emil. *Die Teleologie Kants und ihre Bedeutung für die Logik der Biologie*. Berlin: Borntraeger, 1922.

Vartanian, Aram. "Trembley's Polyp, La Mettrie and Eighteenth-Century French Materialism." *Journal of the History of Ideas* 11 (1950), 259–86.

Vernière, Paul. *Spinoza et la pensée française avant la révolution* 2 vols. Paris: Presses Universitaires, 1954.

Vierhaus, Rudolf. "Bildung." *Geschichtliche Grundbegriffe*. Vol. 1, 508–51.

Vignola, Paul-Émile. "'Seele' et 'Gemut' selon Kant." *Proceedings of the Ottawa Congress on Kant, 1974*. Ottawa: University of Ottawa Press, 1976, 424–31.

Vleeschauwer, Henri de. *La déduction transcendentale dans l'oeuvre de Kant*, vol. 2. Paris, 1936. Reprint: New York and London: Garland, 1976.

Vollrath, Ernst. "Kants Kritik der Urteilskraft als Grundlegung einer Theorie des Politischen." In *Akten des 4. Internationalen Kant-Kongresses, Mainz, 1974*, vol. 2:2. Berlin: de Gruyter, 1974, 692–705.

Vollrath, Wilhelm. *Die Auseinandersetzung Herders mit Spinoza*. Darmstadt: Winter, 1911.

Vorländer, Karl. "Ethischer Rigorismus und sittlicher Schönheit." *Philosophische Monatshefte* 30 (1894), 225–80.

———. "Goethe und Kant." *Kant-Studien* 23 (1919), 222–32.

———. *Immanuel Kant: Der Mann und das Werk*. 2d ed. Hamburg: Meiner, 1977.

———. *Kant-Schiller-Goethe*. Leipzig: Meiner, 1923.

Walker, Mack. *German Home Towns*. Ithaca: Cornell University Press, 1971.

Walsh, William H. "Philosophy and Psychology in Kant's Critique." *Kant-Studien* 57 (1966), 186–98.

Walzel, Oskar. *Das Prometheussymbol von Shaftesbury bis Goethe*. Reprint. Darmstadt: Wissenschaftliche Buchgesellschaft, 1968.

———. "Shaftesbury und das deutsche Geistesleben des 18. Jahrhunderts." *Germanisch-romanische Monatshefte* 1 (1909), 422–25.

Ward, Keith. "Kant's Teleological Ethics." *Philosophical Quarterly* 21 (1971), 337–51.

Warnock, Mary. "Imagination and Perception." In Warnock, ed. *Imagination*. Berkeley and Los Angeles: University of California Press, 1976, 13–34.

Wartenberg, Thomas. "Order Through Reason: Kant's Transcendental Justification of Science." *Kant-Studien* 70 (1979), 410–24.

Washburn, Michael. "Did Kant Have a Theory of Self-Knowledge?" *Archiv für Geschichte der Philosophie* 58 (1976), 40–56.

———. "The Second Edition of the Critique: Toward an Understanding of Its Nature and Genesis." *Kant-Studien* 66 (1975), 277–90.

Weber, Max. "Politics as a Vocation." In Hans Gerth and C. Wright Mills, eds. *From Max Weber:* Essays in Sociology. New York: Oxford University Press, 1961, 120–22.

Weil, Hans. *Die Entstehung des deutschen Bildungsprinzips*. Bonn: Bouvier, 1930.

Weiser, Christian F. *Shaftesbury und das deutsche Geistesleben*. Reprint. Darmstadt: Wissenschaftliche Buchgesellschaft, 1969.

Weldon, Thomas D. *Introduction to Kant's Critique of Pure Reason*. Oxford: Clarendon, 1945.

Westphal, Merold. "In Defense of the Thing in Itself," *Kant-Studien* 59 (1968), 118–41.

Weyand, Klaus. *Kants Geschichtsphilosophie: Ihre Entwicklung und ihr Verhältnis zur Aufklärung*. Cologne: Kölner Universitäts-Verlag, 1963.

White, David A. "The Metaphysics of Disinterestedness: Shaftesbury and Kant." *Journal of Aesthetics and Art Criticism* 32 (1973–74), 239–48.

———. "On Bridging the Gulf Between Nature and Morality in the *Critique of Judgment*." *Journal of Aesthetics and Art Criticism* 38 (1979), 179–88.

Whitney, George T. and David F. Bowers, eds. *The Heritage of Kant*. Princeton: Princeton University Press, 1939.

Wilkerson, T. E. "Things, Stuffs, and Kant's Aesthetic." *Philosophical Review* 82 (1973), 169–87.

Will, Frederic. "Cognition through Beauty in Moses Mendelssohn's Early Aesthetics." *Journal of Aesthetics and Art Criticism* 14 (1955), 97–105.

———. *Intelligible Beauty in Aesthetic Thought from Winckelmann to Victor Cousin*. Tübingen: Niemeyer, 1958.

Willey, Basil. *The Eighteenth Century Background: Studies on the Idea of Nature in the Thought of the Period*. Boston: Beacon, 1961.

Williams, Forrest. "Philosophical Anthropology in the *Critique of Judgment*." *Kant-Studien* 46 (1954–55), 172–88.

Wilson, Kirk D. "Kant on Intuition." *Philosophical Quarterly* 25 (1975), 247–65.

Windelband, Wilhelm. "Einleitung in Kants *Kritik der Urteilskraft*." *A.A.* 5:512ff.

———. *Die Geschichte der neueren Philosophie*. Leipzig: Breithof, 1911.

Wolf, Herman. "Die Genielehre des jungen Herder." *Deutsche Vierteljahrs-schrift für Literaturwissenschaft und Geistesgeschichte* 3 (1925) 401–30.

———. *Versuch einer Geschichte des Geniebegriffs in der deutschen Ästhetik des 18. Jahrhunderts, Bd. I., Von Gottsched bis auf Lessing.* Heidelberg: Winter, 1923.

Wolff, Hans. *Die Weltanschauung der deutschen Aufklärung in geschichtlicher Entwicklung.* Bern: A. Francke, 1949.

Wolff, Robert P. "Kant's Debt to Hume via Beattie." *Journal of the History of Ideas* 21 (1960), 117–23.

———. *Kant's Theory of Mental Activity.* Cambridge: Harvard University Press, 1963.

———. "Remarks on the Relation of the *Critique of Pure Reason* to Kant's Ethical Theory." In Bernard den Ouden and Maria Moen, eds. *New Essays on Kant.* New York: Peter Lang, 1987, 139–53.

———, ed. *Kant: A Collection of Critical Essays.* Notre Dame and London: University of Notre Dame Press, 1967.

Wood, Allen. *Kant's Moral Religion.* Ithaca and London: Cornell University Press, 1970.

———, ed. *Self and Nature in Kant's Philosophy.* Ithaca and London: Cornell University Press, 1984.

Wubnig, J. "The Epigenesis of Pure Reason." *Kant-Studien* 60 (1968–69), 147–52.

Wundt, Max. *Die deutsche Schulphilosophie im Zeitalter der Aufklärung.* Tübingen: J. C. B. Mohr, 1945.

Yolton, John. *Thinking Matter: Materialism in Eighteenth-Century Britain.* Minneapolis: University of Minnesota Press, 1983.

Young, J. Michael. "Kant's View of Imagination." *Kant-Studien* 79 (1988), 140–64.

Yovel, Yirmiahu. "The Interests of Reason: From Metaphysics to Moral History." In Yirmiahu Yovel, ed. *Kant's Practical Philosophy Recon-sidered.* Dordrecht, Boston, London: Kluwer, 1989, 135–48.

———. *Kant and the Philosophy of History.* Princeton: Princeton University Press, 1980.

———, ed. *Kant's Practical Philosophy Reconsidered.* Dordrecht, Boston, London: Kluwer, 1989.

Zeldin, Mary-Barbara. "Kant's Theory of Art and Genius." *International Studies in Philosophy* (1976), 101–14.

———. "The Role of Art and Genius in the 'Vocation of Man.'" In *Akten des 4. Internationalen Kant-Kongresses,* Mainz, 1974, vol 2:1. Berlin: de Gruyter, 1974, 461–70.

———. "The *Summum Bonum,* the Moral Law, and the Existence of God." *Kant-Studien* 62 (1971), 43–54.

Zeller, Eduard. "Lessing als Theolog." In *Vorträge und Abhandlungen* (2. Sammlung). Leipzig: Fues, 1877, 283–327.

Zimmermann, Robert L. "Kant: The Aesthetic Judgment." In Robert P. Wolff, ed. *Kant: A Collection of Critical Essays.* Notre Dame and London: University of Notre Dame Press, 1967, 385–404.

Zocher, Rudolf. "Der Doppelsinn der kantischen Ideenlehre." *Zeitschrift für philosophische Forschung* 20 (1960), 222–26.

Index

Act, aesthetic, 114–15, 119 (*see also* Imagination); cognitive, 49, 54–55, 70, 72, 74, 77, 164, 308, 310, 311 (*see also* Synthesis); practical, 95, 105, 221, 295 (*see also* Freedom; Will)

Action at a distance, 190, 193

Activism. *See* Spontaneity

Actuality (*see also* Existence; Validity), 18–21, 72, 77, 91, 95, 212, 219, 232, 309, 315, 325, 336, 341; objective, 51–52, 68; with validity, 60, 64, 86, 163, 166, 289, 316; without validity, 64, 97, 109, 135, 145, 160, 320

Actualizing the moral law (*see also* Efficaciousness of morality in world of sense), 133, 264–68, 314, 319, 320, 322, 332; and highest good, 323–26, 333–34, 340–41

Addison, Joseph, 26, 28, 277, 355n.68, 356n.98

Adickes, Erich, 39

Aesthetic and ethical, relation of, 3, 273, 278–79, 288, 291, 292–94

Aesthetic vs. logical, 19–21, 48–49, 61, 64, 78–79, 159

Aesthetics, 2, 3, 4, 7, 10, 131, 273, 292

Aesthetics: (critical theory) of 18th century, 5, 122, 273, 277; Kant's "Copernican Revolution" in, 45, 46, 94; and teleology, 88, 151–52

Aggregate vs. system, 160, 171, 173, 174, 268, 304

Agreeable. *See* Pleasant

Akenside, Mark, 354n.62

Allgemeine Deutsche Bibliothek, 233

Allgemeine Literatur-Zeitung, 180, 184, 205, 234

Allgemeine Naturgeschichte und Theorie des Himmels, 19

Allison, Henry, 74, 248, 363n.60, 402n.34

Ameriks, Karl, 48, 55, 71, 369n.54

Analogy, 3, 239, 264, 274–75, 279, 320–21, 324; of judgment of taste and pure moral choice, 7, 89, 93, 278–79, 293; of nature to purpose, 96, 153, 216, 221–22, 315; of reason with organism, 173–74; of symbol to schema, 274, 316

"Analytic of Teleological Judgment," 186, 218, 224, 260

"Analytic of the Beautiful," 2, 4,

ical, 89, 172, 266, 281, 300,
306, 307, 313–19, 321, 327,
346, 419n.61
Auxter, Thomas, 326, 341
Awareness, noncognitive, 81
Awareness: vs. conscious attention, 77

Bacon, Francis, 22, 195
Basedow, Johann, 34
Batteux, Charles, 24
Baumgarten, Alexander, 19–21,
24, 30–31, 46, 48–49, 59, 82,
406n.15; and perfection, 20,
21, 30, 99; and "science of
aesthetics," 20, 30
Bäumler, Alfred, 19, 29
Bayle, Pierre, 243
Beattie, James, 30
Beauty (beautiful), 2, 20–21, 29,
32, 75, 93, 95, 104, 122, 263,
292, 316, 342; in art, 131,
146–47; dependent
(*pulchritudo adhaerens*), 97,
124–29, 146–47, 288, 290–
91, 379n.3; empirical canon
of, 118–19, 139; as enlivening
the mind, 94, 101–2, 117,
118, 282; free (*pulchritudo
vaga*), 125, 291, 379n.3,
411n.60; intelligible, 24, 184;
as mark of immanent determination by mental process,
28, 93, 95, 295; of nature, 5,
131–32, 146, 151–52, 280,
294, 342; and objective perfection, 20–21, 31, 99–101,
184; vs. the pleasant (charm),
101–2, 105–21, 134, 376n.74;
as stimulus to scientific inquiry, 151–53, 280, 383n.11
Beauty, ideal of, 124, 126–28,
134, 146, 288
Beauty as symbol of morality, 7,
14, 268, 273, 275, 277, 280,

288, 289, 291, 293, 294, 328,
342, 404n.62
Beck, Jacob Sigismund, 74
Beck, Lewis, 18, 23, 29, 70, 75,
313, 324–25, 340, 345,
351n.9, 363n.59
Being, original, 35, 230, 232,
239, 244, 250–51, 340, 346;
as intelligent creator, 191,
215, 225, 226, 227, 239, 249,
310, 336 (*see also* Theism);
Spinoza's theory of, 244, 248,
250–59
Being, rational, 307, 314, 317–
18, 319, 321, 322, 323, 344,
346; finite, 94, 268, 299,
313–14, 318, 320, 321, 324,
338
Being-in-the-world (*see also* Human nature), 226, 268, 269,
319, 323, 342
Beiser, Frederick, 228, 235,
348n.21, 351n.50, 399n.6,
403n.55
Belief (*see also* Faith), 78, 234,
238, 240–41, 245, 306,
403n.55
Belief, rational (*Vernunftglaube*),
239–40, 241, 302, 303, 306,
315, 337, 340, 343, 404n.64
Bennett, Jonathan, 69
Beobachten and *bemerken* (*see also*
"Judging, other kind of"), 87,
104
Berlin Academy, 17, 18, 21, 22,
36, 42; 1761–63 Prize Competition, 24, 26, 29–30, 31,
353n.42, 355n.73
Berlin Aufklärung, 11, 22–34,
231, 233–34, 235–36, 329
Berlinische Monatsschrift, 179, 205,
207, 233, 234, 329
Biester, Johann Erich, 233, 235–
37, 403n.55
Biology, science of, 151, 174,

Determinacy. *See* Individuality

Determination. *See* Constitutive
   determination

Determinism, 179, 191, 267, 333

"Dialectic of Aesthetic Judgment,"
   5, 7–8, 122–23, 264, 269, 270,
   287, 302, 303, 344

"Dialectic of Teleological Judgment," 6, 186, 214, 218, 222,
   223, 224, 225, 226, 230, 247,
   248, 260, 318

Dialectical excess, 6, 163, 166,
   176, 222, 226, 251, 260, 270,
   271, 308, 309, 346, 406n.13

Diderot, Denis, 190–91, 394n.42

Dignity of reason, 63, 142, 146,
   167, 199, 314, 317, 346

Disciples of Kant (Kantians), 12,
   14, 232–35, 242–43, 246–47,
   344–45, 351n.50, 404n.78

Discursiveness, 48–55, 61, 159–
   61, 237, 288, 310, 315, 324,
   399n.49; vs. intuitive intellect,
   252–57; and recourse to teleology, 219–27

Disinterestedness of pleasure in
   beauty, 24, 92–93, 108, 125,
   273, 294

Dubos, Jean, 24

Duff, William, 355n.68, 380n.36

Düsing, Klaus, 3, 173

Duty, 32, 255, 264, 268, 291, 297,
   299, 300, 306, 326, 338–39

Eberhard, Johann, 42, 348n.19,
   359n.141, 363n.60

Ectypal nature, 320, 321, 326, 241

Education. *See* Cultivation

Efficaciousness of morality in
   world of sense (*see also* Actualizing the moral law), 265–66,
   295, 299, 306–7, 314, 323, 325

Emotion (*Rührung*), 27–28, 32,
   37, 93, 115, 282, 299

Empiricism, 19, 46, 53, 101, 178,
   195, 388n.2, 419n.61

Encyclopedist, 26, 190

End-in-itself (*see also* Purpose: intrinsic), 99, 306–7, 314–19,
   327, 344, 375n.53, 418n.56

Endowments, natural (*natürliche
   Anlagen*), 200–201, 217–18

Ends, objective, 324, 325, 420n.11

Enlightenment, 8, 17, 21, 22, 24,
   27, 35, 139, 183, 241, 332–33,
   421n.41; British, 22, 24, 29;
   French, 13, 21–22, 23, 24, 183;
   Radical (materialist), 196, 228,
   240, 257, 258; and religious
   tolerance, 11, 241; Scottish,
   422n.43, 422n.45

Enlivening (liveliness) of mind (*see
   also* Spirit), 118, 144–45, 274,
   286, 291, 297–99, 304

Entailment: problem of empirical,
   60–61, 158–61, 260, 343,
   384n.25

Entelechy (*see also* Purposiveness:
   intrinsic), 99, 171

Enthusiasm (*Schwärmerei*) (*see also*
   Fanaticism, religious; *Sturm
   und Drang:* and irrationalism),
   12, 28–29, 33–36, 38, 41, 42,
   44, 178, 184, 232, 233, 236,
   238–39, 240, 246, 247,
   381n.46, 403n.55

Epicurus, 248, 295

Erect posture, 181–82, 199, 204

Ethical turn, 6–8, 129, 248, 259–
   60, 263–64, 265, 276, 306,
   307, 335, 341, 342, 375n.53,
   381n.46, 382n.3, 398n.35

Ethico-theology, 226, 240, 253,
   335, 336, 399n.49

Euler, Leonhard, 120

Evolution: 18th-century theories
   of, 205, 214, 217

Exemplary instance of beauty,
   118–19, 128–29, 139, 141, 145

Good, the, 30, 98, 99, 110, 125, 126, 279, 291, 298, 323; heterogeneity of, 324, 325, 412n.17, 420n.11, 425n.90
Gottsched, Johann, 26
Gracyk, Theodore, 32
Gram, Moltke, 70
Gregor, Mary, 45, 75–76
Ground and consequence, 51, 220–21, 255, 351n.9
Grounding of the Metaphysics of Morals, 157, 175, 186, 242, 300, 307, 310, 316, 318, 319, 321, 326, 345, 419n.61, 419n.63
Guyer, Paul, 70–71

Halle, University of: controversy over Wolff, 11, 17
Haller, Albrecht von, 198
Hamann, Johann, 33–35, 36, 40, 44, 137, 181, 231–34, 241, 242, 355n.64; 355–56n.77, 357n.107, 391n.43, 400n.6, 401n.21, 402n.34
Happiness, 93, 296, 297, 298, 328, 329, 331, 337, 418n.61, 420n.3, 421n.25
Harmony, 85, 118
Harmony of the faculties, 25, 33, 85, 94, 101–2, 116–18, 119, 122, 128, 131, 143, 287–88, 291, 297, 378n.54
Hartknoch, Johann, 9, 156, 389n.10
Hartley, David, 22, 284
Health (*see also* Well-being), 296, 297, 298
Hegel, G.W.F., 14, 141, 333, 344–45, 361n.38, 380n.40, 389n.7, 397n.87, 400n.6, 403n.55, 405n.78, 407n.41, 422n.43
Heidegger, Martin, 69, 397n.87
Hen kai pan, 229–30, 258–59, 400n.12
Henrich, Dieter, 48, 55, 70–71

Herder, Johann, 14, 23, 30, 46, 188, 242, 243, 355n.68, 359n.143, 391n.37, 421n.41, 425n.90; and "beautiful science," 42, 141–42; career of, 35–36; disparagement of Kant, 245, 389n.10, 389n.11; and Hamann, 34–36; on history, 180–81, 330, 396n.75; Kant's rivalry with, 8–10, 39–44, 178–88, 243, 349n.29; and pantheism, hylozoism, 6, 187–88, 199, 203–6, 211, 230, 245, 401n.13; and Spinozism, 229–31, 243–47; and *Sturm und Drang*, 8–10, 12, 35–37, 137–42; Works: *Älteste Urkunde des Menschengeschlechts*, 36, 37, 39–40; *Auch eine Philosophie der Geschichte*, 36; *Gott: einige Gespräche*, 10, 12, 186, 188, 208, 230, 243–47, 258; *Ideen zur Philosophie der Geschichte der Menschheit*, 9, 10, 36, 138, 179, 180–86, 197, 203–6, 207, 243, 330, 332, 389n.7, 389n.8, 391n.44; "Über den Einfluß der schönen in die höheren Wissenschaften," 42; *Über die neuere deutsche Literatur: Fragmente*, 35; *Von Erkennen und Empfinden*, 42, 389n.10
Hermeneutic of suspicion, 425n.89
Herz, Marcus, 80, 233, 235, 236
Highest good (*see also* Actualizing the moral law; Community, ethical; Mankind), 7, 239, 268, 307, 319, 322, 323–26, 333, 419n.63, 419n.3, 421n.25; as moral ideal, 322, 324–25, 326
History, 7, 14, 200, 268, 323, 326–34, 340; German idea of, 13, 330; Kant's philosophy of, 10, 186, 205, 268, 328–29, 344,

423n.57; Kant's rivalry with
Herder over, 10, 178–79, 330–
34, 396n.75
Hobbes, Thomas, 22, 194, 328,
330
Hölderlin, Friedrich, 14, 405n.78
Homer as unschooled genius, 28,
140, 358n.139
Hope, 337, 338
Human experience, complex, 3,
59, 61, 292, 293, 296, 297, 299,
309, 319, 323, 337
Human nature, animal and ra-
tional (unity of man) (*see also*
Being-in-the-world), 42, 62, 93,
268, 293, 302, 306, 411n.1
Humanity, idea of (*see also* Mankind), 63, 280, 285
Humbolt, Wilhelm von, 14
Hume, David, 17, 22, 23, 24, 30,
31, 34, 35, 52, 55, 59, 178, 196,
218, 240, 343, 356n.77,
356n.98, 400n.6, 403n.55
Hutcheson, Francis, 29–30, 31
Huygens, Christiaan, 393n.25
Hylozoism (*see also* Matter vs. life;
Nature: as living whole; Vitalism), 6, 186, 189, 192, 202,
205, 213, 216, 218, 222, 226,
227, 244, 247, 248, 250, 258,
260, 396n.75
Hypotyposis (*see also* Presentation),
273, 321

Iatromechanical approach to biology, 197–98
Idea, aesthetic (*see also* Symbol),
275, 279, 280, 283, 286, 287,
288, 300, 404n.62
Idea, aesthetic normal, 126–29,
134, 285, 288
Idea of reason (rational idea), 79,
126, 164, 172, 176, 240, 339;
vs. ideal, 284–85; and indeterminate concept, 270–71, 274;

and symbolism, 281, 286–89,
304, 321
"Idea for a Universal History," 10,
13, 179, 205, 326, 328, 329,
395n.54, 396n.75
Ideal: of imagination vs. reason,
127, 284–85, 319
Idealism, dogmatic, 60, 131; objective, 302, 345; subjective,
280, 302, 345; transcendental,
53, 67, 230, 367n.15; as unre-
ality, 248–49, 315
Idealism, German, 1, 2, 7, 12–14,
156, 174, 175, 180, 185, 189,
229–30, 301, 305, 330, 334,
342, 344–46, 348n.7, 350n.45,
350n.48, 392n.6, 400n.6,
400n.12, 401n.13, 403n.55,
422n.41, 423n.57, 425n.90,
425n.97; and Spinoza, 14, 229,
231, 257–59, 407n.41
Imagination (*Einbildungskraft*), 29,
44, 50, 82–87, 114, 185, 239,
244, 274, 289, 296, 356n.98,
371n.105, 381n.46; apprehension vs. comprehension, 281–
82; danger in, 33–34, 44; faculty of, 33, 211, 284; as faculty
of presentation (*Darstellung*),
127; following rules without intention, 83–84, 114, 117, 145;
formative vs. synthetic, 366n.7,
372n.121; free play of, 28, 84,
85, 95, 101, 113, 114–15, 116,
118, 121, 127, 128, 131, 135,
145, 292, 297; harmony with
reason in sublime, 280, 281–
84; harmony with understanding in beauty, 84–85, 87, 95,
117, 157, 280, 295; as interpretative, 85; and intuition,
68–69, 76; problem of, 52–53,
61; productive, 114, 284; and
reconfiguration (*umbilden*), 84,
114–15, 121, 127; role in

objective), 60, 63, 70, 74, 82;
ambiguity of validity vs. actuality, 64, 68, 83, 163, 166, 289
*Observations on the Feelings of the
Beautiful and the Sublime*, 31,
276
Odebrecht, Rudolf, 114–15, 284
Ontological argument for God,
18–19, 239, 245, 364n.61
Ontology: dialectical sense of,
163, 176; and existence claims,
49, 57, 172, 212, 239, 308, 310,
313–14, 345–46; Kant's rivalry
with other, 6, 18, 21, 212, 230,
248–51, 260, 302, 342,
390n.26
Openness of Kantian system (*see
also* System [systematicity]: in
Kant's philosophy as a whole),
14, 175, 351n.50
Opus postumum, 413n.60
Organic form (organism): analogy
to reason (purpose), 173–74,
222, 249, 256; analogy to work
of art, 221; definition of, 209–
10, 212–19; as empirical fact,
189, 219–20, 221, 224, 342,
398n.22; and entelechy, 171,
344; ineptness of mechanical
account of, 202, 215–16, 218,
220–21, 225; vs. life, 198, 222,
226; and metaphysical implications, 225–27; as natural
purpose, 98, 215, 221, 222,
224, 263, 327; variation and inherited characteristics, 200–
201, 209, 215–17, 218,
395n.67
Ortega y Gasset, José, 290
Ossian, 27, 36

Panentheism, 229–30, 244, 258,
413n.60
Pantheism (*see also* Panentheism):
and Herder's *Naturphilosophie*,

180, 103, 187, 205, 208, 230,
243–46; Kant's opposition to,
6–7, 186, 191, 208, 218, 246,
259, 260, 264–65, 302, 335;
and materialism (Radical Enlightenment), 196, 257–58,
400n.8; and Spinozism, 14,
187, 218, 227, 229, 243, 250,
257–58, 264–65, 405n.89
Pantheism Controversy, 6, 10–12,
179, 228–48, 274, 340,
349n.40, 352n.13, 400n.6,
401n.13, 401n.21, 403n.55
Paradox of art, grounding, 131–
36, 145, 146, 154, 275
Partiality (*see also* Inclination), 110
Passivity vs. activism in consciousness (*see also* Spontaneity;
Synthesis), 48–50, 52, 68–69,
113–15, 287, 307–8, 309, 311,
314
Perception (*Wahrnehmung*), 66, 68,
72, 75, 79, 81–82, 165, 219,
221, 308
Perfection (*Vollkommenheit*), 20–
21, 99–102, 125–27, 146–47,
221, 252, 272–73, 288, 290–
91; qualitative, 99, 249; quantitative, 99, 249; subjective, 101
Person (personality), 298, 300,
302, 306, 307–8, 317, 325, 326
Phenomenology of subjective consciousness, 45, 51, 52, 61–88,
238, 344, 365n.3, 368n.35
Philosophy, cognitive (theoretical), 47, 60, 265, 339
Philosophy, critical (transcendental), 4, 6, 7, 45, 46, 48, 53, 54,
55, 57, 59, 60, 61, 62, 78, 89,
93, 113, 157, 158, 167, 175,
176, 211, 233, 234, 241, 272,
277, 306, 307, 315, 337, 339,
341, 344, 351n.37, 363n.60,
364n.71, 419n.61, 424n.89
Philosophy, political, 3, 328, 334

Validity, private, 106, 112
Validity, subjective, 72, 78, 82, 96, 176, 224, 291, 316, 339
Validity, transcendental, 56, 59, 111, 168, 270, 310, 404n.64
"Vienna Logic" of Kant, 73
Virgil as learned genius, 28
Vitalism (see also Hylozoism; Matter vs. life; Nature: as living whole), 135, 198, 230
Voltaire, 17, 22, 196, 240, 393n.25
Von deutscher Art und Kunst, 36

Walzel, Oskar, 183–84, 390n.26
Warton, Joseph, 26, 28
"Was heißt: sich im Denken orientieren?" 12, 167, 176, 230, 235, 237–41, 247, 274, 403n.57, 404n.72
Weldon, Thomas, 173
Well-being, feeling of (see also Health), 295–96, 297
"What is Enlightenment?" 13
Whole vs. parts (see also Totality), 51, 218, 220–21, 244, 256–57
Wieland, Christoph, 42, 184, 207
Will: actual (Willkür), 98, 133, 265–66, 295, 296, 299, 307 (see also Desire, faculty of); determinations, objective vs. subjective, 297, 299, 317, 321; free, 260, 264, 295, 299–300, 306, 318, 329, 331 (see also Freedom, practical); holy, 318–19, 324, 419n.61; rational (in-

telligent) (Wille), 133, 221, 226, 295, 319, 325, 327; transcendental explanation of, 90–91
Will, Frederic, 24
Windelband, Wilhelm, 4
Wit (ingenium) as natural talent for similarities, 84
Wizenmann, Thomas, 235, 404n.72
Wolff, Christian, 11, 17–19, 23, 25, 59, 187, 212, 397n.87, 402n.34, 406n.15
Wolffianism, orthodox (see also School philosophy, German), 18–21, 42, 352n.13, 388n.2, 400n.11
Wöllner, Johann V., and Edict of 1788, 11–12, 247, 417n.11
Wood, Allen, 325, 334, 340
World-soul (Weltseele), 183–84, 230, 304, 413n.60
World-whole, idea of nature as a, 79, 176, 184, 226, 271, 281
Worth, moral, 277, 283, 294, 297, 298, 316, 317, 325, 337
Worthiness commensurate with happiness, 338, 339, 424n.89

Young, Edward, 26, 28–29, 34, 355n.64, 380n.36
Young, J. Michael, 75, 76, 84–86
Yovel, Yimiahu, 333, 344, 416n.29

Zeldin, Mary, 325